Volume 11

The Broadman Bible Commentary

EDITORIAL BOARD

BROADMAN PRESS • Nashville, Tennessee

The Broadman Bible Commentary

Volume 11

2 Corinthians-Philemon

Dewey Decimal Classification: 220.7
Library of Congress catalog card number: 78–93918
Printed in the United States of America

Preface

THE BROADMAN BIBLE COMMENTARY presents current biblical study within the context of strong faith in the authority, adequacy, and reliability of the Bible as the Word of God. It seeks to offer help and guidance to the Christian who is willing to undertake Bible study as a serious, rewarding pursuit. The publisher thus has defined the scope and purpose of the COMMENTARY to produce a work suited to the Bible study needs of both ministers and laymen. The findings of biblical scholarship are presented so that readers without formal theological education can use them in their own Bible study. Footnotes and technical words are limited to essential information.

Writers have been carefully selected for their reverent Christian faith and their knowledge of Bible truth. Keeping in mind the needs of a general readership, the writers present special information about language and history where it helps to clarify the meaning of the text. They face Bible problems—not only in language but in doctrine and ethics—but avoid fine points that have little bearing on how we should understand and apply the Bible. They express their own views and convictions. At the same time, they present alternative views when such are advocated by other serious, well-informed students of the Bible. The views presented, therefore, cannot be regarded as the official position of the publisher.

This COMMENTARY is the result of many years' planning and preparation. Broadman Press began in 1958 to explore needs and possibilities for the present work. In this year and again in 1959, Christian leaders—particularly pastors and seminary professors—were brought together to consider whether a new commentary was needed and what shape it might take. Growing out of these deliberations in 1961, the board of trustees governing the Press authorized the publication of a multivolume commentary. Further planning led in 1966 to the selection of a general editor and an Advisory Board. This board of pastors, professors, and denominational leaders met in September, 1966, reviewing preliminary plans and making definite recommendations which have been carried out as the COMMENTARY has been developed.

Early in 1967, four consulting editors were selected, two for the Old Testament and two for the New. Under the leadership of the general editor, these men have worked with the Broadman Press personnel to plan the COMMENTARY in detail. They have participated fully in the selection of the writers and the evaluation of manuscripts. They have given generously of time and effort, earning the highest esteem and gratitude of Press employees who have worked with them.

The selection of the Revised Standard Version of the Bible text for the COMMENTARY was made in 1967 also. This grew out of careful consideration of possible alternatives, which were fully discussed in the meeting of the Advisory Board. The adoption of an English version as a standard text was recognized as desirable, meaning that only the King James, American Standard, and Revised Standard Versions were available for consideration.

The King James Version was recognized as holding first place in the hearts of many Christians but as suffering from inaccuracies in translation and obscurities in phrasing. The American Standard was seen as free from these two problems but deficient in an attractive English style and wide current use. The Revised Standard retains the accuracy and clarity of the American Standard and has a pleasing style and a growing use. It thus enjoys a strong advantage over each of the others, making it by far the most desirable choice.

Throughout the COMMENTARY the treatment of the biblical text aims at a balanced combination of exegesis and exposition, admittedly recognizing that the nature of the various books and the space assigned will properly modify the application of this approach.

The general articles appearing in Volumes 1, 8, and 12 are designed to provide background material to enrich one's understanding of the nature of the Bible and the distinctive aspects of each Testament. Those in Volume 12 focus on the implications of biblical teaching in the areas of worship, ethical duty, and the world mission of the church.

The COMMENTARY avoids current theological fads and changing theories. It concerns itself with the deep realities of God's dealings with men, his revelation in Christ, his eternal gospel, and his purpose for the redemption of the world. It seeks to relate the word of God in Scripture and in the living Word to the deep needs of persons and to mankind in God's world.

Through faithful interpretation of God's message in the Scriptures, therefore, the COMMENTARY seeks to reflect the inseparable relation of truth to life, of meaning to experience. Its aim is to breathe the atmosphere of life-relatedness. It seeks to express the dynamic relation between redemptive truth and living persons. May it serve as a means whereby God's children hear with greater clarity what God the Father is saying to them.

Abbreviations

BBC – *Broadman Bible Commentary*
con. – contra
ERV – English Revised Version
fn. – footnote
Gk. – Greek
IDB – *Interpreter's Dictionary of the Bible*
ICC – International Critical Commentary
KJV – King James Version
LXX – Septuagint
marg. – marginal reading
NEB – New English Bible
RSV – Revised Standard Version
TCNT – *Twentieth Century New Testament*
TDNT – *Theological Dictionary of the New Testament*

Contents

2 Corinthians

G. R. BEASLEY-MURRAY

Introduction

I. Content

The letter has three clearly marked divisions. Chapters 1—7 consist mainly of an exposition of Paul's apostolic ministry. Chapters 8—9 plead the cause of a collection organized among the Gentile churches for the Jerusalem church. Chapters 10—13 defend in strong terms Paul's apostolic authority in face of its denials by people in Corinth.

Paul begins with thanks to God for deliverance from a dreadful experience (of persecution?) in which he had despaired of life (1:3–11). He explains why his intended visit to the church at Corinth was postponed (1:15 ff.): it was to "spare" them. Instead of a further visit he had sent a stern letter, but now that the Corinthians had shown repentance he asks them to relent their discipline of the "offender" (2:1 ff.). Unlike his detractors in Corinth he needs no letters of commendation to them (3:1 ff.); they themselves are a letter from Christ, and he the Lord's amanuensis in writing it. "As Moses hewed the stones and tablets, so we your souls" (Chrysostom's paraphrase). But whereas the law-code brings condemnation, the Spirit bestows life through the gospel. At the giving of the law Moses wore a veil before the people, signifying the transience of its glory. A veil is on the mind of the Jew to this day, and on many a blinded Gentile too, preventing them from believing the gospel. But the God who created light has illuminated our minds through the shining of Christ's glory upon us (3:12 ff.). The afflictions of the present time are as nothing compared with the glory that is coming to us (4:16 ff.). When we "strike tents," i.e., depart from this temporary body, we are to have a permanent house with God, i.e., the resurrection body (5:1 ff.). In the light of Christ's great day, of testing as well as glory, Paul exercises his apostleship (5:11 ff.). It is a ministry of reconciliation, a proclamation of God's reconciling act in Christ. This gospel Paul seeks to live as well as to preach (6:3 ff.). He thanks God for the reconciliation effected between himself and the church in Corinth (7:5 ff.).

The collection organized by Paul (chs. 8—9) shows how seriously he took the request of the Jerusalem apostles that the Gentile Christians "remember the poor" (Gal. 2:10). He incites the Corinthians to worthy endeavor by adducing the generosity of other churches and the example of Christ in his incarnation and redemption.

The spirited defense of Paul's apostolic authority (chs. 10—13) was prompted by the attempts of Jewish teachers to discredit his ministry in Corinth. Their charges that he was cowardly and weak and that he had no right to preach in Corinth are countered one by one (ch. 10). This leads to a passionate answer of fools according to their folly (11:1 ff.). Paul opposes the claims of the "super apostles" of Corinth by recounting his authentic signs of apostleship, namely sufferings borne for the sake of Christ. The Corinthians are bidden to ensure that they themselves are really "in the

1

faith," for when Paul next visits them he will demand from them reality and not a sham faith (ch. 13).

II. Occasion and Purpose

The occasion of the letter was a resurgence of antagonism to Paul's apostolic authority, and its purpose was the vindication by Paul of that authority.

So much is clear; but to reconstruct the events in which the antagonism was expressed and the precise way in which Paul handled it is a difficult undertaking, and there is much disagreement about the matter. The problem is a peculiarly modern one, for early writers were interested only in the doctrinal teaching of this letter, not in the history it reflects. To modern scholars, for whom history is of importance, the problem is of no small interest.

We make a suitable beginning on investigating the circumstances of the letter if we consider who the person was of whom Paul speaks in 2 Corinthians 2:5 f. The man had committed an unnamed offense which had earlier caused Paul much grief. The apostle now urges that the offender has been punished sufficiently and that he be forgiven and restored to fellowship. His former instructions concerning this man had been given to test their obedience, and indeed there was little cause for him to say that he forgave the man, for it was a small matter (2:10).

Earlier expositors assumed that this unknown offender must have been the incestuous man referred to in 1 Corinthians 5:1 ff. The Corinthians appeared to have admired rather than censured this man. Paul had demanded that they should discipline him. Reflection shows however that this identification is well-nigh impossible, for Paul could never have spoken in so casual a manner concerning one guilty of such a grievous offense as that mentioned in 1 Corinthians 5. Moreover in 2 Corinthians 2:9 Paul states that he wrote as he did about the offending person "that I might test you and know whether you are obedient in everything"; in 7:12 "that your zeal for us might be re-

vealed to you"; in 2:10 he speaks of his forgiving of the person "for your sake"; and in 7:11 he declares "at every point you have proved yourselves guiltless in the matter." Could Paul have so written concerning his demand that an incestuous church member be disciplined? In fact the Corinthians had apparently condoned the conduct of this man and regarded his conduct as evidence of their freedom from ordinary moral standards (1 Cor. 5:2–6). They had not been "guiltless in the matter"!

Accordingly, the most natural interpretation of the evidence seems to be that the person wronged was Paul himself. Presumably he had been opposed to his face and insulted before the church by one of its members. Such an incident could not be passed over as of no consequence, for it involved Paul's apostolic authority and message. But once the matter had been put right, Paul would naturally feel at liberty to minimize the offense as of small moment.

That leads to the question, When was the offense committed? It can hardly have been before the writing of 1 Corinthians, for that letter makes no reference to the occurrence. Now there are three references in 2 Corinthians to Paul's visits, or intended visits to Corinth. In each case the language is somewhat ambiguous, as a comparison of the KJV with the RSV will illustrate; but modern scholars unanimously agree with the RSV interpretation. In 2 Corinthians 2:1 Paul writes, "I made up my mind not to make you another painful visit," implying that he had made one such visit. In 12:14 he states, "Here for the third time I am ready to come to you." And again in 13:1, "This is the third time I am coming to you"; and he continues, "I warned those who sinned before and all the others, and I warn them now while absent, *as I did when present on my second visit*, that if I come again I will not spare them."

The combined evidence of these three passages leaves no doubt that Paul paid a visit to the Corinthians after the period when the church was founded, and that that visit was a painful one. It looks as though that was the occasion when he received the grievous insult.

The precise nature of the insult to Paul is beyond knowing. There are, however, scattered throughout the entire letter indications of allegations made against him. His nonfulfillment of promises to spend a long time with the Corinthians are held to show him as fickle (1:15 ff.). He has no letters of recommendation, as he ought to have (3:1 ff.). His preaching is unclear (4:3). He is timid when present and dares to be bold only at a distance (10:1 ff.). He does not really belong to Christ (10:7). He has no right to preach in Corinth (10:13 ff.), even as he knows that he had no right to financial support from the church (11:7 ff.). In fact he is not an apostle of Christ at all (12:12), and there is no reason to believe that Christ ever speaks through him (13:3).

It appears that certain Jewish Christians from Palestine had gained an entrance into the church of Corinth; they claimed to be "superlative apostles" (12:11), and boasted of their Jewish origin, their knowledge of Jesus (as a man?), and their spiritual gifts (12:21 ff.). They appear to have used their position as preachers of the gospel to make money out of their congregations (2:17). They were in the habit of securing letters of commendation from churches, and on the basis of these gaining entry into other churches. This was how they had secured a footing in Corinth, and it is likely that they had persuaded the Corinthians in turn to write letters on their behalf, to be used in other congregations (3:1 ff.). They boasted of their accomplishments and status beyond measure (10:12 ff.). Paul viewed them as preaching another Jesus, another Spirit, and another gospel (11:4), as sham apostles and even servants of Satan (11:13 ff.).

There is no likelihood that these men had been sent by the apostles of Jerusalem to oppose Paul. Nor is there any evidence that they tried to persuade the Corinthians to observe the Mosaic law, so they will not have been identical with the group of Jewish Christians who tried to win over the Galatian churches. Like many Jews of that time they were probably syncretistic, in particular adding to their original Judaism Christianity and Gnosticism. If they were not responsible for the Gnostic tendencies discernible in 1 Corinthians (it is difficult to prove or disprove their presence in Corinth so early), they will have allied themselves with those who held such views and stirred up the opposition to Paul already in the church. While the entire letter is a vindication of Paul's integrity and authority, a plausible suggestion is that the insult which crowned the slanders of Paul's opponents was an accusation by a Corinthian church member in the presence of the church that Paul was organizing the collection for his own benefit with the intention of putting it in his pocket (see 12:16 ff.). It is comprehensible that for Paul that would have been the last straw!

III. Authenticity and Unity

No one today calls into question the genuineness of the letter as a whole. It is passionately and characteristically Pauline; and in any case, as has been observed, no impersonator would have concocted so intricate a set of circumstances as that presupposed in 2 Corinthians. While therefore all agree that the letter comes from Paul, it is nevertheless true that no letter of his has been so dissected and its parts assigned to various occasions as this one. And there are reasons, of course, for such conjectures.

From 1 Corinthians 16:3 ff. it is clear that Paul intended to spend a lengthy time with the Corinthians. In 2 Corinthians 1:15—2:2 he explains why this promise was not kept: it was to spare them. He had paid a lightning visit, presumably to try to set things right in the church, but the visit proved to be disastrous for him and for them. Rather than provoke an even more painful encounter through a third visit he wrote a letter "out of much affliction and anguish of heart and with many tears" (2:4). What happened to that letter? It can hardly be 1 Corinthians, as was once assumed. Apart from all other considerations, if in 1 Corinthians a long visit had been promised, and in the event a short and unhappy visit was paid, which was followed by this painful letter sent to avoid another such visit, clearly this painful letter was written after 1 Corinthians and before 2 Corinthians.

Again we ask, what happened to the letter? Some are content to affirm that it has been lost, and that may be true. Another suggestion, however, has become widely accepted: the "lost" letter is preserved, at least in part, in 2 Corinthians 10—13.

The reasons for this apparently extraordinary suggestion are as follows: (1) A marked change of tone sets in at 10:1. The joy of the earlier chapters and the doxology after appealing for the collection is followed by a fiery apology that not even Galatians can rival. (2) It was curious psychology on the apostle's part to follow chapters 1—9 with 10—13. The earlier chapters express a longing for reconciliation, and indeed breathe gratitude for its establishment, but they are followed by a torrent of reproaches, sarcasm, and warnings that must have almost obliterated his endeavors to consolidate the peace. (3) There are some strange inconsistencies in the present order of chapters. For example in 7:16 Paul writes, "I rejoice because I have perfect confidence in you," but in 12:20 f., "I fear that perhaps I may come and find you not what I wish . . . and I may have to mourn over many of those who sinned before and have not repented of the impurity, immorality, and licentiousness which they have practiced."

(4) Some passages in chapters 1—9 appear to reflect statements made in 10—13. For example: "If I come again I will not spare" (13:2); "I call God to witness against me—it was to spare you that I refrained from coming to Corinth" (1:23). Again: "I write this . . . in order that when I come I may not have to be severe in my use of the authority which the Lord has given me" (13:10); "I wrote as I did, so that when I came I might not be pained by those who should have made me rejoice" (2:3). (5) In chapters 1—9 Paul

declares that he has no intention of commending himself any more (3:1; 5:12), but in 10—13 he does it repeatedly and at length. See especially 10:7, "If any one is confident that he is Christ's, let him remind himself that as he is Christ's, so are we"; 11:5, "I am not in the least inferior to these superlative apostles"; 11:23, "Are they servants of Christ? I am a better one—I am talking like a madman—with far greater labors."

The culminating effect of this evidence is to make at least a plausible case for the view that chapters 10—13 preceded 1—9 in time. There is much in 10—13 which could have been written "out of much affliction and anguish of heart and with many tears." Whether there was more in similar strain in the original letter, and if so how much, we cannot know; but it is understandable that such a letter should have accomplished its purpose and that Paul could have written with such relief as he has in 1—9.

As may be expected, this view has not gone unchallenged. Above all, it has been objected that there is no external evidence for reversing the order of chapters. No early manuscript of the letter gives such an order, neither is there evidence to show that chapters 1—9 and 10—13 ever circulated independently. The difference of tone between the two sections has been accounted for by suggesting that 1—9 was sent to the church as a whole, but 10—13 to a minority that was still rebellious. One must admit, however, that there is not a hint that Paul intended this; on the contrary such a declaration as 11:2 has the whole church in view. Some have thought that after writing 1—9 Paul received grave news from Corinth; or that Titus, who had brought good news to Paul of the Corinthians, departed, and Paul after brooding over the situation gave vent to his feelings; or even that after writing 1—9 Paul had a sleepless night! The reader must judge for himself the likelihood of these explanations.

In the end we have to admit that the case is not proven, but the hypothesis of the reversed order of chapters is attractive. The lack of external evidence ought not to be overpressed, for there are other books of the Bible whose composition is traced without the aid of such evidence (for example, the book of Isaiah and the Gospels of Matthew and Luke). There is reason to believe that 2 Corinthians did not circulate among the churches till long after 1 Corinthians, and this is quite understandable; the church of Corinth was still a flourishing church in the post-apostolic age, and 2 Corinthians was most discreditable to them. "It is impossible to tell how much else of Paul's correspondence with Corinth has either been lost or suffered a fate equivalent to being expunged from the minutes," remarked R. H. Strachan (p. xxii); and one who has had experience of unhappy church meetings will sympathize with that judgment!

It may be asked, however, if chapters 1—9 and 10—13 were separate entities in early Corinth, what made the editor who put them together choose this order? In reply G. Bornkamm [1] pointed out that in early Christian literature warnings against false teachers are often expressed at the end of writings, and this was done with the conviction that the appearance of false prophets is a sign of the last times. He suggested that the editor of 2 Corinthians held to this rule; and by placing the section containing Paul's defense at the end of the letter, he characterized Paul's opponents as false prophets of the end times. The idea is not impossible.

It was earlier hinted that other sections of 2 Corinthians have been separated out as belonging to distinct occasions. Of these 6:14—7:1 has often been assigned to an earlier letter for it appears to interrupt the present context, and it could even be connected with the letter referred to in 1 Corinthians 5:10 f. Some recent scholars advocate the view that 2:7—6:4, the central section of Paul's defense of his apostolic office, was originally a distinct letter and was written when Paul first heard of the appearance

of his opponents but before they had gained their success in the congregation. Chapters 8 and 9 have often been thought to be independent pleas of Paul for the collection; some would assign one or the other chapter to one of the suggested separate sections of the letter (e.g., chap. 8 to the letter of reconciliation, 1:1—2:13 and 7:5 ff.).

Exegetes react variously to these ideas. The English-speaking world has been more cautious in its attitude towards them than the European writers. There is, of course, no question of setting aside Paul's authorship of the letter; it is the original context of the chapters that is in dispute. The present writer inclines to recognize a strong possibility that 10—13 preceeded 1—9 in order of writing, but views the other suggestions as less likely. At best, all such theories can only be viewed as tentative till better explanations of the evidence are forthcoming.

IV. Time and Place

At the time of writing Paul was in Macedonia (2:12). In the beginning of his letter he tells how he had lately been rescued from a terrible danger in the Roman province called "Asia" (in Asia Minor, 1:8 ff.). Shortly afterwards he found himself in Troas, and from there he went to Macedonia to meet Titus (2:12 f.). This situation is often identified with that described in Acts 19—20, where we learn that after the Demetrius uproar Paul left Ephesus ("Asia"), departed to Macedonia, and from there went on to Greece. If that assumption be correct, the Demetrius affair must have involved Paul to a greater degree than Luke's narrative would ordinarily suggest.

First Corinthians is usually dated in the spring of A.D. 55 (cf. 1 Cor. 16:8). Scholars who hold to complicated dissection theories of 2 Corinthians tend to believe that 18 months must be set between the composition of 1 Corinthians and Paul's final letter to Corinth. On the other hand, the journeyings between Ephesus and Corinth by Paul and his companions need not have occupied many months, for the distance was not

[1] "The History of the Origin of the So-called Second Letter to the Corinthians," *New Testament Studies,* 1962, pp. 261–2.

great. Most scholars therefore consider that the events presupposed in 2 Corinthians need not have taken more than six to eight months, and date the letter in the autumn of A.D. 55.

V. *Significance*

Second Corinthians is perhaps the most neglected of Paul's major letters and is read and studied less than his popular shorter letters (Galatians, Ephesians, Philippians). In some ways this is surprising for this letter is the most moving document that Paul has left us. It is the most autobiographical (and therefore the most revealing), and it contains some of his profoundest theological utterances. On the other hand, it must be admitted that the letter is the most obscure of the apostle's writings, alike in its historical allusions, its theological statements, and even its language (as students with a limited knowledge of Greek discover to their dismay!).

Some at least of this obscurity is due to the allusiveness of references to a historical background on which we are very imperfectly informed, but which would have been familiar to the original readers. Paul also expresses his theological ideas at times in a highly compressed manner, and he assumes an acquaintance with presuppositions that often taxes the most erudite student of his writings. For this reason there is wide disagreement on the meaning of his statements about the Spirit in the third chapter of the letter, as also on what he wrote about immortality and the theology of reconciliation in chapter 5.

Above all, however, the form of this letter suffers because Paul wrote much of it against his will. By reason of the accusations of his adversaries Paul found himself under the necessity of doing something that he would never have dreamed of doing in normal circumstances, namely, talk of himself at length. In this very letter Paul states, "What we preach is not ourselves, but Jesus Christ as Lord, with ourselves as your servants for Jesus' sake" (4:5). It is undoubtedly true that normally Paul's all absorbing theme is Christ. But here, like Peer Gynt in Ibsen's play of that name, Paul has to occupy the stage the whole time, and this goes against the grain.

Someone has referred to the letter as "a reluctant confession." [2] The suitability of that description is particularly plain in its latter chapters, where Paul extols his apostolic qualifications, and even his virtues, over against the detractors who boast of their own. In chapter 11 he repeatedly declares that he is "foolish," a "fool," and even a "madman" for talking as he does. At the conclusion of his outpourings on this theme he confesses, almost despairingly, "I have been a fool! . . . For I am not at all inferior to these superlative apostles, even though I am nothing" (12:11). A man who writes under stress of this kind is like a motorist who drives with his brakes on: he's frustrated, and he burns up!

There were the best reasons for the apostle to feel deeply as he wrote the early chapters of the letter. On the one hand he was bursting with relief at the reconciliation that had been effected with the Christian congregation at Corinth. On the other hand he had just come through a fearful experience from which he never expected to emerge alive (1:8 ff.). The passionate recital in chapter 11 of perils and sufferings through which he had passed, with its conclusion, "And, apart from other things, there is the daily pressure upon me of my anxiety for all the churches" (11:28), is strikingly illustrated and brought up to date by his circumstances at the time of writing: a further chapter in his apostolic sufferings and anxieties for the churches has just been added!

Now this painful and almost unbearable predicament of the apostle is that which, under God, gave rise to the most significant feature of the letter. For basically the letter is a dissertation on a single theme—the apostolic ministry. This it is which gives unity to its several parts.

The church needed this exposition of the

2 Von Loewenich, W., *Paul, His Life and Work* (Edinburgh: Oliver and Boyd, 1960), p. 120.

ministry. It is instructive to compare from this viewpoint 2 Corinthians with 1 Corinthians. For the earlier letter has (quite rightly) been characterized as the layman's charter. The chief purpose of its initial discussion about the relations of Paul, Apollos, and Peter to the church in Corinth is not at all to establish their authority in the church, but to appeal to the Corinthians to look to Christ, the Lord of the church, rather than to the ministers he sends them. Thereafter, in the earlier letter it is difficult to find a place for a specialized ministry in the church of Corinth, apart from the gentle plea in 16:15 f. to "recognize" the household of Stephanas. In this letter Paul devotes much space to matters of church discipline and worship, Christian doctrine, and ethics; but in all his discussions on these themes not one reference is made to the role of church officers, not even where demands are made for the rectification of abuses in the church. The impression is conveyed that the church of Corinth is essentially a charismatic community, wherein ministry is that of the membership as a whole under the leadership of the Holy Spirit.

The second letter by no means contradicts the picture of ministry portrayed in the first, but undoubtedly it provides a complement to it. For from first to last the theme in 2 Corinthians is the ministry committed to Paul the apostle, and by implication to his associates also. The emphasis falls on the authenticity of that ministry, its authority, and its role in the new dispensation. Naturally the proclamation of the gospel is stressed as paramount in the apostle's vocation. Paul actually indicates that for him apostleship and message are bound in an indissoluble unity.

In the passage which expounds the doctrine of reconciliation (ch. 5), the ministry of the word is linked with the act of reconciliation wrought by God in Christ. This feature is brought out in the New English Bible rendering: "He (God) has reconciled us men to himself through Christ, and he has enlisted us in this service of recon-

ciliation. What I mean is, that God was in Christ reconciling the world to himself . . . and that he has entrusted us with the message of reconciliation. We come therefore as Christ's ambassadors. It is as if God were appealing to you through us" (5:18 ff.). The reconciling deed finds its complement in the reconciling proclamation, and in both cases it is God who is active through his representatives (Christ on the cross and the apostle in the gospel). On this, E. Dinkler comments, "The proclamation of the event of salvation is nothing additional, but appertains to the Christ event, since God himself instituted the 'ministry,' the 'word of reconciliation' (5:18 ff.). Christ, indeed God himself, meets man in the proclamation, so that the salvation can and must be preached as something present." [3] Needless to say, the power of the proclamation lies not in the person of the preacher but in the action of God in and through the gospel.

Significantly it is precisely in those passages wherein Paul most strongly asserts the genuineness of his apostleship that we find the clearest exposition of its duality, namely, an admixture of humility and authority, of shame and glory, of suffering and vindication. The emphasis in the letter actually falls on the first element, i.e., on the adversity. To Paul that is as much an ingredient in the apostolic ministry as the cross is integral to the gospel. Sufferings rather than visions of the risen Lord are stressed by him as genuine marks of the Lord Jesus; these distinguish true apostleship from false (see 11:16 ff.). True, Paul is prepared to refer to visions granted to him as a mark of special favor (12:1 ff.), but he is aware that his power as an apostle has come not through exaltation of spirit but through weakness that has cast him on the grace of Christ.

Here we clearly recognize that in this letter Paul consistently views his sufferings as *ministry*, not as misfortune. More than once he relates his sufferings to those of Christ for the world. Not that he implies that Christ's redemptive act of reconciliation is

[3] Article "Die Korintherbriefe," in *Religion in Geschichte und Gegenwart*, 3rd ed., IV, 22.

insufficient for its purpose; but he does view his own sufferings as *for others,* as an embodiment of that love of Christ that gives itself for men. This is plain in the exposition of the ministry in chapter 4. The treasure of the gospel is placed in "earthen vessels," such as Paul, "to show that the transcendent power belongs to God and not to us" (4:7). In the discharge of his ministry he is "afflicted in every way . . . always carrying in the body the death of Jesus, so that the life of Jesus may be manifested in our bodies" (4:8 ff.). Paul then continues, "So death is at work in us, but life in you" (4:12). His sufferings are for the sake of his fellow Christians. "It is all for your sake, so that as grace extends to more and more people it may increase thanksgiving, to the glory of God" (4:15). The same principle appears in the opening doxology of chapter 1, following immediately upon the address of the letter (1: 3 ff.).

When we ponder these passages, we begin to understand why Paul places so much weight upon suffering as a mark of genuine apostleship. It is no distorted, masochistic delight of his in suffering for its own sake, but a recognition that a ministry which claims to be apostolic must follow in the footsteps of Christ who gives it, and that the life of such "sent" ones must accord with the gospel which centers on the cross of Golgotha. These are the preachers who know that Christ's power is perfected in weakness, and that when they are weak they are made strong (12:9).

There is room for reflection here on the part of ministers today, who believe that they are called to share in the apostolic task. Has the nature of apostolic ministry changed in the sight of the Lord? Is there not a call for us who preach the gospel to recognise that our vocation includes that of embodying the gospel in a life that does not bypass the hill of the cross?

Naturally, a similar reflection is needed on the part of congregations of Christ's people. Insofar as the apostolic ministry is given to the whole body of Christ, the church as a whole is called to embody its ministry in sacrificial living. Judas is not the only disciple who has shunned the cross. It is of the nature of flesh and blood to do so. The church in history has not been conspicuous for its readiness to shoulder the cross, nor is it more ready to do it today. In a time when the slogan, "The church is ministry," is being heard on all sides, the church would be wise to ponder anew the message of 2 Corinthians, that the ministry it exercises may be apostolic and not spurious.

Outline

I. An exposition of the apostolic ministry (1:1—7:16)
   1. Introductory greeting and thanksgiving (1:1–11)
   2. Paul's relations with the Corinthian church (1:12—2:17)
      (1) The sincerity of his actions (1:12–14)
      (2) The postponement of a visit to Corinth (1:15—2:4)
      (3) The treatment of the offender (2:5–11)
      (4) Thanksgiving for God's leading (2:12–17)
   3. The glory and shame of the apostolic ministry (3:1—6:10)
      (1) The ministries of the old and new covenants (3:1–11)
      (2) The allegory of the veil (3:12—4:6)
      (3) The sufferings, power, and hope of an apostle (4:7—5:10)
      (4) The apostolic gospel (5:11—6:2)
      (5) The apostolic life (6:3–10)
      (6) Appeal for an open heart and separated life (6:11—7:4)
      (7) The joy of restored relationship (7:5–16)

II. The collection for Jerusalem (8:1—9:15)
   1. Examples of generous giving (8:1–9)
   2. The plan for the collection (8:10–24)
   3. An appeal for readiness and generosity (9:1–15)

III. A defense of Paul's apostolic ministry (10:1—13:14)
   1. A rebuttal of allegations (10:1–18)
      (1) Paul's alleged cowardice (10:1–6)
      (2) Paul's alleged weakness (10:7–11)
      (3) Paul's alleged trespass beyond his bounds (10:12–18)

2. Apostolic vindication through foolish glorying (11:1—12:18)
   (1) The apostle's jealous love (11:1–6)
   (2) Paul's refusal of the Corinthians' money (11:7–15)
   (3) Paul's apostolic sufferings (11:16–33)
   (4) Visions and revelations of the Lord (12:1–10)
   (5) The true marks of an apostle (12:11–13)
   (6) Anticipations of a third visit to Corinth (12:14–21)
   (7) Admonitions in view of the third visit (13:1–10)
   (8) Farewell (13:11–14)

Selected Bibliography

BERNARD, J. H. "The Second Epistle to the Corinthians," *The Expositor's Greek Testament*, ed. W. ROBERTSON NICOL, Vol. III. London: Hodder & Stoughton, 1912.

CALVIN, JOHN. *The Second Epistle of Paul the Apostle to the Corinthians and the Epistles to Timothy, Titus and Philemon*. Tr. T. A. SMAIL. Edinburgh: Oliver & Boyd, 1964.

DENNEY, JAMES. *The Second Epistle to the Corinthians* ("The Expositor's Bible.") London: Hodder & Stoughton, 1894.

FILSON, FLOYD V. "The Second Epistle to the Corinthians," *The Interpreter's Bible*, ed. GEORGE ARTHUR BUTTRICK, Vol. X. New York: Abingdon Press, 1953.

HANSON, R. P. C. *II Corinthians* ("Torch Bible Commentaries.") London: S.C.M. Press, 1954.

HERING, JEAN. *The Second Epistle of S. Paul to the Corinthians*. London: Epworth Press, 1969.

HUGHES, PHILIP E. *Paul's Second Epistle to the Corinthians* ("The New London Commentary on the New Testament.") London: Marshall, Morgan and Scott, Ltd., 1961.

PLUMMER, ALFRED. *A Critical and Exegetical Commentary on the Second Epistle of St. Paul to the Corinthians* ("The International Critical Commentary.") Edinburgh: T. & T. Clark, 1915.

STRACHAN, R. H. *The Second Epistle of Paul to the Corinthians* ("The Moffatt New Testament Commentary.") London: Hodder & Stoughton, 1935.

TASKER, R. V. G. *The Second Epistle of Paul to the Corinthians* ("Tyndale New Testament Commentaries.") London: The Tyndale Press, 1958.

Commentary on the Text

I. An Exposition of the Apostolic Ministry (1:1—7:16)

1. Introductory Greeting and Thanksgiving (1:1–11)

¹ Paul, an apostle of Christ Jesus by the will of God, and Timothy our brother.

To the church of God which is at Corinth, with all the saints who are in the whole of Achaia:

² Grace to you and peace from God our Father and the Lord Jesus Christ. ³ Blessed be the God and Father of our Lord Jesus Christ, the Father of mercies and God of all comfort, ⁴ who comforts us in all our affliction, so that we may be able to comfort those who are in any affliction, with the comfort with which we ourselves are comforted by God. ⁵ For as we share abundantly in Christ's sufferings, so through Christ we share abundantly in comfort too. ⁶ If we are afflicted, it is for your comfort and salvation; and if we are comforted, it is for your comfort, which you experience when you patiently endure the same sufferings that we suffer. ⁷ Our hope for you is unshaken; for we know that as you share in our sufferings, you will also share in our comfort.

⁸ For we do not want you to be ignorant, brethren, of the affliction we experienced in Asia; for we were so utterly, unbearably crushed that we despaired of life itself. ⁹ Why, we felt that we had received the sentence of death; but that was to make us rely not on ourselves but on God who raises the dead; ¹⁰ he delivered us from so deadly a peril, and he will deliver us; on him we have set our hope that he will deliver us again. ¹¹ You also must help us by prayer, so that many will give thanks on our behalf for the blessing granted us in answer to many prayers.

Paul's way of beginning a letter sounds strange to us, and even stilted, but he simply followed the standard practice of his time. This was for the writer to announce his name and that of the persons he addressed in the third person, and to follow on with a greeting in the second person. Often the greeting took the form of a pious wish or prayer. What for many was pure formality (like our "Dear Mr. Smith") was taken with intense seriousness by Paul. Every line of the opening greeting of this letter is burdened with meaning.

Paul plunges into the theme of his letter and takes his stance in its very first phrase: *Paul, an apostle of Christ Jesus by the will of God.* That is what all the fuss was about at Corinth! Was Paul an apostle? And who made him one? In the first breath of his dictation Paul declares himself. He is a representative of Jesus Christ—a "sent one." He is no self-made man: *God* appointed him!

Timothy, by contrast, is not an apostle. He is a *brother,* i.e., fellow Christian. The first person plural, *our* brother, indicates a use of the common editorial "we," and it appears throughout the letter. It is a literary device, in part used for the sake of humility, and does not imply the presence of a conjoint author.

With *the church of God . . . at Corinth* are bracketed *all the saints who are in the whole of Achaia.* Because the church is God's church, it is holy (that is what holy means: it denotes that which belongs to God). And such is the name given to Christians: they are *saints,* i.e., holy people, God's people. The term connotes not so much what they are as whose they are. With the Christians of Corinth are associated those of *Achaia.* Strictly speaking, this term should take in the whole Roman province of that name, south of Macedonia. The suggestion then arises that we have before us a circular letter, but the situation is too specific for that. Perhaps, as Tasker comments, Paul "flatters the Corinthians" by this virtual identification of the province with their own city.

Peace was as common a greeting to the Easterner as hello is to the Westerner, and doubtless it often meant no more. But it could include all that we mean by salvation, and that is just what it did mean to Paul.

For which reason he always linked it in his greetings with *grace.* So far as we know, grace had not been a greeting before Paul made it one. It was his favorite word to denote God's gracious action in Christ from the incarnation to the advent in glory. Accordingly one could never wish anyone anything greater than what Paul wished the Corinthians: *grace . . . and peace from God our Father and the Lord Jesus Christ.* He who had that, had all that God could give.

It is striking that the apostle's first utterance after the greeting is a doxology. A sentence or two later he will speak of a dreadful experience which he has lately endured, and which he thought was the end of the journey for him. How easily he might have begun his letter with a sigh! Or he could have reflected sadly on the burdensomeness of life, as in the Chinese drinking song that Mahler set to music, "Dark is life, dark is death." Not so Paul! The skies may be black and the earth totter, but the Lord holds his hand and leads him on. *Blessed* be his name!

But what is his name? *The God and Father of our Lord Jesus Christ.* He is the God whom Jesus revealed in his word and action and to whom he yielded loving obedience every step of his way, the God whom he called *Father,* because he is the unique Son of God. He is the God whom Jesus taught us also to call Father, because the Father loves us, too, and has adopted us into his family (see John 20:17; Gal. 4:4 f.; Rom. 8:14–17). He is *the Father of mercies,* i.e., the merciful God, whose principle of action is mercy (ponder what Jesus thought of this; cf. Matt. 5:48 with Luke 6:36), and *the God of all comfort,* i.e., the God who bestows comfort adequate for every need.

The comfort of God, however, is not bestowed upon us to make us comfortable. It is given so that *we may be able to comfort those who are in any affliction.* Paul is writing as an apostle, called to serve and build up the church of Christ. He is conscious that the Lord does this not alone through the ministry of the word but also through the ministry of suffering. In his experience of this, he learns the meaning and the power of grace in life, and so is able powerfully to testify for the inspiration of God's people everywhere (the way Paul learned this lesson is recounted more fully in 12: 7–10).

Paul describes his sufferings as *Christ's sufferings.* There is a history in this term worth recounting. Pious Jews who looked for the kingdom of God anticipated that the woes or sufferings of the Messiah should precede that kingdom; these were sufferings that men must endure before the Messiah arrived. When the fulfillment of Israel's hope did arrive, the reverse of what they expected happened: the Messiah suffered for them. In the New Testament the sufferings of Christ represent what the Saviour endured to redeem men for the kingdom. With the resurrecton of Christ they constituted a once-for-all event, so decisive that it brought the turn of the ages and the new creation into being. But the-once-for-all event became the pattern of life for the heirs of the kingdom. They are baptized into the dying and rising of the first Easter, that they might exemplify the power of this event every day (Rom. 6:3–11).

Paul speaks of sharing Christ's sufferings; literally, his words may be rendered, "as the sufferings of the Christ overflow to us, so through Christ our consolation overflows too." L. S. Thornton saw in this an instance of the teaching of the New Testament, that the law of the messianic life of suffering is carried over from the Messiah to his people. "There is an overflow of the Messiah's sufferings; and the apostle's afflictions are part of that overflow. Messiahship is rooted in suffering, and this law continues in the church." [4] Observe that the apostle's sufferings are not said to move Christ to pity so that he suffers with the apostle in sympathy. On the contrary, the Lord calls the apostle to enter into the principle of suffering for others that was perfectly embodied

in his atonement, and he grants him to know his own joy in self-giving (cf. Heb. 12:2). In turn the apostle encourages the church also to endure the same kind of suffering, that the Christians too may experience the joy of being a blessing for others (vv. 5 ff.).

This teaching is entirely in harmony with that of Jesus when he warned his disciples of sufferings ahead of them, precisely in the context of Christian witness and service (see Matt. 5:10 f.; Mark 13:9 ff.; John 16: 33). Suffering, it would seem, is part of the church's mission. "No stone of the 'house' can experience another destiny than that which is meted out to the Christ as its corner- and foundation stone," wrote G. Gloege.[5] But that applies to Easter as well as to Good Friday! And so the consolation abounds beyond all desolation.

The precise nature of the unbearable experience in Asia (vv. 8ff.) is not told. The strong language that is used in describing it is hardly met by the supposition of a severe illness, still less by thinking that Paul was *unbearably crushed* by the news of what was happening at Corinth, as some suggest. We know that Paul had a stormy ministry in Ephesus (cf. Acts 20:19; 1 Cor. 15:32). Some such furious onslaught as the Demetrius affair (Acts 19:23 ff.) would suit Paul's statement here. *We felt that we received the sentence of death.* That is a paraphrase, for Paul did not actually say, *We felt that.* He declared that he "had received" the death sentence, that he might set his reliance on God. Like Jesus in Gethsemane, Paul came to terms with death, accepted it from the hand of God, and looked to God for vindication. As many a time before, Paul walked yet again by Calvary's hill, and he experienced a resurrection. He had come to know God as *the God who raises the dead.* That is his name, and that is his character. Every day he repeats the miracle of Easter. Paul anticipates that he himself will experience it again and again in the future.

4 *The Common Life in the Body of Christ* (London: Dacre Press, 3d. ed., 1950), p. 34.

5 *Reich Gottes und Kirche* (Gütersloh, 1929), p. 340.

The principle of v. 11 is to be pondered: when many pray for an apostle, many have cause to bless God for his response to their entreaties. The joy of the man prayed for is multiplied in the joy of those who pray for him. "This," wrote Denney (p. 30), "is the ideal of an evangelist's life; in all its incidents and emergencies, in all its perils and salvations, it ought to float in an atmosphere of prayer." Happy the evangelist and happy the minister who has such partners in prayer! And happy are the partners!

2. Paul's Relations with the Corinthian Church (1:12—2:17)

(1) The Sincerity of His Actions (1:12-14)

¹² For our boast is this, the testimony of our conscience that we have behaved in the world, and still more toward you, with holiness and godly sincerity, not by earthly wisdom but by the grace of God. ¹³ For we write you nothing but what you can read and understand; I hope you will understand fully, ¹⁴ as you have understood in part, that you can be proud of us as we can be of you, on the day of the Lord Jesus.

The conjunction *for* at the beginning of v. 12 indicates that Paul can ask for the prayers of the church at Corinth (v. 11) because he has always pursued his ministry with a clear conscience. But why should he lay such stress on this *boast* of his? Paul attached importance to this feature of his conduct (cf. 2:17), doubtless because it had been denied. His assertion of it in Acts (23:1; 24:16) is instructive, and especially the high priest's order to smite the mouth that uttered the profession of sincerity: the high priest did not believe him, and neither did some people at Corinth.

The reference to the hoped-for intelligibility of his letters in v. 13 provides the clue to the reason for the denial of his sincerity here: it was alleged that Paul was insincere in his letters, that he professed one thing but meant another. On the contrary, says Paul, *we write you nothing but what you can read and understand.* He makes no reservations in what he writes. The Corinthians ought to have known Paul well enough to

refuse the allegations. They *have understood in part*—but only in part! He hopes that eventually they *will understand fully*, and so be as *proud* of him *on the day of the Lord Jesus* as he will be of them. This reflects Paul's characteristic confidence. At the judgment seat of Christ the naked truth about men will become known as their secret thoughts and deeds stand revealed (Luke 8:17; Rom. 2:16). But the apostle is confident that both he and the Corinthians will pass the test and that, when the Lord vindicates him, the Corinthians will be proud of him just as he will be of them. The implication is that if they can but understand him aright, they may be proud of him even today!

(2) The Postponement of a Visit to Corinth (1:15—2:4)

In the belief that the Corinthians shared such an attitude toward him, Paul planned to pay a double visit to Corinth, on his journeys to and from Macedonia, and so give them "a double pleasure" (v. 16). When writing earlier he had anticipated only a single stay with them (1 Cor. 16:5 ff.), which was to take place on his way back from Macedonia. Presumably he had somehow communicated to the Corinthians his change of plan.

¹⁵ Because I was sure of this, I wanted to come to you first, so that you might have a double pleasure; ¹⁶ I wanted to visit you on my way to Macedonia, and to come back to you from Macedonia and have you send me on my way to Judea. ¹⁷ Was I vacillating when I wanted to do this? Do I make my plans like a worldly man, ready to say Yes and No at once? ¹⁸ As surely as God is faithful, our word to you has not been Yes and No. ¹⁹ For the Son of God, Jesus Christ, whom we preached among you, Silvanus and Timothy and I, was not Yes and No; but in him it is always Yes. ²⁰ For all the promises of God find their Yes in him. That is why we utter the Amen through him, to the glory of God. ²¹ But it is God who establishes us with you in Christ, and has commissioned us; ²² he has put his seal upon us and given us his Spirit in our hearts as a guarantee.

The unexpected turn of events, in which the Corinthians manifested their hostility toward Paul, caused him to modify his plan again. A twofold and prolonged visit to Corinth would not have been *a double pleasure,* either for them or for him. This further change of plan brought him sharp criticism: he was charged with saying *Yes and No* in the same breath; that is, he was fickle, covered up his real intentions, and was not to be trusted.

This was a serious allegation, for, if it were established, how could anyone take his preaching seriously? Paul therefore replies, *Our word to you has not been Yes and No.* He here includes the *word* he preached and the *word* he pledged, whether by letter or verbally, concerning everyday affairs. The content of his gospel is *the Son of God, Jesus Christ,* and there is nothing equivocal about him. The coming of Jesus was God's long, loud *Yes* to his purposes of grace and his promises declared in the Old Testament scriptures.

All the promises of God find their Yes in him. All that God had promised to achieve in and for Israel and the whole world, culminating in the kingdom of grace and glory, finds its affirmation and its fulfillment in Jesus. The incarnation, the cross, and resurrection of our Lord, with the gift of the Spirit sent by him from on high, brought into being the kingdom of new life; and its consummation will be effected through him. In recognition of this *we utter the Amen through him;* we own that God has kept his word through Christ and will ever do so. This we do in our meetings for worship as we declare our faith in and gratitude to God in a resounding *Amen.*

Early Christians were renowned for the way they unitedly voiced their *Amen,* and if we could revive the custom today it would undoubtedly be *to the glory of God.* But *the Amen* can be uttered and *the glory of God* furthered by life as well as tongue. This too will have been in Paul's mind. The binding thread of the argument in vv. 15 ff. is the presupposition that Paul could not preach the gospel of God's faithfulness to his pledged word and at the same time be faithless to his own word. The gospel of truth works truth, and the preacher without

truthfulness is the worst of hypocrites. To avoid such a state was Paul's life long concern (1:12 ff.). The like anxiety will be shared by every man who stands in the apostolic succession of proclamation.

Faithfulness in the servants of the word, however, is not only, or even primarily, a matter of their own striving. *It is God who establishes us with you in Christ.* He who "made firm" the pledged word of ancient times in the redemptive action of Christ makes men firm in Christ. The thought is suggested by the association of the Hebrew term *Amen* with the Hebrew verb to confirm, make firm, be trustworthy. In Isaiah 65:16 the phrase rendered "the God of truth" is really the God of the Amen. We say Amen to God and trust him, and he says Amen to us and preserves us.

This God does in a remarkable way: he *has commissioned us* and *he has put his seal upon us.* In so reproducing Paul's words the RSV translators have been influenced by the belief that Paul was speaking of himself as an apostle. But the term *commissioned* here is actually anointed. The connection is perceived if we render, "God establishes us with you in the Anointed One, and he has anointed us," or, "God establishes us with you in the Christ, and he has christed us." How did God anoint Jesus to be the Christ? "God anointed Jesus of Nazareth with the Holy Spirit and with power," said Peter (Acts 10:38). So also it is here stated, "God has anointed us; he has put his seal upon us and given us his Spirit in our hearts," The language clearly extends to every believer.

The Holy Spirit is here said to be given for a twofold purpose: to enable us to serve God and his kingdom, as Jesus did, and to confirm that we shall inherit the kingdom. We are "the Lord's anointed"! United with Christ by the Spirit, we are saved by him to be his instruments of salvation. Both *seal* and *guarantee* are figures to represent the gift of the Spirit himself, rather than gifts from the Spirit. Through him we are "stamped" as belonging to God and reserved for the kingdom of glory (Eph.

4:30).

The term rendered *guarantee* in ordinary speech meant a pledge or down payment on an article with the understanding that the payment of the first installment guaranteed that the rest of the money would follow. The Holy Spirit therefore is God's "down payment" or "first installment" of the kingdom. In the Old Testament prophets the Spirit is promised as God's gift for the coming kingdom (e.g. Ezek. 37:14 f.; Joel 2:28 ff.). The fact that he has been sent by the risen Lord is both a sign that the kingdom has come and a guarantee to those who receive him of participation in the totality of God's salvation when the kingdom is revealed in fulness (Eph. 1:13 f.).

²³ But I call God to witness against me—it was to spare you that I refrained from coming to Corinth. ²⁴ Not that we lord it over your faith; we work with you for your joy, for you stand firm in your faith.

¹ For I made up my mind not to make you another painful visit. ² For if I cause you pain, who is there to make me glad but the one whom I have pained? ³ And I wrote as I did, so that when I came I might not be pained by those who should have made me rejoice, for I felt sure of all of you, that my joy would be the joy of you all. ⁴ For I wrote you out of much affliction and anguish of heart and with many tears, not to cause you pain but to let you know the abundant love that I have for you.

Having given assurance of his truthfulness, Paul now reveals the reason for the nonfullfillment of his promise to make a double visit to Corinth: *it was to spare you.* To emphasize the truth of what he is saying he introduces it with a kind of oath: *I call God to witness against me.* This not only implies that God knows Paul is telling the truth, but it calls on God to take action against him if he is speaking falsehood; and in the biblical setting that is virtually an appeal to God to take his life (cf. Acts 5:1 ff.). That Paul was prepared to use such language shows the strength of mistrust towards him that he knew existed in Corinth. But the motive *to spare you* also indicates the sense of authority that he was conscious of exercising in Christ's name in

the churches (cf. 1. Cor. 4:21).

On the other hand, Paul was equally conscious of the limit of this authority: *not that we lord it over your faith . . . for you stand firm in your faith.* The Lord Jesus is the ground of their faith, he and no other; and he is the Lord over their faith, he and no other. Elsewhere Paul rebukes the man who criticizes his brother in Christ; for there is one alone who is the Master of a Christian, and to him he stands or falls; but indeed the Lord is able to make him stand (see Rom. 14:4). Paul has no desire to usurp Christ's position in the church. On the contrary, *we work with you for your joy.* That is the goal of apostolic labor—joy. "Paul regarded that as an essential mark of the Church," wrote Adolf Schlatter. "If it was lacking, then the message of Jesus had either not been received or it had been given up; if it wavered, then faith also wavered." ⁶

With such a goal before him, Paul was unable earlier to contemplate fulfilling his promise of a double visit to Corinth, for that would have multiplied pain and not joy. *I made up my mind not to make you another painful visit.* Clearly this relates to a recent painful visit that Paul had made to Corinth; it was not the visit on which the church had been founded. This one had proved to be a grievous occasion for them and for him, and he had no intention of precipitating another experience like it. *For if I cause you pain, who is there to make me glad?* asks Paul. The implication of the sentence that follows is that no one can make Paul glad if he causes the Corinthians pain; in such a case he has no joy at all. This meaning becomes clear if, with Jean Hering, we render the latter part of v. 2, "Certainly not the one whom I have pained."

Instead of making a further painful visit, therefore, Paul wrote a painful letter. That this was not to provide Paul with an easy way out of a difficulty is made clear in v. 4; on the contrary, the letter cost him *much*

⁶ *Paulus, der Bote Jesu,* p. 485.

affliction and anguish of heart and . . . many tears. Nor did he write the letter to punish the Corinthians; rather, he says, it was to *let you know the abundant love that I have for you,* and so restore the sundered fellowship and the lost joy.

Denney rightly calls attention to the example here provided of the manner and the motive which a man of God should have when he has to administer a rebuke or discipline God's people: not by fiercely denouncing and assailing them, but to take the way God took in dealing with sin—the costly way of the cross. "Depend upon it, we shall not make others weep for that for which we have not wept; we shall not make that touch the hearts of others which has not first touched our own. That is the law which God has established in the world; He submitted to it Himself in the person of His Son, and He requires us to submit to it" (Denney, p. 70).

He who exercises authority in that way fulfills Christ's word to his own disciples (Mark 10:45) and in his company learns the meaning of redemptive suffering.

(3) *The Treatment of the Offender* (2:5-11)

5 But if any one has caused pain, he has caused it not to me, but in some measure—not to put it too severely—to you all. 6 For such a one this punishment by the majority is enough; 7 so you should rather turn to forgive and comfort him, or he may be overwhelmed by excessive sorrow. 8 So I beg you to reaffirm your love for him. 9 For this is why I wrote, that I might test you and know whether you are obedient in everything. 10 Any one whom you forgive, I also forgive. What I have forgiven, if I have forgiven anything, has been for your sake in the presence of Christ, 11 to keep Satan from gaining the advantage over us; for we are not ignorant of his designs.

The studied ambiguity of Paul's references to the offending church member in vv. 5 ff. and 7:12, and to the offended person in 7:12, is exasperating to the historian trying to reconstruct the story of Paul's relations with the church at Corinth; but for those seeking guidance on how to handle offenders in the church, it is instructive. For Paul

manifests so great a delicacy and tact that it is difficult for us, who are wholly dependent on his writings for our information, to discover who it was who gave the offense and who was offended. This hints where Paul's real concern lay: not on his own vindication but on the restoration of the offender to God and of peace to the church. Once these aims were accomplished the offense could be dismissed.

Until recent times it was commonly held that the offender must have been the man referred to in 1 Cor. 5:1 ff., who was living with his father's wife and whom Paul had demanded that the church should discipline. For a discussion of this matter, the reader is referred to the section in the Introduction relating to the occasion and purpose of the letter. Here we content ourselves with adducing one consideration which makes the proposed identification unlikely.

From 7:12 it appears that the man who had been wronged was alive when Paul wrote this letter. If incest is in view, then the son was actually cohabiting with his father's wife while the father was still living —a most grave state of affairs. Yet Paul declares that in requesting the church to discipline the offender he had neither the sinner in mind nor the one sinned against, i.e. neither the son nor the father, but (in his own words) *that I might test you and know whether you are obedient in everything,* and—still more astonishingly—"that your zeal for us might be revealed to you in the sight of God" (7:12). It is extremely difficult to believe that Paul could have written in such terms about a man guilty of the incest described. Let one compare the sense of moral shock with which Paul wrote 1 Corinthians 5 with the smoothing over of the offense in 2 Corinthians 2:5-11; 7:8-12, and one will surely be compelled to the view that the two situations are unrelated.

The references to the wronged man (7:12), to the pain which was given to Paul himself (2:5), to his own ready forgiveness of the wrongdoer (2:10), and to his motive for demanding rectification of the wrong as a desire to reveal the Corinthians' zeal for him, are all most easily explained if the wronged man was Paul himself. The offense presumably will have consisted of an attack on Paul in public, when his apostolicity was denied, as also his integrity, and possibly even his honesty in money matters (cf. 12:17 f.).

From the mildness of tone in vv. 5 ff. and the call for gentleness in dealing with the offender, we gather that the man had repented of his wrong and that the church was in need of guidance as to how to proceed. In v. 5 Paul does two things: he both lessens the gravity of the offense (*if any one has caused pain;* cf. v. 10 ,*What I have forgiven*), and at the same time extends its scope (*he has caused it not to me, but . . . to you all*), thereby indicating that the whole church had been injured by the offender's actions. *Punishment* has been inflicted *by the majority.* Does this mean that the decision relating to the offender had not been unanimous? If so, we do not know the reason for the difference of opinion, whether some had wished not to inflict discipline on him or some had wished to punish him yet more severely for his wrong. Whatever the truth, Paul views the action that had been taken by the church as *enough,* so the church should now *turn to forgive and comfort him.*

Yet more, Paul writes, *I beg you to reaffirm your love for him.* The term *reaffirm* is significant. It is presumed that the Corinthians had not ceased to love the sinful member, either in his offense or in their infliction of discipline upon him. Yet the discipline could hardly fail to affect the relations between the erring member and the church, and it was desirable that the man should know without doubt the continued love of the fellowship for him.

The reason for Paul's writing his grievous letter had not been that pain might be inflicted upon the man who wronged him, but that the authenticity of the church might be tested and demonstrated: *that I might test you and know whether you are obedient in everything.* Did Paul wish to know whether the Corinthians *were obedi-*

ent in everything to himself? It is doubtful that we should answer yes, without qualification, to that question. Paul speaks of his task as being to "take every thought captive to obey Christ, being ready to punish every disobedience, when your obedience is complete" (10:5 f.). Paul labors to bring men into obedience to Christ (cf. Rom. 1:15), and only insofar as it serves this supreme purpose does he ever ask for obedience to himself. In the light of 10:5 f. it is better to think of his purpose in writing the painful letter as being to test the Corinthians' obedience to Christ.

Anyone whom you forgive, I also forgive. Paul is ready to unite himself with the Corinthians in their forgiveness and in their restoration of the offender. But the force of the sentence that follows should not be overlooked: *What I have forgiven . . . has been for your sake.* It was for the sake of the church that Paul was unable to dismiss the slander of his apostolic office, and was compelled to demand rectification of the wrong; equally, it was for the sake of the church that he pardons the man on his repentance. The wholeness, holiness, peace, and joy of the fellowship was of greater importance than either Paul's status or the offender's folly. For this reason Paul declares the forgiveness of the penitent man *in the presence of Christ.* Both the discipline of sinning church members and the remission of discipline take place in Christ's presence and thereby have his concurrence, authority, and power (cf. 1 Cor. 5:3 ff.).

The clause *if I have forgiven anything* may emphasize the nature of the offense as a church matter: although directed against Paul, the sin was against the church, hence the church's forgiveness was of primary importance and the apostle's concurrence secondary. The NEB however renders the clause, "so far as there is anything for me to forgive," and Plummer describes it as "a gracious parenthesis." It would seem that since the matter had now been completely put right, Paul dismisses it as of small moment. Had the issue been otherwise, naturally the apostle would have made no such comment.

Not the least motive in forgiving the offender and restoring him to fellowship is *to keep Satan from gaining advantage over us.* The *advantage* would have been gained by Satan if the offender had been left unrebuked, and so allowed to exercise unchecked an evil influence in the church. But it would equally occur if the man were treated too harshly, for then he might be lost to the community and to faith. As in converting men from sin, so in restoring the erring church member, God's people need the Holy Spirit's guidance and help to take wise and right actions.

(4) Thanksgiving for God's Leading (2: 12-17)

12 When I came to Troas to preach the gospel of Christ, a door was opened for me in the Lord; 13 but my mind could not rest because I did not find my brother Titus there. So I took leave of them and went on to Macedonia.
14 But thanks be to God, who in Christ always leads us in triumph, and through us spreads the fragrance of the knowledge of him everywhere. 15 For we are the aroma of Christ to God among those who are being saved and among those who are perishing, 16 to one a fragrance from death to death, to the other a fragrance from life to life. Who is sufficient for these things? 17 For we are not, like so many, peddlers of God's word; but as men of sincerity, as commissioned by God, in the sight of God we speak in Christ.

At this point Paul resumes the account of his movements and motives, which so far he has given in mere snatches (1:8,15,23). Surprisingly, however, he again provides no more than a mere fragment of the story. The memory of his anxious days of waiting for Titus, which he now makes known to the Corinthians, leads him to recall the way God removed the burden of anxiety through the coming of Titus. Instead of stating that plainly, he bursts into a doxology of praise to God, who has given him so glorious a ministry and who so wonderfully leads him in it. In turn this gives place to a series of meditations on the nature of the apostolic ministry committed to him (chs. 3—6). Not until 7:5 ff. does he complete the story re-

lated in vv. 12 f. It is extraordinary to contemplate that the heart of this letter, namely Paul's declarations concerning the ministry, is a digression. If that be so, we may thank God for Paul's habit of digressing! It is possible however that Paul intended from the outset to convey the thoughts set down in chapters 3—6, but that he began his letter without any fixed ideas as to the point at which he would introduce them.

From Ephesus Paul journeyed to the seaport of *Troas.* This had been his port of embarkation on his first momentous journey to Macedonia to begin his evangelistic labors in Europe (Acts 16:8 ff.). Evidently he had arranged to meet Titus at Troas on the latter's return from Corinth, but at the same time he planned to use the opportunity *to preach the gospel of Christ* there. The success of the preaching was encouraging: *a door was opened for me in the Lord.* It was none other than the Lord himself who opened up the way for a powerful work through the gospel, and Paul felt a constraint to obey the Lord's leading. *In the Lord* is related to the phrase "in Christ," but it has the implication of necessity for obedience.

Nevertheless, the apostle was torn in heart. He recollects, *my mind could not rest because I did not find my brother Titus there.* The RSV translators have paraphrased here. In this passage *mind* is really *spirit,* and the spirit is that aspect of man's constitution that is responsible to the Spirit of God. What a terrible dilemma, Paul then felt himself to be in! His own spirit tugged him in two directions—to Corinth and to Troas, and God's Spirit pressed on him two concerns—for the lost of Troas who should be won and for the waverers of Corinth who could be lost! In his agony of soul the pastor won the battle against the evangelist. Paul felt compelled to take leave of the Christians in Troas and cross the sea to find Titus in Macedonia.

The change of tone in v. 14, for which no preparation is made in the earlier sentences, finds its explanation in 7:5 ff., the content of which may be presumed to be in Paul's mind at this point. Paul's anxiety is turned into abounding joy through the news which Titus brought of the Corinthians' repentance. The transformation of the scene in Corinth, from one of disorder and disobedience into one of repentance and renewal of love, is typical of Paul's experience of the grace of God in his ministry. He therefore utters a doxology that celebrates the working of God's grace in his ministry: *Thanks be to God, who in Christ always leads us in triumph!* The picture invoked in these words is a stirring one. It is that of the triumphal procession, which in ancient times was accorded to a famous general on his homecoming after years of absence in the field and gaining notable victories. The conqueror would ride in his chariot, accompanied by trusted lieutenants on horses and followed by a train of captives in chains and the spoils of war.

Ironically, one of the best preserved monuments of ancient Rome is the Arch of Titus in the Forum, erected to commemorate his annihilating victory over the Jews and his destruction of the Temple in Jerusalem (A.D. 70). The arch depicts the magnificent triumphal procession that was staged for Titus, and in the procession the seven-branched lampstand, taken from the Temple, is prominently featured. Paul would have been saddened beyond words had he lived to see that arch in Rome, but it would not have made him change a word of what he wrote in this passage. For it gives expression to the central conviction of his life, namely that God has wrought the decisive victory of the ages in the death and resurrection of Christ, and that henceforth history is the scene of God's triumphal march to the final manifestation in glory of the kingdom that Christ has brought.

The apostolic ministry is not merely a witness to that triumph march but is a part of it. It celebrates the victory over the powers of sin and death; and in proclaiming the glorious news it invites men and women to share in the blessings of the deliverance that has been won. This is a magnificent conception of the Christian ministry. It sees the ministry not as a funeral procession on the way to the grave, however incomprehensively gloomy some of the proclaimers may be, but as a triumphant procession from the empty tomb of Christ to his coming in power and glory. Moreover, the Lord who wrought his victory in the turn of the ages, and is to manifest it at the end of all ages, perpetually displays his power in the ministry of his servants, as Paul constantly experienced and as the events at Corinth bore witness. The happy issue of the crisis in Corinth was contemporary evidence that God *always leads* his servants in triumph.

What place does the apostle have in God's triumph march? Calvin, followed by some modern exegetes, thought that Paul had a place in it comparable to that of the victor's associates, who rode by his side in the procession; for Paul, like the commander's officers, had fought great battles and had gained notable victories for the Lord. In a comparable way Christ's ministers at all times take their honored place in the victory procession.

This interpretation is almost certainly mistaken. The only other New Testament passage in which the word (in Greek) "leads in triumph" is found (Col. 2:15) gives it an almost identical significance as it has here. God, through the death and resurrection of Christ is said to have "disarmed the principalities and powers . . . triumphing over them in him" (RSV), or as we could equally well translate, "leading them in the train of his triumph." As the Lord had conquered the spiritual powers and displayed his victory over them, so Christ triumphed over Paul, defeating his obstinate pride and sinful unbelief. He displayed his power in him by transforming his rebellious opposition to a willingness to follow him in love as his adoring servant. It is characteristic of Paul that he should claim, not the place beside the victorious Lord in his triumph march, but that of the opponent who had been overcome—conquered by grace and chained to the Saviour's chariot by a bond of love that answered to the unfathomable love of the Victor.

Through us . . . , adds Paul, *God . . . spreads the fragrance of the knowledge of him everywhere.* The picture of the triumph march is probably still in mind. On those occasions the victor's path was marked by clouds of incense rising from censers burning along the route. So, too, the knowledge of God is spread abroad by the apostolic preachers as they proclaim the victory of the Lord in his redemptive acts and his contemporary presence along the highways of history. In truth, this is a *fragrance* of a costly kind—of freedom, life, and salvation, imparting confidence, joy, and hope. It is to be observed, however, that the apostle not only spreads the fragrance of the knowledge of God through the gospel but is in his own person *the aroma of Christ to God.* In the service of the gospel the preacher and the preaching are inseparably conjoined.

The figure of the triumph march lends itself to such a thought. But we can hardly overlook the well-known biblical concept that an acceptable sacrifice is a fragrance well pleasing to God: "Christ loved us and gave himself up for us, a fragrant offering and sacrifice to God" (Eph. 5:2). The apostolic preacher of the cross is himself, in his proclamation, a fragrant reminder of Christ to God—a humbling thought for any preacher!

But the messenger of Christ is *an aroma of Christ* not only to God but also to men, as he moves among them and bears witness to them. Yet how different are the reactions of men to the aroma of Christ in the gospel and its preachers! To *those who are perishing* it is *a fragrance from death.* It is a reminder of death, it has the odor of death about it. To such people it is as unwelcome as death itself, and is therefore repelled by them as disgusting; but the rejection of Christ in his gospel and messengers leads *to death.* Similarly, the gospel and the preachers of Christ appear to those who are *being saved* as *the fragrance from life*—the aroma from the garden of the resurrection on Easter morning! Their acceptance of the good news leads *to life.* They possess it now,

and they will possess it in fullness on the day of final resurrection, of which Easter is the promise and the pledge.

Such a difference in the effects of the aroma of Christ on people could be compared with the different effects that the fragrance from the censers in the triumph parades must have had on the crowds who welcomed their conqueror and on the hapless victims who were dragged along in the procession: for the crowds it was a fragrance of victory, for the men in chains it was a smell of doom. In view of Paul's application of the figure, it is unlikely that this particular application was in his mind. But there was a view current among the rabbis, according to which the law of God was a medicine for life or a medicine for death (i.e., a poison), the difference being determined by the attitude of its recipients. It was held that when a man studied the law for its own sake it became to him a means of healing for life, but if he studied it for his own selfish ends it became to him a means of death.

If Paul knew that teaching, he would have rejected it, for no man had taken the law more seriously than he did. But he experienced it as a means of death. (Paul actually expounds this theme in the next chapter.) It would be consistent with Paul's teaching elsewhere if he had been acquainted with this element of rabbinic instruction and had claimed for Christ and the gospel what the rabbis had claimed for the law. He himself had received life through Christ in the gospel, and he had witnessed the like effect in the lives of countless others who had received it in faith; but he had also observed violent reactions against the gospel, and above all had been grieved that it had become a supreme stumbling block to Israel (cf. 1 Cor. 1:18 ff.; Rom. 9—11). It was a wonderful privilege to be the means of life for men, but it was a grief to be the agent of their judgment.

It is small wonder that Paul, in horror at the dread responsibility that fell to him as a herald of the gospel, exclaims, *Who is sufficient for these things?* The answer is not given at once, but there can be little doubt that the context demands the answer, Nobody. Any sensitive man is overwhelmed by the thought that he has been appointed to be, in himself and in his message, a means of life to some men and a means of death to others. None but God can enable a man to match the demands of such a ministry (so Paul says explicitly in 3:5).

Nevertheless, Paul recalls that there are men, including preachers who have been active in Corinth, who regard themselves as completely self-sufficient and who pervert the gospel in their ministry. These he calls *peddlers of God's word.* The term *peddlers* brings to mind the thought of hawkers standing at street corners or going from house to house with cheap wares, which they try to talk up with persuasive patter. In Paul's time it especially related to sellers of wine, whether merchants or tavern keepers. The writer Lucian spoke of philosophers who sold the sciences and were like innkeepers who gave bad measure after adulterating and falsifying what they sold. The purpose of adulterating wine of course was to make more money. In using the term *peddlers* Paul will have chiefly had in view men who preached the word of God to make an easy living out of it. So it is clearly in place to observe that such men were ready to accommodate the gospel to make it more acceptable, and so line their pockets more easily.

What an incomprehensible way of life it is, to occupy an office that spells life or death for men and abase it so as to make it like a stand in the gutter for the sale of adulterated Coca Cola at twice the usual price! Such is the effect of a ministry that uses it for self-advantage instead of Christ's glory. In rejecting all such expedients Paul enunciates the ideal for every man of God: *as men of sincerity, as commissioned by God, in the sight of God we speak in Christ.* He who knows that he has been sent by God into the ministry, who exercises that ministry perpetually as *in the sight of God,* and who speaks in the consciousness of being in fellowship with Christ, his life and his Lord,

will find it impossible to be other than a man of sincerity.

3. The Glory and Shame of the Apostolic Ministry (3:1—6:10)

(1) The Ministries of the Old and New Covenants (3:1–11)

[1] Are we beginning to commend ourselves again? Or do we need, as some do, letters of recommendation to you, or from you? [2] You yourselves are our letter of recommendation, written on your hearts, to be known and read by all men; [3] and you show that you are a letter from Christ delivered by us, written not with ink but with the Spirit of the living God, not on tablets of stone but on tablets of human hearts.

[4] Such is the confidence that we have through Christ toward God. [5] Not that we are sufficient of ourselves to claim anything as coming from us; our sufficiency is from God, [6] who has qualified us to be ministers of a new covenant, not in a written code but in the Spirit; for the written code kills, but the Spirit gives life.

[7] Now if the dispensation of death, carved in letters on stone, came with such splendor that the Israelites could not look at Moses' face because of its brightness, fading as this was, [8] will not the dispensation of the Spirit be attended with greater splendor? [9] For if there was splendor in the dispensation of condemnation, the dispensation of righteousness must far exceed it in splendor. [10] Indeed, in this case, what once had splendor has come to have no splendor at all, because of the splendor that surpasses it. [11] For if what faded away came with splendor, what is permanent must have much more splendor.

The question *Are we beginning to commend ourselves again?* is perhaps suggested through reflecting on the immediately preceding statement, which could be regarded as self-commendation (2:14–17; observe especially the contrast in v. 17 between Paul and the "peddlers" of the word of God, some of whom were in Corinth). Still more, the question arose because Paul had written in such a strain at an earlier date. The apostle had been forced to defend himself against attacks on his character and authority. No passage more truly reflects such apostolic self-vindication than chapter 11 of this letter (see the comments on this passage). In contrast however to the self-commendation in which he had been compelled to engage, Paul here scorns the idea that he needed *letters of recommendation* to or from the Corinthians.

Such letters were, of course, common in the early church and were written for the purpose of introducing Christian travelers to churches in areas other than their own (see, e.g., the commendation of Judas and Silas in Acts 15:23 ff., of Apollos in Acts 18:27, of Phoebe in Rom. 16:1 f., and of the two companions of Titus in this letter, 8:18 ff.). Paul's mention of *some* who need letters to and from Corinth may well have reference to the "peddlers" of the word of God (2:17), who had brought letters of this kind to Corinth. That was how they had gained access to the church there, and they sought the like from Corinth for other churches. Since these letters served as authorization of the bearers, Paul's lack of them could have been alleged by his opponents as evidence that he was without authorization from an acknowledged church, and that therefore he was no apostle but a self-appointed preacher, isolated from the churches of Christ.

Paul, on the contrary, was in the habit of emphasising two complementary considerations: on the one hand his gospel was identical with that of the other apostles (1 Cor. 15:3–11), and on the other hand he had been appointed as an apostle by the risen Lord, without the assistance of the other apostles (Gal. 1:1,15 ff.). As he began, so he continued: the signs of his apostleship were provided by the Lord and not by man (cf. Rom. 15:17 ff.). In any case, Corinth was the last place on earth where Paul needed a letter of recommendation. For, said the apostle, *you yourselves are our letter of recommendation.* The Corinthians had experienced the deliverance Christ gives and life in Christ through the ministry of Paul; that was sufficient demonstration that the risen Lord was pleased to use this man as his representative and instrument.

It is possible that the statement of the next verse, *you are a letter from Christ delivered by us,* should be rendered "you are a letter of Christ . . . written by us." This would mean that the Lord fashioned the Corinthians as his living letter through Paul's agency; the Master wrote in the hearts of men through his private secretary Paul. Such a letter was far more effective than any letter of commendation from a church. The Corinthian church was known far and wide, so that Paul could speak of the letter which they were as *known and read by all men.* In contrast to a private letter sent by one church to another, the phenomenon of the church at Corinth was an eloquent testimony to all men to the work of the Lord through his servant Paul. Moreover, they were a letter, written *not with ink but with the Spirit of the living God.* The Holy Spirit is the power of God and the life of God at work in the world. When Christ wrought by the Spirit through the apostle in the lives of the Corinthians, it was a mighty work of transformation and a life-giving operation that took place. That is the kind of letter the Lord writes when he has an amanuensis who knows his weakness, preaches the cross, and casts himself on the Spirit (see 1 Cor. 2:1–5).

The mention of Christ writing through the Spirit in the lives of men reminds Paul of the Scripture that told of God writing words for his people in ancient times, namely, the words of the ancient covenant in the Ten Commandments. For this reason Paul speaks of the Lord writing on *tablets* rather than on papyrus, which was the writing paper of Paul's time. At Sinai God wrote on tablets of stone, and Moses was his chosen messenger; at Corinth the Spirit of God wrote on tablets of human hearts, and Paul was his appointed agent. These words recall a passage in Ezekiel (36:26 f.), which declares that the Lord is to give his people a new heart, replacing their heart of stone with a heart of flesh. Through this work of the Spirit the promise through Jeremiah (31:33 f.) would come to pass. A new covenant would be given when the law would be written on men's hearts and so would become an inward principle instead of an external system of commands.

The contrast between the old covenant and the new is a familiar theme in Paul's writings, but it should not go unobserved that his manner of introducing it at this point implies a contrast between the ministry of Moses and his own ministry. In the immediately ensuing paragraphs this element of comparison becomes explicit, but the use of the plural (we) must not detract from the fact that Paul is writing of his own ministry and its authority in the light of the denial of its validity by his opponents in Corinth. What may be thought to be audacity, in affirming the superiority of his ministry to that of Moses, the founder of the theocracy, is in Paul's mind the outcome of the superiority of the new covenant over the old, which now he proceeds to expound.

If it be charged that this confidence of the apostle is the product of a mind inflated with pride, Paul answers that, on the contrary, it is a *confidence . . . through Christ toward God.* That is, it has been wrought in his heart and mind through Christ, and it is directed wholly towards God. Ultimately, it is a confidence in the truth of the gospel, in the reality of the redemptive power of Christ, and in the effectiveness of the work of the Holy Spirit and his ability to use a man in his service. Paul has already hinted of this in the description of his ministry as a participation in the triumph procession of God in history (2:14 ff.). He now declares that he has neither power nor authority residing in himself. *Our sufficiency is from God*—that is enough for any man!

This sufficiency, however, is not to be thought of in general terms. It is not a pious platitude that any devotee of any religion in the world could make. Quite specifically it is a competence that arises from being a minister of the new covenant. For the great characteristic of this covenant, promised through the prophet Jeremiah as God's gift for the new age (Jer. 31:31 ff.), is that it consists *not in a written code but in the Spirit.* All that one associates with the biblical teaching on the Holy Spirit, as God's power to create and recreate, to reveal and to inspire, to give life and banish evil, all

this is characteristic of the new order. It is this Spirit who mediates the sufficiency of Christ to the ministers of the new order.

Why does Paul introduce the concept of the new covenant at this point? In part, doubtless, because the opponents at Corinth were Jewish teachers, boasting in their Jewish heritage. More important, however, is Paul's mention of the Spirit who inspires his ministry. For the contrast between the old dispensation, of which the chief feature is the law, and the new order, the chief feature of which is life through the Spirit, was at the heart of his teaching; and it was the heart of his own experience of salvation. As a man under the old covenant, Paul had been dominated by the law of Moses. As a man in Christ, his life is dominated by the Spirit. The difference between the two was the difference between life and death.

It requires all of Romans 7 and 8 to understand v. 6. In Romans 7 Paul analyzes his experience under the law, which for him meant a revelation of the evil of his heart, an inability to fulfill God's righteous demand, and so despair, with death as the end. In contrast to this, Christ in the gospel had brought him life, liberation, joy, and power over every force in the universe, and precisely because Christ's order is characterized by "the law of the Spirit who gives life in Christ Jesus' (Rom. 8:2). So in this passage *the written code kills,* because it can only reveal demands which have the effect of condemnation of the guilty. But *the Spirit gives life,* for he mediates the life of the new creation that came into the world through Christ.

The contrast between the ministries of the old and new covenants is developed in vv. 7 ff. It is important to observe that it is not simply the two eras of the old and new covenants that are contrasted, as the term *dispensation* might suggest, nor are law and gospel set against each other in a general way. The term rendered in the RSV by *dispensation* is the common term *diakonia,* which normally means ministry or service; and there is no reason why it should not be so understood here. It is the *ministry* of the law exercised by Moses and the *ministry* of the gospel maintained by Paul which are set in contrast.

To Moses was given the awesome ministry of communicating the law. This was *carved in letters on stone* and, therefore, was and still remains essentially an external command without power to inspire what it demands. Consequently it brought death to those to whom it was delivered. The ministry of Moses therefore was the ministry of death. Nevertheless, despite its grim nature, its inauguration was attended by a manifestation of divine glory, and that glory was extended to its minister. Paul is alluding here to the narrative of Exodus 34: 29 ff., which tells of Moses descending from Mount Sinai with his face shining because of converse with God. Paul never hesitated to acknowledge that the law was given by God, and therefore was holy and authoritative (cf. Rom. 7:12 ff.), and he as freely recognized the glory of him who ministered it.

In contrast however to this service of the law, Paul himself exercised *the dispensation* (ministry) *of the Spirit.* For the gospel was the good news that the Christ of God had brought into being the promised age of salvation, the era of God's saving sovereignty (i.e., the kingdom of God). Accordingly, the ministry *of death* can rightly be offset by the ministry *of the Spirit* since it is the Spirit who bestows life. This ministry also is attended with glory, and the glory is greater than that which was given to Moses, so surely as the gospel is more glorious than the law promulgated by Moses. The face of Paul, or of any other Christian minister, may not shine like that of Moses as he strode down from Sinai, but the glory of their ministry is akin to the glory of the salvation proclaimed in the gospel—hidden till the revelation of the sons of God in the last great day (Rom. 8:19).

The ministry of Moses, as that of his followers, was *the dispensation* (ministry) *of condemnation,* but that of Paul and his fellow preachers of the gospel is *the dispensation* (ministry) *of righteousness.* This comparison follows on the former, and indeed explains it. Because the law brings condemnation to those to whom it is delivered by reason of their nonfulfillment of its demands, it also brings death; but the Spirit establishes a man in Christ and so enables him to participate in the righteousness of Christ. (These contrasting effects of law and Spirit are expounded in detail in Rom. 8:1–11).

It is finally pointed out by Paul that the ministry of the law is temporary; like the glory on the face of Moses, it *faded away* when the gospel came. But the ministry of Christ's good news belongs to *what is permanent.* Once more the whole Pauline message is implicated in his words, for the transitory function of the law is a constant theme in his writings (cf. Rom. 3—4; Gal. 3—4). This stern "schoolmaster" was of the old school indeed, mercilessly flogging men in their consciences and reducing them to despair that at last they might fling themselves in desperation at the feet of him who alone can save (Gal. 3:24). The ministry of the gospel, by contrast, tells of the Christ who introduced the salvation of God's everlasting kingdom, and so it belongs to what endures. Before the splendor of this ministry, the glory of the ministry of Moses pales into nothingness, even as the stars disappear before the sunrise.

(2) The Allegory of the Veil (3:12—4:6)

12 Since we have such a hope, we are very bold, 13 not like Moses, who put a veil over his face so that the Israelites might not see the end of the fading splendor. 14 But their minds were hardened; for to this day, when they read the old covenant, that same veil remains unlifted, because only through Christ is it taken away. 15 Yes, to this day whenever Moses is read a veil lies over their minds; 16 but when a man turns to the Lord the veil is removed. 17 Now the Lord is the Spirit, and where the Spirit of the Lord is, there is freedom. 18 And we all, with unveiled face, beholding the glory of the Lord, are being changed into his likeness from one degree of glory to another; for this comes from the Lord who is the Spirit.

1 Therefore, having this ministry by the mercy of God, we do not lose heart. 2 We have renounced disgraceful, underhanded ways; we

refuse to practice cunning or to tamper with God's word, but by the open statement of the truth we would commend ourselves to every man's conscience in the sight of God. ³ And even if our gospel is veiled, it is veiled only to those who are perishing. ⁴ In their case the god of this world has blinded the minds of the unbelievers, to keep them from seeing the light of the gospel of the glory of Christ, who is the likeness of God. ⁵ For what we preach is not ourselves, but Jesus Christ as Lord, with ourselves as your servants for Jesus' sake. ⁶ For it is the God who said, "Let light shine out of darkness," who has shone in our hearts to give the light of the knowledge of the glory of God in the face of Christ.

A glance at the contents of these two paragraphs shows that the theme of the first is continued into the second. This has given rise to a well-known interpretation of the passage that runs as follows. The passage (4:1–6) is best understood as a refutation of allegations by Paul's opponents in Corinth that the apostle was not open and honest in his preaching: they said that he hid the real nature of his beliefs by deliberate obscurity and made of Christianity a kind of mystery religion.

Paul anticipates this charge in 3:12 ff. in a highly ingenious manner. He refers to a feature of the Exodus narrative which he had just cited. At the time of the giving of the law, Moses put a veil over his face when he finished speaking with the people, but when he returned to commune with God he took it off (see Ex. 34:29 ff. RSV; observe that the KJV of v. 33 is misleading but is corrected in RSV). The inference is that it was not Paul the preacher of the gospel who was afraid to declare the truth of God openly to people but Moses and his Jewish successors in Corinth. Just as Moses did not want the Israelites to perceive that his glory was a fading one and that his ministry was impermanent, so his successors in Corinth were not prepared to declare themselves with candor. Any misunderstanding of Paul's gospel was due to the continued hardness of the Jews and to the activity of Satan.

This is undoubtedly an attractive view and has been adopted by many. Neverthe-

less it creates some difficulties. Above all, if 3:12 ff. were to be interpreted in the light of 4:2, it would link Moses with men who employ *disgraceful, underhanded ways* and who *practice cunning* and *tamper with God's word.* By no stretch of imagination can it be thought that Paul attributed such behavior to Moses. Moreover, those who have suggested this mode of understanding the passage have not always seen that the train of thought in vv. 12 ff. is closely linked with that of the preceding paragraph and that there is really no break. The theme of 3:7–11 is a comparison of the ministry of Moses and of Paul in relation to the two covenants they represent, and this, of course, is also the subject of vv. 12 ff. The allegorical exposition of Moses' use of the veil in vv. 12 ff. is a natural continuation of Paul's employment of the story thus far. We consider, therefore, that it is preferable not to read any secondary considerations into the passage before us and to assume that Paul continues without a break the discussion on which he had embarked in 3:7 ff.

The *hope* referred to in v. 12 appears to combine a confidence as to the glory that attaches to the gospel proclamation in the present with an expectation of a revelation of that glory in the future. The gospel itself has at its heart a manifestation of a glory that has a future, namely, that of the Christ incarnate, crucified and risen, and returning in majesty for the victory of his kingdom. As with the gospel, so with its preachers: whatever their lot in the present, theirs is a glory which will be vindicated in the triumph of their Lord, and therefore they can afford to be *very bold.*

From 3:11 it would seem that Paul viewed the ministry of Moses as linked in a similar manner with the destiny of the law. Moses' ministry was accompanied by a glory that was genuine but fleeting; so also the function of the law that he mediated was God-given, but only for a time. In contrast to the apostolic preacher, who knows that he has God's ultimate word to men which shall stand for ever, Moses was not given such a word for men and veiled his face from their gaze lest they should divine the provisional nature of his ministry through the fading of his splendor. Such is the lesson that Paul draws from the Exodus narrative. We may be sure that he would not have so read it if he had not already come to this understanding of the nature of the law; but having already grasped this truth, he sees it imaged in the Old Testament story.

In a similar manner Paul goes on to extend the allegorical use of the narrative in the light of Israel's actual history and his own experience as an evangelist among them. The veil that was on the head of Moses remains on the Scriptures he gave, as on the rest of the words of God, whenever they are read among the Jews. The context makes it clear that it is not a fault in the words themselves but in the readers and hearers. *Their minds were hardened . . . a veil lies over their minds.* This is the incomprehension not of the unintelligent but of unrepentant minds, calloused through resistance to the familiar. The immedia e reference is to the contemporaries of Moses, who had been busy making a golden calf while Moses was receiving the law and who showed their stubbornness many times thereafter.

Paul knew his Old Testament well enough to know that the same kind of experience was familiar to the prophets (see, e.g., Isaiah 6 and the whole of the book of Jeremiah), and he knew that the same uncomprehending attitude was taken to the ministry and teaching of Jesus (cf. Mark 4:11 f.). Israel's tragedy is that it has possessed words of God (not alone law but also prophets and psalms and the like) that contain declarations of God's demands, and equally of grace and loving kindness and marvellous promises; but the significance of the whole is hidden from the eyes of those who will not see. Experience has shown that it is *only through Christ* that the veil is *taken away.* But he does take it away! Paul recalls the statement of Exodus 34.34: "Whenever Moses went in before the Lord to speak with him, he took the veil off." In

v. 16 Paul generalizes this and declares, *When a man turns to the Lord,* i.e., the risen Lord Jesus, *the veil is removed.* Such a man begins to grasp the purport of words he has known well, so that he understands the real significance of Moses and his law, the fulfillment of the promises in Christ, and the availability of grace today; and then in faith through the Spirit he receives the life of the age to come. Such was Paul's experience. When the scales fell from his eyes, after encountering the risen Lord, he saw not only Ananias properly (Acts 9:18) but still more the Lord in the Scriptures.

The Old Testament did not become the New Testament (the two covenants must not be confused!), but it did become a new Old Testament to Paul. How avidly he read the Scriptures when he realized that he possessed their key in Christ! The experience of the disciples on the Emmaus way (Luke 24:32) and of the apostles in the upper room (Luke 24:44 f.) became normative for the rest of his life. It has been true for multitudes since his day, Jews and Gentiles alike, for whom the Bible as a whole became a new book when they turned to the Lord.

The reason for this universal experience is given in the ensuing words: *Now the Lord is the Spirit, and where the Spirit of the Lord is, there is freedom.* The immediate point of the saying is clear: in the Old Testament the Holy Spirit is especially the Spirit of prophecy, so that he is viewed as the giver of the Scriptures. When a man turns to the Lord Christ, the Spirit whom he has sent removes the veil of incomprehensibility and enables him to understand the Scriptures. That same Spirit gives him *freedom*—freedom above all from bondage to the written code that kills. No longer is he bound to the external command carved in letters on stone. Rather, in the fellowship of Christ and through the new life of the Spirit, he begins to experience the freedom of the emancipated children of God. To elaborate this theme was the purpose of Paul's letter to the Galatians.

While there is general agreement on this understanding of v. 17, the language of the opening clause has occasioned perplexity. What exactly did Paul mean by saying, *the Lord is the Spirit?* Not a few expositors have insisted that the words be taken at their face value, and they have interpreted them as showing that Paul identified the risen Lord with the Holy Spirit. The answer to the question, Who is the Holy Spirit? must be, the risen Christ. To most interpreters this seems an impossible interpretation of the words, not least because of statements that Paul has made elsewhere in his letters to Corinth, especially in 1 Corinthians 12:4–6 and 2 Corinthians 13:14.

An interpretation that has become popular in recent times has found embodiment in the NEB rendering of this verse: "Now the Lord of whom this passage speaks is the Spirit." This views the clause as an explanatory comment on Exodus 34:34: the Lord to whom the Scripture says that Moses turned, and to whom the Jew should turn today for illumination, is the Holy Spirit. As an explanation of the difficulty in the text the rendering above will hardly suffice, for in v. 16 the *Lord* to whom the Jew should turn for the removal of the veil is surely the Lord Christ, as is implied in v. 14. If Paul in v. 17 is intending to identify the person of the Lord in the Exodus narrative, he must mean first of all Christ, and then he proceeds to declare that this Lord Christ is the Spirit. But this sheds no light on how he can call Christ the Spirit.

Most scholars tend to think that Paul is here relating Christ and the Spirit in a dynamic way; that is to say, he is concerned with the working of Christ and the Spirit among men and not their being. Christ is Christ and the Spirit is the Spirit, and Paul has no intention of declaring the one to be the other; but he knows that the Spirit has been sent by Christ and that he is the agent through whom Christ works, so that Christ becomes present through the Spirit's operations. "The Spirit so effectively performs his office of communicating to men the benefits of the risen Christ, that for all intents and purposes of faith the Lord himself is present bestowing grace on his own," wrote Neill Q.

Hamilton.[7] This is true, but it still is not clear that this is why Paul actually made the statement of v. 17.

Perhaps we should look to the context for the needful clue. The theme of the chapter is the contrast between the ministries of Moses and Paul, the old covenant and the new covenant, the law and the gospel. The formative concepts that set in motion the whole train of thought are tablets of stone and tablets of newly created hearts (3:3), and these give place to the opposition of the written code that kills and the Spirit who gives life (3:6). It is not so much law and gospel as law and Spirit that are basic to the discussion. Moses represents the law. Strictly speaking, Paul represents the Spirit, but he forbears to say so. In fact the references to himself in the chapter are strangely indirect, and it is easy to miss them. This doubtless is due to his deference, but it is also demanded by his use of the allegory of the veil in vv. 14 ff.

In his comparison of law and Spirit, therefore, Paul finally *identifies Moses and Christ as the representatives of the two orders of law and Spirit.* Johannes Munck expressed this viewpoint as follows: "Just as he (Paul) might have said, 'Moses is the letter,' so he says here, 'The Lord is the Spirit.' Paul thereby declares which of the two principles Christ represents, and therefore with which one he himself is in a certain sense united." [8] This seems to supply a satisfactory explanation of the mode of Paul's statement, provided we also bear in mind the particular reason that called it forth, namely, Paul's desire to show how a man can advance from incomprehensibility to understanding the word of God, and from bondage to emancipation by the Lord.

Fittingly at this point Paul turns from the consideration of his own ministry to the experience of all believers. The veil is removed from every man who turns to the

[7] *The Holy Spirit and Eschatology in Paul* (Edinburgh and London: *Scottish Journal of Theology*, Occasional Papers, No. 6, 1957), p. 6.

[8] *Paul and the Salvation of Mankind* (London: SCM, 1959), p. 59.

Lord, and so Paul writes, *We all*—apostles and all members of Christ—*with unveiled face, beholding the glory of the Lord, are being changed into his likeness.* The experience of Moses is universalized. Whereas none other of Moses' generation enjoyed his privilege, all Christ's people are granted the like—and more, for they know the life-changing powers of the new age through the Holy Spirit.

Some uncertainty remains, however, as to the precise meaning of the term rendered *beholding.* The interpretation of the word suggested by the RSV rendering is natural enough, and advances from the thought of Moses in communication with God to the Christian gazing on the face of Christ; looking on Christ the Christian is transformed into his likeness.

On the other hand, the KJV follows a well-attested interpretation of the word, "beholding as in a glass" the glory of the Lord. This conveys the notion of an imperfect vision of the likeness of the Lord, for ancient mirrors were made of metal and rarely gave a true image; and we must admit that this conforms to the experience of Christ's people, who are not yet given to see the Lord face to face (1 Cor. 13:12).

There is a yet further possible interpretation, given in the margin of the RSV: *reflecting* the glory of the Lord. Despite assertions to the contrary, this rendering makes good sense in the context. The redeemed people of Christ have had the veil removed from their hearts; they have been granted the privilege of access into his presence, and through their communion with the Lord they reflect his glory to others and at the same time are transformed in their being. Paul adds, *This comes from the Lord who is the Spirit.* In this context that means "from the Lord, whom we experience as the Spirit." The miracle of transformation is wrought by Christ, through whom the experience of the Spirit is gained.

To have received a ministry as great as that described in the preceding paragraphs is to Paul a manifest sign of *the mercy of God.* In the light of that mercy, with its hope of future glory (3:12) and present experience of the Spirit's transforming power (v. 18), Paul affirms, *we do not lose heart* despite the daunting hardships and persecutions which he is called to endure and which he is about to mention in the following paragraph. The *disgraceful underhanded* ways renounced by Paul indicate what men can resort to when they "lose heart" and decline to make a fearless stand for Christ in the world. They adopt subterfuges, become expert in the half truth, and are more adept in the *cunning* that characterizes the devil than the openness that belongs to Christ (cf. the "cunning" that deceived Eve, 11:3).

Worst of all, Paul knows of some who tamper with God's word, a practice to which he earlier alluded (2:17), and which has devastating results. The word of God is then debased to a word of man without power, which leads to destruction instead of deliverance. In contrast, says Paul, *by the open statement of the truth we would commend ourselves to every man's conscience in the sight of God.* There is no need to adapt the truth of God to make it palatable to men. The gospel is truth that shines in its own light. It is reality on which a man can stake his life.

Paul's preaching *in the sight of God* implies that he uttered every word as though he stood before the judgment seat of God. The reality in the gospel demands reality in the preacher. It is directed to the hearer's sense of reality, i.e., to his *conscience.* The preacher's aim is not so much to present arguments to elicit the agreement of reason as it is to penetrate a man's conscience and stir up his will to turn to God. Naturally, *the truth* of the gospel will be made clear in the presentation of the word, but the ultimate strife between the Spirit of God and the spirit of a man takes place not in the sphere of reason but on the battlefield of the will.

Since this is so and because the will of man is constantly perverse, Paul had to admit that a veil can lie not alone on the law, to prevent a Jew from understanding it, but on the gospel, to prevent men from yielding to it (v. 3). While Christ has brought God's last word to man, in distinction from the provisional word spoken through Moses, and its appeal ought to be transparently plain, there are those who stand as uncomprehending about the cross and empty tomb as the Jews stood about blazing Sinai. *Our gospel is veiled . . . only to those who are perishing.* Only! But a terrible qualification is this. Mercifully Paul uses the present tense: those who are blind to the gospel are on the road that leads to lostness; but they have not reached journey's end, and they may yet be guided to the way that leads to life.

How does it come about that men can be so obtuse towards the word of life in Christ? *The god of this world has blinded the minds of the unbelievers* says Paul. The devil has ever been a deceiver, and it is understandable that his activity should be especially directed towards deceiving men regarding the truth of the gospel. This is an aspect of existence which Paul took with deadly seriousness. He would have approved of Goethe's word about Mephistopheles: "People don't know the Devil is there! Even when he has them by the throat!" For if it be true, as Emil Brunner said, "The most important truth about the Devil is this: Jesus Christ has conquered him," [9] it is equally true that the devil is active in endeavoring to keep men from entering into the power of that conquest.

Brunner went on to say: "To believe that wherever the true gospel is proclaimed with power, men will open their hearts without further difficulty is a mistaken optimism. Rather, a living proclamation of the gospel often sifts the hearts of men, and the more powerful the message the more violent is the hostility of the powers of darkness." That is exactly what Paul is saying at this point. The devil belongs to the darkness, but the gospel opens men to the light of God. More explicitly, it unveils before men *the glory of Christ, who is the likeness of God.* The god of this world is a sham deity; he claims the allegiance of men, but "he is a liar and the father of lies" (John 8:44). His malign rule is already broken, and it is due to come to its end (*god of this world* ought to be rendered "god of this *age*"); its effect on men is to drag them down into the devil's darkness.

In contrast to this, the gospel declares *the glory of Christ*—a glory founded in the shame of Christ's cross, vindicated in the radiance of his resurrection, and to be revealed in the splendor of his coming. Its effect is to bestow on men his glorious life. Christ raises men to the heights of his glory. And this he can do because he is *the likeness of God:* unlike the sham god of this age, he is the authentic image and expression of God, so that to see him is to see the Father, and to be in union with him is to be one with God.

If it be true, as is often suggested, that Paul's characterization of the gospel in this whole passage (cf. v. 6) is due to his vision of Christ's glory on the Damascus way, so that for him Christ is essentially the Lord of glory in his exaltation, it should not be forgotten that Paul can also speak of Christ as the "image" of God from all eternity (cf. Col. 1:15), also that the Lord became incarnate as the true image of God, the perfect man born for the restoration of God's image in man (Phil. 2:6 ff.).

How then should Paul do other than *preach . . . Jesus Christ as Lord,* Saviour of men and sovereign of the universe? Far be it from him to exalt himself in place of Christ, even though some of his opponents sullenly suggested that his assertion of authority was sheer self-exaltation. We are *your servants,* he writes (or, as we may render, We are "your slaves"). The Christ himself took the servant's place among men, and his followers should be prepared to occupy it also (cf. John 13:12–17; Phil. 2:5 ff.). Insofar as Christ's ministers share his spirit and walk in his steps, they will carry out their service in a spirit of Christly love for men; but their ultimate motive is *for Jesus' sake.* "Slaves" of the church they

[9] *The Christian Doctrine of Creation and Redemption* (London: Lutterworth, 1952), p. 145.

may be, but they belong to Christ!

Such is the spirit in which the man of God will serve, for the God whose word brought light into being at creation *has shone in our hearts to give the light of the knowledge of the glory of God in the face of Christ.* The glory of the Damascus road shines still. But there is more involved in the language. In the beginning of creation God gave the light through his almighty word, and that word was Christ (cf. 1 Cor. 8:6; Col. 1:15 ff.). He has brought into being a new creation, and in it he has manifested the light of his glory in Christ. That light, however, shines not merely round about men, as the light on the Damascus road, but within them—*in our hearts,* as Paul put it. The saying expresses in personal terms what Paul will later declare in a different way, "If any one is in Christ, he is a new creation" (5:17). The typology of redemption through new creation is at the root of both utterances.

What makes the saying of v. 6 so appealing is its personal character. Doubtless it has an echo in it of the experience of Moses at Sinai, whose face for a while reflected the glory of the vision of God (3:7 ff.). Here we read of God manifesting the knowledge of his glory *in the face of Christ.* The vision of Christ to Paul in part determines the language, but let it be remembered that the face of Christ revealed that glory all along his way, not least as he hung on his cross, as well as when he ascended the throne of God. And that face is known to us as we walk by faith in his company every day. To us is given a fulfillment of the proverb, more profound than anything that could have been dreamed by its compiler: "The path of the righteous is like the light of dawn, which shines brighter and brighter until full day" (Prov. 4:18).

(3) The Sufferings, Power, and Hope of an Apostle (4:7—5:10)

7 But we have this treasure in earthen vessels, to show that the transcendent power belongs to God and not to us. 8 We are afflicted in every way, but not crushed; perplexed, but not driven to despair; 9 persecuted, but not forsaken; struck down, but not destroyed; 10 always carrying in the body the death of Jesus, so that the life of Jesus may also be manifested in our bodies. 11 For while we live we are always being given up to death for Jesus' sake, so that the life of Jesus may be manifested in our mortal flesh. 12 So death is at work in us, but life in you.

13 Since we have the same spirit of faith as he had who wrote, "I believed, and so I spoke," we too believe, and so we speak, 14 knowing that he who raised the Lord Jesus will raise us also with Jesus and bring us with you into his presence. 15 For it is all for your sake, so that as grace extends to more and more people it may increase thanksgiving, to the glory of God.

16 So we do not lose heart. Though our outer nature is wasting away, our inner nature is being renewed every day. 17 For this slight momentary affliction is preparing for us an eternal weight of glory beyond all comparison, 18 because we look not to the things that are seen but to the things that are unseen; for the things that are seen are transient, but the things that are unseen are eternal.

1 For we know that if the earthly tent we live in is destroyed, we have a building from God, a house not made with hands, eternal in the heavens. 2 Here indeed we groan, and long to put on our heavenly dwelling, 3 so that by putting it on we may not be found naked. 4 For while we are still in this tent, we sigh with anxiety; not that we would be unclothed, but that we would be further clothed, so that what is mortal may be swallowed up by life. 5 He who has prepared us for this very thing is God, who has given us the Spirit as a guarantee.

6 So we are always of good courage; we know that while we are at home in the body we are away from the Lord, 7 for we walk by faith, not by sight. 8 We are of good courage, and we would rather be away from the body and at home with the Lord. 9 So whether we are at home or away, we make it our aim to please him. 10 For we must all appear before the judgment seat of Christ, so that each one may receive good or evil, according to what he has done in the body.

It will aid the understanding of this deeply moving testimony of Paul if we bear in mind one feature of the church of Corinth: it knew nothing of persecution. In this it was exceptional among the early Christian churches. The first letter to the Corinthians conveys the impression that, far from feeling the weight of repression, the church was on the best of terms with its pagan environment. Therein lay its danger. It became infected by that environment. In well-known words of James Moffatt, "The Church was in the world, as it had to be, but the world was in the church, as it ought not to be." [10] Consequently, this church's experience and interpretation of the Christian life in the world were very different from those of Paul. There is evidence to suggest that the sufferings of their founder apostle were a perplexity to them, and even a cause of offense (consider, e.g., 1 Cor. 4:8–14).

If we further bear in mind the presence of teachers in Corinth who took good care not to be crucified and who despised Paul for his sufferings, believing themselves to possess a spirituality that removed them from such a low plane of existence as his, we shall see a deeper reason for Paul's exposition at this point. As an apostle of Christ, he was called not only to preach the passion, death, and resurrection of Christ, but also to make them visible in his ministry for Christ and the church.

The *treasure* which Paul, in common with all Christians, possessed is "the knowledge of the glory of God in the face of Jesus Christ" (3:6). That phrase includes the whole gamut of God's revelation and redemption in Christ and the whole breadth of the Christian hope of participation in that glory. But this unimaginably costly treasure has been placed by God *in earthen vessels,* i.e., in people like Paul.

If the primary reference in the apostle's mind is the weakness of his body, it must be remembered that for him the term body can also stand for person, and so it does here. Indeed, the sentences that follow suggest that Paul had in view not only his poor, scarred body and limited, human personality, but his checkered ministry as a suffering servant of the Lord. Just as one might never suspect that a cheap earthenware jar contained priceless gems, so an

[10] *The First Epistle of Paul to the Corinthians* ("The Moffatt New Testament Commentary" [London: Hodder & Stoughton, 1935]), p. xv.

observer looking on this pitiable figure of a man, especially when taken up half dead through stoning or bedraggled from shipwreck, could never imagine that in and through this man the glory of God in Christ was marvelously at work.

Why does God choose such a method of revealing his glory? *To show that the transcendent power belongs to God and not to us.* It does not reside in man—it never has and it never can—to deliver himself from his sin and transform himself into the likeness of God. And if God should use a man to deliver men, this is not because of any ability in the man. That becomes transparently plain when the instrument is an individual with a destiny like Paul's. In this persecuted and downtrodden man there is a *transcendent power* at work, bringing to pass mighty acts through him and making his word powerful to defeat the powers of darkness and to transform lives (see Rom. 15:18 f.; 1 Cor. 2:3 ff.; 4:19 f.; 2 Cor. 10:4 f.). It is the life of the world to come, invading this age through a man who belongs to that world as well as to this.

Because of the duality of Paul's existence —weakness as a man of this world but strength by the Spirit who brings the powers of the world to come—he knows both exposure to the crushing forces of life in this world and the upholding grace of God that continually makes a way out of human distresses. The thought of vv. 8 ff. reminds us of the principle of temptation enunciated in 1 Corinthians 10:13. In vv. 8–9 four kinds of experience are recounted in pairs, in each case the first relating to the weakness of the earthen vessel and the second to the transcendent power at work in him.

The apostle is *afflicted . . . but not crushed;* the picture is that of a man almost overwhelmed by his adversary, yet managing to avoid being hemmed in and finished off (like a boxer hammered by his opponent but refusing to be cornered). He is *perplexed, but not driven to despair.* The word play in Greek (*aporoumenoi* but not *exaporoumenoi*) is difficult to imitate in

English, but after Denney we could render it "hard put to it but not utterly put out"; the wisdom of God is available to us in our times of greatest bewilderment. *Struck down, but not destroyed* recalls Paul's experience at Lystra, when he was struck down by the stones and left for dead, but he revived and continued his ministry (Acts 14:19 f.).

All this is a manifestation of *the death of Jesus,* or more strictly, the "dying" of Jesus. The suffering unto death of the Master, to bring about the salvation of men, is reproduced in his disciple, that he might the more effectively reveal it to men. So surely as God gave Paul a peculiarly profound insight into the meaning of the death of Jesus, so he gave him to lead a life which approximated in a remarkable way the pattern of Jesus' dying. But so surely as God enabled Paul to grasp the significance of the resurrection of Jesus, so he caused the power of the resurrection to be manifested in him—*so that the life of Jesus may also be manifested in our bodies.* This indicates that Paul's following in the steps of Jesus was more than an "imitation of Christ," to use a famous phrase. It was an expression in the Jesus way of the life of Christ within.

His *being given up to death for Jesus' sake* especially relates to his experiences of persecution, when time and again he came near to death. We recall that immediately prior to writing this letter Paul had gone through an overwhelming experience of persecution, in which he had resigned himself to the inevitability of death (1:8 ff.). But his constant deliverances from such situations were examples of the power of the risen Christ, intervening on behalf of his servant. *The life of Jesus* was *manifested* in Paul's *mortal flesh* by its very continuance. It was also manifested in the attitude of the apostle as he cheerfully accepted Christ's cross as his pattern of living, and in the quality of his ministry as the Lord demonstrated the power of his resurrection through him.

The result of such a ministry is *death is at work in us, but life in you.* If we were to be guided by 1 Corinthians 4:8 ff., we could infer that Paul here speaks in an ironical way. As he had there said, "You have come into your kingdom, and left us out, while we are like men sentenced to death," so here he states, "We endure death, but you enjoy life." The intense seriousness of this passage argues against this interpretation; and still more the fact that the sentence continues in vv. 13–15, where Paul emphasizes his unity with the Corinthians in their common destiny in Christ.

If we are to take the cue from the context, it would appear that Paul refers to the different aspects of the Christian calling which have been assigned to the Corinthians and himself. His vocation as an apostle has brought him into a continual sharing of the sufferings of Christ, so that the dying of Jesus for the life of the world is ever and again exemplified in him. The Corinthians have not been set in like circumstances. Had the cult of Caesar worship been pursued in Corinth with the fanatical enthusiasm known in other parts of the world, or if hostile Jewish influence had been particularly strong in their city, things might have been different; but as it was, all was quiet in Corinth. The life of Jesus by the Spirit was manifest among them, not least through the labors of their apostle and his constant travail in spirit on their behalf. But the difference between their lot on earth did not separate them; in Christ they continued to share in the power of his redemption.

At this point Paul cites an Old Testament utterance from a man who had much in common with him: "I kept my faith, even when I said, 'I am greatly afflicted' " (Psalm 116:10). Paul knew that psalm in the Greek version, which may be rendered, "I kept faith, therefore I spoke up, but I was greatly humiliated." The meaning is not greatly different, but the interpretation of "even" as "therefore" makes an interesting difference; the psalmist kept his trust in God, despite his sufferings, and *therefore* he felt compelled to bear testimony to his faith amid suffering.

That is absolutely characteristic of Paul. He was perpetually enduring suffering for the Lord's sake, but he was perpetually maintained in faith. And "maintained" is the right word. For Paul added, *We have the same spirit of faith as he had;* almost certainly "spirit" here means not attitude but the Holy Spirit, who enables a man to step out in faith (1 Cor. 12:3) and who maintains him in faith, come what may. This is all part of the manifestation of the life of Jesus in Paul, even as he carries in his body the dying of Jesus. And he cannot be silent about it but must declare to all men how gracious the Lord is to him.

Paul's experience of the life of Jesus now, which time and again works in him a minor resurrection from the dead, confirms him in his faith that one day he is to experience God's ultimate resurrection power. *He who raised up the Lord Jesus will raise us also with Jesus.* The destiny of humanity is bound up with what God did through the resurrection of the man Christ Jesus (1 Cor. 15:22), how much more that of Christians who, through the Spirit, are united with him to form the Body of Christ? This is a faith that springs not alone from Christ's resurrection but also from his crucifixion. As Paul elsewhere remarked, "He who did not spare his own son but gave him up for us all, will he not also give us all things with him?" (Rom. 8:32). If God could give us Jesus in death, the love of his heart will not stop short of giving us Jesus in life— or, more strictly, to be with Jesus in life. This is the basis of our Christian hope. Our life is in the hands of the God who gave his Son for us and raised him from death to be with him for ever.

He *will bring us with you into his presence.* As in life, so in eternal life, the apostle and his beloved children of faith will not be separated. The resurrection means that God's children will be glorified together (Heb. 11:39 f.), for only in the glorification of the whole body of Christ can any one member find perfection. However different the lives of the apostle and his converts, the grace that sustains and

unites them all will perfect them all, even as that grace will span the ages and present all God's people, that they may be acquitted in judgment and rejoice in the marriage supper of the Lamb.

It is all for your sake, adds the apostle. All his suffering, striving, dying, rising to renewed life is that the Corinthians might be confirmed in grace and attain to glory. *For your sake,* he says, but not for theirs alone: *that as grace extends to more and more people it may increase thanksgiving, to the glory of God.* The ultimate cause of his apostolic labors is for God's sake. As he becomes "a spectacle to the world, to angels and to men" (1 Cor. 4:9), and they see the principle of Christ's dying and rising for their redemption enacted out in him, then more and more people, in Corinth and elsewhere, will join the chorus of praise for love almighty; and the greater will be the glory ascribed to the God of redemption. That is how history will end (Phil. 2:11), and that was the aim of Paul's ministry.

In view of all this—the dying and the rising experienced by Paul, the blessing to others that resulted from it, and the glory of God that is increased by it—*we do not lose heart.* The outcome of a truly apostolic ministry is worth every pain it entails, and Paul is encouraged as he presses on to the goal of his pilgrimage. Yet the end is not indefinitely distant for Paul. While he maintained an undying hope in the coming of the Lord, which could bring him transformation into the likeness of his Saviour without journeying through the valley of the shadow, Paul must have been perfectly aware that the strenuous nature of his ministry was taking a toll on his physical frame. In Denney's pithy comment, "He saw it was killing him." This was no mere biological observation that from youth on we are dying people; it was a recognition that this particular frame was wasting away, like a garment getting worn out through use. But "we do not lose heart"!

Something remarkable is happening to the apostle: *our inner nature is being renewed every day.* That relates simply to the so-called immaterial nature of man, as though Paul had in mind, for example, the sharpening of his intellectual powers as his body grows weaker. On the contrary it is a consolation to be remembered, when looking on our loved ones in their approach to death, that the intellect, like the body, can also waste away as the physical brain deteriorates, without the relationship of the person to God being affected one whit. Plummer points out that the phrase "inward man" (for so *inner nature* may be exactly rendered) is always used in the New Testament in a good sense, and relates to that part of us which is opposed to worldliness and is rooted in God. "It is the highest part of our immaterial being; that which is capable of being the home of the Holy Spirit and of being ruled by him." And this it is which God's new creative activity works on; it commenced in us when we first responded to the Lord's call and experienced the power of redemption (Titus 3:5), and it is to extend to the limit of his creation. We know its action *every day,* and it is to continue working in us till the goal is reached of perfect likeness to the Christ in glory (Rom. 8:29).

In the light of this present action of the Spirit and the goal to which it is moving, Paul characterizes his manifold sufferings as *this slight momentary affliction.* What to onlookers must at times have appeared appalling experiences are viewed by him as *slight* when set in the context of faith and hope. For such experiences prepare for him *an eternal weight of glory beyond all comparison.* The language goes beyond definition, as the apostle vainly tries to describe the indescribable. The real object of hope, as Paul has again and again reminded us, is *glory.* The likeness of God that has been revealed in Christ is being wrought out by God in us and is to be fully bestowed upon us at the consummation of the ages.

That we may entertain a hope to receive that glory is sheer grace. Nothing that we could ever do—though we or Paul or anyone else died a thousand deaths for Christ —could ever enable us to claim that as our due from God. Particularly when we remember that it is *eternal.* And we are creatures of a day! The *weight* of it is out of all proportion to the lightness of our afflictions. Yet it is the afflictions that "prepare" the glory for us. This is not a question of merit. Paul has in view the principle he has enunciated throughout this exposition, that the Christian life is essentially a continuing in the pattern of the death and resurrection by which our redemption was won. It is as we conform to the redemptive pattern of living that the goal of redemption becomes plainer and is assured to us. This is the theme of an early Christian hymn, found in 2 Timothy 2:11 f.:

> "If we died with him, we shall also live with him;
> If we endure, we shall also reign with him."

The doctrine of justification by faith and the prospect of the judgment seat of Christ do not contradict one another, but they do remind us of the intense seriousness that attaches to the life of faith.

What keeps Paul steady and ceaselessly confident in all his afflictions is his habit of looking *not to the things that are seen but to the things that are unseen.* He maintains the attitude of the heroes of faith, whose exploits are recounted in Hebrews 11. Indeed, Paul's language and thought in this passage are remarkably close to the definition of faith in Hebrews 11:1. *The things that are seen are transient,* for they belong to this passing age; *the things that are unseen are eternal,* for they belong to the age to come. They belong, that is, to the kingdom that has been prepared for God's saints from the foundation of the world (Matt. 25:34). On the goal of that kingdom Paul keeps his eye fixed without wavering, as a man in his day plowed a field with an ox and fixed his eye on a distant object (cf. Luke 9:62). And well he might, for it was with a view to the joy of bringing men to that glory that the Son of God "endured the cross, despising the shame, and is seated at the right hand of God" (Heb. 12:2).

The opening conjunction of 5:1 *for* links the succeeding paragraph with what has gone before. It suggests that a further explanation is to be given concerning the confidence to which faith bears testimony (v. 13) and the nature of that "eternal weight of glory" for which the servant of Christ is being prepared (v. 17 f.). The formulation of v. 1 is doubtless inspired by the contrast mentioned in v. 18, between the visible order, which is transient, and the unseen realm, which is eternal. The body in which we spend our life shares in the transience of this age, and so is called an *earthly tent.* It is a flimsy and impermanent thing, and in the biblical perspective it fittingly denotes the dwelling of those who know they are a pilgrim people on the march to a "city which has foundations, whose builder and maker is God" (Heb. 11:10). If and when this tent is *destroyed* (or, as the term may be translated, "taken down") we have a strong, substantial *building from God;* this is a *house,* not a tent, and it is *eternal in the heavens,* not temporary on earth.

So much is clear, but the precise meaning of the sentence is uncertain, and a veritable river of ink has been used in expounding different interpretations of it, along with varied modes of understanding the following verses to which v. 1 supplies an introduction. The chief difficulty is in knowing what the *house not made with hands* is. The most natural interpretation which springs to mind is that it represents the resurrection body which God will provide at Christ's coming. This could indeed be described as *eternal* and *in the heavens,* i.e., with God. Some Jewish writers believed that the resurrection bodies, like everything else belonging to the kingdom of God, actually exist now in heaven; but there is no likelihood that Paul ever held such a view. The present tense *we have* is then regarded as a forceful way of stating the possession of something which is actually future (a use of the present tense common in the N. T., cf. Rev. 22:20). There is much

to be said for this view, and the present writer used to adopt it; but he is less happy about it than he used to be, for reasons which will become clear.

Many expositors strongly urge that the present tense *we have* ought to be allowed its normal meaning here. If that is accepted, the sense of the statement is radically altered. Even so some very different interpretations are advanced on that basis. Some, e.g., maintain that the words imply a resurrection immediately on the death of the body. In that case, Paul must have changed his views about the resurrection. It is claimed that as a Pharisee, Paul held the common Jewish view of a resurrection of the fleshly body; on becoming a Christian, he advanced to the concept of a spiritual body raised from death at Christ's coming, as expounded in 1 Corinthians 15. By the time he wrote this letter, prompted by the terrible experience alluded to in 2 Corinthians 1:8 ff., he had come to believe in a resurrection with Christ immediately on death. This idea of a change of view between the writing of 1 and 2 Corinthians, based on the use of the present tense *we have* in this verse, seems highly dubious to most critics and is less commonly held than formerly.

Accordingly it has been suggested that the *building from God* which *we have* on death must be an embodiment of the soul after quitting the body, anticipatory of the resurrection at the last day, but not the final resurrection itself. It is urged that this is consonant with Paul's teaching generally: at his conversion a man in Christ is raised for life with Christ (Rom. 6:3 ff.), at death he is accorded a richer embodiment of life with Christ, and at the last day the process will culminate in a body sharing Christ's glory. Attractive as this view is, the embodiment after death is nevertheless said by Paul to be *eternal,* not a temporary mode of existence that will yield to something more permanent.

Can it be then that the building from God is not an individual dwelling, but an inclusive one, i.e., for many? In favor of this it should be noticed that the phrase *a house not made with hands* is not intended to compare a future resurrection body made by God with a temporary earthly body, for the latter is also *not made with hands*. The phrase rather contrasts a building made by God with a building made by man, i.e., a heavenly temple with an earthly temple. This has suggested to some that Paul is here speaking of the church as the temple in which we shall dwell in heaven after death since he uses this symbol elsewhere of the church (cf. 1 Cor. 3:11 ff.; Eph. 2:19 ff.), but this is hardly a natural interpretation of the words in this passage.

To conclude, it would seem altogether more likely that Paul has in mind a heavenly temple, in which we shall be at home with the Lord on death. This admirably fits the apostle's reflections in vv. 6–9, and it presents fundamentally the same conception as that found in John 14:1–3 (whether by accident or not, it is also closely related to the Lord's words reflected in Mark 14:58; John 2:19). Whereas in John 14:1 ff. the imagery is that of a spacious home with many rooms in heaven, here the picture is that of a temple in heaven where the Lord and his people may dwell together. Acknowledging that uncertainty attaches to the saying, this interpretation may be adopted as expressing what Paul wished to convey, and it should bring comfort and inspiration to Christ's people to learn of it.

In v. 2 the imagery changes, and the thought progresses. The notion of a building in which we are to live gives place to the idea of clothing which we are to put on, but the metaphor becomes mixed: the apostle longs to *put on* the *heavenly dwelling*. So close is this language to that which is used by Paul in 1 Corinthians 15:53 f., it is difficult to believe that the same thought is not in mind here. At the sounding of the last trumpet "the dead will be raised imperishable and we shall be changed" (1 Cor. 15:52). That is, the dead will rise, and the living will be transformed. It is this transformation of the living which Paul has in view in our passage and for which

he *groans*, i.e., sighs with yearning. He desires to attain the final resurrection, if possible, without the necessity of enduring death.

In rendering v. 3 *so that by putting it on we may not be found naked*, the RSV translators evidently understood *naked* as meaning the condition of being without a body: Paul longed to put on the heavenly dwelling so as not to be bodiless after death. This however entails translating the phrase *ei ge kai* by "so that" instead of "if indeed," whereas the latter is its normal meaning (KJV and ERV, "if so be"; NEB "in the hope that"). Undoubtedly the normal meaning provides difficulties, for Paul could hardly have wished to say that he longed to put on the body of heavenly glory "if indeed after putting it on we shall not be found without a body"! Some early copyists of the New Testament were so puzzled about this that they concluded that Paul could not have written in this manner; they presumed that he wrote not "after putting it on" but "after putting it off" (*ekdusamenoi* instead of *endusamenoi*), and they altered the text accordingly: "in the hope that after putting off this body I shall not be found without a body." In the judgment of the present writer, the RSV translators and the early copyists who altered the text were both unjustified in what they did.

The vital issue is the meaning of *naked*. For the Hebrews, nakedness was especially the condition of slaves and prisoners of war. The prophets referred to nakedness as the result of God's judgment, i.e., by inflicting defeat and humiliation on the nation; and so they conjoined nakedness and shame in their visions of judgment (see especially the terrible description of Israel's judgment in Ezek. 23:22–25). Nakedness, therefore, can represent the condition of a man stripped of his pretensions to righteousness and standing in shame before God in the judgment. It is widely believed that this is the symbolism which was in Paul's mind in this passage. He yearned for the transformation that the coming of the Lord would bring about, but he was also concerned that on that great day he should not *be found,* i.e., by the Judge, as wanting in righteousness, ashamed and rejected as unfit for the kingdom of God. The language finds a close parallel in 1 John 2:28; but the thought is not infrequent in Paul (cf. 1 Cor. 3:10–15; 9:24–27; Phil. 2:12).

The whole train of thought in vv. 1–3 is gathered up in v. 4. *While we are still in this tent, we sigh with anxiety.* The Greek word for *sigh* is the same as for "groan" in v. 2. In the earlier verse the sighing is caused by intense longing on Paul's part, but in this passage it is caused by intense depression. Why depression? Because Paul does not wish to be *unclothed* but to be *further clothed.* As we saw in v. 2, the apostle views death as a burden he would fain be spared. He desires to put on the garment of Christ's resurrection glory at the coming of the Lord, that what is mortal in him *may be swallowed up,* i.e., destroyed by life from Christ. It is striking language, indicating the impossibility of the perishable inheriting the imperishable (1 Cor. 15: 53). The transformation of the living at the coming of the Lord involves a destruction and recreation as radical as death and resurrection. But the operative word is *life.*

The attainment of that life is the destiny of the redeemed children of God. *He who has prepared us for this very thing is God.* How has he prepared us for it? Not simply by creation, but much more by re-creation. This is seen in the very first step the convert to Christ takes, namely his baptism. Its ultimate meaning in Paul's teaching is being clothed with Christ (Gal. 3:27 ff.), and so participating in his death and resurrection (Rom. 6:3 ff.), otherwise viewed as a new beginning of life and renewal by the Holy Spirit (Titus 3:5). The purpose of all this is to attain final resurrection with Christ (Rom. 6:5), and for this *God . . . has given us the Spirit as a guarantee.* The Holy Spirit is essentially the Spirit who belongs to the kingdom of God, the era of resurrection and new creation. In sending him to his people, God has given the first installment of the totality of his salvation, and so a guarantee that the rest will follow.

So we are always of good courage echoes the sentiment of 4:16, "So we do not lose heart," and with similar reason: the apostle knows that he has a glorious destiny, and he is grateful for present grace. The picture of being *at home in the body* and *away from the Lord* has in view the imagery of v. 1. In the body we lead a nomadic existence, dwelling in tents, but the Lord inhabits the eternal temple in the heavens. A double consideration is in mind here: life in the tent cannot give a sense of fellowship with the Lord as immediate as life with him in his temple, and so it is like being *away from the Lord.*

On the other hand, life in the tent is life away from home, for we belong to that heavenly temple which is our real home. The significance of this thought is the greater when we consider who utters it, namely, the apostle whose faith is dominated by the concept "in Christ" and for whom "fellowship" is a key word. Few have more truly known the reality of life in, with, and through Christ as Paul, yet he recognizes that to be in the body involves hindrances to that life so serious as to make existence in the body like life in exile from the Father's house.

For we walk by faith, not by sight. With all Paul's mystic experiences, he knows no relationship with Christ which is not conditioned by faith, and faith has a limitation set to it by God's mysterious providence: it cannot see. Faith learns of grace, responds to the gospel, receives the Spirit, and walks in hope. The grace it sees, the eternal temple in the heavens it cannot see; but neither can it deny the reality of grace and the experience of the Spirit so that it trusts where it cannot see. When the perfect is come and sight is given, will faith be no more? First Corinthians 13:13 suggests otherwise: "There are three things that last for ever, faith, hope, and love" (NEB). This inspired Plummer to comment on the passage, "Here we have faith only, hereafter both faith and sight."

The recognition that existence in the tent

is life away from home enables Paul to overcome his reluctance to experience death: *we would rather be away from the body and at home with the Lord.* Admittedly this takes *courage,* for Paul adopts no sentimental view of death. There is no reason for imagining that he had ceased to view death as "the last enemy" (1 Cor. 15:26), but he knew that he belonged to its Conqueror. Since the Lord had prepared a place for him in his temple, he was willing to forsake his tent house and join the Lord in what he now viewed as his real home.

Again, it is helpful to remember the author's background. If Paul could resolutely set aside his distaste of death, and even welcome it in order to be *at home with the Lord,* it certainly did not occur to him that he would then be sent to bed to sleep till resurrection day. Life in fellowship with Christ was Paul's dominant concern, and for him death now signified fuller introduction to that holy fellowship, as deeper in its quality than the experience of present fellowship as blindness is different from sight. This understanding of death lies at the back of even more famous words of the apostle: "To me to live is Christ, and to die is gain" (Phil. 1:21). That can mean only that for Paul, life is Christ and death is more Christ. Accordingly he, who abominates death, is able to say, "My desire is to depart and be with Christ, for that is far better" (Phil. 1:23). Christ gives victory over death, not only when eyes are closed for the last time and when the last trumpet sounds, but in every moment when the believer is able to echo the apostle's words, "We walk by faith."

It is yet characteristic of Paul that whenever he thinks of the future he remembers that there is to be a judgment. He therefore adds, *So whether we are at home or away,* i.e., in life or in death, *we make it our aim to please him.* The phrase "we make it our aim" is in fact a single verb (Gk.), and its original significance is "we make it our ambition," a meaning which the NEB translators felt it right to retain here (as also in its two other occurrences,

Rom. 15:20; 1 Thess. 4:11). To please the Lord, whether dead or alive, is a good ambition. This was the spirit in which Jesus himself lived (Rom. 15:1–4; Phil. 2:8). The necessity of walking in such steps is emphasized by the consideration, *we must all appear before the judgment seat of Christ.* Every one of us must! Every Christian, every servant of Christ, even the greatest apostle must do so. For resurrection life is wholly the gift of God, as is life in the tent. The Christian looks forward to that day in the tension of a joyful assurance and a recognition that he is in the hands of the righteous Judge.

On that day *each one* will *receive good or evil, according to what he has done in the body.* Who does evil? Only the wicked? Who does good? Only the saints? The issues are in the hands of the omniscient One. What must be recognised by the saints is that some of their works will be exposed as unworthy of servants of Christ and will be destroyed. It behooves the Lord's servant to live at all times in the light of the last day, not alone for his own sake, but because Christ is worthy to be pleased—he who died and rose and comes again that we might receive eternal good.

(4) The Apostolic Gospel (5:11—6:2)

11 Therefore, knowing the fear of the Lord, we persuade men; but what we are is known to God, and I hope it is known also to your conscience. 12 We are not commending ourselves to you again but giving you cause to be proud of us, so that you may be able to answer those who pride themselves on a man's position and not on his heart. 13 For if we are beside ourselves, it is for God; if we are in our right mind, it is for you. 14 For the love of Christ controls us, because we are convinced that one has died for all; therefore all have died. 15 And he died for all, that those who live might live no longer for themselves but for him who for their sake died and was raised.

16 From now on, therefore, we regard no one from a human point of view; even though we once regarded Christ from a human point of view, we regard him thus no longer. 17 Therefore, if any one is in Christ, he is a new creation; the old has passed away, behold, the new has come. 18 All this is from God, who through Christ reconciled us to himself and

gave us the ministry of reconciliation; [19] that is, God was in Christ reconciling the world to himself, not counting their trespasses against them, and entrusting to us the message of reconciliation. [20] So we are ambassadors for Christ, God making his appeal through us. We beseech you on behalf of Christ, be reconciled to God. [21] For our sake he made him to be sin who knew no sin, so that in him we might become the righteousness of God.

[1] Working together with him, then, we entreat you not to accept the grace of God in vain. [2] For he says,
"At the acceptable time I have listened to you, and helped you on the day of salvation."
Behold, now is the acceptable time; behold, now is the day of salvation.

The overriding theme of the central chapters of this letter, namely the authenticity of his apostolic ministry, continues to provide the guiding thread of Paul's thought. Having given some account of the sufferings of his ministry and shown their unity with his proclamation of the death and resurrection of Christ (4:7—5:10), Paul now goes on to expound the heart of the gospel of the cross, but still from the controling viewpoint of his desire to illuminate the nature of his ministry.

Paul begins by indicating the relation of this message to the motives that control him in the exercise of his ministry and to certain charges made against him in Corinth (vv. 11–13). In proceeding to the exposition of his message (vv. 14 ff.) he lightly touches on some of the most profound elements of the Christian faith. The brevity of his exposition and its allusiveness are tantalizing to the exegete and theologian and have led to considerable divergence in the interpretation of the passage. Nevertheless these few verses constitute one of the most important expositions of the message of Christianity in the Bible, and they demand closest attention.

The *fear of the Lord* is one with the "fear and trembling" mentioned by Paul in a not dissimilar context in Philippians 2:12 which is proper to the Christian man as he contemplates the prospect of standing before the judgment seat of Christ (5:10). In this context the words *we persuade men* describe not the apostle's endeavors to persuade men to repent in view of the coming judgment—though of course Paul did that with passionate concern—but his efforts to persuade people, in particular the Christians of Corinth, of his own sincerity as he exercises his ministry. This sincerity had been called in question in Corinth, and Paul protests that insincerity is impossible for one who takes seriously the judgment of Christ. And in truth he takes it seriously: *what we are is known to God*, which suggests that Paul is conscious of the searching scrutiny of his Judge at all times and that he lives in the light of the last judgment every day. God knows all about him, of that he is confident. He can but hope that the Corinthians in their hearts (their *conscience*) know him too, for if they do they will surely acknowledge his sincerity.

To speak even as gently as this brings to mind the old charge, "Self-commendation again!" (cf. 3:1 ff.). "Not so," replies Paul, "we are giving you cause to be proud of us, and ammunition to answer those who are proud of themselves." To appreciate v. 12 fully requires a reading of chapters 10—12. Clearly there was a need for the church members of Corinth to *answer* the people who were proud of themselves, for in their pride these men had attacked Paul. The Corinthians were, therefore, under the necessity of choosing whom to believe, Paul or his detractors. These opponents were evidently the "superlative apostles" mentioned in 11:5, whom Paul does not hesitate to describe as "false apostles . . . disguising themselves as apostles of Christ" (11:13). They prided themselves on *a man's position and not on his heart*, on the impression they made upon men instead of being concerned about their condition before God.

It is likely that a major element in the *pride* of these men, and which was a point at issue between them and Paul, is alluded to in v. 13. But opposite conclusions as to what that issue was have been drawn from the statement. When was Paul *beside* himself, and when was he in his *right mind?* We may rule out as improbable the idea that the former echoes a charge that Paul's attempts at self-vindication were sheer madness, and that he defended them as made for the Lord's sake, while his more sober teaching was for the Corinthians' sake. The term "to be beside oneself" was not infrequently used to denote religious ecstasy. It is suggested therefore that Paul had been charged by the "superlative apostles" with overindulgence in ecstatic experiences in Corinth, notably in the exercise of spiritual gifts in times of worship (cf. 1 Cor. 14:18), and that his critics contrasted his behavior with their own restrained ministry of instruction.

Reflection on the force of the conjunction *for* at the beginning of v. 13, however, will surely suggest that precisely the opposite charge had been made by the false apostles. Priding themselves *on a man's position and not on his heart,* they took delight in manifesting their spiritual powers during the worship of the congregation; they knew that Paul was not in the habit of indulging in religious ecstasy in public (cf. 1 Cor. 14:19), and so they charged him with not being a spiritual man. In their view he was but a tame teacher of pedestrian truths, and since he was without the gifts of the Spirit he was obviously no apostle at all. It is to this criticism that v. 13 is directed.

Paul declares that he knows well enough what it is to experience ecstasy of the Spirit, but he engages in that in the privacy of his communion alone with God; in the congregation, admittedly, he does use restrained speech, but that is for their sakes that they may be better instructed. The principle on which Paul based his action is perfectly illustrated in Corinthians 14:18 f. If it led to misunderstanding on the part of men who were excessively enthusiastic about spiritual gifts and inclined to Gnostic exclusiveness, that was due to fundamental differences between them and Paul, alike in theology and in personal priorities. The two phrases in v. 13 *for God* and *for you* are deeply revealing; concern for the glory of God and the good of others determined Paul's ministry from start to finish.

Where did the apostle learn such selflessness? From the Lord himself. *The love of Christ controls us.* The term *controls,* rather than the familiar "constrains" of the KJV, is important. As this present writer understands the apostle's thought, this clause speaks not so much of the inspiration of Christ's sacrificial love to urge a man to go out into the world and blaze a trail of loving concern for humanity, as of the power of that love to restrain a man from all thoughts of self-advantage and to hem him in to the cross (see the instructive examples of Luke's use of this term in Luke 8:45; 12:50; 19:43). The acceptance of so radical a decision regarding self springs from one's understanding of the significance of the cross.

We are convinced that one has died for all; therefore all have died. Let the reader pause and contemplate those words before reading any further. For they give the plainest, starkest statement in the Bible as to the consequences of the death of Christ, and many students of Paul's writings seem afraid to take it in its stark, plain meaning. Scholars will insist on limiting its meaning, as though it could not apply to all, but only to believers. Or they think that Paul's words here relate to a mystical dying with Christ, or to an acceptance of the ethical norm of Christ's sacrifice, and the like. The present writer has come to the conclusion that Paul's teaching on redemption cannot be understood unless one is prepared to accept this statement in its unvarnished sense. Christ *died for all; therefore, all have died.*

The saying is based on two categories of thought, the significance of which has not always been appreciated. The first is that Christ is the second Adam, who in his birth, life, death, and resurrection stood for the entire race of men. The second is that in all his redemptive actions Christ was the representative of humanity, so that what was done by him for the race could be viewed as done by the race in him. The two concepts are, of course, vitally connected. It is the former which inspires Paul's doctrine of resurrection in 1 Corinthians 15, according to which the resurrection of this one Man entails the resurrection of the whole race. So strong is the unity, Paul declares that the non-resurrection of the race means that Christ could not have risen (1 Cor. 15:13). It is the latter concept which is especially operative here. A simple doctrine of substitution would have led Paul to write, "One man died for all men, therefore all men were spared from dying." The doctrine of representation led him to a step beyond that: "One man died for all men, therefore when he died all men died in him."

It is this view of Christ's death which made possible Paul's teaching on baptism in Romans 6, and to bear in mind that teaching here will save us from some false conclusions; for baptism signifies not simply an acceptance of the belief that Christ died to set the believer free from the death that sin brings, but that the believer participates in the death that Christ died for sin, with the consequence that death to sin and life from death for God's glory become the pattern of living. At this point, however, Paul has not got that far. His concern is the nature of his ministry as a service for others. On the one hand, it is determined by the prospect of the judgment seat of Christ. On the other, it is determined by the cross of Christ.

What ensues? *He died for all, that those who live might live no longer for themselves.* Here the purpose of Christ's dying is alone in view. The mode of appropriating the salvation that he brought about is not in question here. Christ died for men that men should cease to live for themselves. To live for self is the universal bent of humanity. Since Christ gave himself for all men, all should live *for him who for their sake died and was raised.* For the Saviour of humanity is the Lord of humanity; all men rightly belong to him, and therefore all men should serve him. When they live for him instead of living for themselves they do, in fact, live for others. Again, we recall, Paul is expounding the rationale of

his apostleship. He recognizes that Christ died to set men free from their sin and from themselves, in order that they might be enrolled in the service of the Lord which is perfect freedom, and so he sought to shape his ministry in accordance with that principle.

We must stay, however, to ask an important question: Who are *those who live* (v. 15)? The NEB renders the phrase "men, while still in life," and therefore interprets it in a general way, "men in their lifetime." The idea is then that Christ died for men, that men in their lifetime should live for him. Commonly *those who live* are viewed as those who have been spared from death through Christ's dying; in gratitude to the Lord they should henceforth spend the rest of their lives for him.

If there is such a connection of thought between vv. 14 and 15, then we must go further. For the logic of v. 14 is that when Christ died all died, therefore, none escaped death. Here is an example of the allusiveness of Paul's language, to which we earlier referred. He assumes that his readers know not only that in Christ's death and resurrection all men were implicated, since he was the representative of all, but that the proclamation of this message includes a call to believe the good news and be baptized, and so be united to him who died and rose for them. Then they will know in their own lives the power of his death for their sin and the power of his resurrection for their living. It is they who have so received Christ who are thought of in the phrase *those who live.* They *live* by the resurrection of Christ through the Holy Spirit of Christ, and so the purpose of Christ's death is fulfilled in them as they live for their Saviour.

For every man who has been so drawn into the death and resurrection of Christ, life and the world itself have become different: *From now on, therefore, we regard no one from a human point of view.* We would understand Paul's meaning better if we inserted (in thought) the word "merely" here: "we regard no one from a merely human point of view." The "human point of view" is that of the man who belongs to this world alone and who estimates men and things only from the viewpoint of this world. God's new world of redemption and life does not come into his horizon; naturally therefore he cannot take them into account in his reckoning. It is not that this world as such is evil, for God created it, and he made it good. The world is made evil, however, when men cease to lift their eyes on high to the God who created it and withhold the obedience due to him. Life on this latter basis is what Paul calls life "according to the flesh," in contrast to life "according to the Spirit," which is a life that belongs to the new world of Christ's redemptive rule.

In our passage the phrase *from a human point of view* is actually a paraphrase of the Pauline formula "according to the flesh." It is an adequate paraphrase so long as it is borne in mind that the *human point of view* is that of man unredeemed and dependent on his own resources. The man who has died and risen with Christ, however, cannot look on men and the world in this manner. He knows that Christ has brought life and immortality to light through the gospel, and he looks on his fellows as men and women created by God and redeemed through Christ, sons of God through creation and potentially the newborn sons of God in the new creation, if they will but turn to Christ. Those who believe, whatever their status in life—slaves or free, male or female, black or white, rich or poor—the Christian knows them to be fellow heirs with him in the kingdom of God and fellow members of the body of Christ.

The eyes of the believer see every man in a new light. And they see Jesus in a new light. *Even though we once regarded Christ from a human point of view, we regard him thus no longer.* Whether or not Paul ever saw Jesus in the flesh cannot be known. If he had been in Jerusalem at the Passover when Jesus was crucified, it is likely that he would have seen the Lord on his cross; but he could, of course, have been absent from the city on that occasion. If he had seen

Jesus on that dread day, it is strange that he never intimated it in any of his letters that have come down to us. But the sight of Jesus on the cross that Saul the Pharisee would have had and the recollection of it that Paul the apostle would have cherished would have been two quite different things. The same man, the same cross, the same crowd and the same dark sky would have been in view; but Saul would have seen a blaspheming pretender justly suffering the judgment of God, and in wrath his voice would have joined in the curses of the crowd.

But instead, the apostle saw the Christ of God hanging on his cross as the man for all men, bearing in himself the judgment of God for the wickedness of men, and in penitent love Paul asked forgiveness and sought grace to tell the world of so great salvation. It is a monstrous interpretation of the apostle's words to imagine that they were intended to convey a lack of interest in the "Christ according to the flesh," as though he had no time for Jesus of Nazareth, only the Christ of heaven. What Paul declared as belonging to the past was the merely human point of view of Jesus Christ, not the man Christ Jesus himself.

This saying no more hints that the man Christ Jesus is inaccessible to knowledge, or of no importance to us, than it implies that the Christian man is incapable of knowing his fellows or of being interested in them when once he has become a Christian. On the contrary, Paul affirms that the new man sees the world with new eyes, since this world is seen in the light of the world to come, and therefore, it is seen and understood more perfectly. Clearly, this has pertinence to Paul's theme of the ministry of the gospel, for now that Christ has died and risen, Paul (and those who serve Christ as he does) is able to look on men with eyes of compassion and understanding and give himself in loving service for them, as his Saviour did, in order to bring them into God's new world.

It is precisely this new world which is in mind in v. 17. *Therefore* harks back to

vv. 14–15. It is a deduction drawn from the fact that when Christ died the race died, and when he rose a new humanity came into being: *if anyone is in Christ, he is a new creation; the old has passed away, behold, the new has come.* The language is pure eschatology, brought into the life of today. The Bible, both in the Old Testament (e.g., Isa. 65:17 ff.) and the New Testament (e.g., Rev. 21:1 ff.) speaks of new heavens and a new earth which God is to manifest for the setting of his eternal kingdom of blessedness. For the new age of righteousness and life, a new creation is prepared (cf. 2 Peter 3:13).

Accordingly, the concepts of redemption, kingdom of God, new creation—all belong together. The marvellous news which the gospel declares is that through Christ that redemption, that kingdom of God, and that new creation all came into being. When Christ died and rose as the representative of humanity, God's judgment on sin was enacted, the devil was dethroned, the resurrection of the dead began, and the new creation came into being of which he, the Adam of the new humanity, was head and lord. Before ever the gospel was preached, the essential thing happened. In that risen Saviour a new humanity stood in God's new world, the firstfruits of the harvest of mankind (1 Cor. 15:20).

Therefore, if any one is in Christ, he is a new creation. United to the risen Lord, the believer participates in the new creation of which the Christ is the fount and the life. As in the end of time, he who sits on the throne in the heavens will declare, "Behold, I make all things new . . . It is done!" (Rev. 21:5 f.), signifying the passing of the old creation and the coming of the new; so, over him who is united to Christ in penitent faith the cry goes out *the old has passed away, behold, the new has come.* Such a man has stepped from the old world to the new, from death to life, and the purpose of his creation finds its true end. The temporal end of the old creation of course has not been reached, nor the climax of the new creation; but the great thing has happened—in the risen Lord the new world has come into being, and the man in Christ is part of it. Naturally it follows from all this that v. 17 has the strongest ethical implication for the Christian. His life should be radically different—with new moral quality and new spiritual devotion—because "he is a new creation."

All this is from God, who through Christ reconciled us to himself. How else could the new world have come into existence, except through the mighty acts of God the Creator—Redeemer? The whole process of the beneficent divine purpose is due to his gracious activity. Creation comes from the omnipotent and gracious acts of God in Christ, and the new creation proceeds from the omnipotent and gracious action of that same God in Christ. This applies to every step of the redemptive way: from the reconciliation wrought by Christ to the inclusion of a man in the death and resurrection of Christ, his entry into the new creation, his maintenance in grace through life, his maintenance in grace in death, and his attainment of final resurrection for the glory of the consummated kingdom—all is of God through Christ.

At this point, however, Paul singles out one crucial element of God's new creative activity in Christ—that of reconciliation. God *through Christ reconciled us to himself.* This reconciliation had to be achieved in order that there might be a new creation of righteousness and that men might participate in it. Apart from Christ man is alienated from God, doomed to death, and without hope of entering God's new world of life and holiness. Accordingly the God who effected a reconciliation *gave us the ministry of reconciliation.* He made provision that it should be proclaimed to men, that they should experience its power, and so enter the new world.

It was a source of ceaseless wonder to the apostle Paul that God should give to him the awesome privilege of cooperating with him in the work of the reconciliation of the world (cf. Eph. 3:8). It is of the Lord's ordaining that while he brought into being a creation and a new creation without the aid of man, he calls men to become his agents in leading sinful, broken men and women to the Saviour who wrought reconciliation for them and enables them to step into his new world. In the inscrutable providence of God the ministry of reconciliation is the counterpart to the achievement of reconciliation by the Son of God, and without that ministry the achievement does not reach its goal. Only the grace of God could either give such a terrifying responsibility to men or enable them to fulfill it.

What then is the nature of the reconciliation that God wrought in Christ and the ministry committed to Paul and other apostolic men? This forms the theme of v. 19, which virtually restates v. 18, but with significant additions that provide some helpful clues. *God was in Christ reconciling the world to himself, not counting their trespasses against them.* The first thing to note is the parallelism in vv. 18a and 19a.

Through Christ and *in Christ* are parallel expressions; they draw attention to God's operation by the agency of Christ. This strengthens a view long held that v. 19 does not mean primarily that God was in Christ (by incarnation—a fact accepted but not here in question) and that while he was in Christ he performed an act of reconciliation; rather, we must interpret, God was reconciling the world to himself in Christ. That is, God achieved this deed in and through Christ on the cross. But what was the deed of reconciliation? Who was reconciled to whom? and how?

Reconciliation implies a state of hostility brought to an end. Since God is the one who reconciles the world to himself through Christ—and it is never said in the New Testament that man reconciles God to himself—it is natural to presume that God's work in Christ is to remove the hostility in man towards God. Commonly, it is assumed that this is done through the demonstration of God's love that took place in the cross of Christ and the recognition by man of the awfulness of sin in its rejection and murder of the Son of God. This induces in man

repentance, and so he is reconciled to God through Christ. This interpretation, although at first glance attractive and plausible, hardly does justice to the language of this passage or to Paul's teaching on atonement generally, even though many students of Scripture give it their support.

It is worthy of note that some scholars believe that in v. 19 Paul cites earlier Christian confessional language, as he does quite frequently in his letters. Whenever Paul cites earlier writers, it is important to observe his insertions, for they indicate how he interprets what he quotes. The phrase *not counting their trespasses against them* is clearly Paul's own language, and it forms a kind of explanation of what was involved in God's reconciling the world to himself in Christ. It indicates that reconciliation is an aspect of justification; and in Paul's teaching, justification follows on the judgment on sin which Christ endured on the cross and the new relationship made possible through his resurrection (cf. Rom. 3:24 f.; 4:25).

The connection between justification and reconciliation is brought out more clearly in the only parallel to 2 Corinthians 5:19 in Paul's writings, namely, Romans 5:9 ff. According to this passage, justification is "by his blood," i.e., by Christ's death offered to God as a sacrifice for sins. Having been set free from the guilt and power of sin, we shall be "saved from the wrath of God," *for* "we were reconciled to God by the death of his Son." The reconciling death, then, was in relation to the wrath of God. That clearly implies that God was against man in his sin, and it was above all in relation to God rather than man that the reconciling death was suffered. But let it also be kept in mind that God was for man in his sin, even to the point of making reconciliation through his Son. There is a similar connection between reconciliation and Christ's death in relation to judgment in v. 21, for the statement, *For our sake he made him to be sin,* is added as a basis of understanding how the reconciliation came about. The reconciliation came about because Christ bore in himself the judgment for the sin of man. In the man Christ Jesus on the cross men received the judgment on sin, that in the Christ at God's right hand they might become righteous.

These considerations lead to the conviction that God's act of reconciliation in Christ must be viewed as a twofold drawing together of God to man and man to God, not simply of man being drawn to God. Moreover it happened once for all in Christ. In the man Jesus Christ all mankind was represented. In him, the obedient One, mankind bowed to receive the holy wrath of God against sin; in him mankind died to sin; in him mankind was accepted and vindicated through resurrection. In him therefore reconciliation was achieved between God and man and man and God.

It happened! This is why there is a gospel about a finished work of Christ. On the basis of this achievement, Paul and all other ambasadors of Christ are sent with the appeal, *We beseech you on behalf of Christ, be reconciled to God.* This means: "The reconciliation between God and man has been achieved on God's side through Christ; come forward then, lay aside your rebellion, and accept the reconciliation made on your behalf."

Once more we are reminded of the parallel passage in Romans 5:9 ff.: the result of reconciliation by Christ's death is, "We also rejoice in God through our Lord Jesus Christ, through whom we have now received our reconciliation" (v. 11). Christ has wrought the reconciliation with the Father; we on our part are reconciled as we come to God through Christ and accept the proffered peace and forgiveness.

Two lessons are plain in this passage. The first is the seriousness with which God takes sin and the consequent seriousness of the situation of the sinner. Modern man, including the modern Christian man, finds it hard to accept this view. Above all, he dislikes the idea that God can ever be "hostile" toward him in the sense of actively resisting him in his wrath. Consequently Paul's teaching on reconciliation is made into a simple

formula of man's laying down his arms against God. In view of this the reader may fittingly ponder the comment of Adolf Schlatter on this passage.

Since Paul saw in the death of Christ the death that was prepared for him, he recognised that he had God against him. The God who decrees death treats man as his opponent, whom he resists. But out of the attestation of the enmity arises its removal, since God's love caused Jesus to die for all, and the love of Jesus reveals the love of God. Thereby he brings the peace of God to man, his introduction into the fellowship with God. He who is in Christ has God on his side.[11]

That statement may be inharmonious with much modern theology, but it is faithful to the message of Paul and to that of the New Testament writers generally. He who minimizes the wrath of God and the judgment of God in the gospel also fails to understand the breadth and length and height and depth of the love of God declared in the gospel, and in so doing forsakes the company of the apostles who bore testimony to it.

The second lesson of this passage is that entreaty to men to respond to the reconciling act of God in Christ, and so enter into the reconciliation, is integral to the apostolic proclamation of the message of reconciliation. If at one time there was a tendency to regard reconciliation as wholly relating to man's return to God, and therefore not a once-for-all act but a process, there is a contemporary tendency to view reconciliation as wholly independent of the attitude of man. It is argued that since all mankind has been reconciled to God in Christ, it makes no essential difference to the reality of that reconciliation whether men and women know about it or not. All mankind without exception stands reconciled to God; the only difference between the church and the world is that the church knows that the reconciliation has taken place and the world does not. By this view, the preacher's task is to acquaint men of the good news of their reconciliation and to cooperate in all good

11 *Op. cit.,* p. 565.

things with all men, whatever their religion or lack of it, for in Christ all are one.

In view of the foregoing exposition of this chapter, the truth and the untruth of this position should be plain. It is true that a reconciliation has been wrought for every child of man, and neither ignorance nor denial of that can detract from its reality or sufficiency. But it is equally true that every man is under the necessity of recognizing his need of reconciliation by confessing his sin, responding to the call of God in the gospel, and so "receiving the reconciliation."

Such is the implication of vv. 20–21. *We are ambassadors for Christ.* Paul is an accredited representative of the Lord among men. No doubt the apostle is conscious of the rabbinic dictum, "One who is sent is as he who sent him" (cf. Matt. 10:40). Consequently his declaration of the message of reconciliation and appeal to men to be reconciled to God has to be viewed as *God making his appeal through us,* as the very word of Christ. The ambassador's art is diplomacy, and Paul here uses the idea in in its purest form: God "makes appeal" through Paul, and he "beseeches" on behalf of Christ. The news of reconciliation therefore is not merely good news, but urgent news, entailing consequences of highest import for men, indeed of eternal import. So important is it that men receive the news and respond to it, God is prepared to make entreaty of men to take it to themselves and act on it, and Christ beseeches through his representative Paul.

No graver issue can be set before man than for him to learn of the reconciliation achieved by Christ and the necessity for him to end his rebellion against God. And the reason for this gravity is clear: the reconciliation between God and the individual is incomplete so long as the individual withholds repentance, maintains his resistance to God, and declines to acknowledge Christ as Saviour and Lord. A gospel proclamation therefore which does not include God's appeal to men, *Be reconciled to God,* is only half the gospel; and since the omission is so serious, it must be viewed as a misrepresentation of the gospel.

The message and the appeal are alike concentrated in the pregnant statement: *For our sake he made him to be sin who knew no sin, so that in him we might become the righteousness of God.* It is often thought that the opening clause, *he made him to be sin* means that God made Christ to be a "sin-offering." The occurrence of the term *sin* in its usual meaning in the immediately following phrase however makes that suggestion difficult; and in any case there is little evidence in the New Testament to support this interpretation. The analogous language of Galatians 3:13, an equally terrible passage as this, may supply the clue to understanding v. 21. "He became a curse for us" probably means, "he bore the curse for us," i.e., the curse of divine judgment on sin. So here *he made him to be sin* probably means, "he bore the fearful consequences of sin."

The results of sin in human life and society are obvious enough, as Paul was able to demonstrate in the grim descriptions of Romans 1:21 ff. But the ultimate consequences are hidden from human eyes. The clearest and most awful revelation of the results of sin is the cross of Christ. What is visible to the human eye or imagination is shocking enough, in the murder of the one pure man of history, the Son of God himself; but what is hidden from human gaze and understanding, the travail of the Son of God in his soul, cannot be measured. It is dimly guessed in the appalling cry of dereliction from the cross (Mark 15:34). We men and women commit sin. Only the Son of God knew what it was to be *made sin.* But in the bearing of that load he extinguished its destructive force for every man and woman united to him in the Spirit.

In such people what Luther called "the happy exchange" takes place. So sure as Christ took their sin, so they receive in him the righteousness of God, indeed they *become* righteous in God's way. They know not only acquittal at the judgment seat of God but through the Spirit of Christ they become transformed into his image.

Once more the twofold strain of the gospel rings out. The great event whereby the sin of man has been borne away by the representative of mankind has come to pass and stands forever in power. But the release from sin and participation in the righteousness of God in Christ is experienced when men are *in him,* i.e., when they recognise their sinful state, repent and come to God through Christ, and so are united to Christ in the Spirit of faith. Verse 21 therefore implies that the appeal of God in Christ to men, made through the ambassadors of Christ, should run: "The great reconciliation has taken place in Christ; come then to him in whom God has drawn near to man; come to the Christ and lose your burden of sin, gain his righteousness, and enter into peace."

The first two verses of chapter 6 appeal to the Corinthians to receive the grace offered through the reconciliation of Christ, and so enter into his new creation. In the opening phrase of v. 1 the RSV translators rightly add to Paul's original words *Working together,* the expression *with him,* i.e., with God. The context indicates that Paul has in mind his role in the "ministry of reconciliation" (5:18); he who, as Christ's ambassador, entreats men that they be reconciled to God (5:20) cooperates with God in their reconciliation of the world.

But how is it possible to *accept the grace of God in vain?* In various ways. To hear the gospel of God's grace without faith is to forego the grace offered (cf. Mark 4: 14 ff.). It is conceivable that Paul may have suspected that some of the Corinthians had not yet truly experienced the reconciling grace of Christ. To profess faith in the gospel without following it up with a life of faith and obedience towards Christ is also to accept grace in vain. Paul manifests concern for his converts at all times, that they do not confound assurance of God's faithfulness to his word with presumption on man's part (cf. 1 Cor. 15:2). It is also true that Paul was deeply concerned that his converts should not abandon the true gospel for a counterfeit version of it, whether of the kind

that threatened the Christians in Galatia (cf. the solemn words of Gal. 5:2–6) or that which had stirred up the Corinthian church against Paul (cf. 2 Cor. 11:1–4). For the professing Christian, as for the non-Christian hearer of the good news, the sole hope of life is in Christ crucified and risen, hence he must at all times hold "fast to the Head" (Col. 2:18 f.).

The appeal not to *accept* God's grace in vain may have reminded the apostle of a significant Old Testament passage (Isa. 49:8) which tells of the arrival of God's *acceptable time,* i.e., his day of grace. The citation in Isaiah follows closely on the so-called second Servant Song, which announces that the Servant of the Lord is not only to bring Israel back to God but that he is to become a light to the nations and extend salvation to the ends of the earth. In the "time of favor" (translated "acceptable time" in the Septuagint) and the day of salvation, God is to exercise his almighty power to lead his exiles out of their captivity into their homeland where they will find consolation and gladness in his kingdom.

Paul's declaration, *now is the acceptable time; behold, now is the day of salvation,* affirms that the time has now come for the fulfillment of those gracious promises. In this he echoes the teaching of his fellow apostles, which in turn becomes the basic assumption of the entire new Testament: that the promises of God relating to his kingdom have been fulfilled through the redemptive acts of Christ and the outpouring of the Holy Spirit. The emphasis in this passage therefore falls on the word *now* and on its aspect as good news. It is unlikely that Paul is here issuing a warning, as though to say, "Do not decline the grace of God; today you may be saved, but tomorrow will be too late." Rather he affirms, "Rejoice and be glad! The time of deliverance and salvation in God's promised kingdom has come. Open your lives to the flood tide of divine grace. Enter into the reconciliation, and become new creatures in Christ." The sense of wonder implicit in this assertion should be compared with the joyous exultation expressed in Luke 10:17–24, where the Lord himself bids his disciples realize how privileged they are to see and hear things which kings, prophets, and saints of former ages yearned to see but did not see; for to them is given the unspeakable privilege of living in the time of salvation.

(5) The Apostolic Life (6:3–10)

3 We put no obstacle in any one's way, so that no fault may be found with our ministry, 4 but as servants of God we commend ourselves in every way: through great endurance, in afflictions, hardships, calamities, 5 beatings, imprisonments, tumults, labors, watching, hunger; 6 by purity, knowledge, forbearance, kindness, the Holy Spirit, genuine love, 7 truthful speech, and the power of God; with the weapons of righteousness for the right hand and for the left; 8 in honor and dishonor, in ill repute and good repute. We are treated as impostors, and yet are true; 9 as unknown, and yet well known; as dying, and behold we live; as punished, and yet not killed; 10 as sorrowful, yet always rejoicing; as poor, yet making many rich; as having nothing, and yet possessing everything.

The overriding theme of the apostolic ministry is still before Paul's eyes. After expounding the message of reconciliation in 5:11—6:2, Paul now recounts certain consequences for himself of being a preacher of the gospel. The key to the passage is the opening clause of v. 3: *We put no obstacle in any one's way.* This follows directly on the entreaty of v. 1 not to accept the grace of God in vain, for v. 2 is a parenthetical comment which strengthens the appeal there made. Paul has in mind a factor of which ministers of the gospel from his day to our own have been acutely aware, namely, that there is a dread possibility for the gospel of God's grace to be besmirched by its preachers and hence that obstacles be put in the way of men accepting the good news, and so *fault be found with our ministry.*

Admittedly the faultfinding can sometimes be puerile, a mere sop to the conscience of men who reject the word of God, and sometimes it can be downright wicked. Paul had more than his fill of this latter kind

of criticism. It was the cruelty of unscrupulous attacks on him by men who opposed his message and his way of ministry that gave rise to this letter. Nevertheless he was too honest to discount the fact that lack of vigilance on his part could result in the ministry being discredited and men being hindered from turning to Christ.

Accordingly Paul strives to bring about the opposite of disgrace for the gospel and its ministry, namely, to commend them. That is the point of v. 4, *as servants of God we commend ourselves in every way.* What men thought of Paul as an individual was of small moment to him (cf. 1 Cor. 4:3 f.), but insofar as he was identified with the cause of Christ he could not ignore their attitudes. He therefore did his utmost, by speech and actions, to make it easier rather than more difficult for men to receive the gospel. What follows in vv. 4a onwards is a recitation of ways in which Paul sought to commend the gospel.

Inevitably we are reminded of the related description in chapter 4, especially vv. 7–12. In that passage Paul probably had in view the unease with which the Corinthians viewed his fearful experiences of suffering, entailed through his ministry of the gospel, and so he endeavored to show that Christ and his gospel were glorified in his tribulations, for they exemplified the suffering to death and resurrection to life which lay at the heart of the gospel. A similar consideration may be present in this passage also. The ministry committed to Paul entails sufferings of many kinds, but they are neither accidental nor ineffectual, for they are essentially related to the gospel of reconciliation he preaches. The gospel arises in the rebellion of man against God, a hostility which culminated in the rejection of the message of the Christ and his murder. It is hardly surprising therefore if the ambassador of Christ experiences antipathy in his proclamation of the reconciliation offered by God in the gospel. But the story of Jesus became good news only because the Son of God was vindicated in his resurrection; it is therefore wholly consonant with the gospel that the power of God turns the sufferings of Christ's apostle to a means of blessing men. Both aspects of this "commendation" of the gospel are in mind in vv. 4–10, though the element of vindication appears more particularly towards the close of the paragraph as it reaches its crescendo in v. 10.

The first feature mentioned by Paul in his list of ways of commending the ministry is the characteristic Christian virtue of *endurance*. Owing to the persecution which Christians experienced at the hands of ruling authorities, this became a matter of crucial importance to the church. The example of Jesus, who "endured the cross," was continually set before believers (cf. Heb. 12:1–2), and it is likely that the earliest Gospel (that by Mark) took its form, in part at least, to inspire Christians to follow in the footsteps of their Lord and bear their own crosses to the places of execution provided for them by Nero (cf. Mark 8:28–38; 10:35–45; 13:1–37). So here Paul's *great endurance* is particularized in three series of triplets, portraying troubles which befell Paul in the course of his ministry. *Afflictions, hardships, calamities* describe the circumstances in which his ministry was often exercised; *beatings, imprisonments, tumults* denote troubles which are inflicted on him by men in their opposition to his ministry; *labors, watching, hunger* were hardships which Paul voluntarily underwent in carrying out his ministry.

Then follows a list of virtues and various modes of ministry by which Paul seeks to commend the gospel. *Purity* perhaps relates to the discreet way in which Paul behaves towards women whom he had to counsel. *Knowledge* in this context refers rather to his understanding of men than to Christian doctrine. Similarly *the Holy Spirit* is mentioned, not so much in connection with his enabling Paul to perform miraculous deeds and to preach powerfully as with his imparting wisdom to deal with the needs of men (a very important requirement of ministers in their pastoral work). If in v. 7 *truthful speech* is the correct rendering of

Paul's words, it will refer to Paul's endeavor to be accurate and sincere in his preaching. But since the literal meaning of the phrase is "by the word of truth," it could mean the preaching of the gospel itself. The preceding context favors the RSV rendering; the context that follows may be felt to favor the more literal rendering.

The weapons of righteousness for the right hand and for the left are either weapons provided by righteousness or weapons which consist in righteousness— both interpretations suit the context. In any case the *righteousness* in view is not that of man, but God's righteousness that is bestowed through the word of truth and the power of God. God's saving righteousness is both an offensive weapon to overcome sin in man (a weapon *for the right hand*) and a shield against every attack by the powers of evil (a weapon *for the left hand*, in which the shield was always carried).

In vv. 8–10 we come closest to the antitheses of 4:7–12; and as there Paul holds together the hardships which come to him in the course of his ministry and the overruling grace of God which makes of the wrath of men an occasion for his praise. However many lions may attack Paul, the Lord enables him to extract honey from the carcass of every one of them! He exercises his ministry *in honor and dishonor, in ill repute and good repute;* but whatever the conditions, he is not deterred from fearlessly proclaiming the truth which alone has power to save men. The record of Paul's ministry in the book of Acts supplies abundant illustrations of both types of reception which Paul met in his evangelism, and they are spelled out in the contrasts of vv. 8b–10.

We are treated as impostors, he says, as the Corinthians very well knew; for this was the charge laid against him by the "superlative apostles" who sought to undermine his authority in the church of Corinth. *As unknown*—"Who is this man Paul?" asked his detractors. Multitudes in all parts of the Roman world could answer that question in Paul's day, and curiously enough few men in history are so well-known to our age as Paul. *As dying*—whether by sudden onslaught or by persistent overwork day and night—*and behold we live;* for the risen Christ again and again manifests his power to raise the dead in this herald of the gospel (cf. 4:10–12). *As sorrowful*—for Paul had many a heartache through the inconsistencies of his converts (cf. 11:28 f.), and he carried an undying grief for the hardness of his fellow Jews towards the gospel (Rom. 9:2); *yet always rejoicing,* for God constantly led him in triumph in his ministry (2:14), and he knows that the end of all things will be Christ in his glorious reign (1 Cor. 15:25).

As poor—he was not always so, but acceptance of the gospel and the Lord's commission to become its herald involved his forsaking wealth, as all other advantages he had known as a Pharisee (cf. Phil. 3:7 f.); *yet making many rich,* not materially but in an infinitely more important sense, for what can compare with the wealth of God's kingdom which the Christian has already and is to possess in fullness in the future? In this respect the apostle by his sacrificial ministry approximated in a wonderful way the example of his Lord, who "though he was rich, for our sake became poor, so that by his poverty you might become rich" (8:9). The final antithesis, *as having nothing, and yet possessing everything,* forms a fitting climax to Paul's commendation of the ministry, for in it he is associated even more closely with his Lord; yet having Christ he has everything—the world, life, death, the present, the future, and God himself (1 Cor. 3:21 ff.).

(6) Appeal for an Open Heart and Separated Life (6:11—7:4)

11 Our mouth is open to you, Corinthians; our heart is wide. 12 You are not restricted by us, but you are restricted in your own affections. 13 In return—I speak as to children—widen your hearts also.

14 Do not be mismated with unbelievers. For what partnership have righteousness and iniquity? Or what fellowship has light with darkness? 15 What accord has Christ with Belial? Or what has a believer in common with an unbeliever? 16 What agreement has the temple of God with idols? For we are the temple of the living God; as God said,

"I will live in them and move among them,
  and I will be their God,
  and they shall be my people.
17 Therefore come out from them,
  and be separate from them, says the Lord,
  and touch nothing unclean;
  then I will welcome you,
18 and I will be a father to you,
  and you shall be my sons and daughters,
  says the Lord Almighty."

1 Since we have these promises, beloved, let us cleanse ourselves from every defilement of body and spirit, and make holiness perfect in the fear of God.

2 Open your hearts to us; we have wronged no one, we have corrupted no one, we have taken advantage of no one. 3 I do not say this to condemn you, for I said before that you are in our hearts, to die together and to live together. 4 I have great confidence in you; I have great pride in you; I am filled with comfort. With all our affliction, I am overjoyed.

Paul's defense of his ministry is at an end. He has poured out his soul in his exposition of the ministry which he had received from the Lord. How will the Corinthians react to it? Will they reciprocate in a corresponding openness of spirit, or will they manifest narrow heartedness towards him? *Our mouth is open to you, Corinthians.* Paul has held nothing of his mind back, but has used complete candor as he has addressed them. *Our heart is wide*—it stands open to embrace in love every member of the church in Corinth, including those who have caused him most grief. So far, however, the like large heartedness has not been manifested by them. They have been *restricted,* i.e., narrowed, in their affections, leaving little room for the apostle in their hearts. Was this through a lingering resentment on their part that Paul had been so outspoken to them and had made them feel ashamed? Did they still wistfully cling to the ways of the false teachers? Whatever the cause of their restraint, Paul implies that their trouble was basically not intellectual, not a lack of understanding, but a lack of Christian love: *you are restricted in your own affections.* He therefore appeals to them in a manner as if he were talking to children: *In return . . . widen your hearts also.* That is to say, "Play fair, you people! Give the same to me as I give to you!" Or, in Plummer's words, "Repay open heart with open heart."

The immediately succeeding paragraph (6:14—7:1) calls on the Corinthians to separate themselves from all associations inimical to the Christian faith. It is widely believed that the paragraph is in the wrong place. The connection of thought with what has preceded and that which follows is by no means clear, while the context runs smoothly if the passage is omitted (6:13 concludes with the appeal, *Widen your hearts;* 7:2 begins, *Open your hearts to us*).

In this connection attention is drawn to the fact that 1 Corinthians 5:9 refers to a letter written by Paul prior to 1 Corinthians, in which Paul instructed the church not to associate with harlots and the degenerate. It has therefore been suggested that 2 Corinthians 6:14—7:1 may be part of the letter to which reference is made in 1 Corinthians 5:9, and that it was inserted into the present context by someone in Corinth who wished to ensure its preservation. Whatever the merits of the idea that this paragraph may be misplaced, it should be observed that the subject with which it deals is related to that of 1 Corinthians 5:9 but is not identical with it. In the latter passage Paul states that he wrote in his former letter about professing Christians, not about immoral pagans; but 2 Corinthians 6:14 ff. unambiguously has in view immoral pagans, not loose living Christians. It would seem therefore that the letter referred to in 1 Corinthians 5:9 and the passage before us must be dissociated from each other.

There are, of course, many exegetes who defend the view that the paragraph is in its original context. They point out that Paul frequently goes off at a tangent, to return to his subject at a later point; and they consider that an interpolator would have chosen a more obvious place than this one. With this in mind Plummer (p. 205) wrote: "It is not incredible that in the middle of his appeal for mutual frankness and affection, and after his declaration that the cramping constraint is all on their side, he should dart off to one main cause of that constraint, viz., their compromising attitude towards anti-Christian influences. Having relieved his mind of this distressing subject, he returns at once to his tender appeal." Certainty is unattainable in this discussion, and it is not important. What is clear is that no church founded by Paul was in such need of the exhortation in this paragraph as the church of Corinth, whose difficulties in no small measure were due to the disinclination of its members to take a firm stand for the gospel and order their lives in accord with it.

The injunction, *Do not be mismated with unbelievers,* is an attempt to put into English a compound verb which has the idea of being yoked with an incompatible animal. Deuteronomy 22:10, in a context which forbids sowing vineyards with different kinds of seed and mingling different materials in clothes, states, "You shall not plough with an ox and an ass together." The prohibition was later applied among Jews in Palestine to mixed marriages, but not only to them; it was also applied to the association of a teacher with a colleague who held different views. It is likely that Paul had in mind a general application of the metaphor, rather than the sole application to marriage. Moffatt therefore renders the sentence, "keep out of all incongruous ties with unbelievers." The series of questions which follow may then be viewed as reinforcing the reasonableness, not to say necessity, of observing this general rule.

The emphasis in the questions of vv. 14 ff. is on the fundamental incompatibility of that which belongs to God with that which does not submit to his rule. *What partnership have righteousness and iniquity?* The term *partnership* is noteworthy, for it suggests personal relations. Of a truth the righteousness with which Paul is concerned is that which springs from God in Christ (5:21), whereas iniquity proceeds from man in rebellion against God. *What fellowship has light with darkness?* has a similar connotation. For *light* streams from the creative and redemptive speech of God (4:6), while *darkness* is the characteristic of paganism in its alienation from God (cf. Rom. 13:12; Eph. 5:7). *What accord has Christ with Belial?* maintains the same idea of the incompatibility between moral and spiritual opposites; for God's work of delivering men from their iniquity and darkness to gain righteousness and light takes place through Christ, while Belial (= the devil, thought of as the "worthless" one) inspires iniquity, plunges men into darkness, and opposes Christ in the world.

What has a believer in common with an unbeliever? For the former belongs to God, and the latter belongs to the darkness which is under the sway of the devil. *What agreement has the temple of God with idols?* is explained by the immediately following comment, *For we are the temple of the living God.* The idea of the church as a temple is established in Paul's writings (1 Cor. 3: 16 f., referring to the local congregation; Eph. 2:20 ff. to the universal church); and the figure is also applied to the believer (1 Cor. 6:19 f.). In this passage, however, it is the local congregation which is in mind.

To any acquainted with the Old Testament the Temple was the place where the Lord revealed his glory (1 Kings 8:10; cf. Isa. 6:1 ff.), where atonement was made for the sins of the people, and where holy and joyous fellowship was experienced in the festival seasons. Not that any ordinary Jew was ever permitted to enter the Temple itself (v. 16 employs the term *naos,* "shrine," the Temple proper, as distinct from *hieron,* which includes the entire Temple area); but the barriers which kept the people of God from the most holy place are removed for the people of the new covenant (cf. Mark 15:38; Heb. 9:6 ff.; 10:19 ff.). In this new age, therefore, the *temple* signifies the fellowship between the all holy God and his people, in contrast to the "fellowship" which the pagans had in their temples, often sordid and immoral, and with which Paul did not hesitate to associate demonic presence

(1 Cor. 10:19 ff.). Even under the old covenant, to bring idolatrous objects and practices into the Temple was looked on as horrifying (cf. Ezek. 8:3–18, and especially the profanation of the Temple by Antiochus Epiphanes, which ever after became the standing symbol of antichrist; see 1 Macc. 1:41 ff.; Dan. 8:10 ff.; 9:26 f.; 11:31 ff.). To the end of time there can be no compromise between the temple of God and idols.

The promise that the Lord will dwell among his people, as in a temple, cites Leviticus 26:11 f. and Ezekiel 37:27. The latter is especially pertinent to this context, for it is drawn from the climax of Ezekiel's vision of the valley of dry bones, wherein God promises to raise his people from their living death in exile to a resurrection-like life under the rule of the new David. In that time "they shall not defile themselves any more with their idols and their detestable things, or with any of their transgressions . . . I will make a covenant of peace with them . . . and will set my sanctuary in the midst of them for evermore" (Ezek. 37:23 ff.). In the age when that gracious promise is fulfilled, namely the time of the church, it is unthinkable that the Lord's people should again defile themselves with "idols and their detestable things."

Therefore come out from them, and be separate from them, says the Lord. The cry uttered by the prophet of the Exile (Isa. 52:11) demanded that the people of God should depart from Babylon and its unclean things, set out for the land of their fathers, and so receive the salvation which God had prepared for them in his kingdom. The other Old Testament passages echoed by Paul at this point also relate to redemption in the kingdom of God (2 Sam. 7:8,14; Isa. 43:6; Jer. 31:9); they emphasize the same basic thought of forsaking unclean associations with heathenism for the pilgrimage to God's eternal kingdom.

Accordingly the citations are concluded with an appeal: *Since we have these promises, beloved, let us cleanse ourselves from every defilement of body and spirit.* The promises of life with God and his people in the everlasting kingdom are so great, it is unthinkable to contemplate foregoing them by continuing in associations which defile men and rob them of their inheritance. Rather the Christian is called to *make holiness perfect in the fear of God.* That is, he is not only to rid himself of the things which defile, but to see that holy associations take their place, such as are consonant with *the fear of God,* i.e., with reverence for his name and his will. Only by positive action for good as well as negative withdrawal from evil will a man become fit for God in *body and spirit.*

The significance of this last phrase can be overlooked through the rendering of Paul's words in the RSV, for Paul actually spoke of cleansing the defilement of "flesh and spirit." The RSV translators presumably preferred the term *body* to "flesh" here, because they knew that in Paul's writings "flesh" commonly denotes human personality in its creaturely weakness and enslavement to sin, in contrast to "spirit," which is the divine recreative principle of the new order, and which makes the believer a spiritual man. Paul's appeal to be cleansed from every defilement of flesh and spirit clearly shows that he repudiated the Gnostic doctrine that man as "flesh" is incurably evil; on the contrary, Paul implies that man can be cleansed from all the defilements of existence in this world and become acceptable to God through the Spirit. Indeed it is when life in its totality, flesh and spirit, is subjected to the will of God that holiness is made perfect in the fear of God. If this insight is borne in mind, unscriptural applications of 6:14—7:1 will be avoided.

Open your hearts to us takes up again the cry of 6:13, "widen your hearts," and has the same meaning. Paul asks not that the Corinthians will pour out their hearts to him in free and frank confession, but that they will make room in their hearts for him. If 6:14—7:1 is where Paul intended it, the exhortation receives further point; for clearly the Corinthians would have had no room for Paul in their hearts if they had chosen the wrong kind of fellowship; they would now be consorting with iniquity rather than righteousness, with darkness rather than light, with Belial instead of Christ, with the idolatrous world instead of the temple of the living God. But if they have responded to Paul's call for cleansing from defilement, they will surely wish to make room for Paul in their fellowship.

On their part therefore there is no reason for excluding Paul from their affections. Neither is there from Paul's side. *We have corrupted no one, we have taken advantage of no one.* From similar statements of Paul's (e.g., 12:17 f.), it is clear that allegations had been made by some in Corinth that he had in fact corrupted them by his "false" teaching, and that he had taken advantage financially of them. Had the allegations been true, the Corinthians would have had reason to repudiate the apostle; but Paul has shown that they are false. Then there is no room for the Corinthians to withhold from him a place in their affections.

Lest this statement should cause needless discomfort, especially among those who had believed the false reports about Paul, he assures the church of his goodwill: *I do not say this to condemn you.* He has no intention of stirring up old strifes, or of reopening old wounds which now were healing. On the contrary, as he had earlier said, *you are in our hearts* (see 3:2; 6:11 f.); now, however, he adds, what he had not said before, *to die together and to live together.* The bond that links his heart to theirs is so strong, nothing in death or life can destroy it. Naturally this relates to Paul's side of the relationship. Whether the Corinthians could rise to a like expression of affection is doubtful. The apostle had lived so close to his Lord, and had pondered his cross so long, that his heart had been kindled by the fire of love that blazed in the Redeemer's heart (cf. 5:14 f.). So far as he was concerned therefore, it could be said of him regarding his beloved Corinthians, "He will, if need be, die with them, and he cannot live without them. This is the mark of the good shepherd (John 10:12)" (Plummer).

Out of such assurance of unity in heart the apostle now finds it possible to affirm, *I have great confidence in you; I have great pride in you; I am filled with comfort.* How different is that from his earlier expressions of fears for the Corinthians! The issues between them and him have been settled, his pride in them has been vindicated, his anxieties over them have been swept away, and his recent distresses (1:8 ff.) swallowed up in joy. *With all our affliction, I am overjoyed.* By this the Corinthians know that the sundered relations with their apostle, who was their father in God (I Cor. 4:14 f.), have been completely restored and his forgiveness assured. Cold indeed they must have been if after this they did not open their hearts to such a man!

(7) *The Joy of Restored Relationship* (7: 5–16)

5 For even when we came into Macedonia, our bodies had no rest but we were afflicted at every turn—fighting without and fear within. 6 But God, who comforts the downcast, comforted us by the coming of Titus, 7 and not only by his coming but also by the comfort with which he was comforted in you, as he told us of your longing, your mourning, your zeal for me, so that I rejoiced still more. 8 For even if I made you sorry with my letter, I do not regret it (though I did regret it), for I see that that letter grieved you, though only for a while. 9 As it is, I rejoice, not because you were grieved, but because you were grieved into repenting; for you felt a godly grief, so that you suffered no loss through us. 10 For godly grief produces a repentance that leads to salvation and brings no regret, but worldly grief produces death. 11 For see what earnestness this godly grief has produced in you, what eagerness to clear yourselves, what indignation, what alarm, what longing, what zeal, what punishment! At every point you have proved yourselves guiltless in the matter. 12 So although I wrote to you, it was not on account of the one who did the wrong, nor on account of the one who suffered the wrong, but in order that your zeal for us might be revealed to you in the sight of God. 13 Therefore we are comforted.

And besides our own comfort we rejoiced still more at the joy of Titus, because his mind has been set at rest by you all. 14 For if I have expressed to him some pride in you, I was not put to shame; but just as everything we said to you was true, so our boasting before Titus has proved true. 15 And his heart goes out all the more to you, as he remembers the obedience of you all, and the fear and trembling with which you received him. 16 I rejoice, because I have perfect confidence in you.

Paul now calls to mind the occasion of his journey to Macedonia (Philippi?) to meet Titus on his return from Corinth. He had made a brief allusion to this in 2:13, but then had broken off immediately in a doxology to the Lord, who always leads Paul in his triumph train. There is a curious link in the language of the two passages. In 2:13 Paul states that he made a sudden end of his evangelistic work in Troas, because "my mind could not rest," or as it should be rendered more exactly, "I had no rest in my spirit." Here he says, having reached Macedonia, *our bodies had no rest,* or again, more exactly, "our flesh had no rest." Doubtless the terms flesh and spirit are used with freedom, in a popular rather than exact sense. The use of the term flesh in this passage suggests that Paul in his weakness experienced exhaustion due to the strain of the circumstances.

Unlike the "super-apostles" of Corinth, Paul was no superman, but one very much aware of his limitations. *We were afflicted at every turn,* he says; there was *fear within*—anxiety over the situation in Corinth—and there was *fighting without,* i.e., opposition from opponents of the gospel. Paul, we remember, had felt unable to continue his evangelistic task in Troas, by reason of his anxiety for Corinth, and so had crossed the sea to Macedonia in order to meet Titus. But he could not stand idly by in Macedonia while he waited for his colleague. He therefore joined in the work of the Christian community there and naturally must have given a tremendous impetus to the church in those parts. The result was a stirring up of the opposition to the Christians in those parts. Once more Paul had stepped from the frying pan into the fire!

But the pressure did not continue long in this way. *God, who comforts the down-*

cast, comforted us. Paul here cites a sentence from the same paragraph of Isaiah 49 which he had quoted in 6:2. After describing the salvation which God is to bring about through his Servant and the exercise of his miraculous power, the prophet bursts out into a paean of praise: "Sing for joy, O heavens, and exult, O earth; . . . For the Lord has comforted his people, and will have compassion on his afflicted" (Isa. 49:13). It was by like miraculous power that the Lord had brought about the restoration of his people in Corinth; but the "afflicted" whom he had comforted was not the people in Corinth but the apostle who loved them and prayed for them and toiled for their restoration.

God *comforted* him *by the coming of Titus,* both because Titus was dear to Paul, his most trusted and experienced colleague, and by reason of the news he brought from Corinth. Moreover Paul was encouraged *by the comfort with which he was comforted in you.* We need not doubt that Titus had mixed thoughts about the prospect of his visit to Corinth. The church in that city was a troublesome, quarrelsome group, and it had given Paul a terrible time on the occasion of his last visit; the false teachers, with their implacable opposition to Paul, were still in control of the church and would be ready to resist him to the limit. If Paul had fared so badly in Corinth, what chance was there that his representative would do better? Whatever misgivings Titus may have entertained, they were all dissipated on his arrival through the unexpected welcome he received from the Corinthians. *He told us of your longing,* writes Paul, longing, i.e., to see their apostle again; *your mourning,* i.e., of the events that had caused Paul pain and had driven a wedge between them and him; *your zeal,* namely, to rally to the apostle's cause and to vindicate him against those who had opposed him.

This happy turn of events not only brought joy to Paul in the present; it made an end to the tormenting uncertainty he had endured as to whether he had done right in sending the severe letter to Corinth after his disastrous visit to the church. It was not Paul's nature to hurt his friends, nor did he delight in causing grief to a church, least of all to one he loved so dearly as that in Corinth. He was called to be a minister of reconciliation. Should he then have written in such grave terms of rebuke as he had used in writing to Corinth? At one point he wavered and felt that he had made a mistake: *I did regret it.* But the outcome of the letter showed that the regret was needless, for the grief it caused the Corinthians was *only for a while,* and their grief had turned out for their good and not for their loss.

I rejoice . . . because you were grieved into repenting. Repentance in the Bible indicates not a sorrow for sins but a turning from sin to the God who forgives sin and gives grace for righteousness. It is what we commonly mean by the word conversion. For men and women to turn to God is a matter for joy on the part of those who love them, and in this passage Paul consistently distinguishes between the sorrow of the Corinthians and their repentance. The men and women of Corinth certainly experienced grief because of their treatment of their apostle, and they recognized their wrong before God in this matter. But theirs was *a godly grief;* that is, a grief such as God willed, a grief made possible by the work of grace in their hearts.

Naturally the grace of God makes use of instruments for the accomplishment of his purpose. Paul's letter was part of the means to the desirable end, and the ministry of Titus contributed to the same end, but it was the Holy Spirit who applied the word in the minds of the Corinthians and broke down their stubborn hearts, enabling them to perceive afresh the love of Christ in the apostle through whom they had been brought to new birth. They, therefore, *suffered no loss,* but experienced *a repentance that leads to salvation.*

Godly grief is vastly different from *worldly grief;* the former leads to salvation, the latter to death. *Godly grief,* be it remembered, is grief that God inspires and wills. *Worldly grief* is, likewise, grief that is caused by the world. Such grief comes about less through the hard knocks of life —for example, through illness or other forms of adversity—than through men of ill will in their selfishness, jealousy, bitterness, coldness, harshness, even hatred. Many are the pitiable souls who have found this kind of grief from the world too much to endure, and in their grief have ended their lives by their own hand or have languished in a life not worth living. That is the antithesis of grief that comes from God; the latter inspires *a repentance that . . . brings no regret,* for it leads to life (*salvation*), which, like the grief, comes from God; but, unlike the grief, lasts not for an hour but for eternity.

As Paul contemplates the work of grief from God in the Corinthians he rises to eloquence in describing its effects. *What earnestness this godly grief has produced in you.* Earlier they were careless as to their behavior, indifferent as to what the apostle thought, even perhaps indifferent as to what God thought of them, and certainly indifferent as to the gross insult to Paul given by one of their number. Godly grief changed all that. *What eagerness to clear yourselves,* i.e., of the wrong done to the apostle and of indifference to the word of God through him. *What indignation,* that they should have behaved so badly and hurt Paul so much. *What alarm,* in view of their responsibility to the Lord for their actions, whom they must one day face in judgment. *What longing,* to have Paul among them again and to show their love to him. *What zeal,* to vindicate the apostle. *What punishment,* to those who had led the opposition to Paul, above all to the offender who had insulted him (2:5 ff.).

By these means they proved that they were *guiltless in the matter.* They had neither set in motion the original opposition to Paul nor prompted their own member who had brought disgrace upon them all; and having understood the issues, they had now disciplined the offender and de-

clared themselves for the apostle.

That this was in accord with the fundamental attitude of the Corinthians towards him had been the conviction of Paul all along. He after all had been God's instrument to bring them originally to repentance and faith; he had taught them the rudiments of the revelation of God in Christ and nurtured them in the Christian life. He knew them better than they knew themselves! He knew that deep in their hearts there was a genuine love for him, even though temporarily they had been dazzled by the false teachers and affected by their false propaganda. Accordingly, he was now able to say that in writing his stern letter, he had in view not *the one who did the wrong, nor . . . the one who suffered the wrong, but . . . that your zeal for us might be revealed to you in the sight of God.*

Here we take it that when Paul said, *I wrote not on account of . . . but in order that,* he was using the typical biblical mode of stating a comparison, meaning "not *so much* on account of *as* in order that" (cf. the famous statement, "I desire steadfast love and not sacrifice," which continues, "the knowledge of God rather than burnt offerings," Hos. 6:6). Naturally Paul was concerned to see that the offender should be disciplined and come to repentance, as he desired that *the one who suffered wrong* should be vindicated. If, as we believe, the person who suffered the wrong was Paul himself, it is the more abundantly clear that the vindication of the wronged man was secondary to the good of the church. Paul's personal status in Corinth was of small account; it was the gospel which he represented that mattered. In faith that the Corinthians did have a proper estimate of the gospel and that they would acknowledge Paul as a faithful preacher of it, he wrote to make the Corinthians realize where they really stood. The coming of Titus showed Paul that his faith had been vindicated. *Therefore we are comforted.*

A yet further source of comfort to the apostle was *the joy of Titus.* He had been sent on a difficult and delicate task, to ascertain the mind of the Corinthians about Paul after receiving his letter, and to follow up the letter by encouraging a complete reconciliation between the church and the apostle. On the one hand, he knew that Paul's last visit had been a total failure, and it was conceivable that the letter which had been sent could have roused still greater resentment and strengthened the anti-Paul feeling in the church. On the other hand, Paul had assured Titus that Corinth was right at heart, that their recent behavior was an aberration, not a revelation of their real attitude, that the Corinthians would surely receive his letter in a right spirit, and that a visit from Titus would put the finishing touch to the healing of the ruptured relation.

If Titus had gone to Corinth without misgivings, he would have been less than human. But in the event his fears proved groundless. *His mind has been set at rest by you all.* The pride in the Corinthians expressed by Paul to Titus was justified, and Paul was happy to write *I was not put to shame.* In stating this to the church, Paul was able to make a double claim: *everything we said to you was true*—including his proclamation of the word of God, his asseverations as to his authority, his sincerity, and his love for them; and *our boasting before Titus has proved true*—all that he had said to him about the faith of the Corinthians, their sincerity, and the genuineness of their love for him also proved true. So Paul was vindicated, with regard both to the Corinthians and to Titus.

As to Titus himself, as he looks back on his visit to Corinth, *his heart goes out all the more to you,* for *he remembers the obedience of you all, and the fear and trembling with which you received him.* Did Titus, then, act like a tyrant in the church and find the experience enjoyable? By no means! The *obedience* for which he asked will have been in relation to the word of God, to their duty to set right the wrongs they had permitted to be done to Paul, and to discipline the offender. They received

Titus in *fear and trembling,* not unfittingly, for Paul in the first instance had come among them "in weakness and in much fear and trembling" (1 Cor. 2:3). At that time Paul had been anxious that the word of God should not be frustrated by his inadequacy, and he cast himself on the mercy and grace of God, knowing that without them he could achieve nothing. Titus perceived in the way the Corinthians received him as the messenger of the Lord a like attitude, for they submitted to the word of God, they too cast themselves on the mercy of God in respect to their sins and they sought his grace for fuller obedience.

Fear and trembling is a characteristic expression of Paul, expressing the anxiety of a man who knows his limitations to do the will of God, but equally his faith that the Lord is not only Judge but Redeemer and that the grace of God is able to make even him adequate for his task, provided that he rests in faith on that grace. Such an attitude Titus perceived in the members of the church at Corinth, and his heart went out all the more to them.

Paul therefore concludes, *I rejoice, because I have perfect confidence in you.* The statement has more than ordinary interest, for it employs almost exactly the same words (in Greek) that Paul uses in 10:1, but with a quite different meaning. The RSV obscures the connection through its use of different terms. In 10:1 Paul cites, in a parenthesis, a charge made against him by some person or persons in Corinth: "I who am humble when face to face with you, but bold to you when I am away!" The term "to be bold" is that translated in 7:16, "to have confidence" (*tharrein*). Its most common meaning is to have courage (so in 5:6,8). Its secondary meaning depends on what prepositions are used with it. One can speak of being of good courage *in* (= in the case of) a person, and so of having confidence or trust in him; or one may speak of being of good courage *towards* a person, and so against him.

When writing 10:1, Paul cites the reputation he has gained of having courage against the Corinthians—so long as he is away! He took up that matter and dealt with it. Now that peace has been established between him and the Corinthians, he is able to take up the earlier allegation and make it the means of affirming his confidence in them. So the last words of the long, long argument are the Corinthians' own, given back to them with love from their apostle, but with love's new meaning: *I have perfect confidence in you.*

II. The Collection for Jerusalem (8:1—9:15)

In writing to the Galatians Paul tells of the mutual understanding reached between James, Peter, and John on the one hand and himself and Barnabas on the other. The Jerusalem apostles recognized that Paul and Barnabas had been sent by the Lord to the Gentiles, as they had to the Jews. They made one request of them, however, that in their ministry among the Gentiles they should "remember the poor." In recounting this Paul added "which very thing I was eager to do" (see Gal. 2:6–10). The "poor," of course were poor Christians of Palestine, notably in Jerusalem. Paul was eager to carry out this request for obvious reasons. The need at Jerusalem was constant, and it was a clear duty of Christians elsewhere to alleviate it.

Moreover, there was an inevitable suspicion of Palestinian Jewish Christians toward Gentile Christians of other lands because of the nonobservance of the law by the latter (a very difficult thing for Jewish Christians to accept). Especially, suspicion was directed to Paul for his encouragement of this undesirable state of affairs, and it was even rumored in Jerusalem that he tried to persuade Jewish Christians to forsake the law (Acts 21:21 ff.).

The idea of a collection of Gentile Christians for Jewish Christians in Palestine was seized on by Paul. It helped to remind the Gentile Christians of their debt to Jewish Christians and quicken their concern for them; it demonstrated to Jewish believers the love of Gentile Christians for them; it showed the Palestinian church Paul's loyalty to them and affection for them.

The question has been raised, Why were so many poor Christians in Jerusalem? Ever since Augustine it has been common to maintain that this was due to the sharing of goods practiced by the first Christians immediately after Pentecost, prompted by an expectation of a speedy end of the world, and the lesson has been drawn that Christians should not be so foolish. The explanation is dubious. The sharing of goods was never complete, and it was wholly voluntary (the sin of Ananias and Sapphira was not in withholding money, but in lying to the Holy Spirit, Acts 5:3 f.).

It is more to the point to remember that Jerusalem was a center of religious pilgrimage. Like other similar cities it attracted many poor (as Mecca and many Indian cities). For this reason the Jews of the Dispersion regularly sent donations to Jerusalem for poor relief. Many of these indigent people would have been converted through the gospel, and from the first the Christians would have been conscious of their duty to them. The plight of these people would have intensified as soon as the Jewish authorities became hostile to the church in Jerusalem, for they would have cut off assistance to any who joined the followers of the crucified Jesus Messiah. The problem therefore became even more pressing as the years passed. For this reason Paul was asked to "remember the poor," and his collection was the more welcome in Jerusalem.

It is evident that Paul had already endeavored to persuade the Corinthians to play their part in the collection (1 Cor. 16:1). The strained relations between him and them had caused the matter to be neglected; but now that their restoration had been effected, Paul takes up the cause once more and seeks to encourage them to complete the project they had earlier begun.

1. Examples of Generous Giving (8:1–9)

¹ We want you to know, brethren, about the grace of God which has been shown in the

churches of Macedonia, [2] for in a severe test of affliction, their abundance of joy and their extreme poverty have overflowed in a wealth of liberality on their part. [3] For they gave according to their means, as I can testify, and beyond their means, of their own free will, [4] begging us earnestly for the favor of taking part in the relief of the saints—[5] and this, not as we expected, but first they gave themselves to the Lord and to us by the will of God. [6] Accordingly we have urged Titus that as he had already made a beginning, he should also complete among you this gracious work. [7] Now as you excel in everything—in faith, in utterance, in knowledge, in all earnestness, and in your love for us—see that you excel in this gracious work also.

[8] I say this not as a command, but to prove by the earnestness of others that your love also is genuine. [9] For you know the grace of our Lord Jesus Christ, that though he was rich, yet for your sake he became poor, so that by his poverty you might become rich.

Nothing inspires to good endeavor so much as a good example. Paul therefore begins his appeal to the Corinthians to make a worthy collection by citing a notable example of sacrificial giving. *The churches of Macedonia* are those of the Roman province of that name, including Philippi, Thessalonica, and Berea. These churches conspicuously manifest *the grace of God* in the matter of giving. A feature to which Denney drew attention is here worth noting: not once in Paul's exhortations to give does he use the word money. He employs a variety of terms—*grace* (as here), service, a communion in service (*koinonia*), a munificence, a blessing, almsgiving, offering (= sacrifice). Not that Paul viewed money as evil; on the contrary he demonstrates that its use is part of the Christian's outworking of the gospel.

The liberality of the Macedonian Christians was a product of grace. In v. 2 Paul refers to *a severe test of affliction.* From the beginning the Macedonian believers had experienced persecution (see Acts 16—17; Phil. 1:29; 1 Thess. 2:13 ff.), and persecutions involved destruction of property and plundering of goods. What little these people had therefore had become pitifully small, and their plight was desperate. But grace triumphs over such circumstances.

If they knew *extreme poverty* they also knew *abundance of joy;* they gave *according to their means* and even *beyond their means.* What an example to the Corinthians in their relative affluence, their freedom from persecution, and their joylessness, which showed itself in their quarrelsomeness! Paul hesitated to ask the Macedonian Christians to share in the collection, but they actually begged earnestly *for the favor of taking part* in it. And they did this because they had put their priorities right; *they gave themselves to the Lord,* and they gave themselves to Paul and his associates, to carry out whatever service was to be required of them.

In face of such an example Paul urged Titus to complete the *gracious work* he had begun earlier among them, but which had been neglected through the dissensions that had taken place. The Corinthians *excel in everything.* Paul meant that in all sincerity. He had earlier told them that they were not lacking in any spiritual gifts (1 Cor. 1:7). But spiritual gifts are literally "gifts of grace" (*charismata*).

See that you excel in this gracious work also (lit., "this grace") suggests that the grace of God was available to them for generous action among men as well as religious activity in their meetings, but it needed a more responsive attitude on their part. The Corinthians should let their love toward Paul and Titus extend towards the needy—in Palestine and elsewhere. In saying this, Paul issues no *command,* but asks that *the earnestness of others* (the Macedonian Christians) should inspire them to demonstrate that their love, as well as that of the Macedonians, is genuine.

There is a yet greater motive for giving than either the Macedonians' example or Paul's exhortations. It is the *grace of our Lord Jesus Christ.* Grace is the love that stoops to save the undeserving, and in the *poverty* of Jesus it is shown to perfection. For *he was rich*—incomprehensibly so in his life with the Father (Phil. 2:6), as mediator and sustainer of the whole creation (1 Cor. 8:6; Col. 1:15–17). He be-

came poor simply by becoming man, for the difference between divine life and human existence is infinite.

The Christian cannot forget what sort of a man the Son of God became. The hymn of Philippians 2:6 ff. expresses it vividly: "Though he was in the form of God . . . he took the form of a slave . . . he humbled himself, and became obedient unto death, even death on the cross." The stoop from the throne of God to the death on the cross is impoverishment beyond compare. And it happened *for your sake.* No immediate deduction is drawn from this statement. There is no need. For any man who grasps this truth, and has entered into life in God through it, will be grateful. Where gratitude is wedded to *the grace of our Lord Jesus Christ* it issues in readiness for like gracious action, i.e., becoming *poor* to make others *rich.*

2. The Plan for the Collection (8:10–24)

¹⁰ And in this matter I give my advice: it is best for you now to complete what a year ago you began not only to do but to desire, ¹¹ so that your readiness in desiring it may be matched by your completing it out of what you have. ¹² For if the readiness is there, it is acceptable according to what a man has, not according to what he has not. ¹³ I do not mean that others should be eased and you burdened, ¹⁴ but that as a matter of equality your abundance at the present time should supply their want, so that their abundance may supply your want, that there may be equality. ¹⁵ As it is written, "He who gathered much had nothing over, and he who gathered little had no lack."

¹⁶ But thanks be to God who puts the same earnest care for you into the heart of Titus. ¹⁷ For he not only accepted our appeal, but being himself very earnest he is going to you of his own accord. ¹⁸ With him we are sending the brother who is famous among all the churches for his preaching of the gospel; ¹⁹ and not only that, but he has been appointed by the churches to travel with us in this gracious work which we are carrying on, for the glory of the Lord and to show our good will. ²⁰ We intend that no one should blame us about this liberal gift which we are administering, ²¹ for we aim at what is honorable not only in the Lord's sight but also in the sight of men. ²² And with them we are sending our brother whom we have often tested and found earnest

in many matters, but who is now more earnest than ever because of his great confidence in you. ²³ As for Titus, he is my partner and fellow worker in your service; and as for our brethren, they are messengers of the churches, the glory of Christ. ²⁴ So give proof, before the churches, of your love and of our boasting about you to these men.

Paul has refrained from issuing orders to the Corinthians regarding the collection, for a Christian needs no further impetus to generous giving than the example of Christ. Nevertheless, even Christian people need ideas as to how to carry out their good intentions, so Paul now proffers advice.

The first point he makes is a tactful reminder of the uselessness of good intentions which do not issue in corresponding actions. *A year ago* the Corinthians had a desire to participate in the collection. They made a beginning on the project and stopped. Paul urges that the *readiness in desiring . . . may be matched by completing it,* for a will that cannot lead to action is the antithesis of the Spirit-led life. But common sense also has place here. The measure of giving is *what a man has;* a man is not expected to give *what he has not.* It was on this basis that Jesus praised the widow who gave all her living (Mark 12:43 f.); and on this basis many of us stand condemned for what we retain after giving.

On the other hand, there is no question of one group being drained of resources to make it easy for others; the watchword here is *equality.* Christians who have more should give to those who have less. The time may come when the positions will be reversed and the donors become the receivers. God's dealings with the Israelites in the desert illustrate this principle: when gathering the manna those who collected much were not allowed to keep more than the ration, while those who gathered less had their amount made up (Ex. 16:16 ff). That procedure was commanded. The members of the new Israel should carry it out voluntarily, on the basis of mutual love.

Not alone Paul, but Titus also was inspired by the Spirit of God to *care for* the

Corinthians. *Of his own accord* he readily agreed with Paul's suggestion to go to Corinth and help the church there to organize the collection. Observe that under this aspect the organizing of the gift for Jerusalem was out of *earnest care* for the Corinthians: it was for their good! For ungenerous Christians are stunted souls, and neither Paul nor Titus could bear to think of their Corinthian friends being like that.

With him we are sending the brother who is famous among all the churches for his preaching of the gospel. Who is he? We cannot tell. Luke, Barnabas, Timothy, Silas, Mark, Erastus, and a whole number of other friends of Paul have been suggested. Luke's is a particularly suitable name here, for in Acts 20:4 no representative of Philippi is named among the messengers who take the collection to Jerusalem, whereas the next verse uses the term "we," signifying Luke's presence among them. So far as this passage is concerned, however, this identification remains a guess. Of greater moment is the consideration that Titus does not go alone; the sending by Jesus of disciples on mission in twos (Mark 6:7; Luke 10:1) and his promise to be present with two or three gathered in his name (Matt. 18:19) made a deep impression on the church. Companionship in the work of God is of first importance, and the testimony to the gospel is strengthened.

The unnamed brother is appointed not alone by Paul but by *the churches* also. He is to journey with Paul and other messengers to Jerusalem. Undoubtedly Paul intends that the church in Jerusalem should see in these men examples of the fine men of God among the Gentile churches. Their arrival in Jerusalem will be *for the glory of the Lord,* since men will praise God for them, and *to show our good will,* since men will understand that Paul undertook this great task out of genuine concern for them.

Yet further, *we intend that no one should blame us about this liberal gift.* It is notorious how easily troubles can arise over money matters. If Paul had taken the gift of the Gentiles churches alone, questions could

have been raised, both in Jerusalem and among the Gentiles churches themselves, as to whether any of the money had been kept back by Paul. With a group of men above reproach and authorized by the churches bearing the money themselves, no such suspicion could rise.

Yet another unnamed brother is mentioned in v. 22, *tested and found earnest in many matters,* therefore to be trusted in this one. And if people ask questions about Titus and his companions, Paul has a ready answer: *Titus . . . is my partner and fellow worker in your service,* the brothers are *messengers of the churches.* As is well known, the term *messengers* is the usual word for apostles, and apostle means "one sent." The standing of an apostle depends entirely on who sent him and for what purpose. The apostles of Christ had a unique standing, due to their personal association with the Lord and because they were sent by him to perform a unique task in the church. The "apostles of the churches" naturally had a much more limited significance, for their task was simpler; they were appointed to act as representatives of their churches, and on their behalf to hand over to the church of Jerusalem the money that had been collected. Less though that task may be, it is important in God's sight; in virtue of what they are and whom they represent they may be described as *the glory of Christ;* i.e., they are men in whom the Lord's glory is to be seen. Where that glory becomes visible, no task may be viewed as mean.

In the light of these considerations Paul asks that the Corinthians give proof of their *love* and justify his *boasting* about them to his colleagues. Since "he who is sent is as he who sends him," the Corinthians in demonstrating their true nature to the "apostles of the churches" will in effect reveal it to *the churches* themselves.

3. An Appeal for Readiness and Generosity (9:1–15)

¹ Now it is superfluous for me to write to you about the offering for the saints, ² for I know your readiness, of which I boast about you to

the people of Macedonia, saying that Achaia has been ready since last year; and your zeal has stirred up most of them. ³ But I am sending the brethren so that our boasting about you may not prove vain in this case, so that you may be ready, as I said you would be; ⁴ lest if some Macedonians come with me and find that you are not ready, we be humiliated—to say nothing of you—for being so confident. ⁵ So I thought it necessary to urge the brethren to go on to you before me, and arrange in advance for this gift you have promised, so that it may be ready not as an exaction but as a willing gift.

⁶ The point is this: he who sows sparingly will also reap sparingly, and he who sows bountifully will also reap bountifully. ⁷ Each one must do as he has made up his mind, not reluctantly or under compulsion, for God loves a cheerful giver. ⁸ And God is able to provide you with every blessing in abundance, so that you may always have enough of everything and may provide in abundance for every good work. ⁹ As it is written,

"He scatters abroad, he gives to the poor;
  his righteousness endures for ever."

¹⁰ He who supplies seed to the sower and bread for food will supply and multiply your resources and increase the harvest of your righteousness. ¹¹ You will be enriched in every way for great generosity, which through us will produce thanksgiving to God; ¹² for the rendering of this service not only supplies the wants of the saints but also overflows in many thanksgivings to God. ¹³ Under the test of this service, you will glorify God by your obedience in acknowledging the gospel of Christ, and by the generosity of your contribution for them and for all others; ¹⁴ while they long for you and pray for you, because of the surpassing grace of God in you. ¹⁵ Thanks be to God for his inexpressible gift!

It has often been remarked that while Paul's appeal for the collection seems to reach a conclusion at the end of chapter 8, the apostle appears to make a completely fresh start on the subject in 9:1. It has therefore been suggested that the two chapters were written at different times. Those who consider that 2 Corinthians was composed of more than one letter of Paul have various suggestions to make about the relations of these chapters to the constituent parts of the letter and their relative order. In justice it must be said that there is nothing objectionable about hypotheses of this kind; the content of the two chapters is in

no way affected by them, and they can be neither proved nor disproved. It should equally be recognised however that chapter 9 follows on chapter 8 quite naturally. This is obscured in the RSV through its translating the conjunction *gar* in 9 v. 1 as "now" instead of "for." Chapter 9 adduces little that is new. It concentrates on one point, namely that the Corinthians endeavor to ensure that the collection is a generous one. The chapter could have been intended by Paul to take its place in his appeal precisely where it is.

From one point of view *it is superfluous* for Paul *to write . . . about the offering for the saints,* for the Corinthians have long known about it (cf. 1 Cor. 16:1 ff.), and Paul had already told the Macedonian Christians of their readiness to cooperate in it. That Paul should quote the example of the Corinthians when speaking to the Macedonians about the collection (as here), and then in turn cite the sacrificial efforts of the Macedonians to the Corinthians (as in 8:1 ff.) is perfectly comprehensible. It reflects Paul's wisdom in persuading churches to emulate one another, and doubtless it reflects the facts of the case also; for Corinth made a start before the Macedonians, but the latter responded with more generosity.

On the other hand, it is clear that there was a need for Paul to stir up the Corinthians regarding the collection. While they had commenced to organize a collection in the previous year, almost certainly they ceased their efforts later. This was one of the consequences of the upheavals at Corinth, and it must have grieved Paul to learn (from Titus?) that their hostility to him had the effect of depriving the Palestinian Christians of help which the Corinthians could well afford to give.

Paul now writes again, and at length, about the collection and sends *the brethren* to supervise the organization of it (cf. 8:16 ff.). Paul himself will come later, along with the representatives of other churches who are taking their gifts to Jerusalem, and he wishes to ensure that his

boasting about them should not *prove vain
. . . lest . . . we be humiliated—to say
nothing of you.* How dreadful if the
poverty-stricken Macedonians should arrive
at Corinth and find that the church whose
example had been quoted to them had
given a miserly contribution! In such circumstances the Corinthians would stand in
shame, and so would Paul. Therefore he
sends his colleagues in advance to ensure
that the gift of the church in Corinth may
be ready, *not as an exaction*—a gift ex-
torted from them against their will—*but
as a willing gift,* literally a "blessing," issuing from love responsive to divine grace,
which will lead to the joy as well as help of
the recipients.

In vv. 6 ff. Paul enumerates reasons for
generous giving to the cause that is in view.
The first is that giving is like sowing seed;
it produces a harvest. *He who sows sparingly will also reap sparingly.* Whoever
heard of a farmer who was so mean as to
scatter only a few seeds in his field? What a
miserable harvest would be his! So it is in
the realm of giving. To give little is to reap
little—both in one's own life and in that
of others. The same thought is expressed
even more strongly in Galatians 6:7 ff., the
context of which is closely related to this
passage. There is a more profound relation
between a man's giving and his spiritual
welfare than is sometimes realized, and
Paul would have us face the issue in relation to God and his kingdom. Not least
important is the attitude of the giver. To
give *reluctantly* or *under compulsion* is out
of keeping alike with the Christian's experience of God and with the teaching of
the Bible. *God loves a cheerful giver* (from
the Greek translation of Prov. 22:9), and
the Christian knows that that is the spirit
in which God has ever treated his children.

The second reason for openhearted giving
adduced by Paul is God's readiness to provide the generous Christian with means for
generous action. It is tempting to regard
the first clause of v. 8 as relating to what
people are pleased to call the spiritual life,
as though God's power to *provide . . .*

with every blessing in abundance refers to
his imparting of virtues in the hidden life of
the soul. But throughout chapters 8—9 Paul
uses terms like "grace" and "blessing" for
material gifts for distribution, indicating
that the spiritual life and concern for the
ordinary needs of people are inseparable.

In v. 8 the term for *blessing* is literally
"grace" (*charis*), which Paul employs in the
sense of "gracious gift" in 8:4,6–7. The ordinary term for blessing (*eulogia*) occurs
in profusion in 9:5–6. So in v. 8, *God is
able to provide* those material resources
for your own needs, and enough to *provide
in abundance,* i.e., that you may give to
others in a manner which matches God's
abundant giving to you.

Observe however that this is spoken to
Christian people who understand Christian
restraint: *enough* is enough! God does not
promise to provide in such fashion that we
"keep up with the Joneses." Paul's word
enough (*autarkeia*) happens to be a famous
watchword of the Stoics, who used it to denote the sufficiency of a man who needs
little that is in the power of man to give,
for he has enough resources within himself.
Paul therefore uses it especially of contentment (see Phil. 4:11; 1 Tim. 6:6). So here
God gives a man *enough* to have contentment in life and to enable him to be rich
in good works and generous giving.

This conviction is supported with a citation from Psalm 112:9, which fittingly
likens the generous giving of the man who
fears God with a sowing of seed which produces a *harvest of . . . righteousness.* So
also, comments Paul, as surely as God *supplies seed to the sower* and brings from it a
harvest of bread for food, the Lord will
supply you with resources to enable you to
give to the needs of men and will bring
about *the harvest of your righteousness.*

This leads on to yet a third reason for
generous giving. The Lord who enriches his
people with ability for great generosity will
also bring about a harvest of *thanksgivings
to God,* which ultimately will enable the
Corinthians to *glorify God.* That is the final
end of Christian action!

But the way this happens is interestingly described in v. 13. It will happen, says Paul, *by your obedience in acknowledging the gospel of Christ, and by the generosity of your contribution.* The ultimate source of the Corinthians' giving is the gospel, through which not only they but those in Jerusalem have experienced the salvation of God. The Palestinian Christians know, as do the Corinthians, that the gospel is God's power to save men, and they see in the Corinthians' generosity an acknowledgement or a confession of the gospel. It is evident that the concern of the Corinthians for them is an outcome of the grace of God. In turn this concern will evoke from the Palestinians gratitude and love for the Corinthians, which will issue in their longing to see these unknown Gentile brothers and sisters in Christ, and they will pray for them. When this happens, the purpose of the collection will have been reached: God will be glorified in the thanksgivings of many, and the divided Jewish and Gentile churches will abound in love to one another.

In contemplation of so wonderful a result of the love gift of the Gentile churches, Paul exclaims *Thanks be to God for his inexpressible gift!* What is that gift? Is it Christ, whose giving lies at the heart of that gospel which provokes men to give as God gave when he gave up his Son to reconcile divided humanity? Is it the gift of that fellowship in which all men, Jew and Gentile, slave and free, male and female, become one? Is it *the surpassing grace of God,* which produces in the Gentiles the fruit of gracious giving after the pattern of God's own sacrificial giving? It is impossible to tell. The present writer is inclined to the last interpretation, in view of the fact that grace is the key word of chapters 8—9 and that it is the immediate antecedent of this doxology. In the last resort, it does not matter greatly, for it is in Christ that the grace of God has come to us and created the fellowship between God and man which breaks down all barriers and inspires love in action among men. For him, and all gifts in him, *thanks be to God!*

III. A Defense of Paul's Apostolic Ministry (10:1—13:14)

It is patent to every reader of this letter that a marked change of tone and attitude commences at 10:1. The relief and joy of chapter 7, followed by the confident approach of the apostle in chapters 8—9, as he solicits the support of the Corinthian church for the collection for the Palestinian poor, gives way to a vigorous defense of his apostolic authority and attack on those who reject it. While reference is made to a group of individuals who make allegations against Paul (e.g., 10:2, "some who suspect me"; 10:10, "they say . . ."; 10:12, "some . . . who commend themselves"), it is difficult to maintain that this group alone is being addressed in these chapters. On the contrary, the whole church is in the apostle's field of vision (see, e.g., 11:1 ff., 11:7 ff.; 12:14 ff.; 13:11 ff.). To address the whole church was necessary, since apparently it was in danger of being persuaded by the antagonists of Paul. The problems involved in relating chapters 10—13 to chapters 1—9 are discussed in the Introduction, to which the reader is referred.

1. A Rebuttal of Allegations (10:1–18)

(1) Paul's Alleged Cowardice (10:1–6)

¹ I, Paul, myself entreat you, by the meekness and gentleness of Christ—I who am humble when face to face with you, but bold to you when I am away!—² I beg of you that when I am present I may not have to show boldness with such confidence as I count on showing against some who suspect us of acting in worldly fashion. ³ For though we live in the world we are not carrying on a worldly war, ⁴ for the weapons of our warfare are not worldly but have divine power to destroy strongholds. ⁵ We destroy arguments and every proud obstacle to the knowledge of God, and take every thought captive to obey Christ, ⁶ being ready to punish every disobedience, when your obedience is complete.

The language of v. 1 is best explained on the assumption that Paul is citing an allegation of his opponents in Corinth, namely, that he puts on a bold face when he is absent but that he is a weak individual when he comes face to face with people. He is *humble* in the sense of mean and contemptible and *bold* through his letters (see v. 9, which defines perfectly the sense of v. 1). That really amounts to a charge of cowardice. Paul has not the courage to tell people personally what he says when he is far away; there is no reason to fear his threats of a return to Corinth—his next visit will be as disastrous as his last!

In answer to this charge, Paul pleads that he not be placed under the necessity of demonstrating its falsity. Self-assertion is distasteful to him, and he appeals rather to *the meekness and gentleness of Christ* (cf. Matt. 11:29), which he made known to the Corinthians when he taught them the gospel and which he seeks to reproduce in himself.

Paul does not wish *to show boldness* against some who charge him with *acting in worldly fashion.* The references to the world in vv. 2–3 actually employ (in the Greek) Paul's common expression the "flesh": men suspect him of "acting according to the flesh"; on the contrary, though he lives "in the flesh", he does not carry on a war "according to the flesh", for his weapons are not "fleshly" but "mighty through God." It is likely that Paul's opponents had a Gnostic outlook on life and regarded Paul as merely a "fleshly" man and not a man of the Spirit as they. In rebutting their charges Paul keeps to the biblical meaning of his terms: he is not acting "according to the flesh," i.e., like a man left to his own resources and under the dominance of sin. Naturally he shares in the weakness and limitations that are common to humanity, but the conflict he wages is not dependent on the aids available to men limited by this world's horizons. Instead, it is waged with those aids which God supplies.

The passage well illustrates Paul's use of the term "flesh" to denote man's creaturely weakness, liable to the dominance of sin, in contrast to the divine power which is available to the man of faith. *Worldly* weapons need not be evil, but include those which are in man's power, such as eloquence, or-

ganization, propaganda, and the like, which are neutral in themselves, but which can be put to evil use through being made to subserve the selfishness, cunning, and violence of man.

The weapons of our warfare are such as Paul enumerates in Ephesians 6:13 ff., and these have *divine power to destroy strongholds.* What these *strongholds* protect are listed in v. 5, namely *arguments and every proud obstacle to the knowledge of God.* Clearly it is bad arguments, which are employed to resist the knowledge of God, that Paul would destroy, not arguments as such. He would destroy error through the truth of God applied by the Spirit of God; when he comes to Corinth that is what he intends to do with the false doctrines that are being spread by the false teachers. Every *thought* which leads to disobedience to Christ is to be taken captive so that the Corinthians may be set free to obey Christ. For this is the end of thought illuminated by the Spirit of God, namely a life that yields obedience to Christ.

Paul reckons with the possibility that after his arrival in Corinth not all will be willing to receive the truth and obey Christ. When however the church as a whole shows its willingness to render complete obedience to the Lord, he will be *ready to punish every disobedience;* i.e., he will discipline those who reject the truth and refuse obedience to Christ. Such an action is in keeping with the charge laid by Jesus on his disciples regarding admission to and discipline of the church (Matt. 18:18).

(2) Paul's Alleged Weakness (10:7-11)

7 Look at what is before your eyes. If any one is confident that he is Christ's, let him remind himself that as he is Christ's, so are we. 8 For even if I boast a little too much of our authority, which the Lord gave for building you up and not for destroying you, I shall not be put to shame. 9 I would not seem to be frightening you with letters. 10 For they say, "His letters are weighty and strong, but his bodily presence is weak, and his speech of no account." 11 Let such people understand that what we say by letter when absent, we do when present.

Look at what is before your eyes is a call to the Corinthians to use their discernment as to what they have experienced by Paul and his opponents. For there are no hidden factors here, nor is anyone in a position of having information denied to the rest. In particular, *if any one is confident that he is Christ's,* he must recognise that *as he is Christ's, so are we.* The Corinthians themselves can judge of this. Not that it is in their power to discern the secrets of the heart, but the men in Corinth who said that they were Christ's clearly did so in an exclusive sense, above all in relation to Paul: they were Christ's, but he was not. The situation is illuminated by Paul's statement in 1 Corinthians 1:12. The people who claimed to belong to Christ did so over against the followers of the apostles. They believed that they were Christ's in a manner others were not, because they regarded themselves as united to the Spirit of Christ in a unique manner and possessing the gifts of the Spirit in full measure.

By contrast, Paul was a mere man of flesh, confined within the limitations of men of his crude nature and to a ministry of a lower order (10:2 ff.). This was why he was such a very feeble individual; he was incapable of inspiration such as they knew, and he made up for his deficiency by writing violent letters from a distance. At this point Paul's response to their allegations is restrained. He does not deny that these men belong to Christ; he simply points out that if they really are Christ's they will recognize that he belongs to him, too, for their exclusiveness has no basis in reality. The Corinthians' experience of Paul and of his opponents will substantiate that.

Even if Paul were to boast a little too much of his authority, he affirms, *I shall not be put to shame.* The implication is that the Corinthians know that Paul could substantiate his claims. As he pointed out in an earlier letter (1 Cor. 4:19 f.), some people are all talk and have no power, but "the kingdom of God does not consist in talk but in power." The Corinthians have seen the power of the kingdom operative in Paul,

especially in the transformation of their lives through the Spirit of God at work in him (1 Cor. 6:9–11). His authority, therefore, is *for building you up;* it is not *for destroying you,* as the assumed authority of his detractors is threatening to do. He refrains from saying more along this line for he must not frighten them with letters!

That Paul's letters are *weighty and strong* is something which Paul's opponents do not deny. They insist however that the letters do not reflect the man. *His bodily presence is weak, and his speech of no account.* There appears to be an echo here of the impression made by Paul on his initial appearance in Corinth, and perhaps on his second (and disastrous) visit too. Paul himself recounts in 1 Corinthians 2:1 ff. how utterly cast upon the Lord he was constrained to be when he first preached in Corinth; he was with them "in weakness and in much fear and trembling," and was determined to renounce every artifice of speech and wisdom that could becloud the cross of Christ. If he visited Corinth a second time with a like distrust of self, and a readiness to exercise restraint and deal patiently with the recalcitrant Corinthians, there is little cause for wonder that he was misunderstood. "This man is a weakling!" they said. "He has no oratorical power, and he is devoid of Spirit-inspired speech."

Paul replies that there is no cleavage between what he is at a distance and what he is when present, any more than there is between the power of his word in letter and the effectiveness of his action: *what we say . . . when absent, we do when present.* That they will learn, when Paul comes the third time!

(3) *Paul's Alleged Trespass Beyond His Bounds (10:12–18)*

12 Not that we venture to class or compare ourselves with some of those who commend themselves. But when they measure themselves by one another, and compare themselves with one another, they are without understanding.
13 But we will not boast beyond limit, but will keep to the limits God has apportioned us,

to reach even to you. [14] For we are not overextending ourselves, as though we did not reach you; we were the first to come all the way to you with the gospel of Christ. [15] We do not boast beyond limit, in other men's labors; but our hope is that as your faith increases, our field among you may be greatly enlarged, [16] so that we may preach the gospel in lands beyond you, without boasting of work already done in another's field. [17] "Let him who boasts, boast of the Lord." [18] For it is not the man who commends himself that is accepted, but the man whom the Lord commends.

Paul is prepared to be bold in person and in action when next he goes to Corinth, but he confesses that there is a limit to his courage. He cannot bring himself to *class or compare* himself *with some of those who commend themselves.* How have they reached so lofty a self-estimate? *They measure themselves by one another.* They have formed their own ideas as to who are Christ's, and what constitutes spirituality, and all who do not share their views are automatically degraded. In reality such people, by reason of their exclusive concern with their own ideas and experience, cut themselves off from the fellowship of Christ's people and so from sharing in the wider experience of the Spirit granted to the church. Consequently *they are without understanding.*

In contrast to those who so highly esteem themselves, Paul declines to *boast beyond limit;* on the contrary, he adds, we *will keep to the limits God has apportioned us, to reach even to you.* A word play is involved here which is obscured in the RSV, but which the KJV has tried to preserve. The following translation brings out this word play: "They measure themselves by one another . . . but we will not boast beyond measure, but will keep to the measure of the rule God has apportioned to us." Their boasting has gone beyond the limits of reality, and in their ministry in Corinth they have transgressed the limit of God's appointment. Paul on the other hand is prepared to *boast* only of what God has achieved through him, and in his ministry he strictly keeps within the limits which God has appointed for him.

The general sense of v. 13 is admittedly conveyed without the ambiguous term "rule," but in omitting it the RSV translators missed a point which may have been of significance to Paul. For the word can mean "rule" in the sense of a ruler (for measuring and drawing straight lines) and so point to what is ruled off, an area; it can also mean a "rule" or principle of action. Paul exercises his ministry within the limits of a twofold rule, which was prescribed by God: he is commissioned to evangelize the Gentile world (that is his area; see Acts 9:15; Rom. 1:5; Gal. 2:9); and he is sent to preach in places where Christ is not known, hence he is called to be a pioneer missionary (cf. Rom. 15:20). Corinth therefore falls within the orbit of Paul's ministry, appointed him by God, and that is how he came to found the church in that city.

The denial in 14a, *we are not overextending ourselves, as though we did not reach you,* is almost certainly a repudiation of an assertion by Paul's opponents that he had no right to minister in Corinth. They seem to have assumed that the church of Corinth was their peculiar sphere of ministry and that Paul was an intruder. But, said the apostle indignantly, *we were the first to come all the way to you with the gospel of Christ.* There would have been no church in Corinth if he had not evangelized there. In the will of God the Corinthians owed their life in Christ to Paul's missionary labors. The fact that he had been truly sent by God to them was demonstrated in that the Spirit was pleased to work mightily among them through the agency of Paul (cf. 1 Cor. 9:1 f.).

Again, in contrast to the false teachers, who go off without the Lord's commission and fasten themselves on churches like parasites on a body, Paul affirms: *we do not boast beyond limit, in other men's labors.* Paul is a pioneer, blazing a trail for God in those parts of the world which as yet have never heard the gospel. This ministry Paul is anxious to continue. He has spent an inordinate amount of time on Corinth, and he longs to pursue his evangelistic task in further regions. But how can he go on to fresh areas of ministry while Corinth is tottering in its faith? It is *as your faith increases,* he says, that *our field* of operations will be *greatly enlarged* (*among you* is better rendered "by you," i.e., by your assistance). But not till Corinth has been established in the faith and united as a congregation will the apostle feel free to move on to other parts. When that situation is brought about he will *preach the gospel in lands beyond* them.

The identity of these lands is not mentioned by Paul, but without doubt he has in view a long cherished plan to advance to Rome, and from there to go on to evangelize the country which the ancients called "the limits of the world," namely Spain (cf. Acts 19:21; Rom. 15:22 ff). In ministering to those parts he certainly will not trespass *in another's field!* Such a thrust into the unknown will be ministry in accordance with "the measure of the rule God has appointed" him.

It was Paul's happy experience that when carrying out his ministry in obedience to the divine will, it pleased God to cause grace to work through him (see 1 Cor. 15:10 f.). Accordingly he can cheerfully subscribe to the exhortation of Jeremiah (9:24) and *boast of the Lord.* Insofar as the Lord graciously uses him, it is plain that the divine seal is set on his ministry. In the last resort this is the only authorization that matters: not a man's own commendation, but the Lord's attestation, made known through blessing on his ministry. Where such blessing is outpoured, there is a *man whom the Lord commends.*

2. Apostolic Vindication Through Foolish Glorying (11:1—12:18)

(1) The Apostle's Jealous Love (11:1-6)

¹ I wish you would bear with me in a little foolishness. Do bear with me! ² I feel a divine jealousy for you, for I betrothed you to Christ to present you as a pure bride to her one husband. ³ But I am afraid that as the serpent deceived Eve by his cunning, your thoughts will be led astray from a sincere and pure devotion to Christ. ⁴ For if some one comes and preaches another Jesus than the one we preached, or if you receive a different spirit from the one you received, or if you accept a different gospel from the one you accepted, you submit to it readily enough. ⁵ I think that I am not in the least inferior to these superlative apostles. ⁶ Even if I am unskilled in speaking, I am not in knowledge; in every way we have made this plain to you in all things.

Paul is about to indulge in *a little foolishness.* His folly is that of boasting of privileges and achievements as a servant of Christ in comparison with those of other men; this he describes as not only foolishness (11:16 f.) but madness (11:23). Yet the Corinthians have forced him to do it through their readiness to listen to false teachers who maliciously denounce him (12:11 f). Paul therefore demands a hearing: *Do bear with me!*

At once he writes with passion. He is motivated by a *divine jealousy,* i.e., a jealousy such as God feels for his people, for the Lord demands an undivided love and loyalty from those to whom he has given himself (cf. Ex. 20:1-6). Like the steward who found a bride for Isaac (Gen. 24), Paul has taken the part of one who secures a bride for another: he has affianced the church at Corinth to Christ, in prospect of the marriage taking place at Christ's coming in glory—an interesting example of a local church being viewed as a microcosm of the whole church (cf. Eph. 5:25 ff.; Rev. 19:9; 21:9 ff.). The apostle recalls, however, how *the serpent deceived Eve by his cunning* (Gen. 3), and he fears lest the like may happen to this church. As a bride should have eyes for no man other than her bridegroom, so a church should have *a sincere and pure devotion to Christ.*

But such singlemindedness of devotion is threatened when *another Jesus, a different spirit,* and *a different gospel* are presented to the Corinthians. The Jesus who is so preached is, of course, the one Jesus of Nazareth, but he is portrayed in such a different guise that he becomes *another Jesus.* It is almost certainly a Gnostic version of Jesus that is in mind, a Jesus who is a mere vessel for the divine Christ who comes upon him temporarily, a Jesus who could even be cursed (1 Cor. 12:3). The *spirit* preached in such a context is far removed from the Holy Spirit, sent by the risen Lord as a consequence of the redemption he has achieved (Act 2:33; Rom. 8:9 f.), and the *gospel* of another Jesus is equally different, not to be confused with the apostolic gospel proclaimed by truly apostolic men.

In view of this the *superlative apostles*, who in v. 4 are represented as "some one" and in v. 5 are presumed to claim superiority to Paul, cannot be the original apostles of Jesus. They are heretical claimants to the title, and in 11:13 ff. are named false apostles and servants of Satan. These men contrasted Paul's mode of preaching with their own, alleging that he was an amateur (*unskilled* = layman, an untrained man in comparison with the professional) in the art of public speaking, whereas they had been trained as orators. Paul does not contest the claim, but he resists the idea that he is a "layman" as regards knowledge; in this regard he was "an expert and specialist, trained and inspired by the Lord himself" (Plummer).

(2) Paul's Refusal of the Corinthians' Money (11:7-15)

7 Did I commit a sin in abasing myself so that you might be exalted, because I preached God's gospel without cost to you? 8 I robbed other churches by accepting support from them in order to serve you. 9 And when I was with you and was in want, I did not burden any one, for my needs were supplied by the brethren who came from Macedonia. So I refrained and will refrain from burdening you in any way. 10 As the truth of Christ is in me, this boast of mine shall not be silenced in the regions of Achaia. 11 And why? Because I do not love you? God knows I do! 12 And what I do I will continue to do, in order to undermine the claim of those who would like to claim that in their boasted mission they work on the same terms as we do. 13 For such men are false apostles, deceitful workmen, disguising themselves as apostles of Christ. 14 And no wonder, for even Satan disguises himself as an angel of light. 15 So it is not strange if his servants also disguise themselves as servants of righteousness. Their end will correspond to their deeds.

In passing to the subject of money for services rendered to the church at Corinth, Paul touched on a subject about which both the church and his opponents were sensitive.

Paul had *preached God's gospel without cost* to the Corinthians. This was initially possible through his tentmaking. By pursuing this trade in Corinth he abased himself, for in Greek eyes manual labor was degrading for a professional teacher. Paul had done it however that the Corinthians *might be exalted*—that is, raised through the gospel. Was that a *sin?* No, of course not, but it is possible that that idea was sown by Paul's opponents, who charged that his conduct showed a lack of real concern for the Corinthians' welfare.

At this Paul became indignant: *I robbed other churches by accepting support from them;* that is, they paid him, but he *served* the Corinthians! The help provided *by the brethren who came from Macedonia* will have been sent through Timothy and Silvanus, when they returned to Corinth (Acts 18:5). No doubt the Corinthians will have remembered that; Paul was willing to receive money from the Macedonians, but not from the Corinthians! "Correct," said Paul, "and I never will take it from you!" Why should that be so? Is it, as Paul's opponents said, an evidence of his lack of love for the Corinthians? God knows that is a lie! responded Paul.

The reason for Paul's intention to maintain his independence of the Corinthians is indicated in v. 12: *to undermine the claim of those who would like to claim that in their boasted mission they work on the same terms as we.* Paul's independence embarrassed these men, for it set them in a bad light. They will have claimed that they required the support of the Corinthians in order to maintain their advanced spiritual condition and to fulfill their mission; in reality they hoped to shame Paul into taking money as they did, and so remove their unfavorable disadvantage. This Paul clearly perceived, and he declared that he had no intention of becoming as they. On the contrary, he affirmed that these men were *false apostles* and *deceitful workmen*. Yet further: as Christ's apostles are inspired by the Holy Spirit and become transformed by the Spirit into Christ's likeness, so these men were under the inspiration of Satan and had became his instruments of deceit (vv. 14 f.).

It is possible that Satan's disguising himself as an angel of light may allude to a Jewish tradition that Satan appeared to Adam and Eve as a shining angel. In the so-called Apocalypse of Moses (ch. 17), it is said that when conversing with Eve "Satan took the form of an angel and praised God as the angels." But the language could have become proverbial. Paul adds that men who share Satan's propensity to transform their darkness into apparent light will have an end corresponding to their deeds. The language is similar to that in Romans 3:8 and Philippians 3:19. When ministers of Christ pervert the grace into a lie, their sin calls for judgment appropriate to its seriousness.

(3) Paul's Apostolic Sufferings (11:16–33)

16 I repeat, let no one think me foolish; but even if you do, accept me as a fool, so that I too may boast a little. 17 (What I am saying I say not with the Lord's authority but as a fool, in this boastful confidence; 18 since many boast of worldly things, I too will boast.) 19 For you gladly bear with fools, being wise yourselves! 20 For you bear it if a man makes slaves of you, or preys upon you, or takes advantage of you, or puts on airs, or strikes you in the face. 21 To my shame, I must say, we were too weak for that!

But whatever any one dares to boast of—I am speaking as a fool—I also dare to boast of that. 22 Are they Hebrews? So am I. Are they Israelites? So am I. Are they descendants of Abraham? So am I. 23 Are they servants of Christ? I am a better one—I am talking like a madman—with far greater labors, far more imprisonments, with countless beatings, and often near death. 24 Five times I have received at the hands of the Jews the forty lashes less one. 25 Three times I have been beaten with rods; once I was stoned. Three times I have been shipwrecked; a night and a day I have been adrift at sea; 26 on frequent journeys, in danger from rivers, danger from robbers, danger from my own people, danger from Gentiles, danger in the city, danger in the wilderness, danger at sea, danger from false brethren; 27 in toil and hardship, through many a sleepless night, in hunger and thirst, often without food, in cold and exposure. 28 And, apart from other things, there is the daily pressure upon me of my anxiety for all the churches. 29 Who is weak, and I am not weak? Who is made to fall, and I am not indignant?

30 If I must boast, I will boast of the things that show my weakness. 31 The God and Father of the Lord Jesus, he who is blessed for ever, knows that I do not lie. 32 At Damascus, the governor under King Aretas guarded the city of Damascus in order to seize me, 33 but I was let down in a basket through a window in the wall, and escaped his hands.

Paul continues in his "folly," but his heart is torn. He does not wish to be thought *foolish*, but if such is the estimate of him, so be it: he *too* will *boast a little*. The conjunction *too* indicates that his detractors have been occupied in this folly, and the attention paid to them by the Corinthians forces Paul to pursue a like path. What follows is not *with the Lord's authority;* for Christ never boasted, nor did he send his apostles to boast, least of all of *worldly things* (advantages such as those listed in vv. 21 f.). Nevertheless, Paul's *boasting* is of a different order from that of the false apostles. Whereas they gloried in *worldly things* and in successes, Paul recalls experiences of humiliation and suffering for Christ's sake. As in the earlier chapters of this letter, the marks of his apostleship are those in which conformity to the passion of his Lord are most apparent. In the picturesque language of Tasker (p. 164), "He wears his pains like decorations."

Paul excuses his "foolishness" with the comment, *you gladly bear with fools, being wise yourselves,* and heaps up the biting sarcasm in vv. 20 f. It is evident from his words, however, that the false apostles must have exercised a real tyranny over the Corinthians; they made slaves of them, fleecing them of their money and humiliating them (such is the implication of "smiting in the face"). In the light of their conduct Paul apologizes for his weakness in Corinth: he never had the nerve for such behavior.

The list of *worldly things* in v. 22 shows that the "superlative apostles" must have been Jews and that they boasted of their Jewish origins, however much of Gnostic ideas they may have embraced. *Hebrews, Israelites, descendants of Abraham* form a comprehensive description of the Jewish inheritance, of which all Jews were enormously proud. As *Hebrews* they spoke the ancestral language of their people, above all Hebrew, in which the Scriptures were written, as well as Aramaic, which was the living language of this time. *Israelites* represented the nation as the theocracy—chosen people of God. *Descendants of Abraham* characterizes the nation as heirs of the salvation promised to Abraham, which culminated in the Messiah and resurrection to his kingdom. In all these privileges Paul shared. He had been taught the Hebrew Scriptures and spoke Aramaic fluently (cf. Acts 21:40—"Hebrew" really meaning Aramaic); he was a member of the ancient tribe of Benjamin (Phil. 3:5); he was heir to the promises made to Abraham.

With extraordinary candor Paul advances to the claim that he is a better servant of Christ than the vaunted "super apostles" (v. 23); but this is said from the viewpoint of sufferings endured for Christ, not from successes scored for Christ. The *far greater labors* relate to endeavors to take the gospel to men and women throughout the world. Few of the items enumerated in vv. 23 ff. find mention in Acts: many of them will have taken place in the period of Paul's missionary labors prior to the journeys recorded in Acts 12—28 (note that according to Gal. 1:21—2:1 Paul labored for Christ in the regions of Syria and Cilicia for 14 years).

The *forty lashes less one* were inflicted by Jews, in accordance with Deuteronomy 25:3, which forbids more than 40 stripes to be inflicted on a man. The injunction caused the rabbis to limit the punishment to 39 lashes in case of faulty counting. Considering that each occasion of this punishment will have been preceded by an uproar and a trial, Paul's statement gives some indication of the constant furore he aroused among the Jews through his proclamation of the gospel. Beating with *rods* was a Roman punishment and was not administered to Roman citizens; that Paul suffered it, as in Philippi (Acts 16:22), indicates how ineffectual Roman citizenship often was to save him from the malice of brutal magistrates. The *stoning* will have been that which took place at Lystra (Acts 14:19).

The passage goes on to illustrate some of the dangers which came to an itinerant missionary in Paul's day. At that time all traveling was difficult, whether by sea or by land; if the former occasioned shipwrecks, the latter involved crossing powerful rivers with difficult fords. In Paul's case there were constant plots from Jews and Gentiles, to say nothing of encounters with robbers, and—most distressing of all—there was *danger from false brethren.* But there was a *pressure* of a different kind. Not from enemies, but from those for whom he cared most, namely the churches of Christ, particularly those which Paul himself had founded. This pressure will have come about through correspondence and messages from churches, and also from individual Christians, who will have sought out Paul from all quarters, requesting his counsel and help. The *weak* would confess their weakness and look for his sympathy; and those *made to fall,* whether through succumbing to temptation or through the sins of others, caused Paul's heart to burn with indignation.

One more experience is mentioned, in curious isolation, namely Paul's escape from Damascus. Since Luke also tells of it (Acts 9:24 f.), it is likely that it had become well known. Paul himself may have recounted it frequently, as an example of the dangers and humiliations he encountered, and also of the overruling providence of God that preserved him for the furtherance of the gospel.

The asseveration of truth in v. 31 may indicate that the story had become garbled, and Paul here states the truth of what really happened. *The governor under King Aretas* (a title for Arabian kings) *guarded the city of Damascus in order to seize me.* Luke mentions only a plot of the Jews to kill Paul.

It is reasonable to asume that the two groups conspired to take him. Either the governor's troops kept guard over the gates while the Jews searched the city for Paul, or the governor of the Nabateans in the city joined forces with the Jews to prevent Paul's escape. In either case the plot failed, for Paul was enabled by his disciples to make his way in safety from the city. It is ironical that the city to which Paul was making his way to arrest Christians was the scene of this memorable attempt to cut short his career of witness for Christ. Yet the attempt to silence him was as fruitless as his attempt to destroy the church.

(4) Visions and Revelations of the Lord (12:1–10)

¹ I must boast; there is nothing to be gained by it, but I will go on to visions and revelations of the Lord. ² I know a man in Christ who fourteen years ago was caught up to the third heaven—whether in the body or out of the body I do not know, God knows. ³ And I know that this man was caught up into Paradise—whether in the body or out of the body I do not know, God knows—⁴ and he heard things that cannot be told, which man may not utter. ⁵ On behalf of this man I will boast, but on my own behalf I will not boast, except of my weaknesses. ⁶ Though if I wish to boast, I shall not be a fool, for I shall be speaking the truth. But I refrain from it, so that no one may think more of me than he sees in me or hears from me. ⁷ And to keep me from being too elated by the abundance of revelations, a thorn was given me in the flesh, a messenger of Satan, to harass me, to keep me from being too elated. ⁸ Three times I besought the Lord about this, that it should leave me; ⁹ but he said to me, "My grace is sufficient for you, for my power is made perfect in weakness." I will all the more gladly boast of my weaknesses, that the power of Christ may rest upon me. ¹⁰ For the sake of Christ, then, I am content with weaknesses, insults, hardships, persecutions, and calamities; for when I am weak, then I am strong.

Paul deems it necesary to press on with the distasteful business of boasting, and so he comes to *visions and revelations of the Lord* (that is, "from" the Lord). In so doing he manifests an even greater reluctance to describe what is in his mind than before. What he relates has to be wrung out of him, as it were. It is a likely guess that Paul was aware either that the hyper-spiritual, Gnostically inclined leaders in Corinth vaunted their own visions as evidence of their authority, in which case this section has to be set alongside 11:21 ff.; or another guess is that the Corinthians themselves expected him to have such visions, if he were, as he claimed, a man of spiritual power, and then this section stands in contrast to the description of humiliations and sufferings in 11: 23 ff. A confident decision is not possible.

In view of the context and the definition of the theme in v. 1, it is not to be doubted that the *man in Christ* of v. 2 is Paul. He speaks in this oblique way to tone down the "boasting." The date *fourteen years ago* suggests that the vision made a deep impression upon Paul; possibly it occurred at a crucial point in his ministry. *The third heaven* to which he was caught up denotes the highest heaven (despite the speculations of some Jews that there are seven heavens), and this is defined as *Paradise.* The latter term was borrowed from Persia (= *paridaiza*), which meant a walled park, especially the parks of the Persian kings and nobility, and then a park of any kind. It was applied in the Septuagint to the garden of Eden (Gen. 2), and so it came to be used of the habitation of the righteous in the kingdom of God, when the idyllic conditions of Eden would be reestablished (cf. Rev. 2:7; 21:2 ff.). It was used also for the place of the blessed dead as they awaited the resurrection (cf. Luke 23:43). Paul then was granted a vision of the Lord and his saints.

In what circumstance Paul was at that time—*whether in the body or out of the body*—he could not tell; he had lost all contact with the body and the world and everything in it. What he saw and heard were *things that cannot be told*, and *which man may not utter*—a not uncommon conviction for men who have shared such experiences as his (even the Seer of Revelation had a prohibition of this kind laid on him, see Rev. 10:2–4). Paul therefore says no more, either about this experience or of any other like it. Indeed he almost separates the "man in Christ," who had received such blessed visions, from the weak and frail servant of Christ that he was, for this was a privilege not natural to him.

On this two observations may be made. The contrast between Paul, the man of heavenly visions, and Paul, the lowly servant of Christ, is not unnatural to one who strongly distinguished, as he did, between the inward and outward man (see comment on 4:16). Second, Paul for 14 years had carried this secret with him as an inspiration for his faith, but he told none of it, for he was called not to preach visions but Christ crucified and risen. For lesser mortals who do not have *visions and revelations of the Lord* that is no small comfort.

The boasting must cease. It was good neither for the Corinthians nor for Paul. But the Lord who gave the visions gave something else, to keep Paul from a false exaltation of spirit: he gave him *a thorn . . . in the flesh* (the passive *was given* refers to God as the giver). Speculations as to what Paul meant by this are endless, and we cannot review them all. If Paul has in mind Numbers 33:55 (the Canaanites viewed as thorns in the sides of the Israelites), then thorn is a correct rendering of the Greek term here used, *skolops*. It can mean, however, a stake, and was sometimes used by Christians to denote the cross.

More important, it is commonly felt by linguists that *in the flesh* ought to be rendered "for the flesh." If the former is retained, it is likely that a physical disability is in mind, whether eye disease (cf. Gal. 4:13 ff.), or malaria, or epilepsy, or some other distressing condition. If the latter (for the flesh) be in view, then "flesh" refers to Paul in his creaturely weakness, subject to sin, and then a spiritual distress will be in mind. Earlier writers tended to interpret the passage in this way, some thinking of temptations for the flesh (evil thoughts), but more thinking of temptations to despair occasioned by opposition and persecution from enemies of the gospel.

Could the thorn or "stake" denote the re-

curring agony of grief and remorse caused by Paul's former hatred of Christ and his battle against him and his people? It is striking that a reference to this appears in 1 Corinthians 15:9, followed by an affirmation of the power of grace to blot out his sin and fit him for apostolic service; so also in this passage the answer of the Lord to his petitions for the removal of the thorn = messenger of Satan (Accuser!) was an assurance of the sufficiency of grace for him.

We must be content with acknowledging the possibilities of interpretation here and the limits of our knowledge. It is more important to take heed to the message of the Lord (Christ) to the apostle in v. 9: grace blots out all sins and empowers the weakest for the greatest service. Paul's boasting of visions and revelations therefore turns to boasts of *weaknesses* in recognition that *when I am weak, then I am strong.* The completeness of Paul's acceptance of the thorn from the hands of God, and of the truth of the promise that went with it, was, from the human point of view, the secret of his unparalleled achievement.

(5) The True Marks of an Apostle (12:11–13)

[11] I have been a fool! You forced me to it, for I ought to have been commended by you. For I am not at all inferior to these superlative apostles, even though I am nothing. [12] The signs of a true apostle were performed among you in all patience, with signs and wonders and mighty works. [13] For in what were you less favored than the rest of the churches, except that I myself did not burden you? Forgive me this wrong!

In dismay Paul confesses that he has been a *fool* in his utterances—compelled by the lack of understanding of the Corinthians. If his opponents had charged him with being *nothing*—a mere nobody—he agrees; but he is still not inferior to them, for they too are nothing! Yet Paul should have been commended by the Corinthians: for *the signs of a true apostle were performed among you.* What are they? It is tempting to equate them with the *signs and wonders and mighty works* mentioned in the latter part of the sentence, i.e., miracles of healing and the like. Yet the conjunction of v. 11 with v. 12 reminds us of a similar connection of thought in 1 Corinthians 9:1 f.: the Corinthians are the seal of Paul's apostleship, for the Lord worked through him to bring about their conversion. The same idea is expounded in 2 Corinthians 3:1 ff.

So here it should be observed that *the signs of a true apostle were performed . . . with signs and wonders and mighty works.* The former are more inclusive than the latter, for they include miracles of grace wrought in human lives by the Holy Spirit through the gospel; and they were accompanied by miracles of a more external kind wrought by the same Spirit. Observe that an apostle is not an apostle through performing miracles; he is an apostle insofar as he preaches Christ (Schlatter); the reality of his commission is attested in the miracles of changed lives and also, as Paul rejoices, through miracles of other kinds. All these marks of apostleship were witnessed by the Corinthians in Paul. The only thing he denied them was the privilege of paying him a salary. Paul craved their forgiveness for this wrong!

(6) Anticipations of a Third Visit to Corinth (12:14–21)

14 Here for the third time I am ready to come to you. And I will not be a burden, for I seek not what is yours but you; for children ought not to lay up for their parents, but parents for their children. 15 I will most gladly spend and be spent for your souls. If I love you the more, am I to be loved the less? 16 But granting that I myself did not burden you, I was crafty, you say, and got the better of you by guile. 17 Did I take advantage of you through any of those whom I sent to you? 18 I urged Titus to go, and sent the brother with him. Did Titus take advantage of you? Did we not act in the same spirit? Did we not take the same steps?
19 Have you been thinking all along that we have been defending ourselves before you? It is in the sight of God that we have been speaking in Christ, and all for your upbuilding, beloved. 20 For I fear that perhaps I may come and find you not what I wish, and that you may find me not what you wish; that perhaps there may be quarreling, jealousy, anger, sel-

fishness, slander, gossip, conceit, and disorder. 21 I fear that when I come again my God may humble me before you, and I may have to mourn over many of those who sinned before and have not repented of the impurity, immorality, and licentiousness which they have practiced.

As Paul anticipates his forthcoming visit to Corinth he renews his earlier affirmation that he will *not be a burden* to the church, i.e., by receiving contributions from it (cf. 11:9 ff.). In this he is actuated by the best of reasons: *I seek not what is yours but you.* This is not the voice of a proud independence, but the expression of a love that desires to give to the beloved without receiving anything in return. It accords with the parental instinct which Paul, as their father in God, has towards his children, for everybody knows that parents should save up for their children, not children for their parents. Indeed, he will go far beyond opening up a bank account for them: *I will most gladly spend and be spent for your souls,* and that is virtually a readiness to lay down his life for their sakes.

The lack of response among the Corinthians to such love must have been due to the accusation reflected in v. 16: *I was crafty, you say, and got the better of you by guile.* Somebody had suggested that Paul's independence of the church was only apparent, in fact it was pure deceit; he took nothing publicly from the church but collected plenty on the quiet—through his representatives who kept on coming with his letters to Corinth. The reference to Titus in v. 18 ties up with the fact that Titus had been sent by Paul in the previous year to organize the collection for the Jerusalem poor (8:6); it is quite possible that the same person who had made this allegation went on to charge that the collection itself was a swindle, arranged for the benefit of Paul's pocket.12 Paul's answer to such shocking suggestions was to ask which of his rep-

---

12 In the Introduction it is suggested that this allegation may be connected with the insult given to Paul by the "offender" in Corinth on the occasion of his second visit.

resentatives ever did take financial advantage of them at any time. *Did we not act in the same spirit? Did we not take the same steps?* Paul's associates, like Paul himself, all maintained the same scrupulous standards of honesty and refused to take any gifts from the Corinthians for their labors.

Paul makes it clear that in giving this lengthy explanation of his conduct, there is no question of his standing as a defendant before his judges. God is his judge, and Christ has impelled him to speak as he has. Besides, the outpouring of his heart in this letter has not been for his own good, but for theirs: *It is . . . all for your upbuilding, beloved.* This accords with Paul's leading principle of church action: "Let all things be done for edification" (1 Cor. 14: 26). Edification means upbuilding. It is the same word in both pasages. The *upbuilding* of the Corinthians through the ministry of this letter is doubtless felt necessary by Paul, because of the havoc wrought by the false apostles in the church. The fellowship will have been badly disrupted by their contentiousness, and the effects of their teaching will have been serious in the moral realm.

The kind of bitter harvest that Paul fears he may find from such sowing is indicated in the latter part of v. 20. If the items listed are examined, it will be seen that they are precisely the kind of evils that result from the fragmentation of a church fellowship through division. Paul dreads that his next visit to Corinth may be like his last (cf. 2:1), and that it may prove to be a humbling experience for him as that one was. That indeed would be the case if he should find men and women whose repentance of their pagan ways was still incomplete, and church members who had turned deaf ears to his exhortations to turn from heathenism to holiness. If he saw evidence of *impurity, immorality, and licentiousness,* then he would be forced to exercise the kind of discipline demanded in 1 Corinthians 5:1–5, and that would cause mourning, not only to him but to the whole church. The tears of 2 Corinthians were worth while if they prevented the tears of that action.

(7) *Admonitions in View of the Third Visit (13:1–10)*

[1] This is the third time I am coming to you. Any charge must be sustained by the evidence of two or three witnesses. [2] I warned those who sinned before and all the others, and I warn them now while absent, as I did when present on my second visit, that if I come again I will not spare them—[3] since you desire proof that Christ is speaking in me. He is not weak in dealing with you, but is powerful in you. [4] For he was crucified in weakness, but lives by the power of God. For we are weak in him, but in dealing with you we shall live with him by the power of God.

[5] Examine yourselves, to see whether you are holding to your faith. Test yourselves. Do you not realize that Jesus Christ is in you?—unless indeed you fail to meet the test! [6] I hope you will find out that we have not failed. [7] But we pray God that you may not do wrong—not that we may appear to have met the test, but that you may do what is right, though we may seem to have failed. [8] For we cannot do anything against the truth, but only for the truth. [9] For we are glad when we are weak and you are strong. What we pray for is your improvement. [10] I write this while I am away from you, in order that when I come I may not have to be severe in my use of the authority which the Lord has given me for building up and not for tearing down.

Paul's affirmation that he is about to make his third visit to Corinth is followed by an allusion to the Jewish law that *any charge must be sustained by the evidence of two or three witnesses* (Deut. 19:15). Scholars in ancient and recent times have considered that the two earlier visits to the church and the one to come amount to the testimony of *three witnesses,* on the basis of which judgment will be given against the recalcitrant Corinthians. It is an attractive idea, but to many it seems a strained application of the language.

If Paul is not using the Deuteronomic law figuratively, he is speaking with remarkable authority. For in that case he means that when next he visits Corinth, he will observe the biblical principle of judgment and carry out a thorough investigation of what has happened in the church; he will call for *witnesses,* and where there has been proved departure from the word of God he *will not spare* the guilty but will ensure that sentence is passed against them. His reticence to act in this manner in Corinth, particularly on his last visit, has been misinterpreted, so that some in the church doubted whether Christ's power resided in Paul in a comparable way to the spiritual power of the "super-apostles." *You desire proof that Christ is speaking in me.* They shall have it! For some it will be an unwelcome demonstration, as Paul in the power of the Spirit exposes their sin and secures their excommunication by the church.

Paul then draws a parallel between Jesus and himself. By the Father's will Jesus *was crucified in weakness,* but henceforth *lives by the power of God.* So, Paul in union with Christ is weak in his submission to suffering but powerful as the Spirit uses him among men. *In dealing with you we shall live with him by the power of God,* he writes, in reference to his exercise of authority for judgment in the church.

Accordingly the apostle, who has been judged by the Corinthians, turns the tables on them: *Examine yourselves . . . Test yourselves.* The emphasis is on the reflexive *yourselves.* These people had been conducting an examination as to the reality of Paul's apostleship. He bids them carry out a ruthless examination of the reality of their *faith.* They ask whether Jesus Christ is speaking in him. He asks whether *Jesus Christ is in* them. They are concerned about his apostleship. He is concerned about their eternal welfare. If faith is in them, Christ is in them; but if they have no faith, they have no Christ, no God, no hope—nothing! How imperative it is that they should not *fail to meet the test!*

Let none think that Paul is looking forward to arriving in Corinth and passing judgment on those who fail to meet this test. His earnest prayer is *that you may do what is right.* If that prayer is answered, then Paul will *seem to have failed,* for the power of Christ in him to judge degenerate Christians will not be manifest. That however will be no sorrow to him, for his sole concern is to serve the truth of God. The

statement in v. 8, that Paul *cannot do anything against the truth, but only for the truth,* relates to what alone is possible to him as a man in whom the truth of Christ dwells (11.10), and who is called to preach that truth. If it turns out that the Corinthians repent of their wrongs, renounce the falsehoods received from the spurious apostles, submit to the gospel delivered to them by Paul, and acknowledge the legitimacy of his apostleship, then Paul himself must recognize the truth manifest among them and refrain from disciplinary action. To do otherwise would be to act *against the truth.*

In any case, Paul's love for the Corinthians far outweigh his concern for his own standing before men. *We are glad when we are weak and you are strong,* i.e., when the apostle is without opportunity to demonstrate his authority because the Corinthians are spiritually healthy and give no cause for discipline. His aim in his labors among the Corinthians and in his prayers when absent from them is their *improvement.* That includes not alone their advancement in personal holiness, but a growth in grace such as will enable a restoration of relations with one another in peace and love. That becomes clear when it is observed that the noun *improvement* becomes in v. 11 the verb translated as *Mend your ways.* Moffatt brings this out by rendering v. 9*b* as, "Mend your ways, that is all I ask." In v. 11 "mending one's ways" is spelled out in terms of mutual agreement and living in peace in the fellowship of the God of love and peace.

The purpose of Paul's writing this letter is precisely that this may come to pass, for the Lord gave him *authority . . . for building up and not for tearing down.* Such is the purpose for which all ministerial authority is given in the church of Jesus Christ.

(8) Farewell (13:11-14)

11 Finally, brethren, farewell. Mend your ways, heed my appeal, agree with one another, live in peace, and the God of love and peace will be with you. 12 Greet one another with a holy kiss. 13 All the saints greet you.

14 The grace of the Lord Jesus Christ and the love of God and the fellowship of the Holy Spirit be with you all.

Mend your ways takes up the subject of Paul's prayer for the Corinthians in 13:9 (see comment there). The verb occurs in Mark 1:19 of James and John mending their nets. It can therefore appropriately represent the idea of disentangling oneself from that which destroys the spiritual life and setting in order that which is wanting. Since the corporate aspect of Christian relationship is in mind in this context, it here signifies the rejection of that which destroys the fellowship and a healing of breaches made through dissensions.

Where a readiness for harmonious fellowship exists in this way, the presence of *the God of love and peace* is known. And in such a society the ancient custom of greeting with a *kiss* is more than ordinarily appropriate. The kiss as a symbol of love in a fellowship was taken over from the Jews by the churches and incorporated into their public worship as a solemn act, especially in connection with the Lord's Supper. To keep it *holy*, men kissed men and women kissed women, but Cyril of Jerusalem saw a deeper significance in this "holiness": "This kiss is the sign that our souls are mingled together and have banished all remembrance of wrong. The kiss therefore is reconciliation, and for this reason is holy" (cited by Plummer).

It is in the context of a quest for restored relations that we may best understand the benediction of v. 14. The genitives should all be understood in the same way, i.e., as subjective: the prayer is for the gracious action of the Lord Jesus Christ to be directed towards the recipients of the letter, for God's *love* to be freshly known by them, and for the *fellowship* which the Holy Spirit creates to be a reality among them. The quasi-trinitarian language is unmistakable, indicating the threefold mode of apprehending God in thought and in experience, and yet pointing to the unity of the persons in the Godhead.

The order of persons is sometimes thought surprising, and some scrupulous Christians insist on correcting Paul by placing *the love of God* before *the grace of the Lord Jesus* when pronouncing the benediction. Much is made of the point, however, that Christian experience begins with the redemptive *grace* of Christ, and that it is through that grace that we learn of the Father's *love* and experience the *fellowship* of the Holy Spirit. Yet it is possible that a much less weighty theological factor has given rise to the form of the benediction. Most of Paul's letters, including 1 Corinthians, conclude with the simple blessing, "The grace of the Lord Jesus be with you." It would have been quite apt for Paul to end this letter in the usual way, for as Paul himself learned out of profoundest experience, the grace of Christ is enough for anyone and for all.

Yet Paul was writing to a church which had been at serious odds with him, strongly contentious and refusing to cooperate with the other churches in alleviating the poverty of Jerusalem. They needed the *grace* of the Lord Jesus, but they also needed a fresh vision of the Father's *love* and willingness to open their lives in response to it. But more: this was a church which was torn by faction, whose members had ranged themselves contentiously with different apostles, and even against apostles (1 Cor. 1:12). At one point they rejected Paul's authority, and through adherence to the heretical "super-apostles" were in danger of rupturing relations with the rest of the churches of Christ. If ever a church needed to learn afresh the meaning *of the fellowship of the Holy Spirit* it was this one—and not merely its meaning, but its reality.

Accordingly, the benediction which Paul normally pronounced became expanded into a blessing of extraordinary pertinence to the church to which it was addressed. It remains powerfully relevant to Christ's congregations today. Men still need to know that *grace* which stoops to raise men from hell to heaven, the Father's *love* that spared neither the only Son nor himself and still welcomes the prodigal children, and the Spirit's *fellowship* which gathers the separated children of men into one family in Christ.

Galatians

JOHN WILLIAM MacGORMAN

Introduction

Religion as *Evangel* or *Law*—this is the vital issue at stake in the Galatian letter. To be sure, the particular historical form of legalism with which it grappled has long since passed from the scene, itself a remarkable tribute to the effectiveness of this document. No branch of Christendom today is wracked by a controversy over whether or not Gentile converts shall be required to add Jewish circumcision to Christian baptism. For this reason some modern readers may feel that Galatians has historical value only.

Yet Evangel or Law designates the ultimate alternatives in religion at any time. We are never done with legalism as a threat to the gospel of Jesus Christ. Time and again it has been routed only to appear again in new forms. The Reformation was hardly a debate over the Jewish requirement of circumcision, but it was another vast struggle between religion as Evangel or Law. The historical role of Galatians in this later crisis is well known.

The struggle remains a perennial threat because legalism is this world's religion. Legalism is that approach to God which it best understands, for it is but an extension into the religious sphere of the transactional pattern which underlies so much of its social, political, and economic life. Furthermore it leaves the innermost citadels of human pride unshattered.

Few persons have understood as well as Paul the utter incompatibility of religion as Evangel and religion as Law. Having experienced the futility of the latter, he became the greatest spokesman in the early church in behalf of the former. On one occasion in Antioch he seems to have stood alone (Gal. 2:11–14). For him God's supreme revelation was in a Person, not in a code. For Paul right relationship to God came through faith in Jesus Christ, his Son, who died for our sins and was raised from the dead, not through tribal identification or legal conformity. For him ethics was an experience in bearing the fruit of the Spirit, the consequence of an indwelling Presence, not a moral or ritual checklist.

This is why we need to hear what Paul has said in Galatians. It remains one of the greatest documents of the Christian faith, perhaps its most dramatic statement of the religion of the Spirit and its clearest call to freedom. This letter can serve once more as the medium through which God breathes renewal into the life of our churches.

Since God's revelation does not take place in a historical vacuum, we need now to consider the usual questions posed by the study of an ancient letter: authorship, readers, date, and purpose. To these will be added an outline and a selected bibliography.

I. Authorship

There are several evidences in the Galatian letter which point to Paul as the author. First, in the salutation the writer gives his name as Paul (1:1), and later in an emphatic reference he gives it a second time

77

(5:2). Furthermore, there is an extensive autobiographical section in 1:11—2:14 which provides the following information about the writer: (1) Prior to his conversion he was a zealous Judaist, who persecuted the church of God (1:13–14). (2) His conversion included his call to preach the gospel among the Gentiles (1:15–16). (3) His clear call likely occurred in Damascus, as he returned there following a stay in Arabia (1:17). (4) Three years later (seemingly, from the time of his conversion) he made a trip to Jerusalem to see Cephas, and saw James, the Lord's brother, also (1: 18–20). (5) Then he went to the regions of Syria and Cilicia, while the churches in Judea which knew him only by reputation praised God for his conversion (1:21–24). (6) Fourteen years later he went a second time to Jerusalem, taking Barnabas and Titus with him (2:1). During this visit Cephas, James, and John, the leaders, recognized his apostleship to the Gentiles and gave to him and Barnabas the right hand of fellowship (2:2–10). (7) He had a leading role in the church at Antioch, taking precedence over Cephas, Barnabas, and "the men from James" during a time of crisis (2:11–14). The associates named: Cephas, James, John, Barnabas, and Titus; the places visited: Damascus, Arabia, Jerusalem, Syria and Cilicia, Antioch, and Galatia; and the mission assigned: the evangelization of the Gentiles—all point unmistakably to one person, the apostle Paul.

This conclusion finds important corroborative evidence in the book of Acts. Also it is strongly attested in the early canonical lists, the ancient versions, and the writings of the church Fathers. Even among nontraditional scholars Galatians is generally regarded as an authentic letter of Paul.

II. Readers

In the salutation Paul addresses his letter "to the churches of Galatia" (1:2; cf. 3:1). Would that he had added some such qualifying clause as "which are in Pessinus, Ancyra, and Tavium"! Then we would know that he uses the term Galatia in its ethnographical sense, designating the area in north central Asia Minor formerly occupied by the old kingdom of Galatia.

In the third century B.C., wandering tribes of Gauls or Celts from eastern Europe made their way across the Bosporus. They became a threat to the surrounding peoples until subdued and confined in an area which came to be known as Galatia. This vigorous people were destined to play a troubled but significant role in the history of the Anatolian highlands until the death of Amyntas, their last king, in 25 B.C. At this time the kingdom of Galatia, which had grown extensively through the years, came to an end. It was recognized as the Roman province of Galatia, which in turn was enlarged through various annexations before the time of Paul's missionary labors.

Until the last century it was thought that Paul addressed his letter to churches located in territorial Galatia, the more restricted area occupied by the old Gallic tribes. The book of Acts mentions Paul in connection with this territory in two meager references: in 16:6 where it is simply stated that he passed through the region, and in 18:23 where it is said that he strengthened the churches there. Some scholars maintain that the first reference points to the time on the second journey when Paul founded these churches, and that the second describes a return visit on his third journey. Those who hold this view are advocates of the North Galatian hypothesis, e.g., Lightfoot; Moffatt; Feine, Behm, and Kümmel; and Marxsen.[1]

If this is an erroneous historical judgment, it could have been avoided had Paul addressed his readers: "to the churches of

[1] J. B. Lightfoot, *The Epistle of St. Paul to the Galatians* (Grand Rapids: Zondervan, n.d.), pp. 18–85; James Moffatt, *An Introduction to the Literature of the New Testament* (3d ed. rev.; Edinburgh: T. & T. Clark, 1918), pp. 90–101; Paul Feine, Johannes Behm, and Werner Georg Kümmel, *Introduction to the New Testament*, trans. A. J. Mattill, Jr. (14th ed. rev.; Nashville: Abingdon, 1966), pp. 191–93; Willi Marxsen, *Introduction to the New Testament*, trans. G. Buswell (3d ed.; Philadelphia: Fortress, 1968), pp. 45–47.

Galatia, which are in Antioch of Pisidia, Iconium, Lystra, and Derbe." Then we would know that he uses the term Galatia in its political sense, designating the Roman province of his own day. This more extensive area included territory in districts south of old Galatia: Phrygia, Pisidia, and Lycaonia. Here were located the cities just named in our hypothetical address, which Paul and Barnabas both evangelized and revisited on the first journey (Acts 13:13—14:24). Those who hold this view are supporters of the South Galatian or provincial hypothesis, e.g., Ramsay, Burton, McNeile, and Duncan.[2]

The main points in the debate involve Paul's use of terms, the appropriateness of "Galatians" in 3:1 as a designation of the ethnically different inhabitants of the southern districts of the province, and several considerations based upon the Acts account.

Does Paul tend to use terms in their official Roman sense? South Galatianists affirm that he does. They point to such passages as 1 Corinthians 16:19, where he speaks of "the churches of Asia"; 2 Corinthians 8:1, where he mentions "the churches of Macedonia"; and 2 Corinthians 9:2, where he refers in a similar way to Achaia. In these passages Paul is using terms in their official Roman sense. North Galatianists, however, contest this. They insist that in Galatians 1:21 Paul uses Syria in a territorial rather than a provincial sense. They point to 1 Thessalonians 2:14 for a similar use of the term Judea. They note that Arabia in Galatians 1:17 was not the official name for the kingdom of the Nabateans.

Can the term "Galatians" in Galatians 3:1 be an appropriate designation for all of

the inhabitants of the Roman province? North Galatianists claim that it cannot. Marxsen writes: "This can only be a racial term and cannot refer to the inhabitants of a Roman administrative district." [3] Yet South Galatianists are quick to counter this. They insist that if Paul could refer to the churches in Philippi and Thessalonica as Macedonians, he could speak of those in Pisidian Antioch, Iconium, Lystra, and Derbe as Galatians. Donald Guthrie adds: "It is significant that Philippi and Thessalonica were in the province of Macedonia but were in the geographical district whose indigenous people were Thracian." [4]

Advocates of the South Galatian hypothesis appeal to the book of Acts for further support: (1) Whereas there is a minimal reference to Paul's missionary activities in northern Galatia, there is a relatively full account of his work in the south. (2) Among those taking the relief offering to Jerusalem, there are no delegates from the north but there are from the south (Acts 20:4).

Suffice it to say, those holding the opposing view have answers for these claims with some additional ones of their own. The result is an impasse in Pauline studies: the determination of the exact location of the readers of the Galatian letter remains an unresolved problem. Arguments for the South Galatian view seem more cogent, but a consensus is lacking. Though this does not affect our understanding of the essential message of the letter, it does have a direct bearing upon its dating. Since a significant aspect of Pauline studies is the attempt to trace development in his thought, the importance of establishing a chronology for his letters is obvious.

III. Date

From the discussion above it is evident that the North Galatian hypothesis requires a relatively late date, whereas the South Galatian view makes possible, but does not

2 W. M. Ramsay, A Historical Commentary on St. Paul's Epistle to the Galatians (London: Hodder and Stoughton, 1899), pp. 1–234; Ernest De Witt Burton, A Critical and Exegetical Commentary on the Epistle to the Galatians ("The International Critical Commentary"; Edinburgh: T. & T. Clark, 1921), pp. xxi–xliv; A. H. McNeile, An Introduction to the Study of the New Testament (2d ed. rev.; Oxford: Clarendon Press, 1953), pp. 143–46; George S. Duncan, The Epistle of Paul to the Galatians ("The Moffatt New Testament Commentary"; New York: Harper and Brothers, n.d.), pp. xviii–xxi.

3 Op. cit., p. 46.
4 New Testament Introduction: The Pauline Epistles, (Chicago: Inter-Varsity Press, 1961), p. 76.

require, an early date.

Another factor involves the problem of Paul's visits to Jerusalem, as they are recorded in Galatians 1:18—2:10 and Acts 9:26-30; 11:29-30; and 15:1-29. The passage in Galatians records two visits: one to make the acquaintance of Cephas (1:18-20) and the other to resolve the problem of the Gentile mission (2:1-10). However, the Acts account describes three visits, each with important differences from Paul's description. For example, Acts 9:26-30 portrays Barnabas introducing Paul to the apostles, whereas in Galatians 1:18-20 Paul says that he saw only Cephas and James, the Lord's brother. Again, Acts 11:29-30 describes a time of famine, in which the church at Antioch sent a relief offering by Paul and Barnabas. Galatians 2:1-10 reveals no such offering. Finally, Acts 15:1-29 depicts the Jerusalem Council, including a public meeting with the entire congregation, climaxed with the formulation of the apostolic decrees. Galatians 2:1-10 knows nothing of these.

Numerous proposals for reconciling the divergent data have been made. One equates the two visits of Galatians 1:18—2:10 with those of Acts 9:26-30 and 11:29-30. Yet the request that the poor be remembered in Galatians 2:10 is strange indeed, if the passage is to be identified with the "famine" visit. Another equates the visits recorded in Galatians with those of Acts 9:26-30 and 15:1-29, Galatians 2:1-10 providing Paul's account of the Jerusalem Council. This requires Paul's omission of reference to the "famine" visit in a context in which he has placed himself under oath (Gal. 1:20). Others suggest various ways in which the author of Acts has either confused his sources regarding Paul's visits to Jerusalem or has been mistaken regarding the accomplishments of the Council.[5]

[5] For radical reconstructions of Paul's life and ministry see Donald Wayne Riddle, *Paul Man of Conflict* (Nashville: Cokesbury, 1940); John Knox, *Chapters in a Life of Paul* (New York: Abingdon, 1950); Charles Buck and Greer Taylor, *Saint Paul: A Study of the Development of His Thought* (New York: Scribner's, 1969).

All of these proposals have significance for the dating of Galatians. If Galatians 2:1-10 is Paul's account of the "famine" visit of Acts 11:29-30, then it is possible to date the letter before the Jerusalem Council, making it the earliest of Paul's writings. This is Duncan's (pp. xxi-xxxi) position. It makes Peter's vacillation at Antioch more tolerable and explains why Paul makes no appeal to the apostolic decrees in the letter. On the other hand, if Galatians 2:1-10 is Paul's account of the Council visit of Acts 15:1-29, as seems more likely, then a later date is required. Moffatt,[6] a North Galatianist, says that Galatians was written soon after Paul's arrival in Ephesus on his third journey. McNeile,[7] a South Galatianist, says that it was written either shortly before Paul left Ephesus or while en route to Macedonia.

A personal conjecture is that Galatians is not the earliest letter of Paul. Rather it belongs to the same general period as 1 and 2 Corinthians. It seems to be pre-Roman.

IV. Purpose

Soon after the conversion of the Galatians and Paul's subsequent departure (1:6), members of the circumcision party (Judaizers) infiltrated these young congregations. They appear to have been Jewish Christians, whether or not directly related to Jerusalem. For them Jesus was the Messiah of Israel's hope, but circumcision and submission to the Jewish law remained mandatory for all, Gentiles as well as Jews. One needed to believe in Jesus Christ *and* submit to circumcision, in order to be put right with God.[8]

[6] *Op. cit.*, pp. 83-107.

[7] *Op. cit.*, pp. 148-49.

[8] For the view that the Judaizers were Gentile Christians of the Galatian communities, alike reproved by Jewish Christianity and Paul, see Johannes Munck, *Paul and the Salvation of Mankind* (Richmond: John Knox, 1959), pp. 87-134. For the view that they were Jewish-Christian-Gnostics, whom Paul incorrectly understood, see Marxsen, pp. 50-58. For the view that Paul fights a battle on two fronts—against Judaizers and "spiritualistic radicals" or libertines—see James Hardy Ropes. A modification of this position may be found in John Knox, "Letter to the Galatians," IDB, II, 338-40.

To gain leverage for their teaching, the Judaizers claimed that Paul was not a real apostle (1:1), thereby seeking to undermine his authority. They charged that he was a man-pleaser (1:10) who either preached or did not preach circumcision as the occasion demanded (5:11; cf. 1 Cor. 9:19–23). They likely felt that the Gentile converts needed allegiance to the law to keep them from lapsing into pagan immoralities and that Paul's "liberalism" left them in a precarious position.

By the time that the report reached Paul from Galatia, the false teachers were making surprising headway in unsettling the new converts (5:7–10). For some undisclosed reason he cannot or chooses not to return to them. Thus he sends this urgent letter in an effort to stem the tide of their legalistic defection. From first to last his extreme agitation is evident. Omitting the usual amenities from the salutation, he launches immediately into a vigorous defense of his apostleship. He affirms "that a man is not justified by works of the law but through faith in Jesus Christ" (2:16). He warns any who submit to circumcision that Christ will profit them absolutely nothing (5:2). He reminds them that Christian freedom must not be distorted to justify moral license (5:13). Indeed, the one who walks in the Spirit will under no circumstances fulfill fleshly lust (5:16). Even after taking the pen from his amanuensis to make an end of the letter, he can scarcely restrain his arguments (6:11–16). Before a final benediction (6:18) he demands that all men cease troubling him (6:17).

Thus the Galatian letter was written by Paul to defend the gospel of Jesus Christ, the Evangel, from the legalistic perversions of the Judaizers.

Outline of the Letter

Salutation (1:1–5)
I. Personal defense (1:6—2:21)
  1. Amazement at defection (1:6–10)
  2. Affirmation of apostleship (1:11—2:21)
    (1) Conversion and call (1:11–17)
    (2) First visit to Jerusalem (1:18–24)
    (3) Second visit to Jerusalem (2:1–10)
    (4) Crisis at Antioch (2:11–21)
II. Evangel over law (3:1—4:31)
  1. Appeal to experience (3:1–5)
  2. Appeal to Scripture (3:6–18)
    (1) Sons of Abraham (3:6–9)
    (2) Curse of law (3:10–14)
    (3) Priority of promise (3:15–18)
  3. Function of law (3:19—4:7)
    (1) To specify transgressions (3:19–22)
    (2) To prepare for Christ (3:23—4:7)
      a. Law as moral disciplinarian (3:23–29)
      b. Law as guardian (4:1–7)
  4. Folly of turning back (4:8–11)
  5. Appeal to friendship (4:12–20)
  6. Allegorical demonstration (4:21–31)
III. Christian conduct (5:1—6:10)
  1. Remain free in Christ (5:1–15)
    (1) Peril of legalism (5:1–12)
    (2) Peril of libertinism (5:13–15)
  2. Walk by the Spirit (5:16–26)
  3. Heed these commands (6:1–10)
    (1) Restore the fallen (6:1)
    (2) Bear one another's burdens (6:2)
    (3) Avoid censoriousness (6:3–5)
    (4) Share with teachers (6:6)
    (5) Stop deceiving yourselves (6:7–8)
    (6) Do not grow weary (6:9)
    (7) Do good to all men (6:10)
Conclusion (6:11–18)

Selected Bibliography

ALLAN, JOHN A. *The Epistle of Paul the Apostle to the Galatians.* ("Torch Bible Commentaries.") London: SCM Press Ltd., 1951.

BARCLAY, WILLIAM. *Flesh and Spirit.* Nashville: Abingdon Press, 1962.

———. *The Letters to the Galatians and Ephesians.* 2d ed. ("The Daily Study Bible.") Philadelphia: The Westminster Press, 1958.

BLUNT, A. W. F. *The Epistle of Paul to the Galatians.* ("The Clarendon Bible.") Oxford: Clarendon Press, 1925.

BURTON, ERNEST DE WITT. *A Critical and Exegetical Commentary on the Epistle to the Galatians.* ("The International Critical Commentary.") Edinburgh: T. & T. Clark, 1921.

CALVIN, JOHN. *Commentaries on the Epistles of Paul to the Galatians and Ephesians.* Trans. William Pringle. Grand Rapids: Wm. B. Eerdmans Publishing Co., 1957.

DUNCAN, GEORGE S. *The Epistle of Paul to the Galatians.* ("The Moffatt New Testament Commentary.") New York: Harper and

Brothers Publishers, n.d.

LIGHTFOOT, J. B. *The Epistle of St. Paul to the Galatians.* Grand Rapids: Zondervan Publishing House, n.d.

LUTHER, MARTIN. *A Commentary on St. Paul's Epistle to the Galatians.* Trans. Theodore Graebner, 2d ed.; Grand Rapids: Zondervan Publishing House, n.d.

RAMSAY, W. M. *A Historical Commentary on St. Paul's Epistle to the Galatians.* London: Hodder and Stoughton, 1899.

RENDALL, FREDERIC. *The Epistle to the Galatians.* ("The Expositor's Greek Testament.") Grand Rapids: Wm. B. Eerdmans Publish-

ing Co., n.d.

RIDDERBOS, HERMAN N. *The Epistle of Paul to the Churches of Galatia.* ("The New International Commentary on the New Testament.") Grand Rapids: Wm. B. Eerdmans Publishing Co., 1953.

ROPES, JAMES HARDY. *The Singular Problem of the Epistle to the Galatians.* ("Harvard Theological Studies," Vol. XIV.) Cambridge: Harvard University Press, 1929.

STAMM, RAYMOND T. and BLACKWELDER, OSCAR FISHER. "The Epistle to the Galatians," *The Interpreter's Bible,* Vol. X. Nashville: Abingdon-Cokesbury Press, 1953.

Commentary on the Text

Salutation (1:1-5)

[1] Paul an apostle—not from men nor through man, but through Jesus Christ and God the Father, who raised him from the dead—[2] and all the brethren who are with me,
To the churches of Galatia:
[3] Grace to you and peace from God the Father and our Lord Jesus Christ, [4] who gave himself for our sins to deliver us from the present evil age, according to the will of our God and Father; [5] to whom be the glory for ever and ever. Amen.

Paul an apostle—the argument begins dramatically with the second word of the original text! Evidently the Judaizers had sought to discredit Paul's message by denying or depreciating his apostleship. It was an effective use of an old stratagem, and one to which Paul seemed quite vulnerable. He was not one of the twelve chosen by Jesus (Mark 3:14-19; Matt. 10:2-4; Luke 6:13-16; Acts 1:13). Neither did he meet the requirements for apostleship specified in Acts 1:21-22 at the time of the choosing of Matthias: presence with the Lord during his ministry and recognition as a witness of his resurrection. Thus they may well have charged that Paul's claim to apostleship rested on human authority alone.

He affirms, however, that his apostolic commission is *not from men;* it has a greater origin or source than that. Neither

is it *through man;* it has a greater mediator that that. Rather he is an apostle *through Jesus Christ and God the Father who raised him from the dead.* That which constitutes one an apostle is the call of God, and Paul claims this in no lesser sense than that which prevailed with the twelve.

Elsewhere he numbers himself among the witnesses of the resurrection of Jesus Christ (1 Cor. 15:8), but here he does not. In fact, this is the only reference to the resurrection in the entire letter.

The brethren who are with me remain unnamed in the Galatian letter. In other letters he names his associates in the opening verse: Silvanus and Timothy in the Thessalonian letters; Sosthenes in 1 Corinthians; and Timothy in 2 Corinthians, Philippians, Colossians, and Philemon. Nor can we derive help from the concluding verses of the letter, where Paul often makes references to or conveys the greetings of his associates (e.g., 1 Cor. 16:10-20). Here they remain unidentified. Otherwise they might have provided evidence for ascertaining more precisely the historical context of the letter. As it is, we know neither who they are nor the exact location of *the churches of Galatia.* (See the discussion of the North and South Galatian hypotheses in the Introduction.)

The salutation includes a prayer in be-

half of his readers in the form of a benediction. The word translated *grace* is *charis,*
whereas the familiar Greek greeting was
chairein. This feature is impressive in the
original text but is lost in the English translation. It denotes the unmerited favor of
God toward sinful men, which is the basis
for the righting of their relationship to him.
No word lies closer to the heart of the
Christian gospel than *grace.* It distinguishes
it as Evangel rather than as Law or Code.
It is divine gift rather than human achievement. And what a gift! It issues in *peace*
in the lives of those who experience its
reality.

Peace is the translation of the customary
Jewish salutation "Shalom," which was used
both in personal greetings and at the beginning of a letter (e.g., Ezra 4:17). Luther
(p. 15) wrote: "These two terms, grace and
peace, constitute Christianity."

God's grace is mediated to us through
*our Lord Jesus Christ, who gave himself
for our sins.* An impressive feature of the
Galatian letter is its emphasis upon the
vicarious death of Jesus Christ. It was in
our behalf and because of our sins. This
was the message which Paul had preached
to them at the first (3:1; cf. 1 Cor. 2:1–2).
Now he reiterates it in several passages of
his letter (2:20–21; 3:13; 5:11; 6:12,14).

Such an emphasis is understandable in a
letter evoked by the threat of religious
legalism. That Jesus Christ gave himself
for our sins is an affirmation whose full
significance the Judaizers had never
grasped. Legalism never does! It is forever
placing above the cross on which Christ
died an inscription which reads: "Necessary but not enough!" Thus it adds rites
to faith, insisting that faith alone cannot
avail.

But the gospel which Paul preached declared the adequacy of Jesus Christ to save:
he gave himself for our sins *to deliver us.*
This indicates the purpose of his voluntary
sacrifice. The verb translated *deliver* occurs
here only in the letters of Paul. (Elsewhere
in the middle voice it is found in Acts 7:
10,34; 12:11; 23:27; 26:17.) It describes

the accomplishment of Christ's death as
deliverance or rescue. Lightfoot (p. 73)
finds in it the keynote of the Galatian letter:
"The Gospel is a rescue, an emancipation
from the state of bondage."

That from which the death of Jesus
Christ delivers us is *the present evil age.*
To appreciate this reference, one needs to
recall the scheme of the two ages in late
Judaism: the present age and the age to
come. The former is characterized by sin
and death. It is under the sway of the
devil and his evil forces, who hold men in
thraldom (cf. Eph. 6:12). The latter is
characterized by righteousness and life. In
it God, his people, and his ways will be
vindicated forever, and all evil will be vanquished.

Yet one does not need to languish in
the hope of a deliverance reserved for the
future. Jesus Christ has already invaded
this age. In his death on the cross he engaged the evil powers in a decisive struggle, and in his resurrection he triumphed
over them (cf. Col. 2:15; 1 Cor. 2:6–8).
Thus he is able here and now *to deliver us
from the present evil age.*

As this great deliverance is grounded
in *the will of our God and Father,* it is
fitting that these opening verses climax in
a doxology.

In looking back over the salutation, one
should note the following features: (1)
There is no expression of thankfulness for
his readers. This is true of no other letter
of Paul. It reveals the agitation and hurt
he feels in the Galatian defection. (2) The
contents of the letter are presaged here.
The personal apologetic will find a fuller
statement in chapters 1—2; the gospel of
grace will receive a vigorous defense in
chapters 3—4; and Christian conduct commensurate with deliverance from the present evil age will be called for in chapters
5—6.

I. Personal Defense (1:6—2:21)

1. Amazement at Defection (1:6–10)

⁶ I am astonished that you are so quickly
deserting him who called you in the grace of

Christ and turning to a different gospel—7 not that there is another gospel, but there are some who trouble you and want to pervert the gospel of Christ. 8 But even if we, or an angel from heaven, should preach to you a gospel contrary to that which we preached to you, let him be accursed. 9 As we have said before, so now I say again, If any one is preaching to you a gospel contrary to that which you received, let him be accursed.

10 Am I now seeking the favor of men, or of God? Or am I trying to please men? If I were still pleasing men, I should not be a servant of Christ.

This passage reveals much about the crisis in Galatia. It was occasioned by the appearance of false teachers who were preaching *a different* (*heteron*) *gospel.* Paul specifies that their message cannot be regarded as simply *another* (*allo*) *gospel,* for it is completely different. Actually it is a perversion of *the gospel of Christ.* Those who preach it are described as troublers, for they cause much agitation and confusion. The singular form of this same participle (troubling) occurs in 5:10, where Lightfoot (p. 205) thinks that it refers to the "ringleader of this sedition."

The KJV is ambiguous here: "unto another gospel: which is not another." This sounds like double-talk. It derives from the fact that the translators used one English word to render two different Greek words (*heteron* and *allo*). Though these words were often used interchangeably, in the present context they are thrust against each other in such a way as requires a distinctive sense. Thus the "gospel" of the Judaizers was not just another version of the same gospel which Paul preached. It was a thoroughly alien gospel. Grace and law are mutually exclusive.

For their part, the Galatians have shown a surprising readiness to abandon God's call in the grace of Christ.[9] Paul expresses astonishment that their defection is taking place *so quickly.* The prior reference here is not certain. Different interpretations have been proposed: (1) so soon after their conversion; (2) so soon after the arrival of the

false teachers; (3) so soon after Paul's recent visit to them. The first of these seems best to suit the context; yet the others cannot be dismissed. It is even possible to construe the phrase in a nontemporal sense, emphasizing manner, i.e., rashly, but this seems less likely.

The defection of the Galatians is all the more remarkable, since Paul apparently warned them at an earlier time about the threat of those who preach a gospel *contrary to that which you received.*

The passage reaches a climax in the dreadful curse pronounced upon those who pervert the gospel: *let him be accursed.* The Greek word here is *anathema.* It was used in the Septuagint to translate the Hebrew word *cherem,* meaning "a devoted thing." It described that which was so abominable in God's sight that he was glorified in its utter destruction. In Deuteronomy 7:24–26 it was applied to the graven images of the pagan gods of Canaan. In Joshua 6:17–19 it was applied to Jericho and everything in it. The disaster which befell Israel at Ai came because Achan had taken spoils from Jericho into his tent (Josh. 7:1,19–26). Thus the biblical background of the term is awesome. It is doubtful that any English translation captures the fearful dimensions of this concept. Imagine that which is so iniquitous in God's sight that its destruction redounds to his praise! This is the terrible curse which Paul invokes upon those who pervert the gospel (cf. Rom. 9:3; 1 Cor. 12:3; 16:22).

It appears twice in the passage: once in v. 8 and again in v. 9. Again it may seem that Paul is being repetitious, but this is hardly so. To be sure, he uses a conditional sentence structure with an identical conclusion clause (apodosis) in each instance. However, there is a change in the mode of the verb in the "if clause" (protasis) of each verse which modifies the sense significantly. In v. 8 Paul uses the subjunctive mode, describing that which though possible is highly improbable. The RSV captures this sense well by translating: *if we, or an angel from heaven, should preach to you a gospel*

9 Some witnesses omit "Christ"; thus "him who called you in grace."

contrary to . . .

How much likelihood was there that Paul would show up in Galatia saying: "You remember that when I preached the gospel to you at first I told you that faith in Jesus Christ alone was necessary for salvation. Since then, however, I have received a more perfect understanding of the gospel through a lengthy sojourn with the Judaizers in Jerusalem. Now I, too, realize that you Gentiles must submit to circumcision, as well as believe in Jesus Christ, if you are to be saved!"

Or how much likelihood was there that the angel Gabriel would appear in Galatia admonishing: "Have nothing to do with that renegade Paul. Listen rather to the true emissaries from Jerusalem. Faith in Jesus Christ alone avails nothing, but rather such faith coupled with circumcision!"

As improbable as these surmises are, what if they should happen? Paul's devastating answer is: *let him be accursed!*

Observe that Paul makes his apostleship contingent upon his faithfulness to the gospel of Jesus Christ. Conceivably he could change but the gospel does not! No change in his thinking could alter what God has already accomplished for man's salvation through Jesus Christ.

Are there those who tend to rephrase this verse to read: "If the gospel of Christ which was preached by Paul is contrary to that which I have believed, let *it* be accursed?" If so, it is a massive and perilous conceit. The gospel of Christ is not contingent upon any man. Rather, all men are contingent upon God's delivering grace through faith in the crucified and risen Christ as Lord.

Years ago a wise father said to me: "The idols men carve with their minds are as much idols as those they carve with their hands."

In v. 9 Paul uses the indicative mode, describing that which was actually taking place in Galatia. Thus the RSV translates: *If any one is preaching to you a gospel contrary to . . .* Even as he was dictating these urgent lines, the false teachers were perverting the gospel. The indictment remains the same: *let him be accursed!*

Is this bigotry? It all depends. If the gospel of grace preached by Paul and the gospel of law preached by the Judaizers were but alternate versions of the same gospel, then he was bigoted to insist on one to the exclusion of the other. Furthermore, if there are many ways through which a sinful humanity may be put right with God, then it is bigotry indeed to insist on any one of them. But Paul believed that God's way of delivering men from their slavery to sin was through faith in Jesus Christ alone, the only way. Many have a problem with Paul here, not because they fail to understand what he says but simply because they do not believe what he believes. Not all of the *heteron* gospels died in the first century!

Evidently Paul's opponents in Galatia had charged him with trying to please men. Here he points back to the terrible pronouncement in the preceding verses to repudiate all accusations of temporizing. Surely one who seeks to curry the favor of men would not speak in such a manner! Temporizing is not part of the equipment of *a servant of Christ.*

2. Affirmation of Apostleship (1:11—2:21)

The personal apologetic with which Paul began his letter (1:1) is here taken up again and greatly expanded. One must not regard this as a peevish defense of selfish prerogative. Rather his apostleship was so identified with his message that to invalidate the former was to threaten the latter. It was the gospel itself which was at stake in the Galatian controversy.

Though it is evident from 1:1 that the Judaizers claimed Paul's apostleship rested upon human rather than divine authority, no further explanation is given. Who are the men upon whom Paul was supposedly dependent in this regard? Had they heard about his experience in Damascus in which Ananias had laid his hands upon him (Acts 9:10–19)? Or did they point to the men in the church at Antioch who had laid their hands upon him and Barnabas at the outset of their first journey (Acts 13:1–3)? Both of these answers have been proposed, but neither is likely.

If one is to take his clue from this extended passage, he must regard the Jerusalem apostles as those upon whom Paul was supposedly dependent for his apostolic credentials. It was with them that he was being compared so unfavorably. Thus from beginning to end, he declares his independence of the apostles in Jerusalem. Prior to his conversion and call he opposed them, and immediately afterward did not seek them out (1:11–17). Indeed, it was three years before he made his first visit to Jerusalem, at which time he saw only Cephas and James, the Lord's brother (1:18–24). Fourteen years more elapsed before he visited Jerusalem a second time, and on this occasion the leaders there fully recognized his apostleship to the Gentiles (2:1–10). The climax of the passage is reached in Paul's account of the incident in Antioch. Here he was compelled to rebuke Cephas publicly for the crisis he provoked by withdrawing from table fellowship with the Gentile converts (2:11–21).

Thus 1:11—2:21 is a "selected autobiography." It does not purport to be complete. Indeed, one has only to compare it with other autobiographical passages to see how incomplete it is (e.g., 2 Cor. 11: 22–33; Phil. 3:4–11). Instead Paul selected from his religious experience salient features which refuted the Judaizers, who slandered his apostleship as being dependent upon or inferior to the Jerusalem apostles.

Note the progression in the account: from independence of (1:11–24), to recognition by (2:1–10), to rebuke of (2:11–21) the Jerusalem apostles.

(1) Conversion and Call (1:11–17)

11 For I would have you know, brethren, that the gospel which was preached by me is not man's gospel. 12 For I did not receive it from man, nor was I taught it, but it came through a revelation of Jesus Christ. 13 For you have heard of my former life in Judaism, how I persecuted the church of God violently and tried to destroy it; **14 and I advanced in Judaism beyond many of my own age among my people, so extremely zealous was I for the traditions of my fathers. 15 But when he who had set me apart before I was born, and had called me through his grace, 16 was pleased to reveal his Son to me, in order that I might preach him among the Gentiles, I did not confer with flesh and blood, 17 nor did I go up to Jerusalem to those who were apostles before me, but I went away into Arabia; and again I returned to Damascus.**

Paul begins his defense by affirming that the gospel he preaches *is not man's gospel* (lit., "according to man," but the sense is clarified in NEB: "no human invention"). As he has already maintained the divine origin and mediation of his apostleship, so now he affirms the divine nature of the gospel he preaches. It is not man's contrivance; it is God's gracious gift.

In support of this claim Paul states that he *did not receive it from man, nor was he taught it* by man. It was not the Jerusalem apostles who arrested Paul the zealot in full stride with their preaching of the gospel. Rather it was God's *revelation of Jesus Christ* to him. If the genitive here is subjective, then Jesus Christ is the revealer. However, a similar reference in 1:16 argues in favor of the objective sense; thus Jesus Christ is the one revealed.

This verse can hardly mean that Paul's knowledge of the gospel owed nothing to those who were eyewitnesses and followers of Jesus Christ before him (cf. 1 Cor. 15: 3–5). Stamm (p. 454) explains: "He was concerned not to deny that he received the facts about the life, death, and resurrection of Jesus from others, but to defend his interpretation of those facts." Yet perhaps more than an insistence upon the right of interpretation is involved here. In a setting in which his gospel was being depreciated as a human contrivance, he asserts: "It is not! The gospel I preach was given to me by God. He revealed Jesus Christ to me."

The radical change which this confrontation brought to Paul's life is emphasized by the recall of his *former life in Judaism*. This was known to the Galatians. Likely from his own lips they had heard him describe how he had *persecuted the church of God violently* (better, "beyond measure") *and tried to destroy it* (cf. Phil. 3:6; 1 Tim. 1:13; Acts 8:1–3; 9:1–9; 22:2–21; 26:4–23). Because of a surpassing zeal for the ancestral traditions, he was outstripping many contemporaries of like age in his advance in Judaism.

And then it happened! While pressing the persecution of the followers of Jesus Christ, God *was pleased to reveal his Son to me* (lit., "in me," as in the RSV marg.). What a definition of conversion: God's revelation of Jesus Christ, his Son, in us! Nothing less than this is enough; nothing more is possible.

The whole experience is shared with a remarkable restraint, for Paul does not provide many of the details which our historical interest requires. Yet all of the basic elements of the divine encounter are here: (1) God's revelation is of Jesus Christ, his Son. All that went before was preparation for his coming (4:4). We await no other. (2) God's call is a gracious act, rooted in the initiative of his good pleasure. Paul regarded himself as designated from birth to God's service, a conception found in the prophetic tradition of the Old Testament (Isa. 49:1,5; Jer. 1:5). (3) God's redemptive purpose embraces all peoples, Gentiles as well as Jews (3:14,28; cf. Rom. 3:29–30; Col. 3:11). He commissions Paul to preach Christ *among the Gentiles* (cf. 2:7–10).

Following his conversion and call, Paul sought consultation with no man. Neither did he *go up to Jerusalem to those who were apostles before me*. Yet this is exactly what he might have been expected to do had his apostleship in any way been dependent upon theirs. Instead he *went away into Arabia,* a vast desert region east of Damascus which extended southward to the Sinai peninsula. He does not tell us how far he went, how long he stayed, nor what he did before returning *to Damascus.*

In fact, we are left to surmise the reason for the Arabian sojourn. Was it to escape persecution from the Jews in Damascus, who were outraged by his apostasy? Was it to begin his mission of preaching to the Gentiles? If so, his strategy at this time was remarkably different from later, when he made well-populated cities, e.g., Corinth and Ephesus, his missionary base. The passage itself may afford a clue. That he says so emphatically in v. 16 that he *did not confer with flesh and blood* implies that he did seek further communion with God. Thus, like Moses, Elijah, and even Jesus himself, Paul spent time in solitude with God at this crucial stage of his life. The gospel of Christ demanded a radical reversal in his life (cf. Phil. 3:4–11), as indeed it does in the lives of all who take it seriously.

(2) First Visit to Jerusalem (1:18–24)

[18] Then after three years I went up to Jerusalem to visit Cephas, and remained with him fifteen days. [19] But I saw none of the other apostles except James the Lord's brother. [20] (In what I am writing to you, before God, I do not lie!) [21] Then I went into the regions of Syria and Cilicia. [22] And I was still not known by sight to the churches of Christ in Judea; [23] they only heard it said, "He who once persecuted us is now preaching the faith he once tried to destroy." [24] And they glorified God because of me.

Indeed, it was *three years* later before Paul made his first visit *to Jerusalem.* The prior reference here is not certain. It could have been three years following his return to Damascus (1:17), but it seems more likely that it was three years after his conversion and call (1:15–16). In either instance this is hardly the course of action one would expect of a man whose apostleship was dependent upon the Jerusalem apostles.

Paul indicates that the purpose of his trip was *to visit Cephas* (Peter's Aramaic name). This is the only occurrence of the verb *historeō* in the New Testament. In earlier literature it frequently described visits to places of interest or to persons with a view to getting information about them. Thus the translation here is an improvement upon the KJV "see," though it may be inferior to the NEB "get to know."

How much did Paul know about the historical Jesus? Some have interpreted 2 Corinthians 5:16 to mean that Paul placed little value upon the details of Jesus' ministry prior to his passion and resurrection. Yet he knew enough about him and his teachings to prompt a relentless persecution of his followers. Furthermore his letters reflect an adequate understanding of the ministry of Jesus. Can one imagine that Paul spent *fifteen days* with Peter without hearing much personal reminiscence of experiences with Jesus, especially in the very place where so much had happened?

Paul makes a point of the fact that during this brief period he saw *none of the other apostles except James the Lord's brother.* More than likely James became the head of the family surviving Jesus. (In Mark 6:3 and Matt. 13:55 he is listed first among the four brothers and the unnamed sisters of Jesus.) Following a resurrection appearance to him (1 Cor. 15:7), he rose to a place of prominence in the church in Jerusalem. In 2:9 he is named with Cephas and John as one of the "pillars" of the church (cf. Acts 12:17; 15:13–21; 21:17–26). One observes here that the term apostle was not limited to the twelve in the early church.

At this juncture in his account Paul places himself under a solemn oath: *In what I am writing to you, before God, I do not lie!* (cf. 1 Thess. 2:5; 2 Cor. 1:23; 11:31). One wonders why the oath is inserted at this point. Burton (p. 61) can find no reason for such strong language "unless he had been charged with misstating the facts about his visits to the other apostles."

Then introduces a lengthy period following his first visit to Jerusalem, during which Paul was absent from Judea, having no further associations with any of the apostles there. Instead he *went into the regions of Syria and Cilicia.* Thus he was not serving in an area likely for one who had supposedly placed himself under the direction of the twelve. His mission was independent of their authority from the first.

Paul's native city, Tarsus, was located in Cilicia, and Antioch, the third city of the Roman Empire, was in Syria. Since both districts were linked together as one province in Roman administration, it is unwise to make much of the sequence in which they are named here.

As was the case earlier in his reference to a sojourn in Arabia, Paul provides no details of his activities during the lengthy period between his first and second visits to Jerusalem. As the time involved is 14 years (possibly 11), any attempt at the reconstruction of Paul's ministry based upon his letters, the primary sources, faces an extraordinary gap. Even a cursory reading of such a passage as 2 Corinthians 11:22–33 will convince one of how much he does not know about Paul's ministry.

During this time Paul *was still not known by sight* (lit., "by face") *to the churches of Christ in Judea.* The verb here is an imperfect periphrastic, whose sense may be rendered as above (cf. NEB, "I remained unknown"). Rendall (p. 157) takes exception to this translation, insisting that it should be: "I was becoming unknown." That is, at the beginning of this period Paul was a familiar figure in Jerusalem, but during the extended absence he gradually became a stranger to the Judean Christians. This seems strained.

However, they *heard* or kept hearing (also an imperfect periphrastic) that Paul, the former persecutor, was *now preaching the faith he once tried to destroy.* Thus *they glorified God because of me* (lit., "in me," as in the KJV; cf. Matt. 5:16).

Ridderbos (p. 74) contrasts the attitudes of the Judean and Galatian Christians to Paul. The former had suffered so much at his hands; yet they were ready to accept the integrity of his calling and preaching, praising God for the remarkable change in his life. The latter had never known him as a persecutor but only as a fervent evangelist; yet they were so ready to doubt him and his message. Later Paul will ask them with deep personal anguish: "Have I then become your enemy by telling you the truth?" (4:16).

(3) Second Visit to Jerusalem (2:1–10)

¹ Then after fourteen years I went up again to Jerusalem with Barnabas, taking Titus along with me. ² I went up by revelation; and I laid before them (but privately before those who were of repute) the gospel which I preach among the Gentiles, lest somehow I should be running or had run in vain. ³ But even Titus, who was with me, was not compelled to be circumcised, though he was a Greek. ⁴ But because of false brethren secretly brought in, who slipped in to spy out our freedom which we have in Christ Jesus, that they might bring us into bondage—⁵ to them we did not yield submission even for a moment, that the truth of the gospel might be preserved for you. ⁶ And from those who were reputed to be something (what they were makes no difference to me; God shows no partiality)—those, I say, who were of repute added nothing to me; ⁷ but on the contrary, when they saw that I had been entrusted with the gospel to the uncircumcised, just as Peter had been entrusted with the gospel to the circumcised ⁸ (for he who worked through Peter for the mission to the circumcised worked through me also for the Gentiles), ⁹ and when they perceived the grace that was given to me, James and Cephas and John, who were reputed to be pillars, gave to me and Barnabas the right hand of fellowship, that we should go to the Gentiles and they to the circumcised; ¹⁰ only they would have us remember the poor, which very thing I was eager to do.

Paul continues the defense of his apostleship by describing his second visit *to Jerusalem.* Already he has shown his independence of the apostles there by an account of his conversion and call (1:11–17) and of his first trip to the city (1:18–24). In the former none of them had a part, and in the latter he had a limited association with but two of them. Yet in the intervening time he had been preaching the gospel which earlier he had opposed so relentlessly.

The present passage goes beyond the assertion of independence. It describes the full recognition of his apostleship to the Gentiles by the Jerusalem leaders. The occasion followed his first visit by *fourteen years.* This seems to be the most natural

sense of the adverb *then,* which introduces the sequence here as well as in 1:18 and 21. Interpreters may be found who regard Paul's conversion rather than his first visit to Jerusalem as the prior reference (e.g., Calvin, p. 48). If so, 11 instead of 14 years separated the two visits. In either instance this was a lengthy period in which Paul continued to preach among the Gentiles.

Paul makes clear that he *went up by revelation.* It was not in answer to a summons by the Jerusalem leaders. As earlier he had received his gospel "through a revelation of Jesus Christ" (1:12), so now he is prompted by God's disclosure to make this visit to the city. (For a discussion of the problems raised by the accounts of Paul's visits to Jerusalem in Acts, see the Introduction.)

Barnabas and *Titus* are his travelling companions. They were well chosen. Paul was not known personally to the Judean Christians (1:22) and had had limited associations with but two of their leaders (1:18–19). It was otherwise with Barnabas. According to Acts, he enjoyed the esteem of the Jerusalem church: (1) He was regarded as "a good man, full of the Holy Spirit and of faith" (Acts 11:24); (2) he was sent by them to Antioch, to investigate the thriving new work (Acts 11:22); etc. As one who had participated in the evangelization of the Gentiles from the start and as one trusted by all, his presence was needed in this crucial meeting.

Titus accompanied Paul and Barnabas as a trophy of the Gentile mission. Though unmentioned in the book of Acts, he was Paul's "partner and fellow worker" (2 Cor. 8:23; cf. also 2:13; 7:6,13–15; 8:16–17; 12–18; Titus 1:4). As will be seen shortly, the issue of the conference focused in him.

Once there Paul *laid before* the leaders *the gospel which* he had been preaching *among the Gentiles.* The reason for doing so is indicated in a rather unusual clause of negative purpose containing both the subjunctive and indicative forms of the same verb: *lest somehow I should be running or had run in vain* (cf. 1 Thess. 3:5).

Though *trechō* (run) is the same form for
the subjunctive and indicative moods, it is
likely the former here, denoting contingency. However, *hedramon* (run) is an
aorist indicative, referring to the work that
Paul had already done. The clause is somewhat surprising in view of 1:17, where he
makes a point of the fact that he did not
seek out the Jerusalem apostles following
his conversion. Yet it was essential that
harmony and mutual understanding prevail
between them. This is the sense in which
the clause is to be understood, not that it
was within the power of the Jerusalem leaders to invalidate the gospel which he received "through a revelation of Jesus
Christ"(1:12).

The gospel Paul preached centered in
God's call in the grace of Christ (1:6; cf.
3:1). It did not require circumcision. In
fact, Titus was there as a Gentile Christian
who had not submitted to this rite. According to the Judaizers in Galatia, one could
not be saved without it. Now what would
those who were of repute say? [10] The answer is found in v. 3: *Titus . . . was not
compelled to be circumcised, though he
was a Greek.* (This is the first reference to
circumcision in the letter.) Obviously, the
fact that the Jerusalem leaders did not require the circumcision of Titus undercut
the insistence of the Judaizers that the
Galatians needed to submit to it.

It is not as though there were no opposition to this decision, however. There were
those in Jerusalem who sought to compel
the circumcision of Titus. Rendall (p.
158) claims that the struggle over the circumcision of Titus took place in Antioch
rather than Jerusalem. Paul distinguishes
them from the leaders by calling them

[10] Four times in this passage Paul uses this expression. Does he use it in a disparaging sense? For the
view that he does, see C. K. Barrett, "Paul and the
'Pillar' Apostles," *Studia Paulina* (Haarlem: De Erven
F. Bohn N.V., 1953), pp. 1–4. For the view that the
term is a slogan coined by Paul's opponents which he
repeats without any intended irony, see Gerhard Kittel,
"dokeō," *Theological Dictionary of the New Testament*, ed. Gerhard Kittel; trans. Geoffrey W. Bromiley
(Grand Rapids: Eerdmans, 1964), II, 233.

false brethren. By stealth they had *slipped
in to spy . . . that they might bring us
into bondage.* It was their counterparts who
were responsible for the turmoil in Galatia.
The antithesis between Christian liberty
and Judaistic bondage will be developed
more fully in subsequent passages (4:8–11;
4:21—5:1). It is a prominent theme in the
Galatian letter.

At this point it is necessary to take note
of a textual variant which has led some
scholars to conclude that Titus did submit
to circumcision. Some witnesses omit *hois
oude* ("to whom not even") at the beginning of v. 5, yielding the sense that
Titus was circumcised as a concession to
the demands of the extremists. This is Duncan's (pp. 41–48) view (cf. NEB marg.).
According to this view, Titus, as a solitary
Gentile Christian in the center of Jewish
Christianity, submitted to circumcision as
a *modus vivendi*. It was not intended to
become a general rule for all Gentile converts but was rather a practical concession
in a special situation. Later, the Judaizers
distorted what had happened in their reports to the Galatians. They charged that
Paul had been summoned to Jerusalem,
where he was compelled to bow to the
ruling of the apostles there. This proved
that he was an inferior apostle. It also provided the basis for the demand that all
Gentile converts be circumcised.

However, the stronger manuscript support favors the reading reflected in the
RSV translation: *to them we did not yield
submission even for a moment.* What was
at stake was not a temporary or particular expedient but *the truth of the gospel.*
It is not necessary to attribute the inco-
herence of the passage to an embarrassment over what supposedly happened to
Titus in Jerusalem. A more natural explanation—one that does not controvert the
thought-flow of the entire passage—attributes it to an extreme agitation over what
was actually taking place among the
churches of Galatia.

Paul now turns his attention to *those who*

were reputed to be something, i.e., the leaders. As at the end of v. 4, so here there is another break in the grammar of the passage. (These are indicated in the RSV by a dash. The technical term for such grammatical suspensions is anacoluthon.) Paul pauses to observe that human distinctions carry no weight with God, who *shows no partiality.* Then reverting to the thought with which he began v. 6, though altering its grammar, he discloses that the Jerusalem leaders *added nothing to me.* This means that they had nothing to add by way of corrections or amplifications. They had heard the gospel he preached among the Gentiles; they had met Titus as a convert of the Gentile mission; and they were convinced that God was in it. They recognized that the same God *who worked through Peter for the mission to the circumcised worked through me also for the Gentiles.*

By no means does this expression intimate that there were two gospels, one for the Jews and another for the Gentiles. There was only one gospel (cf. Rom. 3:29–30). Neither is this division of labor to be taken so strictly that Paul would never preach to Jews nor Peter to Gentiles. Indeed, Paul often began his labors in foreign cities by preaching to both Jews and Gentiles in the synagogues. A passage like Romans 9:1–5, written comparatively late in Paul's ministry, reveals how poignant remained his concern in behalf of his "kinsmen by race." Likewise, according to Acts 10, Peter evangelized the Gentile Cornelius and his household. This was a working arrangement rather than a strict racial or territorial pact.

The meeting in Jerusalem reached a climax when *James and Cephas and John . . . gave to me and Barnabas the right hand of fellowship.* (Some witnesses substitute *Petros* for *Kēphās* and place it before James, but these are inferior readings.) This action was predicated upon their recognition of *the grace that was given to me.* It signified equality and part-

nership. These men pledged cooperation and mutual support in the one task of gospel witness. Only the main thrust of their labors would be different: *we should go to the Gentiles and they to the circumcised.* It was an appropriate symbol with which to culminate a meeting in which *the truth of the gospel* had been gravely threatened.

The only request made of Paul and his co-laborers was that they should *remember the poor.* Paul needed no persuasion at this point, for it was something that he was *eager to do.* Indeed, he was to canvass the Gentile churches in an effort to gather a relief offering for the poor in Jerusalem (cf. 1 Cor. 16:1–4; 2 Cor. 8—9; Rom. 15: 25–29). Later, at the risk of his life, he was to accompany the delegates with the offering to Judea (Rom. 15:31).

It remains to take brief note of the reference in v. 9 to James, Cephas, and John as *pillars.* Usually this is taken as a designation of those upon whom the greatest responsibility rests, those who hold up the work. However, Barrett argues that the metaphor is eschatological rather than ecclesiastical. He claims that "the Christians in Jerusalem spoke of their leading apostles as 'pillars' because they believed that they occupied (or would occupy) in the temple of the new age positions of fundamental importance and dignity." [11]

(4) Crisis at Antioch (2:11–21)

[11] But when Cephas came to Antioch I opposed him to his face, because he stood condemned. [12] For before certain men came from James, he ate with the Gentiles; but when they came he drew back and separated himself, fearing the circumcision party. [13] And with him the rest of the Jews acted insincerely, so that even Barnabas was carried away by their insincerity. [14] But when I saw that they were not straightforward about the truth of the gospel, I said to Cephas before them all, "If you, though a Jew, live like a Gentile and not like a Jew, how can you compel the Gentiles to live like Jews?" [15] We ourselves, who are Jews by birth and not Gentile sinners, [16] yet who know that a

11 Barrett, *op. cit.,* p. 12.

man is not justified by works of the law but through faith in Jesus Christ, even we have believed in Christ Jesus, in order to be justified by faith in Christ, and not by works of the law, because by works of the law shall no one be justified. [17] But if, in our endeavor to be justified in Christ, we ourselves were found to be sinners, is Christ then an agent of sin? Certainly not! [18] But if I build up again those things which I tore down, then I prove myself a transgressor. [19] For I through the law died to the law, that I might live to God. [20] I have been crucified with Christ; it is no longer I who live, but Christ who lives in me; and the life I now live in the flesh I live by faith in the Son of God, who loved me and gave himself for me. [21] I do not nullify the grace of God; for if justification were through the law, then Christ died to no purpose.

This is a disheartening sequel to the Jerusalem conference, where the efforts of the extremists to compel the circumcision of Titus were repulsed and the Gentile mission was recognized (2:1–10). There Paul received the right hand of fellowship from Peter (2:9); here he takes a public stand against him (2:11). Yet perhaps it was inevitable. The decision in Jerusalem was a compromise rather than a clear break with religion as law. It conceded that Gentile converts did not need to submit to circumcision; it assumed that Jewish converts did. There was an inherent contradiction in this uneasy concord, which assured a subsequent crisis. All that was needed to evoke it was a situation in which a community of Jewish and Gentile believers were confronted by another demand of the same Mosaic law. It happened at Antioch. Christians there were already known as innovators and missionaries.

When Peter arrived in the city, he found Jewish and Gentile converts sharing meals together. This was contrary to Jewish custom. Though the Pentateuch did not prohibit eating with Gentiles, it spelled out a code of dietary restrictions (Lev. 11), whose observance was threatened by social intercourse with them. Furthermore Jewish history had known times of crisis which seemed to make a policy of separatism essential to national survival, e.g., the Babylonian exile, the returns to a religiously corrupted and demoralized homeland, and the enforced Hellenization of the Maccabean period. Thus pious Jews refused to eat with Gentiles.[12]

Yet this long historical conditioning of exclusivism was transcended in the vibrant Christian community in Antioch. Before Peter's arrival Jewish and Gentile believers were together at both the devotional and social levels of their common life in Jesus Christ. Evidently the rightness of it commended itself to him, for he joined them at the tables.

But this was *before certain men came from James*.[13] Their coming precipitated a remarkable about-face in his practice. He began to withdraw and eventually *separated himself* from the common meal occasions. (Both of these verbs are imperfects, connoting a gradual withdrawal or retreat under pressure.) *Fearing the circumcision party* is the reason Paul assigns for Peter's conduct. Paul *opposed him to his face, because he stood condemned* (an effort to render the sense of the pluperfect periphrastic in the causal clause). Actually his actions had condemned him before Paul spoke.

One wonders about the role of James in this incident. Did these men come as his emissaries, carrying out his instructions? Or were they presuming upon their known association with him as leverage for going beyond what he would have approved? Some who are eager to absolve or reduce his complicity point to Acts 15:24 as an example of such an abuse. Yet Peter was no stranger in Jerusalem. He had an adequate basis for evaluating the authenticity of their representation. Furthermore what he was doing clearly went beyond the agreement of the Jerusalem conference, which in no way released Jewish Christians

---

[12] For sources of late Judaism and early Christianity which reveal the Jewish attitude toward eating at Gentile tables, see Dan. 1:8; Tobit 1:10–12; Judith 12:2; Jubilees 22:16; Acts 10:9—11:3; cf. Mark 2:15–17.

[13] Some witnesses have the singular rather than the plural forms for both the indefinite pronoun and verb; thus "before a certain man came." Origen understood this as a reference to James; others, to Peter.

from the requirements of the law.

When reports of Peter's actions reached Jerusalem, James may well have been apprehensive about their implications. Peter's actions were a jolting departure from tradition. James may have felt that Peter was placing a needless obstacle in the way of reaching his own countrymen with the gospel. There may even have been concern lest it prompt the Jewish authorities to adopt some measures of reprisal against the church. At any rate it is understandable that James should have delegated some to investigate the matter.

Of course, one of the hazards of leadership is that it is practically impossible to act privately. A person of less renown might have done what Peter did and hardly been noticed, but not Peter. His presence was missed; his absence understood; his example followed: *with him the rest of the Jews acted insincerely.* (Actually the Greek text is stronger than this: lit., "they played the hypocrite along with him.") With particular chagrin Paul reports that *even Barnabas was carried away by their insincerity* (lit., "hypocrisy"). Since he had been a recognized co-laborer in the mission to the Gentiles, his failure may have dealt the work a greater blow than Peter's. Apparently he never traveled again with Paul, though the latter mentions him with respect in 1 Corinthians 9:6 and Colossians 4:10.

Verse 14 elaborates upon the reproof directed to Peter. It was not exercised over a trifle. As earlier in Jerusalem (2:5), the truth of the gospel was at stake: *they were not straightforward about the truth of the gospel.* Such confrontations cannot be justified over minor scruples, but where the gospel itself is repudiated in the actions of a leader, none is to be spared. Paul rebuked Peter *before them all.* The repair was sought where the damage had been inflicted: both were done publicly. Much moral cowardice hides behind dubious charity, as though silence in the presence of wrong were greater faithfulness to Jesus than its rebuke.

Peter's failure was put into sharp focus

by the question which Paul addressed to him in v. 14b. Observe that he appealed to Peter's former attitude, i.e., the one which prevailed before the arrival of the men from Jerusalem. By controverting his former attitude he was guilty of role playing. Its effect was to *compel the Gentiles to live like Jews.* Peter may have been ready to deny this, affirming that the Gentiles should remain free from the food laws while the Jews observed them. Yet the dimension of compulsion was unavoidable. Intention can not be the final appeal; actual impact has prior claim.

As the paragraph continues, it is impossible to determine where the direct address to Peter ends. The RSV encloses v. 14b in quotation marks but makes no break in the paragraph, as does the NEB. The fact that v. 15 begins with *We ourselves, who are Jews by birth* shows that Paul still has Peter in mind. Yet almost imperceptibly he broadens his discussion to include the religious experience of all Jewish Christians. By the time he reaches the end of the paragraph, the past crisis in Antioch seems to shade into the present one in Galatia.

What has been the religious experience of those who were born Jews, with all of its advantages of special providence and nurture (cf. Rom. 9:4–5; Phil. 3:4–6; 2 Cor. 11:22)? *Gentile sinners* may repeat the designation used by Paul's opponents. (Moffatt sets these words off in quotation marks.) It was the usual term applied by the self-conscious Jew to the uncircumcised. Paul's answer to this question is found in v. 16, truly one of the greatest passages in the entire letter.

Here are some of the fundamental concepts in Paul's thought: (1) *Justified* is a legal term. It means that sinful man is "acquitted" or "set right with God" (RSV marg., "reckoned righteous"). This is no mere legal fiction. (2) *By works of the law* (lit., "by works of law," as there is no article in the original text) designates any religious system, Jewish or otherwise, whose hope for acceptance with God rests upon meritorious obedience to formal statutes. In this letter the phrase has specific reference to the Judaizers, who demanded circumcision of the Gentile converts of Galatia as essential to a right relationship with God. (3) *Through faith in Jesus Christ* describes the way in which God's acquittal is realized in our experience. Faith is more than a statement of belief. It is that kind of belief which commits one's self to God's gracious gift of salvation through Jesus Christ. Years ago I heard the phrase: "Faith is belief—plus yourself!"

The religious experience of those who were *Jews by birth* affirmed that no man can achieve right standing with God *by works of the law.* Thus Paul points out that *even we have believed in Christ Jesus, in order to be justified by faith in Christ.* This is the essential message of Galatians. Three times in v. 16 he reiterates that no one can be justified *by works of the law.* The last of these is a citation of Psalm 143:2 with some modifications. It is introduced to undergird what has been said with the authority of Scripture. The experience of Paul, Peter, Barnabas, and the rest of the Jewish Christians confirmed the failure of religion as *Law* and pointed to religion as *Evangel,* the acceptance of God's salvation through faith in Jesus Christ.

The meaning of **v. 17** remains obscure. The main interpretations are: (1) An objector has taken a true premise and reached a distorted conclusion, which Paul utterly rejects. The true premise is that since we Jews cannot be justified by works of law, we are placed on the same level before God as the Gentiles. The false conclusion assumes the form of a rhetorical question: *Is Christ then an agent of sin? Certainly not!* translates *mē genoito* (lit., "may it not be!"), a strong expression of revulsion which Paul customarily uses in response to such distortions of the truth (cf. 3:21; Rom. 3:4,6; 6:2,15; 7:7,13; 9:14; 11:11). Calvin (pp. 70–72) and Lightfoot (pp. 116–17) hold this view. (2) Burton (pp. 127–30) modifies this by relating it

more closely to the incident in Antioch. That is, an objector claims that while seeking to be justified in Christ, the Jewish Christians in Antioch violated the law by eating with Gentiles. The same rhetorical question is asked. (3) Allan (p. 44) modifies it by dropping the supposed objector and fastening upon the logical inference of Peter's act. It was Christ who led the Jewish Christians to ignore the law in Antioch. By reversing his course Peter implies that Christ has led them into sin, a manifest absurdity. (4) Ridderbos (p. 101) finds here a general objection to the ethical dangers of preaching justification by faith. If, while ignoring the norms of the law, Christians are found living sinfully, even as the Gentiles, doesn't this prove that Christ is a minister of sin? The first two of these interpretations seem more probable, though the exact sense remains uncertain.

Verse 18 counters the preceding verse. By leading the Jews to abandon the hope of justification by works of law, Christ was not serving the cause of sin. Rather the one who reverts to the law, building up again that which he has torn down, proves himself *a transgressor* (*parabatēn,* "a violator of the law," replaces the more ambiguous term *hamartōloi,* "sinners," used by Paul's opponents in vv. 15 and 17). The transgression was in returning to that which had been tried, found wanting, and superseded by faith in Jesus Christ. This is what the Jewish Christians at Antioch had done; this is what the Judaizers in Galatia were doing.

As over against them, Paul gives a moving testimony of his own experience. He says that *through the law* he *died to the law.* He does not explain how the law served as the instrument of his death to it, though Romans 7:7–25 may be the best commentary on this text. Death to law meant that it ceased to have any further claim upon him (cf. Rom. 7:6). The purpose of this was that he *might live to God.* In the strong antithesis of this verse death to law is prerequisite to life to God.

With Christ I stand *crucified* better translates both the word order and tense (perfect). It is a powerfully dramatic statement, one of the many lyrical expressions of deeply personal religious devotion which intersperse Paul's writings. Literalism will lead one astray here; yet identification with Christ in his death on the cross was a vital reality for Paul (cf. 6:14). Here our truest guides will not necessarily be those who can analyze the text faultlessly but rather those who have experienced the reality it describes most fervently. The death which Paul died with Christ on the cross, however, finds him still very much alive. But it is *no longer* Paul living his life, but rather *Christ who lives in me.* Thus Paul's identification with Christ in death has issued in Christ's identification with Paul in life. Now his life is lived *by faith in the Son of God.* He is the one *who loved me and gave himself for me* (cf. 1:4).

Verse 21 sums up the entire passage. Reverting to legalistic works as in any way constituent to the attainment or maintenance of a right relationship to God is to *nullify the grace of God.* It is not to be *straight forward about the truth of the gospel* (v. 14). It is to place "the truth of the gospel" (2:5) in jeopardy. This is the true measure of what had happened in Jerusalem (2:1–10), in Antioch (vv. 11–14), and in Galatia at the time that Paul was writing this letter. Actually, religious legalism of any kind renders meaningless the death of Christ. For if right standing with God were attainable by *law, then Christ died to no purpose.* (The construction here assumes a condition that is contrary to fact, and then draws the conclusion deduced from the false premise.)

In these final verses Paul has moved beyond personal apologetic to the elaboration of the superiority of the gospel of grace to the legalistic gospel of his opponents. This is the great theme that will engage him during the next two chapters.

II. Evangel over Law (3:1—4:31)

Man is not justified by works of law; man is justified by faith in Christ (2:16). This is Paul's insistence in the preceding para-

graph, which serves as a transition to the next major division of his letter. Now he enlarges upon this central theme. He begins by appealing to the Christian experience of the Galatian converts (3:1–5). Then he appeals to Scripture, showing how God's covenant of promise with Abraham has its fulfillment in Jesus Christ and is not abrogated by the giving of the law which intervenes (3:6–18). Having refuted the distortion of the law's role as promulgated by the Judaizers, he proceeds to expound its true provisional and preparatory functions in the divine economy (3:19—4:7). He warns his readers against the folly of lapsing into earlier pagan bondage (4:8–11). In perhaps the most intensely personal passage of the letter he contrasts their former felicity with their present estrangement (4:12–20). Finally, an allegorical interpretation of some familiar Old Testament narrative demonstrates the superiority of grace to law (4:21–31).

1. Appeal to Experience (3:1–5)

1 O foolish Galatians! Who has bewitched you, before whose eyes Jesus Christ was publicly portrayed as crucified? 2 Let me ask you only this: Did you receive the Spirit by works of the law, or by hearing with faith? 3 Are you so foolish? Having begun with the Spirit, are you now ending with the flesh? 4 Did you experience so many things in vain?—if it really is in vain. 5 Does he who supplies the Spirit to you and works miracles among you do so by works of the law, or by hearing with faith?

This passage provides an appropriate sequel to 2:15–21. There Paul drew upon the religious experience of the Jewish converts to refute the legalistic perversion of the gospel. Here he probes the experience of the Gentile converts of Galatia for the same reason. It is remarkable that neither of these passages has any validity apart from the reality of the experience to which the appeal is made.

Paul's intense frustration with his readers is revealed in the derogatory epithet with which he addresses them: *O foolish Galatians!* (Phillips renders this: "O you dear idiots of Galatia," but this seems a bit over-ripe.) This outburst was prompted by the denial of meaning and purpose to the death of Christ to which Paul referred in the preceding verses. It led to the exasperated question: *Who has bewitched you . . . ?* The verb here (*baskainō*) connotes the casting of a spell through the power of the evil eye. There may well be the element of taunt in this question, as Paul is hard pressed to find a suitable explanation for the defection of the Galatians. (The KJV is based upon sources which add the clause: "that ye should not obey the truth," an obvious carry-over from 5:7.)

If only they had kept their eyes on the crucified One! For in Paul's preaching to them *Jesus Christ was publicly portrayed as crucified* (cf. 1 Cor. 2:1–2). The verb here is *prographō*. It is capable of two meanings: (1) "write before" (cf. Eph. 3:3 and Rom. 15:4); (2) "portray publicly" or "placard in public." Rendall (p. 167) opts for the former meaning, referring to some prior document. However, most commentators choose a form of the latter. *Jesus Christ crucified*—had Paul been posting a public proclamation or carrying a placard, this is how it would have read. (The perfect participle emphasizes abiding results rather than simple historical occurrence.) In popular lore one did not come under the power of the evil eye until transfixed by its gaze. Thus if the Galatians had kept their eyes where they belonged, this would never have happened.

In the verses which follow, Paul addresses four rhetorical questions to his readers. They are rhetorical, because he is not actually seeking information. Rather he is making strong assertions in the form of questions. No answers are given, because none are needed.

The first question probes the beginning of their Christian experience. Paul wants to know the circumstances under which they received *the Spirit.* Did it happen as they completed some requirement of religious *law?* Or was its setting entirely different? Did it happen in the presence of gospel proclamation, which was attended

by the kind of *hearing* which issued in *faith?* (Moffatt translates: "by believing the gospel message.") The answer which Paul intends is not spelled out. However, it is anticipated in the question of the preceding verse and assumed as the predicate of the next question.

In v. 3 the antithesis shifts from works and faith to *flesh* and *Spirit.* Granted that Christian experience began in faith-hearing, how is it completed or perfected? [14] Behind this second question we may detect the teaching of the Judaizers. They believed that faith in Jesus Christ was the beginning of that which was completed by submission to circumcision, a rite of the flesh. Both were necessary to a right standing with God. Again Paul invokes the recall of Christian experience to refute this legalistic perversion of the gospel of grace.

The meaning of the third question hinges upon the sense allowed the Greek verb *paschō* in this context. In early usage it meant experience, including everything that happened to a person, whether good or bad. As it developed, the bad sense predominated, i.e., "suffer." In the Septuagint it always describes experience in this unfavorable sense. Against this background, wide variations in the sense attributed to this verse may be found: (1) The NEB renders the verb in a good sense, referring to the benefits described in v. 1–2: "Have all your great experiences been in vain?" (2) The RSV renders it neutrally, specifying neither a good nor bad sense (cf. Burton p. 150). (3) The KJV takes the bad sense: "Have ye suffered so many things in vain?" (Cf. Lightfoot, p. 135.) To be sure, the letter makes no reference to persecutions; yet it is difficult to understand the reluctance to let the usual sense of the word prevail here.

The final words in v. 4 tactfully express the hope that, however threatening, the cause in Galatia is not yet lost.

The fourth question elaborates somewhat

---

[14] The verb is *epiteleisthe.* Ridderbos (p. 114) surmises that the Judaizers may have used this word among the Galatians.

upon the one asked in v. 2. The Spirit received by faith-hearing as Paul preached the gospel had been at work in the lives of the Galatians. There were many manifestations or spiritual gifts (the *charismata;* cf. 1 Cor. 12:4–11,27–30). However, the one specified in v. 5 is the working of miracles. Though an ellipsis leaves the verb understood somewhat in doubt, the sense is clear. Paul wants to know the explanation for God's supply of the Spirit to them and his working of miracles in their midst (lit., "in you"). Is it attendant upon legalistic works or faith-hearing?

The total impact of these rhetorical questions is impressive. Their appeal to experience confirms grace, not law.

2. Appeal to Scripture (3:6–18)

One may wonder why Paul did not rest his case upon the simple pragmatic appeal of the preceding verses (3:1–5). After all, the Galatians had heard the gospel, had responded in faith, and had received the Spirit accompanied by the working of miracles. This had happened before the arrival of the Judaizers with their legalistic perversions of the gospel. It would seem that their experience should have sufficed to protect them against such errors. Yet this was not so, for the Galatians were being unsettled and swayed by the false teachers. More than experiential recall was needed. It was necessary to meet the threat of the Judaizers at the level of the claims they were making upon the basis of Scripture.

A study of the passage reveals that these claims centered in an interpretation of God's dealings with Abraham and his descendants. It involved such questions as: (1) How was Abraham justified before God? (2) Who are his seed who share in the promised blessings? (3) What is the relation of the Mosaic law to the covenant of God with Abraham? One needs to read Genesis 12—17 at this point, for this is where the Judaizers found their arguments. This is also where Paul turns for evidence to refute them.

There are nine references to Abraham in Galatians, seven of which occur in the next 13 verses (3:6,7,8,9,14,16,18,29; 4:22). It should be noted, however, that from here to the end of chapter 4 the argument revolves generally around the questions cited above.

(1) Sons of Abraham (3:6–9)

⁶ Thus Abraham "believed God, and it was reckoned to him as righteousness." ⁷ So you see that it is men of faith who are the sons of Abraham. ⁸ And the scripture, foreseeing that God would justify the Gentiles by faith, preached the gospel beforehand to Abraham, saying, "In you shall all the nations be blessed." ⁹ So then, those who are men of faith are blessed with Abraham who had faith.

How was Abraham justified before God? Who are the seed of Abraham who share in the blessings promised to him? The Judaizers had answers for these questions based upon Scripture, primarily Genesis 12 and 17. In the former chapter God called Abram to leave his father's house for a land to be revealed to him (12:1). He promised him a great posterity (12:2). Abram responded to God's call with obedience (12:4). However, it is likely that the Judaizers dwelt mostly upon Genesis 17. In this chapter God commanded Abram to walk blamelessly before him (17:1). He changed his name from Abram ("exalted father") to Abraham ("father of a multitude," 17:5). He repeated the covenant of blessing to him and his descendants (17:2–9). He demanded circumcision of every male as a sign of the covenant (17:10–11). This included those bought from foreigners as well as offspring (17:12–13). Finally he warned: "Any uncircumcised male who is not circumcised in the flesh of his foreskin shall be cut off from his people; he has broken my covenant" (17:14). That very day Abraham, Ishmael, and every male in his house were circumcised (17:22–27).

Based upon these Scriptures the Judaizers answered the above questions in the following way: (1) Abraham was justified before God by responding to his call with obedience (Gen. 12:4). However, not until he submitted to circumcision was his faith perfected (Gen. 17:1). C. K. Barrett writes: "Current Jewish opinion connected Abraham's circumcision with Gen. xvii. i (Walk before me, and be thou perfect), and drew the conclusion that only with his circumcision did Abraham reach perfection." [15] (2) It is true that all of the nations of the earth will be blessed in Abraham (Gen. 12:3), but this is so only of those who submit to circumcision as the seal of the covenant (Gen. 17:10–14). They alone are his seed, who will share in the blessings promised to him. Since this includes Gentiles as well as Jews, the Galatians need to perfect their faith by being circumcised.

Now observe how Paul seeks to rebut these claims with arguments drawn from the same passage as that used by his opponents (Gen. 12—17). He quotes Genesis 15:6, a passage conveniently overlooked by them, to show that Abraham was justified by faith. This was not faith regarded as a meritorious work and thus rewarded by divine acceptance, as taught by the Judaizers. Rather it was faith expressed as a trusting response to God's call, which *was reckoned to him as righteousness.*

It follows then *that it is men of faith who are the sons of Abraham.* This is the characteristic that distinguishes his seed, regardless of genealogical identities. A circumcised Jew without faith is not a son of Abraham; an uncircumcised Gentile with faith is. Indeed, faith as trusting response to God's call has ever been the way in which men have been put right with God.

The Judaizers had found in Genesis 12:3 evidence to support their view that the blessings of Abraham would fall only upon those who had been incorporated into his posterity by circumcision. Yet Paul cites this same passage as a foretelling of God's intention to *justify the Gentiles by faith.* In this sense *the scripture . . . preached the gospel beforehand to Abraham.*

Abraham had faith, and it is *those who are men of faith* who *are blessed with* him.

One observes that Paul makes no refer-

ence to the teaching on circumcision in Genesis 17:10–14. In fact, he makes no attempt to describe the relation between Abraham's faith and this rite. This is somewhat remarkable, for he does it in Romans 4:9–12. There he points out that Abraham's faith was reckoned to him as righteousness before he was circumcised (4:10). Circumcision was received "as a sign or seal of the righteousness which he had by faith while he was still uncircumcised" (4:11*a*). Barrett writes: "The sign does not effect that which it signifies, but is merely a visible mark, pointing to a truth that exists independently." [16] Its purpose was to make him the father of all who believe, whether uncircumcised Gentile or circumcised Jew (4:11*b*).

(2) Curse of Law (3:10–14)

[10] For all who rely on works of the law are under a curse; for it is written, "Cursed be every one who does not abide by all things written in the book of the law, and do them." [11] Now it is evident that no man is justified before God by the law; for "He who through faith is righteous shall live"; [12] but the law does not rest on faith, for "He who does them shall live by them." [13] Christ redeemed us from the curse of the law, having become a curse for us—for it is written, "Cursed be every one who hangs on a tree"—[14] that in Christ Jesus the blessing of Abraham might come upon the Gentiles, that we might receive the promise of the Spirit through faith.

At this point Paul carries the attack to his opponents. They were claiming the blessings of Abraham upon the basis of works of law. Paul counters by charging that *all who rely on works of the law are under a curse.* This judgment is based upon Scripture, which pronounces a curse upon every one who does not perform all that the law requires (Deut. 27:26). This is the last of the curses to be pronounced from Mount Ebal. Apparently Paul's argument assumes that there are none who render the law the complete obedience necessary to escape its curse (cf. Rom. 3:9,19,23).

As additional evidence from Scripture that *no man is justified before God by the*

[15] *From First Adam to Last* (New York: Scribner's, 1962), p. 37.

[16] *Op. cit.,* p. 38.

law, Paul cites Habakkuk 2:4. This verse has its original setting against the background of the threat of the Chaldean invasion (1:6). The prophet is dismayed that God would permit this wicked nation to swallow up a people more righteous than they (1:13). Thus he takes his place upon the watchtower to see what God will say to him (2:1). The burden of God's disclosure is that "the righteous shall live by his faith," i.e., fidelity or faithfulness. This describes the attitude appropriate to the righteous man in the midst of the contradictions of this world.

In the Septuagint there is a change in pronouns from the Hebrew text which alters its meaning: "But the righteous man will live by my faithfulness."

Paul finds in this verse a scriptural support for his own understanding of justification by faith. However, the five words in the Greek text of his citation are variously rendered. The RSV construes *ek pisteōs* ("through faith") with the subject: *He who through faith is righteous shall live.* (Cf. NEB. This sense would be more obvious if the word order in the Greek text were *ho ek pisteōs dikaios zēsetai;* cf. *hē de ek pisteōs dikaiosunē* in Rom. 10:6.) The KJV construes the phrase with the verb: "The just shall live by faith," which seems the more natural meaning (cf. RSV marg., Moffatt, and Phillips).

Whatever the refinements of combination, these concepts belong together in Paul: righteousness-faith-life.

Law and faith as grounds for justification before God are mutually exclusive. *The law does not rest on faith* (lit., "The law is not by faith"). It does rest on works (cf. Rom. 4:4–5). Again Paul appeals to Scripture in support of his argument: *He who does them shall live by them* (lit., "in them" as in KJV; Lev. 18:5). This is the positive statement of the principle which was stated negatively in v. 10.

Verses 13–14 are introduced rather abruptly into Paul's discussion, having no connecting particle with the preceding statement. They immediately bring the work of Christ to bear upon the plight of those whose disobedience to the law has brought them under its curse (v. 10). In probing the meaning of this remarkable passage, we resort to a catechetical pattern of questions and answers.

First, what is it that Christ has done? The answer is that he has *redeemed us from the curse of the law.* The verb *exagorazō* means redeem, deliver, or secure release for one at a cost to the deliverer. Inasmuch as this passage is directed to those who seek justification before God by obedience to the Jewish law, it would seem that the pronoun *us* would apply to Jews and proselytes only (Lightfoot, p. 139; Duncan, p. 99). The article before *law* favors this understanding. However, Stamm (p. 509) insists that it includes the Gentiles of v. 14 also: "They too were legalists in religion, and Paul regarded legalism as a curse wherever he found it."

Second, how did Christ do it? The answer is by becoming *a curse for us* (cf. 2 Cor. 5:21). Again Paul appeals to Scripture, this time to Deuteronomy 21:23. (He omits "by God" from the Septuagint.) In its original setting the verse does not refer to any form of execution. It rather describes the hideous practice of hanging the body of an executed criminal on a tree. Since "a hanged man is accursed by God," it decreed that his body should not remain thus exposed all night, lest the land be defiled. He is to be buried on the same day that he is put to death. However, Paul finds in this passage scriptural support for his claim that Christ became a curse in our behalf. In the death that he died he took the curse of the law upon himself.

Third, why did Christ do it? The answer is found in two purpose clauses in v. 14. The first one speaks once more of *the blessing of Abraham* as it relates to *the Gentiles.* Already he has introduced Genesis 12:3 into his argument as evidence of God's intention to include them in his blessing upon Abraham (3:8). Now he states that the purpose of Christ's death on the cross is to make the blessing of Abraham available to the Gentiles. The second clause centers in *the promise of the Spirit through faith*. In 3:2 he spoke of this as something that had already happened in the experience of his readers.

(3) Priority of Promise (3:15–18)

15 To give a human example, brethren: no one annuls even a man's will, or adds to it, once it has been ratified. 16 Now the promises were made to Abraham and to his offspring. It does not say, "And to offsprings," referring to many; but, referring to one, "And to your offspring," which is Christ. 17 This is what I mean: the law, which came four hundred and thirty years afterward, does not annul a covenant previously ratified by God, so as to make the promise void. 18 For if the inheritance is by the law, it is no longer by promise; but God gave it to Abraham by a promise.

What is the relation of the Mosaic law to the covenant of God with Abraham? This is another issue in Paul's debate with the Judaizers, which needs to be resolved. Once again he appeals to Scripture as he affirms the priority of promise. The two essential points in his discussion of the covenant are: (1) It antedated the giving of the law by over four centuries. God never intended that the law should abrogate or amend it. (2) It has its fulfillment in Christ.

This is a difficult passage for several reasons. For one thing, its thought is interrupted. Paul introduces an illustration in v. 15, which he does not apply until v. 17. Furthermore, the intervening verse contains some of his boldest handling of the Old Testament text. Also, it is difficult to be certain of his concept in the use of the term *diathēkē*, whether it means a "will" or a "covenant." Indeed, the RSV translates it one way in v. 15 and another in v. 17 (cf. NEB). In the following interpretation this word is taken as a covenant because: (1) This is its consistent sense in the Septuagint, where it frequently translates *berith*. (2) This sense better fits the immediate context in which Paul is discussing God's covenant with Abraham. To be sure, this was the gracious offer of a sovereign God to a man and not a contract equally

dependent upon both parties. (3) This is its meaning in Galatians 4:24.

Paul begins by saying that he is going *to give a human example*, i.e., an illustration from everyday life. He will show that what is true of men in their contractual agreements with each other is even more true of God in his covenantal relationships with men. (See Phillips translation for a rendering closest to the position taken here.) The argument in the passage is *a fortiori*, moving from lesser to greater.

Once a contract has been drawn up and *ratified* by men, *no one annuls* or *adds to it*. The everyday flow of human affairs proceeds on the assumption that men will stand by their solemn agreements. The fact that sometimes they do not is not pertinent to his argument. Every human analogy breaks down when pressed too far.

Verse 16 intervenes the introduction and application of Paul's illustration. Here he affirms that God's *promises were made to Abraham and to his offspring* (lit., seed). The passages he has in mind are likely Genesis 13:15 and 17:7–8, both of which speak of the possession of the land of Canaan. However, Paul's emphasis falls upon the reference to the *offspring*. He makes the point that it is singular rather than plural, ignoring for the time being the collective sense of the word which he himself recognizes in 3:29 (cf. Rom. 4:13–18; 9:8). Then he makes the startling assertion: *which is Christ*. Paul claims that Christ is the *offspring* or seed of Abraham to whom the promise was made.

In v. 17 he applies the illustration introduced in v. 15. If men can be counted upon to honor their contractual agreements, how much more can God be trusted to secure his covenantal promises! God made a covenant with Abraham and his offspring and ratified it. This stood for 430 years before the giving of the law.[17] He did not intend that the law should *annul* the *covenant*

17 This is the duration given in Ex. 12:40 for the sojourn in Egypt. According to the LXX this period includes the time of the patriarchs in Canaan. Gen. 15:13 reads 400 years; cf. Stephen's speech in Acts 7:6.

previously ratified by himself, *so as to make the promise void.*

The Judaizers regarded circumcision as essential for inclusion in the covenanted community. They looked upon the law as the final revelation of God's will for his people. They believed that Jesus was the Messiah of Jewish hope, but this did not remove the necessity for circumcision and keeping the law. These remained mandatory for those who would inherit the blessings of God's promise to Abraham. As they conceived it, law and promise were complementary terms in the divine economy.

In v. 18 Paul counters this view. He asserts that law and promise are antithetical terms (cf. 2:21 and 3:12). To attempt to conjoin them is to misunderstand the role of the law. Rather it is inheritance and promise that belong together. This is confirmed in that *God gave* the inheritance (the implied object of the verb) *to Abraham by a promise.*

3. Function of Law (3:19—4:7)

To this point Paul's discussion of the law has been negative. This was inevitable since he was seeking to refute the errors of the Judaizers. Now he assumes a more positive stance, as he asks: *Why then the law?*

This question introduces one of the most important passages in Paul's writings on this subject. Basically he provides a twofold answer: (1) It was given to specify transgressions until the coming of Christ (3:19-22). Thus it has a provisional status. (2) It was given to prepare God's people for the coming of Christ (3:23—4:7). Thus it has a preparatory function. Two metaphors elucidate this aspect of the law's role: the moral disciplinarian (3:23-29) and the guardian (4:1-7).

(1) To Specify Transgressions (3:19-22)

¹⁹ Why then the law? It was added because of transgressions, till the offspring should come to whom the promise had been made; and it was ordained by angels through an intermediary. ²⁰ Now an intermediary implies more than

one; but God is one.

²¹ Is the law then against the promises of God? Certainly not; for if a law had been given which could make alive, then righteousness would indeed be by the law. ²² But the scripture consigned all things to sin, that what was promised to faith in Jesus Christ might be given to those who believe.

Paul says that the law *was added because of transgressions.* This is a literal translation, but it leaves the meaning in doubt. The reader may conclude: Because there were transgressions, the law was given to hold them in check. Yet this seems to violate the sense of the passage.

At this point it will be helpful to note some references in the Roman letter, ever the best commentary on Galatians. In Romans 5:13-14 Paul discusses the period from Adam to Moses. He says that sin (*hamartia*) was in the world before the law was given, but not transgression (*parabasis*). Evidence of the former was found in the reign of death which prevailed during this time, even when no transgression like Adam's was possible. For there can be no transgression until a standard has been laid down which defines the limits (Rom. 4:15).

The giving of the law provided this standard. It makes clear what sin is by specifying transgressions. In this sense the law converts sin to transgression (cf. NEB). It makes sin and its extent visible (cf. Phillips). It enables men to recognize their sinfulness (Rom. 3:20; 7:7). Duncan (p. 112) says that "men may *sin* in ignorance, but they *transgress* only when they have a recognized standard of what is right, and it was to provide such a standard that the Law was brought in."

Yet this was only an interim function of the law. It was to continue *till the offspring should come to whom the promise had been made.* The recurrence of the term *offspring* as a reference to Christ here helps to refute those who would like to dispatch v. 16 as a scribal gloss.

There seems to be further depreciation of the law in vv. 19b-20. As over against the Judaizers who regarded it as the perfect and direct revelation from God, Paul says that it *was ordained by angels through an intermediary,* obviously Moses. (The tradition associating angels with the giving of the law is found in the Septuagint rendering of Deut. 33:2; cf. Heb. 2:2; Acts 7: 38,53.) The difficult concept may be that whereas the law was mediated by Moses as a go-between for the administering angels and the waiting people, God's covenant with Abraham was given directly. Thus it is the superior revelation.

Has Paul overstated his case? Even when he sets out to discuss the positive role of the law, a depreciation creeps in. Proportion is one of the earliest casualties of sharp polemic. Such an apprehension on his own part may be reflected in the rhetorical question: *Is the law then against the promises of God?* (Cf. Rom. 3:31, where the same measure of concern is expressed lest his exposition of grace destroy the law.)

His answer is an emphatic *Certainly not* (cf. 2:17). He seeks to show the absurdity of such a distortion of his meaning by assuming a false premise and then drawing the erroneous conclusion (cf. 1:10*b;* 2:21*b;* 3:18*a*). The false premise is: *a law has been given which* is able to *make alive.* The erroneous conclusion is: thus *righteousness is by the law.* Of course, the true premise and conclusion are: No law has been given which is able to make alive; thus righteousness cannot be by the law— it is by faith.

It is difficult to know what particular Scripture, if any, has *consigned all things to sin* in v. 22. (The verb *sugkleiō* means imprison or confine. The KJV "hath concluded" is misleading.) Burton (pp. 195–96) thinks it may be Deuteronomy 27:26, which has already been cited in 3:10. Stamm (p. 516) suggests the Old Testament passages which Paul has strung together in Romans 3:9–18. Some have proposed Psalm 143:2, which was cited in 2:16. It is not difficult, however, to discern why Scripture consigned all things to sin, namely, that the promise which is by *faith in Jesus Christ might be given to those who believe.*

(2) To Prepare for Christ (3:23—4:7)

By the use of two metaphors Paul seeks to describe the preparatory function of the law. The first was suggested by the slave (*paidagōgos*) in an ancient household, who —like a custodian—was placed in charge of a boy from about six to sixteen years of age (3:23-29). The second was suggested by the guardian, who was placed over an heir during the years of his nonage (4: 1-7). In both one notes the elements of inferior status and temporal limitation. These are an essential part of Paul's explanation of the role of the law in God's dealings with his people.

a. Law as Moral Disciplinarian (3:23-29)

23 Now before faith came, we were confined under the law, kept under restraint until faith should be revealed. 24 So that the law was our custodian until Christ came, that we might be justified by faith. 25 But now that faith has come, we are no longer under a custodian; 26 for in Christ Jesus you are all sons of God, through faith. 27 For as many of you as were baptized into Christ have put on Christ. 28 There is neither Jew nor Greek, there is neither slave nor free, there is neither male nor female; for you are all one in Christ Jesus. 29 And if you are Christ's, then you are Abraham's offspring, heirs according to promise.

Verses 23–24 describe the situation *before faith came.* Unfortunately, this translation omits the article which appears in the Greek text and invites a misunderstanding. It implies, at least, that faith did not exist prior to the coming of Christ, which is not true. Throughout most of this chapter Paul has been arguing that Abraham was justified by faith. Furthermore he is the father of a large posterity whose distinguishing characteristic is faith. Indeed, any time that a man has been rightly related to God, it has been upon the basis of faith (Heb. 11:2). By the article Paul specifies the faith in Jesus Christ, to which he has pointed in the preceding verse (cf. NEB: "this faith").

Before the coming of Christ, *we were confined under the law* (lit., "we were being held in custody by law"). *Kept under restraint* is the translation of a participle of the same verb in v. 22 which was translated consigned. The element of moral restraint is unmistakable. This confinement looked ahead to the *faith* in Christ, which *should be revealed,* i.e., it was destined to be revealed and was held in readiness for that time.

There is no single word in English which translates adequately the Greek *paidagōgos* (custodian, lit., a "boy-leader"). This is so, because there is no one in our culture who fulfills a comparable role. The KJV renders it "schoolmaster," as does Luther (p. 144–45), but this better translates *didaskalos.* This slave was not the boy's teacher. Furthermore, since taking the boy to school was but one of his important tasks, this ought not to be exaggerated. Rather the *paidagōgos* was entrusted with the moral supervision of the child. He possessed the right of exercising discipline. Blunt (p. 106) observes that he is generally represented on vases with a stick in his hand (cf. Phillips, "a strict governess in charge of us").

Those who use school terms to describe this person's function suggest an educative role for the law in Paul's thinking. Yet it is more likely here that he is thinking in terms of the moral restraints imposed by the law until the coming of Christ. Duncan (p. 122) writes: "It is not as a Teacher that Paul thinks of Christ, but as a Redeemer: the Christian life is not an advanced education, but a deliverance from death into life."

Verses 25–29 describe the situation since the *faith has come* (article in the Gk., as in v. 23). *We are no longer under a custodian* (*paidagōgos*). Instead of being charges under a strict moral disciplinarian, *in Christ Jesus you are all sons of God, through faith.* Thus does Paul seek to refute the claim of the Judaizers that the Gentiles could only be incorporated into the covenant community by circumcision and allegiance to the law.

The only reference to baptism in the Galatian letter is in v. 27. Here Paul uses two analogies: baptism *into Christ* and put-ting *on Christ* (as one puts on a garment). Scholars vary in their understanding of these concepts: (1) Blunt (p. 108) thinks that the first may be the primitive formula of baptism, signifying its aim. Underlying Paul's use of the second, he sees an analogy to the assumption of the *toga virilis,* denoting entrance upon manhood. (2) Stamm (p. 519) speaks of the baptismal water as being charged with the celestial substance of Christ's glorified resurrection body. Thus baptism into Christ denotes immersion in water charged with Christ's spiritual body. (3) Burton (p. 203) describes the first as baptism with reference to Christ and the second as becoming like Christ.

Surely we are to find here an intense expression of union with Christ, a major motif in Pauline thought. The preceding verse has made it clear that it is by faith that we are sons of God. All such have been *baptized into Christ,* which is to *put on Christ,* to be clothed with him. (Rom. 6:3 speaks of being baptized into Christ's death.)

Those who have been baptized into Christ constitute a new solidarity. It is one in which all of the old discriminations are rendered meaningless. There is no place for racial prejudice: *there is neither Jew nor Greek.* The bitterest of the Jewish exclusivists maintained that God's purpose in creating the Gentiles was to provide fuel for the fires of hell. The most exclusive of the Greeks regarded non-Greeks as barbarians, unalterably inferior to themselves. There is no place for social prejudice: *there is neither slave nor free.* After ethnic differences have divided men into various groups, class distinctions tend to erect additional barriers. Some who can recognize *interracial* prejudice seem blind to *intraracial* prejudice. Furthermore there is no place for discrimination upon the basis of sex: *there is neither male nor female.*

There is a thanksgiving in the Jewish Prayer Book, in which one expresses gratitude to God that he was not born a Gentile, a slave, or a woman. These are the very discriminations which Paul repudiates upon the basis of the new solidarity *in Christ Jesus.*

Because this is so, every church ought to become a highly visible demonstration of the power of Christ to recreate a new humanity out of all peoples. It is a complete travesty of the gospel when churches perpetuate the same inequities of society which have brought the modern world so close to disaster.

Once again Paul takes up the theme of *Abraham's offspring.* In 3:6–9 it was stated that men of faith were the true sons of Abraham. In 3:16 Christ was identified as the offspring or seed of Abraham to whom the promises were made. Now in 3:29 *Abraham's offspring* are those who belong to Christ. They are the *heirs according to promise.*

b. Law as Guardian (4:1–7)

¹ I mean that the heir, as long as he is a child, is no better than a slave, though he is the owner of all the estate; ² but he is under guardians and trustees until the date set by the father. ³ So with us; when we were children, we were slaves to the elemental spirits of the universe. ⁴ But when the time had fully come, God sent forth his Son, born of woman, born under the law, ⁵ to redeem those who were under the law, so that we might receive adoption as sons. ⁶ And because you are sons, God has sent the Spirit of his Son into our hearts, crying, "Abba! Father!" ⁷ So through God you are no longer a slave but a son, and if a son then an heir.

Verses 1–2 introduce the second metaphor used by Paul to illustrate the preparatory function of the law. It has been suggested by the use of the term *heirs* in the preceding verse. Thus once more Paul draws upon the day-by-day experiences of men to provide a picture of the point he seeks to make (cf. 3:15).

Principals in the metaphor are: (1) the *heir,* who is a minor; (2) the *guardians* and *trustees,* who have custody of the heir during his nonage; (3) the *father,* who has made the arrangements for the son's inheritance of the estate. The emphasis falls upon the inferior position of the heir during the time of his minority. Literally "he differs

nothing from a slave," *though he is the owner of all the estate.* (The RSV *no better than a slave* can be construed in this sense, but is less clear. The comparison is one of position, not character.) This subjection obtains *until the date set by the father.* At that time the authority of the guardian and trustee comes to an end, and the restrictions made necessary by the former immaturity of the heir are removed. He enters upon his full inheritance as a son. How much greater the position of the son now than when he was governed by legal overseers!

No effort to identify the exact legal procedure suggested by these verses has been successful. The Roman law of a later period made the following provisions for the minor of a deceased father: (1) He remained under the care of a guardian (*tutor*) appointed by the father until he was 14; (2) then he was placed under a trustee (*curator*) appointed by the state until 25. However, these were stipulations of Roman law, whereas Paul describes a situation in which the father defines the terms of the inheritance.

Ramsay (pp. 391–93) finds in the passage a reflection of the old Seleucid law that prevailed in Graeco-Phrygian cities. It was similar to Roman law; yet it permitted the father to appoint by will both the *tutor* and *curator.* However, nothing is said about the real problem of the passage, namely, the setting of the period of guardianship by the father.

Both of these instances presuppose the death of the father. Still another explanation probes the possibility of a special guardianship established during the lifetime of the father. An example of this is found in 1 Maccabees 3:32–33, where King Antiochus placed his son under the care of Lysias before leaving on a Persian campaign. In 1 Maccabees 6:17 Lysias, having learned of the death of the king, set the son upon his father's throne.

These afford some interesting parallels, but they justify no certain claims regarding the source of Paul's legal illustration.

It would seem that he had some definite situation in mind, though Blunt (p. 109) suggests that he may have been thinking rather generally in nontechnical terms, as in 3:15.

The application of the metaphor in the following verses also involves difficulties. What we expect v. 3 to say is this: *So with us; when we were children, we were slaves to* the law. This would be in keeping with the context. From 3:23 on Paul has been describing the function of the law as a preparation for the coming of Christ. Instead the main clause reads: *we were slaves to the elemental spirits of the universe* (cf. Moffatt, NEB, TEV).

Among modern interpreters the last part of v. 3 reflects the most prevalent opinion regarding the meaning of the enigmatic Greek phrase *ta stoicheia tou kosmou* (Duncan, Allan, Stamm). So understood, it designates the spirit beings who were thought by many ancients to indwell and control the heavenly bodies. Thus they held the destinies of men inexorably in their sway, and were dreaded by all.

Advocates of this view emphasize or claim the following: (1) This exact phrase occurs also in Colossians 2:8 and 20, though nowhere else in the New Testament. Here it relates to a context in which Paul mentions "the principalities and powers" (Col. 2:15) and "worship of angels" (Col. 2:18). Thus the term likewise designates cosmical beings or forces. (2) *Ta stoicheia* occurs in 4:9 in connection with the former Galatian bondage "to beings that by nature are no gods" (4:8). (3) The features of Judaism which Paul singles out in the lapse of the Galatians in 4:10 are not circumcision and food laws. Rather they are seasonal observances, which are determined by the movements of the heavenly bodies. (4) In 3:19 Paul associates angels with the giving of the law.

If the view above is the correct understanding of the phrase, then Paul is associating the ritual observances of the Jewish law with the pagan belief in astral deities. He indicts both as slavery to the elemental spirits.

Others propose a very different meaning for the phrase in question. To them it denotes the elementary forms or rudimentary principles of religion, both Jewish and pagan (Lightfoot, Burton, Ridderbos). Thus Phillips renders it "basic moral principles," and Barclay, (*The Letters to the Galatians and Ephesians*, p. 36) "the elementary knowledge which this world can supply" (cf. TCNT: "the puerile teaching of this world"; NEB marg.).

The following claims and counterclaims may be made in behalf of this view: (1) This sense fits the illustration which Paul introduced in vv. 1–2. The rudimentary forms of religion or elementary moral principles relate to the time during which the heir is a minor. ABC's and childhood go together! (2) It is in keeping with the known problem in Galatia and complements the argument up to this point. The Judaizers demanded circumcision and obedience to the law as necessary to the perfection of faith. By asserting the utter incompatibility of works of law and believing the gospel, Paul insisted that such demands constituted a repudiation of faith. To yield to them would be comparable to a son who, having entered upon his full inheritance, insisted upon a return to the bondage of his minority years. (3) The same law which required circumcision and adherence to food laws also specified the observance of special days and seasons (4:10). Admittedly, these were often related to phases of the moon. Yet it seems a most tenuous connection to find here evidence of a relation to the pagan belief in astral deities. Rather they represented more of the weak and beggarly rudimentary principles of religion which belonged to the years of nonage (4:9). One wonders in what sense the awesome astral deities who held all mankind in abject thraldom could be regarded as weak and beggarly! (4) To be sure, in 3:19b Paul invokes the Jewish tradition which associates angels with the giving of the law. Though the reference, including the following verse, is obscure, it seems likely that some depreciation of the law is intended. But it requires some doing to convert these ordaining angels into tyrannizing stargods. (5) In Colossians 2:8 the phrase occurs in a context in which Paul warns against "the traditions of men." In Colossians 2: 20 it occurs in close connection with an admonition regarding "the commandments and precepts of men" (2:22). In each instance "the rudimentary principles of the world" seems to give the sense of the phrase in question. (6) This exact phrase has not been found in any other sources. Thus no claims can be made upon the basis of usage. Since a known meaning of *stoicheia* is "heavenly bodies," one wonders whether the same term would be used to describe the astral deities supposedly indwelling them. (7) In Hebrews 5:12 *ta stoicheia* occurs in a phrase whose full translation is "the first principles of God's word," i.e., the rudiments.

Paul's meaning in this phrase remains problematical. However, the cumulative force of the above arguments merits more consideration than is often allowed by modern writers. If this sense prevails, then Paul is describing the time under the law for the Jews and the pre-evangelical experience of the Galatians as a period of religious nonage. It was a time in which they were governed by mere rudiments. It was both temporary and preparatory; it anticipated fulfillment.

This happened *when the time had fully come* (literally and better, "when the fullness of the time came"; cf. Mark 1:15). This corresponds to *the date set by the father* in v. 2. The period of nonage under the law terminated at the time of God's choosing. This does not presuppose a chronological scheme of successive ages with calculable data in the form of signs, as in Jewish apocalyptic. Nor does it intimate an evolution of ideas which constituted a *preparatio evangelica*, e.g., Greek culture, Roman law, Jewish hope. Duncan (p. 128) writes: "It was not man's *progress* which impelled God to act, but man's *need*." Such elaborations, though interesting, likely over-

interpret the passage. Nor does it resemble the Greek concept of fulfillment as the outworking of an impersonal power governed by necessity. Rather it describes the sovereign decision of a living God, who is mercifully disposed toward us.[18]

At this time *God sent forth his Son.* The preexistent Son was with the Father and was sent into the world by him (cf. 1 Cor. 8:6; Phil. 2:6–7; Col. 1:15–17; Rom. 8:3; Heb. 1:1–2). *Born of woman* indicates the manner of his coming, i.e., he was one with us in our humanity. *Born under the law* further specifies his humanity, i.e., he was a Jew, subject to the law.

A double purpose clause without a coordinating conjunction in v. 5 (cf. 3:14) makes plain God's intention in sending forth his Son. The first clause says that he did this *to redeem those who were under the law.* This is a form of the same verb (*exagorazō*) which Paul used in 3:13 to describe Christ's redemption of those who were under the law's curse. There it was stated that Christ achieved this redemption through his death on the cross. The second clause says that he did this *so that we might receive adoption as sons.* This alters the figure somewhat. Verse 1 described a son during the years of his minority, moving toward the time when he would enter upon his full inheritance. Here one outside the family is adopted into it. It is better to learn to live with such variations in Paul's illustrations than to try to force a consistency that is not there. In both instances they are sons!

The word translated *adoption as sons* is *huiothesian.* It does not occur in the Septuagint and appears in only five passages of the New Testament, all in the letters of Paul (Rom. 8:15,23; 9:4; Eph. 1:5). Some writers say that Paul introduces this metaphor to distinguish between the sonship of Christ and believers, i.e., he is a Son by nature, and we are sons by grace. But this seems strained. In 3:26 believers are designated sons of God without any reference

---

[18] See the article by Gerhard Delling on *plēroō* and related words in TDNT, VI, 286–311.

to adoption.

Our sonship is not merely a formal status. It is an intimate relationship: *God has sent the Spirit of his Son into our hearts, crying "Abba! Father!"* (cf. Rom. 8:15). Some difference of opinion prevails regarding the sense of the Greek word *hoti* which introduces v. 6. The RSV takes it as causal, indicating the reason for the bestowal of the Spirit: *because you are sons.* However, some suggest that it is declarative, indicating the fact of sonship: "that you are sons." Thus the bestowal of the Spirit is evidence of the fact of sonship (cf. Rom. 8:14). The former seems the more natural sense here.

Abba is the intimate Aramaic term for father, which Jesus introduced into his prayers, e.g., Mark 14:36. *Father* translates *ho patēr*, the Greek equivalent of *Abba*. It is interesting that the terms are repeated. Some find in this an early liturgical formula; others, an emphasized entreaty; and still others, a practical translation.[19]

Once again Paul has appealed to a fact of experience to meet the threat of the Judaizers (cf. 3:1–5). They were affirming that the Galatian converts could not inherit the blessings of Abraham apart from circumcision and obedience to the law. Paul points to the presence of the Holy Spirit in their hearts as an evidence of their sonship. Because of what God has done, *you are no longer a slave.* Minority's bondage under the law is over. Christ has come. You are *a son, and if a son then an heir.* Thus does Paul conclude his elaboration upon the meaning of 3:29.

4. Folly of Turning Back (4:8–11)

⁸ Formerly, when you did not know God, you were in bondage to beings that by nature are no gods; ⁹ but now that you have come to know God, or rather to be known by God, how can you turn back again to the weak and beggarly elemental spirits, whose slaves you want to be once more? ¹⁰ You observe days, and months, and seasons, and years! ¹¹ I am afraid I have labored over you in vain.

It was impossible to discuss the meaning of "the elemental spirits of the universe" in the preceding passage without an extensive reference to these verses. Thus a minimum comment will be offered here.

Paul presses his urgent appeal more directly upon the Galatians by recalling their religious experience prior to Christian faith. He describes it as a time of ignorance of God. It was a time of *bondage to beings that by nature are no gods.*[20]

As over against this former ignorance and enslavement, Paul describes the present state of his readers as one in which they *have come to know God.* There is truth in this statement, but Paul immediately thinks of another way he would prefer to put it: having become *known by God* (cf. Rom. 8:28). This relieves any connotation of presumptuousness which the former statement may have. It is less liable to distortion. It recognizes God's initiative in the redemption of men. Stamm (p. 530) comments: "Being known by God is being saved by God's grace."

Thus far the movement in the passage has been from pagan bondage to Christian deliverance. Now Paul comes pointedly to the present threat in Galatia, namely, a lapse into the former bondage: *how can you turn back again?* Whether it involved *elemental spirits* (RSV; cf. NEB, TEV, Moffatt) or "puerile teaching" (TCNT; cf. Phillips, Barclay, NEB marg.) remains uncertain, as indicated above. Yet that to which the Galatians were turning was the demand of the Judaizers that they adhere to the requirements of Jewish law. Verse 10 mentions specifically the observance of special occasions of the Jewish religious calendar: *days, and months, and seasons, and years.* Throughout most of the letter the emphasis falls upon the requirement of circumcision (e.g., 2:3,12; 5:2–12; 6:12–15).

Paul's apprehension regarding the Galatians is great. He fears lest his labors in

---

[19] Joachim Jeremias, *The Central Message of the New Testament* (New York: Scribner's, 1965), pp. 9–30, has an interesting discussion of *Abba*.

[20] That Paul denies *deity* to these pagan gods is obvious, but does he deny *existence* to them? In 1 Cor. 8:4–6 he seems to do this, but in 1 Cor. 10:20 he refers to them as "demons."

their midst prove to be *in vain.*

The shocking feature of this passage is its apparent equation of the threatening Galatian lapse into Jewish legalism with a reversion to their former paganism. In other settings Paul affirms the superiority of Judaism to paganism (e.g., Rom. 3:1–2; 9:4–5). However, here he links both together in a common bondage. The movement from pagan worship to Christian deliverance to Jewish legalism is not faith perfected, as claimed by the Judaizers. It is faith rejected, a reversion to their former enslavement.

5. Appeal to Friendship (4:12–20)

[12] Brethren, I beseech you, become as I am, for I also have become as you are. You did me no wrong; [13] you know it was because of a bodily ailment that I preached the gospel to you at first; [14] and though my condition was a trial to you, you did not scorn or despise me, but received me as an angel of God, as Christ Jesus. [15] What has become of the satisfaction you felt? For I bear you witness that, if possible, you would have plucked out your eyes and given them to me. [16] Have I then become your enemy by telling you the truth? [17] They make much of you, but for no good purpose; they want to shut you out, that you may make much of them. [18] For a good purpose it is always good to be made much of, and not only when I am present with you. [19] My little children, with whom I am again in travail until Christ be formed in you! [20] I could wish to be present with you now and to change my tone, for I am perplexed about you.

This is an intensely personal passage. In it Paul suspends the argument which he has been laboring since 3:6 and will resume in 4:21. It was likely prompted by the exclamatory reference to his labors among the Galatians in the preceding verse. Now he pursues this more intimately.

He recalls the circumstances under which he first preached the gospel to them. An illness had made it a time of great difficulty, but their gracious reception and care had made it easier to endure (vv. 13–14). This fond reminiscence provides the background for his anguished probing of the estrangement that has come between them (vv. 15–16). He does not hesitate to impugn the motivations of the interloping Judaizers (v. 17) nor to remonstrate with his readers (vv. 18–20).

The paragraph begins with a command, whose meaning is obscured by an elliptical construction. Literally it reads: "Become as I, because I also as you, brethren, I beseech you." If we look to the immediate context for a clue to Paul's meaning, it would appear in the first clause that he is urging his readers to adopt his attitude toward the demands of the Jewish law. That is, recognize that it belongs to the period of religious nonage, not to the time since the coming of Christ has brought us into our full inheritance as sons. But what about the causal clause which provides the reason upon which the command is predicated? The main possibilities are: (1) "because I have become a Gentile as you" (cf. 1 Cor. 9:21); (2) "because I was once in bondage to the law as you are now." The former has the advantage of understanding the same verb in the second clause as is present in the first (the Greek text has no verb in the second clause). Some propose a meaning related less specifically to the context. Thus Phillips translates: "I am a man like yourselves."

You did me no wrong also is not clear. Some find here a reflection of a defensive statement from Galatia. Perhaps the Judaizers have claimed that they were not wronging Paul personally in preaching a more authentic gospel (Stamm, p. 533). Or maybe the Galatians have asserted that they were not doing so by accepting it (Burton, p. 237). Some see here a general disclaimer of any grievance against the Galatians for any wrongs done (Duncan, p. 139). Some relate the statement to the treatment accorded Paul on his original visit to Galatia (Ridderbos, p. 165). So far from wronging him, they had treated him well as vv. 13–14 will show. Others think that Paul may be alluding to circumstances unknown to us (Lightfoot, p. 174). Such a variety of interpretations illustrates well the inevitable difficulty of interpreting letters. They always assume a common ground of experience between correspondent and readers which may not be determined by us.

At first is the probable meaning of *to proteron* (cf. NEB "originally"). It simply points to the beginning of Paul's experience with the Galatians. However, others insist that the term designates the first of two visits which Paul supposedly made to Galatia prior to the writing of this letter (cf. TEV "the first time"). Scholars holding the North Galatian hypothesis regarding the location of Paul's readers find in Acts 16:6 and 18:23 references to these two visits. Others holding the South Galatian view tend to ascribe these visits to the outgoing and returning phases of the socalled first missionary journey in Acts 13:4—14:28 (see discussion in Introduction). However, it seems unwise to posit two visits upon such meager evidence.

There is no uncertainty regarding the circumstances which provided the occasion for the evangelization of the Galatians. Paul says that *it was because of a bodily ailment.* Such a statement has prompted several diagnoses. Some have found in v. 15*b* and 6:11 evidence that he suffered from eye trouble. Others suspect malaria, contracted along coastal lands in Pamphylia, from which he sought recourse in the higher altitudes of southern Galatia. Still others opt for epilepsy. Yet all that the text reveals is that while traveling through their territory, Paul suffered from an illness serious enough to require that he stop for care. Certain features of this illness may have constituted a special trial or temptation for the Galatians. (Some sources read *mou* or *mou ton* instead of *humōn;* thus "my trial or temptation.") Even so, they neither scorned nor despised him. Instead they received him *as an angel of God, as Christ Jesus.* They felt themselves fortunate to have him in their midst, no matter what care it involved.

It is against the background of this remarkable reception that Paul seeks to probe the present estrangement. At one time they would not have denied him their very eyes, if possible to give them. Now what has hap-

pened to alter this esteem and their sense of privilege for his presence?

In v. 16 Paul asks whether or not he is the cause of the breach. Yet the question he asks reveals that he scarcely allows this as a serious possibility. There is more rhetoric than inquiry here. It is the sort of question that an offended friend asks when feeling his hurt most deeply. It likely contains exaggeration in the first part: *Have I then become your enemy?* The term may be Paul's alone. It is doubtful that the Galatians so regarded him. It contains an inadmissable ground in the second part: *by telling you the truth.* Couple an exaggerated self-depreciation, which the other would not charge, with a self-condemning ground for the breach, which the other could not admit; then put them in the form of a question which demands a "yes" or "no" answer; and you have the stuff out of which lovers' quarrels are made.

Paul's real opinion regarding the cause of the trouble is revealed in v. 17. It stems from the Judaizers, who are zealously seeking to win the Galatians to their side. Observe that Paul does more than charge them with error; he impugns their motives (cf. 1:7; 2:4–5; 6:12–13). At the same time in v. 18 he seems to defend himself against the possible charge of jealousy.

The paragraph closes with intense expressions of concern for their spiritual welfare and of dismay for their defection. In 3:1 he addressed his readers "O foolish Galatians!" In 3:15 and 4:12 he termed them "brethren." But here he calls them *My little children.* (This is the diminutive *teknia.* Some witnesses have *tekna mou,* "my children.") He invokes the metaphor of birth pangs to describe the anguish he feels, saying that he is *again in travail until Christ be formed in you.* Admittedly the application is confused, giving rise to a variety of translations and interpretations (TCNT: "till a likeness of Christ shall have been formed in you"; NEB: "until you take the shape of Christ"; etc.). Yet as descriptive of the acute distress Paul feels for his readers, it is forceful.

This letter is a poor substitute for the visit which Paul would like to pay to Galatia. He expresses his longing to see them (cf. 1 Thess. 2:17–18; Rom. 15:23; Phil. 4:1). He yearns to alter the *tone* with which he addresses them, but confesses the perplexity they have caused him.

6. Allegorical Demonstration (4:21–31)

21 Tell me, you who desire to be under law, do you not hear the law? 22 For it is written that Abraham had two sons, one by a slave and one by a free woman. 23 But the son of the slave was born according to the flesh, the son of the free woman through promise. 24 Now this is an allegory: these women are two covenants. One is from Mount Sinai, bearing children for slavery; she is Hagar. 25 Now Hagar is Mount Sinai in Arabia; she corresponds to the present Jerusalem, for she is in slavery with her children. 26 But the Jerusalem above is free, and she is our mother. 27 For it is written,
"Rejoice, O barren one that dost not bear;
  break forth and shout, thou who art not in
    travail;
  for the desolate hath more children
    than she who hath a husband."
28 Now we, brethren, like Isaac, are children of promise. 29 But as at that time he who was born according to the flesh persecuted him who was born according to the Spirit, so it is now. 30 But what does the scripture say? "Cast out the slave and her son; for the son of the slave shall not inherit with the son of the free woman." 31 So, brethren, we are not children of the slave but of the free woman.

This is a difficult passage. In it Paul resumes his defense of the gospel of grace which began in 3:1 but was interrupted by the personal appeal of the preceding paragraph. (4:12–20).

Once again he focuses upon the question: Who are the true sons of Abraham (cf. 3: 6–9,29)? However, here his claims are even more sweeping. Not only does he reiterate that the Christian community represents the true Abrahamic lineage, but also he charges that the unconverted Jews are actually the descendants of Ishmael, Abraham's banished son by an Egyptian maidservant. *The Jews are Ishmaelites!* This is the astounding climax that Paul reaches in this passage. To achieve it, he appeals to the allegorical meaning of some familiar Old Testament narrative.

The paragraph begins with a challenge to the Galatians, who are described as those *who desire to be under law.* That they are addressed in this manner rather than as those who are already under law suggests that the defection is in process rather than completed. Paul writes urgently to avert the threatening calamity. Since the Judaizers are basing their claims upon the law, as noted earlier, it is to this source that Paul appeals for their refutation: *do you not hear the law?* (The RSV rightly indicates that the form of the question anticipates an affirmative answer.)

At this point it may be well for the reader to refresh his memory by turning to Genesis 16:1—18:15; 21:1–21. This is the portion of the law which encompasses the pertinent data described summarily in the next few verses.

Abraham had two sons, one by a slave and one by a free woman. Behind this simple statement there lies a poignant story of domestic strife and folly, which Paul does not elaborate. Though his readers are predominantly Gentile, he assumes their familiarity with the narrative. With a remarkable economy he recalls only those features which are essential to his purpose.

At the behest of the childless Sarah, his wife, Abraham fathered a son by Hagar, her Egyptian maidservant (Gen. 16). He was named Ishmael. Physically speaking there was nothing extraordinary about his conception and birth. This is the meaning of the phrase *kata sarka,* which the RSV renders too literally *according to the flesh* (also the KJV: "after the flesh"). Phillips' "in the ordinary course of nature" is preferable (cf. NEB).

Several years later God promised Abraham a son by Sarah, to be named Isaac (Gen. 17:15–21). God specified that it was with him that he would establish his covenant. Physically speaking there was much that was extraordinary about the conception and birth of Isaac. During the normal childbearing years Sarah had been sterile: now "it had ceased to be with Sarah after the manner of women" (Gen. 18:11). Thus *the son of the free woman* was born *through promise.*

To this point the most traditional Jewish contemporary would have found himself in agreement with Paul's account. However, in v. 24 Paul declares that *this is an allegory.* It is important that we grasp his meaning here. He does not intend to deny the historical integrity of the events he has recounted. Nor does he imply that he is merely drawing upon familiar Scripture as the basis for formulating an allegorical illustration. Duncan (p. 144) writes: "By an *allegory* he means something more than an *illustration:* it is a spiritual truth embodied in history, a shadow from the eternal world cast upon the sands of time." It is this deeper meaning already embedded in the biblical text, this prefiguration, that Paul seeks to extricate and interpret for his readers. In doing so he reveals more in common with the rabbinical exegesis of his own day than with the historical exegesis of ours. (See Barclay, *Letters to the Galatians and the Ephesians,* pp. 44–46, for a brief discussion of this point.)

These women are two covenants. This identification introduces the deeper meaning which Paul finds in the biblical narrative. Through v. 27 he draws out this allegorical sense in a series of correspondences, supported by a scriptural citation. This chart makes them more visible:

Hagar, a maidservant	Sarah, the wife
Ishmael	Isaac
Ordinary birth	Extraordinary birth
Sinai: covenant of law	Covenant of promise; cf. 3:15–18
Begetting slaves	Begetting freemen
Jerusalem now	Jerusalem above
They: the Jewish legalists	We: the Christian community

This chart facilitates two observations. First, it shows the basis for Paul's startling conclusion that the Jewish nation, law-bound and Christ-rejecting, are the true descendants of Ishmael. Similarly it visualizes the basis for his claim that the community of faith, Christ-bound and law-transcending, are the true descendants of Isaac. Second, it makes graphic the urgent issue which prompted the writing of this letter. The Galatian converts, by virtue of their faith-response to the preaching of the gospel of grace, belong in the Sarah column as men *born to be free.* Yet due to the infiltration of the Jewish legalists who are perverting the gospel of grace, they are threatening to remove themselves to the Hagar column as men *born to be slaves.* For Paul such a course invites the ultimate disaster which he will state unequivocally in 5:2–4.

There are difficulties in these verses which require further comment: (1) The meaning of v. 25 is obscure. The RSV is based upon textual witnesses which read: *Now Hagar is Mount Sinai in Arabia.* However, the NEB follows other witnesses which read: "Sinai is a mountain in Arabia" (cf. RSV marg.). Obviously it is intended to reenforce the identification of Hagar with the covenant of the law at Sinai in the preceding verse. But its exact sense remains uncertain. Burton (p. 259) thinks it probable that the statement is a scribal gloss. (2) Paul introduces the concept of the heavenly Jerusalem in v. 26 without any explanation. It has a rich background in Jewish thought (cf. Ezek. 40–44; Hag. 2:8–9; Zech. 2; Sir. 36:13–14; Tob. 13:9–18; 14:5; 1 Enoch 90:28–29) and Christian hope (cf. Phil. 3:20; Heb. 12:22; Rev. 3:12; 21:2). (3) The KJV rendering in this verse, "which is the mother of us all," is based upon inferior manuscript support. The RSV correctly reads: *our mother.* (4) Verse 27 introduces a citation from Isaiah 54:1. In its original setting it was addressed to Israel in exile. With Jerusalem in ruins the nation was likened to a desolate woman, without husband or children. However, Israel will not remain so, for God will restore his people to their homeland, to a greater glory than ever. Thus they are to exult. Apparently only one woman is involved in Isaiah's vision: the desolate woman is the one who is to rejoice. But Paul finds in this citation a corroboration for his allegory of Hagar and Sarah. She who had no son gave birth to Isaac, through whom God's covenant promise passed to many, making a large family.

In v. 28 Paul reaffirms the identity of the Christian community with *Isaac* as *children of promise* as the basis for drawing another analogy from the Old Testament narrative. (The RSV *we* in this verse is likely less strongly attested than "you"; cf. NEB.) However, in his reference to the alleged persecution of Isaac by Ishmael he exceeds the explicit scriptural evidence. The Hebrew text of Genesis 21:9 simply describes Ishmael as laughing or jesting. The Septuagint expands this single word to read: "playing with her son Isaac," as does the RSV. Yet since the incident took place on the occasion of a festival honoring the weaning of Isaac and greatly displeased Sarah, some harassment is at least implied. Later a tradition grew, aided by the reference in Genesis 21:20 to Ishmael's prowess as an archer, that he had tried to shoot Isaac with his bow and arrow.

For Paul this persecution of Isaac by Ishmael prefigures the persecution of Christians, the true descendants of Isaac, by the unconverted Jews of his own day, the true descendants of Ishmael.

And what will the outcome be? Again Paul reverts to the Scripture for his answer. He cites Genesis 21:10 where Sarah demanded that Abraham *cast out* Hagar and *her son,* that he not be an heir with Isaac. This prefigures the judgment which Paul sees God bringing upon his unconverted countrymen. They shall be cast out; they will not inherit the covenant of promise.

Read 1 Thessalonians 2:14–16 for a passage which has much in common with this one. Then read Romans 9—11 (especially 9:1–5; 10:1–4; 11:1–36), where Paul discusses the spiritual plight of the Jewish nation with compassion and ultimate hope.

For the third time in this paragraph v. 31 repeats the claim of proper descent (cf. vv. 26,28).

III. Christian Conduct (5:1—6:10)

1. Remain Free in Christ (5:1–15)

The theme remains the same, but now exposition moves on to exhortation, allegory yields to admonition. Since the Galatian converts were *born to be free* (4:31), they ought to *live to stay free.* To do so will require the determination to avoid a lapse into legalism on the one hand (5:1–12) or libertinism on the other (5:13–15). Both are abuses of Christian liberty: the former defaults it, and the latter debases it.

(1) Peril of Legalism (5:1–12)

[1] For freedom Christ has set us free; stand fast therefore, and do not submit again to a yoke of slavery.

[2] Now I, Paul, say to you that if you receive circumcision, Christ will be of no advantage to you. [3] I testify again to every man who receives circumcision that he is bound to keep the whole law. [4] You are severed from Christ, you who would be justified by the law; you have fallen away from grace. [5] For through the Spirit, by faith, we wait for the hope of righteousness. [6] For in Christ Jesus neither circumcision nor uncircumcision is of any avail, but faith working through love. [7] You were running well; who hindered you from obeying the truth? [8] This persuasion is not from him who called you. [9] A little leaven leavens the whole lump. [10] I have confidence in the Lord that you will take no other view than mine; and he who is troubling you will bear his judgment, whoever he is. [11] But if I, brethren, still preach circumcision, why am I still persecuted? In that case the stumbling block of the cross has been removed. [12] I wish those who unsettle you would mutilate themselves!

No paragraph in the letter is more vigorously phrased than this one. It contains urgent appeal (v. 1), dire warning (vv. 2–4), prevailing hope (v. 5), sweeping disclamation (v. 6), probing reminiscence (v. 7), summary indictment (vv. 8–9, 10b), reassuring confidence (v. 10a), outraged apologetic (v. 11), and crude outburst (v. 12). Changes from topic to topic are introduced abruptly.

For freedom Christ has set us free. A glance at the critical apparatus of the Greek text will reveal more textual variants in this verse than can be acknowledged here. The most important of them involve:

(1) whether or not the relative pronoun *hē* (KJV: "wherewith") belongs to the text and, if so, its possible displacement of the article; (2) whether the adverb *oun* (*therefore*) follows the verb *stēkete* (*stand fast*) or the noun *eleutheria* (freedom); (3) the position of the pronoun *hēmas* (*us*). The KJV is based upon a text which has the relative pronoun after *eleutheria:* "Stand fast therefore in the liberty wherewith Christ hath made us free." The RSV translates a better attested text.

The Aland Greek New Testament includes this verse with the preceding paragraph. As such, it constitutes the climax to Paul's allegorical exposition in 4:21–31, which itself culminates his defense of the gospel in chapters 3—4. Indeed, in a remarkable way this verse captures the essential message of the entire letter. It is *for freedom* (the article in the Greek text specifies the freedom described above) that *Christ has set* the Galatians *free*. Thus they are urged to *stand fast* and to refuse to be loaded down or ensnared *again* with *a yoke of slavery* (cf. Acts 15:10). Again Paul equates submission to the demands of the Jewish legalists with a reversion to their prior heathen bondage (cf. 4:9).

The dire consequences for failing to renounce and reject the legalistic perversion of the gospel of Christ (cf. 1:7) are described in ultimate terms in vv. 2–4. Not since 1:8–9, with the exception of 4:30, has Paul invoked such ominous categories of divine judgment. There it was pronounced upon the false teachers; here it is directed to those who seem ready to abandon God's gracious call in Christ (cf. 1:6).

Now I, Paul is a very emphatic way of calling attention to what he is about to say. Actually *now* translates *ide,* an imperative form of *eidon* which has become an exclamatory particle. Literally it means: "See!" (cf. KJV: "Behold"; NEB: "Mark my words"; TEV: "Listen!"; all of which are preferable to the RSV). Added to the emphatic use of the personal pronoun *I* (*egō*) and the insertion of his name (*Paulos;* cf. 1 Thess. 2:18; 2 Cor. 10:1; Col. 1:23; Eph. 3:1), the

exclamatory particle achieves a remarkable impact. Later those listening to the reading of this letter in the churches would sharpen their hearing for what he is about to say.

If you receive circumcision translates the dependent clause (protasis) in a conditional sentence which has (in the Greek) *ean* and the subjunctive. As a mood of contingency, the subjunctive describes an action which is potential rather than actual (cf. 1:8). It is not that the Galatians have actually submitted to circumcision and thus the cause is already lost. It is rather that a situation prevails in which some are inclining perilously toward circumcision and thus need to be warned.

What if these vacillating Galatians finally succumb to the insistence of the Judaistic teachers that they submit to circumcision? Paul's answer is both plain and unequivocal: *Christ will be of no advantage to you.* Again the RSV hardly captures the force of Paul's statement, which reads literally: "Christ will profit you not one thing." A. T. Robertson comments here: "a supposable case, but with terrible consequences, for they will make circumcision a condition of salvation. In that case Christ will help them not at all." [21]

Verse 3 strongly introduces yet another consideration which the Galatians may have failed to take into account: the man who submits to circumcision likewise binds himself *to keep the whole law* (cf. Jas. 2:8–11). One cannot be selective in his obedience. The law is not a cafeteria-line where some items may be chosen and others ignored. To admit its validity with respect to circumcision is to place oneself under its total demand.

You are severed from Christ (cf. NEB: "your relation with Christ is completely severed"). This reiterates and strengthens the statement in v. 2. The Greek verb here is the aorist passive of *katargeō.* By noting its meaning in other Pauline contexts we may enlarge our understanding of its sense here. For instance, it appears in Romans

21 *Word Pictures in the New Testament* (Nashville: Broadman, 1931), IV, 309.

7:2 to describe what death does to a husband's legal claim over his wife: it annuls it. The wife "is discharged from the law concerning the husband." In the application of this marital metaphor in Romans 7:6 it appears again to describe what the death of Christ does regarding the law's claim upon the Christian: it annuls it. He is "discharged from the law." Observe that the movement here in Romans is from law to grace. What does grace do to the law? It annuls it; it severs us from it. In v. 4 the movement is from grace to law. Paul is speaking to those *who would be justified by the law.* (The RSV correctly renders *dikaiousthe* as a conative present, expressing intention.) The Galatian converts are pondering submission to the law's demand for circumcision as necessary to a right standing with God. If they submit, what does the law do to grace? It annuls it; it severs us from it.

It is a strange exegesis which would deny to the verb *katargeō* in Galatians 5:4 the full force of its admitted meaning in Romans 7:6 (cf. Gal. 3:17; 5:11; 2 Thess. 2:8; 1 Cor. 6:13; 13:8–11; 15:26).

You have fallen away from grace. In the Greek text there are three words only: *tēs charitos exepesate.* The noun is an ablative of separation, and the verb is the aorist active of *ekpiptō* ("fall from"). Literally and unmistakably it reads: "From grace you have fallen." (The article specifies God's grace in Christ.)

Religion as Evangel and religion as Law are mutually exclusive (cf. 1:6–7; 3:12). This is Paul's clarion insistence in this passage, as indeed throughout the entire letter. They cannot be conjoined. To turn to law as in any way necessary to effect a right standing with God is to turn one's back upon Christ. It is to become one for whom Christ profits not one thing (v. 2). It is to be severed from Christ (v. 4a). It is to fall from grace (v. 4b).[22] As the present writer understands it, this is Paul's position—nothing less, nothing more.

The first word in the Greek text of v. 5 is the emphatic personal pronoun *hēmeis*

(*we*). It throws the contents of this verse into sharp contrast with v. 4. There Paul has described a hope of righteousness based upon legal-conformity (by the law). Any convert who turns to it will be severed from Christ, will fall from grace. But here he describes a *hope of righteousness* based upon faith-commitment. Initially the Spirit is received through the response of faith to the preaching of the gospel of God's grace in Christ (3:2). Once received, the Spirit in the life of the convert seeks to bring him to completion as a man of faith (3:3). The goal is a righteousness that will stand in that great eschatological day in which God shall judge all men (cf. 5:10, 21; 6:8; 1 Thess. 3:13; 1 Cor. 4:5; 2 Cor. 5:10; Rom. 2:1–11; 8:18–25). At the present time this is a *hope* eagerly awaited. The RSV fails to convey the intensity present in the Greek verb. The NEB is preferable: "we eagerly await" (cf. Rom. 8: 19,23,25). It places a creative tension at the center of life which has remarkable ethical implications. Indeed, one has described hope as the future tense of faith.

By every evangelical canon, v. 6 remains one of the most significant statements ever written (cf. 6:15). The hope of righteousness just attested has provided the background for this sweeping disclamation of all legalism: *For in Christ Jesus neither circumcision nor uncircumcision is of any avail* (cf. NEB: "makes no difference at all"). This indictment embraces both the legalism of performance and the legalism of nonperformance. The former is more easily recognized. Yet the fact remains that it is possible for a man to ground as much hope for acceptance with God in his uncircumcision as another does in his circumcision. For every system of legalistic performance, there is a counter-system of

[22] For a different interpretation of the passage see Kenneth S. Wuest, *Galatians in the Greek New Testament* (Grand Rapids: Eerdmans, 1956), pp. 140–41. He distinguishes between justifying grace (God's judicial act done once for all) and sanctifying grace (the grace for daily living ministered to the Christian by the Holy Spirit). It is the latter, not the former, which is forfeited.

legalistic nonperformance, usually administered by those who regard themselves as the last bastion of evangelical orthodoxy.

Circumcision is a fleshly "is"; uncircumcision is a fleshly "isn't"; both are equally fleshly! Neither matters (cf. 1 Cor. 7:18–19)!

Then what is it that counts? The answer is magnificent, both for its simplicity and profundity: it is *faith working through love.* Faith is glad and trusting response to God's outreaching grace in Jesus Christ. It is dynamic, not static. Faith works (cf. Jas. 2:14–26)! But the medium through which it must operate is love (*di' agapēs*). In 1 Corinthians 13:2b Paul writes, "If I have all faith, so as to remove mountains, but have not love, I am nothing."

This is what counts: *faith working through love.* Allan (p. 79) writes: "It would be well if we had the courage to bring all our ecclesiastical and theological differences into the searching light of this verse." In some cases our religious convocations display *flesh working through pride or hate*—with the added blasphemy that it is done in Jesus' name!

You were running well. Paul used the same verb, as here, several times as a metaphor for Christian service (cf. 2:2; 1 Cor. 9:24–26; Phil. 2:16). Once again he reminisces about the better days the Galatians have known (cf. 4:13–14; 3:1–5). But then something happened to throw them offstride, and Paul wants to know: *Who hindered you?* (The Greek verb means to "cut in" on one.) The tragic consequence of this tactic was that it kept the Galatians *from obeying the truth.*

Of one thing Paul is most certain: *This persuasion is not from him who called you* (actually a present participle, the one who calls you). It does not come from God. What an indictment! For if it does not come from God, from whence does it come? It is quite obvious that the Judaizers were claiming a higher authority for their message than they allowed to Paul. Yet God's call is in "the grace of Christ" (1:6). If this is not the message that comes through, then it does not have God for its source. It is an alien persuasion.

Paul fears that the presence of the Judaizers in Galatia will prove to be an evil influence that permeates all of the churches there. Thus he quotes a proverb: *A little leaven leavens the whole lump.* This is the same saying that he quotes in 1 Corinthians 5:6, where he expresses fear regarding the evil contagion of a case of flagrant immorality in the church. Indeed, with the single exception of Matthew 13:33 (and its parallel in Luke 13:21) yeast is always regarded in the New Testament as a symbol for evil.

A brief reassurance of confidence in his readers intervenes this indictment of the false Jewish teachers. *In the Lord* identifies the ground of this confidence. The RSV translates its substance: *that you will take no other view than mine.* (The words *than mine* do not appear in the original text and somewhat overtranslate Paul's statement.) The last great affirmation of the gospel in the immediate context is in v. 6. Perhaps it is with regard to this that Paul is confident of their agreement.

Paul's distress prompts an even sharper condemnation of the false teachers: *He who is troubling you will bear his judgment, whoever he is.* It seems unwise to make too much of the singular number in the participle and verbs of this verse, as though it suggested a particular individual. The plural of that participle in 1:7 and of a different one in 5:12 argues otherwise.

Paul points to the fact of his persecution as the most obvious refutation of the charge that he *still* preaches *circumcision.* In such preaching *the stumbling block of the cross has been removed* (translated "severed" in 5:4). In 6:12 Paul will charge that the Judaizers preach circumcision "in order that they may not be persecuted for the cross of Christ."

Such calumny evokes from Paul an outburst so crude that the delicate sensibilities of some of his admirers have been offended: *I wish those who unsettle you would mutilate themselves,* i.e., emasculate themselves.

(The KJV misses the point completely, as does Phillips. Cf. NEB: "make eunuchs of themselves"; TEV: "castrate themselves.")

Paul was writing to a people who lived in an area where there were pagan religions in which self-emasculation was practiced, e.g., the Cybele-Attis cult. It was the frenzied rite of sacrifice whereby a man entered the priesthood of the cult-goddess.[23] Thus Paul's outburst is even more shocking than at first supposed (cf. Deut. 23:1). He places Jewish circumcision on practically the same level with pagan emasculation. If *circumcision* is efficacious, then excision ought to be even more so! (Cf. Phil. 3:2-3, where an untranslatable play on the words *katatomēn*, "mutilation," and *peritomē*, "circumcision," nearly equates them.)

(2) Peril of Libertinism (5:13-15)

13 For you were called to freedom, brethren; only do not use your freedom as an opportunity for the flesh, but through love be servants of one another. 14 For the whole law is fulfilled in one word, "You shall love your neighbor as yourself." 15 But if you bite and devour one another take heed that you are not consumed by one another.

A lapse into legalism was not the only threat to Christian freedom among the Galatians. There was also the threat of libertinism.[24] Freed from legal requirements in seeking a right standing before God, some inclined to sit loosely toward moral requirements in their walk among men. Thus Christian freedom degenerated into ethical license, a hideous distortion and, like legalism, also a form of slavery. In at least one respect it is worse than legalism: it makes out that sin is of no consequence or even a good, and in Christ's name it dares to perpetrate that which is totally alien to all that we know of him. Legalism can be, after a fashion, clean; libertinism is usually dirty. There is such

[23] For a graphic description of such a scene see the novel by Sholem Asch, *The Apostle* (New York: G. P. Putnam's Sons, 1943), pp. 298-303.

[24] This led Ropes to conclude that Paul was fighting a battle on two fronts in this letter: against the Judaizers in 3:1—5:10; 6:12-15 and against the "spiritualistic radicals" or libertines in 5:11—6:10; cf. Lightfoot and Stamm.

a thing as "publican's pride," as well as pharisaic pride. Indeed, it represents that form of hypocrisy which is most cherished and least recognized in many quarters of the contemporary scene.

As Christian liberty constituted the basis for Paul's warning against legalism in v. 1, so here in v. 13 it provides the ground for his warning against libertinism. The Galatians are admonished not to use this *freedom as an opportunity for the flesh*. (Originally *aphormēn*, "opportunity," was a military term describing a base of operations, a place from which an attack was launched. In the New Testament it is found only in Paul's letters; cf. 2 Cor. 5:12; 11:12; Rom. 7:8,11; 1 Tim. 5:14.) Rather the freedom they have is *through love* to serve *one another* (cf. 5:6). This is in keeping with the law's summation of our responsibility to others—*love your neighbor as yourself* (cf. Lev. 19:18; Luke 10:25-37; Matt. 22: 34-40; Rom. 13:8-10; Jas. 2:8). This freedom is frustrated when God's people *bite and devour one another* (words describing wild animals fighting). This is libertinism, too. Furthermore, it is a form of it which Paul suspects is prevailing among his readers (*ei*, "if," with the indicative suggests an actual condition). Unless it is stopped, they may be *consumed by one another*.

2. Walk by the Spirit (5:16-26)

16 But I say, walk by the Spirit, and do not gratify the desires of the flesh. 17 For the desires of the flesh are against the Spirit, and the desires of the Spirit are against the flesh; for these are opposed to each other, to prevent you from doing what you would. 18 But if you are led by the Spirit you are not under the law. 19 Now the works of the flesh are plain: immorality, impurity, licentiousness, 20 idolatry, sorcery, enmity, strife, jealousy, anger, selfishness, dissension, party spirit, 21 envy, drunkenness, carousing, and the like. I warn you, as I warned you before, that those who do such things shall not inherit the kingdom of God. 22 But the fruit of the Spirit is love, joy, peace, patience, kindness, goodness, faithfulness, 23 gentleness, self-control; against such there is no law. 24 And those who belong to Christ Jesus have crucified the flesh with its passions and desires.

25 If we live by the Spirit, let us also walk by the Spirit. **26** Let us have no self-conceit, no provoking of one another, no envy of one another.

Is adherence to the law necessary to safeguard the morals of the Galatian converts? Unless supported and guided by the law, will they not lapse into former pagan ways? It is likely that the Judaizers were making such a claim. In their thinking, obedience to the law was the only alternative to a return to old immoralities.

But Paul takes strong exception to this insistence. There is yet another way, the way of the gospel: it is to *walk by the Spirit*. As the Galatians do this, they will most assuredly not be overcome by the pressing desires of their old fleshly nature (vv. 16–21). Rather they will bear the fruit of the Spirit (5:22–26).

Here is a thoroughly evangelical ethic. It is dynamic, spontaneous, and creative. It is not a new legalism, higher than the old. It is living grace expressed in a daily walk.

But I say is a device to call attention to the vital affirmation which follows (cf. 5:2). *Walk* translates a present imperative (this verb frequently found elsewhere in Paul; cf. Rom. 6:4; 8:4; 2 Cor. 5:7; Col. 1:10). As a linear tense, it may be rendered: "Keep on walking." *By the Spirit* may be "in the Spirit," indicating realm (cf. KJV and Phillips). *Do not gratify* is not an adequate translation of the Greek, which is the subjunctive in a clause of emphatic negation. In English two negatives eliminate each other, e.g., "I *don't* want *no* bread" means "I *do* want *some* bread." But in Greek they intensify the negation. Thus the clause should read: "and you certainly will not fulfill" *the desires of the flesh*. Paul uses the term *flesh* in a metaphorical, not in a metaphysical, sense. It designates the lower nature (cf. NEB and Phillips) or ungraced human nature (cf. TEV). The following translation incorporates these points of exegesis: "Keep on walking by (or in) the Spirit, and you certainly will not fulfill the desires of the

flesh." The RSV translates both clauses as commands, whereas the second one is actually a remarkable promise based upon the command in the first.

No Christian is ever overcome by the desires of the flesh *while* walking by the Spirit. However, if his walk becomes sporadic or ceases, anything can happen, and usually does.

Verse 17 elaborates upon the promise of v. 16. It depicts the continuous struggle in the Christian's life between the desires of the flesh and the Spirit. *For the desires of the flesh are against the Spirit. (Desires* in the Greek text is a verb, not a noun; cf. KJV: "lusteth.") Likewise *the desires of the Spirit are against the flesh.* (There is no verb in the second clause, but the parallel structure supports this sense; cf. NEB: "while the Spirit fights against it.") *For these are opposed to each other* describes the relentless warfare, for which there can be no truce.

To this point the meaning of the verse is reasonably clear. However, the sense of the last clause is open to question. First, does it denote result or purpose? The KJV translates the former sense: "so that ye cannot do the things that ye would." The RSV translates the latter: *to prevent you from doing what you would.* Since the Greek *hina* with the subjunctive most commonly denotes purpose, the RSV is preferable. Second, to which of the antagonists in the struggle, flesh or Spirit, does the thwarting apply? Burton (p. 302) says to both: "Does the man choose evil, the Spirit opposes him; does he choose good, the flesh hinders him." But Duncan (pp. 167–68) thinks that this understanding of the passage intimates a standoff, as though flesh and Spirit combatted on equal and consequently indecisive terms. Such a meaning is precluded by the great promise in v. 16, rightly rendered (see above). Thus he concludes that the thwarting applies only to the desires of the flesh, i.e., the Spirit contends against the flesh, to prevent us from being overcome by its desires. Technically either view is possible; yet it seems that the latter overinterprets the passage. (Rom. 7: 15–25 should be read in this connection.)

In a summary statement Paul affirms that those who *are led by the Spirit* (cf. Rom. 8:14) are *not under the law.* (The Greek construction, *ei* with the indicative, denotes an actual, rather than a potential, condition.)

Now the works of the flesh are plain. These words introduce a remarkable characterization of the life that is dominated by the flesh, i.e., ungraced human nature. At least three representative areas of life are included in this list of vices (cf. Rom. 1:29–31; 2 Cor. 12:20–21; Eph. 5:3–5; Col. 3:5–10). They are: sex, worship, and social relationships. Observe that the deeds of the flesh are distortions of impulses or capacities with remarkable potential for good.

Sex.—There is nothing evil in the sexual drive itself. It is not something that man acquired in the fall, but rather is his by virtue of the creation. When its expression is under the sway of the Spirit, it yields indescribable good. It leads to the richness of a love relationship between a husband and wife. It leads to the birth and nurture of children in the home. It remains an important part of that intimate sharing of all life, in which each thrives as a person addressed and cherished.

But what happens when the sex drive is under the dominion of the flesh? It issues in the following: (1) *immorality.* This designates promiscuous sexual intercourse, both pre- and extramarital. (2) *impurity.* This describes moral impurity, a broader term than "immorality." In seven of the nine times that Paul uses it, he associates it with other words denoting sexual wrong, as here. (3) *licentiousness.* The connotation here is utter wantonness in sexual relations, unrestrained by any sense of decency or shame.

At no point did the early preachers of the gospel have greater difficulty in planting a Christian conscience than with regard to sexual relationships. The Graeco-Roman world, which they sought to evangelize, was ridden with sexual dissolution, both

natural and perverted. Often it provided religious sanctions for its degradations, which always seem readily available. Paul labels all such aberrations as evident *works of the flesh.*

It is unthinkable that at the present time there are leaders in major denominations, historically evangelical, who seem bent on redefining adultery, prostitution, and homosexuality as fruit of the Spirit! With high-sounding phrases about love as the only abiding referent and each new situation a context in which to determine the right or wrong of pre- or extramarital sexual conduct, they seem determined to obliterate the very conscience which early Christianity established with such difficulty. Situational ethics too often means selective immoralities!

Worship.—Nothing distinguishes man more than his capacity for worship. As there is a yearning on God's part to reveal himself to man, so there is a deeply implanted need in him to know and worship God. Under the Spirit's sway this leads to deliverance from the present evil age through faith in Jesus Christ (1:5) with all of the meaning and solace of true religion.

But what happens when this basic hunger comes under the dominion of the flesh? It leads to *idolatry,* the tragic spectacle in which men worship the gods of their own creation, whether fashioned with their hands or minds. It leads also to *sorcery,* the practice of magical arts in connection with idolatrous worship.

Social relationships.—Man is a gregarious being. He is endowed with that which impels him to seek companionship and to build communities. Emil Brunner writes: "The whole of human existence is built upon the fact that man cannot live as a solitary individual." [25] Under the Spirit's sway this leads to meaningful relationships, the establishment of community life, and the sharing of skills and goods.

But what happens when this social need

25 *The Divine Imperative* (Philadelphia: Westminster, 1947), p. 211.

is dominated by the flesh? It leads to the following works of the flesh: (1) *enmity* (NEB, "quarrels"). (2) *strife.* In the New Testament *eris* always conveys an evil sense. (3) *jealousy.* In six of the ten times this Greek word appears in Paul's letters it has a good sense (cf. Rom. 10:2; 2 Cor. 7:7,11; 9:2; 11:2; Phil. 3:6). However, here it has a bad connotation (cf. Rom. 13:13; 1 Cor. 3:3; 2 Cor. 12:20). (4) *anger* (NEB, "fits of rage"). (5) *selfishness* (NEB, "selfish ambitions"). Originally the word connoted working for wages. It describes the spirit of partisanship or organized self-interest, (6) *dissension* (NEB, "dissensions"). Literally it means "standings apart." (7) *party spirit* (NEB, "party intrigues"). The RSV translates this word "factions" in 1 Corinthians 11:19, its only other occurrence in Paul. (8) *envy* (NEB, "jealousies"). The KJV adds "murders" here, translating *phonoi*, but this word does not appear in the best manuscripts. It does appear in this sequence in Romans 1:29. (9) *drunkenness, carousing* (NEB, "drinking bouts, orgies").

What a picture of society, ancient and modern, under the thraldom of the flesh!

And the like is a qualifying phrase, which includes all other works of the flesh. After this sordid enumeration, Paul repeats the warning which evidently had been a significant part of his original missionary preaching to the Galatians: *those who do such things shall not inherit the kingdom of God.*

The fruit of the Spirit.—This metaphor is well chosen. Christian ethics are the outworking of an indwelling Presence, not the imposing of a higher legalism. No law has been given which is able to make alive (3:21*b*); it can only instruct, require, and provoke. What is needed is a dynamic commensurate with the demand. For the Christian this dynamic derives from the Spirit who produces his fruit in him (cf. Matt. 7:16–20; Luke 6:43–45; John 15:1–8).

In vv. 22–23*a* Paul describes nine qualities or aspects of *the fruit of the Spirit.* They are: (1) *love.* All that the law requires of us in our relation to others is summed up in the command of love (5:14). This is neither shallow sentiment nor reciprocated benevolence. Its finest description is in 1 Corinthians 13; its finest embodiment is in Jesus Christ. (2) *joy* (from the same root as the word for grace). It is an inevitable concomitant of love. So deep is its wellspring located in God's grace that even the most adverse circumstances cannot stanch its flow. Persecution could not drive it from the early churches (cf. Acts 8:8; 13:52; 15:3), nor could imprisonment deny it to Paul (Phil. 1:4; 4:11–12). (3) *peace.* It is so basic to Christian experience that it regularly appears with grace in apostolic benedictions (cf. 1:3; Rom. 1:7; 1 Cor. 1:3; 2 Cor. 1:2). (4) *patience.* Some are short-tempered, being given to outbursts of rage (cf. v. 20). But the Spirit seeks to make us "long-tempered," a more literal translation (cf. KJV: "long-suffering").

(5) *kindness.* In 2 Corinthians 6:6 this word appears again in conjunction with "patience" (cf. 1 Cor. 13:4, where the verb forms of these same nouns are side by side). Yet it does not designate an innocuous amiability which no wrong can offend. For in Romans 11:22 God is described as one in whom both "kindness" and "severity" may be found. (6) *goodness.* This word occurs only four times in the New Testament, all in the writings of Paul (cf. 2 Thess. 1:11; Rom. 15:14; Eph. 5:9). Phillips translates it "generosity." (7) *faithfulness.* This is the word for faith; yet in this context it denotes the quality of trustworthiness or fidelity. (8) *gentleness.* This word connotes gentle strength, so the KJV "meekness" is no longer adequate. The adjective form of it is applied to Jesus in Matthew 11:29 (cf. Num. 12:3 of Moses). Barclay observes: "Only a man who was *praus* could have both cleansed the Temple of the hucksters who traded in it and forgiven the woman taken in adultery whom all the orthodox condemned" (Barclay, *Flesh and Spirit,* pp. 120–21). (9) *self-control.* This word appears in only two other passages in

the New Testament (Acts 24:25; 2 Peter 1:6). It describes the inner strength by which a man takes hold of himself, refusing to be swept along by errant desires or impulses. It is essential to freedom from the tyranny of the flesh.

Against such there is no law. No law against the fruit of the Spirit! This is hardly remarkable, for society needs no protection from those who bear these qualities. Indeed, *those who belong to Christ Jesus have crucified the flesh with its passions and desires* (cf. 2:20). Rather it is from those who perpetrate the works of the flesh (vv. 19–21a) that society needs protection.

Verses 25–26 seem to provide a transition to 6:1–10. Since the Galatian converts *live by the Spirit,* they are urged to *walk by the Spirit* (*ei* with the indicative, denoting reality). Such a walk affords no place to *self-conceit,* mutual goading, and *envy of one another.*

3. Heed These Commands (6:1–10)

¹ Brethren, if a man is overtaken in any trespass, you who are spiritual should restore him in a spirit of gentleness. Look to yourself, lest you too be tempted. ² Bear one another's burdens, and so fulfil the law of Christ. ³ For if any one thinks he is something, when he is nothing, he deceives himself. ⁴ But let each one test his own work, and then his reason to boast will be in himself alone and not in his neighbor. ⁵ For each man will have to bear his own load.
⁶ Let him who is taught the word share all good things with him who teaches.
⁷ Do not be deceived; God is not mocked, for whatever a man sows, that he will also reap. ⁸ For he who sows to his own flesh will from the flesh reap corruption; but he who sows to the Spirit will from the Spirit reap eternal life. ⁹ And let us not grow weary in well-doing, for in due season we shall reap, if we do not lose heart. ¹⁰ So then, as we have opportunity, let us do good to all men, and especially to those who are of the household of faith.

Paul concludes the main body of his letter with a series of loosely connected commands. Actually there are seven imperatives in these ten verses, and each one deals with some practical aspect of the Christian

life. They may be regarded as an elaboration upon the Spirit-walk which he enjoined in 5:25.

Restore the fallen (v. 1).—What is to be the attitude of a Christian toward another who *is overtaken in any trespass?* The Greek verb is rendered similarly in the KJV (cf. NEB). However, it is capable of another meaning, namely, "to be detected or caught" in the act of wrongdoing (cf. TEV, Phillips, NEB marg.). The word translated "trespass" means, literally, a falling aside.

Paul's answer to this question is found in the command: *restore him.* The Greek verb used appears in Matthew 4:21 and Mark 1:19 to describe fishermen mending their nets. It is used by ancient writers to describe a surgeon setting a fractured limb. It is addressed particularly to those *who are spiritual.* To be sure, all Christians have received the Spirit (3:2), but not all abound in the fruit of the Spirit (5:22–23a). It is the latter who are to be entrusted with the delicate ministry of reclaim.

Such will approach the person in trouble *in a spirit of gentleness* (cf. 5:23). He will have his own conduct under intense personal scrutiny: *Look to yourself.* (At this point the number changes from plural to singular.) *Lest you too be tempted* is an awareness essential to compassion.

Bear one another's burdens (v. 2).—This verse pleads for the reenforcement of those who *bear* heavy *burdens* (weights). In the Greek text it is the reciprocal pronoun, rather than the verb, which appears first in the sentence, a position of emphasis: "One another's burdens bear." To do this is to *fulfil the law of Christ.*

Avoid censoriousness (vv. 3–5).—Pride opposes burden-sharing. It tends to bite rather than to bear, to devour rather than to alleviate (5:15).

Pride is conceit (5:26a). It demands obeisance, the acknowledgment of a superior worth. Where this is not forthcoming, it leads to a round of challenge and counterchallenge, mutual provocation rather than mutual burden-bearing (5:26b).

Envy is the advance guard which pride ever sends forth to scout occupied territory (5:26c). Upon the basis of its reconnoitering the "hot wars" of personal rivalries are waged. It is the antithesis of walking by the Spirit (5:25).

Pride exploits the weaknesses of others to its own advantage. Thoughts of restoring the fallen lie outside its strategy. It is smug, being unaware of its own flaws and vainly imagining itself incapable of the failures so readily seen in others.

Pride is inflated self-estimate. It is the tendency of a man to think *he is something, when he is nothing.* It always creates a credibility gap between self-estimate and actual worth. The illusion is enhanced by the practice of comparing oneself too favorably with others (cf. 2 Cor. 10:12; Luke 18:9–14). By exaggerating one's worth and depreciating that of another, the distortion works from both ends: *he deceives himself.*

The remedy for this game of mirrors comes in the form of a call to rigorous self-scrutiny: *let each one test his own work.* Observe the inwardizing of criteria here. Not the failures of others but the worth of one's own achievements—this is where the test is properly applied. Any consequent sense of well-being will then rest upon the solid foundation of actual accomplishments rather than upon the sordid debris of depreciating comparisons.

Verse 5 is somewhat problematical. It seems to contradict Paul's counsel in v. 2. To be sure, two different Greek words are used in these verses: *barē* above and *phortion* here. Both are translated "burden" in the KJV, whereas the RSV renders the former *burdens* and the latter *load* (cf. NEB: "these heavy loads" and "his own proper burden"). In different contexts *phortion* designates the cargo of a ship (Acts 27:10), the burden of the law (Matt. 23:4; cf. Matt. 11:30), or a soldier's pack. However, it is not possible to draw a sharp distinction between these two words. Yet the context indicates clearly that in v. 2

Paul is thinking of burdens which may be shared and in v. 5 of that which one must bear alone. Walking by the Spirit involves both.

Share with teachers (v. 6).—Here Paul speaks about burden-bearing with a particular reference to the support of teachers (cf. 1 Thess. 2:6,9; 1 Cor. 9:6–18; 2 Cor. 11:7–11; Phil. 4:14–18). This verse provides evidence of the importance placed upon religious instruction in the early Christian congregations. At this relatively early date there were those who devoted enough time to teaching, so that provision for their support became necessary. Upon whom may this responsibility fall more appropriately than upon those who share the benefits of the instruction of such teachers? Thus the one *who is taught the word,* i.e., the Christian message, is to share what he has with the one *who teaches.* In this way each enters into the labors of the other through a mutual sharing of what each can give.

All good things cannot be limited to material support, as though this were the only sharing that could take place. The very indefiniteness of the phrase leaves open the whole broad range of commonality which may bind catechist and catechumen together.

It is interesting to observe what Paul did in various places regarding the matter of financial support. Though entitled to it, he did not always seek or accept it. Among the poor and harassed converts of Thessalonica, he worked night and day while preaching the gospel to them, that he might not add to their economic burdens (1 Thess. 2:9). Because there were those in Corinth who were ready to charge him with preaching for money, Paul refused to accept any support from them (2 Cor. 11:7–11). But when he found a church like Philippi which interpreted financial support as a means of entering into his missionary labors, he accepted it with gratitude and thanked them for being his partners in the gospel (Phil. 4:14–18).

No one ever found Paul making such use of the funds entrusted to him as caused his "partners" to regret their sacrificial giving (cf. 2 Cor. 8:13–14).

Stop deceiving yourselves (vv. 7–8).— This familiar passage begins with an abrupt command: *Do not be deceived* (a present imperative with *mē* prohibiting an action in progress; thus the translation: "Stop deceiving yourselves" or "stop being deceived"). In tone it stands in sharp contrast with the preceding verse, in which Paul has spoken of the mutuality which should prevail between his readers and their teachers. This is why it seems unwise to regard vv. 7–8 as simply an expansion or reenforcement of v. 6. For instance, Lightfoot (p. 219) designates stinginess as the besetting sin of the Galatians. Thus Paul rebukes them for their reluctance to support their teachers in v. 6 and moves on to a general censure of their lack of generosity in vv. 7–8.

The command is supported by a jolting affirmation: *God is not mocked.* (The Greek verb, here only in the New Testament, means lit. "to turn up the nose" at someone, i.e., to treat with contempt. Adapted to our culture, the passage might read: "No man thumbs his nose at God!") This does not mean that it never happens, but rather that it never happens without consequences. Men do mock God, but it is not with them as though they had not done so.

Of what does this mockery consist? The explanation is provided in the words: *for whatever a man sows, that he will also reap.* Here is the law of the harvest applied to the Christian's walk. A man mocks God when he thinks that he can sow *to his own flesh* and not *from the flesh reap corruption.* He mocks God when he interprets the gospel of grace in any way that causes him to trivialize sin in his life, denying its consequences (cf. Rom. 6). He treats God contemptuously when he regards salvation as an immunity to sin rather than as a deliverance from it; when he is confident that no matter how much he sows to the flesh, he will *reap eternal life.*

In 5:17 Paul described the relentless struggle between the flesh and the Spirit in the life of the Christian. In 5:19–21a he characterized the works of the flesh. In 5:21b he repeated the warning given earlier "that those who do such things shall not inherit the kingdom of God." Yet the Galatians seem not to have heard him, for they were still swollen with conceit, striving against and envying one another (5:26). They needed such commands as he sets before them in 6:1–5. Thus he invokes again the categories of flesh and Spirit to reiterate the stern admonition of 5:21b: *he who sows to his own flesh will from the flesh reap corruption.* Similarly as he characterized the fruit of the Spirit in 5:22–23a, so here he reiterates that *he who sows to the Spirit will from the Spirit reap eternal life.*

Men have a respect for nature which they sometimes do not have for God. Whoever heard of a farmer trying to outwit nature by seeking to harvest a crop of potatoes where he had planted buckwheat? In the natural realm the law of the harvest is universally acknowledged: *whatever a man sows, that he will also reap.* Yet men are slow to realize that the same law of the harvest prevails in the spiritual realm. They seem so surprised when having sown rebellion against God, they don't reap a peaceful world; having sown graft, they do not reap stable government; having sown dishonesty, they do not reap integrity in the business community; having sown prejudice, they do not reap goodwill; having sown lust, they do not reap meaningful marriages; having sown escape through alcohol and nicotine, they do not have sons and daughters who shun drugs. This is mocking God, and to mock God is to assure disaster.

Do not grow weary (v. 9).—The harvest metaphor of vv. 7–8 carries over here. It is possible for one to sow well and still not produce a crop. Between planting and reaping there is a time of rigorous toil, in which many obstacles are to be overcome. There is often the temptation to quit, as mounting exhaustion makes the time or possibility of harvest seem remote. What is needed is a persistence commensurate with the exacting demands of the time of cultivation. This comes best to those in whom the hope of the harvest remains fresh.

Paul applies this metaphor to *well-doing*. Here there is a time of enervating toil between planting and reaping also (cf. 2 Cor. 4:8–10). The harvest belongs to those who *do not lose heart*.

Do good to all men (v. 10).—The preceding verse emphasized the season of reaping; this verse emphasizes the season of sowing, i.e., of doing *good*. (The RSV translates *kairos* "season" in v. 9 but "opportunity" in v. 10, thereby obscuring the likelihood that the agricultural metaphor carries over to the present verse.) Both are essential to a good harvest.

To all men is true to the spirit of Jesus Christ, who ate with Pharisees (Luke 7:36–50) and publicans (Luke 15:1–2; 19:1–10) as well as friends (Luke 10:38–42). He defined neighbor as anyone needing our help (Luke 10:25–37). Yet a special sensitivity is to prevail with regard to *those who are of the household of faith* (cf. Eph. 2:19; 1 Tim. 5:8). This designates the intimate unity of all believers, i.e., they constitute God's household through Jesus Christ. A particular awareness of their needs is not a denial of a compassionate concern for all.

This is the last of the seven imperatives in 6:1–10. They bind the passage together, articulating some practical aspects of what it means to walk by the Spirit. They form an appropriate climax to the main body of the letter.

Conclusion (6:11–18)

11 See with what large letters I am writing to you with my own hand. 12 It is those who want to make a good showing in the flesh that would compel you to be circumcised, and only in order that they may not be persecuted for the cross of Christ. 13 For even those who receive circumcision do not themselves keep the law, but they desire to have you circumcised that they may glory in your flesh. 14 But far be it from me to glory except in the cross of our Lord Jesus Christ, by which the world has been crucified to me, and I to the world. 15 For neither circumcision counts for anything, nor

uncircumcision, but a new creation. 16 Peace and mercy be upon all who walk by this rule, upon the Israel of God.

17 Henceforth let no man trouble me; for I bear on my body the marks of Jesus.

18 The grace of our Lord Jesus Christ be with your spirit, brethren. Amen.

A comparison of these verses with the conclusions of other letters of Paul reveals several differences: (1) There are no personal references or greetings (cf. 1 Cor. 16:10–19; Rom. 16:1–23; Phil. 4:21–22; Col. 4:7–17; Philemon 23–24). (2) There is no request for prayer (cf. 1 Thess. 5:25; Rom. 15:30–32). (3) There is no disclosure of travel plans (cf. 1 Cor. 16:1–9; 2 Cor. 13:1–2; Rom. 15:22–29). (4) There is no instruction to greet all with a holy kiss (cf. 1 Thess. 5:26; 1 Cor. 16:20). (5) There is no expression of gratitude for past favors (cf. Phil. 4:10–20).

Instead there is a summons to note that he has now taken the pen into his own hand (v. 11), a restatement of the bitter controversy with the Judaizers (vv. 12–16), a demand that no one deal him further trouble (v. 17), and a brief benediction (v. 18). Thus the conclusion, like the salutation (1:1–5) is noteworthy.

In writing a letter it was Paul's custom to take the pen from his amanuensis and inscribe a personal conclusion (cf. 1 Cor. 16:21; Col. 4:18; 2 Thess. 3:17). Obviously this provided an authentication, but in the Galatian letter something more was involved. Here he calls attention to the *large letters* with which he writes these final words. (The RSV is correct in rendering *grammasin* as a dative or instrumental of manner, calling attention to the distinctive way in which he was forming the Greek characters; cf. NEB and Phillips.) Perhaps the letters were in a cruder stroke than the accomplished penmanship of a professional scribe, serving the function of bold-faced type in modern printing. Thus the boldness of the handwriting at the end matches the boldness of the letter throughout. *I am writing* correctly translates the Greek epistolary aorist *egrapsa*.

The Judaizers are not to be trusted for

several reasons. For one thing, their primary concern is *that they may not be persecuted for the cross of Christ*. Official Judaism would have tolerated as a sect a Christianity that regarded Jesus as the Messiah and demanded circumcision of its Gentile converts. This would have removed "the stumbling block of the cross" (5:11*b*). In fact, it was Paul's refusal to make this demand upon his converts which had resulted in his persecution (5:11*a*). To escape a similar harassment at the hands of their countrymen, the Judaizers were eager to be able to point to a large number of Gentiles whom they had persuaded to submit to circumcision. In this way they would *make a good showing in the flesh*.

Furthermore, Paul charges that *even those who receive circumcision do not themselves keep the law*. The RSV follows the reading *hoi peritemnomenoi*, the present participle. This makes possible a more inclusive reference, i.e., all who accept circumcision. There is considerable support for another reading, *hoi peritetmēmenoi*, the perfect participle. This more clearly designates the Judaizers whom he has castigated in the preceding verse (cf. Matt. 23:1–4). Rather their great desire is *that they may glory in your flesh*.

This is the second time in as many verses that the phrase "in flesh" occurs. It indicates the realm of the physical in which the Judaizers have their ground for glorying. Paul was no stranger to this kind of religion (cf. 1:13–14; Phil. 3:4–6). But now he expresses revulsion in its presence: *far be it from me to glory except in the cross of our Lord Jesus Christ* (cf. Phil. 3:7–11). The KJV translation of *mē genoito*, "God forbid," likely conveys its exclamatory force better than the more literal rendering of the RSV (cf. 2:17).

The meaning of the final clause in v. 14 is somewhat in question. The problem derives from uncertainty regarding the antecedent of the Greek phrase *di' hou*. The RSV regards it as *cross* and so translates: *by which the world has been crucified to me, and I to the world*. The KJV regards

it as "Lord Jesus Christ" and so translates: "by whom . . . ." Since both are in agreement with the relative pronoun, either sense is technically possible, though the former seems more likely. Here is a dying in two directions: the world to Paul and Paul to the world. Nevertheless he lives (2:19–20)!

It is not that the Judaizers gloried and Paul did not. Rather it is that the Judaizers gloried in the flesh of the Galatians, whereas Paul gloried in the cross of the Galilean.

Rightly understood the cross of Christ renders both *circumcision* and *uncircumcision* meaningless. This verse is remarkably similar to 5:6, where the essence of the gospel was summed up as "faith working through love." Here it is described as *a new creation* (cf. 2 Cor. 5:17).

This is the *rule* (lit., "canon") by which Paul would have his readers *walk*. Such a walk distinguishes them as *the Israel of God*, even as circumcision formerly distinguished old Israel. Upon such, *peace and mercy* are rightly invoked (cf. 1:3).

Perhaps mentally and emotionally spent from writing such a difficult letter, Paul draws it to a close by demanding: *Henceforth let no man trouble me*. He refers to his battle scars: *for I bear on my body the marks of Jesus*. The *stigmata* are the scars from beatings, stonings, and other ordeals he has endured in the service of Jesus Christ (cf. 2 Cor. 1:8–10; 6:4–10; 11:23–33). They identify him as either the slave or devotee of Jesus Christ. In a letter in which he has been compelled to affirm the divine authority of his apostleship, he closes with a reference to his battle wounds— they are credentials also.

The final benediction is not remarkable because it contains the expression *with your spirit*, for Philippians 4:23 and Philemon 25 are similar. Rather, it is unusual because the last word before *Amen* is *brethren*. Though this term is common in Paul's writings, in no other letter does it appear in the concluding benediction. It makes an appropriate ending to a letter in which apostolic faithfulness demanded such strong reproof.

Ephesians

RALPH P. MARTIN

Introduction

I. The Purpose of the Letter

No part of the New Testament has a more contemporary relevance than the letter to the Ephesians. Its importance as God's message to the modern church has been recognized by both Protestant and Roman Catholic scholars, and this is especially true when a divided Christendom seeks to find a common ground by participating in a joint study of the Scripture.[1]

The doctrine of Christ and the church is the central ecumenical issue of the mid-twentieth century; and no document of the New Testament speaks more relevantly to this theme. At a different level, academic interest too has focused on this epistle. The older debate of authorship and authenticity has given place to some newer concerns. The issue now is to decide whether Ephesians represents a later development of Christian thinking on the vital topics of Christology and ecclesiology, and whether these features of the letter place it in a period after Paul's lifetime and in the time of an "incipient catholicism." The decisive matter, on which E. Käsemann has laid a probing finger,[2] is the setting of the epistle

in the stream of early Christianity. Does it belong to the closing years of Paul's ministry at Rome and represent "St. Paul's spiritual testament to the Church"[3] as the final summing up of the apostle's life's work and thought? If the answer is affirmative, we shall best look on the epistle as "the crown of Paulinism," in C. H. Dodd's phrase.[4]

Alternatively, European and some American scholars are in general convinced that, on grounds of vocabulary, style, and content, the letter does not come from Paul's hand. Moreover, it contains a body of developed doctrine which places it in a later period than Paul's lifetime, and in a time when the church was growing in self-consciousness as an institutional organization. Features which these scholars appeal to as indications of a later dating and life-setting are: the waning of the eschatological emphases in Ephesians, a highly structured doctrine of the ministry in which Paul's apostleship is venerated, the teaching of the church as Christ's body which is given a near-metaphysical significance, and a moralizing tendency in the realm of Christian ethics.[5]

To anticipate our conclusion, we may say that the truth lies somewhere in the middle between these polarities. The present writer

---

1 "At a particular juncture of time in the sixteenth century, the Epistle to the Romans was rediscovered; now we are rediscovering the Epistle to the Ephesians as a letter speaking to the Church." This quotation of W. Zöllner comes from Y. M.-J. Congar's *Tradition and Traditions* (New York: The Macmillan Company, 1967) p. 346. See also M. Barth, *The Broken Wall* (Philadelphia: The Judson Press, 1959).

2 E. Käsemann, "Ephesians and Acts," in *Studies in Luke-Acts*, ed. L. E. Keck and J. L. Martyn (London: SPCK, 1968), pp. 288–297.

3 J. N. Sanders, in *Studies in Ephesians* ed. F. L. Cross (London: Mowbray, 1956), p. 16.

4 C. H. Dodd, in *Abingdon Bible Commentary* (Nashville: Abingdon Press, 1929), pp. 1224 f.

5 See for example W. G. Kümmel, *Introduction to the New Testament* (London: SCM Press, 1966), p. 257.

has argued [6] that it was a well-known disciple and companion of Paul who published this letter under the apostle's aegis either during his final imprisonment or after his death. He did so by gathering a compendium of Paul's teaching on the theme of Christ-in-his-church; and he added to this body of teaching a number of liturgical elements (prayers, hymns, and confessions of faith) drawn from the worshiping life of the apostolic communities with which he was himself familiar. The purpose of the epistle was to show the nature of the church and the Christian life to those who came to Christ from a pagan heritage and environment, and to remind the Gentile Christians that Paul's theology of salvation-history never disowned the Jewish background out of which the (now predominantly) Gentile church came.

We may well imagine what prompted this manifesto when we study closely the chief emphases of the letter. Two such are the requirements that the call of the Christian life is to the highest levels of morality, both personal and social (4:17 ff.; 5:3,5, 12), and that Gentile believers who enjoy rich privileges as members of the "one body in Christ" can never deny the Jewish heritage of the gospel without severing that gospel from its historical roots. Hence, the epistle's insistence (2:11,12) that the messianic hope meets all the needs of its Gentile readers (3:6). Though they were converted to Christ later in time than their Jewish brethren (1:12,13), they are in no way inferior on that account. Rather the privilege they now have binds them indissolubly to their Jewish fellow-believers; both groups share in the Holy Spirit of messianic promise (1:13; 4:30).

The point seems to be that Gentile Christians, who were streaming into the church, were adopting an easygoing moral code based on a perverted misunderstanding of Paul's teaching (see as evidence Rom. 6:1 ff.).

At this same time, they were boasting of

[6] R. P. Martin, "An Epistle in Search of a Life-Setting," *Expository Times*, lxxix, July 1968, 296–302.

their supposed independence of Israel and were becoming intolerant of their Jewish Christian brethren and forgetful of the Jewish past of salvation-history (see as evidence Rom. 11:33 ff.).

This epistle effectively checks both wrong-headed notions, and does so by displaying the true meaning of Christ's relationship to the church. He is its head and Lord, so requiring loyal obedience and service; he is the bridegroom, seeking a pure bride; and he both Israel's Messiah and the Gentiles' hope, so uniting in himself a new people, both Jews and Gentiles. To be sure, these distinctive features of the letter are not unique to Ephesians, and Paul's disciple has faithfully conveyed the substance of his master's teaching. But he has angled it in such a way that its thrust is set in the direction of some erroneous doctrine and practice which he seeks to dispel. Much of the letter will take on significance if we can endeavor to see it as a magnificent statement of the theme "Christ-in-his-church," yet presented and applied in such a fashion that false ideas and wrong ethical conclusions are rebutted. And as we hear Paul's voice speaking through his disciple we may use the former name in the pages which follow.

II. Some Features

Two features of this epistle stand out clearly. First, except for the closing paragraph in 6:21–22, the argument and appeal of the document are strangely impersonal and indirect. This does not mean that the apostle writes as a detached observer, interested in his readers' problems and needs only at a distance. On the contrary, he expresses great concern over them lest they should succumb to false teachers (4:14) or surrender their ethical ideals by listening to those who would lead them astray (5:6). He rejoices to be assured of their Christian standing (1:15–16) and knows that their faith is well-founded (4:20). As a mark of his confidence in them, he does not hesitate to solicit their prayers on his own behalf (6:19–20).

Yet with all this taken into account, it does remain that the apostle's relationship with his readers is far from intimate. In this way Ephesians contrasts with other Pauline letters like Galatians and Philippians where personal features are pronounced and persistent. Here the apostle has heard of his readers' Christian profession through indirect channels (1:15) and knows that it is only in this way that they have heard of his apostolic ministry for the Gentiles (3:1–2). His bond with his readers is that of an author to the recipients of his letter (3:4) rather than one of firsthand acquaintance.

Indeed, it is a good question whether we do right to speak of Ephesians as a "letter" at all. R. H. Fuller remarks that the document "is really a tract dressed up in epistolary form." [7] This brings us to the second feature which is that of literary usage. Both choice of words and employment of a studied style mark out this epistle as unusual in the Pauline literature.

The vocabulary test shows that there are 38 words which do not appear again in the New Testament, and 44 words which, though they are found elsewhere in the New Testament, are not used in the undisputed Pauline writings. The stylistic peculiarities are even more noticeable. Erasmus was the first to note these features of long, ponderous sentences (1:3–10,15–23); many relative clauses; abstract nouns in profusion; the use of parallel phrases and clauses in close apposition (4:12 f.); the piling up of synonyms connected together by the use of the genitive case (1:19); and the common use of prepositions, especially "in" (see 1:3 ff.). All these traits seem to be far removed from the style of a pastoral letter addressed to the church at Ephesus by the apostle Paul, whose letter-writing habits are known to us from his other epistles and include the use of rhetorical questions and a pointed, direct approach (e.g., Galatians).

At this point we may ask, Is Ephesians

[7] R. H. Fuller, *A Critical Introduction to the New Testament* (London: Duckworth, 1966), p. 66.

addressed to the church at Ephesus? Clearly it is difficult to believe that Paul would write in an impersonal and indirect way to a Christian fellowship he had lived and labored among for some considerable time (Acts 19:10; 20:17–38). On the face of it, this "letter" is no ordinary pastoral address sent to a specific congregation or group of churches.

This fact is confirmed by the textual uncertainty of 1:1. The words translated in KJV "at Ephesus" are lacking in the leading manuscripts and the important Greek papyrus P[46] dated A.D. 200. Moreover, early Christian writers endorse the view that "at Ephesus" was not found in the earliest texts. Two suggestions have been offered to explain this textual irregularity. One possibility is that the letter never had a place-name but was composed as a general tract or essay and not as a letter intended for a particular readership. A second-century scribe is thought to have supplied "at Ephesus" to bring the document which later Christians claimed as a Pauline composition into conformity with the other Pauline letters to the churches of the first-century world.

Against this view and in support of a second submission is the fact that, while the letter does read more like a sermon than a pastoral letter addressed to a church with specific needs, the author does have a certain group of persons in mind and speaks to them in the second person of the verbs he uses (e.g., 5:3 ff.). It is more likely then that this document was composed as a circular letter to the churches in a wide region —Asia Minor is the most probable location, in view of the affinities with Colossians— and either carried from one place to another in the area by a courier or (in view of the later textual authority for the place-name of Ephesus) left by the author with a blank space in the superscription, to be filled in as the messenger handed over the particular copy to the church. There are some difficulties with this reconstruction, but on balance it seems to be the most plausible view.

If we rightly judge the epistle to be an encyclical addressed to the Gentile churches in Asia (3:1), this estimate helps to account for the style which is influenced by a liturgical and catechetical strain. Directly personal allusions may not be expected in a document which is more accurately described as an exalted prose-poem on the theme of "Christ-in-his-church" than a pastoral letter sent to meet the needs of a particular local congregation. The author breaks out into an elevated meditation on the great themes which fill his mind—God's purpose in Christ, his fullness in Christ, Christ's fullness in the church which is his body. Concepts like these lift him on to a plane of rapture and contemplation which is betrayed in his language. His rare terms may well be drawn from the worship of the (Asian) churches. His style is clearly that of a typical early Christian liturgy which shows some of the characteristic features (such as the prolific use of the relative pronoun and the construction with participles, and a fulsomeness of expression) in this epistle.

III. Questions of Authorship

As was said earlier, the question of the authorship is complex and much debated. To be sure, evidence taken from the letter itself (1:1; 3:1) and from the attestation of the church fathers (Irenaeus, Clement of Alexandria, Tertullian) supports the traditional view that this epistle came from Paul's hand. A solid defense of tradition has, in modern times, been made by Ernst Percy,[8] as well as by writers of conservative introductions to the New Testament.[9] For these scholars both unusual vocabulary and exceptional style are no impediment to authenticity, and may be explained by the special circumstances of the nature of the

document. None of the evidence from within the letter points indubitably to a period later than the mid-sixties, and there are points of contact between Ephesians and the earlier Pauline correspondence. F. F. Bruce has argued that ideas which are stated in outline in the earlier epistles are developed and continued in this epistle.[10] On this view, the date of the letter belongs to the period of Paul's imprisonment in Rome, ca. A.D. 60–61, and in view of the many points of similarity with Colossians, especially at 6:21–22 (= Col. 4:7 ff.), it seems clear that both letters were circulated together.

For other commentators, such as F. W. Beare,[11] the main ideas of Ephesians are handled in a way which betrays a distinct shift from the authentically Pauline manner of statement and presentation; and even words which are found to be common to both the earlier and authentic epistles and Ephesians are not used in Ephesians in the same sense. One example is "head," which in Colossians 2:19 refers to Christ's headship over the church, whereas in Ephesians 1:22–23 the headship of Christ is over all cosmic powers. But this piece of reasoning is not too secure in the light of other places where "head-body" metaphor is used both in Colossians (1:18) and Ephesians (4:15–16; 5:23). The following commentary will allude to the various matters on which Beare bases his argument that the ideas of the letter are non-Pauline and therefore come from a time later than the apostle's.

In seeking to evaluate these rival positions, we recognize that substantial evidence of an external character supports the traditional view of Pauline authorship; and this position is maintained by a solid body of opinion today. However, we should give due weight to some difficulties when we examine the evidence of the letter itself.

---

[8] E. Percy, *Die Probleme der Kolosser- und Epheserbriefe* (Lund: Gleerup, 1946). There is a full statement of Percy's case and a critique thereof in J. C. Kirby, *Ephesians, Baptism and Pentecost* (London: SPCK, 1968), pp. 18–40.

[9] For example, by D. Guthrie, E. F. Harrison, and W. L. Lane, *The New Testament Speaks* (New York: Harper and Row, 1969).

[10] F. F. Bruce, "St. Paul in Rome 4: The Epistle to the Ephesians," *Bulletin of the John Rylands Library* 49, 2, 1967, 303 ff.

[11] F. W. Beare in *The Interpreter's Bible* (Nashville: Abingdon Press, 1953), XI, 599*a*. See also C. L. Mitton, *The Epistle to the Ephesians* (Oxford: Clarendon Press, 1951).

On a third possibility, which we have adopted, the teaching of the epistle is Pauline but the composition and style of this letter were entrusted by the apostle to a colleague and amanuensis. Paul's use of a secretary in other places is attested in Romans 16:22, and one submission is that Paul left Tychicus to put together this Ephesian epistle.[12] Our option is for Luke [13] in view of the various links between his writings in the Gospel and Acts and this epistle. But even more important than this hypothesis is the understanding which supports it concerning the ruling purpose of the letter and its relevance to a situation in the Gentile churches of Asia Minor in the period immediately following Paul's death.

IV. *Central Ideas of the Letter*

As a document addressed to a perilous situation, this letter is full of Christian instruction of great importance. The author is gripped by what is virtually a single theme which runs like a thread through his treatise. He marvels, as a true disciple and follower of the great apostle in whose name he writes, at the grace of God which has brought into being a united church. In this Christian society Jews and Gentiles find their true place (2:11–22). The unity of this universal society which is nothing less than Christ's body (1:23; 3:6; 4:4; 5:30) is his great concern (4:3 ff.). He starts from the premise of "one new man" (2:15) in

12 See G. H. P. Thompson's Commentary in the *Cambridge Bible Commentary* (Cambridge: University Press, 1967), pp. 17–19. The name of Tychicus as collector and editor of the Pauline corpus as well as responsible for the compilation of Ephesians had earlier been suggested by W. L. Knox, *St. Paul and the Church of the Gentiles* (Cambridge: University Press, 1939), p. 203; and C. L. Mitton, *op. cit.*, pp. 27, 268. Among those sympathetic to the notion that Paul used a secretary who was given freedom to assemble materials which became our Ephesian letter are M. A. Wagenführer, P. Benoit, "L'horizon paulinien de l'épître aux Ephésiens," *Revue biblique*, 46, 1937, pp. 342–361, 506–525, and A. Wikenhauser, *New Testament Introduction* (Dublin: Herder and Herder), 1958, p. 430.

13 For details we may refer to the article in *Expository Times*, lxxix, July 1968, pp. 300 ff., with its acknowledgment to Peter Rhea Jones, now of The Southern Baptist Theological Seminary, Louisville, Kentucky.

which a new humanity has been created by God through Christ's reconciling work on the cross (2:16). By this achievement in relating man as a sinner to God, Christ has brought Jews and Gentiles into God's family (1:5; 2:19; 4:6; 5:1) as brothers. The coming into existence of this one family where all barriers of race, culture, and social status are broken down is the wonder which fills his vision. The earlier Pauline teaching of Galatians 3:28–29 and 1 Corinthians 12:12–13 is now filled out and its lessons drawn and applied.

But there is a new slant put upon the apostolic teaching, which marks a novel phase of development in the doctrine of the church. One factor is the way in which Christ and his church are regarded as a single entity. The head-body metaphor which is familiar to us from the earlier Pauline letters takes on a new dimension in that the head becomes inseparable from the body. In 1 Corinthians 12 Paul had insisted on the indivisibility of the body, which is made up of many members (cf. Rom. 12:4 f.). But in Ephesians (notably in 1:22 f.; 4:15 f.; 5:30) the head and the body are inextricably united and interdependent.

Another important statement about the church's nature comes in the attributing to it of a sort of transcendental status. The church shares the heavenly life of its exalted Lord even now in this age (1:22; 2:6; 5:27), and the distinctive features of the church in this epistle are akin to those classically stated in the creed "I believe in one holy, catholic, apostolic church." That is, there is a timeless, idealistic quality about the church's life which says more about what the people ought to be than what they actually are in this present world.

Yet the epistle knows that the church lives an empirical life in this world and that its readers face pressing dangers. They are counseled against allowing their pre-Christian moral standards to decide and control their present conduct (4:17 ff.). They are put on their guard against pagan teachers who would undermine the Christian ethic they accepted as part of their new life in Christ (5:3 ff.). Baptism is appealed to as a dramatic summons to rouse from moral stupor and a call to walk in the light of holy living (5:14).

The seductions of those who were leading the readers astray with empty words (5:6) and causing them to be tossed about by crafty dealings (4:14) suggest the presence of a type of Gnostic teaching. Basic to the Gnostic world-view was a dualism which drove a wedge between God and his creation and regarded the latter as alien to him. It insinuated that men could safely ignore the claims of morality and (in a strange paradox with both elements attested in second-century Gnosticism) either indulge their bodily appetites without restraint or treat their bodily instincts with contempt. Thus both libertinism and asceticism are logical consequences of the principle that God is remote from matter and unconcerned about what men do with their physical life.

Paul is moved to give warning against a cluster of evil practices (5:3,5,12) and to argue for resistance to the pull of degrading influences (2:3). He is equally concerned to defend the value and dignity of marriage against those who, from false ascetic motives (cf. 1 Cor. 7; 1 Tim. 4:3) would depreciate the marital state. But his real answer to these false notions and practices is to deny outright the dualistic basis of the teaching. This denial is carried through by an insistent statement of the church's heavenly origin and earthly existence. The incarnation of Christ and the elevation of redeemed humanity are two powerful facts to which he appeals for his conclusion that heaven and earth have been brought together into harmony (1: 10).

By the same token of cosmic unity, the Gnostic tenet of mankind as held in the grip of a relentless and pitiless fate is effectively challenged and overthrown. The answer to this element in Hellenistic religion is found in the eternal purpose of God, whose will embraces those very cosmic powers—the aeons—which first-century man most feared (3:11). It was the divine plan in Christ that these spiritual beings which Greek astral religion thought of as holding men's lives in thrall have lost that hold upon men and women (3:9–10). For God has raised his Son from death's domain and placed under his feet the entire universe, including these cosmic agencies (1: 21 ff.). He has exalted the church, too, above these powers and so lifted Christians beyond the range of cosmic tyranny and bad religion (1:22; 2:1–10; 5:8,14,27).

Christ's victory at the hands of God, who raised him from death, is at the very heart of the theology and cosmology of the epistle. But the question presses, How do believers come to share in this conquest over evil powers? The New Testament answer is that in baptism they "put off" the old nature (4:22 ff.) and so die to the rule of these malevolent powers (Col. 2:20); and at that time they "put on" the new man with his Christlike qualities. This feature explains both the hinge—represented by the baptismal chant of 5:14—on which Paul's practical and hortatory counsels turn (5:3 ff.) and also the admonitions he addresses to his readers to be renewed in the image of the new Adam (4:17 ff.).

The experience of baptism (in 5:26) marks the start of a new life of holiness to which this epistle summons its readers. Paul warns them to shun the specious doctrines of Gnostic libertinism with its disparagement of the body and calls them (in 6: 10 ff.) to stand manfully against those evil powers which are ranged against them. They are potentially defeated foes of the church, but victory will come only as Christians are diligent in the use of the armor God has provided and prove the reality of their conversion and baptism by standing firm in the Lord.

In summary, the epistle teaches the cardinal doctrine of the God who is all-powerful and all-wise in his loving design for the world. Christians, who share the risen life of Christ, are raised above the pitiless control of cosmic forces which would treat men as playthings of "fate" and "luck." [14] Equally they are lifted onto a high plane of noble living which opposes all that is sensual and debasing. The conflict they engage in is a sign of the reality of their new life, begun in the conversion-baptism experience.

The church is the historical witness to God's renewing purpose. Originally centered upon Israel, a nation elect for the sake of mankind, that purpose now embraces the Gentile peoples. Both races find their focal point of harmony and understanding in the creation of a new society, "one new man" (2:15), neither Jew nor Greek but Christian. Here is the clear articulation of Paul's thought in 1 Corinthians 10:32 and the foundation of the later Christian claim that the church forms a "third race" of men, who, reconciled to God through Christ, are united in a new way to realize a new society of men and women and to be a microcosm of God's ultimate design for a broken and sinful race.

Outline

I. Address and salutation (1:1–2)
II. The purposes of God in eternity and time (1:3–14)
    1. The Father's choice (1:3–6)
    2. The Father's plan accomplished in Christ (1:7–10)
    3. The Holy Spirit's ministry (1:11–14)
III. Paul's intercession for the church (1:15–23)
    1. Prayer for illumination (1:15–19)
    2. The exalted Christ and his church (1:20–23)
IV. The church's history—past, present, and future (2:1–10)
    1. Humanity outside of Christ (2:1–3)
    2. Humanity in Christ (2:4–6)
    3. What it means to be in Christ (2:7–10)

V. The unity of the church (2:11–22)
    1. The Gentiles before and after Christ's coming (2:11–13)
    2. Jews and Gentiles are now one body —in Christ (2:14–18)
    3. The one church on the one foundation (2:19–22)
VI. Paul's apostleship and his prayer for the church (3:1–21)
    1. Paul's calling and how he understood it (3:1–6)
    2. Paul's calling and how he fulfilled it (3:7–13)
    3. Paul's prayer for the church (3:14–21)
VII. The church's vocation as Christ's body (4:1–16)
    1. The church's calling in the light of its unity (4:1–6)
    2. Christ's gift and the church's gifts (4:7–12)
    3. The church's path to maturity (4:13–16)
VIII. A statement of the Christian's personal conduct (4:17–32)
    1. Some principles which govern Christian conduct (4:17–24)
    2. A continuation of Christian social ethics (4:25–32)
IX. The Christians' conduct in the world (5:1–20)
    1. Love excludes lust (5:1–7)
    2. Light banishes darkness (5:8–14)
    3. Wisdom corrects folly (5:15–20)
X. Christ, the church, and the family (5:21—6:9)
    1. Marriage in the light of the sacred marriage of Christ and the church (5:21–33)
    2. Family duties (6:1–4)
    3. Relations of masters and slaves (6:5–9)
XI. The Christian's warfare and the apostle's plea (6:10–20)
XII. Personal remarks and final greetings (6:21–24)

Selected Bibliography

Commentaries on the Epistle

BEARE, F. W. "The Epistle to the Ephesians," *The Interpreter's Bible*, Vol. XI. Nashville: Abingdon Press, 1953.

BRUCE, F. F. *The Epistle to the Ephesians.* London: Pickering and Inglis, 1961.

DIBELIUS, M. *An die Epheser.* Revised by H. GREEVEN. ("Handbuch zum Neuen Testament.") Vol. 12. Tübingen: J. C. B. Mohr, 1953.

---

14 On the present-day meaning to be drawn from Paul's use of first-century astrology and mythology, see F. F. Bruce, "St. Paul in Rome 3: The Epistle to the Colossians," *Bulletin of the John Rylands Library* 48, 2, 1966, 284 f., and Jung Young Lee, "Interpreting the Demonic Powers in Pauline Thought," *Novum Testamentum*, XII, January 1970, 54–69.

FOULKES, F. *The Epistle of Paul to the Ephesians* ("The Tyndale New Testament Commentaries.") London: Tyndale Press, 1963.

JOHNSTON, G. *Ephesians, Philippians, Colossians and Philemon* ("The Century Bible," new edition) London: Thomas Nelson, 1967.

MASSON, C. "L'épître de Saint Paul aux Ephésiens," *Commentaire du Nouveau Testament.* Neuchâtel: Delachaux et Niestlé, 1953.

ROBINSON, J. ARMITAGE. *St. Paul's Epistle to the Ephesians.* London: James Clarke, 1904.

SCHLIER, H. *Der Brief an die Epheser.* Düsseldorf: Patmos, 1957.

SCOTT, E. F. *The Epistles of Paul to the Colossians, to Philemon and to the Ephesians* ("The Moffatt New Testament Commentary.") London: Hodder & Stoughton, 1930.

THOMPSON, G. H. P. *The Letters of Paul to the Ephesians, to the Colossians and to Philemon* ("Cambridge Bible Commentary.") Cambridge: University Press, 1967.

Other Studies in Ephesians

BARTH, M. *The Broken Wall.* Chicago: The Judson Press, 1959.

BRUCE, F. F. "St. Paul in Rome 4: The Epistle to the Ephesians," *Bulletin of the John Rylands Library.* Manchester, 49. 2, 1967.

CROSS, F. L. (ed.) *Studies in Ephesians.* London: Mowbrays, 1956.

GOODSPEED, E. J. *The Meaning of Ephesians.* Chicago: University Press, 1933.

HANSON, S. *The Unity of the Church in the New Testament: Colossians and Ephesians* Lund: Almquist and Wiksells, 1946.

KIRBY, J. C. *Ephesians, Baptism and Pentecost.* London: Society for Promoting Christian Knowledge, 1968.

MITTON, C. L. *The Epistle to the Ephesians.* Oxford: University Press, 1951.

PERCY, E. *Die Probleme der Kolosser- und Epheserbriefe.* Lund: C. W. K. Gleerup, 1946.

Commentary on the Text

I. Address and Salutation (1:1-2)

[1] Paul, an apostle of Christ Jesus by the will of God,

To the saints who are also faithful in Christ Jesus:

[2] Grace to you and peace from God our Father and the Lord Jesus Christ.

Following the pattern both of letter writing practices in the ancient world and of his own earlier correspondence with the churches, Paul begins the letter with his own personal name. Abundant evidence of the format of ancient letters has been provided by the discovery of papyrus fragments preserved in the sands of Egypt.[1] From these we know how ordinary individuals conducted their private correspondence in the first centuries of the Christian era. But in Paul's case there is a new factor. He writes in full awareness of his office as *an apostle of Christ Jesus.*

By this self-description he is appealing

[1] See an account of these discoveries in A. Deissmann's classic, *Light from the Ancient East* (London: Hodder and Stoughton, 1927).

to his writing as authoritative, for apostleship meant the exercise of a God-given authority within the life of the churches (cf. 2 Cor. 13:10). That authority came from the risen Lord, who appointed the apostles as his representatives through whom he was to lay the foundations of his church. Our understanding of the nature of the apostolic office and function is considerably helped by what we read on the subject in this epistle (cf. 2:20; 3:5; 4:11 f.).

Paul boldly included himself as an apostle on the basis of his having seen the living Christ (cf. 1 Cor. 9:1). It is significant that he qualifies his claim to apostleship with the words *by the will of God.* In that phrase he acknowledges that his calling is not self-derived nor conferred upon him by other Christians. Rather his apostolic authority and status are traced solely to the call and commission that came to him at the time of his new life in Christ (see the accounts in Acts 9:15-16; 22:14-15; 26:16 ff.; Gal. 1:15-17). Then he heard from the risen Lord words of appointment to be his servant and missionary to the Gentiles. So Paul confidently lays claim to the title *apostle* (lit. "one sent on a mission"), for he cannot doubt the reality of Christ's appearing to him. Moreover, this call gave him assurance of his vocation as missionary to the Gentiles, and it is important for him to give evidence of his credential in a letter which wrestles with the tension between Jews and Gentiles in the church (cf. 3: 1 ff.)

Paul greets his readers whom he does not know personally (cf. 1:15) under the titles of their Christian profession. They are *the saints (hagioi)* and the *faithful in Christ Jesus.* Much discussion has been centered on these titles, raising the question of how they go together in the verse. Compare Colossians 1:2 where the meaning is simpler. One view is to take the Greek word (*pistos*) rendered *faithful* in an adjective sense to mean then that Paul is addressing "the saints who are also believers in Christ Jesus," but this is a doubtful exegesis in view of the absence of a definite article before *pistois.*

The key phrase which qualifies both "saints" and "faithful" is *in Christ Jesus.* The phrase with variants occurs 35 times in the epistle and is full of rich meaning. Both preceding terms have roots which go back deep into the Old Testament. Israel was called to be a holy (*hagios*) people (Ex. 19:5–6; Lev. 19:1–2; Deut. 7:6; 14:2) and faithful in the service of the Lord. This concept of dedication is basic to the biblical teaching on holiness. As Israel was chosen by God to be his own people, the same call goes out to the new Israel of the Christian church. Israel's destiny as both a holy and faithful nation is handed on to the church whose life is found *in Christ Jesus.* That phrase is normally taken in the sense of in union or fellowship with Christ; and this is a true meaning. Only by a faith-union with Christ can believers know how to discharge their calling as *saints* and *faithful* disciples.

But recent interpreters are more inclined to give a corporate overtone to the phrase,

thus making it stand for "in the community of Christ, the church." [2] Such a meaning would give excellent sense here and underline what is the ruling theme of the entire letter. Israel's vocation as God's elect, holy, and witnessing people is passed on to a united company of believing people, both Jews and Gentiles, who find their true calling by sharing in Christian fellowship the unity they have in Christ as his people, "one new man" (see 2:15; 4:1–6,25).

This interpretation serves a second purpose which runs through the epistle. Paul is insistent that the church of the new covenant cannot dissociate itself from its ancestral past in the Jewish faith and Israel's salvation-history. The use of cultic terms like saints and faithful is a quiet reminder to his readers that "in Christ" means inseparable and necessary links with God's ancient people.

For the omission of "at Ephesus" from the RSV, see the Introduction.

Grace and *peace* are parts of a familiar Pauline prayer (cf. 1 Thess. 1:1; 1 Cor. 1:3; Gal. 1:3; Phil. 1:2) in which both the words and the sequence are important. We enjoy peace with God on the ground of his gracious act of redemption in Christ (Rom. 5:1–2). *Grace* is the action of God's loving concern to win men and women back to fellowship with himself; and this he has done in his Son. The firstfruit of the new relationship in which the believer stands is *peace.* From its Old Testament ancestry (Heb., *shalom*) this Greek word takes on the distinctively Christian dress of an enrichment of life, covering body, mind, and spirit, which is possible when we live in communion with God our maker and redeemer.

Both gifts are ascribed to God and the Lord Jesus Christ as joint-authors. By sure Christian insight, even in the apostolic age, the foundations of the creedal **doctrine of the Godhead** are being laid.

---

[2] There is a popular treatment of this by A. M. Hunter in *Interpreting Paul's Gospel* (London: SCM Press, 1954), pp. 37 f., 99 ff.

II. The Purposes of God in Eternity and Time (1:3–14)

There are two ways in which these stately verses may be approached. We may discover in them a trinitarian pattern corresponding to the purposes and activities of the members of the Christian Godhead. Thus the passage speaks of the Father who chooses his people in love (vv. 3–5). The one in whom the church is chosen is Christ the Son, who is also the Redeemer at the cost of his sacrificial death (v. 7). It is the Holy Spirit who applies the work of Christ to the church and so makes real in human experience the eternal purpose of the Trinity (vv. 13–14). Paul is here, on this view, laying the foundation on which the later church erected the creedal statement of "one God in three Persons." [3]

An alternative proposal suggests that Paul's thought flows along temporal channels as he views the entire range of God's redeeming purpose from a past eternity (v. 4) to its future realization (v. 14). On this understanding Paul is concerned to show how the plan of God which was conceived in his eternal counsel was brought to actuality in his Son's achievement of human redemption. By this one act in history (v. 7) the forgiveness of sins is secured for all believers (v. 13) who are brought to faith by their hearing the gospel and responding to it. The transition from historical redemption to its application in personal experience is made by the work of the Spirit who gives to the believer now (v. 13) a foretaste of his completed salvation (v. 14).

However, these two approaches are not mutually exclusively; and it is possible to hold that Paul is expressing a rudimentary trinitarian belief through a chronological pattern. On balance, the second suggestion is to be preferred, especially if the formal structure of the passage is taken from the Jewish prayer-pattern known as berakah

(lit. blessing). [4]

God is blessed as the giver of blessings. These noble acts are enumerated as election, adoption, redemption and forgiveness, revelation, and the gifts of the Spirit. But whatever the formal similarity between Jewish and Christian benedictions, the important distinctive in the latter should be noted. God's goodness to his church is focussed in Christ. It is in him that every spiritual good reaches his people because it is in him that God's final purposes for the universe are summed up (v. 9). The constant repetition of the phrase "in him" should be carefully noticed, with the center point of Paul's statement of salvation-history coming in v. 7. The thought in these verses is so concentrated that we do well to subdivide the section.

1. The Father's Choice (1:3–6)

[3] Blessed be the God and Father of our Lord Jesus Christ, who has blessed us in Christ with every spiritual blessing in the heavenly places, [4] even as he chose us in him before the foundation of the world, that we should be holy and blameless before him. [5] He destined us in love to be his sons through Jesus Christ, according to the purpose of his will, [6] to the praise of his glorious grace which he freely bestowed on us in the Beloved.

Paul breaks out in an exultant doxology in praise of God as the Father of our Lord Jesus Christ, his beloved Son. He recalls that all spiritual benefits are placed at the disposal of the church which exists in and draws its life from its head, Christ, who now reigns in the heavenly places (cf. 1:20; 2:6). The oneness of the risen Christ and his people is the foundation of Pauline confidence, and this staggering thought evokes his praise.

The church now lives in Christ because of God's premundane choice which ensures that men and women who hear the gospel through the apostolic witness and preaching

---

[3] Other allusions to a trinitarian pattern in the New Testament teaching are mentioned by J. N. D. Kelly, *Early Christian Creeds* (London: Longmans, 1950), pp. 22 f.

[4] Modern study of this passage, which began with T. Innitzer in 1904, received great impetus from Lohmeyer's classification of the verses as poetic and liturgical based on Jewish synagogue practice. See J. C. Kirby's *Ephesians, Baptism and Pentecost* (London: SPCK, 1968), pp. 126 ff.

will respond in faith (cf. 2 Thess. 2:13). Here we confront the mystery of divine election which runs through much of the New Testament. Some guidelines of interpretation may be helpful. The New Testament writers proclaim God's electing mercy not as a conundrum to tease our minds but as a wonder to call forth our praise. They offer this teaching not as an element in God's character to be minimized but as an assurance that our lives are in his powerful hands rather than in the grip of capricious fate, which was a fear first-century man knew well. And the doctrine is never stated as an excuse for carelessness in spiritual matters, but always as a reminder that Christians have a moral responsibility "to confirm [their] call and election" (2 Peter 1:10) by following the highest ethical standards. We are chosen *that we should be holy and blameless.*

God's electing purpose is an expression of his *love* (RSV is here better than KJV and NEB which take "in love" with the previous verse) and has as its design the fulfillment of his plan that there should be many sons in his family, who all share the likeness of their elder brother (Rom. 8:29; cf. Heb. 2:10). Election through divine love is linked with the description of Jesus as *the Beloved.* This title recalls Mark 1:11 as an appellation for the Messiah in Jewish literature (see J. A. Robinson's note, pp. 229 ff.); but the closest Old Testament background reference is Genesis 22:1–8; which Paul also has in mind in Romans 8: 32. Through the Son, God's grace is conveyed (cf. John 1:17).

2. The Father's Plan Accomplished in Christ (1:7–10)

⁷ In him we have redemption through his blood, the forgiveness of our trespasses, according to the riches of his grace ⁸ which he lavished upon us. ⁹ For he has made known to us in all wisdom and insight the mystery of his will, according to his purpose which he set forth in Christ ¹⁰ as a plan for the fulness of time, to unite all things in him, things in heaven and things on earth.

When Paul mentions that divine grace has been displayed, this prompts him to a larger treatment of the theme. Sonship and membership in God's family are made possible on the ground of redemption. But this deliverance is not effected without cost, for it is by the offering of *his blood* (i.e., his life given gladly in obedience to the Father's will) that Christ obtained his people's liberation from the tyranny of evil and gave them the assurance of pardon. The background to this idea of sin as a taskmaster and tyrant is clearly supplied in the Old Testament. Israel was a captive nation in Egypt and cried out for God's deliverance (Deut. 15:15).

Redemption and forgiveness are but part of the entire work of Christ. What the apostle terms *the mystery of his will* embraces the universe in its scope, for it is *a plan for the fulness of time.* That means it is a plan which God will fulfill in his own way and according to his invincible will. The nature of that plan is now stated. It has as its great objective the summing up of all things in Christ. This is a difficult phrase, but it probably means that in Christ the entire universe finds its full explanation and rationale. Christ gives meaning to life when we perceive that he is not only the source and sustainer of the universe's structure and fabric (as in Col. 1:15 ff.; cf. John 1:3–4; Heb. 1:2–3); but as the destined Lord of creation he is the goal towards which the whole creation is moving. It is the magnificent vision of the cosmic Christ which fills Paul's mind in these verses. He gives Christ the freedom of the universe and depicts him as creation's goal (A. M. Hunter).

The occasion of this teaching may well be sought in a dangerous threat to the Christian faith which showed itself in Asia Minor in Paul's day. Evidence for this is provided by his epistle to the Colossians. False teachers were evidently claiming a secret instruction which was open only to a privileged few who enjoyed the possession of the clue to an understanding of the universe. They congratulated themselves on their self-styled wisdom, insight, knowledge, and access to "the mystery" which unlocked the door to the universe's dark secrets. And they were intent on guarding all this private information and keeping it within the circle of initiates. In a word, they were Gnostics priding themselves on the acquisition of a knowledge (*gnosis*) which gave them the key to the riddle of life.

Paul counters this specious pretension. By deliberately availing himself of the very terms and language they were using, he opposes the false teachers. The secret of the divine purpose is in Christ, and it is an open secret accessible to all who believe in him. It is and remains a *mystery* in the sense that no human intelligence could have guessed what God intended to do in Christ, but it is now revealed to Christians (see 3:3–6). Its content is "the inclusion of the Gentiles as well as the Jews in a common hope in Christ" and, even more, "the unification of humanity in the Christ" (J. A. Robinson). This specific content drawn from 3:3–6 suggests that the false teachers were Jewish Gnostics who made much of their exclusivist claims and dismissed God's purpose for the mass of unenlightened men. Paul knows that Christ is a universal Saviour, and that the divine scheme embraces the world.

We should interpret v. 10 in this light. Christ performs his God-appointed role on a cosmic scale by gathering the fragmented parts of human life into a whole. He forms a uni-verse out of a disparate collection of what appear to be alien elements. The Gnostic errorists doubtless (like their counterparts in the second century A.D.) drove a wedge between heaven and earth and taught that God has contempt for alien matter. Paul's reply is that the cosmic Lord who came from God to man is now exalted to the divine presence, and so has bound heaven and earth together into a unity. There is no aspect of human society and human life outside the scope of his redemptive work, and no hostile force in heaven or hell which can frustrate God's eternal purpose (Rom. 8:38–39).

3. The Holy Spirit's Ministry (1:11–14)

[11] In him, according to the purpose of him who accomplishes all things according to the counsel of his will, [12] we who first hoped in Christ have been destined and appointed to live for the praise of his glory. [13] In him you also, who have heard the word of truth, the gospel of your salvation, and have believed in him, were sealed with the promised Holy Spirit, [14] which is the guarantee of our inheritance until we acquire possession of it, to the praise of his glory.

The apostle's mind turns to consider the process by which God's saving design comes to effectual outworking in human lives. He joins together both himself as representing the Jewish people who had long been sustained by the hope of Messiah's coming and his readers who were of Gentile origin. Now in Christ these ethnic and religious connotations have lost their meaning. Both Jews and Gentiles are "members of the same body" (3:6), a worldwide church, though they did come into that body from different cultures.

The way to Christ, however, is the same for both Jews and Gentiles. The outline is described in vv. 13–14. Hearing *the word of truth* (i.e., the gospel as Paul proclaimed it, cf. Col. 1:5) is the first step. It is followed by a trustful acceptance of him of whom it speaks. The next term is "sealing," which is associated with the Holy Spirit and refers—in the judgment of this writer—to baptism as the outward attestation of the Christian's resolve to follow in the way of Christ and in the fellowship of his church (cf. 4:30; the term seal is a common designation in later times for the work of the Spirit in baptism).[5] The Holy Spirit gives to the person who is newly baptized his own witness in terms of an assurance that

---

[5] See G. W. H. Lampe, *The Seal of the Spirit* (London: Longmans, 1951). Not all interpreters accept this identification. See, for a contrary view, J. D. G. Dunn, *Baptism in the Holy Spirit* (London: SCM, 1970), p. 160, who makes the seal to refer to God's gift of the Spirit without reference to water baptism.

he belongs to God's people as Israel was God's inheritance under the old covenant cf. Col. 1:12; Acts 20:28; I Peter 2:9). The indwelling of the Spirit is again compared in v. 14 with Israel's experience. The Jews of old became God's elect nation by adoption and the covenant relationship but did not enter their full possession of the divine promises until the time of Joshua and the conquest of Canaan. The Christian receives the "first installment" (*arrabōn*, which the RSV in v. 14 translates *the guarantee*) at conversion and awaits the final consummation of God's purpose in the confidence that "he who began a good work in you will bring it to completion at the day of Jesus Christ" (Phil. 1:6). The gift of the Spirit in present experience is a token (2 Cor. 5:5) of his salvation which will be completed at the resurrection (Rom. 8:23). Clearly Paul's thinking about the church as God's inheritance is governed by Old Testament categories, as is clear from his use of a Greek term (*klēronom-*) [6] which the RSV obscures by its various translations in vv. 12,14,18. The ERV of v. 11 gives the more literal rendering: "in whom also we were made a heritage." His thought goes back to Deuteronomy 32:9. And this Pauline discussion makes a distinctive contribution to the main purpose of the letter, which is to show how the church of Jesus Christ has inseparable roots in the Israel of the Old Covenant.

III. Paul's Intercession for the Church (1: 15–23)

In this section Paul expresses his gladness that the readers of his letter have come to share in the blessings of God's saving plan which he has described in the previous paragraph. And for Paul the most characteristic way in which he expresses his confidence in a group of fellow Christians is to pray for them. In fact, the mention of

---

6 See the full study of this word in Paul by James D. Hester, *Paul's Concept of Inheritance: A Contribution to the Understanding of Heilsgeschichte* (Edinburgh and London: Oliver and Boyd, 1968).

prayer sends Paul off on a lengthy statement which runs on to the end of the chapter division.

It seems clear that Paul does not know his readers personally (v. 15); and in this respect they are like the Colossians (Col. 1:3–4; 2:1). But the news of their *faith* in Christ and its expression in active *love* to their fellow believers has reached him at a distance. This fact alone is conclusive proof, says Masson, that he is not writing to the church at Ephesus in which he had labored for three years.

Some important manuscripts as well as P [46] omit the words *and your love*. If this omission is accepted, the text then reads: "as I have heard of your faith in the Lord Jesus and in all the saints." This view is taken by E. F. Scott, who also wishes to understand *faith* in the sense of fidelity or loyalty. But a novel reconstruction of the text such as he proposes is without parallel in other Pauline writings, except perhaps Philemon 5. It is better to explain the omission in some manuscripts of the three words as accidental, as the eye of the scribe passed over from one Greek word to another, overlooking the intervening word (Greek *agapēn*) which comes as a second word in a series of three words. This slip (known as haplography) would adequately explain the omission. Moreover, the interlocking of "faith . . . and love" is a factor in Christian living by which Paul set a considerable store (Gal. 5:6).

Paul often delighted to recall his links with his Christian friends expressed in the words *remembering you in my prayers* (e.g., Rom. 1:9; Phil. 1:3; Col. 1:3; 1 Thess. 1:2–3; 2 Thess. 1:3). What is new here is the way in which he goes on to give the full content of that prayerful remembrance. The interesting point to observe is that this content is expressed in terms of knowledge and that Paul's prayer shades off into a magnificent theological statement (vv. 20–23) of God's purpose in the resurrection and exaltation of Christ as the church's Lord and head. We may use these two divisions to mark out the parts of what is in the Greek one long, involved sentence.

1. Prayer for Illumination (1:15–19)

15 For this reason, because I have heard of your faith in the Lord Jesus and your love toward all the saints, 16 I do not cease to give thanks for you, remembering you in my prayers, 17 that the God of our Lord Jesus Christ, the Father of glory, may give you a spirit of wisdom and of revelation in the knowledge of him, 18 having the eyes of your hearts enlightened, that you may know what is the hope to which he has called you, what are the riches of his glorious inheritance in the saints, 19 and what is the immeasurable greatness of his power in us who believe, according to the working of his great might

Knowledge in this context is not a loose and general term, as though it stood for *savoir faire* and acquaintance with all manner of topical interests and subjects. Paul is thinking about the highest form of understanding, which is to know God. But how can finite man comprehend the infinite? He needs above all else the right receptivity and ability to know God. And so the prayer opens with a request that calls upon God to grant the requisites for the acquirement of this knowledge: *a spirit of wisdom and revelation.* Both terms are to be seen on an Old Testament background (e.g., Job 28:12 ff.; Jer. 9:23 ff.) and underline the biblical teaching that *wisdom* does not come by human ingenuity and cleverness in excogitating divine truth from man's mind, but it is the gift of God (Luke 10: 21). *Revelation* is the name for this gracious self-disclosure of God who always takes the initiative in this action. He prepares human minds to receive the revelation; and this receptivity is expressed in terms of illumination: *the eyes of your hearts enlightened* is a pictorial way of stating what illumination means. (There are literary parallels in Greek philosophy and the Jewish religious tradition of Philo; but the Old Testament provides some close analogies in Psalms 13:3; 19:8; 119:18. The most interesting comparison, however, is the blessing in Dead Sea Scroll 1QS 2:3: "May he enlighten your heart with life-giving wisdom and grant you eternal knowledge.")

Added to a request for knowledge of God is a petition that to the enlightened minds of the readers God would make known *the hope to which he has called you* (cf. the identical phrase in 4:4). The calling is his summons to salvation (as in Phil. 3:14) rather than his appointing his servants to some specific task, though the latter idea is found elsewhere in Paul.

A third constituent in the apostle's prayer touches upon the theme of the church's wealthy *inheritance* as the people of God's new covenant just as Israel was the Lord's inheritance (Deut. 33:3–4). This idea of Christians as God's heritage looks back to 1:12,14 and forward to Paul's exposition of the church's enrichment by the exaltation of Christ. Words for *power* are piled up in an impressive, if bewildering, array in v. 19. Indeed, the sentence construction is so complex and involved that translation into English is almost rendered impossible. No fewer than four words for power are joined together. F. F. Bruce asks, Why this attempt to exhaust the resources of language to convey something of the greatness of God's power? Because, he replies, Paul is thinking of one supreme occasion when that power was exerted.

2. The Exalted Christ and His Church (1:20–23)

20 which he accomplished in Christ when he raised him from the dead and made him sit at his right hand in the heavenly places, 21 far above all rule and authority and power and dominion, and above every name that is named, not only in this age but also in that which is to come; 22 and he has put all things under his feet and has made him the head over all things for the church, 23 which is his body, the fulness of him who fills all in all.

That supreme occasion is beyond dispute the raising of Jesus from the dead, seen here as the signal display of divine power. Note that the emphasis falls on what God did: "he raised Christ" is a better way of stating the resurrection than "Jesus rose." Resurrection by itself, however, does not tell the whole story of God's purposes through Christ's victory. The raising of the crucified Lord was followed in the biblical pattern of events by his elevation to God's *right hand in the heavenly places*. The enthronement of Christ is one of the most heavily documented elements in New Testament teaching about Christ's person and place, for which Psalm 110:1 provided the chief starting-point (see Acts 5:31; 7:56; Rom. 8:34; 1 Cor. 15:25; Col. 3:1; Heb. 1:3; 8:1; 12:2; Rev. 5:1–14; as well as the classic statement in Phil. 2:9–11).[7]

The significance of this passage lies in the way Paul relates God's power in the mighty event of the resurrection to the supply of all needed grace made available to the church. The imagery of such phrases as God's *right hand* and *sit . . . in the heavenly places* is obviously pictorial. But the motive which governs Paul's use of these terms is definitely and concretely practical.

Exaltation at God's right hand expresses in picture language (drawn from Psalm 110:1) both the world dominion of the messianic King and the enjoyment of a dignity which comes from sharing the throne of God himself.[8]

But the lordly Christ is master not only of the visible world of nature and men. He has command of all the spirit-forces which were thought to control the destiny of men in antiquity as star deities. Christ, Paul teaches, is Lord of all the cosmic agencies that men may care to name because he is both their creator (Col. 1:16) and rightful ruler (Phil. 2:9–11). His name excels all these forces, both *in this age* and *in that which is to come*, i.e., throughout the entire time span of the universe, which embraces the two ages of Jewish apocalyptic

thought. We may recall 4 Ezra 7:50: "The Most High created not one age but two." Paul declares that both the old age up to Christ's coming in the incarnation and the messianic era, begun at the resurrection and to be openly manifested at the Parousia, are alike under the lordship of the cosmic Christ.

Nor is this all that is bound up with the Easter vindication of Christ. He has been accorded an authority by God to exercise *de facto* rule over those spiritual powers which until his victory at the cross and empty tomb held men in bondage (Gal. 4:3; Col. 2:14–15). *He has put all things under his feet* again draws upon pictorial imagery which in turn utilizes the Old Testament language. Genesis 1:26 and Psalm 8:6 speak of man's dominion over nature, but Hebrews 2:5 ff. gives indication that early Christians took this promise to be specially applicable to Jesus as the last Adam. Here Paul follows the same line of reasoning as in 1 Corinthians 15:24–25, and reaches forward in anticipation of Christ's final triumph which faith claims now as a present reality. How to bring together the future hope of 1 Corinthians 15 and the "realized eschatology" of this present verse which teaches that all is already subject to Christ's dominion is not easy, but one answer may be given.

It may be that v. 22*a* is a projection into the future of the final victory of the cosmic Lord but which appears to the vision of the worshiping church an already accomplished fact. The reason for this possibility lies partly in the liturgical strain which sounds through these verses and allows some scholars to label v. 20–23 as "a kind of hymn, celebrating the power of Christ's exaltation," after the manner of Colossians 1:15–20 and Philippians 2:6–11.[9]

The other possible reason for taking the

---

7 The present writer may refer to his book *Carmen Christi: Philippians 2:5–11 in Recent Interpretation and in the Setting of Early Christian Worship* (Cambridge: University Press, 1967), pp. 229–283, for a treatment of the enthronement of Christ.

8 See for important conclusions from the background material in Jewish thought the articles in *Theological Dictionary of the New Testament*, ed. G. Kittel and G. Friedrich, trans. G. W. Bromiley (Grand Rapids: Eerdmans, 1964, 1965) II, 39; III, 1089.

9 C. F. D. Moule writes: "At moments of Christian worship, time and space are obliterated and the worshipping Church on earth is one in eternity with the Church in the heavenly places" (*The Birth of the New Testament*: [London: A. and C. Black, 1962], p. 102). See further discussion in R. P. Martin, *Carmen Christi*, pp. 266–270.

universal sway of Christ's triumph to be proleptic is seen from the second half of the verse. God has made him *head over all things for the church.* Clearly this is meant by Paul to be an already achieved purpose. "All things," i.e., all those demonic forces which militate against Christ's lordship and seek to destroy the church, are now subject to Christ's control. The verse is an assurance that there is no part of the created order which is capable of such evil machinations and destructive tendencies; and this confidence falls into line with Matthew 16: 18–19 and Romans 8:35–39.

Mention of Christ's headship over these cosmic powers recalls to Paul that Christ is also (in a different sense, however) head of his people. They are *his body;* and that means the church is the instrument of his purpose in the world (Rom. 12:4 ff.; 1 Cor. 12:12 ff.).

That much is clear, but the idea which is uppermost in Paul's mind is rather derived from the special sense of *head . . . for the church, which is his body.* S. F. B. Bedale [10] has shown that this phrase carries the sense "ruler of the church"; and this is exactly Paul's intention. He wants to show that Christ has authority in his house, just as the head controls the movements of the human body (so 5:23 ff.).

The phrase which completes the sentence, *the fulness of him who fills all in all,* though it is much controverted, confirms this understanding. The problem with verse 23*b* lies in the Greek participle rendered "who fills." The question posed is, Is it Christ that fills the church, or the church that fills Christ as his complement? Stig Hanson [11] has offered conclusive proof for preferring the former alternative. He concludes: "all that Christ has from God, the power, the gifts, the grace, He passes on to the Church. . . . The Church has nothing to give Christ of herself, by which what is lacking in Him could be filled up. Instead,

it is the Church that is filled with Him (3:19), becoming a partaker of all that He owns and is, for the purpose of continuing His work."

This exegesis of a problematic verse may be supplemented by the contribution of J. A. T. Robinson.[12] He maintains that, while it is the church which is receiving gifts from the ascended Lord, the Lord himself is equally receiving the complete fulness from the Father. This is not to say (as J. Armitage Robinson does) that Christ is in a measure incomplete without the church, but it is to stress the close union between Christ and his people which is a constant theme in this epistle as well as the parallel witness of Colossians 2:9–10.

IV. The Church's History—Past, Present, and Future (2:1–10)

This passage takes a broad sweep in its survey of the plight of human life outside of Christ and untouched by the influence of his gospel; and then it goes on to relate Christ's coming to the great changes which have occurred in the human condition because of what God in Christ has done by that coming. The section is really a contrast which puts side by side the former state of the apostle's readers (vv. 1–3) and the new life in Christ which has become theirs (vv. 4–10). The hinge is at verse 4*a*: "But God, who is rich in mercy. . . ."

The RSV supplies the verb, *and you he made alive* in v. 1 from v. 5, which is the natural procedure to adopt. In this way we are to regard the intervening verses as a preliminary digression which prepares the way for the triumphant announcement of the steps God has taken to meet the needs of man as a sinner, whether he is a Gentile (vv. 1–2) or a Jew (v. 3).

The connecting link with chapter 1 is a continuation of Paul's thought. He has demonstrated the superlative act of power in God's raising his Son from the dead (1:19 ff.). Now, he proceeds to show that

---

[10] In *Studies in Ephesians,* ed. F. L. Cross (London: Mowbray, 1956), pp. 69 f.

[11] S. Hanson, *The Unity of the Church in the New Testament: Colossians and Ephesians* (Lund:ASNU 14, 1946), pp. 126 ff.

[12] J. A. T. Robinson, *The Body* (London: SCM, 1952), pp. 68 f.; a similar view is taken by Dale Moody in *The Hope of Glory* (Grand Rapids: Eerdmans, 1964), 143 f.

the same power is at work in vivifying the spiritually dead and raising them to new heights of life in Christ and with Christ. The closest parallel is Romans 6:1–11, though John's Gospel contains some comparative teaching (e.g., John 5:21–25).

1. Humanity Outside of Christ (2:1–3)

[1] And you he made alive, when you were dead through the trespasses and sins [2] in which you once walked, following the course of this world, following the prince of the power of the air, the spirit that is now at work in the sons of disobedience. [3] Among these we all once lived in the passions of our flesh, following the desires of body and mind, and so we were by nature children of wrath, like the rest of mankind.

The sorry plight of erstwhile pagans (who are now incorporated into the one church of Christ) is fully detailed in these verses (cf. 4:18). The root cause is alienation from God which results in condemnation, which in turn issues in spiritual death; and death characterized the whole of their pre-Christian experience (see Col. 2:13; Rom. 5:21; 6:23; 7:11,13). The two terms *trespasses* and *sins* are not to be treated as separate items, sharply to be distinguished. Rather, as H. Schlier observes, we see here a case of a doubling up of expression such as a preacher might use to enforce his point!

There follows a threefold characterization of society in Paul's day, as Graeco-Roman life is viewed from a Christian viewpoint. The first phrase is literally "according to the age (*aiōn*) of this world order" (*kosmos*). It suggests that human life is seen under the malign influence of celestial powers which hold man in tyrannical grip (so Gal. 1:4; 4:3; Col. 2:8; Heb. 2:15).

The possibility that there is a personal figure standing behind the term "aeon" (suggested by W. L. Knox) [13] is confirmed

by the next descriptive phrase, *the prince of the power of the air.* This description answers to the devil who, as ruler of demonic agencies in the upper regions of the sky (in ancient thought), controls human action by goading men into sin. In the cosmology of the Hellenistic age the interstellar space, especially that between the moon and the earth, was thought to be the place of constant demonic activity, with baneful effects upon all earth-dwellers (cf. English word "lunacy" from Latin *luna* = the moon). While we now have to reject the cosmology, non-human evil influences of a personal character (cf. Tillich's demonic) upon human life are only too well known, producing all manner of mental and spiritual derangements and widespread social consequences.

As a further elaboration of malevolent evil powers Paul mentions *the spirit that is now at work* among men who, like Satan, are paying the price of their disobedience to God. Satan's downfall in Jewish angelology was linked with his refusal to obey God. His rebellious spirit is still active in men who have pitted themselves against God in their blindness (2 Cor. 4:4).

The sad fruit of this disobedience to God's gracious will for mankind is seen in the moral turpitude of society. Paul's lists of vices in Romans 1:18–32 and Galatians 5:19 ff. are a realistic commentary on the moral state of the ancient world, from a Christian standpoint. And his readers, like the Corinthians (1 Cor. 6:5–11), had known the worst of contemporary life before their deliverance from evil and experience of new life in the church. Perhaps the saddest of all descriptions is the solemn sentence: *by nature children of wrath.* This is a Hebraic term, meaning "deserving of God's judicial condemnation." There is no support here for the notion of original guilt or for thinking of wrath as a fitful or vindictive emotion unworthy of God. It declares the objective fact that men are (outside of Christ) under divine judgment by reason of moral choices they have made, and these in turn are dictated by their warped nature (see Rom. 1:18–22).

---

13 W. L. Knox, *St. Paul and the Church of the Gentiles* (Cambridge: University Press, 1939), p. 187. The translation then runs: "in obedience to the aeon, or controlling spirit, of this world." Alternately, the term means the *Zeitgeist* or "spirit of the age" in a general, cultural sense. But the reference in 6:12 tells against this view.

2. Humanity in Christ (2:4–6)

⁴ But God, who is rich in mercy, out of the great love with which he loved us, ⁵ even when we were dead through our trespasses, made us alive together with Christ (by grace you have been saved), ⁶ and raised us up with him, and made us sit with him in the heavenly places in Christ Jesus,

The darkness of hopelessness and desperate needs serves only as a background to make the love and grace of God shine more brightly. The sentence which marks the turning point in the story is v. 4, which highlights these attributes of God, chiefly that he is *rich in mercy*. This phrase, borrowed from the Old Testament (Psalm 145:8), is the antithesis of divine wrath. The evidence of God's loving concern which does not leave man to perish is seen by Paul in a double action. God has both made alive the spiritually dead and raised up those who were held down by the servitude of that death. In effect, God has done for Christians (vv. 5–6) what he has already done for Christ (1:20); and this is one illustration which this epistle gives of the intimate bond uniting Christ and the church. Paul's language here is rich in the use of verbs with the preposition "with" (Greek *sun*) and even to the extent that he employs verbs like *made us alive together with* which are not previously found in Greek literature and not attested again in later Christian writers.[14]

The verbs for vivify and raise up are found together in John 5:21 and Romans 8:11, with God as the subject. And this confirms the view that both acts are uniquely predicated of God (as in the Old Testament and the synagogue liturgy, where it is God alone who can both quicken and raise up the dead). But there is this distinction. While in the Old Testament teaching the raising of the (physically) dead is in view, here it is a spiritual renewal that is stressed.

The best parallel to Paul's thought here is one by contrast, namely Galatians 3:21. The very thing which the law cannot do—

give life to those dead in their alienation from God—is achieved in the gospel (2 Cor. 3:6). And this promise is bound up with Christ's own resurrection which, in turn, was followed by his exaltation. So believers are lifted up *with him* to a new plane of living by sharing his life (so 1 Cor. 6:17).

The *heavenly places* is a phrase which runs like a thread through this epistle (found at 1:3,20; 2:6; 3:10; 6:12) and has been the occasion of much speculation [15] as to its background, ranging from a view that the spirit-world of star worship is in mind (so Reitzenstein) to Odeberg's taking the phrase in a general sense to mean "spiritual condition." The truth seems rather to be that the phrase signifies "the realm of ultimate realities beyond the visible, empirical world" (N. A. Dahl) where Christ's presence is known by the church in its antagonism with spiritual malevolent powers. Believers are already raised up to an elevation where Christ is as part of their new life. Hence v. 5,8 can employ the perfect tense of the verb to be saved. Usually this is taken as a mark of non-Pauline authorship, for the apostle normally uses only a simple past tense (Rom. 8:24) or a present (1 Cor. 1:18). But Schlier defends the use of the perfect here as part of the epistle's design to see the church's salvation in its total aspect, as already fully achieved.

3. What It Means to Be in Christ (2:7–10)

⁷ that in the coming ages he might show the immeasurable riches of his grace in kindness toward us in Christ Jesus. ⁸ For by grace you have been saved through faith; and this is not your own doing, it is the gift of God—⁹ not because of works, lest any man should boast. ¹⁰ For we are his workmanship, created in Christ Jesus for good works, which God prepared beforehand, that we should walk in them.

In spite of this tendency in the letter, the futuristic element in salvation is not altogether neglected. The purpose of God's

---

14 R. Bultmann in *TDNT*, II, 875.

15 See H. Schlier's excursus in his commentary, pp. 45–48.

action in lifting the church out of the condemned realm of sin and death into Christ's heavenly presence is one which only the future will disclose. For it is with the consummation of his redemptive plan *in the coming ages* that the full extent of his bounty will be known. The time-scheme, "this age–the age(s) to come," is taken from Jewish thought and picks up the idea from 1:21.

Indeed, Paul can sum up the entire process of past, present, and future in a creedlike, pregnant epitome. Salvation is complete (hence the perfect tense *you have been saved*) in the sense that no defect or inadequacy mars God's purpose; it originates in the grace or saving love of God expressed to sinners; and it enters human experience by the receptivity of faith or trustful acceptance. And the creedal language suggests that Paul is giving expression to a perspective which views reality "under the aspect of eternity" and views the continuing experience of Christians as an already accomplished fact.

This entire process is God's doing, as 2 Corinthians 5:18 insists, not man's, and it comes to him as a freely offered gift (Rom. 6:23). *This* renders the Greek neuter pronoun and cannot look back in agreement with *faith* (a Greek feminine noun *pistis*), however true it may be that we come to believe only because of God's prevenient or causative grace. It is the whole gamut of salvation that forms the antecedent of this word, as in the reference to 2 Corinthians 5:18.

Paul gives a rationale for his teaching on *sola gratia, sola fide* (by grace alone, by faith alone). No person can be allowed room to contribute to his own salvation, else there would be ground to *boast*. This word means more than proud assertiveness in biblical thought; it stands as a synonym of confidence in one's native prowess or spiritual competence (cf. Psalm 97:7 and Isa. 42:17). And it represents the exact opposite of self-distrust which casts itself on God and his mercy. So Philippians 3:3–11.

Why does Paul insist in v. 10 that this teaching needs a counterbalancing emphasis? It is clear from Romans 6:1 ff. that his gospel of free grace and simple trust can be misrepresented. H. Schlier correctly observes that Paul has to combat two errors. Against those who looked to their attempts at self-righteousness as a way of salvation— what Schlier calls *moralismus*—Paul contends that God's acceptance is freely given to the undeserving. But Paul's teaching is travestied when righteousness of living and a high moral tone to life become forgotten on the mistaken assumption that Christians can live carelessly, claiming that if they sin their lapses only give the grace of God more room for display. This false reasoning lay at the center of a later gnosticizing (Schlier's term is *Gnostizismus*) tendency to treat Christian morality loosely (see for evidences in Rev. 2:14 ff., 20 ff.; 2 Peter 2:2 ff.; 17 ff.).

Hence the apostle sounds the call for *good works*, not as a ground for claiming God's favor (a bid denied in v. 9), but as the necessary consequence of the readers' new life in Christ as his new creation (2 Cor. 5:17). Titus 2:14 is the best commentary, though here Paul's thought is picturesque. *Workmanship* is a Greek word (*poiēma*) from which the English "poem" comes, and the practical application of this truth to Christian conduct and social influence in the world is seen by the word *walk* (a conscious contrast with the same term in vv. 2–3 where the Greek is translated "we once lived").

V. *The Unity of the Church* (2:11–22)

A new section begins with v. 11. This paragraph forms an extended exposition of the theme of the church's essential oneness in spite of the barriers of race and culture which kept the Jews and the Gentiles (i.e., non-Jewish nations) apart in the ancient world. The kernel of Paul's argument may be found already in 1 Corinthians 12:13; Galatians 3:28; and Colossians 3:11. What is singular about the present passage is the way that Paul fills out his earlier discussions and does so in some unusual ways. The reference in v. 15 to the canceling of the law has suggested to some scholars a novelty of thought which betrays a non-Pauline conclusion. Paul in Romans 10 speaks rather of Christ as fulfilling the law and so achieving its consummation, not abrogating its authority—which possibly is the very false teaching Paul is being accused of in the church which cherished the warning of Matthew 5:17–19.

One reason, however, for the fuller treatment here may be that Paul is drawing upon material which derives from Christian public worship. Recent study has detected in this paragraph evidence for the presence of a number of what appear to be baptismal hymnic fragments. On this view, Paul is incorporating this accepted liturgical teaching in order to spell out fully the importance of the church's unity, which was a pressing pastoral concern in the Asia Minor churches of Gentile composition.

Before commenting on the individual parts of this section, we should note what lies at the center of the apostolic argument. See v. 14: *He is our peace, who has made us both one.* A single programmatic statement like this is important, since it combines within itself elements taken from the surrounding verses. And these may be tabulated: (1) the enmity between Jews and Gentiles has now been overcome and pacified; (2) the disparate segments of the divided first-century world are now called to a harmonious amity within the fellowship of the Christian church; and (3) both Jews and Gentiles in losing their ethnic and cultural identity gain something in return which is far better, namely a place in Christ's body, as Christ's body, so forming a new race of men. Later Christian writers therefore call men and women in the church a "third race," neither Jews nor Gentiles but Christians. And, says Paul, they also gain an unsurpassed privilege of access to God, which they could never know in its depth in their previous and unreconciled state.

No passage of the New Testament could be more relevant to the second half of the twentieth century than this magnificent statement of the one hope for the human race. The world we know is fallen, divided, and suspicious. Paul holds out the prospect of a reconciled, unified, and amicable society, whose microcosm is seen in the church of God's worldwide, transnational, and reconciling family.

1. The Gentiles Before and After Christ's Coming (2:11–13)

[11] Therefore remember that at one time you Gentiles in the flesh, called the uncircumcision by what is called the circumcision, which is made in the flesh by hands—[12] remember that you were at that time separated from Christ, alienated from the commonwealth of Israel, and strangers to the covenants of promise, having no hope and without God in the world. [13] But now in Christ Jesus you who once were far off have been brought near in the blood of Christ.

The appeal is directed specially to non-Jews, who were the apostle's readers in this epistle. They were presumably Gentile Christians in Asia Minor; and as such they are bidden to reflect on what their spiritual condition was in their pre-Christian days. They were classed by the Jews as uncircumcised and so standing outside God's covenant with Israel. *In the flesh* is Paul's irony, referring to the physical-surgical operation which made circumcision the badge of Jewish profession. Conversely *uncircumcision* (lit., "foreskin") is mentioned in the Old Testament (Jer. 9:26) of nations outside of Israel. But that same Old Testament verse points forward to a distinction within the Jewish people which Paul uses in his argument in Romans 2:25–29. His concern was a spiritual circumcision (Gal. 6:15; 1 Cor. 7:19), of which the outward sign is baptism (Col. 2:11—"a circumcision made without hands," i.e., of God, who thus confers upon Christian believers the title, "the true circumcision," Phil. 3:3).

What was the state of Gentiles, from a Jewish point of view? Paul takes the Jews' place and gives a threefold reply. They were (1) lacking in any hope of a Messiah. Indeed, the usually attested Jewish hope of the Messiah's coming entailed the destruction of the Gentile foreigners or at best their subjugation to Israel (see *Psalms of Solomon,* an intertestamental Pharisaic book written about 50 B.C.). Then (2) Gentiles suffered a deprivation in that they did not have right of citizenship within the elect nation. This is the understanding of *alienated from the commonwealth of Israel* offered by C. Masson; and it is confirmed by v. 19. Privileges and advantages of belonging to the most favored nation on earth are described glowingly by Paul elsewhere (Rom. 3:12; 9:4,5; Phil. 3:5 ff.).

(3) The saddest misfortune of all is in the words *having no hope and without God in the world.* The two parts of this phrase go together. But they need to be carefully understood. "Without God" does not mean a denial of his existence. There were very few atheists (in the modern sense) in the ancient world. Rather, the thought is that men outside of the church lack a true knowledge of the one God of the Judeo-Christian tradition and so commit themselves to "religion" (like Paul's designation in Acts 17:22). The multiplicity of ancient pantheons of gods and goddesses coupled with a prevailing tendency to despair (cf. Gilbert Murray's phrase "failure of nerve" used of Hellenistic society) quite naturally led to the sad condition of hopelessness. Paul's answer to both problems is found in a knowledge of the true God whose Son has opened a new era for the Gentiles.

Two expressions in v. 13 stand out in a carefully constructed sentence. *But now* answers to the phrase "at one time" and "at that time"; and *in Christ Jesus* fills the lack suggested in the phrase *separated from Christ* to show how the Gentiles' position has changed with their inclusion in the covenant of grace.

The contrast *far off—brought near* is borrowed from Isaiah 57:19 in the Greek Old Testament. But the novelty in Paul's statement comes in his declaration that the means by which underprivileged Gentiles have come into the inheritance is the Messiah's death on the cross. So the intention

of this verse is clear. Access to God is now freely available to all, irrespective of their former racial and cultural impediment. What remains to be explained in detail is the effect this transformation should have on the societal relations of men within the church.

2. Jews and Gentiles Are Now One Body— in Christ (2:14–18)

14 For he is our peace, who has made us both one, and has broken down the dividing wall of hostility, 15 by abolishing in his flesh the law of commandments and ordinances, that he might create in himself one new man in place of the two, so making peace, 16 and might reconcile us both to God in one body through the cross, thereby bringing the hostility to an end. 17 And he came and preached peace to you who were far off and peace to those who were near; 18 for through him we both have access in one Spirit to the Father.

Messiah in the Old Testament carried one title among others: "Prince of peace" (Isa. 9:6). The Hebrew term for peace (*shalom*) means much more than an absence of hostility, like an armed truce; it connotes well-being and security at every level. So *peace* in the Pauline text should carry a double sense. In uniting sinners to God and by canceling the enmity set up by sin, Christ has also brought Jews and Gentiles together in a unity and amity otherwise unknown in the first-century world. Reconciliation is the theme of this short paragraph. But it is another dimension of the reconciliation referred to elsewhere in Paul. In Romans 5:1–11 he is concerned with man's relationship to God; here he is interested to state the application of Christ's work in his breaking down *the dividing wall of hostility* between the two rival groups, as in Galatians 3:28 and Colossians 3:11. *Both* (a recurring term in vv. 14,16, 18) are united as *one.*

That *wall* poses an exegetical problem. What precisely is in the apostle's mind as background? Obviously the metaphor speaks of separation and alienation between opposing groups (cf. Winston Churchill's now famous description of an "iron curtain" between West and East, and the historical witness of the Berlin wall). But is there a more exact use of this metaphor?

The commonest illustration of the imagery behind the phrase is the Temple balustrade which separated the Court of Gentiles and the Court of Women in the Jerusalem Temple (Josephus, *Antiq.* 15:11; *Jewish War*, 5:5). This fence with its warning inscription [16] served to remind the non-Jews that they must keep their distance from Israel's sacred shrine (see Acts 21: 27 ff. for an example of the Jewish fear of a trespass). This barrier, v. 14 declares, has been broken down in the sense that access to God is no longer restricted to Jews and their cultic observance.

M. Dibelius, however, asks a question of this interpretation: Would the Gentile readers in Asia Minor have understood this allusion? This query leads him and many contemporary German scholars to think that the background reference in the verse is to Gnostic images of a wall which separates the aeons and divides the heavenly *plērōma* from the earthly world. On this view, the allusion is to the Gnostic redeemer's re-entry from the terrestrial zone (to which he has descended on his mission) to the celestial regions. He has gone back to his heavenly world, and his flight path (to use the modern term from space exploration) necessitated a breaking down of all hindrances which stood in his route. This piece of cosmic movement was taken by the Gnostics as a symbol of the way in which man's access to the heavenly regions was opened as he followed the ascending redeemer. Against this view F. F. Bruce has offered a telling criticism by observing that the barrier in the Pauline text is a vertical one denoting a division between two groups of people resident in this world rather than

a horizontal division between the upper and lower world.[17] And the verb *broken down* refers more naturally to a vertical fence.

In the judgment of this writer, it is best to take another line and regard the *wall* which set up *hostility* as a covert allusion to the Mosaic law and its scribal interpretation. On a Jewish understanding of the law (preserved in the *Letter of Aristeas,* a Jewish second-century B.C. document), the intention in God's granting his law to Israel was to protect the nation from the Gentiles and so indirectly to prevent the Gentiles from having access to God because of Judaism's particularism. There is confirmation of this background if we take the verb *broken down* to mean that the law's enactments as a way of salvation are now abolished, i.e., rendered void. The law's abrogation was necessary for the creation of a universal church.

Furthermore, verse 13 speaks of the Gentiles as *far off,* and this description is best taken to imply that, from a Jewish rabbinical point of view, the Gentiles were kept at a distance from Israel which alone was a people near to God (Psalm 148:14). *Peace* was needed to unite two alienated religious groupings—and Christ's cross has effected just that. Indeed, the key thought of the whole passage is found here: *one new man in place of the two,* i.e., one Christian church instead of two ethnic groups of Jews and Gentiles separated by an "iron curtain" of animosity.

The way in which the reconciliation is accomplished is now set out in v. 15a which requires some detailed exegesis. Jesus as Israel's Messiah is credited with *abolishing . . . the law,* i.e., removing its validity as a way of saving righteousness, because only thus could a universal salvation be offered to those who never had the law. Again we are reminded of Matthew 5:17 as a possible polemic to this position which

---

[16] See the discussion by E. Bickermann, *Jewish Quarterly Review*, 37 (1947), 387 ff. An inscription of the warning reads: "No man of another race is to enter within the fence and enclosure round the Temple. And whoever is caught will have only himself to thank for his ensuing death."

[17] F. F. Bruce, *Bulletin of the John Rylands Library* (Manchester), 49, Spring 1967, 316.

goes beyond Paul's statement in Romans 10:4.[18]

Thus Christ is the creator of a new race in which age-old distinctions of nationality have lost their relevance and force. The *one body* can hardly be a reference to the crucified body of Jesus, as some commentators both ancient (like Bengel) and modern (Schlier) have insisted. More likely the allusion is to the church as Christ's body as in 1:23 and 4:4,16 (so E. F. Scott, S. Hanson, and C. Masson). The sense will then be that when he died his purpose was to embrace the disparate sections of humanity in that saving deed and in reconciling men, without distinction, to God to kill the hostility which up to that point in history had kept them apart and at war. Whether the reconciliation is that between races or between men and God need not be decided exclusively. Paul's thought surely includes both, argues W. Foerster.[19]

He came in the person of his apostolic messengers who carry the gospel of peace (Rom. 10:15), which is freely offered to all races, both Gentiles formerly *far off* and Jews formerly *near* to God as his chosen race. Acts 2:32, which uses the same Old Testament scripture in Isaiah 57:19, shows the beginning of the breaking down of this rigid distinction, so fundamental to rabbinic Judaism.

Up to this point, Paul's thought has lain in the past tense. He was dealt with God's past action in breaking down obstacles to a worldwide reconciliation. Now he offers as a clinching summation of his argument the experimental reality of what every Christian knows to be true: *through him we both have access.* United in fellowship, Jews and Gentiles in Christ discover their oneness in a common and free access to God by the Holy Spirit who is the author of unity within the church (so 1 Cor. 12:

13). For this statement of a functional Trinity within the Christian Godhead we may compare 1 Peter 3:18.

3. The One Church on the One Foundation (2:19–22)

19 So then you are no longer strangers and sojourners, but you are fellow citizens with the saints and members of the household of God, 20 built upon the foundation of the apostles and prophets, Christ Jesus himself being the cornerstone, 21 in whom the whole structure is joined together and grows into a holy temple in the Lord; 22 in whom you also are built into it for a dwelling place of God in the Spirit.

So then is a phrase which often in Paul's writing draws out a consequence from a previously established fact or conclusion (Rom. 5:18, etc.). Possibly he has a vivid, concrete expression of Christian fellowship in mind, such as a common table fellowship in which believing Jews and Gentiles met in celebration of the Lord's Supper. The Gentiles were not in any way inferior, nor is their admission to the church a grudging one as though God had allotted them only second-class status within the covenant community. Rather, they were welcomed, by God, as full members, *fellow citizens with the saints.* The latter term probably stands for Jewish Christians, as often in Acts as well as Romans 15:25. Both classes constitute *the household of God* as a single entity, members of one society with equal rights and privileges.

The church as a house is clearly taught in Hebrews 3:6, but the inference is found in Paul at 1 Corinthians 3:10,16 where the text has in view one special house, namely, God's holy house, his temple. That this is Paul's application of the house-imagery is clear from v. 21. Christians are likened to living stones (as in 1 Peter 2:5) built into the framework which in turn rests upon a foundation which is Christ (1 Cor. 3:10) and which is laid by the apostles and prophets (so NEB).

There is an alternate way in which v. 20 may be understood, for the Greek is ambiguous. *Apostles and prophets* are gen-

---

[18] See C. F. D. Moule, "Obligation in the Ethic of Paul," in *Christian History and Interpretation: Studies Presented to John Knox,* ed. W. R. Farmer, C. F. D. Moule, and R. R. Niebuhr (Cambridge: University Press, 1967), pp. 401 ff.

[19] *TDNT,* Vol. II, 415.

erally agreed to mean Christian leaders in the New Testament church, the second term referring to such prophets as Agabus (Acts 11:27 ff., 21:10). But even with this general agreement the text could be read in the sense that these men formed the foundation of the church, as in Revelation 21:14. Some scholars argue for this view, which is opposed directly to what Paul says about Christ as the foundation stone in 1 Corinthians 3:10. So, they infer, we have in Ephesians a doctrine of the ministry which belongs to a later, more institutional structure of the church, and so coming out of a post-Pauline period. But this insistence on the apostles and prophets as themselves being the church's foundation is not without dispute, and the NEB translates otherwise: "the foundation laid by the apostles and prophets."

Christ's designation as *foundation* is equally capable of diverse interpretation. J. Jeremias argues for the meaning "coping stone" which unites all sections of the (completed) building, but this verse has been effectively challenged.[20] The traditional view of cornerstone, derived from Isaiah 28:16, is best, with a recognition given to Whitaker's argument that, in ancient building methods, the cornerstone had special importance as the stone used by the architect-builder to determine the "lie" of the whole building. So Jesus Christ is the pattern by which the life and growth of his church are shaped by God.

The result of the church's being settled on and determined by the foundation stone is next given. The church is a building but not in any static or inanimate sense. It is more like a living organism (Paul's verb being a change of metaphor) which takes shape by the Spirit's guidance through the circumstances of history. The *holy temple* recalls Solomon's Temple (1 Kings 6—8), which was a dwelling place he desired to erect for God. The New Testament counter-

20 See R. J. McKelvey, *The New Temple* (Oxford: University Press, 1969), pp. 108 ff., 195 ff., for the discussion and references to Jeremias and G. H. Whitaker, *The Expositor* 8 (1921), 470 ff.

part to this aspiration finds fulfillment in a temple made without hands, a spiritual body of men and women in whom God's Spirit dwells (1 Cor. 3:16). The Qumran community looked forward to a new temple to supersede the Jerusalem cult and ritual. That hope was amply fulfilled in Christ and his church in which God now finds his habitation. Not in a material shrine or a renovated cultus but in the lives of his consecrated people, God lives and shows himself to our world.

VI. Paul's Apostleship and His Prayer for the Church (3:1–21)

Paul held his commission to be Christ's special messenger to the Gentiles in high regard. Yet he found it needful repeatedly to assert his entitlement to the name apostle as much as he found that assertion a personally distasteful task. The truth was that his apostleship was repeatedly called in question and attacked by his opponents within the churches. And after his lifetime the same spirited defense of Paul's apostolic office and mission was made by his disciples. In the section covered by these verses (especially vv. 1–13), we have to ask ourselves whether these statements of Paul's apostleship read more naturally as his own spoken claim to be Christ's representative to the Gentiles offered as proof of his credentials, or whether we are listening to the claims made on Paul's behalf after his death by some admiring disciple writing "out of love for Paul" (*amore Pauli*, in the later Christian phrase). In other words, this chapter poses the issues of authorship and purpose of the epistle in an acute form. We are called to find some account of the autobiographical posture Paul adopts in these paragraphs.

The autobiography, in fact, at v. 9, merges into a statement of the content of his preaching in the light of the special destiny which he was charged to fulfill (vv. 3–6). The important statement of vv. 5–11 is given for the effect of showing that Paul's apostolic ministry to the Gentiles is based on the place which it has in the economy of God's saving purpose for the world through the church.

The personal note creeps in again as an interlude (vv. 7–8). It is resumed again as Paul offers a memorable pastoral prayer for the Christian congregations in the world (vv. 14–19). This concludes with an equally notable doxological ascription of praise (vv. 20–21).

1. Paul's Calling and How He Understood It (3:1–6)

¹ For this reason I, Paul, a prisoner for Christ Jesus on behalf of you Gentiles— ² assuming that you have heard of the steward-ship of God's grace that was given to me for you, ³ how the mystery was made known to me by revelation, as I have written briefly. ⁴ When you read this you can perceive my insight into the mystery of Christ, ⁵ which was not made known to the sons of men in other generations as it has now been revealed to his holy apostles and prophets by the Spirit; ⁶ that is, how the Gentiles are fellow heirs, members of the same body, and partakers of the promise in Christ Jesus through the gospel.

Paul's personal name is intended to give emphasis to the prayer which will follow in vv. 14–21. In fact, there is no matching verb to follow the name until v. 13, which introduces the prayer. Likewise, the mention of him as a *prisoner for Christ Jesus* is not a piece of self-advertisement but a reminder to his readers (or else, his disciple's reminder) of his credentials as apostle *on behalf of you Gentiles,* as in 2 Timothy 2:9–10.

Paul writes to a company of believers to whom he is unknown (1:15). Nevertheless he assumes that it is certain that they have heard of his ministry (3:2) and his commission of special responsibility in God's plan (1:10) to bring into being a worldwide church (3:9) composed of believing Jews and Gentiles.

The apostle came to understand the truth of God's intention early in his Christian life (see Acts 9:15–16; 22:21; 26:17) and refers to it in the term *revelation.* This reference harks back to the Damascus road encounter with the living Lord and its sequel (Gal. 1:16). Then he was given

some insight into the divine purpose for the church and his life, and he has outlined in the previous part of this letter (2:13–22) the basis for his mission to the Gentiles. This explains the tense of the verb *I have written* (Gk. *proegrapsa*), which is to be regarded as epistolary aorist. That is, the writer puts himself in the place of his readers at the time when the composition is actually read by them. So the notion of an earlier letter to which this verb is then made to refer (suggested by E. J. Goodspeed) is not required. Paul has in view what he has just written (so Schlier, who illustrates *briefly* by referring to Heb. 13:22; 1 Peter 5:12).

The *mystery* (cf. 1:9) in v. 4 relates to the inclusion of the Gentiles in a church wherein all barriers of race are broken down (see on 2:14,17,18). Earlier periods of history even within the life of the Jewish people, failed to recognize the embracing purpose of God, although hints had been given as, for example, in the promise to Abraham (Gen. 12:1–3), which Paul exploits in his argument with the Judaizers at Galatia (Gal. 3:8,9). What was once hidden and unrecognized, namely, that there should be one, holy, universal, apostolic church, is now entrusted to the preachers of the Gentile mission by the Holy Spirit.

Alternatively, v. 5 reflects the conviction of a post-Pauline group that only the apostolic preachers of the Pauline churches had grasped the truth of a world church, and it is *their* claim (in the phrase *holy apostles and prophets*) that they stand in succession to those preachers on whom they confer an aura of sanctity in the title *holy.* This phrase is appealed to as evidence of the "incipient catholicism" reflected in this letter. But this argument is not decisive, and *holy* may be used simply to distinguish Christian leaders (as in 2:20) from the "sons of men" (mankind in general) in v. 5.

By contrast with 2:12,19, which depicted the sad condition and bleak prospect of Gentiles outside the national covenant, those same disinherited and disadvantaged races are now in Christ sharers in all the blessings promised to the Jews (1:18). The wealth of their new inheritance is spelled out clearly by the use of a triad of terms all of which have the same prefix (Gk., *sun*). J. Armitage Robinson aptly translates: "The Gentiles are now co-heirs, concorporate, co-partakers of the Promise." It is a fine statement of the *gospel* of a universal society of Christian brotherhood.

2. Paul's Calling and How He Fulfilled It (3:7–13)

⁷ Of this gospel I was made a minister according to the gift of God's grace which was given me by the working of his power. ⁸ To me, though I am the very least of all the saints, this grace was given, to preach to the Gentiles the unsearchable riches of Christ, ⁹ and to make all men see what is the plan of the mystery hidden for ages in God who created all things; ¹⁰ that through the church the manifold wisdom of God might now be made known to the principalities and powers in the heavenly places. ¹¹ This was according to the eternal purpose which he has realized in Christ Jesus our Lord, ¹² in whom we have boldness and confidence of access through our faith in him. ¹³ So I ask you not to lose heart over what I am suffering for you, which is your glory.

For the accomplishment of his God-appointed service (of which 2 Tim. 1:11 speaks) Paul, like all who are called to Christ's service in his church in every age, needed the gift of divine *grace*. This is a multipurpose word in Paul's vocabulary. In 2:5 it speaks of the unmerited love and mercy of God shown to needy men. But here the thought is different. As in 2 Corinthians 12:9, it stands for divine power for the enablement of God's work in service. So Paul the *minister* (*diakonos,* our word "deacon"; but here more general for any Christian servant of God) is glad to be equipped for the work of the ministry.

In a telling snatch of personal autobiography and self-revelation, Paul confesses to his own inadequacy and need. The Greek text offers an interesting sidelight on this. With the use of a reinforced superlative rendered in the RSV *the very least of all the saints* (lit. lower than the lowest of all God's people), he reflects on his past life as a persecutor of the church (Acts 8:1; 9:1; Gal. 1:13,23; Phil. 3:6; 1 Tim. 1:13). If the sight of his painful past infamy flashed at that moment before his mind's eye, this may explain a phrase of self-depreciation which C. L. Mitton regards as "calmly deliberate, even self-conscious and a little theatrical." ²¹

The apostle, moreover, rejoices in the supply of God's power to enable him to achieve his task of preaching *to the Gentiles* a message which he characteristically describes as *the unsearchable riches of Christ.* The adjective rendered *unsearchable* is found only once again in the New Testament. At Romans 11:33 it describes the unfathomable ways of God.

A further purpose in v. 9 expresses the precise content of that untracked wealth in Christ. As in 1:18 the Pauline thought embraces a variety of metaphors. There is a rich vein of spiritual truth waiting to be discovered and appropriated—and then, shared with others. But both Christian preachers and those to whom they go as ambassadors need illumination to give them the capacity to appreciate what these riches are. So Paul's apostolic task is to enlighten all men by the unveiling of God's redemptive plan, once concealed (v. 5) but now brought out into the light. This is the *mystery* (see comment on 1:9,17); and the church on earth, under Paul's leadership, is summoned to be a witness to it and at the same time a vehicle of it to the nations.

The church's gospel is addressed to men and women. But there is another dimension in Paul's thinking, expressed in vv. 9–10. And he writes of it in a way which has puzzled commentators and exegetes. The dimension takes in a nonhuman, cosmically oriented realm of angelic intelligences,

²¹ C. L. Mitton, *The Epistle to the Ephesians* (Oxford: University Press, 1951), p. 15. The congruence of this statement of Paul's humility with his other personal remarks in 1 Cor. 15:9 and 1 Tim. 1:12–16 lays a basis for any realistic assessment of the ministerial office, as the present writer has argued in the book *My Call to Preach,* ed. C. A. Joyce (London: Marshall, Morgan and Scott, 1968), pp. 61–67.

known as *the principalities and powers.* [22]

These spiritual agencies also receive the news of Christ's victory, and are held not only in wonder but subjection. For the gospel message reaches them only to sound their defeat (cf. 1 Cor. 2:8; Col. 2:15) and announce that the action of God in Christ for salvation has a cosmic ramification; it has brought to an end the malign regime of these spirits and their tyranny in the shape of "fate" and astrological fear over human life (see comment on 1:21–22).

Certainly later in the letter Paul will write realistically of the church's conflict with these (potentially defeated) enemies (6:12). They are thought of here, however, as already subjugated in *the eternal purpose* of God because to them God's wisdom in Christ's cross displays his *manifold* (lit., multi-colored) *wisdom,* to dazzle them by its sheer simplicity and apparent weakness (1 Cor. 2:6 ff.).

But this weakness of God (1 Cor. 1:25) which allowed his Son to be crucified by the design of these agencies (2 Cor. 13:4) was the divine strategy, for "he lives by the power of God" to receive their homage as the cosmic Christ, Ruler of all creation (Phil 2:9–11).

Admittedly the language, concepts, and imagery of vv. 9–11 are difficult to hold together in a realistic way, and there is need to see the relevance of Christ's control of all alien powers in the universe which would threaten and terrify human life. Yet Paul never loses sight of the role of *the church* on earth in all this cosmic, even dualistic, picture language; and at v. 12 the scene switches to the church on earth as Christians are reminded that "they owe to Jesus Christ their Lord the distinctive characteristics of their new spiritual state" (Masson) *through our faith in him.* In this way Paul has extracted the spiritual and

practical value for believers from a cosmically oriented background, and brought the truth of Christ's supra-terrestrial work to a personal application in his doctrine of reconciliation and fellowship with God. As in the earlier allusion (2:18), for Paul the chief element in this dramatic presentation was that no hostile power can separate the church from God the Father, since Christ's triumph over all the enemies first-century man most feared spells the end of fate's control over man's destiny.

At v. 13 the RSV offers one possibility of translation out of many. The exegetical difficulty centers on what is the proper subject of the verb *lose heart.* The Greek is cryptic and compressed; and it could mean that Paul is asking his readers to pray that he will not become discouraged, as in 2 Corinthians 4:1,6, which have the same verb. Otherwise, it may yield the sense that they themselves may not become despondent because of his imprisonment on their behalf (3:1). On balance, the present RSV reading seems best.

3. Paul's Prayer for the Church (3:14–21)

14 For this reason I bow my knees before the Father, 15 from whom every family in heaven and on earth is named, 16 that according to the riches of his glory he may grant you to be strengthened with might through his Spirit in the inner man, 17 and that Christ may dwell in your hearts through faith; that you, being rooted and grounded in love, 18 may have power to comprehend with all the saints what is the breadth and length and height and depth, 19 and to know the love of Christ which surpasses knowledge, that you may be filled with all the fulness of God.

20 Now to him who by the power at work within us is able to do far more abundantly than all that we ask or think, 21 to him be glory in the church and in Christ Jesus to all generations, for ever and ever. Amen.

In any event, Paul is requesting the prayers of his readers partly on the ground of the freedom of access to God which they, as Gentiles, now enjoy; and partly because they have a special place in his ministry. He is "their" apostle, and so he can confi-

22 Two monographs with roughly the same title taken from this text may be mentioned for further elucidation: G. B. Caird, *Principalities and Powers* (Oxford: University Press, 1956); H. Schlier, *Principalities and Powers in the New Testament* (Edinburgh-London: Thomas Nelson, 1961).

dently count on their intercession for him.

The opening words of vv. 14–15 take us back to v. 1, which they complete by adding the necessary verb. This understanding is to be preferred to the view which links v. 14 with v. 13. It is best to see a resumption of the apostle's thoughtful concern for his readers as he speaks of his prayer to the Father for them. Nor should we miss the intensity of his regard expressed in the posture of prayer: *I bow my knees.* Jews normally stood to pray (Matt. 6:5; Luke 18:11,13). Kneeling for prayer was a sign of great urgency and distress.[23]

Again, we should not overlook the appellation *Father,* which is the distinctively Christian name for God, derived from the example of Jesus (Mark 14:36) and his teaching (Luke 11:2). His Aramaic term *Abba* (meaning "dear Father") secured a firm place in the liturgical language of Gentile churches, as in Asia Minor and elsewhere (Rom. 8:15; Gal. 4:6).

God as Father sets a pattern, for his fatherhood is the archetype of all family life, according to v. 15. The exact interpretation of the verse is, however, in doubt. It seems that Paul is consciously mindful of the distinction drawn in Jewish literature between two aspects of divine fatherhood. The rabbis spoke of "the upper family," meaning the world of angels. This matches Paul's designation *every family in heaven.* And they alluded to Israel as "our family." The Pauline phrase *on earth* is best understood in this light, as the apostle's bold appropriation of a title proudly claimed by Jews, but which he reinterprets in the light of 2:18. Both Jews and Gentiles now make up God's family in the fellowship of a united, single church.

The content of this petition is twofold. He prays for the empowering of the Holy Spirit, whom he calls in to fortify the Christian's "inner life" especially in time of trial (see Col. 1:11; Phil 1:19). The best commentary on *inner man* is 2 Corinthians 4:16.

The complementary member of this petition is an invocation of the indwelling Christ who comes to make his home (Gk. *katoikeō,* which looks back to 2:22, where the noun is "dwelling place," *katoikētērion*). This correspondence between v. 17 and 2:22 confirms the view that there is no great difference between the action of the Spirit on the inner man and Christ's habitation in believers' hearts. C. Masson aptly cites A. Monod on verse 17*a:* "It is the same grace seen from another side."

The indwelling Lord is the assurance of the Christian's moral strength (Phil. 4:13). Certain consequences follow from the fulfillment of the apostle's prayer which has, as its frontispiece, a combination of metaphors which are also found together at 2:21 and Colossians 2:7. *Rooted* is a horticultural term denoting the firm bed in which plants are set. *Grounded* (from the verb *themelioō;* cf. the Greek noun *themelios,* meaning foundation, in 2:20) borrows from the language of architecture, and ensures a strong base on which a superstructure rests and rises. *Love* (i.e., God's love for the church, as in Col. 2:7) is both the soil in which the plant thrives and the firm ground on which the building stands.

Metaphors from the physical world now give way to images drawn from the intellectual and moral universe. The verbs *comprehend* and *know* are combined with little distinction of meaning, except that the qualifying phrase added to the *with all the saints* ("all God's people," NEB) is a reminder that this knowledge is not reserved for any special class of Christians, as the Gnostics were later to claim. Nor does Paul know of any private mystical experience in isolation from the company of believers in the church's fellowship.

The objects of knowledge for which he prays are (1) God's redemptive plan in all its richness and profundity and (2) Christ's love of which this redemptive enterprise is the consummate expression. Indeed, so amazing is that love which God's purpose for his church in the world reveals that it

[23] See R. P. Martin, *Carmen Christi: Philippians 2:5–11,* pp. 264 f. for the significance of this posture with reference to biblical and extra-biblical literature.

eludes our full grasp. Just because it is so variegated (a thought suggested by *the breadth and length and height and depth,* which is a poetic way of enlarging upon the infinite variety of God's purpose),[24] it *surpasses knowledge.* Yet at the same time its attraction beckons us on to a progressive experience as we are more and more filled "up to the measure of" God's fullness. This is the force of the Greek preposition *eis* (RSV, *with*) in verse 19*b*.

A splendid doxology comparable with Romans 16:25 ff.; Hebrews 13:20–21; and Jude 24 f. rounds off the apostolic prayer. It celebrates the church's confidence that God is both able and willing to do all that Paul's prayer asks for. Indeed, by the use of a rare adverb (Gk., *huperekperissou: far more abundantly*—a translation like "infinitely more" as popularly used brings out the real sense of this adverb), Paul expresses the thought that God's intention is to exceed by his answer even the far-ranging petitions of his prayer and even the aspirations which have prompted them. Martin Luther somewhere offers the dictum that we pray for silver, and God gives us gold.

The secret of this confidence is that God's power is *at work* in the church in which his fullness dwells by the presence of Christ and the Spirit (2:22; 3:17). And Paul knows that secret in his own life (Col. 1:29). Fittingly, at the close of this lofty thought, praise is ascribed to God who is present both in Christ (uniquely so, since he is the embodiment of deity, Col. 2:3) and the church (which, as Christ's body, is intimately associated with him, 1:23; 4:15–16; 5:30). But for Paul in this letter Christ and his church are not two separate entities but are so closely conjoined that it would be permissible to write of one corporate whole, Christ-in-his-church. It is be-

cause of this indwelling and empowering presence that *glory* can be offered to God eternally.

VII. The Church's Vocation as Christ's Body (4:1–16)

So far in his address to his Gentile congregations Paul has expounded the way in which God's purpose was conceived and executed. In a sentence, this says that believers have been brought from death to life; and both Jewish and Gentile Christians form one, single church. Furthermore, this intention of God to have one people corresponding to one head, Christ, was realized chiefly through Paul's mission—though the plan stretched back to God's eternal decree. Now Paul is able to look back on the accomplishment of that mission during his lifetime of Christian service.

But the ideal of one head–one body needs an empirical application to the churches which are made up of ordinary men and women in the world of Greek and Roman culture. So, from the exposition of the place of the church in God's redeeming purpose for the world by the preaching of the gospel, Paul now turns to the practical outworking of this ideal in everyday living. To use a technical but useful expression, his concern in the remainder of the letter is with "exhortation" (*parenesis*) and "encouragement" (*paraklēsis*).[25]

This division of the letter helps our understanding. Having laid a foundation in a theological exposition of the theme Christ-in-his-church, Paul now takes up his practical purpose as he sets before his readers the guidelines of Christian conduct and deportment in the world. But before he gets involved with details, he must first give an overall picture of what is to be the church's calling in the world. This is the particular interest of 4:1–16.

Because this section functions as a frontispiece to the balance of the letter, its structure must be noticed here. The charac-

---

24 These terms became familiar names for "the eternal dimensions of the Deity" in Gnostic religion (G. Johnston, *Commentary,* "The Century Bible" [London: Thomas Nelson, 1967]), ad loc. But it would be unneccessary to find a background to this text in this astrological vocabulary in spite of the formal similarity. See the cautions offered by W. L. Knox, *St. Paul and the Church of the Gentiles* (Cambridge: University Press, 1939), p. 192 n.1.

25 For these terms in the New Testament literature, we may refer to A. M. Hunter, *Paul and His Predecessors,* 2nd ed. (London: SCM Press, 1961), ch. 6.

teristic note is struck in v. 1 as Paul calls his readers to be true to their destiny in the light of the following: (1) Their place within a church which by definition is one (vv. 2–6); (2) yet unity does not mean a monochrome, deadpan uniformity, which would be true if the church were a thing, an inert and static object. (3) But the church is an organism, pulsating with life and made up of living persons who are responsible for growth of character and personality, according to their use of the gifts which Christ has bestowed (v. 7). (4) His purpose is that the church shall reach "mature manhood" (v. 13), and to that end he has prepared gifts to be exercised through his servants (vv. 8–12). (5) The church's progress is marked by a growth out of infancy into maturity as it takes on the character of its head, Christ (vv. 14–16).

1. The Church's Calling in the Light of Its Unity (4:1–6)

¹ I therefore, a prisoner for the Lord, beg you to lead a life worthy of the calling to which you have been called, ² with all lowliness and meekness, with patience, forbearing one another in love, ³ eager to maintain the unity of the Spirit in the bond of peace. ⁴ There is one body and one Spirit, just as you were called to the one hope that belongs to your call, ⁵ one Lord, one faith, one baptism, ⁶ one God and Father of us all, who is above all and through all and in all.

Therefore connects Paul's appeal with what has gone before (as in Rom. 12:1; Col. 3:1; 1 Thess. 4:1). The Christian's *calling* is God's summons to him answered at conversion (Phil. 3:14); and his response is to be worked out in his subsequent behavior patterns. *Lead a life* is literally "walk," which picks up the Hebrew idiom for everyday conduct (cf. Psalm 1). *Worthy* (cf. Phil. 1:27) shows the connection between God's plan and the Christian's acceptance of it, spelled out in terms of his daily living. For the same ethical incentive, we may compare Colossians 1:10; 1 Thessalonians 2:12.

The tone and temper of the believer's life and deportment are set out in v. 2. The

moral qualities therein described are best understood as the fruit of the Spirit in view of Galatians 5:22–23. They are completed by the encouragement Paul gives *to maintain the unity of the Spirit* (i.e., the unity the Spirit makes possible by his activity within the church, as in v. 4 and 1 Cor. 12:13) *in the bond of peace.* Two matters are stated here. First, there is a unity which the Holy Spirit creates. Second, Christians have a responsibility to cherish it by their harmonious relationships. *In the bond of peace* is a phrase which denotes how the unity is preserved; it is "made fast with bonds of peace" (cf. NEB) forged by the reconciling work of Christ himself.[26]

Verses 4–6 further define what the Spirit's gift of unity implies; and they do so by a series of creedlike formulations, all of them being given emphasis by the repetition (seven times) of the term *one.* Moreover, the three parts of v. 4 are matched by corresponding partners in the next verse, thus forming a triad of couplets. We can best display this diagrammatically:

one body (the church)—*one Lord* (the church's head)

one Spirit—*one faith* (as he calls men to acknowledge Jesus Christ: 1 Cor. 12:3, and baptizes them into one body: 1 Cor. 12:13)

one hope (accepted by the confession of baptism)—*one baptism*

After this trinity of unities Paul seals this creedal statement with a trinitarian reference to *one God* who is known in his self-revelation as Father *above all,* as Son *through all* (the preposition answers to concept of mediation, as in 2:18), and as Spirit who is *in all* the family of God.

This triad and its subsequent trinitarian statement is often regarded as an early Christian baptismal creed enshrining the chief elements of a confession of faith made in baptism. The new convert renounced the

26 So S. Hanson, *op. cit.* p. 149. Cf. 2:17. This view is to be preferred to the translation which makes the bond one of concord between Christians (so W. Foerster in *TDNT,* I, 417).

worship of many gods in his adherence to one Lord.

The convert made profession of his acceptance of *one faith,* originally in its elemental form, Jesus Christ is Lord (1 Cor. 12:3; Rom. 10:9). It was later expanded in more specific terms.[27] The occasion on which this confession was made was baptism, here called *one baptism* [28] in contrast to the diverse lustrations of pagan mystery religions, or possibly Jewish proselyte baptism (as in Heb. 6:2) or even a deviationist baptismal practice like that adopted by John's disciples near Ephesus in Acts 19: 1-7.

One God (v. 6) picks up the Old Testament and Jewish creedal statements of the unity of God (Deut. 6:4 f.), but Christianizes it by the addition of the name *Father.* The latter is the distinctive title of God revealed in Jesus and understood by *us all* (i.e., Christians), though the Greek word rendered "us" is a scribal addition absent from the best texts. It has probably crept in from 1 Corinthians 8:6. Nonetheless the following word *all* (Gk. *pasin*) is certainly to be understood here as a personal not a neuter reference (so Masson).

2. Christ's Gift and the Church's Gifts (4:7-12)

[7] But grace was given to each of us according to the measure of Christ's gift. [8] Therefore it is said,
"When he ascended on high he led a host of captives, and he gave gifts to men."
[9] (In saying, "He ascended," what does it mean but that he had also descended into the lower parts of the earth? [10] He who descended is he who also ascended far above all the heavens, that he might fill all things.) [11] And his gifts were that some should be apostles,

---

[27] For examples of the later expanded versions, see R. P. Martin, *Worship in the Early Church* (Old Tappan, N. J.: Revell, 1964), pp. 53-65.
[28] Much has been made of this phrase in support of a notion of a general baptism of mankind at Calvary by O. Cullmann, *Baptism in the New Testament* (London: SCM Press, 1950) and J. A. T. Robinson, "The One Baptism" in *Twelve New Testament Studies* (London: SCM Press, 1962), pp. 158-175. There is an effective reply to this proposal, from a Baptist standpoint, by W. E. Moore, "One Baptism," *New Testament Studies,* 10, 1963-64, pp. 504-516.

some prophets, some evangelists, some pastors and teachers, [12] for the equipment of the saints, for the work of ministry, for building up the body of Christ,

The grammatically singular word *gift* in v. 7 is the key to this difficult passage. It needs to be interpreted along with the term *grace* in the same verse. *Grace* is not an allusion to 2:6,8 but rather to those other places in Pauline writing where the same Greek expression (*charis*) refers to the Spirit's gifts to the church (Rom. 12:3 ff.; 1 Cor. 12:4 ff.). What Paul has here in mind is the part which all Christians are to play in the life of the body of Christ. There are no exceptions, for all in the church are the members of his body and as such endowed with some gift-by-grace (*charisma*). It is the ascended Lord who has bestowed these gifts by first sending his gift par excellence, namely, the Holy Spirit (see John 7:39; 20:22; Acts 2:33). The bestowal of the Holy Spirit at Pentecost is in view in the aorist tense of the verb Paul uses (assuming that the verb expresses punctiliar action), *was given.* The tense looks back to a particular occasion when the exalted Lord gave to his church, though some commentators prefer to find a subjective element in the occasion behind the verb *was given,* at baptism.

The Scripture citation which follows poses a number of difficulties. While it derives from Psalm 68:18 (LXX, Psalm 67: 19), the reading does not conform to the Hebrew text. Rather it adapts the original in such a way that the resultant text closely follows the reading of the Syriac version known as the Peshitta:

"Thou didst ascend on high,
And take captivity captive;
And thou gavest gifts to men."

Another version, similar to this one, is found in the Aramaic paraphrase version known as the Targum. This shows that the sense of "he gave to men" (in contrast to the LXX, "thou didst receive") was an old Jewish interpretation on which Paul is evidently drawing in this citation.[29] The Targum refers the text to Moses as the one who gave the law to men.

The apostle's application of this text is to Christ's ascension. Scholars are, however, divided over the logical connection between the descent and ascent of Christ. The point at issue turns on whether the description he *descended into the lower parts of the earth* relates to Christ's coming from heaven to earth in the incarnation (so NEB) or to a descent to the underworld after his death (see NEB marg.).

G. B. Caird[30] has offered an attractive, third possibility. He interprets the "descent" which follows—in his view, chronologically —the ascent of Christ as the coming of the Holy Spirit at Pentecost. At that time, in the realistic way of 2 Corinthians 3:17 (cf. John 14:15–18) the Lord returned to earth, laden with gifts for his church. Acts 2:33 speaks of the Holy Spirit as the gift of the exalted Lord. It is he—and not Moses, as in the Jewish Targum—who has inaugurated the new age of grace (cf. John 1:17), and it is he who has given to the church all the varied ministries which serve to upbuild the church's life (vv. 11–12). The thrust of this use made of the Old Testament is clear. Christ's enthronement over the universe leads to the imparting of the Spirit (see for a parallel connection John 16:7); and with the gift of the Spirit all the gifts of Christ to the church are enfolded, ensuring that nothing needful is lacking for the equipment of the church's life and witness. To confirm this interpretation we may comment that v. 11 should literally be translated: "And it was he [Gk. *autos*, as an emphatic pronoun—the One who fulfilled the prediction of Psalm 68] who gave." The grace-gifts of v. 7 are now spelled out in terms of the church's ministries.

Apostles and *prophets* hold first place in the list, as in 1 Corinthians 12:28 (cf.

Didache 11:3). The reason for this prominence is given in 2:20, namely that these leaders in the early church bore witness to the incarnate and risen Lord and were the vehicles through which he continued to express his mind to the church. *Evangelists* were men like Philip (Acts 21:8) and Timothy (2 Tim. 4:5) in the apostolic church, though the term denotes a function more than an office.[31]

The construction of the phrase *pastors and teachers* with one definite article in the Greek to cover both words is interesting. It suggests that there were two functions shared by the same individuals, whose chief task is described in Acts 20:28. These men would be local congregational leaders in charge of established churches which had been brought into existence by the preaching of the apostles and others. We may compare Acts 14:23 where "elders" corresponds to those church leaders addressed by Paul in Acts 20:17.

From vv. 12–13 Paul makes it plain that the bestowal of Christ's gifts of the ministry has a specific purpose in view. This is that all God's people (called here *the saints*) may be equipped by the functions which his servants perform in order that they in turn may discharge their service as Christians in the world. The consequence is that by this interplay of a regular ministry, ordained and appointed by the Head of the church, and the rank and file of the church, Christ's body may be built up. This is a complicated thought, but it is necessary to express it in this way, if we would do justice to the subtle use of prepositions in this short passage. The RSV, by its punctuation, tries to respect these usages. To be sure, there is room for diversity of opinion even so. A possible view sees the task of the apostles, etc., (v. 11) as one of equipping Christians in general for their work of service so that

29 For a fuller discussion of these textual problems, see E. E. Ellis, *Paul's Use of the Old Testament* (Edinburgh: Oliver and Boyd, 1957), pp. 15 f.

30 "The Descent of Christ in Ephesians 4,7–11" in *Studia Evangelica II*, i (Berlin: Akademie-Verlag, 1964), pp. 535–545.

31 So G. Friedrich (*TDNT*, II, 733 ff.). The discussion of church ministries by A. Harnack in his *Mission and Expansion of Christianity* (New York: G. P. Putnam's Sons, 1908), I, pp. 319–368, is still worth mentioning. He discusses also the later meanings given to "evangelists" in Eusebius, *Church History* III. 37.2; V. 10.2.

the latter may build up Christ's body.

Alternatively, we may follow S. Hanson [32] and accept that the drift of Paul's thought is rather that it is the apostolic ministry which prepares God's people and in so doing it edifies the whole body. This makes the apostolic work a necessary part of the church's ongoing life and would accord with a more developed structure of organizational pattern of church and ministry which is found in subapostolic writers like I Clement and Ignatius. C. Masson accepts this setting for the doctrine of the ministry in Ephesians, remarking that in this epistle *the saints* do not edify the church, but are themselves edified (see on v. 16).

3. The Church's Path to Maturity (4:13–16)

13 until we all attain to the unity of the faith and of the knowledge of the Son of God, to mature manhood, to the measure of the stature of the fulness of Christ; 14 so that we may no longer be children, tossed to and fro and carried about with every wind of doctrine, by the cunning of men, by their craftiness in deceitful wiles. 15 Rather, speaking the truth in love, we are to grow up in every way into him who is the head, into Christ, 16 from whom the whole body, joined and knit together by every joint with which it is supplied, when each part is working properly, makes bodily growth and upbuilds itself in love.

The "unity of the Spirit" (v. 3) is a present experience shared by Christians as they reflect on their common allegiance to one Lord. But *the unity of the faith* is clearly here an object of hope one day to be attained. The work of the ministers who are Christ's gifts to the church has this end in view, namely that the church will be built up until its final state is reached. That goal is denoted by the phrase *mature manhood* (Gk. *anēr teleios*, complete man) and is reached as Christians make progress in their united understanding of and laying hold on the riches which are theirs in Christ. The connecting word *and* is best interpreted as explanatory, so that *the unity of the faith*

consists in a deeper insight (Greek *epignōsis*, which RSV translates *knowledge*) into Christ himself as the embodiment of God's treasure (cf. Col. 3:2; and we may refer to earlier verses in this epistle, 1:18; 2:4; 3:8) and the supplier of the church's needs as its Head (1:22–23).

The master theme of these verses is growth. But Paul is concerned that this enlargement of the church shall be along right lines, by an increasing approximation of believers to the likeness of Christ. He ensures that the believers shall do just this by inserting the phrase *to the measure of the stature of the fulness of Christ.* The Greek term rendered *stature* could be translated "age," which would link up with the idea of maturity and prepare for the ensuing thought of v. 14, but the picture of physical growth by the church's expansion seems the dominant image in the passage as a whole. *The fulness of Christ* recalls to the readers the availability of his grace and resources which are made over to the church to aid its growth until it reaches his designed end, which is a fully completed church embodying all his fullness. [33]

Certain tests of the church's increasing maturity are given in vv. 14,15. Christians will no longer remain infantile. The word *children* means infants, and stands in contrast to *mature manhood* in v. 13. Nor will they be lacking in stability when subjected to stress and strain. The description *tossed to and fro* may suggest a nautical picture of a ship battered by angry seas (Luke 8:24 speaks of "raging waves," using the same Greek word). Nor will believers be led astray into false teaching which heretical leaders will seek to promote (see Heb. 13:9; Jude 12 for similar wording). At the back of these errors are men who cherish evil designs and practice underhand ways. Second Corinthians 2:17 offers a parallel

---

32 S. Hanson, *The Unity of the Church in the New Testament: Colossians and Ephesians* (Lund: ASNU 14, 1946), p. 157.

33 C. Schneider (*TDNT*, II, 943) writes: The church's "perfect form is achieved when all who are appointed to it by the divine plan of salvation belong to the church. The emphasis is in the words *all we.* The Church, which is the body of Christ, represents in its perfected form the *plērōma* (fullness) of Christ."

with its allusion to Jewish teachers who later in that epistle are branded as "crafty" (2 Cor. 11:3). Paul himself had been accused of this practice of cunning ways (2 Cor. 4:2), and here he returns to self-defense by an oblique assertion of his own orthodoxy.

One final metaphor of the church's life in the world completes the presentation. The call to *grow up* is the most natural way to round off the section. This growth is to be *in love* which goes better with the verb to *grow up* than with *speaking the truth.* The reason for this choice is that the Greek verb rendered *speaking the truth* (*alē-theuontes*) means "dealing truly" (ERV marg.). The translation "practicing the truth" is preferred by some commentators, citing Galatians 4:16 (RSV marg.). In either case, the operative phrase is "in love," which defines the attitude of Christians in their social and personal relationships. It suggests a combination of concern for others in need and a care which expresses itself in tangible help. The church's striving for social justice in the world as God's instrument is certainly a necessary part of its vocation. And such a clarion call saves the definition of "growing up into Christ" from lapsing into a sentimental and unrealistic pietism.

Guided by Colossians 2:19 we may interpret the line of thought in v. 16 as the supply the church receives from Christ its head. That simple idea is, however, compounded by the strange paradox of associations which suggest a double movement. As the church derives its life from him who supplies all its need, its growth is naturally from him. But Paul adds the notion that the church grows toward Christ. This striking combination of ideas which are difficult to conceptualize should put us on our guard against expecting a neat, logical analogy between Christ's body and the human body (based on our recall of 1 Cor. 12:14 ff.). Apostolic teaching here is more complex than in the Corinthians passage; and the understanding of the church's life and progress toward Christ is hardly compatible with the hope of an *immediate* end-of-the-

age scheme which includes such ideas as the catching up of the church out of the world (1 Thess. 4:16–17) or even the eschatological prospects in Colossians 3:4. Some scholars drive this shift of emphasis on eschatology to the point of affirming that ecclesiology in Ephesians has replaced eschatology, especially Masson when he writes: "Already united with Christ as the body to the head, the church grows toward Christ. The church no longer expects him to come to it" (*L'épître aux Ephésiens,* p. 199). This implies that while the hope of a final consummation of all things is not in any way denied, the expectation of an *imminent* return of Christ is not prominently in view in this epistle.

Summing up a difficult verse, made even more complex by some turgid Greek constructions, we may remark that (1) Christ's body is made up of many members (Rom. 12:4–5; 1 Cor. 12:12) who, although different in obvious ways, yet are part of one body, which is the universal church. In 2:21 it is likened to a holy temple built by many stones. (2) The church grows by the action of Christ on its behalf. And he exerts a unifying action on the body by means of his work through *every joint* which he supplies. This last thought takes us back to v. 11 and makes possible the equation of *every joint* with Christ's gift of the ministry. Christ works through the ministers; and they in turn have a responsibility to see that *each part is working properly.* That is, each church member fulfills his task in the life of the corporate whole.

(3) By this chain reaction of Christ-his-ministers-his-people, the whole body is edified as *love* becomes the "atmosphere" in which this process of mutual encouragement and responsibility is exercised, with each part of the church playing the role appointed for it. Christ the head imparts his risen life and bestows by the Spirit his gifts of ministries. His ministers fulfill their mission by equipping the saints (v. 12) and being the ligaments (the Greek *haphē* is a medical term) of the church's cohesion to Christ and one another. Christ's people

make the contribution (which is the sense of the Greek *meros,* RSV *part*) needful for Christ's design to be realized for the body's upbuilding and growth into him. And above all, it is a growth in love (cf. 1 Cor. 8:1).

VIII. A Statement of the Christian's Personal Conduct (4:17–32)

Scholars have in recent years devoted a good deal [34] of attention to the ethical teaching of the New Testament. One fruitful line of enquiry has been a comparative study of the various motifs which are found as an encouragement to Christian morality, both personal and social. One of these ethical principles is the contrast between the old life characterized by pagan ways, and the new outlook and behavior pattern which Christians accepted at their conversion and baptism, which marked a clean break and a new beginning. Second Corinthians 5:17 states the contrast clearly. Elsewhere, in Paul, it is expressed by the phrase, "no longer . . . but now." A second ethical command to which the apostle appealed with great effect is couched in the form, *Put off the old nature . . . put on the new nature;* and Galatians 3:27 roots this call in the baptismal experience.

This section of the letter in which Paul turns more specifically to the actual congregations of the Gentile churches in Asia Minor illustrates both types of moral appeal. Formerly his readers adopted the only way of life they knew, namely the pagan outlook and practice vividly depicted in vv. 17–19. But at conversion they exchanged—for many of them in a dramatic renunciation—these evil practices and took on a new deportment which vitally affected their character and manners. Verses 28–32 powerfully recall the change with an insistent summons not to relapse into former ways. The other appeal (put off . . . put on) is expressed in the terms Paul uses (vv. 22–25) and has an obvious, pointed application to Christian conduct which exemplifies the

[34] Cf. the pioneer study by P. Carrington, *The Primitive Christian Catechism* (Cambridge: University Press, 1940).

new life imparted by the living Christ to his people.

1. Some Principles Which Govern Christian Conduct (4:17–24)

[17] Now this I affirm and testify in the Lord, that you must no longer live as the Gentiles do, in the futility of their minds; [18] they are darkened in their understanding, alienated from the life of God because of the ignorance that is in them, due to their hardness of heart; [19] they have become callous and have given themselves up to licentiousness, greedy to practice every kind of uncleanness. [20] You did not so learn Christ!—[21] assuming that you have heard about him and were taught in him, as the truth is in Jesus. [22] Put off your old nature which belongs to your former manner of life and is corrupt through deceitful lusts, [23] and be renewed in the spirit of your minds, [24] and put on the new nature, created after the likeness of God in true righteousness and holiness.

The Gentile (i.e., pagan, whether pre-Christian or non-Christian) way of life is painted in some sombre colors which recall Romans 1:18–32. Paul fastens on the root cause of the idolatry and excesses which disfigured life in the first-century Graeco-Roman world with a pointed allusion to idol worship in contemporary religion. *Futility* suggests this, meaning the veneration of dead vanities (Acts 14:15, which picks up the Old Testament condemnation of worthless, lifeless idols, Psalm 115). Idolatry can take on several forms and the worship of idols can be expresed in erroneous thinking and wrongful desiring (Col. 3:5) as well as overt acts. "Depraved reason" (NEB) sums up the root of what leads to idolatry, as in Romans 1:28.

Two consequences follow. Unregenerate man has his understanding (of spiritual realities) darkened, and he suffers alienation from God caused by his culpable ignorance and refusal to submit himself to God. This process of resistance leads inevitably to a deadness and insensitivity to God, called by Paul *hardness of heart.*

Man's relationship with God as a sinner has its direct repercussions in his daily behavior and his relations with his fellowmen. Verse 19 pointedly indicates that a *hardness of heart* to God shows itself in a moral insensibility which in turn produces a lax moral code and a sensual gratification of all the appetites without restraint or consideration of others. *Greedy* represents a Greek noun (*pleonexia*) often linked with immoral ways (1 Cor. 5:10–11; 6:10; Col. 3:5), and this may be sensed here especially as *licentiousness* (NEB, vice) and *uncleanness* have just been mentioned. And the association of *pleonexia* with irresponsible sexual excess in 5:3 confirms this interpretation.

Verse 20 implies a contrast which the RSV fails to bring out. We should paraphrase: "But that way of life doesn't fit in with a life in Christ." That life was begun when the readers became disciples of Christ; hence the descriptive reference to learning Christ (cf. Matt. 11:28–30).

This mention of "discipleship" (which is the Latin equivalent of the Greek verb in v. 20 meaning to learn) might lead us to anticipate an enlargement of the theme of Christian instruction given to new converts prior to their baptism and admission to the church fellowship. This is precisely what we have in v. 21. Paul is pointing out the incompatability of pagan habits with the new life in Christ whose moral teaching is recalled as the basis of his readers' catechesis before they entered upon the privileges of church fellowship.

So much seems clear. But how could it be that they heard about Christ and were taught in him? The answer must lie in some catechumenate in which these new converts were trained as in the school of Christ.

Further, what does *as the truth is in Jesus* mean? We may either regard this phrase as an assurance that under Paul's tutelage, represented by his disciple in the Gentile mission, they really learned of "the authentic Christ" (so Masson) or follow the suggestion of Charles A. Scott [35] that this closing part of v. 21 should be linked with the call to abandon old ways. Support for this exegesis is found in 2 Corinthians 6:14, and in Paul's allusion to Christ's subjugation of the flesh in Colossians 2:11,15.

The *old nature* which dictated the tendencies of the believers' *former manner of life* (cf. 1 Pet. 1:18) is the willing victim of a seduction which appeals to it and leads it into evil desire. Such a seduction is made all the more easy because man's nature inherited from Adam is (according to Paul) twisted and so a prey to evil. Genesis 3 is possibly in Paul's mind (cf. 2 Cor. 11:3) in addition to the rabbinical teaching on the "evil propensity" which goads men into sin.[36]

The summons at v. 22 to put off the old nature as a suit of clothes is shed may sound like a counsel of despair, impossible of fulfillment, for fallen man is in a helpless plight. But Paul's appeal is to Christians who have known the renewal of the Spirit which, begun decisively at conversion, is a process to be continued. Hence the present tense of his admonition which calls upon his readers to be *renewed* in their minds (thus answering the need stated in vv. 17–18) by the action of the Holy Spirit. This interpretation requires us to take *spirit* as a reference to the Holy Spirit and not the human spirit. An index of the choice to be preferred is the observation that the Greek term for "spirit" (*pneuma*) is never used in Ephesians of man's spirit; and we may compare the similar wording in Titus 3:5.

Grace like nature abhors a vacuum. To divest oneself of evil habits is not enough —see the poignant, parabolic illustration of the folly of a negative religion in Matthew 12:43–45. Putting off the old nature must be followed by the donning of *the new nature,* imparted at the new birth by the Spirit and to be increasingly recognized as the dominant moral force in the Christian's life as he faces an inner conflict. We may compare Galatians 5:16 ff., which contain many of the key terms of this section. Paul's

[35] *Christianity According to St. Paul* (Cambridge: University Press 1961), p. 86.

[36] On the place of this rabbinical idea in Paul's anthropology see W. D. Davies, *Paul and Rabbinic Judaism*, 2nd (London: SPCK, 1955), pp. 20 ff.

call in v. 24 is another way of expressing the exhortation of Galatians 5:25. The new birth and the Spirit's control restore the image of God in man broken by sin (Gen. 1:27), and so give back to the sinner, now redeemed by Christ and renovated by the Holy Spirit, what he lost in Adam, namely *righteousness* (i.e., a right relationship with his creator) and *holiness* (i.e., a moral requisite for fellowship with a holy God) demanded by the truth of God. This verse well exemplifies the descriptive caption suggested by George Johnston: "The character of the New Adam." [37]

2. A Continuation of Christian Social Ethics (4:25–32)

[25] Therefore, putting away falsehood, let every one speak the truth with his neighbor, for we are members one of another. [26] Be angry but do not sin; do not let the sun go down on your anger, [27] and give no opportunity to the devil. [28] Let the thief no longer steal, but rather let him labor, doing honest work with his hands, so that he may be able to give to those in need. [29] Let no evil talk come out of your mouths, but only such as is good for edifying, as fits the occasion, that it may impart grace to those who hear. [30] And do not grieve the Holy Spirit of God, in whom you were sealed for the day of redemption. [31] Let all bitterness and wrath and anger and clamor and slander be put away from you, with all malice, [32] and be kind to one another, tenderhearted, forgiving one another, as God in Christ forgave you.

With v. 25 Paul begins a section which applies to concrete situations the principles stated earlier. Opposed to truth-telling, which is the mark of a life fashioned on likeness to God, is lying. This practice has to be discarded. Two reasons are given. First, lying is condemned in the Old Testament (Zech. 8:16 is quoted in Paul's words); second, failure to honor one's word leads to a breach of Christian fellowship because it breeds distrust and suspicion, and so destroys the common life in the body of Christ (Rom. 12:5) by which *we are members one of another.*

Verse 26 contains a Pauline text which has become proverbial—and misunder-

[37] G. Johnston, *op. cit.,* p. 20.

stood. The difficulty is cleared up if we remember that in the Greek language used in the New Testament times (so called *koinē*) the imperative mood expresses not only a command but also a requirement or a concession. Applying this rule we can see that Paul is not advocating anger but drawing a line: "You may be angry . . . if you can't help it, but do not sin thereby." His chief concern is to prevent anger from becoming an obsession. When that happens, the devil finds a loophole, for the evil one uses all devices, even by exploiting our good intentions and social concerns, to bring the church into disrepute. Hence in v. 27 Paul's name for the enemy is *diabolos* (lit., slanderer) in place of the apostle's more usual title for Satan. Second Corinthians 2:5–11 gives an apt example of the way he works in this way by leading to an excess of zeal and turning a righteously indignant attitude in the presence of evil and injustice into a fixation.

Let *the thief* renounce his occupation is the ringing call of v. 28, now that he has become a new man in Christ. Again, refusing to stay with a negative warning, Paul remarks that the Christian will have a social conscience for the needs of the poor, especially within the fellowship of his new circle (Gal. 6:10).

Words are an index of character (Matt. 12:34). *Good* words are to be chosen over *evil talk* (the same Greek adjective *sapros* is found in the record of Jesus' teaching just quoted). But how may we discern the good? The criterion is simple: Do our words build up the hearer's character and make him a better man for his having heard our speaking? Do they meet his need (*as fits the occasion* is a paraphrase of this requirement)? And do they in this way "bring a blessing" (so NEB) by supplying that need?

By contrast, foul or inappropriate language is not only an insult to the hearer. It saddens the Holy Spirit by wounding him and denying in practice the meaning of his indwelling and sanctifying presence in the believer which is a token of the

Christian's final redemption (see 1:13–14). Acts 5:1–11 provides a sad and salutary lesson of this type of speech, and is the counterpart of Paul's reminder (in 1 Cor. 8:11–13) that causing one's fellow Christian to stumble is to inflict a wound on Christ himself in his body, the church.

Mention of the misuse of the tongue leads on to a full statement of vices to be avoided and virtues to be cultivated, with the use of the spoken word running through all these admonitions (vv. 31 f.). *Malice* (Gk. *kakia,* evil) is the parent of the unhappy brood of earlier terms for quarrels and contention. But, as befits that new quality of life in Christ (Gk. *Christos*), the Christian should seek to be kind (Gk. *chrēstos*) with a compassionate and forgiving disposition which is based on the simple but amazing fact that this is the attitude which has been shown him in God's forgiveness, offered *in Christ.* We may compare 2 Corinthians 5: 19 for the sense of this phrase. Matthew 6: 12 shows how quickly this interconnection between God's forgiveness of sinners and their resultant treatment and acceptance of others became embedded in the catechetical and liturgical life of the churches.

IX. *The Christians' Conduct in the World (5:1–20)*

If we may rightly detect a change of perspective and proportion at this point in the epistle, we may describe the change as one from the Christians' behavior within the church fellowship to that of their bearing and actions in the world of society around them. From this standpoint we may pick out some of the salient features of Paul's guidance.

He is addressing his readers as God's *children* and his chosen people. But both these appellations need the tacit understanding that Christians' lives are set, not in isolation from the world of men, but in the midst of a society which is alien to God and hostile to the Christian spirit (cf. 2 Cor. 6:14 ff.). Even though they are God's children and *saints,* they live in a wicked world where the pressures of conformity

and solicitation to evil are very real and have to be resisted. Hence the warning of v. 6 rings out: *Let no one deceive you,* and the call of v. 7 sounds forth to Paul's readers: *Do not associate with them.* The antidote to these viruses to which the body of Christ in the world is exposed is hinted at by Paul in a number of his references in this section.

In addition to the ethical maxims we have already noted (for instance, the contrast *once you were darkness, but now you are light*), Paul recalls the churches to their God-appointed destiny as children of light who, at the commencement of their new life as believers, have been brought into the full light of Christ. Verse 14 is a stirring baptismal chant. They are followers of wisdom whose integrity shows up the folly of an immoral and materialistic society around them (vv. 15 ff.). They are men and women whose lives reflect a dependence on God and who turn to him in grateful acknowledgment of his goodness (vv. 4, 19, 20), both in private life and public worship.

In all, the Christian life in this section is shown to possess a distinctive ethos and pattern, and is intended to be both a challenge to contemporary society and a rebuke of it. But Paul offers no mandate for Christians to contract out of the world as though they were ascetics or fanatics. His moral guidelines which combine both a situational and prescriptive element are constructed on the implied assumption (explicitly drawn in 1 Cor. 5:10) that it is possible to live the full Christian life "in this world" (Titus 2:12).

1. *Love Excludes Lust (5:1–7)*

[1] Therefore be imitators of God, as beloved children.
[2] And walk in love, as Christ loved us and gave himself up for us, a fragrant offering and sacrifice to God.
[3] But immorality and all impurity or covetousness must not even be named among you, as is fitting among saints. [4] Let there be no filthiness, nor silly talk, nor levity, which are not fitting; but instead let there be thanksgiving.

5 Be sure of this, that no immoral or impure man, or one who is covetous (that is, an idolater), has any inheritance in the kingdom of Christ and of God. 6 Let no one deceive you with empty words, for it is because of these things that the wrath of God comes upon the sons of disobedience. 7 Therefore do not associate with them,

Paul has issued a summons to emulate the forgiving spirit (4:32). Forgiveness, however, is supremely the divine trait, and it follows that the whole of life should be based on the example of God's love in all its facets. Indeed, Christian character finds its pattern and exemplar in God himself, the Father (3:14–15; Matt. 5:48).

Beloved children finds its natural sequence of thought in reference to the Father's beloved Son (1:6), who in turn demonstrated his love for the church as well as his loving acceptance of the Father's will by his self-giving on the cross.

A fragrant offering and sacrifice is a phrase couched in the language of the Old Testament ritual. Perhaps the KJV, which renders the first part "sweetsmelling savour" as a literal translation, captures the sense of the Mosaic sacrifices (Ex. 29:18, 25) more adequately. Elsewhere, the phrase is used by Paul of the church's gift to himself (Phil. 4:18). Here the terms of reference are different, and highlight the pleasing nature of Jesus' self-surrender on Calvary as an offering acceptable to God. Additionally the cross has the effect of eliciting from believers a desire to "live in love" to him and their fellow Christians. In 2 Corinthians 5:14–15, Paul elaborates and enforces this truth.

What that "life in love" means is now explored. In a statement of astringent ethics (vv. 2 ff.) Paul reflects the need for the church to retain its identity in the contemporary world, and by the purity of its life to give no countenance to the immoral practices which were the accepted norm of Graeco-Roman society. The words *silly talk* and *levity* are to be taken not as condemning lighthearted merriment or good-humored fun. But in association with *filthiness* (lit., grossness, baseness in the sense of coarseness of speech) these terms refer to slanderous name-calling and flippant buffoonery (Masson's word) which goes beyond the bound of good taste. The best commentary on *silly talk* is Matthew 5:22: Jesus threatened a fearful penalty to the man who sneers at his brother, "You fool!" —and thus abuses the image of God in him.

Part of the illicit use of words is the unbridled descriptiveness of evil which leaves nothing unsaid and little to the imagination. Paul's remark (both at v. 3b and again in v. 12) that there are some items of man's underworld which are better left in darkness stands in contrast with the present-time trends of a permissive society. "Western culture, in all the mass-media, calls a spade a spade with a crudity that is corrupting. The present age has a filthy tongue" (G. Johnston).

On Christian lips the note of praise to God and appreciation of what is noble and wholesome in life (see Phil. 4:8) is more appropriate. *Thanksgiving* covers both sides of a healthy alternative to evil speaking.

Paul continues to pinpoint some of the excesses of his contemporary culture. The way in which these warnings are introduced in vv. 5,6, and 7 makes it clear that his readers are in danger of being led astray and are exposed to moral danger. The inference from these stern admonitions is that the Gentile churches in Asia Minor at the time of the epistle's composition and circulation were giving hospitality to ideas and practices which Paul regarded as alien to the gospel and a distortion of his moral teaching that Christians are summoned to high ethical standards. An antinominian spirit which rejected the claims of the moral law on the ground of a supposed freedom from the law had evidently crept in. Signs of this perversion of the Pauline doctrine of "free from the law" are seen in Romans 3:7–8; 6:1 ff., and the Asia Minor churches seem to be the special target of these false teachers, as we can see from the state of those churches in Revelation 2—3. A suitable "life-setting" of the warnings in this section is one of the few aids we possess for sketching a background to the Ephesian letter as a whole.

No immoral or impure man recalls similar warning passages in 1 Corinthians 6:9–10; Galatians 5:21; Hebrews 13:4; Revelation 21:8; 22:15. *Covetous* usually refers to a possessive spirit, which is the trait of a man who wants to acquire material wealth for its own sake. This is the sin of idolatry, as in Colossians 3:5. In the context of the types of sin mentioned here, however, "covetous" may imply immoral excesses (as in v. 3) which are produced when men live for the gratification of their appetite and become idolaters not in sense of being worshipers of idols but in the sense that "appetite is their god" (Phil. 3:19 NEB).

All classes of moral perversion fall under a severe rubric of judgment. Such practitioners are excluded from God's kingdom and the realm of Christ's rule in the church. This is the serious consequence of playing fast and loose with God's moral law. Paul does not mince his words; and we can only account for this in view of the contrary views of a relaxed morality to which Christians were listening. Therefore, *let no one deceive you.* Whether these sentiments are directed against pagans who were urging believers to do what they did or misguided Christians who were leading others astray cannot be decided with certainty. *Sons of disobedience* picks up a phrase from 2:2–3 in reference to the pagan world, but Paul seems to have his eye more intently fixed on evil influences within the churches.

The sad effect of this bad religion which has infiltrated into the church is that Christians are being duped into thinking that they can live indifferent moral lives and be no better than *the sons of disobedience* who stand under sentence of *the wrath of God.* The latter phrase (akin to what is described in 2:3) means God's holy displeasure at moral evil—and is especially directed against those who lead others into disgraceful and debased practices, as in the teaching of Jesus (Matt. 18:5–9).

Sons of disobedience is an Old Testament expression for men of disobedient

character. What is reflected is not simply misdirected zeal or harmless neglect but a willful infringement of God's law (Rom. 1:32). Hence the call follows that Christians should not parley with these false teachers.

2. Light Banishes Darkness (5:8–14)

⁸ for once you were darkness, but now you are light in the Lord; walk as children of light ⁹ (for the fruit of light is found in all that is good and right and true), ¹⁰ and try to learn what is pleasing to the Lord. ¹¹ Take no part in the unfruitful works of darkness, but instead expose them. ¹² For it is a shame even to speak of the things that they do in secret; ¹³ but when anything is exposed by the light it becomes visible, for anything that becomes visible is light. ¹⁴ Therefore it is said,
"Awake, O sleeper, and arise from the dead, and Christ shall give you light."

The pagan world is what Christians formerly were—children of darkness. But by God's grace the church has been brought into the light (1 Peter 2:9). The calling of believers then is to live as *children of light,* that is, true to their place in the divine family. Paul is drawing upon common teaching which evidently found a firm place in early Christian catechesis, i.e., instruction given to new converts in preparation for baptism and church membership. We may refer to Romans 13:12; 2 Corinthians 6:14; 1 Thessalonians 5:5; John 12:35 f.; 1 John 1:5 f. In fact, the terminology is broader in range than the biblical literature.

Children of light was a self-description claimed by the people of the Dead Sea scrolls (1QS 3:13 ff.) in their hatred of the "sons of darkness." ³⁸ Their withdrawal to the Qumran monastery in the Judean wilderness was a protest movement, for which the New Testament ethical teaching offers no parallel. Christian *children of light* are to let their light shine amid the society of men and women (Matt. 5:16; Phil. 2:15); they have no mandate to become recluses

³⁸ We refer to the discussion, "The Epistle to the Ephesians in the Light of the Qumran Texts," by K. G. Kuhn in *Paul and Qumran* ed. J. Murphy-O'Connor OP (London: Geoffrey Chapman, 1968), pp. 115–131.

cut off from the world of ordinary people.

Verse 9 forms a parenthetic note to show what are the qualities of living in the light. Observe that the KJV's translation "fruit of the Spirit" is based on a secondary textual reading which is influenced by Galatians 5:22. Moreover, the sense of the context requires some allusion to *light* as the contrast light-darkness runs through this section up to v. 14.

The "intention to please God in all things" (as William Law phrased it in his book, *A Serious Call to a Devout and Holy Life*, 1728, a writing which had a decisive impact on John Wesley) is a Pauline ethical rubric, found at v. 10 and often elsewhere (Rom. 12:2; 14:8; 2 Cor. 5:9; 1 Thess. 4:1; Col. 3:20). It is a reminder that Christian ethics cannot be stereotyped as a legalistic bundle of prohibitions couched in harshly negative and restrictive terms. Rather, in its essence Christian morality represents a positive ambition to be pleasing to a loving God whose character his children long to share (5:1).

Not only do Christians steer clear of evil practices and pursuits. They have a responsibility to show up by a contrasting style of life the nature of the world around them, its moral climate and its culpability. *Expose* may at first sight suggest a censorious and judgmental attitude which Jesus opposed (Matt. 7:1–5). But this is not necessarily so, and the verb is best understood in reference to what follows in vv. 12–13. Christians as children of light in the world cast an illuminating beam into the dark corners of human society where evil practices are conducted in the darkness of secrecy. Paul has in mind the immoral and magical pursuits practiced in the so-called mystery religions. Christian influence has a reproving effect as Christ's light shines "not merely 'to display,' but 'to show to be evil,' so that we do best to keep to the rendering 'to correct,' especially as deeds and doers are closely related." [39]

[39] F. Büchsel in *TDNT*, II, p. 474. We may compare John 3:20 for this sense of the verb "to expose" (Gk. *elenchō*).

The encouragement given in these verses to a quality of living as befits children of light is strengthened by the citation of a hymn of three lines:

"Awake, O sleeper,
From the grave arise.
The light of Christ upon you shines."

The setting of this exhortation is most likely that of baptism, which was frequently known in the later church as a person's "enlightenment" and depicted as the rising of the convert from the death of sin into union with the living Lord (Rom. 6:4 ff.). Paul harks back to this experience as a reminder to his readers that they should now make good their baptismal profession by walking in Christ's light and by stirring themselves to active witness. [40]

3. Wisdom Corrects Folly (5:15–20)

[15] Look carefully then how you walk, not as unwise men but as wise, [16] making the most of the time, because the days are evil. [17] Therefore do not be foolish, but understand what the will of the Lord is. [18] And do not get drunk with wine, for that is debauchery; but be filled with the Spirit, [19] addressing one another in psalms and hymns and spiritual songs, singing and making melody to the Lord with all your heart, [20] always and for everything giving thanks in the name of our Lord Jesus Christ to God the Father.

The church's witness is now the subject of apostolic admonition, which here takes a positive turn. In the earlier verses (vv. 3–13) his directions have been mainly negative and intended to warn the churches of the threat of complicity with evil in the world.

Now he issues a call to wisdom which is set over against the folly of a pagan environment. The path taken by *wise* men

[40] The introductory phrase "it is said" (lit., he/it says) must relate to a Christian hymn, and cannot support an implied citation of a saying of Jesus or an Old Testament quotation. The verse is labeled hymnic because the words are arranged in rhythmical form, so producing a three-line stanza (not as in RSV a two-line verse). See further for a bibliography of modern discussion on this verse, R. P. Martin, *Worship in the Early Church*, 1964, pp. 47 f., 104, and article "Aspects of Worship in the New Testament Church," *Vox Evangelica* (London: Epworth Press, 1963), pp. 19 f.

has to be understood on its Old Testament background where wisdom is not an intellectual achievement but an attitude to life. It begins with a knowledge of God and an avoidance of all that displeases him (as in Job 28:28; Psalm 1; Prov. 4:5 ff.; 8:1 ff.)

The practice of wisdom in everyday conduct involves specific moral activities and enterprises. First, there is the buying up of every chance: *making the most of your time* (cf. Rom. 12:11, NEB marg.). The language here is borrowed directly from the commercial vocabulary of the marketplace (Gk. *agora*). The verb is *exagorazomenoi* where the prefix *ex* denotes an intensive activity, a snapping up of all the opportunities which are available. The Christian's stewardship of time as God's precious and priceless commodity is the simple teaching here, with a call to invest our energies in occupations which are worthwhile.

Part of this call springs from the recognition that the *days are evil.* This may mean days which precede the final crisis of the end of the age (so E. F. Scott) or, more generally, the character of the age in which the church has to contend with evil powers. The continuance of the second idea in 6: 11–12 supports the latter exegesis.

In the next place, there is a summons to self-understanding in the light of God's will, which is the outstanding mark of a wise man who lives in fellowship with God (2 Tim. 2:7). One sure way of disrupting that fellowship and refusing to accept God's will comes in a blurred vision in turn caused by an abandonment of self-control. Verse 18 highlights the danger of intoxication through which the vigilance of the moral censor is lifted and a gate opened to immorality. The Christians' avoidance of profligacy (here rendered *debauchery*) was the occasion both of the amazement and hostility of pagan neighbors for whom carousing was part and parcel of life (1 Peter 4:4). The warning *do not get drunk with wine* quotes from Proverbs 23:31 (LXX). It touched upon a very real peril confronting Christians in a pagan culture.

In a daring contrast Paul goes on to apply the lesson. Let the infilling you seek be one of the Spirit, not of wine. And as drunkenness is a common occurrence in the world around you and overindulgence in wine a daily experience, let the fullness of the Holy Spirit be your constant preoccupation. *Be filled* is a present tense, indicating a continuing experience. But the entire phrase here poses a teaser for the translator. Paul's Greek is compressed. C. Masson rightly remarks: " 'By the Spirit' is too precise. 'In the Spirit' is too vague. We propose: 'seek the fullness which the Spirit gives.' " This rendering is preferable to the final alternative: "become full of the Spirit" of which J. Armitage Robinson says, "Such an injunction however has no parallel: had this been the Apostle's meaning he would almost certainly have used the genitive" instead of the preposition *in* (*en*) and the dative.

One hallmark of the Spirit's filling will be a desire to give vocal expression to the heart's devotion *to the Lord* by the use of canticles and songs which the Spirit inspires. The classification of these songs into Old Testament psalms, Christian hymns used in early church worship, and anthems employed by the heavenly worshipers as in the scenes of the book of Revelation (5:9; 14:3; 15:3) is popularly made. But it is too neat. Probably distinctively Christian compositions are intended for all three types, especially if the adjective *spiritual* (i.e., inspired by the Spirit) covers all the preceding terms as the Greek will allow.[41]

By the use of these verbal articulations Christians both edify one another (implied in *addressing one another*) and give vent to their emotional stirrings by the spiritual exercise of thanksgiving to God (v. 20). Paul has a congregational assembly in mind (as in 1 Cor. 14) rather than acts of private or family worship. The thanksgiving is the church's corporate response to the good-

---

[41] A full discussion of the background here and the place of the rubric in verse 19 in the development of church worship is offered by the present writer in *Worship in the Early Church*, chapters 4 and 12.

ness of God, and so forms a bridge which links the ethical teaching of these verses with what follows in the letter.

X. Christ, the Church, and the Family (5:21—6:9)

Mention of the church at worship invites a consideration by Paul of the place of women, first in the church service and then, as a natural sequel, in the domestic relationship with their husbands and family. From this opening statement of the true ordering of the husband-wife relationship the apostle proceeds to draw the analogy of Christ and the church. He uses Genesis 2:24 as a text applicable first to human relations but also—and for him more significantly—prefiguring the nuptial union between the heavenly Bridegroom and his bride the church, which is one with him (5:31).

It will be helpful if we set down in advance of a detailed commentary the four lessons he draws from the correspondence between the Christ-church parallel and the man-woman relationship.

First, Christ is the head of the church, his body; and in the ordering of creation man occupies a place of headship over woman (1 Cor. 11:3; 1 Tim. 2:13).

Second, Christ requires the obedience of his people who are rightly subject to him (v. 24). The inference is made that woman too is to be dependent upon man in all things (v. 24) and not simply in the arrangement of public worship, to which v. 22 refers. Such is the view of this writer, though others may legitimately hold a contrary view (see further discussion below).

Third, Christ has set his love upon the church and shows the extent of that love in all he has done for the church's redemption (vv. 25 ff.). While much of this section belongs uniquely to the Christ-church nexus, the chief point is made in verse 28: let husbands love their wives with a love that is akin to his love.

Four, Christ who looks upon his church as a part of himself, as his body, cares for

it (vv. 29–30). In the marriage bond, too, the husband has a responsibility for his spouse.

Verse 33 sums up the Pauline discussion on the note of "respect" (Gk. *phobeō*) of the wife for her husband. It cannot be accidental that the opening verse of Paul's discussion (v. 21) also used this word in its noun form to show the "reverence" (Gk. *phobos*) of the church for Christ. This is an example of the rhetorical device of *inclusio* by which the opening and close of a discussion match and so form the terminal points of a section of classical prose. But its value here is more than literary. It shows that the paragraph division should come after v. 20 (as in RSV) and make v. 21 an integral introduction to the treatment on the theme of Christ and the church. But v. 21 is best isolated as a separate paragraph (so NEB), so functioning as a bridge between the verses which have gone before and those which come afterwards. The reason lies in the absence of a verb from the Greek of v. 22. Clearly that verb must be carried over from v. 21, as in the RSV, which inserts: *Wives, be subject. . . .* The submission of v. 21 looks back to the description given of the structure of the church at worship (vv. 19–20) and forward to the attitude of a woman to her spouse, which is voluntary on her part and not the result of the husband's overbearing action. But Paul may be easing his way into that latter discussion by remarking in v. 22 that it is in services of public worship that a woman ought to be submissive to her husband, as in 1 Corinthians 14:34 which uses the same verb and 1 Timothy 2:11 which uses a cognate noun. The need to set Christian worship on a right basis is the starting point for his treatment of the analogy between Christ and the church, just as in 1 Corinthians the excess of spiritual gifts (1 Cor. 12) prompts his instructions about the unity of the body.

The call to submission has a wider frame of reference, however. Many interpreters relate its primary application to the total or general husband-wife relationship. Codes of "household duties" (*Haustafeln* [42]) covering both domestic and social relationships were not uniquely Christian, but could be paralleled in the world of the first century. Paul, along with other New Testament writers, may have borrowed the framework, but he has filled it out in a distinctively Christian way by inserting such phrases as "in the Lord" (6:1; cf. Col. 3:10) and by drawing upon Old Testament teaching (6:2–3) to buttress his appeal. His concern for family life is a logical deduction from the teaching on the husband-wife relationship and goes back to his earlier premise of the divine Father who calls his people into his family as children of his love (5:1; cf. 3:14–15).

With these backgrounds in Paul's ecclesiology and his use of ethical framework, we may proceed to examine the substance of his teaching.

1. Marriage in the Light of the Sacred Marriage of Christ and the Church (5:21–33)

21 Be subject to one another out of reverence for Christ. 22 Wives, be subject to your husbands, as to the Lord. 23 For the husband is the head of the wife as Christ is the head of the church, his body, and is himself its Savior. 24 As the church is subject to Christ, so let wives also be subject in everything to their husbands. 25 Husbands, love your wives, as Christ loved the church and gave himself up for her, 26 that he might sanctify her, having cleansed her by the washing of water with the word, 27 that he might present the church to himself in splendor, without spot or wrinkle or any such thing, that she might be holy and without blemish. 28 Even so husbands should love their wives as their own bodies. He who loves his wife loves himself. 29 For no man ever hates his own flesh, but nourishes and cherishes it, as Christ does the church, 30 because we are members of his body. 31 "For this reason a man shall leave his father and mother and be joined to his wife, and the two shall become one." 32 This is a great mystery, and I take it to mean Christ and the church; 33 however, let each one

of you love his wife as himself, and let the wife see that she respects her husband.

Verse 21 is, as we have seen, a link uniting two sections (5:19–20 and 5:22–33). Christian forbearance in worship finds a specific illustration in the attitude of women both in congregational assembly and within the marriage union. In the last named area the man-woman relationship leads Paul to expatiate on the way in which Christ and the church are united. Headship belongs to both Christ and man-as-a-husband (Greek *anēr* is used, not the generic term for man as *homo sapiens, anthrōpos;* but the usage is not hard and fast, as the occurrence of *anthrōpos* in the Old Testament quotation in v. 31 shows).

Christ is the church's head because it is likened to a body, as earlier Pauline teaching had insisted (Rom. 12:4–5; 1 Cor. 12:12 ff.).[43]

What is novel comes in the additional phrase: *and is himself its Savior.* The designation of Jesus as Saviour, so popular in Christian hymnody and devotion, is singularly absent from Paul. Its chief occurrences are in the Pastoral epistles, but it is attested only in Philippians 3:20 and here in the church letters. Some special explanation is therefore sought. Dibelius-Greeven in their commentary suggest that this addition to the analogy is an afterthought because woman is not saved by man. But there may be a special sense of the verbal noun. Guided by 1 Timothy 2:15 we may propose here the sense of the verbs "protect, preserve." The meaning is then that Christ looks after the church's welfare; and this idea would prepare for vv. 29–30 in the comparison.

In everything does not perhaps mean to imply an unreasoning and harsh subjection on the part of woman as may be thought at first glance. More likely it is added to extend the limited reference of the submis-

---

[42] This expressive German term derives from the ground-breaking study of K. Weidinger, *Die Haustafeln. Ein Stück urchristlicher Paränese,* "Untersuchungen zum Neuen Testament" (Leipzig: J. C. Hinrichs, 1928).

[43] The origin of this teaching has been traced most suggestively to Paul's Damascus road encounter where he saw that in persecuting the church (Christ's body) he was wounding Christ himself (the head): Acts 9:4–5; cf. 1 Cor. 8:12.

sion given in v. 22. That verse talks about a woman's dependent place in public worship (as in 1 Cor. 14:34; 1 Tim. 2:11). Now Paul wishes to broaden the scope of this dependence. It is time for him also to say what submission means. Verse 25 defines the true meaning of obligation, expressed by the verb rendered *be subject;* it is an obligation in love. The husband's love is patterned on the greater love of Christ for his bride.

The church as Christ's spouse is so unfamiliar a thought that its correct setting and milieu should be noticed. He refers to it in 2 Corinthians 11:2–3 (cf. Rev. 19:7 ff.; 21:2), drawing on the same Old Testament background. In particular he is fixing attention on Yahweh's marriage with Israel described in Hosea 2:16; Isaiah 54:4 f.; 62: 4 f.; Ezekiel 16:7 f. The rabbis took these passages and used them to eulogize the covenant between God and his people at Sinai in terms of a marriage contract. The Torah or law of God received by Israel as the foundation of the covenant became that contract. Moses was the one who led the bride to God, the divine husband. In Christian terms, Christ's relationship to his bride, the church, became for Paul one further way of saying that the age of the Torah had given place to the new age of the Messiah's fulfillment. The apostle himself plays the role of the lawgiver Moses in leading Christ's spouse to him (as in 2 Cor. 11:2; cf. John 3:29).

The heavenly Bridegroom's actions for his bride, the church, are traced back to his love and self-giving on the cross. *Loved* and *gave himself* are two verbs which also go together in Galatians 2:20.

The purpose and effect of Christ's work on behalf of the church are expressed in terms of sanctification. But the sense is not quite the same as the one normally associated with that term in dogmatics. Rather the verb carries the sense that the church is taken out of the sphere of sin and placed in that of the divine holiness as Christ lays claim to the church as his own possession. (For this use of the verb "to sanctify"

meaning to consecrate by committing the life to God, see John 10:36; 17:17; see also Jer. 1:5; Ecclesiasticus 49:7.) The means by which this transference is accomplished is then cryptically described as *having cleansed her by the washing of water with the word.* All agree that the birth of the new people of God is intended by this phrase, and there is no less general agreement today that Paul has the baptismal cleansing in view—though there is a minority view that spiritual renewal is alone meant (cf. John 13:10) without reference to water baptism. *The washing of water* recalls the reference in Titus 3:5, but more especially 1 Corinthians 6:11 where washing and sanctification are side by side. *With the word* is a puzzle. The Greek phrase *en rhēmati* (in a word) is even more mysterious than the English. One emendation has been proposed with the suggested reading *en haimati* ("with [his] blood"). But this is a desperate expedient. Nor is there much help from the suggestion that *washing* and *word* go together as a reference to prenuptial bridal baths and the marriage vow, a practice familiar among Greeks and Jews.[44]

Rather the *word* must refer to either the proclamation of the gospel which led to response in baptism, or (more likely) the convert's affirmation of faith at baptism, mentioned in Acts 22:16 and illustrated in the question-and-answer dialogue of Acts 8:36 ff. (see Western text, printed in KJV; RSV marg.). In the later church there grew up an elaborate arrangement for the interrogation of the candidates for baptism [45] and to each inquiry a suitable reply was expected. Quite probably Paul's phrase relates to this situation.

Verse 27 looks forward to the ultimate realization of Christ's purpose when the bride will at length be ready to meet her spouse. That this is a future event afar off seems clear, and is fastened upon by those scholars who point to a period in New

44 See A. Oepke's discussion, *TDNT,* IV, 296 ff.
45 See R. P. Martin, *Worship in the Early Church* (1964), pp. 60 f. for examples.

Testament historical and theological development when the imminent return of Christ was no longer anticipated. At some later time the church will attain its full *splendor* as *holy* and *without blemish*. From 1:4 we can observe how this later verse contemplates the actualization of God's plan for the church which was conceived in a past eternity. It would confirm the view that what is described in this elaborate analogy of a sacred marriage is nothing less than the pairing of God's original plan for the new creation and its fulfillment at the end-time.

From a magnificent theological statement of Christ and his bride the author slips into the lower gear of a pointed application (vv. 28–33). We may wonder why this lengthy enforcement of the teaching is now made, especially as some parts of it (vv. 29,33) seem to smack of utilitarian ethics and a naive altruism. There must be a historical reason behind this section. Some commentators find it in the unusual need for catechetical instruction about marriage (cf. Heb. 13:4) or the apostle's profound sense of the church as a sacred, corporate mystery based on Old Testament ideas (in Hos. 2:2 ff.; Isa. 54:4 f.) which were spiritualized and idealized by Philo (*De Cherub* 13). More probable is the view that Paul's readers were falling victim to a gnosticizing belief that marriage was inherently defiling and that the celibate state was per se virtuous (cf. 1 Tim. 4:3).

The apostle is driven to make this counterblast by the necessity of exalting marriage as God-intended. And this he does by the use of the *great mystery* uniting Christ and his bride, the church. The underlying motif is that the messianic age has already dawned and this means that the Messiah and his bride are being united in anticipation of the day when the marriage feast will be celebrated (Rev. 19:7,9).

With v. 28 the application begins. The strange wording *as their own bodies* which is used of the husbands' love of their wives is probably to be explained by the desire to keep close to the analogy of the preceding verses. Christ loves his body with which he is so closely joined that it may be thought of as part of himself. We may recall Acts 9:4:"Why do you persecute me?"—a question spoken in reference to Saul's hostility to the church-he was attacking.

The two positive verbs in v. 29, *nourishes and cherishes* are borrowed from the language of the nursery (as in 1 Thess. 2:7). They denote great solicitude and tender regard. When used of a husband's care of his wife, they imply "protection, affection, and tangible and practical maintenance" (Masson). This is true when Christian marriage rises to the heights set by Christ's care for the church.

A citation from Genesis 2:24 (slightly different from LXX) is taken by Paul *to mean Christ and the church*. Jesus used this Old Testament verse (in Mark 10:7 f.) to establish the permanent nature of the marriage bond, and earlier Paul had marshaled the text as an argument against the practice of cult prostitution (1 Cor. 6:16–17). Now he follows through the insight accorded him into the nature of the church (3:4, which also speaks of the *mystery*, that is, God's plan for the world through the church, 1:9). He applies the Old Testament text analogically to the union not of man with woman but of Christ and his body which is one with him. Whether there is a polemical slant involved in the disclaimer *and I take it* is not clear. Is Paul inferring that his interpretation has to overcome rival views? Some scholars [46] believed that Paul was deliberately opposing a Gnostic speculation which in the classical systems of the second-century heresy produced a complex teaching on the "pairing of aeons," likened to a marriage and ostensibly based on Genesis 2:24. But this background seems a long way removed from this part of Ephesians.[47]

Verse 33 sums up. It looks back to the preceding verse which is archetypal and exemplary. From the nexus Christ-the-

46 e.g., H. Schlier in his earlier book *Christus und die Kirche im Epheserbrief* (1930), pp. 60–75.
47 So E. Percy, p. 327.

church, Paul argues to the ideal husband-wife relationship, and not vice versa. This is an important observation which accounts for two parts of the teaching often misunderstood. He calls wives to be subject to their husbands, for the church is rightly under the control of Christ. Also this is why he "never tells wives that they are to love their husbands. . . . The reason is that which he gives: Christ loves the church, but it is for the Church to obey and submit to Christ." [48]

2. Family Duties (6:1–4)

[1] Children, obey your parents in the Lord, for this is right. [2] "Honor your father and mother" (this is the first commandment with a promise), [3] "that it may be well with you and that you may live long on the earth." [4] Fathers, do not provoke your children to anger, but bring them up in the discipline and instruction of the Lord.

From the true basis of family life in marital union, attention is switched to family relations as *children* are called to accept their place in obedience to parents. It is *right*, that is, in line with God's will (as in 4:24) that they should. The addition *in the Lord* (not present in Col. 3:20) modifies the command and at the same time supplies a Christian motivation and inspiration spelled out in the next verse.

This further reason for children to be obedient to their parents is supplied by a quotation from Exodus 20:12, part of the Decalogue with which is then joined an adaptation of Deuteronomy 5:16. This latter text stands itself under the influence of Deuteronomy 22:7 in the Pauline citation. Nor is this complex "conflation" of Old Testament verses the only problem in the passage. How are we to understand *first commandment* (contrast Matt. 22:37–38)? The answer must be that the requirement to *honor your father and mother* is the first section of the "Ten Words" to have a promise attached, or else and more likely, that *first* is not a reference to numerical order but is used adverbially in the sense, "a

very important commandment." A similar usage with the same Greek word is discovered at 1 Corinthians 15:3 where the term is to be rendered "of first importance."

Next come the father's duties which are displayed both negatively and positively. First, there is a warning against the practice of irritating children. This could be by nagging at them and so leading them to exasperation and hostility. Second, there follows an injunction to train them in disciplinary education. This latter phrase is the best way to join together the two Greek words *paideia* (which means properly education by discipline) and *nouthesia* (education by instruction). The subjects taught in this school of spiritual and moral education may be epitomized in a single curricular interest: the Christian life, what it is, and how it is to be lived, which is the wide-ranging meaning of the phrase *of the Lord.*

3. Relations of Masters and Slaves (6:5–9)

[5] Slaves, be obedient to those who are your earthly masters, with fear and trembling, in singleness of heart, as to Christ; [6] not in the way of eye-service, as men-pleasers, but as servants of Christ, doing the will of God from the heart, [7] rendering service with a good will as to the Lord and not to men, [8] knowing that whatever good any one does, he will receive the same again from the Lord, whether he is a slave or free. [9] Masters, do the same to them, and forbear threatening, knowing that he who is both their Master and yours is in heaven, and that there is no partiality with him.

This section of the "household code" treats of a very real problem for first-century Christians in their social responsibilities. The church was born into a society in which human slavery was an accepted institution sanctioned by law and unquestioned even by high-minded moralists. The problem was not one of an acceptance of the institution per se or how to react to a demand for its abolition (which not even the epistle to Philemon hints at), but the way slaves were to accept their status and the treatment Christian slave-owners were to give to slaves in their control. Modern readers of these verses need to recall the historical circumstances of the first-century

[48] C. Chavasse, *The Bride of Christ* (London: Religious Book Club, 1939), p. 77.

world and be on their guard lest they ask questions of the New Testament Scripture which do not come within the purview of the latter. Slavery is a case in point. Otherwise we shall be amazed that the Pauline call is one to obedience and not to revolt.

This latter course would have been suicidal as W. Bousset has perceptively noted: "Christianity would have sunk beyond hope of recovery along with such revolutionary attempts; it might have brought on a new slave-rising and been crushed along with it. The time was not ripe for the solution of such difficult questions." [49]

Verse 5 sounds a note which is characteristic of the New Testament generally with its summons to acquiescence and not protest. Instead the sting is partly drawn from the inhuman practice by the slaves' attitude as Christians. *As to Christ* holds a distinctively Christian sound, thereby transforming all work and recalling the teaching of Matthew 25:31 ff. Service to others in the name of Christ puts a new face on what we do as we serve other people for his sake.

The same thought is repeated in the following two verses, which are built around the consciously attempted play on words: *Slaves . . .* [be] "slaves" (RSV marg.) *of Christ.* What it means to be a slave (Greek *doulos,* as in v. 5) of Christ is spelled out in this short section. It entails serving him by doing the will of God *from the heart,* that is, not in a dilatory or listless fashion but rather *with a good will.* The commentary of Dibelius-Greeven cites an interesting payrus dated a century or so later than Paul, in which there is a parallel to this phrase. A slave is set free in his master's will because of his "cheerfulness and affection" shown in the way he has served the family. Now the deceased owner acknowledges this in an act of manumission which bids the slave go free. Not all slave owners were the monsters of popular imagination,

however degrading the principle of the institution seems to us today. Service *with a good will* would sometimes bring its reward. In this context the Pauline phrase must carry this sense: work with an eagerness "which does not wait to be compelled" (J. Armitage Robinson).

Present opportunities of service, though set within the limited bounds of the master-slave relationship, are lifted by Paul onto a higher level in v. 8. All worthwhile enterprise and helpful response to need point ahead to the future when Christ, the Servant of God and man par excellence (Luke 22:27), will assess the worth of the Christian's life at his judgment-seat (see 1 Cor. 4:5; 2 Cor. 5:10; Rom. 14:12). Here is a prospect awaiting all Christians irrespective of their social status. The undertone, however, is a pointed allusion to those who have broader fields of opportunities. They will be held responsible for what they have done with those opportunities, and this seems clearly to switch attention from the slave to his master as *free* man and so able to utilize more of his time and energy for doing good and helping others.

So the discussion moves on to consider the slave owners. They too are bidden to act in a way which befits their Christian calling. There is a caution registered against an overbearing disposition and a reminder that, though they are *Masters* (Greek *kurioi*) of their slaves, they too have a heavenly *Master* (Greek *kurios*). He cannot be bribed or corrupted in any way. *Partiality,* i.e., favoritism which can be bought by a gift, is an Old Testament term used, for example, in 2 Chronicles 19:7. In fact, the Greek word (lit., favorable regard) is patterned on the vivid Hebrew phrase which denotes an openness to be persuaded shown by a facial expression.

Colossians 3:25 uses the same idea of impartiality but in a different context. There it is a call to slaves not to exploit their Christian owners—a slant perhaps inspired, as E. Percy [50] suggests, by the case of

[49] W. Bousset, *Die Schriften des Neuen Testaments* (Göttingen: Vandenhoeck and Ruprecht, ii, 1929), p. 101.

[50] *Op. cit.,* p. 402.

Onesimus, who had cheated and run away from his master Philemon at Colossae. By contrast, the teaching in Ephesians is "situationless" and so transposed into a more general ethical rubric.

XI. The Christian's Warfare and the Apostle's Plea (6:10–20)

¹⁰ Finally, be strong in the Lord and in the strength of his might. ¹¹ Put on the whole armor of God, that you may be able to stand against the wiles of the devil. ¹² For we are not contending against flesh and blood, but against the principalities, against the powers, against the world rulers of this present darkness, against the spiritual hosts of wickedness in the heavenly places. ¹³ Therefore take the whole armor of God, that you may be able to withstand in the evil day, and having done all, to stand. ¹⁴ Stand therefore, having girded your loins with truth, and having put on the breastplate of righteousness, ¹⁵ and having shod your feet with the equipment of the gospel of peace; ¹⁶ above all taking the shield of faith, with which you can quench all the flaming darts of the evil one. ¹⁷ And take the helmet of salvation, and the sword of the Spirit, which is the word of God. ¹⁸ Pray at all times in the Spirit, with all prayer and supplication. To that end keep alert with all perseverance, making supplication for all the saints, ¹⁹ and also for me, that utterance may be given me in opening my mouth boldly to proclaim the mystery of the gospel, ²⁰ for which I am an ambassador in chains; that I may declare it boldly, as I ought to speak.

In this concluding admonition the reality of the church in the world is faced. Paul issues a call to steadfastness under trial and a summons to prepare for conflict. The church's enemies, however (as Paul knows well), are not simply the human agents which oppress Christians. Behind them he sees the malign forces of evil. The assaults of demonic powers require heavenly aid to repel; and it is the apostle's conviction that God has placed at the Christians' disposal all that is needed to resist such an attack. In particular, the various pieces of armor are listed in detail. This description is drawn from the equipment worn and used by the Roman soldier who is ready for battle. A representative soldier may well have been at Paul's side as he wrote or dictated

the letter, for he speaks of himself as "an ambassador in chains" (v. 20). As a Christian apostle he looks to his friends in the Asian churches to stand by him with their prayers, for he is a special target of attack and so in special need of encouragement which their intercessions can bring (vv. 18–19). As a personal plea, he confesses that he wants to be faithful in the discharge of his apostolic work (v. 20; see 3:8,13 for similar pleas in this letter).

The two exhortations of verse 10 are set side by side and interpret each other. The interposing and is explanatory. The NEB helpfully runs the two stirring calls together: "Find your strength in the Lord, in his mighty power." The three Greek terms rendered be strong (endunamousthe), strength (kratos), and might (ischus) are all variants of the idea of power, and recall a similar piling up of synonyms in 1:19. What this exhortation means is then specified, as Paul moves into a discussion of the armament God makes available to the Christian warrior. The battle motif is now introduced.

The key to the interpretation of the next few verses lies in the phrase armor of God. It is clear that the Christian lives in a kind of no-man's-land between the opposing forces of God and the devil. He is called to align himself with God and against his enemy. But how? By taking the armor of God. This phrase could mean either "the armor which God provides" or "the armor which God wears," depending on the type of genitive construction meant. Parallels in Isaiah 59:17 and the Wisdom of Solomon 5:17–20 make it certain that the second interpretation is to be preferred. The armament with which the Christian soldier is to gird himself is nothing less than the armor God puts on (figuratively) in his war against evil.

The enemy, in the Christian contest, is the devil described in his capacity as slanderer (Greek diabolos). In that sense he is the sworn foe of the church which cannot be neutral in any case (Rev. 12:10), in view of the evil machinations of the devil and his minions. The same Greek word rendered here *wiles* is found in 4:14. Paul, like the writer of Revelation 12:10, had a vivid picture of the personal agent of evil before his eyes, especially in his enmity to the saints of God, even though both Scripture writers draw upon terminology from a Jewish apocalyptic world view.

Paul lifts the veil and permits his readers to see the transcendental dimension of the church's struggle in the world. On the level of history that struggle is between men of goodwill and men of evil disposition. But Paul dismisses this account as too simplistic. The conflict at its in-depth level is not against human powers: *flesh and blood* (see Matt. 16:17; Gal. 1:16 for the phrase understood in the sense of men and women). Rather it is directed against the real power behind the persecutors on earth, demonic agencies which, according to 1 Corinthians 2:8, were primarily responsible for Jesus' death. Caiaphas, Herod, and Pilate were the historical instruments of these malevolent angelic powers, says Paul.

The spiritual hierarchy of evil is depicted in some detail. *Principalities* and *powers* are terms used elsewhere in Paul for the orders of creation of which Christ is both the origin and the head (Col. 1:16). They are thought of as having detached themselves in rebellion against the cosmic Lord and so being in active opposition to him and his people. But he dealt them a mortal blow on the cross (Col. 2:15) and their doom is writ. His final word (1 Cor. 15:24) will quickly slay them.

In the interim between the cross and resurrection and the Parousia they have power to harass the church but not to destroy it (Rom. 8:38).

World rulers belong to the same company, but the derivation of the term is not certain. It is attested as an astrological term in Greek writers yet absent from the Septuagint and Philo. A good clue would be that the rabbis used a Semitic form of the word to denote the angel of death.[51]

51 Strack-Billerbeck, i, p. 145; ii, p. 552.

Later Gnostics within Christendom applied the word to the devil. Irenaeus says of the Valentinians: "the devil they call kosmokrat." Paul's word is plural, however, and probably denotes evil forces which are as implacably opposed to the church as *darkness* is opposed to light. This contrast picks up the earlier teaching of 4:18; 5:7 ff. with its stark antithesis of darkness versus light. There may be a further application. The aim of "kosmokrats" is to hold men in the darkness of their ignorance of God and his truth as in 2 Corinthians 4:4–6.

The final member in this cluster of malevolent agencies is *the spiritual hosts of wickedness in the heavenly places.* The nearest parallel to this phrase is 2:2. In both texts the church's conflict is located in the upper air regions. But this is precisely the region where the sphere of Christ's rule (1:20) is found, where there is witness made to the church's proclamation of the gospel (3:10) and from which as from a fountain head (1:3) blessings flow from God to his people. We should, therefore, not hesitate to regard the phrase as metaphorical and designed to speak to first-century man on his own wave length by reassuring him that the place from which evil spirits came to assault him was no longer filled with horrendous influences but had known Christ's victory over all fears even if there is continuing hostility. The message of v. 12 is therefore one of hope. In spite of the tremendous evil of which these demonic powers are capable in their attempt to destroy the church, the assurance is given that because "these powers are competing with God" (Thompson, p. 94) and the church already victorious in Christ now ascended to heavenly places, they are doomed to failure and ultimate defeat. The language and ideology may be conditioned by the world outlook and pressing forebodings of Hellenistic man, but the principle underlying this message is timeless and especially pertinent to our day.

Because of the church's confidence in its struggle against a foe which is already under sentence of doom—this is the logical connection of *therefore*—the Christian soldier is bidden to take up his battle position with high courage. He is enheartened to stand his ground *in the evil day,* that is, in an age when the pressure of persecution against the church is mounting (see 5:16). Some commentators take this to specify the eschatological stress which will precede the Parousia of Christ; but the reference is too vague to attach this meaning to it—as this writer understands it.

Having done all carries the natural sense of a total preparedness to meet the enemy when a fresh onslaught is expected *in the evil day.* But Paul's Greek verb may take on another flavor. It is just possible that what is intended is a secondary meaning, attested by Herodotus, of "having defeated all." The *all* will then look back to the spiritual hosts of v. 12. Either way, the important part of the clarion call is clear: get ready for battle and be ready when the fighting breaks out.

Paul spells out the responsibility the soldier has. He must equip himself adequately for the fray. But as the armor is God's (v. 11), no provision is lacking and no part of his body is unprotected. Like Achilles' armor fashioned by the gods (Homer, *Iliad* 18, lines 478–616), the Christian's protection as he meets his enemy is adequate. Yet he has the responsibility to use it.

This description (vv. 14 ff.) evidently has its model in the Roman soldier on duty. The belt was a sign of this, and a mark of active service. The Romans spoke of *miles accinctus,* meaning a soldier at the ready with his belt (Latin *cingulum*) fastened in position (Tacitus, *Annals,* 11.18).[52]

The *breastplate* imagery is taken from Isaiah 59:17 (cf. Wisdom 5:18). Paul's reference to *righteousness* follows the prophetic sense of vindication and action which redresses all wrong. It is the picture of God's servant doing battle for social justice in the world of perverted values and

flagrant crime against humanity. *Feet* need shoes for marching as God's kingdom does not come without long, painful effort. There is equally an Old Testament background in Isaiah 52:7 which is in the apostle's thoughts as he writes Romans 10:15. Then, well-equipped feet will mean promptitude of service in evangelistic and social endeavor, as Christians carry the *gospel of peace* (Old Testament *shalom* means the well-being of the whole man, body, mind, and spirit: see note on 1:2).

Above all is as ambiguous in English as in Greek (*en pasin*). Does the phrase mean "with all these" (NEB) or, "to cover all the parts of the body"? The second idea is certainly possible because it is matched by Paul's choice of a Greek word for *shield* (Gk. *thureos*). The Latin equivalent of this is *scutum,* which was specially valuable as a soldier's defence against flaming darts. *Scutum* "was a large quadrangular shield devised to catch and extinguish ignited arrows" (G. H. P. Thompson, *op. cit.*). In the spiritual warfare it is the *shield of faith* in God's final victory, already achieved in principle by Christ's resurrection and exaltation over all evil powers (1:20–22) and made available to give the Christian victory over evil now. The *flaming darts of the evil one* (i.e., the devil) are best understood as satanic designs aimed at destroying the Christian's faith (2 Thess. 3:3).

Two further items of equipment make up the balance of the soldier's dress. The *helmet of salvation* is drawn from Isaiah 59:17 (perhaps in direct contrast is Wisdom 5:19: God wears a helmet of doom). In these texts Yahweh wears a helmet on his head as he goes forth to vindicate his oppressed people. The rabbis, however, applied this thought to the Messiah's work, and Christian interpretation of the Old Testament may well have followed suit, as we know was the case with a similar passage in Isaiah 11:1–5. Taking the helmet then means availing oneself of all that Christ in his saving work offers.

The sword is wielded with cutting power when *the word of God* is preached. This

---

[52] Details of the Roman soldier's equipment are discussed by A. Oepke in *TDNT,* V, 295–315. There are further parallels in the paramilitary organization of the camp at Qumran in the Dead Sea scrolls. See K. G. Kuhn's additions to *TDNT,* V, 298–300.

seems a clear reference to Isaiah 11:4 which describes the conquests of the Messiah (cf. Rev. 19:15) and recurs in Hebrews 4:12. The Greek *rhēma theou* rendered *the word of God* omits the definite article, a fact which suggests a LXX usage where the term relates to some words spoken by God himself. An apt illustration of what this verse implies is seen in the story of Jesus' temptations. Full of the Holy Spirit he met the enemy's insinuations with some appropriate part of Scripture which then became to him *the sword of the Spirit* (Luke 4:1–13).

Although it has no counterpart in a soldier's equipment, the continued list of *prayer and supplication* are evidently intended to be included in Paul's catalog. The link thought which suggests this continuation of the items the Christians have at their disposal is *the Spirit* who inspires Christian prayer (Rom. 8:26 ff.). In the vocabulary of prayer there is a word for general prayer (Gk. *proseuche*) and a term for the offering of some specific request (Gk. *deēsis*). The same conjunction of terms is found in Philippians 4:6 and 1 Timothy 5:5.

Paul now itemizes one object of Christian supplication, namely *for all the saints,* who form God's people of the new covenant (1:1). The call to intercession for fellow Christians requires the twin virtues of watchfulness and perseverance. The first word appears in the passage (Mark 13:13; Luke 21:36) dealing with the disciples' alertness in an eschatological setting, but it is not restricted thereto and may just as well be applicable to any crisis in life which may break on us without warning. Jesus in Gethsemane issued the same call, as reported in Mark 14:38. This latter sense is confirmed by the back reference to *pray at all times,* which is best taken to mean "at every critical time" in life rather than "maintain a constant attitude of prayer" (as in 1 Thess. 5:17).

The second word is a summons to persistence lest our hearts and spirits grow weary when there is no immediate answer to our prayer. The cognate verb "to persevere" is found in this sense in Colossians 4:2; Romans 12:12; Acts 1:14.

From the general admonition Paul moves on in v. 19 to a particular need which centers on himself, as in 2 Corinthians 1:11. There is difference, however. Where previously his requests for prayer have been set in a personal framework (his safety, his relations with the churches), now the plea is connected directly with the apostolic ministry committed to Paul as apostle to the Gentiles (3:1). Some scholars catch here the accent of the Pauline disciple voicing the need for the churches' prayers that the same apostolic mission, begun by Paul and continued by his followers, may not be retarded by timidity or wither through an indifference to the truths represented uniquely by Paul in his lifetime. But the close parallel with Colossians 4:2–4 makes this view less than certain.

The plea in vv. 19–20 is for cooperation in prayer that Paul's ministry of preaching *the mystery of the gospel*—a term explained in this letter as the uniting in one church of both Jews and Gentiles—may be fulfilled. For such a task he needs above all else courage in time of trial, for he is a prisoner whose witness must not be muted. He is Christ's *ambassador,* i.e., personal envoy (2 Cor. 5:20), but unlike a court personnel he enjoys no diplomatic immunity. Quite the contrary; he is *in chains* (Col. 4:18, cf. Acts 26:29).

XII. Personal Remarks and Final Greetings (6:21–24)

21 Now that you also may know how I am and what I am doing, Tychicus the beloved brother and faithful minister in the Lord will tell you everything. 22 I have sent him to you for this very purpose, that you may know how we are, and that he may encourage your hearts.
23 Peace be to the brethren, and love with faith, from God the Father and the Lord Jesus Christ. 24 Grace be with all who love our Lord Jesus Christ with love undying.

Verses 21–22 contain "the most extensive

verbal connection" (in the phrase of Dibelius-Greeven) between Ephesians and Colossians. Colossians 4:7–8 should be compared. Tychicus is the informant of Paul's immediate circumstances to the Asian churches; and he is warmly commended with the apostle's fine character reference. By bringing news of Paul's situation in Rome, he will put fresh heart into these Christians. This is the plain sense of vv. 21–22. But it is not quite as simple as this, and the RSV inserts a space between vv. 20 and 21 to mark a distinct break and change of subject in the letter. The Greek text accentuates the same change. The unusual phrase *you also* poses a difficulty, for Paul seems to have another group in mind with whom he is linking the addressees of Ephesians. We may speculate that Paul wrote two conclusions (here and Col. 4:7 f.) at the same time, hence their verbal agreement, or that this ending was later appended when the circular letter was directed and despatched to the church at Ephesus, being derived from Colossians. Or perhaps it is a later addition borrowed from Colossians by Paul's disciple to illustrate the kind of care the apostle exhibited for his churches in the Gentile mission. The disciple feels able in good conscience to use his master's vocabulary since he has the precedent of Colossians in front of him as he compiles this Pauline mosaic.

What I am doing is not to be taken literally, as though Tychicus were to take back a verbal cine-film of Paul in person and how he filled his days. The NEB captures the Greek idiom with the translation, "how I am" or, as colloquial English says, "how I am getting on" or asks, "How are you doing?"

Tychicus is described as a *faithful minister*. The term may have a general sense, meaning helper or a specific one, with the nuance suggested by 3:7. If the purpose of the appendix (vv. 21–22) is to endorse the ministries of the post-Pauline missionaries, the latter translation may be preferred, but this is uncertain.

I have sent him is too literal a version. The Greek aorist tense is "epistolary" (see comment on 3:4). The NEB improves with its rendering "I am sending." This makes it clear that Tychicus is to be the bearer of the letter to its destination; and he will be able to give a personal report of the apostle's condition and so encourage the churches.

The closing greeting is slightly longer than in other Pauline letters (e.g., Phil. 4:23) and couched in more general terms by the use of an impersonal term (*the brethren*) instead of the normal "you." But the authentic Pauline note is struck with the prayer for God's *grace* to be with the universal church described as *all who love our Lord Jesus Christ with love undying.* The letter which began with a salutation of grace and peace now closes with the same blessing in inverse order and with the addition of love and faith. All these are hallmarks of the Pauline theology, the stock-in-trade of his theological vocabulary.

The one exception, however, stands out unmistakably. *With love undying* represents the Greek *en aphtharsia* (there is no word for love in the original). This phrase is literally "with immortality," and *aphtharsia* is not common in Paul. The "immortality" could go with *grace* as the theme of Paul's prayer for his readers. So the NEB which renders: "Grace and immortality," but the order of the words is against this construction. Dibelius-Greeven suggest a different interpretation by taking the preposition in a local sense: the Lord Jesus Christ who (lives) in imperishable (glory). In support of this view James 2:1 as well as 1 Timothy 1:17 may be cited. And the solemn character of the conclusion supports this notion. The epistle which began with the church's blessings "in heavenly places" (1:3), where the enthroned Christ rules (1:20) and to which he calls his people (2:6), concludes fittingly on the same note. The church is directed to love him as the exalted head as a people already joined with him in his heavenly realm.

Philippians

FRANK STAGG

Introduction

That Philippians was written by Paul is virtually unquestioned. Traditionally it has been grouped with Colossians, Philemon, and Ephesians as belonging to Paul's "Prison Epistles," letters thought to have been written from Rome during Paul's two years or more there under "free custody" (*libera custodia*) or house arrest (cf. Acts 28:16,30 f.). Questions most debated today are its structural unity, the place of its origin, and the source and meaning of the Christological hymn in 2:5–11.

Many scholars find Philippians to be a composite of two or more letters, while others of equal competence see it as a structural unity with no more than characteristic Pauline digressions. The ancient tradition of Roman origin was first challenged in 1731 by Oeder of Leipzig (Martin, p. 25) and continues to be an open question today, alternatives being found in Caesarea, Ephesus, or some unknown city. Theologically, most attention centers in the so-called kenotic passage (2:5–11). Even the dominant mood of the letter is debatable, for it is by no means certain that John A. Bengel did it justice in his oft-quoted claim, "The sum of the epistle is, 'I rejoice, rejoice ye.'" Scholarship today is concerned about the letter's unity, but the letter itself is concerned throughout for the unity of the Philippian church, a note equally as strong as the joy note.

I. Paul and the Philippians

According to Acts 16:12–40, Paul and his missionary companions founded the church during his so-called second missionary journey (*ca.* A.D. 49), having answered a call at Troas to enter Macedonia to help there. The church was born in a situation of crisis, knew hardship and persecution from its inception (cf. 1 Thess. 2:2), proved to be most loyal to Paul (cf. Phil. 4:14–16), and possibly was the church dearest to him.

Philippi received its name from Philip II of Macedon, father of Alexander the Great. It was situated on the site of an earlier settlement known as Krenides (Springs). Originally a Thracian village, it was strengthened in 360 B.C. by a settlement of Greek families from Thasos. In 357 Philip stationed a Macedonian garrison there, making it a military stronghold to protect the nearby gold mines. Later, the mines exhausted, it was important for guarding the great Egnatian Way which connected East and West. In 146 B.C. it became a part of the Roman province of Macedonia. Its primary importance dates from 42 B.C., at which time it was the scene of battle in which Antony and Octavian (later known as Augustus Caesar) defeated Brutus and Cassius, thus prevailing over the Republican generals who had opposed Julius Caesar's ambitions. This opened the way for the founding of the Roman Empire.

Antony settled a number of veterans in Philippi and gave the city the status of a colony, i.e., a military settlement with exceptional civic privileges. In 30 B.C. Octavian, having defeated Antony and Cleopatra at Actium, added some Latin-speaking settlers to Philippi. The new emperor now named the city Colonia Augusta Julia Philippensis (F. W. Beare, p. 6).

Philippi remained a Roman colony when Paul first entered the city. Its military and Latin character is reflected in the attitude of Paul's first opponents there, men who thought of themselves as Romans (Acts 16:21). Its variety of religions and cults added to its pagan nature. Gods from Thracia, Greece, Rome, Anatolia, Syria, and Egypt were worshiped there. Along with the wide variety of religious cults were many private clubs, economic and burial. Judaism, too, was represented, but it seems to have been of minimal strength.

There is no conclusive evidence of a Jewish synagogue in Philippi. Paul and his companions seem to have been in the city for some days before they were able to locate a little band of worshipers who gathered for prayer alongside the river and outside the city gate (Acts 16:12–13). Some see this gathering as a "mission synagogue." A woman of Thyatira of this little group was converted and seems to have become the chief support for Paul and his companions. Lydia seems to have been neither Jewish born nor a proselyte, but rather a God-fearing Gentile woman attracted first to Judaism and then to Christianity. But this little band of people proved to be unusually courageous, loyal, and generous as they lived and worked under the pressures of anti-Semitic prejudice (Acts 16:20). They remained consistent in giving Paul financial and moral support, from the earliest months of their existence as a church up till the time of special generosity which largely occasioned Paul's writing the letter before us (1:5; 4:15–18).

II. Attestation of the Letter

Philippians seems to have been quoted in 1 Clement, written from Rome in A.D. 96. Clement's "in the beginning of the gospel" seems to reflect Philippians 4:15; "If we walk not worthily of him" is strikingly like 1:27, especially in Greek; and there

seem also to be reflections of 1:10; 2:15; and 2:5 ff. The cumulative force of these apparent citations suggests that Clement knew this epistle (Lightfoot, p. 74). Ignatius in his letter to the Romans (ii) reflects 2:17 in his "poured out as a libation to God." In his epistle to the Philadelphians (viii), his admonition to "do nothing from party spirit" seems to come from 2:3, as does "nor from vainglory" earlier in his epistle (i). In his epistle to Smyrna, Ignatius derives "being perfect be ye also perfectly minded" from 3:15. Polycarp is the first explicitly to refer to Paul's having written Philippians, as seen in his own letter to the Philippians (iii, xi). Actually, he said that Paul "wrote letters" to the Philippians, apparently more than one. He seemingly reflects the text of Paul's Philippians 2:2–5,10,16; 3:18; 4:10; and possibly 1:27. The second-century Jewish-Christian work entitled *The Testaments of the Twelve Patriarchs* seems to borrow from Philippians 1:8; 2:6–8,15; 3:21. Our letter was included in the earliest known Christian canon, that of Marcion (*ca.* A.D. 150) and in the Muratorian Fragment, which preserves the canon recognized in Rome about A.D. 200. The letter is quoted as Paul's by Irenaeus, Tertullian, and Clement of Alexandria.

III. The Question of Literary Unity

The most difficult critical question is that of the literary structure of Philippians, whether a unity or a composite. Except for Polycarp's reference to Paul's having written "letters" to the Philippians, the evidences are internal. Scholars are almost evenly divided on the question, and the issue is inconclusive. Only on dogmatic grounds may one close the debate in favor of either the letter's unity or composite nature. This writer feels that the case for a composite of two or more letters is strong but indecisive. The burden of proof must rest with those who contest its unity, and proof falls short of conclusiveness. Even those who see Philippians as composed of two or more fragments hold that the components are Paul's own writing, with the possible exception of 2:5–11. This latter is considered by many to be a pre-Pauline "hymn," but few would hold it to be an interpolation (see comment on 2:5–11).

The strongest case for the interpolation of a fragment from another letter can be made following 3:1. For many scholars the gulf between the serene mood of 3:1a, "Rejoice in the Lord" and the scathing words of 3:2, "Look out for the dogs, look out for the evil-workers, look out for those who mutilate the flesh," is too great to bridge. The recurrence of "finally" (to loipon) in 3:1 and 4:8 may indicate conclusions to two letters.

Stephan Le Moyne (Varia Sacra, II.332, 343) suggested that two letters were combined in our Philippians, observing the fact that Polycarp in his own letter to the Philippians (iii) said that Paul wrote "letters" to them. Heinrichs (Koppe's New Testament, 1803) proposed that 1:1—3:1 was written to the church in general and that 3:2—4:20 was written to the rulers of the church, with 4:21–23 being the conclusion to the earlier letter (cf. Lightfoot, p. 68). This hypothesis has been explored in various forms for nearly two centuries. A modern example is Edgar J. Goodspeed's proposal that 3:2—4:2 was the earlier of two letters, written soon after Epaphroditus arrived from Philippi with gifts, and 1:1—3:1 was the latter, written as Epaphroditus was at the point of returning following a long and near fatal illness.[1]

Although the arguments for interpolation are weighty, they are not decisive. Polycarp's reference to letters may be erroneous or a misreading of 3:1.[2] The repetition of to loipon is not decisive, for it may mean "for the rest" or "as to what remains" as well as "finally" (cf. 1 Thess. 4:1; 2 Thess. 3:1). The phrase may mark no more than a transition, not necessarily the conclusion of a writing.

More substantive is the abrupt shift of tone and subject matter after 3:1a. This could indicate an interpolation. Although no extant manuscript gives a variant to the familiar text, there are literally hundreds of thousands of textual variants in biblical writings, and some of them are extensive (e.g., Mark 16:9–20). Since there are many known textual disturbances, one may not a priori rule out the possibility even where extant manuscripts give no such evidence. But the case for interpolation is weakened by the failure of scholars after almost 200 years of study to reach agreement on the number of interpolations or even on the extent of the suspected interpolation beginning in chapter three.[3] These examples do not exhaust the theories of partition. Should not the "seams" between letters be more apparent? Among modern scholars who have seen Philippians as one single letter without interpolations are M. Dibelius, C. H. Dodd, G. S. Duncan, E. Haupt, W. G. Kümmel, E. Lohmeyer, and E. F. Scott.

A colleague, Professor Harold S. Songer, suggests that more plausible than interpolation is the possibility of an excision or loss of some part of the letter following 3:1 (cf. Lightfoot, pp. 136–140). This would account for the rough seam at the beginning of the omission with no equally apparent seam at the end of the lost section. An insert into the middle of a paragraph would cause two seams, but the loss of the end of a paragraph would cause only one seam.

3 Some critics see an interpolation consisting of 3:2—4:3, some of 3:2—4:1 (McNeile-Williams, J. Weiss), some of 3:2—4:20 (Goodspeed), some of 3:1b—4:9 (Friedrich). Some see Philippians to be composed of three Pauline letters: 4:10–20/ 1:1—3:1; 4:2–9,21–23/ 3:2—4:1 (Beare); 4:10–23/ 1:1—3:1; 4:4–7/ 3:2–4,8 f. (Schmithals); 1:1—3:1; 4:4–7,21–23/ 3:2—4:3/ 4:10–20 (Bornkamm); 4:10–20/ 4:10–20/ 1:1—2:30; 4:21–23/ 3:1—4:9 (Rahtjen). Willi Marxsen sees three letters: A: 4:10–20; B: 1:1–3:1; 4:4–7,21–23; C: 3:2–4, 8–9 (Introduction to the New Testament, tr. G. Buswell (Philadelphia: Fortress, 1968), p. 62. See also W. G. Kümmel, ibid, pp. 235 f.

1 Introduction to the New Testament (Chicago: University of Chicago Press, 1937), pp. 90–96.
2 W. G. Kümmel, Introduction to the New Testament, 14th rev. ed., of the Paul Feine-Johannes Behm Einleitung, tr. A. J. Mattill, Jr. (Nashville: Abingdon, 1966), p. 236.

Few of Paul's letters have escaped theories of extensive interpolation and/or abridgment (cf. 2 Cor. especially). It may be that modern editors are trying to impose upon Paul literary standards by which he was never bound. Paul acknowledged roughness in speech (2 Cor. 11:6), and roughness may also have characterized much of his writing. He was capable of elegant style, but he seems to have cared little for it. His emotional involvements were strong, and his style often reflected his strong and changing moods and emotions. Moreover, 3:7-14 appears to look back to 2:5-11, tying together the two passages most often disputed.[4] In view of these facts and of the indecisiveness of partition theories, it is thought best here to try to understand the letter as it has come to us, not in terms of highly questionable reconstructions.

IV. Place and Date of Writing

The tradition that the letter was written in Rome is traceable to the second century Marcionite prologues, in which it is said that the apostle wrote the Philippians "from Rome, from prison, by Epaphroditus." In the fourth century, Chrysostom linked Philippians, Ephesians, Colossians, and Philemon as Paul's imprisonment letters, all written from Rome. This position remained unchallenged until the eighteenth century and continues to be maintained by scholars like Beare, Dodd, Guthrie, Heard, Jülicher, Rahtjen, and J. Schmid. In 1731 Oeder of Leipzig and then in 1799 H. E. G. Paulus proposed Caesarea as the place of origin; and in 1897 (and in 1923) Adolf Deissmann suggested Ephesus, followed by H. Lisco in 1900. No scholar contests that the letter came out of an imprisonment. From Acts 23:23—26:32; 28:14-31 we know of imprisonments in Caesarea and Rome. An Ephesian imprisonment is a possibility but cannot be demonstrated.

The terms "praetorian guard" (1:13) and "Caesar's household" (4:22) seem to point to Rome. In Rome Paul was under house arrest but was guarded by soldiers, apparently under the praetorian guard. But praetorium can refer to situations outside Rome. The term was first used for the tent in which the praetor and his people lived when encamped, and later it came to designate the official residence of the governor (cf. Matt. 27:27; Acts 23:35). The term may refer to praetorian barracks, but since imperial soldiers were found throughout imperial provinces, no conclusion may be reached as to the reference in Philippians. The same inconclusiveness pertains to Caesar's household, which may refer to emancipated imperial slaves in Rome or elsewhere.[5]

The distance between Philippi and the place of origin is a factor. It is possible that four trips are implied between the Philippians and Paul's place of imprisonment: (1) news of Paul's imprisonment reaching Philippi, (2) the coming of Epaphroditus with gifts from Philippi, (3) the report in Philippi of the illness of Epaphroditus, and (4) Epaphroditus' learning that the Philippians were concerned for his health. Travel between Philippi and Ephesus would be much easier and quicker than to either Rome or Caesarea. On the other hand, the known imprisonments were sufficiently long in Rome and Caesarea to allow for four trips, if such is indeed implied.

It is argued that when Paul wrote the letter to the Romans, he planned to visit them on his way to Spain (15:28), but that Philippians reflects no such plan. This argument has little force; for, if written from Rome, several years of imprisonment in Caesarea and Rome along with other changes could easily have altered his plans. The longing to see old friends again could easily turn his attention to Philippi from whatever imprisonment he may have been writing.

The conditions of Paul's imprisonment as reflected in Philippians are congenial to

---

4 G. S. Duncan, "Letter to the Philippians," IDB (Nashville: Abingdon, 1962), III, 791.

5 Marxsen, op. cit., p. 65.

what is known about the Roman house arrest. Paul was awaiting a trial which could issue in execution or release. There is no evidence that he faced the danger of execution at Caesarea, and nothing is known about an Ephesian imprisonment. Paul's freedom to write a letter like Philippians, possibly with the help of an amanuensis, answers to the freedom of his house arrest in Rome. The need for such help as was provided by the Philippians is more understandable at Rome than in Ephesus, a base of operations for nearly three years. At Caesarea it seems that help would have been nearer at hand than Philippi. That his internment "served to advance the gospel" (1:12) in so significant a way speaks more for Rome than for Caesarea or Ephesus.

A major argument in dating and locating Philippians is its comparison with Ephesians, Colossians, and Philemon on the one hand and with letters to the Thessalonians, Galatians, Corinthians, and Romans on the other. It is claimed by some that the affinities are closer to the latter group, thus suggesting an early date for Philippians. By any dating Philippians stands loosely to the other so-called Prison letters. It could have been from the same imprisonment but at a different time, either before or after the other three. Although it is often assumed that the opponents of chapter 3 are Judaizers, this is not clear. They could have been Jewish Christians or non-Christian Jews. There are also some evidences of a "perfectionist" group of pseudo-spiritualists among Paul's opponents. There is no evidence that problems with Judaizers or super-spiritualists, reflected especially in the Corinthian letters, faded away before Paul's imprisonment.

If Philippians was written from Ephesus, the date was about A.D. 54–55. If from Caesarea, the date was about 56–57, although exact Pauline chronology eludes us. If from Rome, the date could be the late fifties or early sixties, depending upon the date given for the succession of Felix by Festus. With all considered, the Roman imprisonment remains the best probability, but the question must remain open as we await further light.

V. Occasion and Purpose

Since the time of John A. Bengel (d. 1752) Philippians has been known as the joy letter: *summa epistolae; gaudeo, gaudete* ("The sum of the letter is, I rejoice, rejoice ye."). But this overstates the case. The note of joy is emphatic (16 times), and it is highly significant in that it is sounded out of an imprisonment and prospect of possible death and is proclaimed to a church that has known persecution and hardship all its days. The joy note is there, but there is an equally strong note of concern over "grumbling" and "questioning" (2:14) and actual rupture of fellowship in the church (4:2 f.). Paul had known the agony of the earlier Corinthian divisions, and his mission to Jerusalem with the offering from prevailingly Gentile churches had been designed to bring Jewish and Gentile Christians into a stronger fellowship. There is no evidence that the church at Philippi had reached a critical stage of disunity, but Paul certainly saw this as a threat and sought to head it off (cf. 1:27; 2:1–4).

If it may be assumed that alongside his gratitude for the Philippians and joy in their virtues there was also grave apprehension over signs of growing conflict and disunity within the church, many passages in Philippians take on new meaning, also more continuity within the letter becomes apparent. Paul already had seen that behind all the surface problems at Corinth was the root problem of self-centeredness, the world's false wisdom of self-trust, self-love, and self-assertion. Against this he had proclaimed God's wisdom, the love that reached its highest manifestation of self-denial and self-sacrifice in the cross. Do not these very presuppositions shine through Philippians? Behind the quarreling of Euodia and Syntyche (4:2) was selfishness. Behind the grumbling and ambitions of those who would "mutilate the flesh" (3:2) and behind the preaching from "envy and rivalry" and from "partisanship" (1:15,17) was the same self-centeredness (2:1–4).

Against this poorly motivated preaching, whether at Rome or elsewhere, and against the selfishness asserting itself in Philippi, Paul offered the example of Christ (2:5–11), the example of Timothy (2:19–24), and the example of Epaphroditus (2:25–30). To this he also adds his own example in turning from selfish goals to the claims of Christ (3:4–21).

Paul's primary appeal for renunciation of the egocentricity behind the grumbling, contentions, and division is with a view to having the mind of Christ Jesus (2:5–11). Those who reject the "example theory" wrongly interpret the passage as concerned chiefly with humility. Were this the burden of the passage, it would follow that to try to be humble is self-defeating. But the concern is at most only incidentally with humility. What is held up for example is the disposition of Christ to relinquish his privileged rights in his concern to serve God and man. It is this example of utter self-denial and self-sacrifice which the Philippians need. How could Euodia and Syntyche continue their quarrel in the presence of him who surrendered his rights and privileges for the sake of others. This "hymn" is not an interpolation; it is germane to the basic concern of the letter. Its precise nature and meaning will be analyzed in the commentary.

Against this background, the examples of Timothy and Epaphroditus are clearer as to meaning. The one thing which Paul commends in Timothy is his being "genuinely anxious" for others and his refusal to look after his "own interests" (2:20 f.). What is stressed about Epaphroditus is his risking his life to complete the Philippians' service to Paul (2:30).

The immediate occasion of the letter was to acknowledge the generous Philippian ministry to Paul, to deal with incipient problems of division, and to warn against the serious threat of some "evil-workers"

(3:2), the precise nature of whose character and message is not clear. It is a letter of joy and gratitude. It is also a letter of distress, concern, and apprehension.

Outline

I. Introduction (1:1–11)
  1. Greetings (1:1–2)
  2. Thanksgiving and prayer for the Philippians (1:3–11)
II. Victory out of suffering (1:12–30)
  1. The gospel preached in prison (1:12–14)
  2. Friends and foes aroused to new effort (1:15–18)
  3. Willingness to live or die for Christ (1:19–26)
III. Plea for unity grounded in the mind of Christ (1:27—2:30)
  1. First exhortation: living worthily of the gospel through unity and courage in the face of hostility (1:27–30)
  2. Second exhortation: unity and self-abnegation with supreme example: the mind of Christ (2:1–11)
  3. Third exhortation: working out their salvation (2:12–13)
  4. The example of Paul: poured out as libation (2:14–18)
  5. The example of Timothy: concern for others (2:19–24)
  6. The example of Epaphroditus: life risked for others (2:25–30)
IV. Warning against a distorted religion (3:1–21)
  1. Confidence in the flesh *versus* the knowledge of Christ (3:1–11)
  2. Threat of false perfectionism (3:12–16)
  3. Threat of libertinism (3:17—4:1)
V. Appeal to unity and peace (4:2–20)
  1. Euodia and Syntyche (4:2–3)
  2. The peace of God (4:4–7)
  3. What to take into account (4:8–9)
  4. Paul's response to the Philippians' gifts (4:10–20)
VI. Concluding greetings and benediction (4:21–23)

Selected Bibliography

BARTH, KARL. *The Epistle to the Philippians.* Tr. J. W. LEITCH. 6th ed. Richmond: John Knox Press, 1962.

BEARE, F. W. *The Epistle to the Philippians.* ("Harper's New Testament Commentaries.") New York: Harper & Brothers, 1959.

BEASLEY-MURRAY, G. R. "Philippians." *Peake's Commentary on the Bible.* New York: Thomas Nelson & Sons, 1962.

DIBELIUS, M. *An die Thessalonicher*, i, ii; *an*

die Philipper. ("Handbuch zum Neuen Testament.") 3rd rev. ed.; Tübingen: Mohr, 1937.

DUNCAN, GEORGE S. *St. Paul's Ephesian Ministry.* New York: Charles Scribner's Sons, 1930.

KENNEDY, H. A. A. "The Epistle to the Philippians," *The Expositor's Greek Testament.* London: 1903.

LIGHTFOOT, J. B. *St. Paul's Epistle to the Philippians.* 4th ed. London: Macmillan and Co. 1896.

LOHMEYER, E. *Der Brief an die Philipper.* ("Kritisch-exegetischer Kommentar über das Neue Testament"). 9th ed. rev. by W. SCHMAUCH. Göttingen, 1953.

MARTIN, R. P. *The Epistle of Paul to the Philippians.* "Tyndale Bible Commentaries." Grand Rapids: Wm. B. Eerdmans, 1959.

————, *Carmen Christi: Philippians 2:5–11 in Recent Interpretation and in the Setting of the Early Christian Worship.* ("Society for New Testament Studies.") Cambridge: University Press, 1967.

MICHAEL, J. H. *The Epistle of Paul to the Philippians* ("The Moffatt New Testament Commentary.") New York: Harper and Bros., 1928.

SCOTT, E. F. "The Epistle to the Philippians," *The Interpreter's Bible.* Nashville: Abingdon Press, 1955.

SYNGE, F. C. *Philippians and Colossians.* ("Torch Bible Commentaries.") London: SCM Press, 1951.

VINCENT, M. R. *The Epistle to the Philippians and to Philemon.* ("The International Critical Commentary.") Edinburgh: T. & T. Clark, 1897.

Commentary on the Text

I. Introduction (1:1–11)

1. Greetings (1:1–2)

¹ Paul and Timothy, servants of Christ Jesus, To all the saints in Christ Jesus who are at Philippi, with the bishops and deacons;
² Grace to you and peace from God our Father and the Lord Jesus Christ.

The first word in 13 New Testament writings is *Paul.* In one of his earliest letters (2 Thess. 3:17) Paul indicated that his letters could be recognized by his own autograph, meaning probably that where an amanuensis was used (cf. Rom. 16:22) he would at some point take the pen in hand and thus authenticate the letter as his own (cf. Gal. 6:11; Philemon 19). It does not follow that Paul wielded the pen at the outset of each letter, but he did begin each letter with his own name. His name does not again appear in the letter and there is no special authentication (as in 2 Thess. 3:17; Gal. 6:11; Philemon 19), but there is no serious question as to the Pauline authorship of the letter, although many scholars hold it to be a composite of two or more Pauline letters (see the Introduction). Verses 1–2 are in the letter form

of the first century.

Timothy is associated with Paul, but it does not follow that he coauthored the letter. In 1:3 Paul says "I" and in 2:19–23 he refers to Timothy in the third person. Paul first met Timothy in Lystra or Derbe (Acts 16:1; 20:4) and there enlisted him as a fellow worker. Timothy became one of Paul's closest and most trusted companions (2:19–22). From Acts we learn of their work together in Macedonia (18:5; 19:22), Corinth (18:5), and Ephesus (19:22). Timothy was with Paul in Corinth when he wrote each Thessalonian letter. He was with Paul at Ephesus prior to his writing 1 Corinthians (4:17; 16:10) and when he wrote 2 Corinthians (1:1), probably from Macedonia. Timothy joined Paul in greetings to the Romans, probably from Corinth (Rom. 16:21). He was associated with Paul in the salutations of Colossians (1:1) and Philemon (1). If Philippians and these other prison letters were from Rome, there is no supporting evidence that Timothy was there with Paul. If written from Ephesus, there is supporting evidence both for their being together there and for Timothy's being sent to Macedonia (Acts 19:22) from Ephesus (with Erastus, not Epaphroditus as in Phil. 2:19,25).

Servants translates *douloi,* literally, "slaves." Behind Paul's usage may be the Old Testament picture of God's chosen servants as his accredited messengers (cf. Ex. 14:31; Num. 12:7; Psalm 105:26; Amos 3:7; Jer. 25:4; Dan. 9:6,10). The Septuagint renders the Hebrew *'ebed* by *doulos,* and the latter term may thus lose its picture of servitude for one of dignity. The term was obvious to Greeks but seldom used by Jews in a religious sense except as a term of honor. Paul's meaning is best seen from his own writings. He saw Christians as belonging to Christ by virtue of redemption (1 Cor. 6:20; 7:23). His correlative for Christians as slaves is Christ Jesus as *Lord,* thus acknowledging that total submission to the will of Christ is proper to the Christian (Beare, pp. 50 ff.). Paul often introduced himself as an apostle of Christ Jesus, but apparently he did not recognize Timothy as an apostle (cf. Col. 1:1). *Saints* is Paul's usual designation for Christians. The term points to our being set apart by God and unto him, covenant people of God. The term applies to all Christians, not to a select few of special spirituality or moral excellence. Saints are such by divine calling, and they are also ones who on their part have called upon the Lord Jesus Christ (1 Cor. 1:2 f.). Divine initiative in calling and human response in faith, both belong to one's becoming a saint. Saints in the New Testament are the eschatological people or "the saints of the Most High" of Daniel 7:18,27.

In Christ Jesus is a basic Pauline concept, found repeatedly in this letter. The phrase as nearly as any other reflects the heart of Paul's understanding of Christian existence. To be "in Christ" is not only to be bound to him individually by faith, trust, and commitment; but it is to be bound together with his people. To be "in Christ" is the opposite of being "in sin" or "in Adam" (cf. 1 Cor. 15:22). Those addressed reside *at Philippi,* a city in Macedonia (see Introduction), but their distinctive existence is *in Christ Jesus.*

Bishops and deacons refer not so much to offices as to functions or responsibilities in the church. *Bishops* translates the Greek term *episkopois,* literally, "overseers." The plural indicates that as yet there was no "monarchical bishop" at Philippi. Also, "bishops" and "elders" were probably interchangeable terms as seems true in Acts 20:17,28 ("guardians" translates *episkopous*) and Titus 1:5,7. More than a half century later Polycarp of Smyrna wrote of "presbyters" (elders) and deacons in the church at Philippi, with no mention of bishops, but in Clement of Rome (*ca.* 96) the terms bishops and elders are still interchangeable. There were senior men of the church who, as in the Jewish synagogues, were accorded a special supervisory role by the congregation. The deacons were another group of men who may have had special assignments in connection with the material needs and responsibilities of the church. Their work may have been patterned after that of the seven of Acts 6:1–6, but the latter are not called deacons.

Grace . . . and peace are early Christian greetings, possibly combining the Greek form of greetings (*chairein*) with the Hebrew *shalom* (peace). If so, the pagan Greek *cheirein* (hail!) has been changed to its cognate *charis* (grace). The whole Christian existence is one made possible only by the grace of God. *Peace from God* is not the world's escape from war but that reconciliation to God and with oneself and with others brought about for those who entrust themselves to God. Jesus knew God as *Father* and came that we may so know him. *Lord Jesus Christ* brings together three basic understandings. *Jesus* means "Yahweh saves." Paul uses the term for the earthly and the risen Christ. *Christ* means "anointed" and designates Jesus' function as the one in whom the kingdom of God has come. *Lord* gives further emphasis to what is implied in *Christ.* It is his authority to rule. The New

Testament knows nothing of his being Saviour (Jesus) without first becoming Lord. The monotheism of the Old Testament is retained, and in Jesus Christ is seen not only God's authority but his presence.

2. Thanksgiving and Prayer for the Philippians (1:3–11)

³ I thank my God in all my remembrance of you, ⁴ always in every prayer of mine for you all making my prayer with joy, ⁵ thankful for your partnership in the gospel from the first day until now. ⁶ And I am sure that he who began a good work in you will bring it to completion at the day of Jesus Christ. ⁷ It is right for me to feel thus about you all, because I hold you in my heart, for you are all partakers with me of grace, both in my imprisonment and in the defense and confirmation of the gospel. ⁸ For God is my witness, how I yearn for you all with the affection of Christ Jesus. ⁹ And it is my prayer that your love may abound more and more, with knowledge and all discernment, ¹⁰ so that you may approve what is excellent, and may be pure and blameless for the day of Christ, ¹¹ filled with the fruits of righteousness which come through Jesus Christ, to the glory and praise of God.

Thanksgiving (vv. 3–8).—Paul begins with a strong note of thanksgiving and joy, prompted by all his *remembrance* of the Philippians. This note is so strong throughout the letter that since Bengel (d. 1752) it has been known as the "joy letter." But a parallel note, just as strong and significant, may be found, even though Paul seems to insert it with maximum tact (see Introduction). This is the note of deep concern for the unity of a church which already is seriously threatened but not yet hopelessly broken. The studied repetition of *all* or *you all* (cf. 1:1,7,8,25; 2:17; 4:21) underscores the letter's major concern to secure the unity of the church (cf. 1:27; 2:1–4; 4:2–3,5, 7,9) as Paul seems to intimate that he makes no difference between persons or parties in the church (Lightfoot, p. 81). Joy is not the sum of the letter. Joy and concern for unity or joy and concern for the overcoming of the self-centeredness behind disunity come closer to being the sum of the letter.

Paul gives thanks in particular for *partnership in the gospel. Partnership* translates *koinōnia,* a highly significant term in the New Testament, variously translated as "partnership," "communion," or "fellowship." The basic idea is that of having something in common or jointly. Paul saw the life which we share together in Christ to be the *koinōnia* of God's Son into which we are divinely called (1 Cor. 1:9). This fellowship is also known as the *koinōnia* which is of the Holy Spirit (2 Cor. 13:14). Paul also uses the term to portray a common task or work, as the collection for the poor among the saints at Jerusalem (2 Cor. 8:4; 9:13). In Philippians some cognate form of *koinōnia* appears in 1:5; 2:1; 3:10; 4:15 (rendered respectively as partnership, participation, share, and partnership).

From their earliest days until the writing of this letter, the Philippians had had partnership in the gospel. They had sent material help more than once while he labored in Thessalonica (4:16), at which time the church in Philippi could not have been more than a few months old. The most recent expression of their partnership in the gospel was the help sent through one of their number, Epaphroditus (2:25; 4:18).

Verse 6 expresses Paul's conviction that God, i.e., *he who began,* will complete what he began, but it also reflects Paul's awareness that the Philippians were not perfect and that they needed to be reminded of this. The Philippians themselves or someone seeking to influence them may have been overconfident about their need of being made better. In 3:12–16 Paul emphatically denies that he himself has reached perfection, probably with a view to disturbing their complacency about their imagined perfection. Along with Paul's concern over their disunity is his dissatisfaction with their satisfaction over their spiritual state.

The *good work* which God began in them and will complete may be their inward spirituality or their outward cooperation with Paul in the furtherance of the gospel. Since Paul is so high in his praise of their outward performance in missions, it is likely that the *good work* which needs completing is their inner spirituality. That God will *bring it to completion* implies that he is at work to this end now but that the work will not be completed until *the day of Jesus Christ.* This *day* is eschatological, at the end of history. In the Old Testament the day came to be described by the prophets (cf. Amos 5:20; Zeph. 1:15) more and more in terms of judgment. In the New Testament the emphasis upon judgment is not lessened, but greater attention is given to the day as one of salvation. Both judgment and redemption are seen as beginning in life but consummated only at *the day of Jesus Christ.* Both have a commencement, continuance, and consummation (cf. Michael, p. 13).

Paul may expect the Parousia to come in the lifetime of the Philippians. Earlier he seems clearly to have expected "the coming of the Lord" during his own lifetime (1 Thess. 4:15; 1 Cor. 15:51). In Philippians he sees that he may die before that coming, but it does not necessarily follow that he has surrendered his earlier expectation that the Lord would come to his generation.

What Paul thinks it *right* for him to *feel* about the Philippians is not clear. He could mean his affection for them or their progress toward completion. Possibly he had in mind something more inclusive: his thanksgiving, joy, intercession, and confidence (Barth, p. 18). He holds this to be right because he *holds* them in his *heart.* The clause *because I hold you in my heart* could be read "because you hold me in your heart." The construction is peculiar to Greek, with no English parallel, an infinitive followed by two accusatives (objective case in English). The Greek reads literally, "because of the having me in the heart you." Probably the RSV is correct in its rendering. *You all* is probably a deliberate reminder that he excludes none from his own heart, implying that

they should exclude none (cf. 2 Cor. 6:11–13; 7:2).

Paul's further reason for finding it right that he have confidence in their ultimate perfection, at the day of Jesus Christ, is the fact that all of them have been *partakers* with him of grace. They have had *koinōnia* with him in God's grace, and this has come to special expression in connection with Paul's imprisonment (see Introduction as to the place of his imprisonment). Since Paul was on trial for his life, anyone who identified with him ran the risk of suffering his fate. To risk this, as was true of Epaphroditus, was a manifestation of God's grace at work in them. Once again, Paul includes *all* in this recognition.

Defense and confirmation seem to be technical legal terms (Moulton and Milligan, *Vocabulary,* p. 108). The meaning of *defense* is obvious. *Confirmation* probably meant vindication of one's claims. Paul's trial is also the trial of the gospel, and he expects it to be not only defended but vindicated (see Moffatt translation). By *imprisonment* Paul alluded to an actual arrest, but by *defense and confirmation* he does not necessarily refer to stages in a Roman trial, even though legal terms are used. He probably had in mind his whole ordeal, one which the Philippians were sharing with him in sympathetic concern and action. In so doing they were participating with him *of grace.* Paul chose not to call it an ordeal but an expression of God's grace that he permits his servants to suffer for the gospel (cf. 1:29).

In saying *I yearn for you,* Paul probably means simply that he wants to be with the Philippians. His *witness* to this longing is God. Paul often invoked God as his witness (Rom. 1:9; 9:1; 2 Cor. 1:23; 11:31; Gal. 1:20; 1 Thess. 2:5,10). Here there is no suggestion that the Philippians doubt his word. It is in *affection* which comes from *Christ Jesus* himself that Paul yearns for them. *Affection* translates *splagchnois,* a Greek term designating the nobler viscera (heart, lungs, liver) and not the *entera,* the lower viscera or intestines (Lightfoot, p. 84). The inelegant and inexact "bowels" of the KJV goes back to John Wyclif's rendering of the Latin Vulgate's word *viscera* (Michael, p. 19). "Heart" comes close to being the English counterpart to Paul's Greek term, i.e., the seat of the emotions in popular thought.

Prayer (*vv. 9–11*)—Paul does not deny that the Philippians have *love*, but he sees it to be deficient, possibly against the pride of some that they lack nothing. To Paul *love* (*agapē*) is the "more excellent way" (1 Cor. 12:31), the supreme gift or fruit of the Spirit (Gal. 5:22; 1 Cor. 13). It is the disposition to relate to others for their good, regardless of cost or consequence to oneself. It is the opposite to self-centeredness. Paul prayed for a growing abundance of love for the Philippians. Especially was he concerned that their love be enlightened, for goodwill is not enough. The desired growth in love related particularly to moral insight, *knowledge and all discernment*. The word here for *knowledge* is *epignōsis*, which sometimes is distinguished from *gnōsis*, the latter being simple knowledge and the former signifying thorough or complete knowledge. The distinction here probably is not to be pressed. *Discernment* signifies insight or perception. In this context, love is seen as ideally having the moral instinct to perceive what is right. Of course, love is to be informed. Love's disposition is to trust and to understand, but it also must be informed if it is to function adequately.

The Greek of v. 10 has several ambiguities. *Approve what is excellent* may also mean to "prove by testing the things that differ" or to "distinguish the things which differ." Of course, the RSV rendering presupposes the alternate, for one cannot meaningfully "approve what is excellent" unless he can distinguish the things that differ. A parallel appears in Romans 2:18, where the meaning seems to be, "You distinguish the things that differ," but usage is ambiguous there also. However translated, Paul's concern is for enlightened

moral discernment, "a sense of what is vital" (Moffatt), which leads to right moral choice. Quarrelling Philippians needed to know what mattered and what did not. The desired result is that the readers be pure and blameless at the final judgment, *the day of Christ.*

Two images are brought together by the words rendered *pure* and *blameless*. The first refers to precious metal (there were once gold mines at Philippi) purged of all dross. The second may refer to a traveler unhindered in his journey (Scott, p. 27), or it may refer to one who has not hindered others. "Pure" translates *eilikrineis*, the etymology of which may be "to judge in the sunlight," but this is uncertain. Whatever the etymology, Paul's usage seems to mean unmixed or pure. Moffatt holds closer to the possible etymology in his rendering "transparent." The other image, *aproskopoi*, may mean not stumbling or not causing others to stumble (as in 1 Cor. 10:32). Either meaning suits the context. "Blameless" opts for the second meaning, not causing others to stumble.

Righteousness is seen not as the *fruits* themselves but as that which produces the harvest which comes about *through Jesus Christ* and unto the *glory and praise of God*. Righteousness is both right standing with God and also the creative work of God as he makes men righteous—of course involving the free response of men. This is divine work, not man's own work, and it is more than merely counting righteous one who is unrighteous. Paul does not here spell out what are the *fruits* of righteousness (cf. Gal. 5:22). God's glory is his character manifested in redemption, and his *praise* is man's recognition of that character (Michael, p. 26).

II. Victory Out of Suffering (1:12–30)

1. The Gospel Preached in Prison (1: 12–14)

¹² I want you to know, brethren, that what has happened to me has really served to advance the gospel, ¹³ so that it has become known throughout the whole praetorian guard

and to all the rest that my imprisonment is for Christ; 14 and most of the brethren have been made confident in the Lord because of my imprisonment, and are much more bold to speak the word of God without fear.

Paul's "gaol becomes a pulpit," his bonds a novel form of preaching (Synge, p. 24). Those responsible for Paul's imprisonment had sought thus to silence him, but their strategy backfired. They unwittingly gave him a new pulpit, a new forum, a new audience. The gospel was actually advanced by what happened to him. *Happened* translates a phrase which more literally means "the things pertaining to me." It is best rendered "my circumstances" (cf. Eph. 6:21; Col. 4:7). Paul does not attribute his imprisonment to God or say that in itself it is good. His claim is that there has been salvage value from it; God has used it for good (cf. Rom. 8:28).

Advance translates a word which literally means "to cut in front of," possibly but not certainly used for cutting a way before an army to further its march (Vincent, p. 16). The idea here is that of progress, possibly with the further nuance of "pioneer progress" (cf. 1:25; 1 Tim. 4:15).

Praetorian guard is probably the correct rendering of *tōi praitōriōi*, but the precise meaning cannot be established. The term originally designated the tent of the praetor ("first") or general of a Roman army, i.e., the headquarters. The word came to be used variously for the residence of the governor of a province (as in Matt. 27:27; Mark 15:16; John 18:28,33; 19:9; Acts 23:35) and for the praetorian guards in Rome or elsewhere. This latter, a body of men rather than a place, is probably Paul's meaning (cf. Lightfoot, pp. 97–102). Reference could be to the main imperial guard in Rome, about 9,000 soldiers, or to some small detachment as at Ephesus or Caesarea. *All the rest* refers to all others, pagans or Christians, who were in some way in touch with Paul's imprisonment. These had come to know that Paul was not under arrest for some crime but because of

his relationship with Christ. It is not said that any became Christians, but this may be implied in 4:22.

Paul indicated the influence of his imprisonment upon Christians as well as upon outsiders. Christians could have been frightened into silence because of the arrest of the great apostle. Instead, they were moved to speak out more boldly. It is not implied that they were silent prior to this but rather that though already vocal they became bolder. It was not because they did not realize the seriousness of Paul's arrest but that they found new incentive and courage from Paul's boldness. Paul so transcended his circumstances (cf. 4:11–13) that they dared to declare the gospel without fear of consequences. There is strong manuscript and patristic evidence that the words *of God* were added to the simpler *the word*. If so, the addition makes explicit what was implied.

2. Friends and Foes Aroused to New Effort (1:15–18)

15 Some indeed preach Christ from envy and rivalry, but others from good will. 16 The latter do it out of love, knowing that I am put here for the defense of the gospel; 17 the former proclaim Christ out of partisanship, not sincerely but thinking to afflict me in my imprisonment. 18 What then? Only that in every way, whether in pretense or in truth, Christ is proclaimed; and in that I rejoice.

Paul's imprisonment moved many to new efforts in preaching Christ, but with no uniformity of motive. Some preached from *envy* and *rivalry*, others from *good will*, presumably toward Paul. There is no hint that Paul's rivals were considered heretical, Judaizers or Gnostics. In question was not the soundness of their gospel but their motives. These may have been jealous of the attention given Paul, even as a prisoner. This would be more likely in Rome, where Christianity had preceded Paul by some years and Paul's coming could pose a threat to their leadership. This also accords with the charge of partisanship, a group outside Paul's following.

Presumably Paul's opponents thought

that their success would *afflict* Paul by making him jealous. To the contrary, Paul could *rejoice* that they at least proclaimed Christ, even if for unworthy motives. This is not to discount the importance of motive, but it is to recognize that the gospel has its own power even when proclaimed by people lacking in motive or character.

3. Willingness to Live or Die for Christ (1:19–26)

[19] Yes, and I shall rejoice. For I know that through your prayers and the help of the Spirit of Jesus Christ this will turn out for my deliverance, [20] as it is my eager expectation and hope that I shall not be at all ashamed, but that with full courage now as always Christ will be honored in my body, whether by life or by death. [21] For to me to live is Christ, and to die is gain. [22] If it is to be life in the flesh, that means fruitful labor for me. Yet which I shall choose I cannot tell. [23] I am hard pressed between the two. My desire is to depart and be with Christ, for that is far better. [24] But to remain in the flesh is more necessary on your account. [25] Convinced of this, I know that I shall remain and continue with you all, for your progress and joy in the faith, [26] so that in me you may have ample cause to glory in Christ Jesus, because of my coming to you again.

Paul was confident that his ordeal of imprisonment and his harrassment by partisan Christians would end in victory. *Deliverance* translates *sōtērian*, normally rendered "salvation." Deliverance is not an adequate translation, especially if it suggests deliverance from imprisonment. Paul had no settled feeling about that and did not make it primary. Possibly he means deliverance from any weakness under trial, but probably he means salvation in its fullest, eschatological sense (cf. 1:28). He is quoting the Septuagint version of Job 13:16, where Job looked confidently to his ultimate vindication. Paul is confident that whether released or executed he will know the fullness of the salvation which already for him has begun and which is to be consummated at the final judgment in "the day of Christ."

For the victory expected, Paul is dependent upon *the help of the Spirit of Jesus Christ. Help* translates a word normally rendered "supply." The Greek allows for either of two ideas, either that which the *Spirit of Jesus Christ* supplies or that the Spirit is that which is supplied, depending upon whether the genitive form of Jesus Christ is objective or subjective. Probably the genitive is subjective and the reference is to what the Spirit supplies. Paul makes no distinction between the Spirit of Christ and the Spirit of God (Rom. 8:9), presumably meaning the Holy Spirit in each expression. The *help* or supply provided by the Spirit includes courage and strength to meet the demands upon him. Paul relied, too, on the prayers of intercession of his friends in Philippi. God does not require to be informed of need or forced to give (Matt. 6:8), but prayer is an opening of channels of reception between man and God as well as man and man.

Verse 20 indicates that Paul's primary concern is not with the outcome of his trial, whether *life* or *death*, but with his own manner throughout the ordeal, that he not be put to shame by any failure in courage. The RSV probably has missed the force of the verb in its rendering: *that I shall not be at all ashamed.* The verb is passive. Paul does not want to be *put to shame* by faltering in any way. It is his *eager expectation* (*apokaradokian* pictures one with head stretched out, as peering ahead) and *hope* that he not only be not put to shame but that *Christ will be honored.* Paul does not want to be a hero. He wants to meet his fate, whether life or death, with such dignity and spirit that all may see what Christ means to him. *Full courage* may more literally be rendered "in all boldness." The Greek word first expressed freedom in speech and then came to designate the boldness or openness in general which characterizes a free man.

The oft-quoted v. 21 shows Paul at his best. He stood before life and death and found both inviting. His mood is the opposite of Hamlet's "To be or not to be, that is the question." Hamlet found life such a disillusionment that he considered suicide, yet the unknown realm of death was so foreboding that he drew back. Paul did not desire death as escape from life. He saw death as entrance into the greater fullness of a life that already was full (Beare, p. 62). Whatever life may mean to others, to him it was Christ, i.e., Christ gave life its meaning for him and apart from Christ it had no meaning. Death meant not loss but *gain,* for the good life he now knew in Christ would be not only continued but heightened. This verse seems not to imply an "intermediate state." It is precarious to argue the point, for that is not Paul's subject here; but it is hard to see how death would be gain if it led to an intermediate state, especially if disembodied!

The grammar in v. 22 is somewhat broken, reflecting Paul's own wavering before the inviting options of life or death. The RSV seems to have captured the meaning of 22*a*. If Paul is released, that can issue only in more fruitful work. His one interest in release would be to continue his ministry. The RSV has improved on the KJV's "I wot [know] not" in 22*b*. *Gnōridzō* in the New Testament seems always to mean make known (cf. 4:6; 1 Cor. 12:3; 15:1; Gal. 1:11). The verb for "know" is *ginōskō.* Even better than *I cannot tell* is "I do not make known." The point is that Paul turns from the matter of choosing between life and death. That is not his choice to make. Even if he has a preference, his answer would be "No comment."

Paul does concede two tugs at his heart. Were he alone involved, death would offer the better option. *To depart* translates a Greek term which was used for the loosing of a ship from its moorings and also for breaking camp or "striking tent." The term came to be a metaphor for death (2 Tim. 4:6). Paul could have had the nautical or military usage in mind, but he was more prone to use the latter than the former (Vincent, p. 28). Paul saw death as like breaking camp in order to move on (cf. 2 Cor. 5:1). For him this would be better, but he saw that to *remain in the flesh* was

more necessary for the Philippians. Paul felt that a church threatened with disunity and overconfidence and by eager, coercive persons (cf. 3:2) needed his help.

Hard pressed between two translates a difficult phrase. His was not a dilemma of being trapped between two fates from which he desired escape. It was the happier lot of being confronted with two attractive options. He felt the gravitational pull of both this life and the next. It seems then that even as he faced the choices but chose to forego the right to choose, a new sense of direction came to him. Precisely when he refused to make known his choice, willing to accept life or death, the conviction came that he would be released in order to continue his ministry. He would see the Philippians again. They would know further *progress and joy in the faith* and would find new occasion *to glory in Christ Jesus* because of his coming to them again. *Coming* translates *parousia,* a term used for the ceremonious and joyous arrival of a king or governor into a city. Paul could use the term for Christ's eschatological coming (1 Thess. 3:13), but he could also use the term for any presence or arrival (1 Cor. 16:17). In 2:12 *parousia* is opposite to *apousia* (absence) and simply means presence.

III. Plea for Unity Grounded in the Mind of Christ (1:27—2:30)

This is the first major appeal in the letter and reflects one of its primary purposes. Apparently division in the church had not reached a critical stage, but one was in the making. Euodia and Syntyche, once co-workers, were now openly divided (4:2), and already there was "grumbling" and "questioning" in the church (2:14). If Philippians is actually later than the Corinthian correspondence, as assumed here, Paul already had known the painful experience of seeing a church riddled with dissension and division. In the section before us he exhorts to unity and appeals to the supreme example of Christ as well as to the examples of Timothy, Epaphroditus, and himself for the self-abnegation which undercuts the egocentric striving behind divisions.

1. First Exhortation: Living Worthily of the Gospel Through Unity and Courage in the Face of Hostility (1:27-30)

27 Only let your manner of life be worthy of the gospel of Christ, so that whether I come and see you or am absent, I may hear of you that you stand firm in one spirit, with one mind striving side by side for the faith of the gospel, 28 and not frightened in anything by your opponents. This is a clear omen to them of their destruction, but of your salvation, and that from God. 29 For it has been granted to you that for the sake of Christ you should not only believe in him but also suffer for his sake, 30 engaged in the same conflict which you saw and now hear to be mine.

Let your manner of life translates one Greek word (*politeuesthe*), which literally reads, "Let your citizenship be." Twice in Philippians Paul appeals to the fact that our true citizenship is a heavenly one (cf. 3:20). Philippi was a Roman colony, its inhabitants being citizens of Rome with legal rights as though they lived on Italian soil although living in Macedonia.[6] By analogy Paul applies this to Christians, who living in this world have their true citizenship in heaven (cf. Heb. 13:14). He does not mean that a Christian is without obligations to this world or that he is to view it as of no significance. Paul did take seriously the here and now. But the point is that our ultimate citizenship is heavenly and that we are now a colony of heaven on earth. Ultimate allegiance is to be to God, and we are to live now in this world in a way worthy of our heavenly citizenship.

To live *worthy of the gospel of Christ* is defined in terms of unity in *spirit* and *mind* as we strive together for the *faith of the gospel.* This is no requirement of dull uniformity or loss of individual identity; it is an appeal for oneness in spirit and in

[6] K. Lake and H. J. Cadbury, *The Beginnings of Christianity* (London: Macmillan, 1933), IV, 190.

purpose. *The faith of the gospel* may to some extent imply basic doctrinal agreement, but the stress is not on this if it is implied at all. *The faith* came later to stand for the content or teaching of Christianity and may tend in that direction even here, but it still stands chiefly for the trust and commitment which the gospel awakens (Michael, pp. 67 f.).

In quick succession Paul employs a military term, *stand firm,* and then one envisioning a team of athletes *striving side by side* (*synathlountes*). Firmness and dauntless courage are to be blended with unity in their preaching the gospel and resistance of evil.

Not frightened picks up a term sometimes used for the shying of a startled horse. Paul may use the term to imply that the opponents try to strike terror in the Christians' hearts and throw them into panic (Beare, p. 67). Christian fearlessness in the face of opposition is an *omen* or token of the opponents' *destruction* and of the Christians' *salvation.* These are not two omens or tokens but one. The opponents' failure to strike fear in the hearts of the Christians foreshadows their ultimate defeat and ruin as well as the ultimate triumph of the Christians.

Destruction and *salvation* (cf. 1:19) are both eschatological, pointing to final destinies in the judgment, not to the immediate outcome of persecution (Beare, p. 68). *That* which is *from God* does not refer directly to any one word in the Greek sentence but to the whole idea of the eschatological result of present persecution and fearlessness. That is, God controls the history which brings rebellion to final judgment and faithfulness to a completed salvation.

Paul traces to the grace of God (*granted* is the verb that corresponds to the Greek noun for grace) two great privileges: to *believe* in Christ and to *suffer for his sake.* To believe is to trust, and this is a privilege opened up to us by God's grace. Belief or trust is not imposed upon us, for resistance to God's grace is possible; but except for the initiative of God's grace, faith would not be a possibility to us. It is significant that Paul sees suffering for Christ also to be a provision of God's grace. He does not see it as a price paid for the privilege of faith but as a gift of God's grace. This is not mere theory for Paul. It is existential or experiential. It belongs to Paul's existence as a Christian to suffer for Christ, and he is grateful for the privilege (cf. Acts 5:41).

Conflict translates *agōna,* from which comes our word for agony but a Greek term in Paul's day for an athletic contest. Paul sees the Philippians as having entered into the very contest in which he is engaged, a common struggle with the pagan forces which oppose them, whether in Rome, Philippi, or elsewhere. In Philippi they *saw* him flogged and jailed (Acts 16:22 f). They *now hear* of his present *conflict* and imprisonment.

Verse 29 accepts suffering as Christian privilege. Verse 30 moves on to show that more than passive suffering is proper to the Christian. He is to be actively engaged in the great contest with evil. Already Paul had affirmed that the weapons of our warfare are not carnal but that they are mighty for the overturning of evil (2 Cor. 10:4). In a real sense the *conflict* is not optional, for Christian existence itself contains within itself something that is in inescapable conflict with the evil world (Michael, p. 72).

2. Second Exhortation: Unity and Self-abnegation with Supreme Example: the Mind of Christ (2:1–11)

¹ So if there is any encouragement in Christ, any incentive of love, any participation in the Spirit, any affection and sympathy, ² complete my joy by being of the same mind, having the same love, being in full accord and of one mind. ³ Do nothing from selfishness or conceit, but in humility count others better than yourselves. ⁴ Let each of you look not only to his own interests, but also to the interests of others. ⁵ Have this mind among yourselves, which you have in Christ Jesus, ⁶ who, though he was in the form of God, did not count equality with God a thing to be grasped, ⁷ but emptied himself, taking the form of a servant, being born in the likeness of men. ⁸ And being found in human form he humbled himself and became obedient unto death, even death on a cross. ⁹ Therefore God has highly exalted him and bestowed on him the name which is above every name, ¹⁰ that at the name of Jesus every knee should bow, in heaven and on earth and under the earth, ¹¹ and every tongue confess that Jesus Christ is Lord, to the glory of God the Father.

This is a close-knit paragraph, with everything conjoined and interwoven (Barth, p. 49). It continues the admonition begun in 1:27. It appeals first for unity and then for the self-abnegation supremely exemplified in Christ, the indispensable foundation to unity.

Self-abnegation is not used here to mean self-hatred, self-despising, or rejection of self. What is meant is the refusal to let personal interest or advantage govern the course of one's life.

Unity and self-abnegation (vv. 1–4).— Paul clearly recognizes that the success of his appeal is dependent upon the actuality of the Philippians' existence in Christ. Given that, there is hope for the response he seeks. His appeal for unity and self-abnegation rests upon the reality of the *encouragement* which is in Christ, the *incentive* which arises out of love, *participation* in the Holy Spirit, and *affection and sympathy* in his readers.

Encouragement renders *paraklēsis,* a term most elusive as to precise meaning. Literally it is a "calling alongside." "Advocate" is derived from the Latin equivalent. The calling alongside may be with a view to admonition, defense, exhortation, consolation, or comfort. One is tempted here to render it "summons," i.e., "If there be any summons (calling alongside) in Christ." So understood, Paul would be basing his appeal on the presupposition that the Philippians are answerable to Christ and that they do answer to his summons, in this case to unity and self-abnegation. Paul's intention probably is to remind them of the strength (comfort) which is available to them in Christ.

Love is seen as providing *incentive* for the desired goal of unity, humility, and concern for others. *Love* (*agapē*) for Paul is the disposition to relate to another for that one's good, regardless of cost to oneself. *Incentive* seems to satisfy the context here, though the Greek word can mean persuasion.

Participation is hardly adequate to translate *koinōnia*. Paul's term is a basic one in the New Testament, pointing to a common or shared life. Here it is to have "koinonia" or partnership with the Holy Spirit, although *spirit* could but probably does not refer to the human spirit.

Affection and sympathy point to the tender compassion which properly comes from the heart. Problems at Philippi require not so much instruction as right will or spirit. Dissension and division are not insurmountable problems where one answers to or is strengthened by Christ, where there is the incentive of love, where there is fellowship with the Spirit, and where there are the hearts of compassion.

Paul's plea seems at first glance to be that his own *joy* be brought to fullness, but his first concern is for the unity of the church. His joy will be in their *being of the same mind,* i.e., having the same basic disposition or purpose. It is dependent upon their *having the same love.* The phrase *being in full accord* renders the one word *sumpsuchoi,* "knit together in soul."

The twice repeated call in 2:2 for their "minding the one thing" is spelled out in vv. 3–4. It is to be freed of selfishness and concerned for the *interests of others.* It is to be free of *conceit* and to be characterized by *humility. Selfishness* and *conceit* may be rendered partisanship or factionalism and *vain* ambition. The only rivalry which is proper in Christians is that in which each seeks to outdo the other in esteeming the other. One is not to be concerned about receiving honors or advantages for himself. He is to be concerned that his brethren be honored and served.

The example of Christ (*vv. 5–11*).— Many scholars see 2:6–11 as a hymn, possibly pre-Pauline and at least older than the Philippian letter. This theory may be true, but it is weakened by the fact that there is no agreement as to the poetic structure of the "hymn." J. Weiss, the first to see the passage as poetic, found it to consist of two strophes of four lines each. Hans Lietzmann arranged it in 17 lines. E. Lohmeyer arranged the passage in six strophes of three lines each. M. Dibelius finds vv. 6–8a to be one strophe of seven lines and 8b–11 to consist of four stanzas of three lines each. L. Cerfaux arranges the hymn in three stanzas of four, five, and six lines progressively. J. Jeremias proposes that the entire hymn consists of couplets, arranged in three stanzas of four lines each. To obtain the balanced symmetry which he finds, he has to excise various phrases. R. P. Martin sees a hymn composed of six couplets, so arranged that they could be chanted antiphonally.[7] C. H. Talbert, in a convincing demonstration, proposes a structure of four strophes of three lines each, uneven as to length and marked by inner parallelisms and repetition of key terms.[8]

It is strange that scholars are so sure of the hymnic nature of the passage and so unsure of its poetic structure. Furthermore, vv. 1–4, seem to be as poetic as 6–11. The RSV may be correct in its paragraphing of vv. 1–11 as a unity, and vv. 6–11 may never have had a separate existence. The concern throughout is for "single mindedness" (2:2) and that this "mind" be that of Christ (2:5).

To be rejected is the widely held position that 2:6–11 is an adaptation of an old "redemption myth" from Hellenistic (syncretistic) religious thought, possibly Iranian, in which the heavenly redeemer descends from heaven and then ascends victoriously into heaven, opening the way for his followers (Beare, p. 75). On this

---

[7] *Carmen Christi,* pp. 36 f. This whole paragraph draws upon a much fuller discussion by Martin of the major interpretations of Phil. 2:5–11. *Carmen Christi* is to date the most comprehensive study of the passage for background, major options, and bibliography. A simpler yet serviceable study is that of A. M. Hunter, *Paul and His Predecessors* (rev., London: SCM Press, 1961), pp. 39–44.

[8] "Pre-existence in Philippians 2:6–11," *Journal of Biblical Literature,* 86:2 (1967), p. 147.

view, Paul or more probably one of Paul's disciples adapted the myth and applied it to Christ. Thus understood, 2:6–11 is seen strictly as soteriology (how the Redeemer enables his followers to ascend into heaven) and concerned with neither Christology nor ethics. Scholars taking this approach reject the view that the "hymn" offers Christ as a moral or ethical example.

Talbert [9] cogently argues that vv. 6–7 refer not to the pre-existence of Christ but to the earthly life of Jesus. This first strophe (vv. 6–7b) is paralleled by the second strophe (vv. 7c–8), this latter unquestionably speaking of the earthly, human existence of Jesus. So understood, these two strophes (vv. 6–8) affirm that in his earthly existence, Jesus took a course opposite to that of the first Adam. Whereas the first Adam tried to snatch equality with God, Jesus (the second Adam) *emptied himself* or "poured out his life" to God in the service of man.

This passage is not in the judgment of this writer the adaptation of an old Hellenistic hymn about a Redeemer who descended and then ascended; instead it is a Christian "hymn" (probably Paul's own composition for this very context but possibly pre-Pauline) about the Servant nature of the earthly Christ Jesus. Somewhat similar to 2 Corinthians 8:9, it does call for the awakening in the Philippians of the mind of Christ, that mind already being in them if they, indeed, are in Christ Jesus.

To sum up: vv. 1–4 appeal to something already in the Philippians (the strength of Christ, the incentive of love, the fellowship of the Spirit, tender compassion); v. 5 assumes that "in Christ Jesus" they have the mind of Christ; and vv. 6–8 explain that this mind that is in Christ Jesus (the earthly, not pre-existent) is that of the Servant who pours out his life to God in the service of man. The appeal is that they be what they are, that the mind of Christ already in them be activated in their re-

lationships with one another, particularly as in self-abnegation they resist the temptation to seek their own glory and rather give themselves to one another in a common life of love and service.

Paul's major appeal is that the disposition or *mind* which governed Christ also govern his people. The passage is not a loose-fitting insert but intrinsic to the context. It arises out of what precedes and governs or at least prepares the way for all that follows (E. F. Scott, p. 47). Humility belongs to the *mind* to which Paul appeals, but that is not what is stressed. It is the self-abnegation or self-sacrifice which stands over against a self-seeking which is raising its ugly head in Philippi.

The grammar in the Greek text of v. 5 is baffling. There is no verb in the last part of the verse. There is no Greek behind the RSV *you have,* although that may be a proper understanding of Paul's intention. In the usual understanding (KJV), Paul is asking the Philippians to have in themselves the mind that is in Christ Jesus. Many interpreters will prefer this interpretation. However, the RSV is probably nearer Paul's meaning, with its seeming redundancy; *Have this mind . . . which you have.* Already there is in them a *mind* which is theirs because they are *in Christ Jesus.* The appeal is that they activate or reactivate this mind among themselves. *In Christ Jesus* thus does not directly refer to the *mind* that is in Christ Jesus (KJV) but to their being in Christ. In short, they are to have among themselves, in their relationships within the church, the mind which already they have as ones who are in Christ. They are encouraged to put into practice in the life of the church the disposition engendered in their hearts by communion with Christ (Michael, p. 85). Although *in Christ Jesus* probably refers to the Philippians' being in Christ and not to Christ's own mind, the verses which follow do lay bare this mind or disposition of Christ. And, on this basis, many interpreters prefer the view in the KJV rendering.

Verses 6–7 are usually taken to refer to

9 *Op. cit.,* p. 153.

the preexistence of Christ, at which time he consented to leave his heavenly state for an earthly one. This passage gave rise to "kenotic" Christology (*kenōsis* is Greek for emptying), that in some sense the pre-existent Christ surrendered his divinity in order to become man. But how could God divest himself of deity? Christ's divinity is not a cloak which may be taken off and later be put back on. One may surrender privileges or give up a favorable situation, but he cannot lay aside his nature. The chief weakness of the *kenōsis* theory is that it is unreal and meaningless. Christ did not and could not empty himself of his divinity, in preexistence or otherwise.

If, as is improbable, vv. 6–7 refer to Christ's preexistent state, *emptied himself* must mean something less than that he gave up his divinity. So understood, it probably means that he gave up his privileged estate in heaven for an humble one of privation and sacrificial service on earth. Talbert [10] cites the obvious difficulties in the view that preexistence is meant in vv. 6–7. This would see incarnation as *kenōsis* (empty-ing) rather than *epiphany* (divine mani-festation) as elsewhere in Christian hymns (cf. John 1:1–18; 1 Tim. 3:16). Nowhere else in early Christianity is Christ seen to make a preexistent decision. On the view of preexistence, *emptied himself* is normally understood as the giving up of divinity for humanity. One is almost driven to the po-sition that the *exalted* state (v. 9) is higher than the original, preexistent *form of God*. These difficulties disappear if verses 6–8 are seen to refer to the earthly existence of Christ Jesus rather than to preexistence.

Talbert [11] makes a forceful case for parallelism between verses 6–7b and 7c–8. The latter verses unquestionably refer to the earthly existence. He sees a reflection of the typology in which Christ is the second Adam, reversing the mind and de-cision of the first Adam, who did try to be equal with God (Gen. 3:5).

In the form of God could apply to Jesus'

[10] *Op. cit.*, p. 141.
[11] *Op. cit.*, pp. 147 ff.

preexistent or earthly state. *Form* translates *morphē*, a term which normally stresses the relationship between outer shape and inner reality, the inner nature showing itself in the outer form. In the Septuagint *morphē* is often interchangeable with the *likeness* (*homiōma*) of v. 7. Christ did not have to give up *the form of God* (i.e., lay aside his divinity) in order to take *the form of a servant*. If preexistence is in Paul's thought, Christ's becoming man did not mean that he ceased to be God. If his earthly existence is Paul's reference, then *emptied himself* refers to his pouring out of his life to God in humble, obedient, self-denial, refusing in any way to act selfishly. His *kenōsis* (emptying) was not the sur-render of divinity but the acceptance of servanthood. The thought is similar to that of 2 Corinthians 8:9, "He became as poor as a beggar" (Beare, p. 81).

Grasped or clutched is the probable meaning of the Greek term which the KJV renders "robbery." Adam tried to be equal with God (Gen. 3:5), but Jesus relin-quished privileges and powers which rightfully belonged to him. He came not to be served but to serve, even at the cost of his life (Mark 10:45). *Morphē* is used again, the outer shape of the servanthood of Christ reflecting his actual, inner nature. His servanthood was not an act. It was his true existence.

Being born may over translate *genomenos*. This participle may have the force of either being or becoming. It may refer to the incarnation or may refer to Christ's assuming the lowly, servant role during his earthly existence. In the phrase *in human form* the Greek word is *schēma* rather than the earlier *morphē*. If *schēma* differs from *morphē*, it is that the former does not necessarily imply correspondence between the outer expression and the inner reality. *Morphē* is the stronger term, usually stressing the correspondence. *Schēma* does not deny the correspondence, but does not stress it. It is highly im-probable that in saying, as a literal trans-lation would have it, "in fashion being found as a man," Paul implies that Jesus was only a seeming (docetic) man. To Paul, both the divinity and humanity of Jesus Christ were real. Emphasis, some suggest, may fall upon *being found,* i.e., that this is how men "found" him, as only a man (Scott, p. 50), though this is forced.

The humility of Christ is made explicit in v. 8, opening the way for the declaration of the subsequent exaltation. It does not follow that humility is the essence of the mind of Christ or that it is chiefly humility which Paul seeks to awaken in the Philippians. The essence of that mind was his disposition not to grasp at equality with God but rather to be *obedient unto death.* Although not explicit, presumably it is obedience unto God to the point of death that Paul means. Scholars who see a pre-Pauline hymn here, hold that Paul added *even death on a cross.* The cross is at the heart of Paul's preaching, and the phrase is undoubtedly his, pointing up not only the kind of death Jesus died but the fact that there was no limit to his self-abnegation or obedience to God. That this prose is an addition and not original to the "hymn" is a conjecture that cannot be proven.

Verses 9–11 form the second part of the "hymn," describing the exaltation of one whose complete self-abnegation led to the cross. Jesus had taught others that life is found by losing it and that just as one who exalts himself is humbled so the one who humbles himself is exalted (cf. Matt. 23:11). Of course, he did not mean "the pride that apes humility." To pretend humility with a view to glory is simply another form of selfish pride. What Jesus taught others he himself incarnated. God *highly exalted* the one who was willing to be self-denying, humbled, and obedient.

In biblical thought *name* does not just distinguish one individual from another, but it reflects character and status (Beare, p. 86). The name given him, *the name which is above every name* presumably is *Lord.* This is the Septuagint term for Yahweh. *Jesus Christ is Lord* is probably the earliest Christian confession. It recognizes that God's sovereignty, the kingdom of God, comes ultimately in God's Anointed (Christ) who is one with Jesus. *Jesus* means "Yahweh saves," and is the name for the earthly one in whom salvation comes to us. This very Jesus who did not grasp but who poured out his life in obedience to God and in sacrificial service is Christ and Lord. God exalted the one who emptied himself. God made Lord the one who took the form of a slave (cf. Matt. 28:18).

The assurance that *every knee* shall bow and *every tongue* confess may look two ways. It may reflect the divine offer of redemption to all God's creation. It more likely means that God's kingdom will be absolute in that the lordship of Christ must eventually be acknowledged everywhere. All will submit because they must (Isa. 45:23). There is a sense in which the kingdom of God is not dependent on human response. God is king without man's consent. The kingdom of God comes, even where men resist (cf. Luke 10:11). So here, the gospel is that all may know the joy of the kingdom which comes in God's Christ. But the truth remains, he is Lord, whatever our response. Our passage does not guarantee universal salvation. It does promise universal lordship of Christ, his enthronement.

God's *glory* is his character manifested in redemption. The lordship which finds fulfillment in Jesus Christ is not competitive with that of *the Father.* God is one God, and it is he who confronts us in Jesus Christ. Every knee must ultimately bow *in the name of Jesus,* but it is to God that each shall bow (cf. Eph. 3:14).

This profound Christological passage is not an exercise in theology for its own sake. Theology is meaningful only as it affects character and life. Paul's concern is not with theology itself but with the existence of the Philippians. How can they cling to their little ambitions and persist in their petty quarrels if they confess Jesus Christ as their Lord (Scott, p. 50). The *mind* which they have in him is that of humble

self-abnegation and obedient service, not
of self-seeking ambition.

3. Third Exhortation: Working Out Their Salvation (2:12–13)

¹² Therefore, my beloved, as you have always obeyed, so now, not only as in my presence but much more in my absence, work out
your own salvation with fear and trembling;
¹³ for God is at work in you, both to will and to
work for his good pleasure.

The burden of this paragraph is the plea
that the Philippians *work out* their *salvation.* They are encouraged to work out
what is already there. That they work *out*
what God worked *in* does not capture
Paul's picture. In the verb form, *out* is an
intensifying preposition, as in the expression
"to work out a problem." It is to complete
or bring something to its goal. Paul does
not specify what precisely he means, but
the context offers some clues. His appeal
has been self-abnegation and sacrificial
service, rather than self-seeking and empty
boasting (2:1–4).

The continuing burden of the letter is for
just this practice among themselves of the
"mind" which they have in Christ. In
3:7–11 is given his own experience of sur-
rendering all that he once saw as "gain"
for the sheer privilege of knowing Christ
Jesus as Lord. It was precisely in sharing
in Christ's suffering that he found assurance
of sharing in his triumphant resurrection.
He presses on to the goal which Christ has
set for him, a life of triumph through seeming defeat, of life through what takes the
outward shape of death (3:12–21). Just
as Christ's exaltation followed upon his
humiliation and sacrificial service, and just
as Paul finds his own course to be on this
pattern, so the Philippians are called upon
to *work out* their *own salvation,* not in
selfish bickering and glory seeking but in
putting into practice among themselves the
mind which they know in Christ Jesus.
Your own salvation refers not so much to
individual salvation as to that of the whole
community. It is the quality of their
corporate life that most concerns Paul.
Even so, the corporate life is the composite

of individuals and the desired quality depends on individual response. This in itself
is a personal challenge.

The heavy demand for salvation thus
wrought out is not utopian nor impossible.
They are not left to their own resources for
it. Salvation is God's work from beginning
to end—which requires that it become
man's willing and determined response from
beginning to end. He initiates and completes; he gives the resources for the goal
to which he calls. His demands are first of
all his gifts. God gives himself, becoming
in us a transforming presence. *God is at
work in you.* He is there both *to will* and
to work. He awakens in one the will and
incentive to salvation. He supplies through
his own indwelling the energy for it. *To
work* translates *energein,* from which comes
our word for energy. Salvation is God's
work, but it is never imposed, never coercive; always God works within man's
willingness (1 Cor. 15:10; Gal. 2:20).
Salvation is God's gift but also his demand
(see on "Matthew," BBC, Vol. 8, p. 64 f.).

Fear and trembling are not cowardly fear
or mistrust. They refer to awe and reverence in the presence of God. The nearness
of God, actually working in us and among
us, is not to become a familiarity in which
God is thought of as just one other among
us. Although nearer than a brother, he is
not just a brother. He is God. *Fear and
trembling* are also appropriate to the primary importance and eternal significance of
the kind of existence which may be called
salvation.

Paul may have modeled this appeal on
that of Moses' farewell charge to Israel
(Deut. 33:1–5). If so, his absence refers to
his prospective death rather than his just
being geographically away from Philippi.
The point is uncertain and not to be
pressed, for he did expect soon to be with
them again (2:24).

4. The Example of Paul: Poured Out as a Libation (2:14–18)

¹⁴ Do all things without grumbling or questioning, ¹⁵ that you may be blameless and inno-

cent, children of God without blemish in the midst of a crooked and perverse generation, among whom you shine as lights in the world, [16] holding fast the word of life, so that in the day of Christ I may be proud that I did not run in vain or labor in vain. [17] Even if I am to be poured as a libation upon the sacrificial offering of your faith, I am glad and rejoice with you all. [18] Likewise you also should be glad and rejoice with me.

It is not enough to *do*. One must *do all things* in the right spirit. There is always the danger that the zealous man turn into a zealot or that the fighter for truth and right turn into a wrangler (cf. Barth, p. 55). *Grumbling* translates an onomatopoetic word, one that mocks or mimics, like the English "murmur" or "mutter." *Questioning* is too weak a rendering for *dialogismōn*. In this context, the reference is to arguments, disputing, or wrangling. The term may even mean resort to court litigation (cf. 1 Cor. 6:1–11). Paul wants the Philippians to be free of both private murmurings against one another and public disputes. The church is not to be a gossip club nor a debating society. Both words, *grumbling* and *questioning*, describe some aspects of a self-assertive temper (Beare, p. 92), the opposite to the mind of Christ.

The Philippians are to be in but not of the world (cf. John 17:15). They are to live responsibly in the world but with a different kind of existence. As *children of God* they are to be a striking contrast to the world about them. They are to be *blameless and innocent*. Paul does not see them as perfect, but perfection is the proper goal for God's children (cf. Matt. 5:48). He does not claim perfection as an attainment for himself, but it is his goal (3:12). By *blameless* Paul means that they are not to leave themselves open to reproach. Probably he has in mind the community as a whole rather than the individual. *Innocent* is literally "unmixed," like wine that is not diluted or metal without alloy.

In a world that is *crooked* and *perverse* they are to be *without blemish*. This was not an attainment at Philippi, but it was a proper goal. Their grumbling and dis-

puting are the blemishes against which Paul warns here. In this world of darkness they are to *shine as lights*. Although Jesus warned against religious performance to be admired by men, he also called his followers to live in open goodness before God and the world, letting the light of their good works shine before men (Matt. 5:16). *Lights* (in the N.T. only here and Rev. 21:11) renders the Greek word used almost exclusively for heavenly bodies, stars or luminaries (Lightfoot, p. 115). Paul may be thinking of the stars as giving guidance to sailors at night, but probably his point is simply the contrast between light and darkness.

The *word of life* is probably the gospel. It is not likely that Paul is using "word" for Christ as in John 1:1. Most of the New Testament had not yet been written, so he could not have meant the Bible as we now know it. *Holding fast* probably captures Paul's meaning, although holding forth or profferring is possible. They are not to relax their grip on the truths which they have received (Michael, p. 108). The idea here is not so much that they preach the gospel as that they remain true to its light.

Should they thus prove to be true, Paul's labor will be vindicated in the *day of Christ*, i.e., at the final judgment (cf. 1:6,10). If they hold firm, he may take pride in his own work as not having been in *vain*.

Paul anticipates that his lot may be martyrdom, and he entertained hopes of seeing the Philippians again. On the other hand, he had experienced too many beatings and threats to his life to fail to realize that he could be put to death by some court or mob. He did not seek death, nor did he have a morbid fear of it. He was prepared for life or death (1:21). Should martyrdom come, it would be his *libation* added to their *sacrificial offering*.

A libation was a drink offering, usually a cup of wine, poured out in connection with the offering of a victim on an altar. Paul may think of his own outpouring of life as secondary to the primary sacrificial service of the Philippians. If so, it was proper and beautiful for him to think of it this way, whatever the relative measure or merits of their respective ministries. If he should be called upon thus to pour out his life, he wants no pity or sorrow. It will be for him gladness and joy, and in it he wants them to be glad and rejoice. This joyous outpouring of life is a proper response to Christ's own outpouring of his life in obedient service and in death (2:6-8).

Sacrificial offering is literally "the sacrifice and priestly service." The two Greek words are governed by only one article and probably form only one conception (Michael, p. 110). What is meant by their *faith* is not clear. The genitive is probably subjective and not objective. It is not the offering up of their faith but a sacrificial offering of themselves arising out of their faith, their trust or commitment to Christ.

5. The Example of Timothy: Concern for Others (2:19-24)

¹⁹ I hope in the Lord Jesus to send Timothy to you soon, so that I may be cheered by news of you. ²⁰ I have no one like him, who will be genuinely anxious for your welfare. ²¹ They all look after their own interests, not those of Jesus Christ. ²² But Timothy's worth you know, how as a son with a father he has served with me in the gospel. ²³ I hope therefore to send him just as soon as I see how it will go with me; ²⁴ and I trust in the Lord that shortly I myself shall come also.

Paul projects in several stages plans relating to himself and the Philippians. Epaphroditus will bear the letter to Philippi (2:25); he hopes to send Timothy as soon as the outcome of his trial is indicated (2:23); and Paul trusts that he himself may visit them later (2:24). It is urgent that the Philippians be relieved as soon as possible in their anxiety about the reported illness of Epaphroditus (2:28). Timothy will have a dual ministry of serving the Philippians (2:20) and then, hopefully, of bringing back news to cheer Paul (2:19).

Timothy was one of Paul's most devoted and trusted friends (see comment on 1:1).

He also was well known to the Philippians. He had accompanied Paul on his first visit to Philippi (Acts 16:1 ff.). He had preceded Paul there from Ephesus on Paul's second known visit there (1 Cor. 16:10). They knew his *worth*, i.e., his tested character. In sending Timothy, Paul is assured that they know that he is no poor substitute but one who comes as near to representing Paul as is possible.

Paul's primary concern in sending Timothy is that he *may be cheered by news* from them. It does not follow necessarily that Paul expects to find them in such a state as to give him cheer. There are too many evidences of grumbling, disputing, disunity, and open tension as between Euodia and Syntyche (4:2). Timothy's mission is to bring about a happier situation in Philippi, and thus afford Paul the *cheer* he awaits.

Paul has available no one who is so qualified for this delicate mission as Timothy. He embodies the "mind" the Philippians need to gain. *I have no one like him* translates an ambiguous clause. Literally it reads, "I have no equal-souled" or "like minded" one. This has been understood to mean, I have no one equal "to me in soul," i.e., "like me." The grammar favors another meaning: "I have no one like him." Beare (p. 96) suggests, "I have no one to match him" or "I have no one else who can fill my shoes, for the task in hand."

It is Timothy's spirit which so suits him for the task in Philippi. He will be genuinely anxious for their welfare. There is nothing phony about his concern; it is authentic (cf. 1 Tim. 1:2, where the genuineness of Timothy is praised). Others may selfishly *look after their own interests*, but not Timothy. He has the self-abnegation already commended, the mind which one may be expected to have in Christ Jesus (2:5). He will look after their interests because he seeks the things of Christ. He *has served* the gospel with Paul. *Served* is literally "slaved." This may look back to 2:7, where it is said that Christ Jesus took the form of a servant or slave.

Paul likens Timothy to his son in the ministry, but he associates himself with Timothy in their servanthood: *he has served with me.* His next mission will be to bring about a new mind of self-abnegation and unity in Philippi. In the presence of Timothy, can they continue their wrangling and self-seeking?

Does Paul mean that absolutely all those near him are self-seeking? This must in some sense be modified, for already he has acknowledged some who preach Christ out of good will and love (1:15 f.). Possibly Paul means that he has available no one so suited to the mission to Philippi as Timothy. The mission would involve days or weeks, depending upon whether from Rome, Ephesus, or Caesarea. One going would have to leave business and possibly family. But chiefly, few so possess the mind of Christ as does Timothy, and that mind is what the Philippians need.

6. The Example of Epaphroditus: Life Risked for Others (2:25-30)

25 I have thought it necessary to send to you Epaphroditus my brother and fellow worker and fellow soldier, and your messenger and minister to my need, 26 for he has been longing for you all, and has been distressed because you heard that he was ill. 27 Indeed he was ill, near to death. But God had mercy on him, and not only on him but on me also, lest I should have sorrow upon sorrow. 28 I am the more eager to send him, therefore, that you may rejoice at seeing him again, and that I may be less anxious. 29 So receive him in the Lord with all joy; and honor such men, 30 for he nearly died for the work of Christ, risking his life to complete your service to me.

Epaphroditus is unknown outside this passage. He is not to be confused with Epaphras of Colossians 4:12. These are two forms of the same name, but the persons seem to be different. The name is derived from the Greek goddess Aphrodite. Many pagan converts continued to use familiar pagan names. Epaphroditus is introduced as Paul's *brother, fellow worker,* and *fellow soldier.* The first term would apply to any Christian. *Fellow worker* may refer to his early association with Paul in Philippi.

Soldier is not to be taken in a literal sense for either. Both were companions in conflict as Christian soldiers. Paul made extensive use of military terms, but he transmuted all into spiritual forces. He affirmed that we are not engaged in a "worldly war" and "the weapons of our warfare are not worldly" (2 Cor. 10:3 f.).

Epaphroditus is also introduced as the Philippians' *messenger and minister* to Paul's need. *Messenger* translates the Greek word for "apostle," but it is not used in the sense employed for the twelve or for Paul. He was an *apostle* of the church, one sent on a specific mission by the church and authorized to act for the church within the limits of that commission. *Minister* renders a word for "priestly service," but he was not a priest in the technical sense. In a metaphorical sense he did complete a priestly service (v. 30) in behalf of the Philippians (cf. Vincent, p. 71). The Greek term is made up of two words, one for people (our "laity") and one for work. It could refer to public, social service, but probably the meaning here is priestly service. Paul sees services as ordinary as supplying material needs or looking after a brother in jail as a priestly or religious service. Nothing is secular when in Christ's name one serves another at any level of need.

Paul felt it necessary to send Epaphroditus at once to Philippi, to relieve their anxiety over Epaphroditus, who was *distressed* as he learned that they had learned of his own recent illness. Paul, too, wanted relief, knowing that the Philippians and Epaphroditus were anxious about one another.

One cannot settle the question about how much distance separated Paul and the Philippians. There seem to have been at least four trips: (1) news had reached Philippi of Paul's imprisonment, (2) Epaphroditus had been sent with aid to Paul, (3) news of Epaphroditus' illness had reached Philippi, and (4) he had learned that they knew about his illness. This amount of travel may imply that the distance was not so great as to Rome or

Caesarea. On the other hand, if the distance were short enough to permit a quick trip there would have been little call for all the discussion about his return (Beare, p. 98).

Not only had Epaphroditus been *ill, near to death,* but he seems to have exposed himself to some risk which almost cost him his life. *Near to death* is literally "next door neighbor to death." *Risking his life* is the language of gambling. He hazarded or gambled his very life. He took a calculated risk of life, staked his life, in his effort to do for Paul what the Philippians could not do themselves. He did this to *complete* their *service,* literally to "bring to fullness" what was lacking in their "priestly service" to Paul. Lack does not imply neglect or anything blameworthy on the part of the Philippians. It refers to what could be accomplished only through personal presence and attention.

Paul does not explicitly hold up Epaphroditus' self-abnegation and sacrificial service as an example to the Philippians, but the suggestion is easily implied. How can they persist in their divisive quarreling in the presence of one of their own who gambled his very life in his devotion to both Paul and his own church? They are exhorted to *receive* Epaphroditus and to *honor such men.* There is no way in which they could so honor him as by emulating his own generous, sacrificial spirit.

IV. Warning Against a Distorted Religion (3:1–21)

1. Confidence in the Flesh versus the Knowledge of Christ (3:1–11)

¹ Finally, my brethren, rejoice in the Lord. To write the same things to you is not irksome to me, and is safe for you.
² Look out for the dogs, look out for the evil-workers, look out for those who mutilate the flesh. ³ For we are the true circumcision, who worship God in spirit, and glory in Christ Jesus, and put no confidence in the flesh. ⁴ Though I myself have reason for confidence in the flesh also. If any other man thinks he has reason for confidence in the flesh, I have more: ⁵ circumcised on the eighth day, of the people of Israel, of the tribe of Benjamin, a Hebrew

born of Hebrews; as to the law a Pharisee, ⁶ as to zeal a persecutor of the church, as to righteousness under the law blameless. ⁷ But whatever gain I had, I counted as loss for the sake of Christ. ⁸ Indeed I count everything as loss because of the surpassing worth of knowing Christ Jesus my Lord. For his sake I have suffered the loss of all things, and count them as refuse, in order that I may gain Christ ⁹ and be found in him, not having a righteousness of my own, based on law, but that which is through faith in Christ, the righteousness from God that depends on faith; ¹⁰ that I may know him and the power of his resurrection, and may share his sufferings, becoming like him in his death, ¹¹ that if possible I may attain the resurrection from the dead.

A major turn in the letter is obvious at this point. *Finally* translates *to loipon,* which recurs at 4:8. If *finally* is the intended meaning, then Paul either reopened the letter at 4:8 for a fresh subject or something has been inserted into (or dropped out of) chapter 3. It is questionable that *finally* correctly interprets Paul's intention in the letter before us. The phrase may intend to register no more than a transition, not a conclusion (it means henceforth in 1 Cor. 7:29; 2 Tim. 4:8; and elsewhere in the N.T.). In 2 Corinthians 13:11 *loipon* seems to introduce a conclusion; but in 1 Thessalonians 4:1 it is followed by two chapters, and in 2 Thessalonians 3:1 by a whole chapter, with a variety of subjects in each case.

The problem of literary structure has been reviewed in the Introduction. Arguments can be made for the insertion of material from some otherwise lost Pauline letter or for the loss of a part of the original letter, leaving a rough seam at 3:1. In view of the thousands of textual disturbances reflected in the extant manuscripts of the New Testament, most of them minor but some as extensive as the long ending to Mark's Gospel (16:9–20), one may not rule out *a priori* the possibility of a major textual disruption in Philippians, so early that no extant manuscript preserves the original form. On the other hand, no theory of insertion or deletion has been conclusively demonstrated. It is even more precarious to try to reconstruct the "original" text from internal evidence alone.

All in all, it seems best to try to understand Philippians as it has come to us in the manuscripts. Chapter 3, with the possible exception of v. 1, is of one piece, and the polemic with which it begins (3:2) and closes (3:18 f.) is interwoven with his plea for Christian maturity, preparing the way for chapter 4 (Scott, p. 72). Emphasis upon the importance of being right "minded" (3:15), upon "example" (3:17), upon "suffering" (3:10), and upon the "cross of Christ" (3:18) is the strongest kind of internal evidence that chapter 3 is continuous with chapter 2.

Rejoice probably translates Paul's intention in 3:1*a* (as in 2:18; 4:4), although many contend for "farewell" as the meaning.[12] In 2:18 *chairete* can only mean rejoice. In 4:4 it may mean farewell. In 3:1*a*, coupled with *in the Lord,* it surely means rejoice and not goodbye.

What does Paul mean by *the same things?* Some see this to belong to a part of another letter inserted here or to something which dropped out of the present letter. Assuming the basic structural unity of Philippians, with only another example of the roughness of style which Paul himself conceded (2 Cor. 11:6), we may look within the letter itself for clues. The most likely reference is to the duty of rejoicing (cf. 2:18,28; 3:1; 4:4) and to the danger of dissensions (cf. Lightfoot, p. 123).

To keep writing about these things, however repetitious, is for Paul not *irksome,* and for them it is *safe.* It does not cause him weariness, and it is something upon which they may safely rely. Joy belongs properly and essentially to Christian discipleship, and grumbling and wrangling contradict it. Enough is at stake that Paul risks repeating himself. It is no burden to him, and it is a safeguard for them (Barth, p. 92).

Verse 2 comes as a jolt, so rough that

many conclude that the section it introduces comes from another letter, a later insert into Philippians. It begins a strong warning against the threat of some form of Judaism, either Christian or non-Christian (3:2–11). Both the charges Paul makes against those labeled *dogs, evil-workers* and those who *mutilate the flesh* and the way he describes his own conversion experience point unmistakably to something Jewish. Scholars are divided over this question, and it cannot be answered conclusively. The *dogs* could be non-Christian Jews trying to proselytize Christians or they could be Judaizers, i.e., Christians who insist that Christ does not free us from the Jewish law, including circumcision.

Possibly a stronger case can be made for Paul's opponents being Judaizers than Jews or Gentile proselytes, converted first to Judaism and then to Christianity. He would have less justification for invective against Jews, who, if sincere, had the same right as he to seek converts, than against Christian Jews (or Christian Gentiles) who reverted to legalism after encountering the freedom in Christ (cf. Gal. 1:6; 3:1 f.; 5:1). Paul was extremely harsh with any Christian who seemed to "Judaize." He could be very tender toward unbelieving Jews, whom he yet loved as his kinsmen (cf. Rom. 9:1 ff.). We know that there were Judaizers who dogged Paul's footsteps in Galatia, Syria, and elsewhere. It does not follow necessarily that they actually had reached Philippi, but they were at work here and there.

Look out for the dogs may be understood in terms of a Gentile or Jewish background. It may echo the familiar Latin sign, *Cave canem* ("beware the dog"), but more likely Paul is throwing back at Jews their term for Gentiles, calling them dogs. The term is harsh, however used. Possibly Paul reserves it for religious fanatics determined at any cost to impose their partisan ways upon the people. The harsh term may reflect the growing tension between Jewish and Gentile Christians within the church and/or between synagogue and church. This

12 Cf. E. J. Goodspeed, *Problems in New Testament Translation* (Chicago: University of Chicago Press, 1945), pp. 174 f.

tension reached the breaking point in the years leading up to the first Jewish-Roman War (A.D. 66–70). From that point on, Christianity moved deeper into the Gentile world and farther from Judaism. A movement which initially had been thoroughly Jewish became almost exclusively Gentile by the end of the century. Feelings ran high on both sides through the various stages of conflict, tension, and rupture. Possibly more serious effort has been made at constructive dialogue between Jews and Christians since World War II than from the first century to the twentieth.

It is often stated that *dogs* were unclean to Jews, but this is not unqualifiedly true. In the Pharisaic book of Tobit, Tobias had a dog which followed him on his famous journey. The Jews seem to have had dogs as pets (cf. Matt. 15:27). Probably dogs were not unclean as such, but were often considered defiled because of their eating habits. Paul may see the legally or ritually based "cleanness" of his opponents to be itself unclean. *Evil-workers* and *those who mutilate the flesh* refer to the same people as those called "the dogs." Their threat is not persecution but seduction. They seek to win Christians back to Judaism or, probably, to transform Christianity back into Judaism (Barth, p. 92). They all *evil workers* in that they are "busybodies" whose "busy work" only diverts their victims from authentic to inauthentic values, from realities to shadows.

Those who mutilate the flesh translates one Greek term (*tēn katatomēn*), "the concision" or "the incision." This is an obvious parody on *peritomē*, "circumcision." Physical circumcision had served as a sign or symbol of one's belonging to the community of God, but to ascribe to it saving value was to distort its meaning. To try to elevate it to a saving sacrament was to demote it to simply a mutilation of the flesh. According to Acts 16:3, Paul circumcised Timothy; but when circumcision was made a test of salvation or table fellowship, he stood firmly in the position that "circumcision is nothing, and uncircumcision is

nothing" (1 Cor. 7:19). Could not more careful attention to Paul's cogent distinction between circumcision in heart and that in flesh and his refusal to let the latter be made a test of salvation or table fellowship instruct us with respect to baptism today?

Paul made much of the distinction between the artificiality and superficiality of "circumcision in the flesh, made by hand," and the reality of "circumcision in heart" (cf. Rom. 2:25–29; Eph. 2:11; Col. 2:11). A priest could effect circumcision in the heart. This spiritualizing of circumcision did not begin with Paul but within pre-Christian Judaism, going back at least to Jeremiah (4:4). In Deuteronomy (10:16; 30:6) circumcision of "the foreskin" of "the heart" is joined to the great commandment to love God with all one's being. Philo took the position that a convert may not need to be circumcised.

In v. 3 Paul makes two basic claims: (1) we are the *true circumcision* and (2) our confidence is *in Christ* rather than *in the flesh.* The first is the claim that true Judaism finds its fulfillment in Christ and survives there. The second is the claim that Christ is wholly sufficient for salvation, requiring no supplement out of man's own virtue or effort. By *flesh* Paul means here man in himself, apart from God. Sometimes he uses flesh in the literal sense (cf. 1 Cor. 15:39) and sometimes for the whole person (cf. Rom. 3:20; 1 Cor. 1:29; Gal. 1:16; 2:16). More often, by flesh Paul alludes to man's weakness or distance from God, man as unredeemed (cf. Rom. 7:5; 8:4–5,13; 2 Cor. 1:17; 5:16; 10:2–3). Here it describes man relying upon his own privileges and achievements, confident that he can establish himself with God (cf. Rom. 10:3).

Over against *the flesh,* i.e., self-love, self-trust, self-assertion, is *Christ.* We offer him our religious service or *worship,* and our *glory* or confident boast is in him, not in ourselves. This we do *in spirit,* as contrasted with *flesh.* Some manuscripts have "Spirit of God," meaning that it is by the Holy Spirit that we are able to shift from confidence in our works to confidence in

Christ's work. The oldest extant copy of Philippians (P[46], early third century) has neither "in spirit" nor "in the Holy Spirit." Some manuscripts have "in God." Probably P[46] preserves the original reading, all the others being explanatory glosses.

One may renounce only what he has; one cannot give up what he does not have. Paul was in position to declare how void of value was much that he once prized as primary. His was not the jealousy of a "have-not" (Barth, p. 95). He knew by firsthand experience what it is to trust in seeming religious advantages, virtues, and achievements. He could more than match his opponents on their own ground (cf. 2 Cor. 11:18—12:11). He could boast of having more reason for *confidence in the flesh,* but all such confidence was worthless.

What Paul meant by *flesh* is illustrated in vv. 5–6. He was *circumcised on the eighth day,* this in keeping with the Jewish law (Gen. 17:12; Lev. 12:3). Ishmaelites were circumcised at age 13, and proselytes at the time of their conversion. Paul had the induction rite of a native-born Jew. He was of *the people of Israel* (cf. Rom. 11:1; 2 Cor. 11:22). Israel was the covenant name for God's people. Paul's family had not lost track of its tribal identity, knowing that they were of *the tribe of Benjamin,* the tribe which, along with Judah, remained loyal to the Davidic line under Rehoboam (1 Kings 12:21 ff.); and with the tribe of Judah it had returned to Palestine after the Exile (Ezra 4:1). Of course, Benjamin was a child of Rachel, Jacob's favorite wife. Paul was a *Hebrew born of Hebrews,* probably a reference to his family's retention of their ancestral language, Hebrew or Aramaic (cf. Acts 21:40; 22:2; 26:14). Although he grew up in a Greek city and was exposed to Hellenistic culture, he remained basically a Hebrew.

The above four "gains" belonged to Paul's heritage, not choice. The three following were his choosing. He was a *Pharisee* with respect to *the law.* The Pharisees were a religious party which emerged out of the Jewish conflict with the Seleucids in the Maccabean period. They were laymen who became experts in the Mosaic law and champions of the traditions of Israel. Paul belonged, it seems, to the more liberal school of Pharisaism, that of Hillel and not Shammai, being a student of Gamaliel (Acts 22:3).

As to zeal, Paul once could boast that he was *a persecutor of the church* (cf. Gal. 1:13 f.). It is inescapable, that Paul once considered such persecution a virtue, and it was at that time so esteemed in Judaism. Both Judaism and Christianity have a record of religious persecution, both as aggressors and as victims. Each has attained its best under persecution, and each has sunk to its lowest in persecuting others. The Old Testament and noncanonical Jewish literature preserve Israel's own record of persecuting her own finest prophets as well as many non-Jews. Christianity likewise has martyred some of her own finest and has persecuted non-Christians from time to time. "The pot cannot call the kettle black." Both religions have betrayed themselves, their God, and the world far too often in resort to brute force and coercion instead of love's way of the suffering service which culminated in the cross. Before Paul met Christ he was the persecutor; afterwards he was the persecuted, even in Philippi (Acts 16:16–40).

As to righteousness, i.e., that *under the law,* Paul was found *blameless.* This was legal righteousness, measured by compliance with the Mosaic law as interpreted by the Pharisaic tradition. In meticulous detail, the Pharisees had interpreted the Mosaic law and applied it to every area of life. The basic motive was no doubt good, but when they tended to "measure themselves by one another" (2 Cor. 10:12) the process became quite deceptive. Does not each community tend to grade itself by its own mores? Sincere people can be so fooled by their own examinations that they can even kill other people and think they do God a service (John 16:2). Saul the Pharisee, zealous for the law, meeting so fully the religious standards of his group that he was considered blameless, could at the same time persecute people of a different religious stance!

When Paul came to know Christ Jesus, many of his values were reversed. What he had cherished as *gain* suddenly became *loss*. One whom he had despised became his *Lord*. Duncan [13] is surely right in seeing unmistakable links between 3:7–14 and 2:5–11 (further evidence of the originality of chapter 3 to the letter). Just as Christ had gained all in relinquishing all, so Paul found his greatest gain precisely at the point where what formerly he had considered *gain* became *loss*. That life is found by losing it, is not just a saying (Matt. 10:39); it is the very heart of the kind of existence Jesus had and which he offers us. It is the deepest truth he taught, and the hardest for us really to believe and accept.

Knowing Christ Jesus as his *Lord* came to be of *surpassing worth*. To know in this usage is more than an intellectual attainment. It is a knowledge which masters heart and will as well (Beare, p. 114). There is a kind of knowledge in which a personal subject masters an object. This is knowledge of a thing. In this relationship, the subject masters the object, but the object does not know the subject. Knowing Christ is more than knowing about him. It is the knowledge that a subject has of a subject. It is the personal acquaintance which is possible when person meets person in an atmosphere of love and trust, where there is acceptance and commitment. We may know Christ because he first knows us (cf. Gal. 4:9). Revelation is not primarily God giving us facts but God giving us himself. The knowledge Paul has in mind is that which is possible when faith responds to revelation.

To know Christ Jesus as *Lord* is to come under his claim as absolute and ultimate. It is to submit to the kingdom of God (God's sovereign rule) as it confronts us in the one whom he has anointed (Christ) to rule. One cannot know Jesus (Yahweh

[13] *Op. cit.,* p. 791.

saves) as Saviour without knowing him as Christ (anointed to rule) the *Lord*. It is like the kingdom of heaven, it costs everything and is worth everything (Matt. 13:44 f.).

When Paul *suffered the loss of all things* for Christ, he was not giving up things until then counted evil or worthless. These were his former treasures, and things prized most highly by his family and friends. But in the presence of Christ all was reversed. His heights became abysmal, his assurance lostness, his light darkness, his plus a minus (Barth, p. 97). What became *loss* was not his former wickedness but his former "goodness." Barth (p. 98) states it forcefully: because of Jesus Christ "the lofty is humbled, the solid shattered, assurance dispelled, man in his self-made goodness exposed, Israelitic man in the splendour of his religious system declared guilty before God."

Paul came to count *as refuse* what he had trusted and cherished. *Refuse* translates a word for "street-sweepings," "table scraps," or "excrement." The context would permit table scraps thrown to *the dogs* (*skubala* is from *es kunas balein*, to throw to the dogs, according to Moulton and Milligan), but the precise analogy remains uncertain. By any interpretation, the term is one of contempt, applied to his former assurance, self-righteousness, and zeal.

Paul's surrender of legalistic self-righteousness did not result in antinomian libertinism. Freedom from legalism did not mean lawlessness. *Righteousness* remained his consuming goal. But in Christ he came to have a new understanding of righteousness, both as to its content and the means for obtaining it. *A righteousness of my own* had formerly been his goal. It would be his virtue and his achievement. This proved to be not only unattainable, but it actually led him into pride and haughty zeal that persecutes others. In Christ he sought the righteousness which is *from God* and which is received through the channel of *faith*. It is God's achievement, not man's; and it is achieved in one who has the openness of faith to receive Christ into his life as a living, transforming presence. This is what it is to be *in him* or to have "Christ in you" (Col. 1:27).

Righteousness is not forensic or merely imputed righteousness. Neither righteousness nor justification (cognates in Greek) is to be understood solely as a forensic term from the law courts, but as a term with roots in the Old Testament, where righteousness and salvation are often synonymous (Synge, p. 42). It is true that God accepts sinners even while they are yet sinners; but this is not to say he accepts sin. A physician accepts a patient, but not disease. He accepts the patient with a view to freeing him of the disease. God accepts the sinner with a view to making him righteous. *Righteousness* is not only a new relationship with God; it is also a new kind of existence, a new quality of life—of attitude and action—rightness within one's life and in his conduct. It is the triumph of good over evil, not as man's doing but as God's work.

This righteousness will be perfected only eschatologically, at the Parousia of Christ; but it is already underway as the creative work of God. Paul is emphatic that *righteousness* has nothing to do with "lawlessness" (2 Cor. 6:14). To him "goodness" is not a bad word; it belongs to "the fruit of the Spirit" (Gal. 5:22). Salvation throughout the New Testament is God's gift and demand. In it man's one part is the openness of *faith*, to receive God's gifts and to yield to his claims.

In v. 10 Paul returns to the momentous decision to surrender all to Christ in order to *know him*. The two sides of this knowledge of Christ would be the sharing of his *resurrection* and *his sufferings*. To live with Christ, one must die with him (cf. John 12:24 f.; Rom. 6:1–11; Gal. 2:19 f.). One cannot go back to Golgotha, but the Christ who conquered there can come to us and enable us to become *like him in his death* and thus to know his kind of existence, partially now and completely in *the resurrection from the dead.*

It may be observed in vv. 10 f. that resurrection is mentioned twice, *his resurrection* and *the resurrection.* Before we are able to *share his sufferings* (cf. Col. 1:24) or become *like him in his death,* he the risen One must come to us. It is in his power alone that we can "be crucified" or "die to live." But *in him* we can share in his suffering and can look ahead to the resurrection which for us is yet future. The life now transformed and empowered by being *in Christ* is a significant reality, but it also looks ahead to the resurrection which must be understood as bodily, whatever the nature of that body is to be (cf. 1 Cor. 15:35–50).

Becoming like him in his death is tied closer to 2:6–11 than this translation reveals. It is being conformed to his death. Paul can find life only by pouring it out to God for others, just as Christ poured out his life. It is the opposite of snatching at life and its privileges. To *know him* translates an aorist infinitive, but this does not rule out progressive action, as Beare (pp. 122 f.) holds. The aorist is simply non-descriptive and may cover any kind of action, despite the fiction of "point action" which otherwise enlightened grammars continue to maintain (cf. John 2:20, where an aorist refers to 46 years of Temple building, and Luke 19:13, where waiting disciples are commanded to "carry on business until I come," an aorist being employed.).[14] To *know him* is to get to know him and also to keep on knowing him.

2. Threat of False Perfectionism (3:12–16)

12 Not that I have already obtained this or am already perfect; but I press on to make it my own, because Christ Jesus has made me his own. 13 Brethren, I do not consider that I have made it my own; but one thing I do, forgetting what lies behind and straining forward to what lies ahead, 14 I press on toward the goal for the prize of the upward call of God in Christ Jesus. 15 Let those of us who are mature be thus

14 The aorist may treat an action as a point, but that does not mean that it is in itself point action (cf. A. T. Robertson and W. H. Davis, *A New Short Grammar of the Greek Testament* (New York: Harper & Row, 1933), p. 295.

minded; and if in anything you are otherwise minded, God will reveal that also to you. [16] Only let us hold true to what we have attained.

What Paul has just written about "gain" and "loss" and about the goal of "the righteousness of God" seems to remind him of two threats which imperil the Philippians.[15] On one side is the threat of a false "perfectionism" (3:12–16) and on the other the threat of antinomian libertinism (3:17—4:1). The former could have its roots in legalism (passing easy, external tests) or some form of Gnostic "spirituality." The latter is a distortion of the idea of grace, seeing it as license or freedom from moral restraint. Religion is always threatened by these fallacies, resulting in either "the pride, superficiality, and irrelevance of legalism or the moral breakdown and ethical irresponsibility of the license which masquerades as liberty" (Stagg, "Matthew," BBC, Vol. 8, p. 61).

Paul rejects outright any claim that he is *already perfect.* Some at Philippi seem to suffer the illusion that they are perfect. Not only is the ultimate goal of attaining to the resurrection from the dead yet ahead, but even the goal attainable in this life is before him, not a past achievement. The race toward that goal has not been finished. There is no safety or wisdom in letting up. To do so would be like a runner pulling up short of the finish line. He must *press on . . . forgetting what lies behind and straining forward to what lies ahead.* This is the *one thing* upon which he concentrates. There is no Greek verb behind *I do.* Paul's words are abrupt, staccato, *but one thing,* reflecting his strong emotion as he thinks of the situation (Martin, *Philippians,* 153).

By *what lies behind* Paul seems not to refer to his former Pharisaic values, already given up as "loss" or "refuse." He is referring to that part of the Christian course already run. He cannot rest on his laurels. Past achievements are not enough. There

15 Duncan, IDB, p. 789.

is no place to stop in a race yet unfinished.

The *goal* toward which he continues to strive is the fulfillment of *the upward call of God in Christ Jesus.* Christ has laid hold upon him, calling him to a certain kind of existence. Paul's goal is to attain to the goal Christ has for him. Perfection is the goal, though unattained. It is his goal, however elusive. But he is equally concerned to avoid the illusion of actual attainment of the goal.

To make it my own probably means "to appropriate," "to grasp," "to seize tight hold of" (Michael, p. 158). Christ had "grasped" Paul; and *because* of this, Paul wants to grasp or appropriate the "perfection" which is Christ's goal for him. New Testament writers are not afraid of perfection as a goal (cf. Matt. 5:48). It is any claim that one has achieved it that is denounced (1 John 1:8–10). Conversion is a radical break with the past, but it is a beginning and not an end. Salvation has a beginning and a goal, but it is known in one's lifetime as a process. Paul could write of "those who are perishing" and of "us who are being saved" (1 Cor. 1:18).

Possibly *goal* and *prize* are two ways of expressing the same thing. In Paul's day, the prize, usually a wreath, awaited one at the finish line; but goal was not a technical term for the end of a race. The goal or prize toward which Paul strives is *the upward call of God in Christ Jesus.* He probably means not his call as an apostle (cf. Rom. 1:1; 1 Cor. 1:1) but the call to discipleship, the calling which he shares with all God's people. All Christians are "saints by calling" (1 Cor. 1:2).

Mature (teleioi) seems to capture Paul's thought in v. 15, even though the Greek word is a cognate of the one rendered *perfect* in v. 12. Although moral qualities are not excluded, Paul employed *teleios (telos* means end or goal) for the mature (1 Cor. 2:6) as contrasted with "babes in Christ" (1 Cor. 3:2). To be *thus minded* means to have the point of view which Paul has just claimed for himself. Paradoxically, one can be perfect (*mature*) only if he disclaims perfection as an attainment and affirms it as a goal (cf. Barth, p. 111; Beare, p. 131).

The *mature* are those who *hold true* to what they *have attained. Hold true* means "to stand in line" or "to march in line." There must be no divergence to left or right from the path which has brought them to this point, but they must press on in this direction (Barth, p. 112). Philippians are admonished to remain faithful to this attitude or point of view, a condition for further progress. They are neither to forget the goal as the demand under which they live nor to suffer the illusion that they have attained it. God's further light is available to those alone who remain open to it (cf. Matt. 13:9,12; John 9:39).

That there were those *otherwise minded* follows from Paul's strong disclaimer of having attained perfection and the paragraph following, in which antinomianism is exposed. The "mind" which Paul commends, perfection or maturity as a constant goal but not a vaunted attainment, is available to all who are open to it, for *God will reveal* it. The Greek word behind *minded* is a term prominent throughout the letter (1:7; 2:2,5; 3:19; 4:2,10). To be *otherwise minded* is more than an intellectual difference; it is to have a different outlook and attitude (Martin, *Philippians,* p. 155).

3: Threat of Libertinism (3:17—4:1)

17 Brethren, join in imitating me, and mark those who so live as you have an example in us. 18 For many, of whom I have often told you and now tell you even with tears, live as enemies of the cross of Christ. 19 Their end is destruction, their god is the belly, and they glory in their shame, with minds set on earthly things. 20 But our commonwealth is in heaven, and from it we await a Savior, the Lord Jesus Christ, 21 who will change our lowly body to be like his glorious body, by the power which enables him even to subject all things to himself.

1 Therefore, my brethren, whom I love and long for, my joy and crown, stand firm thus in the Lord, my beloved.

Having stressed perfection as the proper goal for discipleship and having warned against the presumption of having attained it, Paul now turns to the danger of giving up all such aspiration, presumably in the name of liberty which is actually perverted into license.

Some would connect *the enemies of the cross of Christ* with "the dogs" of 3:2, but this is not probable. If "the dogs" are non-Christian Jews, we know nothing about Paul which prepares us for his describing them as follows in this paragraph. If, as is likely, "the dogs" of v. 2 are Judaizers, the description here does not fit them, except by undue forcing of the analogies in v. 19. Paul may have seen the *end* of the Judaizers as *destruction,* but it is not likely that *the belly* is a veiled reference to their food laws or that *their shame* refers to Jewish embarrassment over their circumcision, especially when they went to the baths. The *enemies* of v. 18 are not likely to be "the dogs" of v. 2, despite Barth (p. 113 f.) and other commentators.

Paul begins his new appeal by offering himself, and possibly others as *an example.* He begs his *brothers* to become "imitators together" (*summimētai*) of him. They also are encouraged to *mark,* i.e., fix their attention upon, *those who so live* as does Paul (and possibly others). It is uncertain whether *us* is a true plural over against the singular *me* (v. 17) or if it is a polite plural by which Paul refers only to himself.

It may seem that Paul is immodest in offering himself as an *example,* but what he says must be interpreted in the light of vv. 4–14. His only boast is in Christ. He claims no virtues or achievements of his own. He disclaims having attained his goal in Christ. It is in his commitment to the "upward call" that he can offer himself as an example. The Philippians are challenged to join together in following his *example* in commitment to the goal of perfection with no boast of achieving it.

The *many* who *live as enemies of the cross of Christ* are identified as to destiny and character but not otherwise. It is not possible to identify their place of residence, whether in Philippi or elsewhere. Since they are *many* and Paul has *often* warned against them, possibly they are not limited to any one place. We already have suggested that they are not "the dogs" of v. 2. They seem not to be Jews or Judaizers. They most likely are within the church, whether of Jewish or Gentile origin. Paul's *tears* could reflect his sorrow over such lives within the church or his anxiety for the damage they may do to others.

The enemies of the cross of Christ are described as to their fate and their character. Their *end* is *destruction*, i.e., ruin. The primary reference is eschatological, to their final judgment; but their quality of existence is already one of ruin. That *their god is the belly* points most likely to the sensuality which the libertines sought to dignify as their liberty. *Belly* may point to gluttony, drunkenness, or preoccupation with the physical and material. Some in the early church thought of themselves as "spiritual," having a special knowledge of God, and claimed to be above sin. They held that they were essentially "soul" or "spirit" and that the body was only a temporary house, with no enduring value. Those holding such a dualism, spirit as good and matter as evil or worthless, became either ascetic or libertine. The ascetics called the body evil and tried to suppress it. The libertines called it insignificant, and claimed freedom to do as they pleased with it.

That *they glory in their shame* is again best understood in terms of libertinism. These "spiritual" people could even take pride in what ordinarily is considered *shame*. At Corinth, e.g., there were those who were "arrogant" or "puffed up" in pride with respect to one of their members who was "living with his father's wife" (1 Cor. 5:1 f.). Presumably, they saw this as a sign of their being so "spiritual" as to be above normal restraints. Although such people called it spirituality, Paul saw them as having *minds set on earthly things*. They were not spiritual but rather carnal (cf. 1 Cor. 3:1-3).

These are *enemies of the cross* in that they reject its principle of self-abnegation and self-sacrifice for that of self-assertion and self-indulgence. It is that "their whole life is antagonistic to the cross" and that they are "neutralizing the influence of the cross as a renovating principle" (Michael, p. 174). Their *minds* are not the mind which one has in Christ (2:5).

In contrast to the antinomian preoccupation with *earthly things* is the heavenly citizenship of those in Christ. *Commonwealth* (*politeuma*) is a cognate of the Greek word behind "your manner of life" (1:27), the basic idea being "citizenship." The idea that our true home is heaven even while on earth was a widely held one among early Christians, as seen in the New Testament (cf. Gal. 4:26; Eph. 2:19; Heb. 11:13,16; 1 Peter 2:11). The idea may have had special appeal and meaning in a city like Philippi, a Roman colony. Although living in Macedonia, they were citizens of Rome with the privileges and responsibilities of Romans (cf. 1:27).

The grammatical antecedent to the *it* from which *we await a Savior* may be either *commonwealth* (singular in form) or *heaven* (plural in Greek). It probably is pedantic to insist with some that commonwealth (our capital city) must be the antecedent. It is probably from *heaven* that *a Savior* is awaited. "Savior" is not a frequent title in the New Testament (24 times). Except for the Pastoral letters, the term appears in Pauline writings only here and in Ephesians 5:23. In the Pastorals it is ascribed to God and to Christ Jesus. Its infrequent appearance may be because of its usage for pagan gods and for the Caesars. Here it is used with reference to the time of the final deliverance of God's people, whether the Parousia or a bodily transformation coincident with death. Paul saw salvation as a dynamic process within this life (1 Cor. 1:18), its completion belonging to the future (Rom. 13:11). He thought not so much of our "going to heaven" as of Christ's coming to us *from it* (heaven) (Beare, 138), whether at the Parousia or at the time of the Christian's death.

The final act of redemption is that of the *body* (and the creation, according to Rom. 8:19–23). The New Testament doctrine is not immortality of soul but resurrection of the body. This follows from the biblical view of the wholeness of man, body being essential to his person. *Lowly body* refers to its humble state as compared with its future state as a *glorious body* (cf. 1 Cor. 15:35–50). "Vile body" is the unfortunate rendering of the KJV, and it has contributed to the fallacy that the body is necessarily evil or worthless. The body is to be neither despised nor worshiped; it is to be respected (1 Cor. 6:19 f.). The risen body is to have both continuity and discontinuity with the present body. Its precise nature remains a mystery to us, but by the *power* of God it will be like the *glorious body* of Christ. That is enough to know, to give us encouragement to stand firm in the *Lord.*

We await a Savior is generally understood to refer to the Parousia, and that may well be. However, there is no explicit reference to the Parousia in the passage and nothing absolutely requires it. Paul could have in mind the coming of the Lord to each Christian at the time of death, then and there changing the *lowly body* into one like *his glorious body.* If so, 3:20–21 expands 1:21–23, both envisioning a bodily transformation at the time of death. Against this, vv. 20–21 seem to refer to one coming and not many.

There is much speculation over Paul's understanding of the Christian dead, whether they are given their resurrection bodies at the time of death or must await them at "the Parousia of the Lord." It seems clear that when he wrote 1 Thessalonians he expected to be among those who would be living at the Parousia and who would be transformed without having to experience death (1 Thess. 4:15,17), while others are described as "those who are asleep" (4:13), "those who have fallen asleep" (4:14), and "the dead in Christ" (4:16) and awaiting resurrection. He writes that "the dead in Christ will rise first" and then "we who are alive, who are left, shall be caught up together with them in the clouds to meet the Lord in the air" (4:16*b*–17). In sum, at this point (when he writes 1 Thess.) Paul expects to live until the Parousia and receive his new body without experiencing physical death, but those who die before the Parousia must await the Lord's return before they are raised (cf. also 1 Cor. 15:51 f.).

In a recent study, Charles Buck and Greer Taylor [16] have contended that Philippians was written after 1 Corinthians but before 2 Corinthians 1—9 and that at some point Paul had come so close to death that he was compelled to rethink the relationship between physical death and one's resurrection. They hold that Philippians 1:12–14,19–24 is a vivid description of what later is alluded to in 2 Corinthians 1:9, "We felt that we had received the sentence of death." These writers hold that in Philippians Paul retains his view that those who are yet alive at the Parousia are transformed without knowing the experience of death and that this older view is reflected in Philippians 3:20–21. They hold that because Paul now sees the likelihood of his own martyrdom before the Parousia he has given up his former belief that Christians who die before the Parousia must await the Parousia to be resurrected, this view being reflected in 1:23.

In dating Philippians before 2 Corinthians 1:9, Buck and Taylor put too much weight on the possibility that 2 Corinthians 1:9 looks back on Philippians 1:12–14, 19–24, but they are doubtless correct in understanding Philippians as allowing for no "intermediate state," that those who die are at once with the Lord (1:23) and that others in their lifetime *await a Savior* who will change the *lowly body*, without the experience of death, *to be like his glorious body* (vv. 20–21).

Two points remain problematic. In Phi-

[16] *Saint Paul, a Study in the Development of His Thought* (New York: Charles Scribner's Sons, 1969), pp. 68–81.

lippians 1:20–22 Paul is prepared for a death which results in his being immediately with Christ, but in 3:20–21 he seems to expect to live until the Parousia, if indeed this latter passage refers to the Parousia. In 1 Thessalonians there is some hint that even at that writing Paul did not see the Christian dead as having to wait for their new bodies. At least he saw them as already with God, for "God will bring with him those who have fallen asleep" (4:14). There is no conclusive evidence that Paul ever envisioned an intermediate or disembodied state for the Christian dead. There is no trace of it in Philippians.

All scholars recognize the difficulty of correlating 1:21–23 with 3:20–21 and 4:5. Some see an unresolved tension in Paul's own thought with the result that Philippians contains two distinct views. They hold that Paul's earlier view that he will live until the Parousia and escape death by experiencing a bodily change at the coming of Christ survives in 3:20–21 and 4:5, even though in 1:21–23 he already has set forth his newer expectation of death before the Parousia, with an immediate reception of his heavenly body. Others admit conflicting views but say that this is because Philippians is a composite of at least two letters, with the two views representing different stages of Paul's development.

Although a strong case may be made for either of the above views, there are other possibilities. In 1:21–23 Paul may express his expectation of martyrdom with an immediate translation into his bodily presence with Christ; in 3:20–21 and 4:5 he may have in mind others who will live on until the Parousia, at which time they will experience a bodily change without death. But in these latter passages Paul does seem to include himself. It may be that in 1:21–23 he expresses his readiness for death (with immediate bodily change) even though, as 3:20–21 and 4:5 show, he still tends to think in terms of an imminent return of Christ and his own escaping of physical death. At least, in Philippians

Paul makes no place for a bodiless state. Either one dies and is immediately with the Lord, or he lives until the Parousia and is translated then.

V. Appeal to Unity and Peace (4:2–20)

1. Euodia and Syntyche (4:2–3)

² I entreat Euodia and I entreat Syntyche to agree in the Lord. ³ And I ask you also, true yokefellow, help these women, for they have labored side by side with me in the gospel together with Clement and the rest of my fellow workers, whose names are in the book of life.

Paul now makes explicit a problem implicit throughout the letter. Only after carefully laying a foundation did he approach it directly. Division in the church seems not yet to have become acute, but throughout the letter are hints of "grumbling" and "questioning" (2:14) and the need of being "in full accord and of one mind" (2:2). A falling out between *Euodia* and *Syntyche* is more than just a private quarrel.

Nothing more is known of *these women*. It is futile to try to identify them. The cause or nature of their difference is not known, only the fact of it, but that in itself is a serious matter. Paul does not take the side of either. He appeals directly to each *to agree in the Lord.* The phrase parallels that of 2:2; they are to be of the "same mind." They are to be one in spirit and purpose, not necessarily in thought.

The *true yokefellow* is not otherwise identified, and again it is futile to speculate. "Yokefellow" may be a proper name, but there is no trace elsewhere of such a name. *Help* is literally "take hold together with," i.e., help them help themselves. They once had *labored* with Paul and others *in the gospel. Clement* is otherwise unknown, not likely to be the well-known Clement of Rome (*ca.* 96). Other fellow laborers are unnamed here, but their names are written in *the book of life.* This is a Jewish and Christian way of referring to the faithful who are secure in God's care (cf. Ex. 32:32 f.; Psalm 69:28; Luke

10:20; Rev. 3:5). It is not clear whether these are yet living or dead. Not to be excluded is a possible reference to the whole church as those *whose names* are in the book of life and who are responsible for the unity of the church.

2. The Peace of God (4:4-7)

⁴ Rejoice in the Lord always; again I will say, Rejoice. ⁵ Let all men know your forbearance. The Lord is at hand. ⁶ Have no anxiety about anything, but in everything by prayer and supplication with thanksgiving let your requests be made known to God. ⁷ And the peace of God, which passes all understanding, will keep your hearts and your minds in Christ Jesus.

The note of joy runs throughout the letter (cf. 1:4,18,25; 2:2,17,18,28,29; 3:1; 4:1,4,10). However, the letter is not all joy, for this note is set over against *anxiety* as well as discord and disunity. *Rejoice* translates a term which may also be rendered "farewell," but in the sense of "God be with you" (shortened in English to goodbye). But *rejoice* best captures the meaning here.

The Greek word behind *forbearance* has no single equivalent in English. It could be rendered gentleness, considerateness, thoughtfulness, moderation, or graciousness. The Christian's gentleness should be apparent to pagan as well as fellow Christian.

The Lord is at hand can be understood as meaning near, and this certainly has valid application in the light of what immediately precedes. Possibly it is better understood eschatologically. Paul means more than a sense of his presence, as important as that is. Early Christians had a vivid expectation of the return of Christ. To them the Parousia was imminent. *Marana tha!* (Our Lord, come!) was an Aramaic prayer which survives in the Greek New Testament (1 Cor. 16:22; cf. Rev. 22:20). Although Christ has not yet come in the expected sense, Christian theology must be one of hope as well as faith. God is in our future as well as in our past and present.

Anxiety is distraction, being "pulled apart" or "going to pieces." Jesus warned against anxiety (Matt. 6:25-33). What is meant is not properly rendered "Take no thought" or "Be careful for nothing." We are not taught to neglect present or future or to be indifferent to difficulties, threats, or dangers. There are problems in the world, and we are to take these seriously. But anxiety is destructive, not creative. It is faithless, fruitless, and evil. Its antidote is the *thanksgiving* out of which one lives in openness to God, grateful for life and all its provisions and open to what more God has to give.

Prayer is the general term for addressing God, whether in thanksgiving, worship, confession, petition, or intercession. The English word means "asking," a pitiful reduction of the biblical concept of *proseuchē* (*prayer*). *Supplication* is a more limited term, used for requests made of God or man. Prayer is more than asking, but it may ask. Faith may ask, but it never demands. To ask is to trust the other. To demand is to trust oneself. It is proper to let our *requests be made known to God.* It is not that God requires to be informed or to be begged. It is that we need to ask, to come to grips with our needs, recognize and acknowledge them.

The peace of God is first of all the peace which God possesses and then the peace which he bestows (Beare, p. 147). This peace cannot be imposed, but it belongs to all who open themselves to God in *thanksgiving* and *supplication.* This peace *passes all understanding.* This may mean that it offers more than we can devise or that it is unfathomable. It is beyond the mind's power to attain, understand, or imagine, but not beyond God's power to give. It is the sense of acceptance, the assurance, the poise, the serenity which one may know within, whatever the situation without. *Keep* renders a word for "guard," a military term. God's *peace* is a garrison to protect us against all threats. This does not mean that it is compromised; it is enjoyed while at war with evil.

3. What to Take into Account (4:8–9)

⁸ Finally, brethren, whatever is true, whatever is honorable, whatever is just, whatever is pure, whatever is lovely, whatever is gracious, if there is any excellence, if there is anything worthy of praise, think about these things. ⁹ What you have learned and received and heard and seen in me, do; and the God of peace will be with you.

Paul again employs a term which may mark a turn in thought, "for the rest," or a conclusion, *Finally* (see comment on 3:1). He has not as yet introduced his last major subject, his gratitude for their gift. The several factors which cause some scholars to consider Philippians a composite letter may only reflect Paul's indifference to modern principles of logic, sequence, coherence, etc. He was writing to inform and to persuade, not to entertain with literary effect.

The eight virtues mentioned were familiar and accepted in pagan society. With the exception of *gracious*, each is found in the Septuagint (Martin, *Philippians*, 171). The terms are not distinctively Christian and are not extensively used in the New Testament. *True* means just that, in the widest sense of the word. *Honorable* is what is worthy of honor or reverence. *Just* refers to what is upright or righteous. *Pure* means stainless, not just chastity (Lightfoot, p. 159). *Lovely* is love-inspiring, pleasing, attractive, or worthy of being loved. *Gracious* (*euphēma*) is not passive, "well-spoken of," but active, "fair-speaking," or that which puts the most favorable construction on anything (Lightfoot, pp. 159 ff.). Moffatt renders it "high-toned," with the primary meaning of "well-speaking." It is the disposition to upgrade rather than downgrade.

Shifting to a conditional sentence, Paul admonishes his readers to *think about these things*, wherever there be *any excellence* or *anything worthy of praise*. Our translation is inadequate, for Paul means more than meditation. *Think about* is really to reckon or take into account, not just reflecting upon but allowing the things

considered to affect one's course of action. *Excellence* is moral excellence, goodness. *Worthy of praise* probably to Paul would be what God praises.

Paul goes beyond the injunction to take account of basic moral and ethical virtues. He counsels his readers to act, do! Attention has been given so exclusively to Paul's teaching that salvation is the gift of God's grace rather than reward for man's merit that this side of his teaching is neglected. Paul did stress the demands of salvation as well as the gift. He urged action or practice, as did Jesus before him. They are to *do* all that they have *learned, recieved, heard,* and *seen* in him.

4. Paul's Response to the Philippians' Gifts (4:10–20)

¹⁰ I rejoice in the Lord greatly that now at length you have revived your concern for me; you were indeed concerned for me, but you had no opportunity. ¹¹ Not that I complain of want; for I have learned, in whatever state I am, to be content. ¹² I know how to be abased, and I know how to abound; in any and all circumstances I have learned the secret of facing plenty and hunger, abundance and want. ¹³ I can do all things in him who strengthens me.

¹⁴ Yet it was kind of you to share my trouble. ¹⁵ And you Philippians yourselves know that in the beginning of the gospel, when I left Macedonia, no church entered into partnership with me in giving and receiving except you only; ¹⁶ for even in Thessalonica you sent me help once and again. ¹⁷ Not that I seek the gift; but I seek the fruit which increases to your credit. ¹⁸ I have received full payment, and more; I am filled, having received from Epaphroditus the gifts you sent, a fragrant offering, a sacrifice acceptable and pleasing to God. ¹⁹ And my God will supply every need of yours according to his riches in glory in Christ Jesus. ²⁰ To our God and Father be glory for ever and ever. Amen.

These 11 verses are a carefully worded expression of appreciation for a gift which Paul had received from Philippi through Epaphroditus. It rivals Philemon for its brilliance in handling a delicate matter with tact, insight, and force of expression. In these verses Paul walks a chalk line which avoids ingratitude on the one hand

and dependence on the other. Positively, he expresses profound gratitude for generous and meaningful gifts and at the same time maintains his independence of external support. His ultimate resources are within himself, these not of himself but of Christ; and in Christ he has a sufficiency which has a sovereign independence of all circumstance, whether plenty or poverty, whether surrounded by friends or abandoned.

Why this expression of appreciation comes so late in the letter and why so late in time cannot be explained. Much time has elapsed since Paul received the gift. Word of the critical illness of Epaphroditus had reached Philippi, and he had learned of their concern for him (see comment on 2:25–30). Is this Paul's initial acknowledgment of the gifts?

Some hold that vv. 10–20 belong to an earlier letter of thanks, not original to this letter (so Beare, p. 150). Another view is that this is not Paul's first expression of thanks but that it presupposes an earlier one, in a letter now lost to us. Michael (pp. 209–214) argues for this view, holding that the Philippians had been offended because Paul's first response had seemed to lack due warmth of appreciation. The view is argued cogently, but it is quite hazardous to read as much between the lines as is thus required. Another possibility is that Paul had communicated his appreciation, orally or by letter, but now he returns to the subject, either because he feels that he has not yet fully expressed his feelings or as a part of his continuing burden to activate "the mind" already present in the Philippians (see comment on 2:5).

Paul rejoices because they have *revived* their *concern* for him, expressed in their gift through Epaphroditus. He hastens to explain that they have been guilty of no neglect, only having lacked opportunity. *Revived* translates a term used for a tree putting out new growth in the spring, governed by the season. Here had been no negligent delay, only lack of opportunity. This could mean that they wanted

to give earlier but lacked resources. Probably it means that they had been cut off from Paul, either not knowing his whereabouts or unable to reach him, entirely possible in view of imprisonments, shipwrecks, etc. The "mind" of concern was there all the time, and now there is *opportunity* for its reactivation.

From expressing his appreciation, Paul turns to the matter of his own contentment or sufficiency and his source of strength. He wants at one and the same time to assure the Philippians of his gratitude and his independence. He does not *complain of want,* i.e., lack. He has *learned* through experience to be *content,* whatever his *state,* i.e., condition. He has known the extremes of abasement and abundance.

Content (autakrēs) is a Stoic term (our "autocratic"), but Paul gives it Christian meaning. Stoic self-sufficiency was their basic pride, independence of all external circumstances. The Stoics solved the problems of life by renouncing all desire or want. They would strive but with an indifference to result, as playing a game with "counters" instead of money. Their strength was within themselves. Paul's contentment (lit., sufficiency) was not in himself. It flowed into him from Christ. It was only *in him who strengthens* that he could *do all things.* Verse 13 reads, "As to all things I am inwardly strong in the one empowering me." Christ was the source of his strength to rise above *plenty* or *hunger, abundance* or *want.* He had *learned* this *secret* by experience. He borrowed a word from the mystery religions here, for *learned the secret* means to be "initiated." He had been initiated into Christ's secret about living triumphantly above changing circumstance (cf. Matt. 11:28–30).

Paul was neither an ascetic who despised the material things of life nor a materialist who lived for such values. He could enjoy the physical and material things when they came to him. He could get along without them when deprived of them. He sought neither poverty nor wealth. Drawing upon inner resources which were his in Christ, he found meaning and fulfillment as his outward circumstances changed from day to day.

In vv. 14–16 Paul turns again to appreciation for their gift. *Kind of you* is literally "you did well" or even "you did beautifully." *To share my trouble* is literally "having fellowship with my affliction." They did more than send gifts. They entered into his sufferings in a meaningful *koinōnia*. Their recent gift was no isolated matter, for they had *entered into partnership* (*koinōnia* again) with him from the days of his Macedonian ministry (cf. 1:5). This was a *partnership* in *giving and receiving*. *Beginning of the gospel* is from their perspective, i.e., from the time they knew the gospel. They had sent to his need *in Thessalonica*, at a time when the church in Philippi could hardly have been more than a few weeks old (cf. Acts 17:2). *Once and again* means at least twice, possibly more.

In vv. 17–20 Paul returns to the theme of his independence. He did not seek any *gift* from them (cf. 2 Cor. 12:14). He did *seek the fruit* or "interest" abounding to their account (*credit*). Although the terms are commercial, he means the spiritual gains which accrue to them as they give so generously. Whether or not he received a gift was unimportant, but that they wanted to give was all-important. He uses another commercial term for a receipt in saying, *I have received* (*apechō*) *full payment*. He had more than enough. The value of their *gifts* went far beyond the material. Because of the spirit in which they had given, they were a *fragrant offering*, a *sacrifice acceptable, pleasing to God*. This is sacrificial language, reflecting the dimension of worship in true Christian giving. Their gifts were an outpouring of themselves in sacrificial service, the essence of the "mind of Christ."

Paul has confidence that *God will supply every need* they have, just as his needs have been met. This certainly does not mean that selfish desires will be met. It is no assurance of material wealth. Paul has just declared his independence of external things. Surely he must mean just such fulfillment as he has known, even in the extremities of life. Again, the source of fulfillment is in *Christ Jesus*. And the measure of God's supply is the immeasurable *riches* of his *glory* made manifest in Christ.

VI. Concluding Greetings and Benediction (4:21–23)

21 Greet every saint in Christ Jesus. The brethren who are with me greet you. 22 All the saints greet you, especially those of Caesar's household.
23 The grace of the Lord Jesus Christ be with your spirit.

The letter is completed with various greetings and a benediction. The *saints* include all Christians. The *brethren* probably include Timothy and other associates. *Caesar's household* was a term for people in government, from slaves to high ranking officials (Lightfoot, p. 169–76). Although by the end of the century there were converts close to the imperial family itself, Paul's reference is probably to civil and/or domestic servants, even slaves. Those referred to may have had special ties with the Roman colony of Philippi. Those of *Caesar's household* could be in Rome or elsewhere.

The letter closes with a benediction. Paul presumably expected the letter to be read before the assembled church. It may be in deliberate support of his overriding concern for unity that he prays for Christ's *grace* to be with their *spirit*. *Your* is plural but *spirit* is singular. They are to be united in one spirit.

Colossians

R. E. O. WHITE

Introduction

History has a way of focusing renewed attention upon varying parts of Scripture. Man's new awareness of the universe around him lends new force to the central message of Colossians. For here Christ is set forth in a cosmic context, as he through whom the universe came to be, upon whom its coherence depends, for whom it was created, and in whom alone it will be restored to its primeval harmony.

So Paul answers the earliest of many attempts to relegate Christ to some subordinate role. He reaffirms the divine *fullness of Christ* as the key to all the *fullness of life* in Christ. This is the letter's permanent value, making Colossians both a theological feast and a spiritual tonic.

The focal point is 2:6–7. To this Paul gently leads, through thanksgiving and prayer which prompt profound reflections on the person of Christ, and a declaration of his pastoral concern. Firmly he recalls to spiritual reality, and to what is truly profitable. Life in, and for, the inexhaustible Christ is then movingly analyzed in rich detail (see Outline).

Personal references and greetings close a letter which, while everywhere concentrated upon its immediate, local purpose, yet by its emphasis upon the fullness of Christ and the Christ-filled life continues to be relevant and rewarding to Christians in every place and every age.

I. The Church at Colossae

The ancient Phrygian city of Colossae had forfeited its former glory to its growing neighbors in the Lycus valley, Hierapolis 13 miles to the northeast and Laodicea 10 miles to the west. But it was no backwater. Standing on the trade route between the five-road junction at Laodicea and the pass through the snowcapped Cadmus range, Colossae welcomed streams of travelers bringing to the valley news and currents of thought from east and west.

Greek colonization explains the language of the letter—and possibly the love of philosophic speculation against which it warns. Josephus says that Antiochus transplanted 2,000 Jewish families into the district from Mesopotamia. The Babylonian Talmud complains of their addiction to wine and baths! For good and ill, the church at Colossae was subject to strong Jewish influence. In addition, Phrygia was part of the Roman province of Asia, with its capital at Ephesus, 100 miles west of Colossae.

But beneath Greek, Jewish, and Roman influences lay the native paganism, probably animistic. A river disappearing underground, a petrified waterfall, sulphur springs, a "poison gas" chasm, and earth tremors (which finally destroyed all three cities in the later years of Nero) all demanded explanation and evoked a fearful awe. Later, Jewish angelology lent new names to old superstitions. The church Council at Laodicea, in A.D. 363, testified to the persistence of "the secret idolatry" of angel worship in Phrygia.

Paul passed "through the upper country" of Phrygia to come to Ephesus (Acts 18:

23; 19:1). His mighty three-year mission to Ephesus ensured that "all the residents of Asia heard the word of the Lord" (Acts 19:10,26). Among these were Philemon, Archippus, and Epaphras, almost certainly a citizen of Colossae (4:12). The name Epaphras is a shortened Epaphroditus, but too common to support identification with the messenger from Philippi (Phil. 2:25).

It was from Epaphras that the Colossians had learned the grace of God (1:7); he evangelized Colossae as Paul's representative. Epaphras had "worked hard" also "for those in Laodicea and in Hierapolis" (4:13) when he visited the apostle to report upon their progress and their problems (1:8; 4:12). The theory that a rift had arisen between Epaphras and the church is discussed in the commentary (see comment on 4:12–13).

Epaphras was Gentile (4:10 f.). It is not surprising therefore that the church also appears predominantly Gentile, as 1:21,27; 2:13; (perhaps 1:12), the scarcity of Old Testament allusions, and the kinds of vice named in 3:5–7, all imply. Only passing reference is made to the Jewish-Gentile controversy (3:11; 4:11); it was not a living issue at Colossae.

II. The Author

The opening and closing verses affirm, and tradition accepts, that Paul wrote this letter, though doubts have been raised. Supposedly "un-Pauline" details of style include labored sentences, 25 new words, overworking the preposition "in" (e.g., 1:9–23; 2:9–15), and fondness for phrases like "reward of the inheritance," "body of flesh," and "hope of glory." It has been replied that these features are most frequent where Paul is dealing with the Colossian problem, even borrowing heretical terminology—naturally they would not be found elsewhere; also that Paul deliberately uses here a sustained liturgical style. Others point to the natural development of Paul's thought and even to the influence of prison surroundings.

But this mechanical computing of grammatical details assumes that Pauline authorship means Pauline penmanship. We know that Paul employed amanuenses (Rom. 16:22), only occasionally taking pen in hand for closing words. Custom confirms this; his physical affliction may have required it. It is idle to speculate just how detailed was Paul's dictation.

Guthrie and Bruce discuss and dismiss theories of a shorter Pauline Colossians, interpolated by the author of Ephesians, as Moffatt had done, calling it "filagree-criticism." [1]

Colossians is included in the Pauline corpus from earliest references. Allusions to it in Ignatius, Polycarp, Barnabas, and Justin Martyr are very debatable; but it is cited in Irenaeus, the Muratorian Canon, Clement of Alexandria, Marcion's list, Origen, and included in second-century Old Latin versions.

The unbroken tradition of Pauline authorship, the close link with Philemon (than which no epistle is more surely Paul's), and the "thoroughly and characteristically Pauline theological background" [2] outweigh literary hesitations for most scholars. The only real issue is whether the error presupposed in the letter demands a post-Pauline date: this will be examined below.

Paul's circumstances are unclear. He is a prisoner (4:10; 4:18), but whether in Rome, Ephesus, or Caesarea remains unsolved. Most scholars still decide for Rome, but with many hesitations. Those who accept the Roman origin usually identify the occasion with Acts 28; estimates of its date then vary from A.D. 59 to 62–63.

III. The Colossian Heresy

The error troubling Colossae plainly involved both Jewish and pagan elements. Unmistakably Jewish elements are the stress upon sabbaths, circumcision, the

---

[1] D. Guthrie, The Pauline Epistles (London: Tyndale Press, 1963), p. 168. F. F. Bruce (see bibliography), pp. 171 f. J. Moffatt, Literature of the New Testament (Edinburgh: T. and T. Clark, 1912), p. 157.

[2] Guthrie, op. cit., p. 170

law, and probably the references to keeping festivals and new moon holy days; 3:11 and 4:11 also seem to presuppose a Judaist source of disagreement.

Unmistakably pagan elements include a "philosophy" depending upon plausible methods of reasoning resting upon human tradition, rather than upon logical demonstration and revelation. The worship of angels (as distinct from belief about them as in Jubilees, Tobit, and Ascension of Isaiah) probably reflects the widespread pagan fear of heavenly beings, elemental spirits of the universe. Of these beings, the sun, moon, and stars were in some sense the material embodiment. Ruling the earth, they should be placated, especially on their appointed seasonal occasions, by self-abasement and rigorous devotions.

The prohibition of certain foods could be a Judaist trait, but the reference to drink and the association with ascetic repression of the body suggest a pagan dualism, as do the phrases "inheritance in light," "dominion of darkness," and "kingdom of the Son." The emphasis upon visions, also, could be Jewish (e.g., the Book of Enoch); but those of which the errorists boast (2:18) are essentially sensuous, not spiritual, and appear to convey occult meanings needing interpretation. This recalls the trance-revelations promised in pagan cults.

The stress laid by the errorists upon wisdom resembles Proverbs, Wisdom of Solomon, and Sirach; but its exclusiveness (opposed in 1:26 ff.; 3:11) and the derogatory expressions in 2:4,8 suggest instead a Gnostic intellectualism.

Gnosticism was a climate of thought as widespread as evolutionary theory is today. It probably came into prominence in the first century or earlier and reached its zenith in the second. It combined philosophic speculation, superstition, semi-magical rites, and sometimes a fanatical and even obscene cultus. Ideas common to its many forms include: salvation by knowledge (*gnosis*)—the enlightened are "advanced Christians"; dualism—everything spiritual is by nature pure, everything material is by nature irretrievably evil, including the world and the body. God therefore is far off; the gulf between him and the world is filled by a chain of beings of descending spirituality. The body, the tomb of the spirit, may be rigorously suppressed or indifferently indulged as irrelevant to the life of pure spirit.

Being extremely intellectualistic, and therefore individualistic, Gnosticism cultivated an enlightened elite, for whom alone salvation was possible, and despised all others. The earlier Gnosticism reinterpreted Christianity and sought to "improve" it, offering to make Christians "perfect"; later, the bitterest antagonism developed.

Additional hints of such Gnostic ideas at Colossae are seen in phrases which were to become watchwords of later Gnostic systems: the "secret" or "mystery," the "fullness," knowledge (five times), and two or three others. Gnostic denials of the full incarnation of deity in Jesus find forceful reply in chapters 1 and 2. Any early signs of Gnostic "moral indifferentism" would be well answered by the blunt counsel of 3:5 ff.

But that Jewish and Gnostic elements should appear interwoven in one heresy (see 2:14 f.) has constituted matter for a century's debate. For the Gnosticism we know most about dates from the second century A.D. and was anti-Jewish, while orthodox Judaism was fiercely resistant to all compromise with paganism.

Some therefore deny any reference in Colossians to Gnosticism, holding that the Jewish idea that angels mediated the law expressed only extreme reverence for the law and that assertions of Christ's superiority to angels merely emphasize his superiority to the law. But angel worship in chapter 2 implies more than this; and insistence upon Christ's superiority to "thrones, dominions, authorities," suggests that they are personal, nearer to polytheism and Gnostic dualism.

Acts tells of Jews who practiced magic (Acts 13:6; 19:13 ff.) and of Simon Magus, long afterwards held the father of Gnosticism. Some features of the Colossian heresy are found mingled with Judaism in Galatians 4:3, 9–10, while traces in Timothy, John, 1 John, and Revelation show Gnostic ideas on the fringe of Jewry in Asia Minor during the second half of the first century.

Lightfoot in 1875 compared the Colossian error to Essenism, which did combine meticulous observance of the Jewish Torah and strict sabbatarianism with severe monastic asceticism, worship towards the sun, and an elaborate doctrine of angels. Abbott (see his discussion, pp. liv-lvii; his conclusion, pp. xlviii f.) thought the false teachers in Colossae claimed exclusive insight into the world of intermediate spirits, by the favor of whom (given the required austerity and humiliation before angels) new revelations ("visions") could be obtained: "it might be called Gnostic Judaism."

C. F. D. Moule (p. 31) likewise speaks of a "theosophy" of a Jewish-Gnostic type. Bruce (p. 166) appears satisfied that incipient forms of Gnosticism were current within Judaism in the first century A.D. Oscar Cullmann [3] thinks the Colossian heresy attempted to mix philosophical speculation tainted with Gnosticism with the gospel, as preliminary forms of Gnosticism existed previously in Hellenized Judaism. A. M. Hunter [4] finds strong evidence of this in John's Gospel.

Guthrie [5] cites with cautious approval W. D. Davies for the "many features common to the Colossian heresy and the Qumran sect," and R. M. Wilson for the character of the Scrolls as "pre-Gnostic." Qumran taught that to be a "son of light" meant absolute obedience to the law of Moses, in a legalism exceeding even the tradition of the elders: this may illumine 1:13; 2:14; 2:21 ff.

In this growing climate of opinion, it is not surprising that R. H. Fuller [6] roundly holds that the Christology of Colossians is slanted against Gnostic ideas, that the "philosophy" opposed is the syncretistic mythology of Gnosticism, that the cultic observances referred to recall Gnostic hierarchies, and that the ascetic prohibitions arise from Gnostic dualism.

Much of the discussion clearly reduces to the definition we give to Gnosticism. Certainly, the developed Gnostic systems described and opposed by the church Fathers were second-century phenomena. But preliminary Gnosticism, proto-Gnosticism, was an atmosphere, a varied and amorphous syncretism, long before it became a rationalized system; and its leading ideas were of considerable age.

In the end, we must describe the Colossian error in general terms, as a version of the Christian faith distorted and obscured by conceptions of a Gnostic type, which infiltrated the church by way of an already unorthodox Judaism.

Its effect was to loosen men's hold on the Christ of whom they had first been taught (2:19; cf. 2:6–7); to obscure, even to deny, the uniqueness of the ascended Lord, the *only* mediator, through whom they had once entered into freedom. Paul's answer is a Christology of truly cosmic proportions. He insists on the fullness of deity indwelling Christ; on his preeminence in creation over thrones, dominions, and principalities (1:16); on his headship over them in status (2:10); and on his victory over them at Calvary (2:15). His argument is that to doubt the fullness of Christ is to miss the fullness, richness, and sufficiency of the Christian life.

IV. Relation to Other Literature

The relation of Colossians to Ephesians and to Philemon must be left to the introductions to those epistles in this volume. Colossians 3:8—4:12 echoes very closely

[3] *The New Testament* (London: SCM, 1968) p. 76 f.

[4] *According to John* (London: SCM, 1968) pp. 27 ff.

[5] *Op. cit.*, p. 165.

[6] *Critical Introduction to the New Testament* (London: Duckworth, 1966), p. 60.

similar teaching found in epistles otherwise as different as Romans, Thessalonians, Ephesians, James, Hebrews, and 1 Peter, all of which reproduce five main themes in similar order. The source of this pattern of early catechetical instruction on conversion, baptism, and church membership lies in Jewish synagogue education, transformed by Christian experience and enriched with treasured words of Jesus. By echoing here this widely used syllabus of thought, Paul shows he can assume that at Colossae as elsewhere this primitive apostolic catechesis is already well known: he is but expounding that which they had already learned, as they were taught (1:7; 2:7).[7]

In 1:15–20 certain peculiarities of language, the elevated style, the loose attachment to its context, and the closely parallel structure in two strophes have suggested that Paul is using and adapting an early Christian hymn to Christ (cf. Eph. 5:14; Phil. 2:6–11; 1 Tim. 3:16). Much used to be made of the "too advanced" Christology of Colossians, although the ideas presented are only a more systematic exposition of teaching already given in 1 Corinthians 8:6; 1:24; 2:6–10 and Romans 8:19–22. But if Paul is quoting, then this advanced Christology is seen to be rooted in the thought and worship of the primitive, pre-Pauline church, though developed and completed, doubtless, as Paul thought out his own response to Gnostic misrepresentations.

Outline

Selected Bibliography

ABBOTT, T. K. *Epistles to the Ephesians and to the Colossians.* ("The International Critical Commentary.") Edinburgh: T. and T. Clark, 1897.

ASHBY, E. G. *A New Testament Commentary,* ed. HOWLEY, G. C. D., BRUCE, F. F., and ELLISON, H. L. London: Pickering and Inglis, 1969.

BARCLAY, WILLIAM. *Letters to Philippians, Colossians and Thessalonians.* ("Daily Study Bible.") Edinburgh: St. Andrews Press, 1959.

BEET, J. A. *Commentary on St. Paul's Epistles to the Ephesians, Philippians, Colossians and to Philemon* (3rd ed.) London: Hodder and Stoughton, 1902.

LIGHTFOOT, J. B. *Epistle of St. Paul to the Colossians.* London: Macmillan, 1875.

MOULE, C. F. D. *Colossians and Philemon.* ("Cambridge Greek Testament Commentary.") Cambridge: University Press, 1957.

MACLAREN, ALEXANDER. "Colossians and Philemon," *The Expositor's Bible,* VI. London: Hodder and Stoughton, 1890.

PEAKE, A. S. "Colossians," *The Expositor's Greek Testament,* III. London: Hodder and Stoughton, 1903.

SCOTT, E. F. *Colossians, Philemon and Ephesians.* ("The Moffatt New Testament Com-

---

[7] See P. Carrington, *Primitive Christian Catechesis* (Cambridge: University Press, 1940); E. G. Selwyn, *First Epistle of Peter* (London: Macmillan, 1949 Essay II); R. E. O. White, *Biblical Doctrine of Initiation* (Grand Rapids: Eerdmans, 1960), ch. 10 and "Additional Note 7," and literature there cited.

mentary," 7th ed.) London: Hodder and Stoughton, 1948.

SIMPSON, E. K., AND BRUCE, F. F. "Ephesians and Colossians," *New International Commentary on the New Testament.* Grand

Rapids: Eerdmans, 1957.

WILLIAMS, A. L. *The Epistles to the Colossians and to Philemon.* ("The Cambridge Greek Testament.") Cambridge: University Press, 1907.

Commentary on the Text

Introduction (1:1-14)

1. Address, Greeting (1:1-2)

¹ Paul, an apostle of Christ Jesus by the will of God, and Timothy our brother,

² To the saints and faithful brethren in Christ at Colossae: Grace to you and peace from God our Father.

The word *apostle* establishes Paul's right to address his readers, though strangers. *By the will of God* sets his authority upon its true foundation, not Paul's superiority but God's appointment; while associating Timothy with himself as *brother* robs the assertion of any personal pride.

Though *Gentiles,* the Colossians are *saints,* i.e., separated unto God, part of the holy people. *Brethren,* as a term for religious relationship, is far older than Christianity and needs the defining addition *in Christ* to specify the Christian brotherhood. When the Jew Paul uses it of Gentiles, it gains yet further significance. *Faithful brethren* at once precludes any suspicion that Paul writes in criticism or is moved by rumor. *Grace* (favor— "the smile of God," as J. A. Beet calls it) is in Greek a pun upon a familiar pagan greeting. *Peace* echoes the familiar Jewish "shalom." The greeting is, unusually, from *God our Father* only—perhaps because addressed expressly to *brethren* in the one multiracial family of the one *Father.*

Saints towards God and *brethren* towards each other, the readers live simultaneously *in Christ* and *at Colossae.*

1. Thanksgiving for Experience (1:3-8)

³ We always thank God, the Father of our Lord Jesus Christ, when we pray for you,

⁴ because we have heard of your faith in Christ Jesus and of the love which you have for all the saints, ⁵ because of the hope laid up for you in heaven. Of this you have heard before in the word of the truth, the gospel ⁶ which has come to you, as indeed in the whole world it is bearing fruit and growing—so among yourselves, from the day you heard and understood the grace of God in truth, ⁷ as you learned it from Epaphras our beloved fellow servant. He is a faithful minister of Christ on our behalf ⁸ and has made known to us your love in the Spirit.

Paul offers thanks for the Colossians' fruitful response to the gospel, which, he insists, they had accurately understood from the first. At the same time, he subtly prepares for the warnings about error which he has to offer and throws the strong shield of his commendation over their pastor, *Epaphras,* and his account of the Christian faith.

The occasion of Paul's thankfulness is the common Christian report which he has *heard* (repeated in v. 9). The gospel's *fruit* among them is analyzed into the familiar triad of *faith* toward Christ, *love* toward their fellow Christians, and the *hope* which is their final reward. These three essential elements of the Christian life occur together elsewhere in Paul (1 Cor. 13:13; 1 Thess. 1:3; 5:8; Gal. 5:5 f.; Rom. 5:1-5; Eph. 4:2-5), in Hebrews (6:10-12; 10:22-24), and in 1 Peter (1:3-8;21-22), from which A. M. Hunter argues that the formulation is pre-Pauline.[8]

Faith and *love* comprise all Christian good, relating the Christian to both God and man. For all its preoccupation with

[8] *St. Paul and His Predecessors* (London: SCM, 1961 ed.), pp. 33-35.

Gnostic intellectualism, Colossians leaves no doubt that it is to *faith* that knowledge comes (1:23; 2:5,7,12).

The love which you have for all the saints suggests that the Colossians were known for hospitality shown to believers traveling the great eastern road. In Colossians, as in Ephesians, Paul has the unity of the church much in mind: such *love* is its bond (3:14 f.).

Love in the Spirit (or spirit: no article in Greek) in v. 8 may introduce the only reference to the Holy Spirit. To understand this as "spiritual love," opposed to "fleshly love," seems pointless here. Paul conceives the Spirit as indwelling the Christian community and being "grieved" by antisocial behavior (Eph. 4:25–32; Gal. 5:13–26; 1 Cor. 12—14). In such a context, *love in the Spirit,* love in (a Christian) spirit, and *love . . . for all the saints* amount to the same thing.

Hope here is not the virtue, hopefulness, but the thing hoped for, *laid up . . . in heaven,* "future, hidden, secure" (Scott). Does Paul represent the hope as the reason (or ground) of the Colossians' faith and love (so ancient Greek commentators, and many moderns)? Or does he give thanks that those possessing *faith* and *love* have so great a hope (so Abbott, commenting that of all graces love is the least self-seeking)? Neither faith nor love can be sustained by the calculating hope of reward. It is specifically for the assured outcome that Paul gives thanks: he sees their eager response to the gospel as promise, preparation, and foretaste of coming glory (1:12,27).

Beside recalling all that is permanent (1 Cor. 13:13) in Christian life, this triplet of excellences perfectly describes the three dimensions of Christian experience, as it reaches upward to God, outward to the brethren, forward to God's future. So wonderfully does God break into the narrow cell of individual life and liberate the soul into all the freedom of the redeemed.

With consummate tact, Paul closes his thanksgiving with the remark that their pastor had made known their high attainment and maturity, lest anyone at Colossae should suppose some ill report by Epaphras. Their pastor had in no way denigrated his people!

A delicate and disarming opening, it yet hints of warnings to come. The phrase, *God, the Father of our Lord Jesus Christ,* introduces the unique dignity of Christ which the letter will expound. God is truly known as Father only to those who hold fast to an adequate view of Christ as Son (cf. Matt. 11:27; 1 John 2:23).

Again, *the gospel* which they had *heard* was *the word of the truth* (cf. Eph. 1:13), not human philosophy, profitless speculation, or the empty deceit of visionary "revelations." It was the gospel they had *heard before,* no novelty, but vindicated in experience; no localized, sectarian fashion of thought, but proclaimed *in the whole world,* as effective far beyond their familiar valley as it had been among themselves.

Nor had they misconceived the gospel, so as to need now some more perfect teaching: they had accurately **understood** it to be no mere theory or human code (con. 2:8) but a message concerning the free *grace of God* (con. 2:14,20 ff.) It had proved its value in two ways:

First, in *bearing fruit* among them in approved character and conduct (con. 2:8, 23; cf. Matt. 7:15–20; John 15:8). *Faith in Christ Jesus* and *love . . . for all the saints* are precisely the points in which Christianity differed from its Gnostic perversion (see Introduction).

Second, by its power of development. *Growing* in richness and depth as faith matured, the gospel needed no supplementing by human philosophy. Both the fruitfulness of the gospel and its power of growth may echo the Greek of Mark's parable of the sower, perhaps glancing at Gnostic misuse of that traditional saying of Jesus. *Growing,* however, is sometimes taken as growing in influence, making many converts. Would Paul appeal to the popularity of any teaching as evidence of its truth? Verse 10, the echo of the sower, and the Gnostic claim to more advanced teaching favor Maclaren's interpretation: "The word long since heard . . . will open out into all new depths, and blaze in new radiance as men grow. It will give new answers as the years ask new questions."

On Paul's testimony to Epaphras, see the comment on 4:12 f. Paul stresses Epaphras' faithfulness, both to Christ and (apparently) as Paul's own delegate. The Colossians need no new instructors: they have been soundly taught.

Paul's sensitive, purposeful introduction provides (1) a succinct description of what is central in the Christian life—faith, love, and hope; (2) a stimulating description of the gospel by which that life is kindled—as true, universal, fruitful, growing; and (3) a satisfying description of the Christian minister—as a faithful servant of Christ, beloved colleague, and utterly loyal to his own people.

3. Prayer for Knowledge (1:9–14)

⁹ And so, from the day we heard of it, we have not ceased to pray for you, asking that you may be filled with the knowledge of his will in all spiritual wisdom and understanding, ¹⁰ to lead a life worthy of the Lord, fully pleasing to him, bearing fruit in every good work and increasing in the knowledge of God. ¹¹ May you be strengthened with all power, according to his glorious might, for all endurance and patience with joy, ¹² giving thanks to the Father, who has qualified us to share in the inheritance of the saints in light. ¹³ He has delivered us from the dominion of darkness and transferred us to the kingdom of his beloved Son, ¹⁴ in whom we have redemption, the forgiveness of sins.

The good report has prompted not only thanksgiving but prayer, *from the day* Paul *heard of it.* To his prayer, the most intellectual, even "Gnostic," Christian could say Amen. For Paul asks for their continual increase in *knowledge . . . wisdom and understanding.*

The structure of Paul's long sentence implies that this is the one thing Paul asks: the purpose of his request is a life

well-pleasing, analyzed in four descriptive phrases. Paul prays for them *knowledge,* not of mysteries or of speculative doctrines, but of God's *will.* Barclay well remarks that this is the true goal of all praying, but we so often plead "Thy will be changed" instead of "Thy will be done."

The *wisdom* Paul asks is neither "fleshly" (as ministering to pride, 2:18), nor mere show (2:23), nor worldly (1 Cor. 2:5 f.), but *spiritual,* i.e., an insight into spiritual truth, perception of spiritual values and priorities, and the vision of spiritual ends (cf. 1:28; 2:3;23; 3:16; 4:5).

The *understanding* Paul seeks for his readers is the ability to apply spiritual principles to practical situations. Once, Paul would have sought *the knowledge of* God's *will* in a written code; now he seeks it in the knowledge of God's mind, wisdom to discern the right, and understanding to apply it to new problems in developing ways—i.e., in Christian instruction, Christian insight, and Christian common sense.

Christians inclined to Gnosticism would be less pleased by Paul's insistence that the sole purpose of wisdom is *a life worthy of the Lord, fully pleasing to him.* For *life* Paul uses the customary Hebrew "walk," and he requires that it be right in the sight of the Lord. *Worthy* obviously does not mean deserving, but fit, competent, corresponding to God, the gospel, the call, and the Master (1 Thess. 2:12; Phil. 1:27; Eph. 4:1). Never worthy to be saved, we strive to become worthier of him who saved us in our worthlessness.

To be *fully pleasing to him* means to be satisfying to God in every way (cf. 3:22; Eph. 6:6; Rom. 15:1–3). The life thus divinely approved is described in four parallel phrases: (1) *Bearing fruit in every good work* may have special significance for the errorists (see comment on 1:6), but in apostolic thought the quality of *fruit* reveals, in trees and men, the quality of the life within; while in contrast with "works," fruit suggests good deeds as the natural, spontaneous overflow of the good Spirit within (Gal. 5:22; Matt. 7:16 ff.; John 15:1–8; Luke 13:6 ff.) The fivefold *all* (vv. 9–11 in Greek) cannot be accidental: the character issuing from knowledge of God's will should be of maximal, not of minimal, dimensions.

(2) *Increasing in the knowledge of God* is not repetition. In v. 9 Paul prays for the knowledge of God's will; here he is thinking of deep and growing intimacy with God's character, ways, faithfulness, and love. Some take Paul to mean growing *by* the knowledge of God: more probably he means that the Christian filled with the knowledge of God's will and so living worthily of the Lord will continually advance in the deepest wisdom of all—the personal knowledge of God himself that is the inmost secret of Christian life. Knowledge of God and obedience to God deepen each other: contrast John 7:17 with 13:17.

(3) *Strengthened with all power according to his glorious might* reminds us that moral power is at least as important as moral understanding. Until the moral direction of life is decided by *belief* and the moral resources released by *decision*, knowledge of the good life remains barren. Neither ancient nor modern Gnostics may welcome the thought, but knowledge and wisdom are not enough.

But even knowing the right and having power to do it are not the whole of life. Adversity, opposition, and sacrifice have to be faced. The strength of the *worthy* life is shown in *endurance*, or fortitude, maintaining the right against all odds; and in *patience*, the capacity to bear with people without being embittered. Unlike Stoic self-mastery, Christian strength rises even to *joy*. Such Christians are more than conquerors: they possess that tenacious and cheerful buoyancy which made the apostolic church, even in that Roman world, invincible and indestructible. Such unconquerable courage manifests *his glorious might* as clearly as does spectacular achievement.

(4) *Giving thanks to the Father* describes the prevailing feeling-tone, the profound sense of privilege, which possesses the redeemed heart (cf. 1:3,12; 2:7; 3:15,17; 4:2). In the New Testament generally, thankfulness is a master motive of the Christian soul. When man serves God no longer through fear, or the pursuit of merit, the one utterly un-self-seeking constraint that sustains all endeavor is simple thankfulness to him who loved us and gave himself for us. The only answer appropriate to grace is gratitude.

He has qualified us to share in the inheritance of the saints in light: the inheritance promised to Abraham, the allotment to Israel of portions in the Promised Land, the chosen people being *qualified* by divine choice, experience, and covenant to be his saints—into the spiritual fulfillment of all this the Gentile Christians have entered. "God gave you title" (as Abbott renders it) to a portion (Deut. 10:9) no longer in darkness but in the light of his holiness and favor.

The Qumran community spoke much of the inheritance of God and of the war of light with darkness. Paul's phrasing here may well allude to the Judaist-Gnostic heresy troubling Colossae (see Introduction): the Colossians already possess what the errorists offer, are already qualified saints of Israel, needing neither circumcision (2:11) nor human approval (2:16; for the main thought, cf. 1 Cor. 10:1–8; Rom. 9:6 ff.).

Moreover, as Israel was delivered from Egypt and transferred to Canaan (and as the Jews of Phrygia had been forcibly transferred to their new homes there; see Introduction), so the Colossians had been freed from the domain—*delivered . . . from the dominion*—of hostile demon powers (Eph. 6:12; Luke 22:53) and transplanted into a kingdom of light and love. Perhaps the Exodus metaphor for conversion was once as familiar as new birth, new creation, and death-resurrection. For the *kingdom* of Christ, cf. 1 Corinthians 15:24; Ephesians 5:5; for Christians as already in light, cf. Ephesians 5:8; 1 John 1:5–7; 1 Peter 2:9 and the reference to Qumran above. Note too the curious relationship to Acts 26:18, to which the key seems now lost. Paul's main point is clear: Why should the Colossians fear or placate the very powers from which Christ has already delivered them?

Like Israel, too, the Colossians *have redemption*, the regular word for the exodus from Egypt and later for the return from the exile in Babylon. Perhaps in contrast with current ideas of "enlightenment" as all-important, Paul identifies *redemption* with *forgiveness of sins*. That is the release and liberation most necessary for sinful men. Whether or not the reference to purchase by ransom, by the blood of Christ, is part of the text here (as in Eph. 1:7), the thought would surely be in Paul's mind.

The Colossians, then, have abundant reason to be thankful. And that undergirding gratitude will sustain the whole Christian character—fruitful, intimate with God, and strong—which shall be worthy of the Lord and filled with awareness of God's perfect will. A great prayer to offer for one's friends, and for oneself!

I. The Fullness of Christ Affirmed (1: 15–23)

1. In Relation to God (1:15–20)

[15] He is the image of the invisible God, the first-born of all creation; [16] for in him all things were created, in heaven and on earth, visible and invisible, whether thrones or dominions or principalities or authorities—all things were created through him and for him. [17] He is before all things, and in him all things hold together. [18] He is the head of the body, the church; he is the beginning, the first-born from the dead, that in everything he might be preeminent. [19] For in him all the fulness of God was pleased to dwell, [20] and through him to reconcile to himself all things, whether on earth or in heaven, making peace by the blood of his cross.

The closing words of the thanksgiving have brought Paul to Christ and so to one great theme of the letter, the fullness of Christ. Fifteen tremendous assertions comprise "the great Christology," Paul's exploration of the cosmic Christ. On the advanced thought and poetic form of the passage, see the Introduction. But we miss Paul's meaning if we forget that he wrote with severely practical purposes—to instruct a questioning faith and to enrich daily Christian life.

Paul's theme is the preeminence of Christ, first in relation to God. In all that concerns man's knowledge of God, Christ is without peer. He is the Son (1:13), in whom God's character is reproduced, God's life incarnate: preeminent in relationship. He is the beloved (1:13), on whom God's love is set, in whom he is well-pleased: preeminent in God's heart. He is the King (1:13), to whom God has given the name above every name: preeminent in status and authority. He is Redeemer, too (1:14), the channel of God's saving purposes and the bearer of their cost: preeminent in responsibility.

And in all this Christ is *the image of the invisible God*. The word image is used of the Logos in Philo; of wisdom in Wisdom of Solomon 7:26; as here in 2 Corinthians 4:4; of a stamp upon a coin in Matthew 22:20; of a statue in Revelation 13:14. Barclay adds examples meaning portrait, especially pen-portrait; Moule contrasts Exodus 20:4 with Genesis 1:27. Clearly, likeness, representation, and manifestation are implied: Christ makes the invisible God visible in human flesh. He is preeminent in revelation.

So Paul refutes the Gnostic assertion that Christ was but one in a whole series of emanations mediating between God and the world. He is without rival in bringing God to man and man to God. This unparalleled truth about Jesus is urgently relevant today. As our one world draws together in its planetary home, his is the only conception of God that could ever satisfy all races and types of men; as human knowledge expands to the horizons of space, his is the only vision of God that could be reconciled with our new understanding of the universe. Christ is not only preeminent, but unique, in all that makes God real to man in every age.

2. In Relation to the Universe

Christ is preeminent here, too: *the first-born of all creation.* Grammar and context exclude Christ from among created things, but the meaning of *first-born* is less clear. Peake argues for the meaning of "dominion, rulership," a messianic title in Hebrews 1:6 and Psalm 89:27. So Bruce equates it with "heir of all things" in Hebrews 1:2. Abbott, Williams, and the NEB margin, however, stress Christ's priority in time (so first-born is used in 2 Sam. 19:43, LXX; Luke 2:7; Rom. 8:29; Rev. 1:5). Verse 18 may use the title thus, though as Moule suggests, both prior to and supreme over could be intended; cf. "his is the primacy" (NEB).

In him all things were created . . . through him: the parallel with wisdom in Proverbs 8:22 ff. is close, as it is in John 1:1–18 and Hebrews 1:2; which echo Paul. With *in him,* Abbott well compares the phrase *in him* used constantly of the Christian life. Only in him does church or creation have any being: he is the necessary environment of both, the mediator alike of creation and redemption. *Through him* makes Christ the agent by whom, as well as the sphere within which, all things came to be.

The broken sentence (v. 16) well illustrates the thrust of the passage against Gnostic opposition. The rival thrones and authorities of which the errorists made so much are after all Christ's creation. Christ, not the angels, is Lord of the material creation. Paul adopts, without explanation, the current terminology about various ranks of angel powers. Williams and Peake reject Lightfoot's idea that Paul lists these titles with "impatience"; but the varying order—and especially the addition of "every name that is named" in Ephesians 1:21 ("You name it, he's above it!")—support the suggestion.

Christ is the goal, as well as the origin, of creation: *all things were created . . . for him* to fulfill his aims, serve his purpose, and promote his glory. Not the history of Israel only, but all time tends toward Christ. Though the final goal of all things must be the glory of God, the mediate goal and the full meaning of that glory are defined in Christ. The universe knows no higher End than he.

Moreover, every created thing depends for its existence upon something that existed before it: but he is *before all things,* self-existent, dependent upon nothing save upon the Father. *Before* can be purely temporal (in which case *is* must be timeless), or causally prior, or (Moule) superior in rank. Williams remarks that only in a Being who *is,* independently, can all things be created and sustained: which is surely what Paul means.

In him all things hold together, literally, "stand together," cohere. "He maintains in being what he has brought into being" says Bruce; "in him [all things] have their unity and meaning," says Scott. Once more Paul echoes what had been said of wisdom (Wisd. Sol. 1:7; Wisd. Sirach 43:26). He means at least that he through whom all things were created now also holds all things in being (so Heb. 1:3). But there is implied too the suggestion that he imposes upon all things their pattern and inner coherence, and so their meaning. In the last resort, it is the presence of Christ in history that makes the universe intelligible.

Paul has still to add that Christ will *reconcile* all things. This stupendous vision of the universal Christ has much meaning for a world reaching deeply into space and standing bewildered before the immensity of things. Ours is the Christ who was God's agent in creation, who stands behind and ahead of the universe, who gives to the universe coherence, and to whose authority and saving purpose at the last all existing things will bend. He who makes all things new also makes all things meaningful.

3. In Relation to the Church

Christ is preeminent, further, in the church: *the head of the body.* The metaphor of *the body*, traced by some to Stoicism and by others to Jesus (Mark 14:22), develops greatly in Paul's usage (1 Cor. 12:12 ff.; Rom. 12:4 f.; Eph.). The interpretation of *the head* as a directing brain is probably anachronistic. If a parallel with Adam as head of the race is implied, the thought of the church's origin in Christ may be present. But the head's position, the location of sight and hearing, and the fact that wounds to it are more likely fatal, sufficiently explain the usage in all languages for "chief, prior in rank." This meaning seems required in 2:10 (see comment on 2:15).

The beginning may mean simply that Christ is the church's origin (NEB); but it is an idea upon which early Christians loved to dwell (cf. dayspring, alpha, author of faith, morning star, beginning of the creation of God, firstfruits from the dead, prince of life). The phrase here relates Jesus to the new creation as John 1:1 relates him to the old.

Paul seems to imply that Christ is head and origin of the church because he is the *first-born from the dead*, first to break the bands of death, and leading many sons to glory; first in time and rank in the resurrection, as he is in creation (v. 15; cf. Rev. 1:5). The identity of the preexistent (v. 15 f.), incarnate and crucified (v. 20), and risen (v. 18) Christ is assumed as self-evident.

To understand *that in everything he might be pre-eminent* as the purpose for which he is *head, beginning,* and *first-born* seems tautological as a statement of fact: it has more point as a statement of what should be—God has made him head and beginning so that he might be absolute and unrivalled in the loyalty and love of hearts that adore him. "He is supreme in the universe: he has to become supreme in relation to the church" (Peake)—especially perhaps in the church at Colossae.

Verses 19-20 sum up this breathtaking Christology. Unfortunately they bristle with questions. *The fulness* (Paul's complete phrase) was in Gnostic thought the divine "plenitude," the total of divine emanations, agencies, energies, which filled the void between pure spirit and the material world. Paul asserts that all the activities of God are displayed in Christ. The Gnostics conceded that God was "in some manner present in Jesus" (Scott); Paul insists that Christ in his own person represents the "fulness." Moule, Williams, Abbott, and the RSV, in varying phrases, understand this to be "the fullness of deity"; the NEB has "the complete being of God" (cf. 2:9).

Instead of *the fulness . . . was pleased to dwell* (Abbott, Moffatt, RSV), some prefer "God was pleased that all the fullness should dwell in Christ" (Williams, citing 13 NT parallels; Scott, citing rabbinic idiom; Bruce). This prepares better for *and through him to reconcile*. But it is not precisely what Paul wrote and appears to make the fullness of deity in Christ to depend on the Father's "pleasure." Others therefore take *fulness* as the fullness of grace which enabled Christ *to reconcile*—without help from angelic mediators (Peake).

But the limitation to fullness of grace is alien to the context; *dwell* (i.e., permanently) seems directed at the Gnostic idea of Christ's temporary deity; and Williams draws attention to the echoes, in "beloved Son" and "pleased," of the baptism and transfiguration stories. The NEB paraphrase seems therefore to capture Paul's meaning, though it misses the deliberate use of the Gnostic catchword, *fulness:* "in him the complete being of God, by God's own choice, came to dwell." Paul's exalted conception of Christ's person could scarcely find more adequate expression than in this single sentence.

As to Christ's work: the reconciling mediation of Christ is as timeless and universal as his creative mediation (v. 20 repeats v. 16). The cross, too, has cosmic significance (Eph. 1:10; 2 Cor. 5:19; 1 John 2:2); and a rare word shows that its reconciling work is complete. Moule takes *blood* as sacrificial; Barclay sees in it the final proof of the love (Rom. 8:32) that reconciles; but Scott holds that Paul means Christ died on the field of battle fighting man's enemies, and his death was the stroke of victory. This is the metaphor of 2:15, but it does not explain either reconciliation or peace in this passage. *Blood of his cross* is not so much a mixed metaphor as a highly condensed one. The cross is a gibbet; the blood-shedding is doubtless Christ's death thereon; the interpretative naming of that event as "blood making peace" is the essence of the idea of atoning sacrifice.

It seems clear that *to reconcile . . . all things . . . in heaven* tilts at the Colossians' reverence for spiritual beings and authorities: so far from supplementing Christ's work, they too need reconciling, and by Christ. *All things . . . on earth* tilts at the dualism, and possibly the exclusiveness, of the Gnostic outlook. But precise exposition is much debated, perhaps because Paul is once more using the language of his opponents.

Among many suggestions, tenable interpretations seem reducible to three. (1) *All things . . . in heaven* means nature, and Paul is repeating Romans 8:20 f. But there nature is delivered from corruption, not reconciled, at peace. Moreover, v. 16 tells against this explanation. (2) Scott thinks of Christ destroying the divisive forces of a universe at war with itself by breaking the principle of evil upon the cross. More personally expressed, *all things . . . in heaven* includes the devil and evil angels, or demon powers (Eph. 1:20 ff.). But did Paul expect such universal reconciliation, and through the passion of Christ in human nature? (3) *All things . . . in heaven* may mean angelic beings, and all other opposing forces, which will be subdued to unity, rather than reconciled to fellowship and peace—as in 2:15. This is "reconciliation through subjugation," peace compulsorily imposed (Bruce cites 1 Cor. 15:28). Is the unusual word for reconciliation due to this less familiar idea of imposed unity (despite its use in v. 22)?

This third interpretation is in line with Ephesians 1:10 (cf. Eph. 3:10; Phil. 2:11) where the whole universe is to regain its lost unity in Christ, the shattered, fragmented, alienated chaos resulting from man's fall being reduced to the order, beauty, and design which God originally intended. But the words *reconcile . . . peace . . . blood of his cross* scarcely suit the idea of final subjection.

One suspects a double intention of Paul: those who consent will be reconciled into peace through the sacrifice of Christ; those who resist will be vanquished into submission through the victory of the cross (2:15). Either way, Christ is preeminent in this also, that he, unaided, will bring the whole creation, including the spiritual hierarchies, back to the God who made it, (not, probably, *to himself*)—and made it in Christ, through Christ, and for Christ.

Such is Paul's exposition of the towering greatness, the inexhaustible fullness, of the cosmic Christ. He is without peer, needing no angelic assistants, alike in creation and in redemption. Paul's immediate purpose is urgently relevant and practical: in him dwells the fullness—you have come to fullness of life in him, needing no Gnostic supplements. We may note too, with Moule, the connection Paul maintains between creation and redemption: Christ is not the antithesis to nature but its completion and meaning. God's world is one. Because Christ was maker, origin, coherence, and reconciler of *all things*, we can keep him out of nothing. All that concerns us, including (as Paul will show) home, family, work, and public life, must be kept in living relationship with him, as the rightful Lord of all things.

But the ultimate implications are just as urgently relevant, perhaps especially so in our generation. The cosmic fullness of Christ means for us that wherever man goes on earth or in space, he will still be confronted by Christ's challenge and ideal. Whatever man discovers will still bear the marks of the creative Mind, as Christ has helped us to read them. However clever man becomes, he will still need Christ's grace to make him good. And however far he flees to the horizons of the universe, no immensity of distance shall separate him from the love of God which is in Christ Jesus, our Lord.

The humanist Christ is insufficient. In an age of space exploration, when the heart hungers for a more adequate conception of God, and the practical problems of life on earth seem insoluble, only the cosmic Christ of Colossians will serve our need.

4. In Relation to Experience (1:21–23)

21 And you, who once were estranged and hostile in mind, doing evil deeds, 22 he has now reconciled in his body of flesh by his death, in order to present you holy and blameless and irreproachable before him, 23 provided that you continue in the faith, stable and steadfast, not shifting from the hope of the gospel which you heard, which has been preached to every creature under heaven, and of which I, Paul, became a minister.

Our outline is mere convenience: Paul's thought is uninterrupted. The Colossians have already proved for themselves the truth he has been expounding. They have been reconciled, and should allow no teachers of novelties to cast doubt upon their past experience.

The alienation in which the gospel first found the readers was threefold, religious (*estranged*), psychological (*hostile in mind*), and moral (*doing evil deeds*). *Estranged* is translated "alienated" in Ephesians 2:12; 4:18. It has echoes of not belonging to the family (Matt. 17:25 f.), of being unknown (John 10:5), of being immigrants in a foreign land (Acts 7:6; Heb. 11:9); of men deprived of their rights (Beet) and banished (Alford). The "political" overtone of the word recalls v. 13 (and local events, see comment on v. 13).

Bruce rejects Maclaren's "not aliens, as though it were an original condition, but alienated, as having become so"; but Paul does use a verbal form and not an adjective. Paul surely means *estranged* from God, and not from Israel, as Moule suggests.

Hostile in mind may continue the po-

litical metaphor—"enemy aliens." Beet, following Meyer, argues (mainly from Rom. 3:24; 5:10) for "having to reckon with God's hostility." But most hold that the following words require an active meaning, "hostile towards God," an attitude expressed in worthless deeds. The *evil deeds* both express and, by accumulated guilt, confirm the estrangement from God.

The divine reaction is likewise threefold: *he has now reconciled, in his body of flesh,* and *by his death.* Paul appears to have moved unconsciously to Christ (RSV) rather than God (NEB; see v. 19) as the immediate agent of the Colossians' salvation. *His body of flesh* here and in 2:11 is explained by Bruce as "physical body" (citing Qumran commentary on Hab. 2:7); the NEB has "his body of flesh and blood" (con. Phil. 3:21).

But why is this phrase employed? To tilt against the idea that disembodied angels assisted in reconciliation (Peake, Abbott)? To stress incarnation, against Gnostic tendencies (Bruce, Ashby)? Because for Paul sin had its seat in the flesh, and Christ must conquer it there (Scott)? To imply sacrificial meanings (note *present you holy;* cf. Rom. 8:3; 1 Peter 2:24)? Or is it not simply to anchor the reconciliation objectively in gospel history, against the Gnostic intellectualism which made reconciliation a matter of knowledge and initiation? For Paul, reconciliation with God had to be wrought by God in the flesh of the incarnate Christ by means of death (cf. Rom. 3:25), "making peace by the blood of his cross."

The saving transformation experienced by the Colossians has, again, religious, psychological, and moral implications, directly opposed to the moral indifferentism of the Gnostic. *To present* may be sacrificial (cf. Rom. 12:1; *holy* and "without blemish" were originally ritual expressions). It may be bridal (Eph. 5:27; 2 Cor. 11:2); or judicial (Acts 23:33; *blameless* = unimpeached). It may connote presentation at court to a monarch or other person of dignity (Luke 2:22). The use of the word in Romans 6:13,16 f.; 12:1 supports the interpretation of it as a present experience.

Most commentators, however, refer the presentation to the Parousia or the judgment (citing 1 Cor. 1:8; 2 Cor. 4:14; Jude 24; Rom. 14:10; Eph. 5:27 and 2 Cor. 11:2 are more debatable). On this view the presentation is a distant consequence of the reconciliation: 1:22 and 28 appear to support this interpretation, as does the warning against losing this hope through disloyalty.

But this makes the purpose of the reconciliation very remote from the readers' present experience, to which Paul had been appealing. The true antithesis to being formerly *estranged, hostile,* is to be now, in this life, presented before God, acceptably, unrejected; to be "brought into God's presence" (as NEB translates the same word in 1 Cor. 8:8). On this view, the presentation is not the consequence but the meaning of reconciliation: the enemy alien is presented at court. To be legally *blameless* ("unaccused" rather than faultless), *irreproachable* before God now (cf. Rom. 8:33 f.), is thus the precise equivalent of justification, being reckoned righteous; and to be presented is the equivalent of that "access" of which Paul made so much (see comment on 2:13).

Even those commentators who defer the presentation to the last day nevertheless add "Christ has changed alienation into glad friendship" (Maclaren); "those once far away . . . brought close, those who used to be at war . . . at peace" (Bruce). Paul's appeal is not that the Colossians shall be prepared for judgment day but the much more urgent and relevant plea that they shall not be robbed of their present daily experience of acceptance with God.

The condition of so remaining in reconciliation is to *continue in the faith, stable and steadfast,* and *not shifting from the hope of the gospel* to some other, deceitful, hope. *The faith* is probably not orthodoxy but the personal faith already commended.

Stable and steadfast are building metaphors: Paul was fond of the figure of "edification." Is there a third metaphor in *not shifting?* The NEB ("never to be dislodged") takes it as passive (so Peake), referring to outside forces that tend to remove them from the foundation laid by Epaphras. Is there a neat allusion to the earth tremors familiar at Colossae? (Moule, cf. Matt. 7:24 ff.). Paul's expression suggests confidence that the condition will be fulfilled: but "with these words Paul approaches the definite aim of the letter" (Scott).

Even the gospel, which has effected all this, gets its threefold description. It is no new version of Christianity, such as they are being urged to accept, but that *which you heard:* let them be loyal to their spiritual origins. Nor is it any private, sectarian, intellectually exclusive doctrine, but that *which has been preached to every creature under heaven* (cf. 1:6). "Only the truth is universal" (Beet). Maclaren thinks we need not be pedantic about literal accuracy; Bruce thinks Paul indulges in "prophetic prolepsis"; others think that the gospel was preached to all strategically. A one-letter emendation would change the phrase to "every region" (cf. Rom. 15:18 f.) It may simply be rhetorical.

Of which I, Paul, became a minister. So Paul introduces himself, to go on to speak of his pastoral concern. It is scarcely an appeal for personal loyalty, since Paul was not known at Colossae; nor an appeal to the evidential value of his conversion. Nor was Paul throwing his apostolic authority on the side of Epaphras, for *minister* means just servant (Mark 10:45). Paul concludes the appeal by reminding that this gospel which had transformed their lives was what he himself had received, submitted to, and experienced: "It is older than I, not my invention; I am myself its captive, and its servant."

Everything, therefore, should impel the Colossians to adhere to the true message— their past experience of its saving power, their present need of steadfast patience to maintain that experience still, and simple loyalty to the gospel so commended by its primitive purity and universal appeal. Paul's exploration of the fullness of Christ in thought, and their own proving of it in experience, point clearly to the same duty: Hold fast to what you were originally taught.

II. The Fullness of Christ Appealed To (1:24—2:23)

1. Appeal Tactfully Prefaced (1:24—2:5)

(1) Paul's Charge to Gentiles (1:24-29)

24 Now I rejoice in my sufferings for your sake, and in my flesh I complete what is lacking in Christ's afflictions for the sake of his body, that is, the church, 25 of which I became a minister according to the divine office which was given to me for you, to make the word of God fully known, 26 the mystery hidden for ages and generations but now made manifest to his saints. 27 To them God chose to make known how great among the Gentiles are the riches of the glory of this mystery, which is Christ in you, the hope of glory. 28 Him we proclaim, warning every man and teaching every man in all wisdom, that we may present every man mature in Christ. 29 For this I toil, striving with all the energy which he mightily inspires within me.

Paul moves tactfully towards his urgent message by first justifying his addressing at all a church he did not found. His justification is twofold: his intense vocational interest in the welfare of all the Gentile churches (vv. 24–29); and his intense pastoral concern for his present readers especially (2:1–5).

The basis of Paul's vocational interest in the Colossian church is (1) his *divine office* or stewardship (cf. Luke 16:1 ff.; 1 Cor. 4:1 f.) in the church, including Colossae (*for you*) and all *the Gentiles;* and (2) his special responsibility *to make the word of God fully known,* in particular *this mystery, which is Christ*—the message which the Colossian heretics challenge. On both grounds he cannot ignore what is happening at Colossae. He can *rejoice* to suffer for them, with *toil* (athletic *striving* as in 1 Cor. 9:25; Col. 4:12), working by Christ's strength for them. He is not interfering but sharing their problems.

The meaning of the paragraph is thus clear, though three expressions require explanation. (1) Whether the background to v. 24 is Paul's intense distress at Ephesus (2 Cor. 1:8 ff.; 1 Cor. 15:32), or his prolonged imprisonment at Caesarea and then Rome, any thought that his suffering supplemented the otherwise incomplete atonement of Christ would contradict everything Paul (and the whole NT) declares about the completed work of Christ.

Christians certainly share Christ's afflictions (Mark 10:29; John 16:1 ff.); and Christ suffers in the suffering of his church (Acts 9:4)—but would Paul *rejoice* in the continued suffering of the ascended Christ? The idea that the post-Calvary sufferings of the "corporate Christ" in his persecuted body, the church, completes the "birth pangs" of the messianic age (Matt. 24:6; Luke 21:9;24), reads very much into Paul's words.

That whatever *is lacking* is supplied by Paul's sufferings suggests that it is not Christ's afflictions, but Paul's, or the church's, which are incomplete—though that is not exactly what Paul says. Suffering is not here valued for its own sake, morbidly: it serves the Gentile cause, or that of the whole church. The saying sets all persecution, undeservedly endured, in the double light—shared by Christ, vicarious in benefit. It is certain that the full measure of suffering needed to establish Christ's Kingdom has not yet been endured. Is that what Paul wishes to complete?

Paul pressed toward the goal of more perfect identification with the sufferings of Christ (Phil. 3:8–14). Crucified with Christ, bearing about the dying of the Lord Jesus (2 Cor. 4:10), dying daily, he longed to be brought nearer yet into the fellowship of Christ's sufferings. Insofar as his present affliction contributes toward that and benefits the churches, he can truly rejoice. If this is Paul's meaning, the form of expression may be due (as Moule suggests) to his use of a Gnostic catchword ("that which is lacking") which does not accord easily with Christian ideas.

(2) The concept of a *mystery,* hidden from some people, or for some time, but now made known, is inseparable from any

religion claiming divine revelation (cf. Dan. 2:17–23; Matt. 13:11–16; 16:17; John 14:17). The Qumran community claimed such secrets; and paganism, in the mystery religions, offered the intellectual satisfaction of an elect coterie "initiated" into divine secrets, under seal of secrecy on pain of death. Paul uses the technical term in Philippians 4:12; 1 Corinthians 2:7, and the word *mystery* ten times in Ephesians— Colossians (cf. also Rom. 16:25; 1 Cor. 13:2; 4:1). It would be familiar in the Jewish-Gnostic atmosphere at Colossae, though Paul gives it specifically Christian meaning, as something formerly concealed but now revealed, even proclaimed.

The gospel secret hidden, either since eternal *ages* and the human *generations* that followed, or from heavenly hierarchies known as ages or generations (Scott; cf. 1 Cor. 2:7 f.), is now made manifest to *every man.* The universality of the gospel which in Galatians Paul vigorously asserts against racial and religious exclusiveness, he here asserts against intellectual exclusiveness: "an intellectual aristocracy is the most exclusive of all" (Maclaren). Equally apt is the emphasis on instructing *every man* "in all the ways of wisdom" (NEB). All the truth of God for all the people of God, comments Bruce; and Barclay well recalls that neither Jew nor Gnostic had place for *every man.*

(3) The secret is the presence of Christ among the Gentiles, incorporating them into Israel by the preaching of the Messiah to Gentile hearts. This is no anticlimax (as Scott suggested), at any rate for Jews, nor is it contrary to Ephesians 3:6. The argument whether Paul means *Christ* among *you,* collectively (Lightfoot, Abbott, Moule, NEB marg.), or *Christ in you,* mystically, (Peake, Scott, Williams, cf. 3:16), is a little unreal. Paul knew no other way by which the living Christ could be present among the Gentiles collectively but by indwelling individual believers. That this is their *hope of glory* confirms the deeper thought (cf. Eph. 3:17).

The divine *glory* combines the visible radiance of God's majesty and the moral splendor of God's character. This glory man, made in the image of God, was destined to share (Psalm 8:5), but fell short of it (Rom. 3:23). Man's recovery of the lost image and glory (Rom. 5:2; 8:29; 2 Cor. 4:6) doubtless includes "the external glory of the heavenly state" (Williams; cf. 3:4); but since man lost it through sin, its recovery also has a moral and spiritual implication (cf. 2 Cor. 3:18). The rabbis explained the lost glory as the reflection of God's glory on Adam's face. Moses' face shining in converse with God, and the Christian stories of the transfiguration and of Stephen, illustrate the thought.

The fact that Christ is in us, here and now, as our life (3:4) is assurance that even Gentiles can attain that *glory.* That is the unexpected wealth within this mystery (a favorite metaphor with Paul: 2:2; Eph. 1:7,18; 2:7; 3:8,16; Rom. 11:33). With such a conception of his vocation, and of his pride in it, the Colossians could not wonder that Paul felt obliged to concern himself with their welfare.

Paul's sense of ministerial vocation wonderfully balances suffering and toil with privilege and joy; the sense of being specially set apart with the sense of being servant of all men; he is separated from ordinary tasks, but not from ordinary people. Equally impressive here is his analysis of the ministry, as the sharing of riches (cf. Luke 12:42)—the rich secret of the good life, namely Christ—by preaching, teaching, and pastoral counseling; aiming in all ministerial activity to *present every man mature in Christ* whether now (Moule, cf. *present* in Rom. 12:1), or at the Parousia (1 Thess. 2:19).

(2) Paul's Concern for Colossae (2:1–5)

1 For I want you to know how greatly I strive for you, and for those at Laodicea, and for all who have not seen my face, **2** that their hearts may be encouraged as they are knit together in love, to have all the riches of assured understanding and the knowledge of God's mystery, of Christ, **3** in whom are hid all the treasures of wisdom and knowledge. **4** I say this in order that no one may delude you with beguiling speech. [5] For though I am absent in body, yet I am with you in spirit, rejoicing to see your good order and the firmness of your faith in Christ.

Beside his vocational interest, Paul feels also intense pastoral concern for both the churches he addresses (4:16; see Introduction). His striving (see 1:29) doubtless includes prayer, solicitude, talk far into the night with their pastor, and the present letter. But behind these lay a whole career of Gentile evangelism.

Paul's immediate concern is *that their hearts may be encouraged.* One source of such strengthening is a renewed unity in the face of the divisive tendencies of the false teaching—*knit together in love* (cf. 2:19; 3:14) rather than "instructed in love." A second source of strengthening will be a settled conviction, filling and enriching (see comment on 1:27) the mind. Paul probably means here, as in Ephesians 3:18, that such wealth of Christian insight is attained only in close-knit fellowship "with all the saints."

The knowledge of God's mystery, of Christ may be a third source of strength; more probably it describes the understanding they need, and may have, in preference to any new philosophy. As to what *God's mystery* or open secret (see comment on 1:26) is, "there are few places in the NT where the MSS differ so widely" (Scott). Copyists made ten or twelve attempts to smooth an obscure phrase, but in view of 1:27 most interpreters equate the *mystery* with Christ himself. Really to know him in whom all the secret of God has been clearly and completely revealed is indeed to possess *all the riches of assured understanding.*

In 1:27 the mystery consists in Christ indwelling Gentiles; here it is Christ *in whom are hid all the treasures of wisdom and knowledge.* Once again the metaphor of wealth occurs, here recalling Proverbs 2:1-5: Christ has become to Christian minds all that wisdom was to Old Testament sages. He is the wisdom of God (1 Cor. 1:24,30); in him all intellectual wealth is ours.

The treasures of wisdom are *hid* in Christ. Gnostics regarded apostolic teaching as too elementary, the mere ABC of religious wisdom; profounder insights from their own apocryphal ("hidden") books were needed by the intellectually mature. Paul replies that the full meaning of Christ is not disclosed to the superficial; it is *hid.* Scott says that both *wisdom* and *knowledge* imply perceiving deeper reality underlying appearances. In Christ an infinite treasury of wisdom (Eph. 3:8; 1 Cor. 2:6 ff.) waits to be explored by patient meditation and advancing maturity. It is needless, then, to seek more truth elsewhere: having Christ, the Colossians have all they can require.

"What I mean is, Let no one talk you round" (Moule, Bruce) *with beguiling speech,* fallacious reasoning in specious language. The danger that overshadows the readers is at last named. And because "warning so easily passes into scolding" (Maclaren), Paul urges once again his personal concern, before stating bluntly the essential burden of his message (2:6-7).

Though I am absent in body, yet I am with you in spirit means more than "thinking of you, wishing I were there." Paul is imaginatively identified with them so as to rejoice with them in their loyal adherence to the truth: 1 Corinthians 5:3-5 provides a vivid contrast. Confident that the Colossians have not yet shifted "from the hope of the gospel which [they] heard," he generously expresses "the joy with which from his prison, he traveled in spirit across mountain and sea, and saw them in their quiet valley, cleaving to the Lord" (Maclaren).

Before sharpening his warning, he commends their *good order and the firmness of* their *faith in Christ.* The terms were originally military: "your orderly formation or array, unbroken ranks, solid phalanx." Some translate this with building metaphors, "firm structure, bulwark, solidity of a stable construction," recalling 1:23. But others take the words quite generally for the steadiness and solid front (Moffatt) which their faith has so far enabled the church to present.

One might search the New Testament for a finer analysis of the pastoral charge. Paul feels for these distant, unknown Colossians as every true pastor feels for his people. He desires for them encouragement, to hearten the worker and revive the smoking flax of faith; unity, that they might build a fruitful partnership; and assurance in the faith to give steadiness of mind. Moreover he is their loyal defender, even to the point of indignation with those who would beguile them. No modern minister is only a pastor: but such are the demanding dimensions of the pastoral ministry—to encourage, reconcile, instruct, and defend the people committed to his Christlike concern.

2. Appeal Forthrightly Stated (2:6–7)

6 As therefore you received Christ Jesus the Lord, so live in him, 7 rooted and built up in him and established in the faith, just as you were taught, abounding in thanksgiving.

The focal point of the letter, stating Paul's purpose in writing, is brief and clear; but every word must be allowed its full weight. We note again the anxiety not to offend: the Colossians had been well taught, and truly (cf. 1:7); also the further reference to thankfulness as prophylactic against deviations (see on 1:12).

The appeal is for consistency: *as you received . . . so live. Received* is a technical term (in Greek) for the perpetuation of traditional teaching by formal instruction (cf. 4:17; 1 Cor. 11:23; 15:1–3; 2 Thess. 3:6; Rom. 6:17 for similar use; *taught* is a different word). Paul insists that his gospel is the original message shared by all the churches. The content of that common tradition is *Christ Jesus* as *the Lord*, not mere doctrine. An unusual turn of phrase makes the title almost a creed. It is the confession required of disciples by Jesus (Mark 8:27–30), and of converts by Peter (Acts 2:21,36,38; cf. 15:17). It is Paul's message (Acts 18:5) and the basis of salvation (Rom. 10:9; cf. Phil. 2:11; 1 Cor. 12:3). It is the basis therefore of baptism (Acts 8:16,37, marg.; 22:16; cf. James 2:7;

in this context cf. Luke 6:46; Matt. 7:21). The same insistence upon the primitive Christian confession, aimed likewise at Gnostic denials, occurs in 1 John (2:22 ff.; 3:23; 4:15; 5:5–13).

Although some take the phrase as a double affirmation, "Jesus is the Christ and Lord," as Lightfoot said "the central point of the Colossian heresy was the subversion of the true idea of Christ." The order of Paul's words leaves little doubt that he is reiterating the earliest Christian faith, that Jesus, who appeared as Messiah, is truly the divine Lord—with all the wealth of meaning expounded in chapter 1.

Christ, rightly conceived, being the content of the true tradition, the necessary corollary to receiving it is to *live in him*. Paul uses the ancient Hebrew ethical term for behavior, "walk" (cf. 1:10; 4:5; Eph. 5:2; 1 John 1:7). Every step of the Christian's way should be within the encompassing circle of Christ.

The four metaphors—*live* (walk), *rooted, built, established*—clash literally but are relevant spiritually. A safe daily walk demands a heart securely rooted. The Colossians have been *rooted* (Paul's tense) in Christ as soil: both stability and nourishment are implied (for illustration, cf. Psalm 1:3; Mark 4:6; Eph. 3:17; Col. 1:10). Now, they must be continually *built up* (again Paul's tense). This figure may add, to the natural growth of *rooted*, the thought of personal effort: a progressive stability is clearly implied.

The walk is within Christ, the tree is rooted in Christ, the house rises upon Christ: but the resulting establishment is *in the faith* (*just as you were taught* makes this meaning likelier than "by your faith"). *Established* has a legal association, of guaranteeing a purchase, confirming testimony or an oath (Heb. 2:2 f.; 6:16). Those walking, rooted, and built up in Christ show themselves confirmed in a valid faith.

Such an appeal could not be more forthright. Well instructed to begin with, and already responding in great fruitfulness, the Colossians need to continue as they have begun. Their original faith needs no supplementing from alien sources in Gnostic novelties. Instead, they need to consolidate their gains, matching a growing apprehension of Christ to all his unexplored, inexhaustible fullness. That should, and it surely will, make them overflow *in thanksgiving.*

3. Appeal Firmly Enforced (2:8–23)
(1) As Recall to Experience (2:8–15)

[8] See to it that no one makes a prey of you by philosophy and empty deceit, according to human tradition, according to the elemental spirits of the universe, and not according to Christ. [9] For in him the whole fulness of deity dwells bodily, [10] and you have come to fulness of life in him, who is the head of all rule and authority. [11] In him also you were circumcised with a circumcision made without hands, by putting off the body of flesh in the circumcision of Christ; [12] and you were buried with him in baptism, in which you were also raised with him through faith in the working of God, who raised him from the dead. [13] And you, who were dead in trespasses and the uncircumcision of your flesh, God made alive together with him, having forgiven us all our trespasses, [14] having canceled the bond which stood against us with its legal demands; this he set aside, nailing it to the cross. [15] He disarmed the principalities and powers and made a public example of them, triumphing over them in him.

Paul spells out the concise appeal of 2:6 f. in three ways: by recalling the readers to the fullness of experience they have already received (as the reiterated past tense emphasizes); by recalling them from idle speculations to realities of religious life; and by recalling them to life consistent with what they profess.

Their rich experience stands in clear contrast to the predatory nature of the errorists' *philosophy. See to it that no one* (a particular plunderer?) *makes a prey of you* (carrying you as booty into slavery) takes up the thought of their rich treasure (1:27; 2:2 f.), and prepares for the thought of liberation (13 f.; 20 f.). The means of that spoliation is a philosophy both unprofitable and untrue, though beguiling (2:4).

Paul first dismisses that specious make-believe as (1) entirely man-made, in no way derived from authentic gospel tradition

(2:6); (2) as demon-inspired—*according to the elemental spirits of the universe.* Some understand "elements of the cosmos" as the mere rudiments of religion (e.g., 2:16,20–22; see NEB marg.), ironically contrasted with the advanced teaching the Gnostics claimed. Others (RSV, NEB, Scott, Bruce, Peake) take the phrase with 1:16; 2:10,15–20; Galatians 4:1–8 and understand it to refer to spirit-beings (see Introduction on the Colossian heresy). The make-believe is (3) *not according to Christ* —for Christian hearts, this is condemnation enough. But Paul underlines the foolishness of turning to weak and beggarly elemental spirits (Gal. 4:9), in whom divinity is thinly distributed, when we have Christ, in whom *the whole fulness of deity dwells bodily* (i.e., totally, wholly; rather than "incarnate" or "in glorified humanity"). He is *the head* of all heavenly beings, *all rule and authority,* headship implying as in 1:18 supremacy and no more.

Having the full Christ, we *come to fulness of life in him,* not of course fullness of divinity, but "all that anyone not only can need, but also can have" (Williams). This has been the Colossians' experience: it needs no supplementing by a pagan and profitless mythology, only progressive exploration throughout the Christian life.

Paul then itemizes six constituents of that total Christian experience. (1) Whether the errorists pressed *circumcision* as a divine command, as a prophylactic against fleshly sin, as a talisman against evil spirits, or as the badge of superiority of Jewish teachers, the issue had clearly been raised. Paul's reply is not that circumcision is nothing (Gal. 5:6; 6:15; 1 Cor. 7:19), but—surprisingly—that they had been *circumcised,* not physically (*without hands,* cf. Eph. 2:11) but spiritually; not with the circumcision of Moses but with that *of Christ.*

In conversion, they had put off not merely a symbol of the flesh in which sin dwelt, but the whole body of the flesh, the sensual self with all its works (3:9). The *circumcision of Christ* was not his own, for that was with hands. Bruce and Moule take this as his putting off the body in crucifixion (cf. 1:22), a somewhat complicated allusion. The reference is, surely, to the initial renunciation of the flesh in Christian conversion—essentially, Christian repentance. Though this is called *circumcision without hands* only here, it echoes Deuteronomy 10:16; Jeremiah 4:4 and parallels; Romans 2:29; Philippians 3:3.

Since the meaning of circumcision has been fulfilled in the Colossians' experience, and the status it confers is already theirs (see comment on 1:12,27), to submit to the outward rite would be a base denial of what Christ had done for them.

(2) The occasion of this Christian circumcision was their baptism (so the Greek implies), when *the body of flesh* was not only cut off but *buried* with Christ and the convert was *raised with him* to resurrection life. Baptism, by immersion, the symbol of death and burial, and faith as "the instrument by which the benefit to be obtained in baptism is received," are all assumed (Williams, Beet, Peake, Moule, Scott, Bruce). As in Romans 6, Paul can take for granted such a baptism and such an interpretation of it, even in a church he had not visited.

The death-resurrection metaphor of conversion is much more familiar than circumcision. On its negative side—repentance— it derives from Mark 8:34, dramatically reinforced after Calvary by the sense of sharing Christ's own death to sin (Rom. 6:1–11; Gal. 2:20). Paul does not here mention Christ's death: burial is the obvious disposal of the body put off in Christian circumcision. On its positive side, the metaphor represents the Christian rising with Christ from death to victorious life by faith. "It is this trust in God which gives meaning and efficacy to the baptismal rite," says Scott, and Moule agrees; but here, as in Romans 4:17,24; 6:8; 10:9, it is specifically faith in the divine power which raised Christ. This positive, dynamic, life-affirming aspect of Christian baptism is too often forgotten.

The close association of baptism and cir-

cumcision in this passage has led to the curious equation of the two in the church's thought, and the substitution of baptism for circumcision in church practice towards infants. This interpretation makes inexplicable the use of both rites together by Jews, by Jesus, by some early Christians (as at Galatia), and by Paul (Acts 16:3). It makes nonsense of Peter's refusal to eat with uncircumcised Christians, if their baptism was the equivalent of circumcision. It raises the unanswerable question why Paul did not use this direct and sufficient argument in his polemic against circumcision,— and indeed why he contended at all against the imposition of circumcision on his converts, if it was merely to substitute an equivalent rite.

But the argument totally misrepresents Paul. He does not equate, or even compare, circumcision and baptism: he contrasts them. More strictly, he contrasts the literal circumcision made with hands with the spiritual circumcision *made without hands* in the convert's putting away of the *flesh;* and then he says that that happened in baptism. Thus, Christian baptism is sufficient; it has accomplished, *through* the convert's *faith,* all that circumcision imperfectly signified, the putting away of the flesh. No further ascetic or renunciatory rite is necessary, or would be meaningful. To equate the baptism efficacious through faith with literal circumcision, in order to apply a baptism without faith to infants, makes nonsense of Paul and of logic.

(3) Verse 13 asserts, not again the deliberate death to sin of the convert (v. 12), but the already subsisting death in sin, and in alienation from God, of the sinful pagan. In Paul's language, the man *dead* in sin may be *made alive* through death with Christ to sin: the meaning of death subtly changes as the spiritual situation is expounded. The two causes of spiritual death are sins or false steps, blunders; and literal *uncircumcision,* here indicative of the readers' former alienation from the commonwealth of Israel as strangers to the covenants of promise. Ephesians 2 elabo-

rates both points. Peake takes *uncircumcision* as a metaphor for sensuality (NEB, "morally uncircumcised"). But Paul is arguing that the Colossians' spiritual circumcision in Christ has made their literal uncircumcision of no account.

The Colossians have thus experienced a double quickening: both as sinners and as aliens; they have been *made alive* to God and to God's people, Israel. He who quickens *together with him* must be God; whether the subject changes to Christ between vv. 13 and 15 is very difficult to decide.

(4) Assured forgiveness is an essential element in Christian experience. "To a man doomed to die, pardon is life" (Beet). Paul's word came to mean free, generous forgiveness both of debt (Luke 7:42 f; see comment below on v. 14) and of sin; but its root idea is of being favored (3:13; cf. 2 Cor. 12:13; Luke 7:21; Acts 3:14; 25:11,16). Paul was ever deeply moved by the thought of being granted access into the favor of the Most High (Rom. 5:2; Eph. 2:18). As so often, he breaks the thread of the passage to include himself; and he remembers how complete God's pardon is—*all our trespasses.*

(5) The Colossians have experienced liberation from the law. The trespass canceled, *the bond* registering the obligation is first obliterated and then removed out of the way, being nailed *to the cross.* Whether the hostile "handwritten document" was an unpaid bond for debt (cf. Matt. 6:12; 18:23 ff.) or an accusation of offense like that nailed above Christ, seems to make little difference. It enshrines the enmity of the law (Rom. 3:19; against Gentiles, Rom. 2:14 ff.; cf. Gal. 3:13, "curse of the law"; Rom. 7:7–14) with all its detailed demands and accusations; but it has been removed (Rom. 10:4; 7:1–4; Gal. 3:24 f.) Christ has (in accord with current practise for reusing expensive papyrus) washed the gum and soot inkmarks from the document; he has taken it out of our way; and he has nailed it up publicly, as so canceled, upon his cross (the allusion

to Mark 15:26 is almost irresistible). Why, after such liberation, should Christians become subject again to human "regulations"?

(6) We take v. 15 to describe a sixth element in Christian experience, though its terms are ambiguous. *Disarmed* may mean discarded, divested (cf. 2:11; 3:9; 2 Cor. 5: 4; Zech. 3:1 f.); the subject may be either God, or Christ; *the principalities and powers* may be evil forces or good angels (so Williams, citing 1:16; 2:18 and taking "Head" in 2:19 and 1:18 as "leader, nourisher," not simply as supreme.)

Two main lines of interpretation are possible. First, Christ then divested himself of the angels who had attended his ministry, being able to do without them (cf. Matt. 26:53). Or, God divested himself in Christ of the "robe" of mediating angels: the law being abrogated, the angels who mediated it and who wielded it over men have lost their place (cf. Acts 7:53; Gal. 3:19 f.; Heb. 2:2 and context; so in substance, Beet, Alford, Williams, Peake). The "parade" of triumph is then a procession in which priests and others were exhibited with pleasure. On this interpretation, v. 15 elaborates the Christian's freedom from the law affirmed in v. 14.

Second, the RSV understands that God spoiled and disarmed evil spiritual forces and made a public parade of them in Christ. Or, Christ discarded the hostile forces (NEB) in his cross; or, divested himself of his body, his human nature through which evil forces beset him. Either way, evil is overcome, and the cross itself is a military triumphal procession.

This is a bold paradox, but the *Christus Victor* interpretation of the death of Christ is wholly in line with John 12:31; 14:30; 16:11; Ephesians 4:8; Hebrews 2:14. It may derive from Luke 10:18; 11:14–22; it is expressed clearly in 2 Corinthians 2:14 and Ephesians 4:8—though the captives there are willing converts, not demonic powers. Ephesians 1:21; 3:10 and Romans 8:38 give ample warrant for taking the *principalities and powers* as evil forces to be overcome: he through whom **they** were created (1:16) and who is their supreme head (2:10), is also their conqueror (Eph. 1:20 ff.). (So, in substance, RSV, NEB, Moule, Bruce, Scott).

On this interpretation, the Colossians have experienced a second liberation, additional to freedom from the law: liberation from bondage to demonic powers (2:20). So vv. 14–15, together, meet the two sides of the Colossian heresy (see Introduction), strongly confirming this view.

Uncertainty about details must not obscure the richness of Paul's analysis. The recall to experience is cogent. On the one hand, the successive statements about what Christ has done further expound his divine fullness and sufficiency as Saviour. On the other hand, the sixfold statement of what Christians have received through him is a secure basis from which to reject every suggestion that human philosophizing has anything to offer to men and women so abundantly privileged.

(2) As Recall to Realities (2:16–19)

16 Therefore let no one pass judgment on you in questions of food and drink or with regard to a festival or a new moon or a sabbath. 17 These are only a shadow of what is to come; but the substance belongs to Christ. 18 Let no one disqualify you, insisting on self-abasement and worship of angels, taking his stand on visions, puffed up without reason by his sensuous mind, 19 and not holding fast to the Head, from whom the whole body, nourished and knit together through its joints and ligaments, grows with a growth that is from God.

As the basis of religious life must lie in experienced salvation, so the content of religious faith must consist, not of theories, visions, self-invented disciplines, but of real events and substantial facts. In no realm is the shadow so easily mistaken for the substance as in religion. Paul passes therefore from analyzing a valid spiritual experience to its expression in realistic religious practice. There may be a reference also to the divisive tendencies of all such speculative, emotional self-will: for Paul emphasises the whole body, nourished and knit together.

Let no one continue to pass judgment on you . . . let no one disqualify you. The usual method of propagandists of some "advanced, spiritual" theosophy is to unsettle tender consciences, creating discontent and guilt, then to play upon that dissatisfaction with specious promises of great blessing to be obtained through some new deviation. Paul urges that the Colossians shall refuse such assessments of their spiritual condition. They are to hold fast to the Head and remain part of the whole body whose growth . . . is from God. He adds some trenchant criticisms of the man-made substitute, "religiousness," being pressed upon the Colossians.

Let no one continue to pass judgment on you implies that someone is doing so. Asceticism, rather than ritual uncleanness, is the issue (on the Judaist elements of the heresy, see Introduction). All Judaism was prophetic, the foreshadowing of the gospel that was to come, and so of necessity was temporary. To understand what is to come as still future, destroys Paul's argument. To understand substance (body) as the church, or the glorified body of Christ, misses the emphasis of the paragraph, well summarized in the NEB, "the solid reality is Christ's" (cf. Heb. 8:5; 10:1 ff.). Paul does not say, let no one observe these prophetic customs: he merely forbids any to sit in judgment upon others in such matters (cf. Rom. 14:1–13).

"Let no one rob you of your prize" (ERV) preserves Paul's metaphor of the game's umpire passing judgment. Beet explains the lost prize as eternal life (Phil. 3:14; 1 Cor. 9:24). Most scholars accept disqualify you (1 Cor. 9:27; Rev. 3:11). There follows a fourfold description of the Colossians' self-appointed judges.

(1) They are described as insisting on self-abasement and worship of angels—an almost unintelligible phrase—otherwise rendered "delighting in humility," "self-conscious humility," "voluntary humility," and even "disqualify you of his mere will." Further doubt arises if self-abasement is taken, as in Hermas, for fasting, asceticism.

Paul may be describing that willful, exaggerated "humility" which says it dare not approach God except through hosts of intermediary beings (see Introduction on Colossian heresy; cf. Heb. 1:4 f.). *Worship* here refers to the external religious cultus (cf. Acts 26:5; James 1:26 f.): exaggerated self-abasement usually breeds ritualism and an emphasis upon mediation.

(2) They are described as *taking* their *stand on visions*. Much erudition is spent to defend "poring over, investigating, exploring, interpreting, trying to enter into some vision," or "dwelling in, invading, taking a stand upon, parading their boasted visions." Either way, the heretic overvalues his private emotional experiences and illuminations, as compared with the common experience of the historic faith (cf. Jer. 23:25 ff.; John 3:11; 8:38).

This interpretation concedes that the critic has visions. Abbott thought that Paul spoke ironically, confusing some early scribe, who inserted "not seen" (KJV). This would be a strange charge to make for one who lived by faith (Peake)! Most scholars, with strong manuscript support, omit "not." A more modern emendation redivides the text, obtaining "treading upon the empty air," i.e., baseless speculations. Ramsay, followed by Scott and Bruce, tells of an inscription using the word as a technical term of the mystery religions—"having received the Mysteries, he entered in" (was initiated). Bruce says: "taking his stand on what he has seen in the Mysteries." Moule finds this reference difficult and farfetched. It seems probable that throughout this passage Paul deliberately quotes the heretics' terms in ironic tone. He scorns the Gnostic claim to supernatural visions which confer greater certainty and illumination than the apostolic gospel of the fullness of Christ could bestow.

(3) The judges in Colossae are described as *puffed up without reason by* their *sensuous mind*—literally, inflated as with bellows (cf. 1 Cor. 8:1; 13:4; hence "bursting with conceit," NEB). *Without reason* because Paul will concede no pride of

intellect whatsoever, university man though he is (see 1 Cor. 1:18–29). That "humility" must be false which masks intellectual arrogance (for *sensuous mind*, cf. Rom. 1:28; Eph. 4:17; but opposite, Rom. 7:22,25). So far from intellectualism and asceticism purifying the flesh, they are governed by it, ministering to self-absorption, spiritual pride, and sense-bound piety.

(4) They are described as *not holding fast to the Head*—the culminating accusation. It is irrelevant to identify the *joints and ligaments* by which the *body* of the church is united and nourished or to discuss Paul's acquaintance with physiology. The church is a body, organically united and nourished by its firm adhesion to its living Head; it is no bundle of faggots (Maclaren) mechanically held together by a common creed or theosophy. Divisiveness means starvation, and stuntedness: only by holding fast to the unity of the whole with the Head can *growth that is from God* be known. Whether this is "growth such as God requires" (Peake) or "such as God gives" (1 Cor. 3:6; cf. Eph. 4:15 f.), the ironic contrast with the growth that is merely inflation is unmistakable.

(3) As Recall to Consistency (2:20–23)

20 If with Christ you died to the elemental spirits of the universe, why do you live as if you still belonged to the world? Why do you submit to regulations, 21 "Do not handle, Do not taste, Do not touch" 22 (referring to things which all perish as they are used), according to human precepts and doctrines? 23 These have indeed an appearance of wisdom in promoting rigor of devotion and self-abasement and severity to the body, but they are of no value in checking the indulgence of the flesh.

The errorists' failure to hold fast the Christ they once grasped frames the appeal that the Colossians act consistently with their experience. (On *elemental spirits*, see comment on 2:8). Paul means that, as to die with Christ is to die to sin, law, self, flesh, and world, so also it is to die to the former bondage to elemental powers of the universe. Why then let people dictate to you how to placate them? Echoing 2:14,

Paul holds all such *regulations* abolished. The prohibitions cited are childish in tone, but they were evidently the means by which the world-spirits exerted their power, either through dread or as "angels of the law." So the Colossians were brought again into the bondage from which Christ had released them.

Moreover, submission to such *regulations* shows exaggerated concern with things essentially trivial, because perishable; and that for the sake of merely human authorities. The former point Paul expresses elsewhere (1 Cor. 6:13; cf. 8:8), as did Jesus more forthrightly (Mark 7:18 f.). The latter point reproduces Isaiah 29:13 in such close resemblance to Mark 7:5–8 that Peake and Abbott suggest Paul had Christ's discourse in mind. At least we can say that Paul uses against Judaist-Gnostic ritual asceticism a form of argument already familiar at Rome and claiming dominical authority.

Paul's final thrust against the heresy is a direct denial of its claim. It fails utterly to accomplish what it sets out to do—to liberate the divine spark, the spirit, from the "grave" of the flesh which imprisons it. Gnosticism is entirely ineffective by the supreme test of all religion, the subjugation of the flesh to the higher life of the spirit.

The way in which Paul says that is so obscure that many either emend the text freely, abandon it as corrupt, or assume that Paul is using his opponents' terms. Paul concedes that the heresy has a reputation for intellectualism (though not well founded, his Greek implies). "It makes a favourable impression" (Bruce) in *promoting rigor of devotion*, a self-imposed worship (Abbott), "will-worship," literally. Paul probably coined a word to describe worship not required by God but willfully self-invented and self-imposed. Doubtless the reference is to angel-worship, with self-abasement (v. 18).

Severity to the body refers to the sterner, ascetic side of Gnosticism (see Introduction). Rigorous devotion, mysticism, abasement, self-mortication, never fail to impress those who measure religion by its forms

and its pain. Paul agrees it is all impressive: he adds devastatingly that nevertheless all are valueless in dealing with that flesh which the Gnostics said was the spirit's declared enemy.

The RSV rendering of the closing words chooses two doubtful translations (honor translated as *value* in the sense of efficacy; *indulgence* could as well be "reasonable satisfaction, repletion"); and it imports one word, *checking*, for one which normally means "towards" (but 3:13; 3:19 support this). It probably represents Paul's meaning (Bruce, Moule, Barclay); for it seems unlikely that Paul would close his argument by saying these practices show no honor to the body in satisfying its reasonable wants. He means at least that Gnostic prescriptions fail to subdue the fleshly nature; he may mean that Gnosticism actually serves to indulge the flesh, pampering its sensuousness, emotion, and pride.

Paul's recall to experience, to reality, and to consistency, combined with severe criticisms of the heretics, comprise a powerful negative exhortation. He turns now from negative warning, even more from negative attempts to deal with the flesh, to present the positive Christian truth. The consistent consequence of dying with Christ is, not to live any longer in the world, subject to the spirits, but to seek the things that are above, and enjoy the fullness of life hid with Christ in God.

III. The Christ-filled Life (3:1—4:6)

1. Focused upon Christ (3:1–4)

[1] If then you have been raised with Christ, seek the things that are above, where Christ is, seated at the right hand of God. [2] Set your minds on things that are above, not on things that are on earth. [3] For you have died, and your life is hid with Christ in God. [4] When Christ who is our life appears, then you also will appear with him in glory.

Paul turns from expounding the fullness of Christ, sufficient answer to the doctrine of the heretics, to describing the fullness of the Christian life, sufficient antidote to their alluring promises. And first, he emphasizes that the full life is focused entirely upon the full Christ. Having died with Christ and having been buried with Christ, we now have been raised with Christ; we are hid with Christ, and we *will appear with him. Christ,* in fact, *is our life.*

The brief, rich paragraph mingles statement, exhortation, and promise in three encouragements to "live up" the Christian life to its height.

The first encouragement is to focus life's aim upon Christ. They *have been raised* (answering 2:20, as in 2:12–13): to *seek the things that are above* is but to be consistent with their own experience. Christ is *seated at the right hand of God* (cf. 1:18; 2:12): *to seek the things that are above* is but to be consistent with their own conviction that Christ was raised far above all earthly things.

This is the strongest of all appeals to be "spiritually minded," i.e., to orientate all life's goals by the ascended Christ and to focus one's emotive drives upon all that belongs to God's right hand. Prohibitions, visions, ascetic negations never succeed; though whether *then* refers *things . . . on earth* back to the precepts of 2:16 ff. is doubtful. For *things . . . above* does not mean heavenly precepts, nor the blessings of heaven (Beet), but "the whole higher realm" (NEB), including the enthroned Christ and all things ultimate, essential, and transcendent (Matt. 6:19,33; 7:7; sufficiently illustrate).

Psalm 110:1 was a constant proof text of early apologetic (Acts 2:34 and 11 parallels). It is cited here, not to indicate the place of power from which Christ can supply grace (Williams), but as evidence of Christ's supremacy over all powers (2:10). *Seated* expresses rest after conflict; *the right hand of God* declares the resulting authority and power (cf. 1:18; Eph. 4:10; Phil. 2:9).

But those who have risen with Christ, too, must realize their ascension (Peake; so Eph. 2:6). The death and resurrection with Christ which is the ground of salvation, and which in baptism becomes the analogy

of spiritual experience, is also the pattern of Christian ambition. The ascension of Christ, and of the Colossians, has happened at a definite moment (*If* expresses not doubt but logical sequence, "as surely as"; cf. 2:20): these two asserted facts carry the ethical exhortation between them, *Seek.*

The second encouragement is to focus the *mind* upon Christ, including affections, will, disposition. The importance to Paul of what fills the Christian's mind may be gathered from Romans 8:5 ff.; 12:3–4, 16; 1 Corinthians 13:11; Philippians 2:5; 3:19; 4:8 f. Here he urges that the seeking of things above will be sustained only by a mind nourished upon things above. Where Christ our treasure is, there should our hearts be also.

Again two assertions carry the exhortation. *You have died* in baptism (see comment on 2:12) to the things of earth (in 2:20 "to the elemental spirits"; in Gal. 6:14 to the world; in Rom. 8:5 to the flesh; cf. Phil. 3:19). Perhaps Paul alludes especially to those earthly rules and practices which obsessed the Colossian heretics. If the reference is to earthly things generally, it is not for any evil inherent in them (recall 1:16,20), but because to treasure them in preference to things above is shameful and impoverishing (Phil. 3:19; Matt. 6:19).

Moreover, *your life is hid with Christ in God. Hid* may continue the baptismal metaphor (Dodd, Moule, Barclay): whereas pagans spoke of death as a hiding in the earth, the Christian claims instead to be hidden in Christ. But Scott replies that it is the new life which here is hidden. Many commentators speak of Christian life as hidden for security, "beyond the reach of harm" (Bruce). What becomes then of the warnings of the epistle and of the promised manifestation? Safety, in this letter, lies not in concealment but in "holding fast to the Head." Besides, is Christ hid in God for safety? The thought of the Christian's hidden resources is more persuasive: having died to the world we draw our inspiration from heavenly places and obey a heavenly throne. Thus the Christian life is beyond the world's understanding (John 14:17,22; 15:18–21; 1 John 3:1*b*). So understood, 3:3 reiterates 2:3 and 2:9 f., and is differently expressed in Ephesians 2:6.

But we should not miss the intended contrast with the Gnostic claim to a hidden mystery, an inner life beyond the understanding of the common believer. Paul says the risen life belongs already to that invisible, eternal realm to which Christ belongs. Why be so fascinated with a mere spurious mystification? (2:18). He has previously insisted on the hidden mystery now revealed to Christians (1:26) and on the hidden riches awaiting discovery in Christ (2:3); here, in the same sense, he urges that the deepest sources of Christian life itself are likewise hidden—with Christ in God.

Having died to earthly things and enjoying a life whose inner resources spring among heavenly things, we should find it no effort to fix our whole mind and disposition where our true life belongs.

The third encouragement is to focus our hope upon Christ: and this is carried by three assertions. Christ will appear, will be openly made known (so in John 21:1; 14; 1 Cor. 1:7; 2 Thess. 1:7; 1 Peter 1:7). The earliest, dramatic form of the eschatological hope is here affirmed, though with no hint of time or manner. As Paul turns from past to future, from experience known to the end anticipated, all is once more focused upon Christ. Our future is bright with his appearing.

And Christ *is our life*—not simply our eternal life (Meyer), or the giver of life, but the essence of life. "To me to live is Christ" (cf. Phil. 1:21; Gal. 2:20; 2 Cor. 4:10 f.; 1 John 5:12). Like the disciples at the ascension, "faith stands gazing into heaven . . . feeling that the best part of its true self is gone with him" (Maclaren). This is the most succinct assertion of a truth everywhere in the New Testament, that the Christian life is life utterly concentrated upon Christ, dying, risen, alive, glorified, and coming.

And again, we *also will appear with him in glory.* "As surely as your life is hidden with Christ while he is hidden, so shall you be manifested with him when he is manifested" (Williams; 1 Thess. 4:13–18; 1 John 3:2; and 1 Cor. 15:51–56). Baptismal identification with Christ in death, burial, resurrection, and ascension is consummated by appearance with him in glory. More is implied than "the righteous blazing forth like the sun in the kingdom of their Father," more even than immortality in a spiritual body no longer hindered by the flesh (Scott). Included also is the recapture of the glory lost in the fall: the outshining image of God perfectly reflected at last in the world he created (see comment on 1:27; cf. Rom. 3:23; 8: 19 ff.).

The Christ-filled life, then, is life filled with Christ: its aim, its mind, its hope so taken up with Christ that all *things . . . on earth* shrivel to dwarfed significance. This is what Paul means by "holding fast the Head." It is paradoxical: like Christ, the Christian has died, yet remains vigorously, buoyantly alive. He is "dead" upon one level, in one set of relationships, by a deliberate act of identification with Christ who died to and for sin; he is alive upon another level, in other relationships, by deliberate appropriation of Christ who is his life. This paradox is continued, and sharpened, in detailed analysis in 3:5–17.

Scholars of every denominational loyalty find (as we have seen) that 2:11—3:4 is full of profound baptismal significance. Scott remarks how much Paul rests upon the Colossians' experience of baptism, unfolding its obligations. Barclay insists that "the Christian cannot rise from baptism the same man as he went down into baptism." Most agree that, according to Paul, the literal and objective death and resurrection of Christ is appropriated subjectively, by the Christian, in a faith which identifies him (1) with what Christ did as his substitute, on his behalf, so that he need not do it again, and (2) with what Christ did as his representative, on his behalf, so that he must do it likewise. This two-fold faith is expressed in baptism, as both a trust in Christ's death and resurrection for the sins of the world and an identification with Christ's death and resurrection in a total change of attitude—towards sin, self, and the world, on the one hand, and towards God, Christ, the Christian fellowship, and the world to come, on the other.

That double identification, however, though a real event in the believer's life-history, irrevocably expressed in baptism, has constantly to be reaffirmed. In 2:8–23 (with 3:2–3) Paul calls for the constant reaffirmation of the Christian's death with Christ to the law, to all spiritual bondage, to the elemental spirits of the universe, and to things on the earth. In 3:1–4 he calls for the constant reaffirmation of the Christian's resurrection with Christ to a risen life focused upon the ascended Christ as its aim, resource, secret, and hope. The urgent pleas of the next two paragraphs follow naturally. Reaffirming your death with Christ, "put to death . . ."; reaffirming your resurrection with Christ, "put on then . . ."

2. Putting Off Things Unchristian (3:5–11)

[5] Put to death therefore what is earthly in you: immorality, impurity, passion, evil desire, and covetousness, which is idolatry. [6] On account of these the wrath of God is coming. [7] In these you once walked, when you lived in them. [8] But now put them all away: anger, wrath, malice, slander, and foul talk from your mouth. [9] Do not lie to one another, seeing that you have put off the old nature with its practices [10] and have put on the new nature, which is being renewed in knowledge after the image of its creator. [11] Here there cannot be Greek and Jew, circumcised and uncircumcised, barbarian, Scythian, slave, free man, but Christ is all, and in all.

The Christ-filled life obviously cannot at the same time be filled with Christless things. The triple assertion that Christians "have died" followed by exhortation to *put to death . . . what is earthly* seems to some too violent a metaphor, "an abstract theological idea which does not fit in with the facts of life" (Scott; on the inherent paradox, see preceding comment). But Paul well knew that although conversion involved a total change of moral direction, it was no prescription for instant holiness (cf. Phil. 3:12). It is not only that the Christian lives on two planes at once (Bruce); or that he is called to become in fact what he is ideally (Scott); or that the death to the old and life to the new, ideally complete at conversion, has to be realized gradually (Peake); but that the radical change already experienced in the inward nature has to be wrought into character and wrought out in conduct (Maclaren).

It is wrong to suggest that what happens in conversion is "only" a change of status, "in principle." The aorist tense constantly marks that radical reorientation, as a death, a "putting off" of the former self, a turning around, a new birth, at a definite point in experience, and having permanent consequences. But the new self, willing new things, enshrining a new nature, accepting new resources, and living in a new world (in Christ), must now build the new character appropriate to this change, and "work out . . . salvation."

What is earthly in you too smoothly paraphrases Paul's "your members which are upon the earth." Identification of the Christian's "members" with the sins to be put to death is awkward: it seems to mean that the believer, dead to sin in his inmost self, must now proceed to reckon dead (so Rom. 6:11; 4:19) every separate and outward part of himself, each individual member so far as it is identified with sin. The translation "mortify . . . your members" (KJV), and the whole ascetic tradition of physical self-mortification which appealed to it, certainly misrepresents Paul. The members are in apposition to the vices which follow and define them. If the physical limbs were intended, "which are upon the earth" would be pointless.

In the same vigorous metaphor Jesus had spoken of the need, in crises of temptation, to cut off the hand, pluck out the eye. Paul goes further. For him, the members are parts of that body of sin, flesh, death, which makes man vulnerable to evil and which becomes the dwelling place and vehicle of sin (Rom. 6:6; 7:24; cf. 7:17 f.; 6:19; 7:5,23; Col. 2:11). The metaphor, identifying the body and its members with the sin which uses them, is no more "violent" than those in 1 Corinthians 6:15; Romans 8:13.

The list of sins to be put to death covers the prevailing Gentile evils, sensuality and covetousness. The former proceeds from the outward act to the inward state of mind (as does the Sermon on the Mount, ;Ashby)—fornication, indecency, lasciviousness, and lust. The latter, "the constant greed for more," acquisitiveness, is set beside plundering and robbery in 1 Corinthians 5:10; 6:9 f.; but elsewhere it is insatiable greed for sensual pleasure (1 Thess. 4:3 ff.; Mark 7:21; 2 Peter 2:14; [?] Rom. 7:7 ff.). The close parallels in Ephesians 4:19; 5:3 ff. support this interpretation here.

Which is idolatry would then link insatiable sensuality with ritual prostitution associated with idol worship (cf. Eph. 5:5; and the close connection in Gal. 5:19–20). Most scholars however interpret *idolatry* here as "making a god of earthly things" (cf. Matt. 6:24), worship pursued as a means to prosperity (Barclay), making a god of gain (Ashby). Williams, more persuasively, takes the comment as summarizing both sins, sensuality and covetousness, as together the characteristic sins of paganism.

On such things *the wrath of God is coming.* Of course divine vindictiveness is excluded, but to talk of an abstract principle of retribution or the disaster evil provokes does not evade the fact that the present and future consequences of sin, in a moral universe which God made, are divine judgments. Paul is sure of this (Rom. 1:18 ff.; Gal. 6:7) and equally insistent that the sin of Christians is not exempt (1 Cor. 6:10; Gal. 5:21).

Retaining (with Beet, Abbott, and Barclay) the marginal phase at v. 6 "upon the sons of disobedience" (Bruce and NEB omit as probably from Eph. 5:6) would require "among whom you once walked" (as Eph. 2:2 f.). This might explain Paul's "you also" (with other Christians) *put . . . away*—better company demands conformity to better manners! The painful reminder in v. 7 is meant to awaken penitence, perhaps revulsion.

The language here, *put . . . away . . . off . . . on,* has a threefold background. Clothes represent conduct in Job 29:14 (Psalm 35:26; Isa. 11:5) and the figure recurs repeatedly (Rom. 13:12,14; Eph. 4:22,25; 1 Thess. 5:8; Gal. 3:27; Rev. 3:4,18). Maclaren well remarks that "habit" means both costume and custom. But baptismal allusion is clear, too: whether to new baptismal garments (Bruce), or to the new robe given to initiates in the mystery religions (Scott), or simply to the unclothing and reclothing of those baptised by immersion (Moule, Barclay).

The terms are also key words of the primitive catechesis. Others in this passage are "be subject" (3:18), and be watchful (4:2). (So Bruce and Moule; see Introduction.) This fact makes the baptismal allusion still more significant. The Colossians are being reminded of their earliest instruction when first they knew Christ.

This may explain the unexpectedly elementary exhortations (vv. 8 f.). Anger (whether smouldering *anger* or blazing *wrath*), *malice, slander* against men or God, abusive language, lies, are not what we expect of Christians at any stage. The veneer of Christian manners on converts so new seems to have been very thin: perhaps harsh things had been said during heretical controversies.

Three "speaking sins" are mentioned: "What floods of idle words, foul words, words that wound . . . deluge the world," exclaims Maclaren. Jesus (Matt. 12:36) and James (3:1 ff.) treat the evil as seriously as does Paul. The second list of sins (vv. 8 f.) emphasizes the importance of charity, as the first (v. 5) urged chastity. We shall see that the social content of these exhortations may have especial significance.

The paradox noted on 3:1 ff. continues in *put . . . away . . . put off . . . seeing that you have put off.* As *the old nature* (lit., "man"; cf. Rom. 6:4; Eph. 4:22 ff.) denotes the former self, now dead and buried in Christian conversion, so *the new nature* denotes the new self emerging from baptism in newness of life. Beet points out that a third, "neutral personality," is implied, which puts off and on the old and new character. "I myself change myself," says Maclaren.

There are too many echoes here of the Adam story to be accidental: *image* (cf. Gen. 1:27), *knowledge* (cf. Gen. 2:17), and the recovered glory (see comment on 3:4). The story is everywhere in Paul (Rom. 5:14 ff.; 7:7–13; 8:20 ff.; 1 Cor. 15:21 ff.,45 ff.), and it adds overtones to his words about a new creation, a perfect man, a new humanity. Here he means that the deeds and practices of the old Adamic humanity have no rightful place in the new humanity which derives its nature from Christ.

Scott sees here once more the language of baptism: it is the individual's death to one type of humanity, and his resurrection into another, that enables him to be transformed into a useful member of a group. Hence the antisocial nature of the sins here forbidden: all are sins against fellowship—e.g., *Do not lie to one another* (see comment on v. 11). This thought of the Christian man, as saved out of isolation into fellowship, becomes the central theme of Ephesians (cf. 1:10; 2:11 ff. etc.).

Four things, however, are said of *the new* man which the Colossians *have put on.* (1) It *is being renewed,* continually, day by day (2 Cor. 4:16). As the old man grows increasingly corrupt (Eph. 4:22), and the self that died with Christ must undergo repeated mortification (v. 5), so the new self experiences perpetual renewal —*is . . . renewed.* So in Romans 6:4 we rise to walk not simply in new life but in newness.

(2) The new man is renewed with a view to *knowledge* (literally; Moule compares Heb. 6:6). Progressive increase in knowledge is implied, and earlier references (1:9,27; 2:2 f.) sufficiently illustrate Paul's meaning. The knowledge Adam fatally sought in wrong ways (Gen. 2:17; 3:1–6) is given to the new man—and that without any spurious Gnostic fantasies!

(3) The new man is created, as Adam was, in God's image (Eph. 4:24); but as that image is known to us in Christ, we may speak of his image as the pattern (1:15; Rom. 8:29; 2 Cor. 3:18). In other words, believers "put on Christ" (Gal. 3:27; Rom. 13:14). What was lost in Eden is recovered in Christ.

(4) The new man, like Adam, is created for fellowship. Antisocial feelings and talk are out of place because the old racial, religious, and cultural barriers have gone in Christ. *Greek and Jew* embodied racial antipathy; *circumcised* symbolized religious antagonism; *barbarian* expressed Greek contempt for the uncultured; *Scythian* was the synonym for "savage"; the *slave,* a mere living tool, had neither rights nor place in that society. Yet all might sit together in any Christian congregation. The barriers were down: to all alike Christ was *all* that mattered. *Christ is all* and is *in all*—therein a totally new and imperishable bond of social unity had come into being. (In Gal. 4:6 this phrase is analyzed, and in 1 Cor. 15:28 it is used of God himself.) Colossian Christians must beware a heresy that reintroduced those racial and intellectualist barriers that Christ had destroyed.

New men must live up to their new humanity, putting off things Christ-less and putting on Christ.

3. Putting on Christ (3:12–17)

[12] Put on then, as God's chosen ones, holy and beloved, compassion, kindness, lowliness, meekness, and patience, [13] forbearing one another and, if one has a complaint against another, forgiving each other; as the Lord has forgiven you, so you also must forgive. [14] And above all these put on love, which binds everything together in perfect harmony. [15] And let

the peace of Christ rule in your hearts, to which indeed you were called in the one body. And be thankful. [16] Let the word of Christ dwell in you richly, as you teach and admonish one another in all wisdom, and as you sing psalms and hymns and spiritual songs with thankfulness in your hearts to God. [17] And whatever you do, in word or deed, do everything in the name of the Lord Jesus, giving thanks to God the Father through him.

Here is the exact converse of v. 5: those who have already *put on the new nature* in principle, in a radical change of moral direction, are now urged to put on every separate item of the new character, in five detailed exhortations. So Paul gives practical and pertinent meaning to the idea of putting on Christ, and continues to echo the baptismal catechesis.

A prior question arises as to whether the main bearing of these exhortations is individual or social. Unquestionably, the qualities required are in the heart (v. 15). In v. 16 Paul wrote "sing in your hearts," though the distinctions named seem pointless if the reference be only to the silent singing of the happy Christian heart. There are seven indications that Paul is thinking of these personal qualities as expressed in social relationships within the church.

(1) All the virtues singled out in vv. 12–14 are those demanded in social life, and are the direct opposites of the vices of v. 8. (2) The reference to mutual *complaint* emphasizes this. (3) To Christ's *peace* they were called *in . . . one body.* (4) Teaching, admonishing *one another,* is plainly a matter of collective life, and so probably is (5) the singing. (6) Verse 14 probably describes *love* as binding all Christians *together.* (7) The introductory words stress that the Colossians are collectively the elect people of God (see comment on 1:12 f.). Israel's election was for service among the nations; holiness was the condition of that service; and later prophets insisted that God's love, or covenant mercy, was its basis. To apply all this to Gentiles was near-blasphemy in Jewish ears, but to Paul it provided an additional motive for living as worthy members of the divine society.

It is surely evident that Paul is working out the implications of putting on the new humanity, by reviewing the several spheres in which the convert finds himself: here the church, then below in the home, in employment, in private devotion, and before outsiders. The peace of the community, the Word finding expression in the worship of the community, and the common activities of the community (v. 17)—all reveal the new quality of life of the new humanity in its social expression. Together, as well as individually, the Colossians are to put on Christ.

Put on the character of Christ.—Community life, shared by individuals of varying gifts, experience, and background, yet bound together in God's service, demands the social lubricants listed in vv. 12 f. The sympathetic spirit (in Rom. 11:22, opposed to severity), generosity of mind, a non-aggressive reaction, patience in the face of injury or insult, and forbearance—the willingness to bear with others' idiosyncrasies for the sake of fellowship—all are simple things, yet immensely valuable in Christian cooperation. They are not the negation of strength but its perfection, as we observe them in the character of Christ.

Put on the example of Christ.—Where actual injury (Onesimus' stealing?) or offense (the heretics' activities?) have given rise to just complaint, fellowship will depend wholly upon the willingness to forgive. But a disposition toward reconciliation, rather than towards revenge, is rare: a new and potent motive is therefore introduced—*as the Lord has forgiven you.* Christ's forgiveness is both model and motive (Beet); and the echo of Matthew 6:12,15; 18:23 ff. is so clear as to raise the question whether Paul is commenting on these sayings. (Paul's curious "forgiving yourselves" may be stylistic, but suggests the mutual benefit of a forgiving spirit exercised within the Christian community).

Put on the law of Christ.— *Love* completes the Christian's social equipment.

Plainly vv. 12–14 is no "mental parenthesis" (Beet) but the application of v. 11 to the divisiveness of the Colossian heresy. Does *above all* mean "to crown all" (NEB), "over all as a silken sash or belt" (Williams, Maclaren), or, more probably, "most important of all"? This echoes Romans 13:8 ff. (cf. 1 Cor. 13:1–3; Gal. 5:14 f.) and implies an appeal to the law of Christ (Gal. 6:2; Matt. 22:34 ff.; John 15:12). And what is bound *together?* Surely not *everything;* nor "all the virtues," despite Moule's attractive parallel of Christ the principle of coherence in character with Christ the principle of coherence in the universe (1:17). *Love . . . binds* all people *together* in Christ: a few manuscripts have "bond of unity" (cf. Eph. 4:3).

Paul means that the perfection, or maturity, which the heretics promised is to be attained only in the corporate experience of those who are bound together in love, not driven apart by intellectual pride and divisive teachings. How stunted mere sectarianism makes a man! Paul's Greek could imply that the total social disposition (vv. 12–14) is the bond of united spiritual perfection, not some imagined intellectual secret shared by the enlightened. In any case, the supreme law of Christ is the secret both of corporate unity and of spiritual perfection: so the whole New Testament insists.

Put on the peace of Christ.—The peace which Christ knew and bestowed (John 14:27; Matt. 11:28 f.) is to *rule* the Christian heart. Paul probably meant simply "Let peace direct and discipline your conduct," though the origin of the word, drawn from the prize-givings in the games stadium ("Let Christ's peace be arbiter," NEB) lends vividness to the appeal. *To which . . . you were called in the one body* clearly implies that the preservation of peace in the community is to be a factor, a controlling motive, in deciding actions and settling disagreements among brethren. The inner peace is to be a collective responsibility and a social concern.

Be thankful in v. 15 is so closely parallel to thankfulness in vv. 16–17 and in 1:3,12; 2:7; 4:2 that one seems compelled so to translate Paul's expression. Yet the parallel is less close in the Greek; and the context, the precedent of Proverbs 11:16 (LXX), and some support from Colossians 4:6 encourage the rendering "be agreeable, pleasant, good-natured." Only those who have not tried to do Christian work alongside unpleasant, disagreeable Christians could say that such an exhortation would be unnecessary, or "very weak" (Williams). Both inward peace and community peace depend very much upon the effort to be agreeable.

Put on the word of Christ.—Like peace, the indwelling *word* is both individual and social. *The word of Christ* is more probably the teaching of Christ, or the message about him, than some inward motion of the Spirit, "an admonitory inner voice" (Lightfoot). The three explicative participles—teaching, admonishing, singing—leave little doubt that Paul is thinking of the corporate worship of the church.

Praise, like *the word,* must move the individual heart. But again the distinction of three types—sacred song, festal praise, solemn ode—and the setting of singing alongside mutual exhortation point unmistakably to worship meetings.

From the beginning, says Barclay, the church was a singing church (cf. Eph. 5:19 f.; 1 Cor. 14:26), and the frequent snatches of hymnody in the New Testament confirm the fact. Though Bruce cites Tertullian for mutual teaching through antiphonal songs (cf. Eph. 5:19), it seems better, with Williams, to take teaching, admonishing, and singing as successive elements of early Christian worship. Theophylact understands that the singing is to be gracious (singing sweetly; cf. comment on v. 15; Luke 4:22) rather than grateful (cf. 1 Cor. 10:30). Grateful is more probable here, though there is no need to dismiss the other suggestion so curtly as Williams does: "Paul is not training a choir!" Christian praise should be worthy of Christ.

In all wisdom may describe the word of Christ (1:9; Eph. 1:9), or (as here in RSV and 1:28) it may emphasize the need that where heresy has already divided the fellowship, any mutual instruction and admonition needs to be very carefully and tactfully offered.

If in the worship, exhortation, and song, the word about Christ's riches (1:27; 2:3; Eph. 3:8) is allowed to *dwell . . . richly* within the Colossian church, there will be neither need nor opportunity for heresy to offer spurious "advanced" experiences.

Put on the name of Christ.—The context suggests that both the words and the deeds that Paul has in mind are those of the Christian community, but the daily conduct of individual members is of course part of that total church activity. Its sustaining motive, as so often in this letter, is to be gratitude. Its quality is to be determined by *the name of the Lord Jesus.* Deissmann offers examples in support of the interpretation "representative" of Christ. *Lord* suggests that all must be done in obedience to Christ's authority, as by slaves (3:23). "In honour of the Name" (Jerome) reflects 1 Corinthians 10:31. Perhaps the baptismal overtones persist, and the memory of being baptized into the name = into the ownership of Christ, is subtly appealed to.

Do everything in the name of the Lord Jesus provides a succinct formula for a Christian situational ethic: "everything in love" would be another formula. It embraces all possible avenues of Christian behavior, and all conceivable situations demanding Christian reaction, under the single principle: what is worthy to set Christ's name to. That in itself consecrates all living.

A life so adorned with the character of Christ, modeled on the example of Christ, subject to his law of love, ruled by his peace, indwelt by his word, dedicated to worthily bear his name, has indeed *put on the new nature, renewed after the image of its creator.* A Christian and a church, so characterized, are surely sharing the Christ-filled life.

4. Living for Christ (3:18—4:6)

(1) In Domestic Situations (3:18—4:1)

[18] Wives, be subject to your husbands, as is fitting in the Lord. [19] Husbands, love your wives, and do not be harsh with them. [20] Children, obey your parents in everything, for this pleases the Lord. [21] Fathers, do not provoke your children, lest they become discouraged. [22] Slaves, obey in everything those who are your earthly masters, not with eye-service, as men-pleasers, but in singleness of heart, fearing the Lord. [23] Whatever your task, work heartily, as serving the Lord and not men, [24] knowing that from the Lord you will receive the inheritance as your reward; you are serving the Lord Christ. [25] For the wrongdoer will be paid back for the wrong he has done, and there is no partiality.

[1] Masters, treat your slaves justly and fairly, knowing that you also have a Master in heaven.

The abruptness of descent from high theology and ethical analysis to domestic matters is best explained by the familiar pattern of catechesis which Paul is following (see comment on 3:5 ff.). But it is also natural for Paul to pass from the convert in the church to his home, daily work, private devotions, and his life before the world.

Living for Christ in the domestic situation affects marital, parental, and employer-servant relationships—the last covering here the slave within the household. Christians were as well aware as Jews and Stoics that character training begins at home.

The emphasis in the primitive catechesis upon "subjection," reflected here in the greater attention to the duties of wife, child, and slave, arises partly from the basic concept of sin as self-will, which needs to be subjected to God's law (Judaism), to God's kingdom (Jesus), to the lordship of Christ (Paul).

The subjection of the wife, doubtless inherited from Judaism, has nothing to do with supposed male superiority. It arises from the necessary and natural responsibility for protection and provision that falls to the husband during woman's vulnerable years of child-bearing. So it is explained in Ephesians 5:23 ff. And so Paul's word implies not submission (contrast "obey" in vv. 20,22) but acceptance of rank, or function (1 Cor. 11:3; for the word cf. Luke 2:51; 1 Cor. 15:28; Rom. 13:1 ff.) *In the Lord* raises natural necessity to what *is fitting* in a life ruled by Christ.

In 3:20 (Gk.) and 4:17 *in the Lord* is urged as a motive. Ephesians 6:1 and 1 Corinthians 7:39 use the phrase as a limitation, which would imply here that the wife is not subject against her conscience. Perhaps as in Philemon 16,20, it means "in a Christian context." An orderly Christian home was, and is, a powerful testimony for Christianity. Scott wonders if a bid for woman's "emancipation" had brought reproach upon the Colossian church.

But not only the natural order of function is upheld; the principle of reciprocal obligation (Barclay), implying that subordinates, too, had moral rights in Christ, is Christianity's contribution to each of these relationships. The responsibility of the husband (itself a new thought) is raised to a Christlike, self-giving love, subjection to which is no indignity. Ephesians 5:25 ff. works out the new concept in detail. The single prohibition—against harshness (bitterness in Rev. 8:11)—safeguards the weaker partner against overbearing strength, the danger inherent in the marital situation.

The obedience required of *children* (lit., young children) is that of discipline rather than rank. No limitation is mentioned (cf. Eph. 6:1 f.): while in place of divine law and family welfare the motive urged is to be pleasing "in" the Lord (literally). Is this an appeal to the child's wish to be popular in Christian circles? Moule understands it as "pleasing to God," in contrast to v. 22.

The submission which is pleasing in the child is pitiable in the young adult. It is a grave parental failure so to crush

the emerging strength and independence of the young as to leave the adolescent vulnerable to every evil pressure and exploitation. Hence, addressing parents (*fathers* = parents, Heb. 11:23), Paul demands understanding, stressing the danger of provoking exasperation (NEB; so Paul's word is used in 2 Macc. 14:27). Is there in this plea a reminiscence of childhood in a strict Jewish home in heathen Tarsus, full of allurements forbidden to a Jewish boy?

Within the home was the slave. The recent incident with Onesimus, possibly the presence of many converted slaves at Colossae, drew extended attention to their Christian duty. Paul's basic principle (3:11) and his attitude over Onesimus might appear to condone indiscipline towards Christian masters (cf. 1 Tim. 6:1 f.; Titus 2:9 f.) It was socially, and apologetically, essential for the early catechesis to give clear guidance—note the appeal to what is already known, 3:24; 4:1.

The general counsel *obey . . . your earthly masters* was the only practicable advice, if slaves in some pagan households were not immediately to be put to death and if the church were not to court disaster as a revolutionary emancipation movement. But every other phrase here relieves the harshness of the situation.

The master is only an *earthly master.* Slavery is a physical, social, temporary condition in this world order. In mind and ultimate destiny the slave is already Christ's freeman.

The service of slaves need not be cringing or resentful. A generous, free, magnanimous spirit (so *singleness of heart* in Acts 2:46; 2 Cor. 8:2, etc.), offering the day's work *as serving the Lord and not men* could transform slavery into vocation. Jesus uses this argument for translating compulsion into freedom by willing acceptance (Matt. 5:40 f; cf. Eph. 6:7; 1 Cor. 7:21 ff.; 9:15 ff.). *Eyeservice, as men pleasers* thus means not "doing only what superficially pleases" but "working only when the master watches," fearing displeasure. The NEB "put your heart into it as if you were doing it for the Lord" misses Paul's reiterated point that the day's work, done willingly with integrity, is in fact done for the Lord, as an example of Christian honesty and a testimony to Christian grace (so 1 Peter 2:18 ff.).

That is why the heavenly *Master* will reward the slave, as no earthly master did. The slave usually possessed nothing, certainly no rights of inheritance: the Christian slave shared the inheritance of Israel (cf. comment on 1:12; Eph. 6:8). But he who rewards integrity punishes *the wrong-doer.* Is this an encouragement not to be disheartened by injustice—the master will be punished one day? Would Paul make that appeal to vindictiveness? Is it a warning to masters (so Eph. 6:9; but why did it not follow Col. 4:1)? Or is it a warning to slaves not to presume upon the leniency of a Christian master by assuming that God is on the side of the oppressed even in wrongdoing? Paul would remove the weak excuse that a "mere slave" could not be blamed for lack of moral responsibility.

Paul does not attack slavery: he transforms it. The slave knows himself the Lord's freeman, transfigures his situation by acceptance, uses it to serve Christ, and looks beyond the earthly master, free of indignity and full of hope.

That a reciprocal duty is imposed upon the master at all is a radical advance upon common custom. *Treat your slaves justly and fairly* redefines the slave as one having a right and a claim. *Fairly* avoids the peril of claiming "equality": Paul's word is nearer "equity," the opposite of tyranny, temper, and caprice. Charity, says Maclaren, likes to come in and supply wants which would never have been felt had there been equity.

You also have a Master in heaven redefines the master as one having only relative power, no absolute possession. The *Master in heaven* is pattern and judge of the master on earth. Being master alike of owner and slave, he makes them equal

whether they acknowledge it or not. In the bearing of Christ's lordship upon each member of a Christian home, there is emphatically no partiality.

(2) *In Private Devotions (4:2–4)*

> 2 Continue steadfastly in prayer, being watchful in it with thanksgiving; 3 and pray for us also, that God may open to us a door for the word, to declare the mystery of Christ, on account of which I am in prison, 4 that I may make it clear, as I ought to speak.

The necessary private resources by which to live for Christ, perhaps as the only Christian in a pagan household, would be found only in prayer. For most early Christians, poor and illiterate, even scriptural aids to devotion were not available: hence the counsel to *continue steadfastly in prayer.*

God cannot be coerced by our much speaking (Matt. 6:7), but our persistence demonstrates our sincerity and purifies our desire. Jesus stresses such persistence (Luke 18:1–7; cf. 11:5 f.), and so does Paul—at all seasons (Eph. 6:18), being constant (Rom. 12:12), unremitting (1 Thess. 5:17). Only a heart thus habitually open and responsive to things above will safely withstand the pressures of things on the earth.

Being watchful in it again recalls Jesus (Luke 12:35 ff.; Mark 13:32 ff.) and perhaps also some apostolic reminiscence of Luke 9:32; Matthew 26:40 ff. It has been suggested that Paul urges we should keep awake while praying (Barclay), or "pray with mind awake" (NEB), "watchful in the act" (Abbott). But the echo of the primitive catechesis (see comment on 4:8; cf. 1 Cor. 16:13; 1 Thess. 5:6 ff.; 1 Peter 5:8) suggests that Paul's appeal is that we should keep alert and vigilant with the aid of prayer (cf. Luke 22:45 f.).

Private prayer, however persevering, is impoverished if it descends to endless asking for things, forgetting *thanksgiving.* It is no less impoverished if it becomes selfish. Paul would have the Colossians link their daily prayer with God's work in all the world: both for Christian colleagues —*pray for us also*—and for the cause, *that God may open to us a door for the word,* even *in prison.* The burden of the prayer should not be for release but for grace to take the presented opportunity and the gift to *make . . . clear* the secret of life in Christ (cf. 1:26).

That prayer opens doors is a frequent New Testament theme (Acts 14:27; 1 Cor. 16:9; 2 Cor. 2:12; Eph. 6:19 f.). It may be however that Paul is here thinking of the *answer* (v. 6) he must make before his judges. Even so it is not of his safety that he thinks, but of the cause, that his explanation of the reason why he is in prison may be persuasive to court, jailers, and fellow prisoners (cf. Phil. 1:12 ff.) Answering as the representative of Christ and of the church, he needs and deserves their full prayer support.

Such concern for the world and such fellowship with God's servants in distant places, make every Christian's daily prayer time a direct contribution to the ongoing purposes of God in history. Such outgoing prayer binds in one cause the leaders in the front line of the kingdom and the humblest saint in obscure places faithfully upholding them in intercession.

(3) Before Outsiders (4:5-6)

⁵ Conduct yourselves wisely toward outsiders, making the most of the time. ⁶Let your speech always be gracious, seasoned with salt, so that you may know how you ought to answer every one.

Church, home, work, and private devotions do not exhaust the theaters of Christian conduct: the Christian life has a public circumference. Here living for Christ demands wisdom, opportunism, graciousness (especially in conversation), and readiness to testify in apt and appropriate ways.

An ex-Pharisee, Paul knew the temptation of all dedicated groups to scorn or patronize "outsiders." Elsewhere he calls for obvious honesty of purpose (Rom. 12:17; 1 Thess. 4:12), for peaceableness

(Rom. 12:18), and intelligence (1 Cor. 14:23 ff.). More often he urges wisdom, as here (so Eph. 5:15). This is the fourth sphere in which wisdom is required, according to this epistle (cf. 1:9,28; 3:16). Jesus, too, advised us to live among men wise as serpents. Maclaren remarks that Paul advised walking in wisdom: he abhorred walking in craftiness.

Paul may have been thinking of the unwise aggressiveness, self-righteousness, and denunciation, too often shown to unbelievers; more probably, he is concerned with the wisdom required to testify effectively (cf. 4:4). Our paramount duty towards them that are without is to bring them in.

First, we are to seize every opportunity, at any cost, which is the way Paul expresses *making the most of the time.* Paul's word suggests cornering the market in opportunity, or buying back the present time from its evil obsessions into usefulness again (cf. Eph. 5:15 f; Rom. 13:11; 1 Cor. 7:29). So Christ "bought back" us from the curse (Gal. 3:13). We all live, constantly, in strictly measured days and must grasp the fleeting moment.

Second, we shall be wise in testifying if we *let* our *speech always be gracious, seasoned with salt.* More clearly than in 3:16, "gracious" (really, grace) here has its classical meaning: pleasant, agreeable, charming disposition, sweetness and courtesy of conversation (see Psalm 45:2; Eccl. 10:12—which could be in Paul's mind). Some, underrating the value and perhaps the rarity of that virtue, press for more theological meanings: talk with saving grace; conversation full of the gospel; avoiding all corruptness of speech (cf. Eph. 4:29; Matt. 5:13). Such meanings are not excluded, but those who can only "talk religion" to the unbeliever, and that not always graciously, may need to be told to speak *with* grace as well as *of* grace.

In Greek, "salty speech" often meant witty, epigrammatic conversation. *Seasoned* (cf. Mark 9:50) might imply piquant, pertinent, interesting speech, not empty insipidity. Admittedly the sole aim is not to please men, and there are limits to agreeableness. But though the Christian will be discriminating in talk, he need never be dull. There is immense difference between the incessant declaiming of the religious bore, and the gracious, pungent conversation that converts.

Third, wisdom in testifying will *know how . . . to answer every one*, each type differently, each case appropriately, each individual personally. Jesus (Matt. 10:19) and Peter (1 Peter 3:15) stress readiness to answer the outsider. To know the right time to speak demands patience; to understand the person addressed demands sympathy; but such gracious, effective testimony is the final test of living for Christ before the outside world.

Conclusion (4:7–18)

1. Paul's Messengers (4:7–9)

⁷ Tychicus will tell you all about my affairs; he is a beloved brother and faithful minister and fellow servant in the Lord. ⁸ I have sent him to you for this very purpose, that you may know how we are and that he may encourage your hearts, ⁹ and with him Onesimus, the faithful and beloved brother, who is one of yourselves. They will tell you of everything that has taken place here.

Paul leaves his two messengers to convey personally the news the Colossians were anxious to receive (cf. Phil. 1:12). Mutual understanding, then as now, depends upon close personal contact, which Paul is ever eager to maintain.

Tychicus appears to be a trusted personal "assistant" (cf. Acts 13:5; 20:4) and delegate (2 Tim. 4:12; Titus 3:12). An Asian, he was the obvious choice for distributing letters to his home district. Maclaren pleasantly notes that it took the great apostle and the humble Tychicus to get this precious missive to its destination. That *Onesimus*, a runaway slave and possibly also a thief, had been converted during Paul's imprisonment and was returning to his master, was probably part of *everything that has taken place* which the messengers would explain. Paul delicately

refrains from comment, finely assuming that Onesimus will be welcomed, and commending him as *faithful*, now, and *beloved*, and a *brother*.

Who is one of yourselves, usually understood as informing the Colossians that Onesimus was of Colossae, seems entirely unnecessary. Paul must mean "count him one of you henceforth, for such he is" (cf. 4:12). Involved in the many theories surrounding Onesimus is the suggestion that he became the bishop of Ephesus referred to by Ignatius, the first collector of the Pauline letters, and so the first to take steps towards the formation of the New Testament. The discussion is fascinating, but inconclusive (see the Introduction to Philemon).

2. Greetings, Instructions (4:10–17)

¹⁰ Aristarchus my fellow prisoner greets you, and Mark the cousin of Barnabas (concerning whom you have received instructions—if he comes to you, receive him), ¹¹ and Jesus who is called Justus. These are the only men of the circumcision among my fellow workers for the kingdom of God, and they have been a comfort to me. ¹² Epaphras, who is one of yourselves, a servant of Christ Jesus, greets you, always remembering you earnestly in his prayers, that you may stand mature and fully assured in all the will of God. ¹³ For I bear him witness that he has worked hard for you and for those in Laodicea and in Hierapolis. ¹⁴ Luke the beloved physician and Demas greet you. ¹⁵ Give my greetings to the brethren at Laodicea, and to Nympha and the church in her house. ¹⁶ And when this letter has been read among you, have it read also in the church of the Laodiceans; and see that you read also the letter from Laodicea. ¹⁷ And say to Archippus, "See that you fulfil the ministry which you have received in the Lord."

Aristarchus, a "Dispersion Jew" of Thessalonica (hence his Gentile name), is usually with Paul in trouble (Acts 20:4; 19:29; 27:2): "clearly a good man to have about in a tight corner" (Barclay). *Fellow prisoner* (cf. Philemon 23) is taken as a metaphor by Moule and (apparently) NEB— "Christ's captive like myself." If the word still meant "war-prisoner" this must be the meaning, and the thought resembles 2 Corinthians 2:14; Ephesians 4:8 ff. Others think Paul's situation precluded a metaphorical meaning. It would certainly seem strange to distinguish only certain Christians as Christ's captives. Those who take the word literally suggest that either compulsorily (as Paul's servants) or voluntarily (as remaining his faithful companions) Epaphras and Aristarchus took turns to share Paul's imprisonment.

The repeated plea that Mark be welcomed *if he comes* suggests some reluctance on the church's part. The story in Acts 13:13; 15:36–40 could have been known at Colossae, but it happened some 12 years before, and plainly Paul and Mark are now on excellent terms. Another possible explanation is Mark's close connection with Peter, and so perhaps (in Colossae's eyes) with the Judaist opponents of Paul. It is idle to speculate who had given the previous *instructions,* or why mention of Barnabas should commend Mark at Colossae. Had Barnabas been there?

Paul's *if he comes* appears fulfilled in 2 Timothy 4:11; 1 Peter 5:13, where Mark seems to have connection with Asia (cf. 1 Peter 1:1) and to be with Peter in Rome. We would give much to know the background. It seems significant that here Mark and Luke—the prime evangelists—are together, with the apostle.

Of *Jesus, called Justus,* "made immortal in three words" (Maclaren), we know only that he was a Jew, a Christian, whose epithet suggests uprightness (or strictness; cf. "James the Just")—whether as a rigorous Christian or a scrupulous Jew.

Paul certainly means that of the Jewish Christians these only have been his *fellow workers* (KJV, ERV are wrong in translation and in fact). The reference to this continuing coolness between Paul and the Jewish party could have been occasioned by the mention of Mark. Like Philippians 1:15–16; 3:2 ff. it prevents our supposing the old Galatian controversy dead. *Comfort* (in Gk.) is said to be a medical term—"a cordial to me": Paul's patriotism would find the support of Jews especially sustaining. The rare Pauline reference to

the kingdom (cf. 1:13; Acts 28:23,31) is likewise appropriate—it was in the transformed messianic hope that Paul found his deepest concord with his fellow Jews.

The Colossian pastor, *Epaphras,* evidently does not intend to return with Tychicus (see Introduction: The Church at Colossae). *One of yourselves,* here, clearly contrasts Epaphras with the Jewish Christians. The reiterated commendation, underlining 1:7, has suggested he needed Paul's support, and the assurance of his constant concern could well be an answer to doubts in the Colossians' minds (see below). *Remembering you earnestly* and the NEB, "praying hard," are weak versions of Paul's "agonizing" or "wrestling"; Gethsemane, and even Peniel (Gen. 32:24 ff.), may be in Paul's mind.

The content of Epaphras' prayer "glances back at the main object of the letter" (Scott). He asks that they may maintain their position (cf. Eph. 6:11,13), *perfect, mature,* needing no Gnostic supplements to complete their experience; *fully assured,* convinced, needing no Gnostic illumination to complete their faith (cf. 2:2; Rom. 4:21; 14:5). Standing *mature . . . in all the will of God* may be a reminder that the Christian needs no Gnostic or legalistic additions to the wisdom and understanding available in Christ (1:9 f., 2:3).

He has worked hard again says less than Paul's "labor, toil, often with distress." Scott conjectures that some special task on behalf of Colossae brought Epaphras to Rome, perhaps some injustice to be righted, possibly even to seek help after the great earthquake which affected Colossae about this time, and evoked widespread charity. Others understand the exertions to be in prayer.

It is this strong word, together with Paul's emphatic commendations (1:7; 2:6; and here) and the phrase of unexpected force, "I bear witness concerning him" (cf. Rom. 10:2; Gal. 4:15), which has suggested some rift between Epaphras and the church, so that he remains with Paul and Archippus takes over his leadership.

Discussing this, Moule thinks it more natural to take the reference as to pastoral concern, comparing 2 Corinthians 11:28 f. Certainly, if Epaphras had been deposed, or replaced, we would have expected more comment than v. 17.

The position revealed in the letter, a new, persuasive version of the gospel being opposed to that which Epaphras had taught, with the church hesitant and confused, sufficiently explains why Paul throws behind Epaphras his own authority and confidence. To support and vindicate the faithful messenger was to Paul an important means of maintaining the truth of the message. (On Laodicea and Hierapolis, see comment on 2:1 and Introduction).

Setting *Luke* among his Gentile colleagues, and calling him *the beloved physician,* Paul tells us more about him than any other source, except inferences from Luke's own writings. He attended constantly upon Paul, and *beloved* may express heartfelt gratitude for personal medical care. The exact order of words supports "Luke, the doctor, our dear friend."

Demas (cf. Philemon 24) may be mentioned last, and without comment, because he penned the letter (Bengel), not because he already betrayed incipient disloyalty. The joining of Demas here with Mark and Luke tends to support identification with the Demas in 2 Timothy 4:10, evidently a Thessalonian. On the same assumption, Maclaren contrasts Luke and Demas: setting out from the same point, traveling side by side, subject to the same training, alike in contacts with the magnetic Paul, yet at the end wide as the poles asunder. "Circumstances are mighty: the use we make of circumstances lies with ourselves."

The brethren at Laodicea were clearly associated with those at Colossae in some intimate way, but to speak of a congregation of the Colossian church meeting at Laodicea probably introduces a later distinction. (On "ecclesia" for the local housegroup, cf. Acts 12:12; 1 Cor. 16:15,19; Rom. 16:5,23.)

Nympha and the church in her house
(or "his" or "their" house) remains as unclear to modern scholars as to the early copyists; "house of Nymphas and his wife" seems the likeliest meaning.

On the circulation and public reading of the epistles, cf. 2 Corinthians 1:1; 1 Peter 1:1; 1 Thessalonians 5:27. *The letter from Laodicea* cannot be one Paul wrote from Laodicea (he had not been there), nor a letter by the Laodiceans (Paul would hardly commend it in this way), but a letter of Paul's sent to Laodicea, now to be exchanged for the present epistle. An existing letter with this title is usually discounted as a collection of Pauline phrases, fabricated under the impulse of this verse: it may be seen in Barclay.

Some think the epistle lost; others, discounting ancient identifications with Hebrews and 1 Timothy (see after 6:21 in KJV), identify it with Philemon or Ephesians. Barclay thinks the former an attractive possibility, as does Knox (summarized, with Goodspeed's modified view, in Moule, pp. 14 ff.). Knox suggests that our Philemon was sent to Archippus, real owner of Onesimus, but via Philemon the overseer of the Lycus Valley churches, as an act of courtesy. Thus it would reach Archippus at Colossae *from Laodicea.* The *ministry* which Archippus is charged, in the presence of the church, to *fulfil* is then the releasing of Onesimus. Moule finds this unconvincing. Goodspeed thinks Philemon originally stood in the Pauline corpus as "Laodiceans," until that church fell into disrepute (Rev. 3:16).

Marcion thought *Laodiceans* was our Ephesians. This is probably the prevailing view. If Ephesians is a circular letter, travelling in the order of the churches in Rev. 2—3, it would reach Colossae *from Laodicea.* Oscar Cullmann thinks this identification explains much—the similarity of Ephesians to Colossians (time and situation being so closely related), why Tychicus carried both, and several puzzling details in Ephesians. But Bruce thinks Ephesians later than Colossians (so not mentioned in Col.); and if Paul wanted the Colossians to read Ephesians would he not simply send them a copy? The mystery of the Laodicean epistle remains.

Archippus was probably the son of Philemon and Apphia (Philemon 2). Whether he "ministered" at Hierapolis, Laodicea, or Colossae, it seems strange to address him through the Colossian members (cf. Phil. 4:2). The word for *ministry* can imply service as a deacon, or apply more widely (Acts 12:25). Both Paul's "take heed" and the message sent recall the tone of the Pastorals. Was Archippus a very young minister whom the church is urged to encourage, not criticize, while Paul himself assures him that his ministry was received not merely from his parents and friends but with Christ's authority?

3. Signature (4:18)

¹⁸ I, Paul, write this greeting with my own hand. Remember my fetters. Grace be with you.

The personal signature authorizing the work of the amanuensis is already, within Paul's lifetime, a necessary safeguard against forgery (2 Thess. 3:17; 2:2). *Remember my fetters* may be a request for prayer (cf. 1 Thess. 1:3), an explanation why he is not visiting them, or a reinforcement of his counsel—"not a plea for sympathy but a claim to authority" (Barclay).

So closes a brief but great letter. After the immense range of high theology in chapter 1, the forthright argument of chapter 2, the lofty spiritual and ethical appeal of chapter 3, followed by detailed instructions about daily life, we feel in these concluding glimpses into apostolic conditions the warm response of Paul to those who encouraged him and his own concern for Christians in distant places. Paul's great gospel of the fullness of Christ, imparting fullness of life, was finding effective expression in the little house-churches and personal ministries which, in the plan of God, were the channels of that fullness to a thirsty world.

1-2 Thessalonians

HERSCHEL H. HOBBS

Introduction

1. Historical Background

Thessalonica was the principal and capital city of Macedonia. Its original name was Therme, after the hot springs in the area. In 315 B.C. Cassander rebuilt the city and named it Thessalonica after his wife, the daughter of Philip of Macedon and the half-sister of Alexander the Great. Since 42 B.C. it had been a free city in the Roman Empire. Among other things this meant that no Roman garrison was quartered there, and it enjoyed the privilege of self-rule within the framework of the laws of the Empire. This rule was of "the people" (Acts 17:5) under the leadership of politarchs (Acts 17:6, "city authorities"). At one time Luke's accuracy in using this word for the rulers was questioned. But an inscription found in Thessalonica affirms it.

Thessalonica was located on the Thermaic Gulf. Its excellent harbor had been the naval headquarters of Xerxes in his invasion of Europe. In Roman times it was the site of great dockyards. The city was also on the Egnatian Way, Rome's highway linking Europe and Asia.

The main street of the city was this highway. This sea and land location meant that it was a great trade center. Coupled with this was the fertile soil, forests, and mineral deposits of the region. It is understandable, therefore, that it was so important a city then, and that the modern, thriving city of Salonika is still there. In ancient times it was said that "so long as nature does not change, Thessalonica will remain wealthy and prosperous."

Paul came to this city on his second missionary journey, probably in A.D. 50 (see Acts 17:1–9). The presence of a synagogue showed that there were Jews in the city. This is understandable due to its commercial status. Luke says that Paul spent three sabbath days debating with them out of the Scriptures with reference to the death and resurrection of Christ. He proclaimed Jesus to them as the Christ. The result was that some Jews joined with Paul and Silas. Also "a great many devout Greeks and not a few of the leading women." According to Sir William Ramsay (p. 227) women enjoyed a higher status in Macedonia and Asia Minor than elsewhere. The devout Greeks were "God-fearers." Disillusioned by idolatry and low moral standards of the pagans, they were attracted to the monotheism and high moral standards of the Jew. As God-fearers they were studying the Jewish religion but had not yet adopted it as their own. One barrier to this final step probably was the legalism of the Jewish faith. So they were readily attracted to Paul's gospel of freedom.

This aroused the jealousy of unbelieving Jews. They resented losing these God-fearers. They also rejected Paul's message about Jesus being the Christ. So using "wicked fellows of the rabble" they incited a riot against Paul and his company. Failing to find them at the home of Jason, their host, they brought Jason and some

257

other of the brethren (Christians) before
the politarchs. They accused Jason of har-
boring men who taught sedition by saying
that Jesus was another king or Caesar.
Therefore, the politarchs took "security"
from Jason and the others, and let them go.
This security probably was their promise
to keep the peace and perhaps not to harbor Paul and his company.

Thinking that it was best for Paul and
his group to leave Thessalonica for the
time, they sent them away. After a brief,
successful ministry in Beroea, Jews from
Thessalonica descended upon that city
"stirring up and inciting the crowds" (Acts
17:13). Thus Paul left there for Athens,
with Silas and Timothy remaining in
Beroea. However, upon arriving in Athens
Paul sent word for them to join him there.
Timothy came to Athens only to be sent
back to Thessalonica to bring word to Paul
as to conditions there (1 Thess. 3:1-5).
He feared that persecution by the Jews
might disrupt the new converts.

However, due to his experience in
Athens, Paul left for Corinth ahead of
schedule. Silas and Timothy came to him in
Corinth. Their coming greatly strengthened
Paul in his work there (Acts 18:5; 1 Thess.
3:6 ff.).

II. Authenticity

1. 1 Thessalonians

The authenticity of this epistle was
challenged by both the Tübingen and
Dutch schools. But with few exceptions it
is accepted by modern scholarship as genuinely Pauline. F. C. Baur and his followers
questioned the epistle on three grounds:
(1) differences in style and vocabulary
from the Corinthian epistles, Romans, and
Galatians; (2) absence of Old Testament
citations; and (3) absence of the predominantly Pauline ideas (justification by
faith, the Judaizer controversy, and matters
relating to eschatology).

However, these objections have been
largely refuted. For instance, Werner Georg
Kümmel (p. 185) insists that the vocabulary
and style are Pauline. No writer after Paul's

death would have attributed to him his
expectation to see the return of the Lord.
The apocalyptic thoughts of the epistle are
found in 1 Corinthians 15:23 ff., 51 ff.
Certainly the occasion of the epistle would
determine the form and explain any supposed differences. No writer is bound to a
set style and vocabulary. The Judaizer
controversy was not an issue in Thessalonica as it was in Corinth.

The external evidence is strong for the
epistle's authenticity. It is included in Marcion's collection of Paul's works (ca. A.D.
140); it is referred to in the Muratorian
Canon (ca. 180); and it is quoted by name
by Irenaeus. Both Clement of Alexandria
and Tertullian regarded it as Pauline. And
it is included in both Old Latin and Old
Syriac Versions, according to Donald Guthrie (p. 182), who also notes that there are
some reasons to hold that Ignatius cites
1 Thessalonians 2:4 (cf. Leon Morris,
p. 16).

The internal evidence is equally as strong
for Pauline authorship. The church organization is simple, which argues for an early
date. The eschatology reflects a time within
the apostle's life. The language and thought
are Pauline. The situation in Thessalonica
is one to be expected from Acts 17.

Certain problems have been envisioned in
attempting to harmonize the epistle (2:7-
11) with Luke's account of the founding of
the church in Thessalonica. Some insist that
the author's relationship to the church calls
for a longer stay than the three sabbaths
or weeks of Acts 17:2. They point to the
author's word about laboring with his own
hands for support. Also the point is made
that the gifts from Philippi (Phil. 4:15 ff.)
suggest a longer period in Thessalonica.
Morris (p. 17) suggests that Philippians
4:16 probably does not mean that help was
sent to Paul twice while in Thessalonica.
The Greek phrase *hapax kai dis* appears to
mean "more than once," and with *kai* pre-
fixed it will signify, "both (when I was) in
Thessalonica and (*kai*) more than once
(*hapax kai dis*, when I was in other places)
you sent. . . ."

Even if this not be the case, there is no real conflict between the two passages. Acts mentions only Paul's work in the synagogue. It is possible that he spent additional time probably working among the Gentiles as such. Ramsay (p. 228) suggests a stay of about six months in Thessalonica. C. G. Findlay sees this as an extreme view, but agrees that the time was months rather than weeks.[1]

Another problem has to do with the converts in Thessalonica. It is objected that Acts does not mention those won from idolatry (1 Thess. 1:9). However, these could be the God-fearers. Ramsay (p. 227) suggests from certain manuscripts that the non-Jewish element in the synagogue (Acts 17:4) may have included God-fearers and other Greeks or pure pagans. In either case the objection seems to be untenable.

A third problem relates to the movements of Silas and Timothy. Acts 18:5 says that they rejoined Paul at Corinth. However, 1 Thessalonians 3:1 ff. shows that Timothy was with Paul in Athens. Acts 17:15 says that Paul sent for Silas and Timothy to join him in Athens. Timothy did so, but no mention is made of Silas in that regard. After Timothy returned to Thessalonica Paul departed for Corinth where he was joined by both of his helpers (Acts 18:5). Thus the seeming discrepancy disappears.

Morris (p. 18) quotes Clogg (*An Introduction to the New Testament*, London, 1940, p. 21): "Discrepancies of this nature prove little except that the authors of Acts and of 1 Thessalonians wrote independently of each other."

Therefore, the weight of evidence strongly favors the Pauline authorship of this epistle. It is so held by this writer.

2. 2 Thessalonians

Like the first epistle this one has been strongly assailed by the Tübingen school. Questions were raised concerning supposed differences between the two epistles: es-

chatology, tone, and readers. It was said that the former holds to an imminent return of Christ, but that the latter does not. Conditions concerning the "man of lawlessness" suggest a delay of the Parousia (2 Thess. 2:1–11). Also emphasis was placed on a difference in tone: the former is more friendly than the latter. A difference in readers was supposed: Gentiles in the former and Jews in the latter. Second Thessalonians was said to assume a greater knowledge of the Old Testament (cf. 1:6–10; 2:1–12).

However, it has been noted that most apocalypses contain the idea of imminency and of certain preparatory signs.[2] The fact that 1 Thessalonians does not mention these signs is offset by the fact that the writer had spoken of these while in Thessalonica (2 Thess. 2:5). The situation of 2 Thessalonians calls for a sterner approach than that in the former epistle. But the friendly note is present in the latter also (2 Thess. 1:3 f.; 2:13—3:5). The matter of different readers is subject to serious question. Certainly one may assume that the Gentile Christians were familiar with the Old Testament teachings which Paul had expounded (Acts 17:2–4). This would be especially true of apocalyptic matters. Guthrie (p. 187) points out that Mark 13 contains such and that it "is generally reckoned to have been written for Gentiles."[3]

On the positive side the external evidence for 2 Thessalonians being Pauline is better attested than that of 1 Thessalonians. It is included in both the Marcionite Canon and the Muratorian Fragment. Polycarp, Ignatius, and Justin all seem to have known it. Irenaeus quotes it by name. From that time on it was universally accepted by the ancients.

The internal evidence is just as strong. In the latter epistle the author was dealing with special problems as to the second

---

[1] *The Cambridge Greek Testament for Schools and Colleges,* 1 and 2 Thessalonians, 1911, 1. 22.

[2] Kümmel, p. 188; Guthrie, pp. 185 ff.; Morris, pp. 20 ff.; McNeile, pp. 128.

[3] The date of Mark is probably later. But its use of apocalyptic language assumes that its readers could understand it.

coming. These called for a more commanding tone and for more detail. Certainly the style and vocabulary are as Pauline as in the former epistle (Kümmel, p. 189). The author's emphasis upon his signature certainly should bear weight (2 Thess. 3:17).

It may be concluded, therefore, that despite problems raised by some, both of the Thessalonian epistles were written by the apostle Paul. This is the position largely held by modern scholarship.

III. Situation and Date

Assuming that Paul wrote both of these epistles, what situation prompted him to do so? What was his purpose? Some scholars suggest that 2 Thessalonians actually preceded 1 Thessalonians. But as will be seen later their arguments are inconclusive. For that reason the epistles will be considered in their canonical order.

As previously noted Paul and his company left Thessalonica in an atmosphere of persecution from the Jews. In view of his subsequent experience in Beroea, Paul had every reason to believe that the young converts in Thessalonica continued to endure hardships. When Timothy joined him in Athens he sent his young helper back to Thessalonica to ascertain conditions there. Later Silas and Timothy joined him in Corinth. Paul was overjoyed and strengthened to hear of the steadfastness and activity in the faith of the believers in Thessalonica. So immediately he wrote 1 Thessalonians. In it he expressed satisfaction as to their state. He answered certain charges made against him by the Jews, exhorted the Christians to persevere in the face of their difficulties, and declared the superior morality of the Christian faith over that of pagans. He sought to calm anxieties related to the return of the Lord, and then dealt with certain other matters involved in the church's life.

Shortly thereafter Paul received word that the first epistle had not had the desired effect. So he wrote a more demanding letter. This one dealt mainly with the problems relative to the Lord's return. It is possible that someone had sent a communication purported to be from Paul. Or he may have merely anticipated such. At any rate he signed the letter so as to assure them that it was authentic.

Places other than Corinth have been suggested as Paul's location when he wrote these epistles (e.g., Ephesus). But the evidence for Corinth is strong. The dates of the epistles hinge upon this. Assuming Corinth as the place, what would be the dates?

The most exact date in Paul's chronology places him in Corinth. He was arrested and brought before the proconsul Gallio (Acts 18:12 ff.). An inscription at Delphi tells of a question referred to the Emperor Claudius by Gallio. It is dated in the twelfth year of the emperor's tribunical power and after his twenty-sixth acclamation as emperor. This would be before his twenty-seventh acclamation which was dated before August 1, 52 A.D. So the inscription was dated prior to this date. Proconsuls usually took office in midsummer and served for one year. Some scholars date Gallio's arrival in Corinth as A.D. 52. Others date it one year earlier so as to allow time for his inquiry to reach Claudius prior to 52. The date of Paul's appearance before Gallio hinges upon this matter. Apparently it was shortly after Gallio's arrival.

It would seem that Paul had been in Corinth for some time when this took place. Perhaps it was near the end of his 18 months there. Depending upon whether one dates Gallio's arrival in A.D. 51 or 52, this would mean that Paul arrived in Corinth in either A.D. 50 or 51. Ramsay (p. 254) thinks that he arrived in September, 51.[4] Either date is possible.

It is highly probable that Paul wrote 1 Thessalonians shortly after his arrival in Corinth. Which would mean either A.D. 50 or 51. And assuming that 2 Thessalonians came either a few weeks or even

---

[4] Guthrie, p. 181 (holds to A.D. 51); Morris, p. 15 (holds to A.D. 50); James Moffatt, dates it probably near A.D. 53; Robertson, Word Pictures, suggests either 50 or 51.

months later, this would mean either late 50 or 51 or early 51 or 52. This writer is inclined toward the earlier date for Paul's arrival. Perhaps the two epistles should be dated in the latter half of A.D. 50.

If this be true then these are probably the earliest of Paul's writings which have been preserved. Some scholars date Galatians at A.D. 49. But it likely came later. Some date James very early and others very late (see "James," BBC, Vol. 12). If James be dated early, it is likely that 1 Thessalonians was the second New Testament book to be written, with 2 Thessalonians following shortly thereafter.

IV. The Order of the Epistles

Traditionally the epistles have been accepted in their canonical order. But some scholars have insisted that the order should be reversed. This was first suggested by Grotius (1640) and later championed by Baur (1845). This position has been held by certain modern scholars (Guthrie, p. 191). For the most part modern scholarship holds to the traditional order.

However, it will be well to examine the reasons for reversing the order. It is argued that the length of the former epistle, not historical sequence, determined their order in the canon. This is an arbitrary argument unsupported by any real evidence. Again, it is contended that nothing in 1 Thessalonians could cause the misunderstanding evidenced in 2 Thessalonians. But 2 Thessalonians 2:5; 3:10 imply that this misunderstanding grew out of Paul's oral instruction. Furthermore, it is held that the eschatology in 2 Thessalonians is not as refined as that in 1 Thessalonians. But would Paul change his mind so quickly? This matter has been touched upon previously. This group also sees the trials in Thessalonica as being over in the former epistle, but seem to be yet ahead in the latter epistle. The former was designed to encourage, but gives no hint that other trials will not come. Indeed, the situation in Acts favors the idea of continuing problems. It is further suggested that the problems in Thessalonica were well

known in the former but came as a new development in the latter epistle. Also it is insisted that 1 Thessalonians 4:10–12 needs 2 Thessalonians 3 to be understood. But, to the contrary, it may be said that problems touched upon in the former epistle were dealt with in more detail in the latter. The problem had deepened by the time Paul wrote 2 Thessalonians.

Certain references in 1 Thessalonians 4:9,13; 5:1 are seen as concerning matters mentioned in a previous communication. But these could refer to oral reports brought by Silas and Timothy. Paul's personal word in 2 Thessalonians 3:17 is used as proof of a previous letter by Paul. However, 2 Thessalonians 2:2 could refer to false letters purported to be from Paul. This could well explain his personal word in 3:17. Finally, it is suggested that Timothy took a letter from Paul when he returned from Athens to Thessalonica. It is held that this letter could be 2 Thessalonians. This is nothing more than conjecture. The fact that Timothy was the coauthor of both letters, not the bearer of them, rules out this idea.[5]

The evidence points decisively to the canonical sequence as the proper one. Paul wrote 1 Thessalonians to deal with certain matters. When this epistle did not have the desired effect, he wrote 2 Thessalonians. In them one sees Paul as a missionary pastor wrestling with the problems of this infant congregation. In so doing he speaks to all churches in all ages of Christian history.

Selected Bibliography

AIRHART, ARNOLD E. *The First and Second Epistles to the Thessalonians.* ("Beacon Bible Commentary.") Kansas City: Beacon Hill Press, 1967.

BAILEY, JOHN. W. "Introduction and Exegesis of 1 and 2 Thessalonians," *The Interpreter's Bible.* Nashville: Abingdon Press, 1955.

BARCLAY, WILLIAM. *The Letters to the Philippians, Colossians, and Thessalonians.* Philadelphia: The Westminster Press, 1959.

BLAILOCK, E. M. *Cities of the New Testament.* Westwood, N. J.: Fleming H. Revell Com-

[5] See Kümmel, pp. 186 f.; Guthrie, pp. 190 ff.; Morris, pp. 27 ff.; Moffatt, pp. 10 f.; McNeile, pp. 129 ff.

pany, 1965.

CLARKE, JAMES W. "Exposition of 1 and 2 Thessalonians," *The Interpreter's Bible.* Nashville: Abingdon Press, 1955.

ELLICOTT, CHARLES JOHN. *Commentary on the Epistle to the Thessalonians.* ("Classic Commentary Library.") Grand Rapids: Zondervan Publishing House, 1957.

ERDMAN, CHARLES R. *The Epistles of Paul to the Thessalonians.* Philadelphia: The Westminster Press, 1961.

FRAME, JAMES EVERETT. *A Critical and Exegetical Commentary on the Epistles of St. Paul to the Thessalonians.* ("The International Critical Commentary.") Edinburgh, T & T. Clark, 1912.

GUTHRIE, DONALD. "The Pauline Epistles," *New Testament Introduction.* Chicago: Inter-Varsity Press, 1968.

KÜMMEL, WERNER GEORG. *Introduction to the New Testament.* Nashville: Abingdon Press, 1966.

LINEBERRY, JOHN. *Vital Word Studies in II Thessalonians.* Grand Rapids: Zondervan Publishing House, 1961.

MORRIS, LEON. *The Epistles of Paul to the Thessalonians.* ("Tyndale Bible Commentary.") Grand Rapids: Eerdmans Publishing Company, 1965.

MCNEILE, A. H. *An Introduction to the Study of the New Testament.* London: Oxford University Press, 1953.

MOFFATT, JAMES. "The First and Second Epistles to the Thessalonians," *The Expositor's Greek Testament.* Grand Rapids: Eerdmans Publishing Co., 1951.

ORR, JAMES. "Man of Sin," *The International Standard Bible Encyclopaedia,* Vol. III. Grand Rapids: Eerdmans Publishing Co., 1949.

RAMSAY, WILLIAM M. *St. Paul the Traveller and the Roman Citizen.* Grand Rapids: Baker Book House, 1960.

ROBERTSON, A. T. *Word Pictures in the New Testament,* Vol. IV. Nashville: Broadman Press, 1931.

STAGG, FRANK. *New Testament Theology.* Nashville: Broadman Press, 1962.

TOD, M. N. "Thessalonica." *The International Standard Bible Encyclopaedia,* Vol. V. Grand Rapids: Eerdmans Publishing Co., 1949.

VINCENT, MARVIN R. *Word Studies in the New Testament,* Vol. IV. Grand Rapids: Eerdmans Publishing House, 1946.

WALKER, ROLLIN HOUGH. "The First Epistle of Paul to the Thessalonians." "The Second Epistle of Paul to the Thessalonians." *The International Standard Bible Encyclopaedia,* Vol. III. Grand Rapids: Eerdmans Publishing House, 1949.

Commentary on 1 Thessalonians

Outline

I. Signature and address (1:1)
II. Present situation in Thessalonica (1: 2–10)
  1. Basis of thanksgiving (1:2–4)
  2. Entrance of the gospel into Thessalonica (1:5)
  3. Response to the gospel (1:6–10)
III. Reminders of the past (2:1–16)
  1. Difficulties in witnessing (2:1–2)
  2. Paul's defense of conduct and motives (2:3–12)
  3. Paul's commendation of the Thessalonians (2:13–16)
IV. Present relationship to the Thessalonians (2:17—3:13)
  1. Paul's desire to visit them (2:17–20)
  2. Timothy's mission to Thessalonica (3:1–5)
  3. Timothy's report to Paul (3:6–8)
  4. Paul's joy and prayer (3:9–13)
V. Practical exhortations (4:1–12)
  1. Christian example (4:1–2)

  2. Moral purity (4:3–8)
  3. Brotherly love (4:9–10a)
  4. Honest endeavor (4:10b–12)
VI. Problems concerning the Lord's return (4:13–5:11)
  1. Living and dead (4:13–18)
  2. Times and seasons (5:1–3)
  3. Children of light (5:4–11)
VII. General matters (5:12–22)
VIII. Conclusion (5:23–28)

I. Signature and Address (1:1)

¹ Paul, Silvanus, and Timothy,
To the church of the Thessalonians in God the Father and the Lord Jesus Christ:
Grace to you and peace.

In keeping with ancient custom Paul began the epistle with a signature followed by the address. It is characteristic of all his writings. While he associated Silvanus and Timothy with him in the epistle, it is definitely Pauline. Their inclusion reflects their relation to the church in Thessalonica, and the fact that they shared in Paul's concern and agreed with his statements.

Since the trouble in Thessalonica involved Paul's character and motives rather than his authority, he made no mention of his apostleship (cf. Rom. 1:1; 1 Cor. 1:1; 2 Cor. 1:1; Gal. 1:1; Eph. 1:1; Col. 1:1; the Pastoral epistles; absent from the Thessalonian epistles, Philippians, and Philemon). The absence of this speaks for his personal relationship with this church.

Silvanus (called Silas in Acts) was a prophet and a trusted member of the church in Jerusalem (Acts 15:22,27,32) sent to Antioch to affirm the letter from the Jerusalem Conference. Later Paul chose him to accompany him on his second missionary journey (Acts 15:40). He was imprisoned with Paul in Philippi (16:19 ff.). From Acts 16:37 it appears that Silas, like Paul, was a Roman citizen. He was with Paul in Thessalonica and Beroea (Acts 17:4,10).

From Athens Paul sent for Silas and Timothy (Acts 17:15). No mention is made that Silas went to Athens; but he later joined Paul in Corinth (Acts 18:5; 2 Cor. 1:19). He is probably the Silvanus mentioned in 1 Peter 5:12. Luke used the name "Silas," while Paul and Peter used "Silvanus."

Timothy is first mentioned in Acts 16:1. He was the son of a Greek father and a Jewish mother. Perhaps Paul won him to Christ during his first missionary journey. Apparently from Lystra, he was also well regarded by the Christians in Iconium (Acts 17:2). Since he was a half-Jew Paul circumcised him before taking him as a companion in the work (Acts 17:3). The fact that Timothy had not been circumcised as a child suggests either strong resistance to it on the part of his father or lack of strong conviction on the part of his mother—perhaps both. Later Paul refused to circumcise Titus, a full Greek (Gal. 2:3). Timothy's circumcision was designed

to make him acceptable to the Jews among whom he would serve.

No mention is made of Timothy during the Macedonian ministry until Acts 17:14 where he is mentioned along with Silas. But it is implied that he had been with Paul and Silas in the founding of the churches in Philippi, Thessalonica, and Beroea. The fact that Paul sent him to Thessalonica (1 Thess. 3:1–2) shows his standing in that church. Along with Silas he was active in Paul's Corinthian ministry (cf. Acts 18:5; 1 Cor. 16:10; 2 Cor. 1:1,19; Rom. 16:21). Unlike Silas, he is also mentioned in Paul's later ministry (Phil. 2:19 ff.). Two of Paul's epistles were written to him. John W. Bailey (p. 254) notes that Timothy is mentioned more frequently as an associate of Paul in his travel and work than any other person in the apostle's letters.

The fact that Silvanus is mentioned before Timothy in this address suggests that he was the elder of the two. Although Paul dictated this epistle, he included Silvanus and Timothy, not as subordinates, but as fellow laborers in the work (cf. Rom. 16:21).

To the church ("the called out ones") *of the Thessalonians.* The word rendered *church* (*ekklēsia*), in the basic meaning of the Greek, referred to any group of people "called out" to form an assembly. It had a political connotation in Acts 19:32, 39,41. Also, it had a Hebrew background and connotation. It was used in the Septuagint to render *qahal* referring to the congregation of Israel assembled before God in the wilderness. Both *ekklēsia* and *qahal* connote a calling. In the Hebrew-Christian sense it denotes God's people. This idea is preserved in the English "church," which seems to be from *kuriokos,* "belonging to the Lord." The church, local or universal, is God's people, by his calling and creation. Jesus used this word to describe his church (Matt. 16:18; 18:17). In the New Testament it is used a few times to refer to all the redeemed of all the ages (cf. Eph. 3:10). The vast majority of uses, as here, is with reference to the local church (cf.

Gal. 1:2, plural). The singular form is never used to refer to a body of churches in a given area or in the modern sense of a denomination.

In God the Father and the Lord Jesus Christ. In the Greek text there is no definite article before *in* (*en*) or *Lord,* or *en* before *Lord.* This shows that this phrase is a unit instead of a double antithesis to "pagan" and "Jewish" respectively. Moffatt notes that *in . . . Christ* identifies this as a Christian assembly rather than a pagan or Jewish one. Morris points out that *in God the Father* is peculiar to the address of the Thessalonian epistles among Paul's writings. His favorite phrase is "in Christ." This statement speaks of the oneness of God the Father and the Lord Jesus Christ. Indeed, "and" may read "even."

The names *Lord Jesus Christ* are significant. *Christ* is the official title of God's Anointed. *Jesus* is his historical, human, and saving name. *Lord* is used as the equivalent for Jehovah. When used of Jesus in the purely Christian sense it is used in this regard. Prior to their becoming Christians, pagans had used "Lord" of Caesar; the Jews had used it of Jehovah. In their Christian relationship they saw Jesus Christ as Lord or as the full revelation of God. Being *in* the Father and the Son shows their intimate relationship with God.

Grace to you and peace. This greeting peculiar to both Thessalonian epistles is the shortest in Paul's writings. It reflects both the Greek (grace) and Jewish (peace) forms of greeting. Some scholars relate this combined greeting to Numbers 6:24–26. Others see it as simply inclusive of Greek and Jewish Christians among his readers. In either case it is distinctly Pauline. Charles R. Erdman (p. 32) regards this form of greeting as having been coined by Paul. It expresses the Christian experience as *grace* from the Father and *peace* in the Son. In a very real sense both resulted from one's experience with God in Christ. *Grace . . . and peace* from God was at the heart of Paul's Christian experience, and in that order.

II. Present Situation in Thessalonica (1:2–10)

From his signature and address Paul plunged immediately into the body of his letter. His heart overflowed with joy and love because of their loyalty to him and to the gospel. Here one sees the heart of a pastor bound with ties of love to those who had responded to his ministry.

1. Basis of Thanksgiving (1:2–4)

> ² We give thanks to God always for you all, constantly mentioning you in our prayers, ³ remembering before our God and Father your work of faith and labor of love and steadfastness of hope in our Lord Jesus Christ. ⁴ For we know, brethren beloved by God, that he has chosen you;

In ancient literature it was customary to follow a greeting with an expression of thanksgiving. However, this should not be viewed as a mere form on Paul's part. He was genuinely thankful for the Christian graces and steadfastness of these converts under trial.

The plural form of the verb *give thanks* includes Paul, Silvanus, and Timothy. In the present tense it connotes repeated or habitual action. They were in the habit of thanking God *always for you all.* "For you all" is inclusive of the entire church fellowship. "For" means about. Robertson says that they encircled all of them in a prayer of thanksgiving. This speaks also of the unity within the church. At this point they were no problem to the apostle. *Always* does not mean that the writers were constantly on their knees. Thus it should not be taken literally. This should warn against conflict over the question of taking the Bible *literally.* It should be taken *seriously,* sometimes literally and sometimes not. The question is as to what the writer means. They lived in the atmosphere of prayer. And from time to time when they prayed they were thankful for the Thessalonian Christians.

Constantly mentioning you in our prayers. Again, they did this when they prayed. The Greek text reads "making mention." Robertson raised the question as to their having a prayer list. But the number would not have been so great that they could not pray for them individually and by name. Or it could mean prayer for the group.

The KJV couples *constantly* (without ceasing) with "remembering." Probably it belongs with "mentioning" as in the RSV. But, as Moffatt notes, either way it does not seriously affect the final meaning. "Constantly" renders an adverb from the verbal adjective meaning "not leaving off." It is used in the New Testament only by Paul (1 Thess. 1:3; 2:13; 5:17; Rom. 1:9), and always in connection with prayer.

In their prayers they remembered before God the Father their *work of faith and labor of love and steadfastness of hope in our Lord Jesus Christ.* The word rendered "work" connotes the general idea of work or business, daily tasks or employment. Whatever they did, it was a work characterized by faith. It was the activity which faith inspired.

Paul's great emphasis was upon salvation by grace through faith apart from works (cf. Rom. 4). But it was a faith which produced works (Eph. 2:8–10). There is no conflict between Paul and James (2:14 ff.). A faith that saves will produce good works as evidence of salvation. It is that kind of faith which saves (James 2:14*b*). Indeed, Paul speaks of faith that works through love (Gal. 5:6).

Labor of love. Labor means toilsome, wearisome work. It is laborious toil done for love's sake. The word rendered "love" (*agapē*) connotes the love which characterizes God's nature (1 John 4:8). Basically it means a state of absolute loyalty to its object (cf. Rom. 5:8). Here it has the connotation of Christian love, above all other types of love. It is a love which has its origin in God's nature. In response to it man so loves God. And in Christ the Christian reaches out in love to all men. It has both a horizontal and a vertical dimension. It is best epitomized by the cross. So having yielded to God's love, the Chris-

tians at Thessalonica gave themselves to others in a laborious toil characterized and inspired by love.

Steadfastness of hope. Steadfastness (patience) does not connote a negative, passive acquiescence. Its content is a positive, active, manly endurance. This word is found in the papyri to connote an athlete or soldier who could endure his opponent's attack, yet possess reserve strength with which to countercharge to victory. In military life it was a citation like a medal of honor. This patience was characterized by hope. It endured in hope or assurance of victory. This was especially meaningful in the situation in Thessalonica (vv. 5 ff.). Note the three Christian virtues: faith, love, and hope (cf. 1 Cor. 13:13).

These graces were exercised *in our Lord Jesus Christ.* This is an objective genitive meaning that these graces were, literally, "in the Lord of us Jesus Christ." It has the sense of "in Christ." Some relate this only to the last of these graces. But it makes even better sense to relate it to all three. The whole of the Christian life is lived in Christ. He inspires work of faith, labor of love, and steadfastness of hope. This hope looks to the return of the Lord when he will right all wrongs and reward his own.

Brethren beloved by God is a true reading (cf. KJV). *Brethren* as used here is a purely Christian term. The New Testament does teach that men are a part of humanity and as such should be the object of love on the part of all other men, including Christians. But brethren in the Christian sense are those who have become sons of God through faith in God's Son. "Brethren" in this sense is used 21 times in this epistle (singular and plural nine times in 2 Thessalonians), showing the warm relationship between Paul and his readers. Morris notes God's power to cause this Pharisee to love these Gentiles thus. *Beloved* renders a perfect passive participle of *agapaō;* this was an expression of completeness, a love which began in the past and continued to the present and into the future.

For we know . . . that he has chosen

you (lit., knowing . . . your election). In Greek, knowing is a perfect passive participle of *oida* from *eidō*. The root meaning of this verb is to see as by perception. In Greek the word *ginōskō* means to know by experience. *Oida* means to perceive that knowledge until it becomes a conviction of the soul. So Paul had a complete conviction about the Thessalonians that they were chosen of God. It was based upon the evidence of their genuine faith and fervent ministry for Christ. They were known by their fruits.

Chosen may be rendered "election." They were elected of God to salvation. There are generally two views as to the meaning of election. One view emphasizes the sovereignty of God to the neglect of the free will of man. It sees the arbitrary election of some to the exclusion of others. Another view sees God taking the initiative in salvation with man free to choose. To this author, this is the preferred view. God always takes the initiative, whether it be in creation, revelation, or salvation. E. Y. Mullins sees election as meaning that God has chosen the means whereby to save men and a people to propagate the gospel that saves. Man is free to choose in both cases, but is responsible for his choices.[1] Mullins summarizes: "Election is not to be thought of as a bare choice of so many human units by God's action independently of man's free choice and the human means employed. God elects men to respond freely. He elects men to preach persuasively and to witness convincingly. He elects to reach men through their natural faculties and through the church, through evangelism and education and missionary endeavor. We must include all these elements in election. Otherwise we split the decree of God into parts and leave out an essential part" (Mullins, p. 347).

Paul's most complete treatment of election is in Ephesians where he shows God electing individuals to salvation and those receiving it as a people, the church, as elected to propagate the plan of salvation. In Ephesians 1:3–13 Paul used "in Christ" or its equivalent ten times. The sovereign God elected to save all who are in Christ. Free man chooses or refuses to be in Christ through faith in him. Such a view respects both God's sovereignty and man's free will.

Of course, an omniscient God knows who will receive or reject. But foreknowledge of an event does not cause it. The Thessalonian Christians had responded favorably to God's elected plan of salvation and to his elected purpose that they should propagate the plan (cf. vv. 7 ff.). It is no wonder that Paul was thankful. Their faithfulness gave him courage for his ministry in Corinth.

What one church does, good or bad, affects the cause of Christ favorably or unfavorably wherever its influence is felt. No Christian lives in isolation. The fellowship of believers binds all church members together in privilege and responsibility.

2. Entrance of the Gospel into Thessalonica (1:5)

5 for our gospel came to you not only in word, but also in power and in the Holy Spirit and with full conviction. You know what kind of men we proved to be among you for your sake.

Paul's assurance of the election of the Thessalonian Christians was based upon the gospel which they had heard and to which they had responded in faith. This is seen in the word *for*. This word could mean because or how that. In this context the former seems to be the sense.

Our gospel is not a gospel contrived by Paul and his companions. It is the good news of salvation which God provided in Christ. It refers not to the act of preaching but to its contents. In this same letter Paul spoke of the "gospel of God" (2:2,8,9) and the "gospel of Christ" (3:2; cf. 2 Thess. 1:8). God is the ultimate source of the gospel; Christ is the center of it. But Paul,

---

[1] *The Christian Religion in Its Doctrinal Expression,* (Nashville: Baptist Sunday School Board, 1917), Chapter XIV.

Silvanus, and Timothy had believed it. They knew its effect and power, and were committed to preach it. They were so involved in it that they could speak of it as "our gospel." And they were debtors to share what they had received (cf. Rom. 1:14).

They brought the gospel to Thessalonica *not only in word,* human reasoning or eloquence, *but also in power and in the Holy Spirit and with full conviction. Power* does not refer to miracles but to the transforming power of God. This was wrought in the Holy Spirit, not by man's devices. *Conviction* may better read "assurance" (much assurance). Moffatt notes that the omission of "in" before assurance links this thought with Holy Spirit as one idea. Thus this thought complements power. The apostle and his aides had full assurance that in the Holy Spirit the gospel was a transforming power. They preached it, and the response of their hearers affirmed this.

Know renders *oidate* (see comment on 1:4). On *what kind of men we proved to be among you* Erdman comments, "The hearers could testify 'what manner of men' the apostle and his friends had shown themselves to be, how full of the Holy Spirit, how evidently sent of God to secure his purpose and to accomplish his work of grace and love" (Erdman, p. 35).

3. Response to the Gospel (1:6–10)

⁶ And you became imitators of us and of the Lord, for you received the word in much affliction, with joy inspired by the Holy Spirit; ⁷ so that you became an example to all the believers in Macedonia and in Achaia. ⁸ For not only has the word of the Lord sounded forth from you in Macedonia and Achaia, but your faith in God has gone forth everywhere, so that we need not say anything. ⁹ For they themselves report concerning us what a welcome we had among you, and how you turned to God from idols, to serve a living and true God, ¹⁰ and to wait for his Son from heaven, whom he raised from the dead, Jesus who delivers us from the wrath to come.

The response which the Thessalonian Christians made to the gospel is a further proof to Paul of their election. As Paul and his friends had preached the gospel in power and assurance by the Holy Spirit, so had these Christians received it and had been transformed thereby. They not only became "followers" (KJV) but *imitators* of them *and of the Lord.* The Greek word is *mimētai* (imitators; note "mimics"). This word appears only six times in the New Testament. All but one (Heb. 6:12) are by Paul (cf. 1 Cor. 4:16; Eph. 5:1; 1 Thess. 2:14). The key to all these is 1 Corinthians 11:1: "Be imitators of me, as I am of Christ." One need have no fear in imitating another who imitates Christ. Such should be a challenge to every pastor and, indeed, to each Christian.

Specifically how did they imitate Paul and the Lord? They did this by receiving the gospel *in much affliction, with joy inspired by the Holy Spirit. Affliction* renders a Greek word meaning to be in a tight place. The verb form was used of grapes being crushed in the press. Here Paul spoke of the trials endured by both him and his company (2:2), and of those inflicted by the Jews upon the Thessalonian Christians (2:14; 3:2–5,7; 2 Thess. 1:4). They suffered while Paul was there and after he left. Both the evangels and the evangelized imitated the Lord. Jesus suffered in his trials with the Jews during his ministry (2:14–15). Of course, Jesus' death was redemptive suffering. But they suffered in order to be true to him.

And as Jesus rejoiced in his sufferings before and on the cross (cf. Heb. 12:2), so Paul and these believers suffered in *joy inspired by the Holy Spirit.* There is no natural joy in tribulation as such. But to suffer for Christ with a purpose does bring joy to the Holy Spirit and from the Holy Spirit. Jesus never promised freedom from tribulations. But he gives joy and victory in them (John 16:33). Moffatt (p. 24) calls *affliction . . . joy* a "paradox of experience"—and further: "The gladness of the primitive Christian lay in the certainty of possessing soon that full salvation of which the Spirit at present was the pledge and foretaste." Morris (p. 38 f.) quotes Martin

Luther: "If Christ wore a crown of thorns, why should His followers expect only a crown of roses?" The answer is obvious. But it is also true that through the Holy Spirit Christ gives a peace which the world cannot give or remove (John 16:22).

The result of the faithfulness of these Christians was that they became *an example* (type) to all the other *believers in Macedonia and in Achaia* (Greece). Robertson (p. 12) points to the singular "example" and the plural "you". The former looks at the church as a whole; the latter suggests the individuals in the church. The Greek text has the definite article before both Macedonia and Achaia, treating them as separate provinces, as was true (Robertson), but forming the whole of Greece (Morris).

But Paul said even more. The gospel had *sounded forth,* not only in the above-mentioned areas, but *your faith in God has gone forth everywhere*—literally, "your faith the one toward the God" or the true God. It had gone forth (perfect tense of completeness) in every place. This may be seen as hyperbole, but a "pardonable" one (Moffatt). Morris notes that Aquila and Priscilla had come from Rome to Corinth just before Paul wrote this letter (cf. Acts 18:1 ff.). Had they heard about this Thessalonian faith even in Rome? If it were known there, it would certainly be known elsewhere. Morris' point would depend upon the time factor as to the length of Paul's stay in Thessalonica. But such widespread knowledge among believers would not be impossible. "Everywhere" (in every place) certainly means a widespread knowledge. Thessalonica's location on the Egnatian Way would contribute to this. The Thessalonians had used to advantage their strategic location. Certainly this knowledge had preceded Paul wherever he had gone since leaving Thessalonica, as is shown in verses 8-9.

Sounded forth calls for attention. It translates a perfect form of the verb *exēcheō,* found only here in the New Testament, to sound as a trumpet, to thunder, to re-

verberate like an echo.[2] Note that "echo" comes from this verb. It is not amiss to liken this sounding forth to a modern broadcasting station. Moffatt translates this, "The word of the Lord has resounded from you." Phillips: "You have become a sort of sounding board from which the Word of the Lord has rung out from you . . . everywhere the report of your faith in God has been told, so that we need not mention it." What a noble tribute to a church committed to evangelism and missions!

The result of this echoing of the gospel was that wherever Paul had gone (Beroea, Athens, Corinth) he found that the good news had preceded him. Rather than having to tell others about the church in Thessalonica, they were reporting about it to him. Moffatt: "People tell us of their own accord about the visit we paid to you." Usually bad news about a church travels fast, but in this case it was good news.

The good news was *how you turned to God from idols, to serve a living and true God. Turned* translates a compound verb *epi* and *strephō,* denoting an intensive, definite turning from something to something. Figuratively it involves a change of mind or a course of action, especially in one's relation to God.[3] In this sense it is akin to repentance.

They turned "to" (*pros*) God "from" (*apo,* away from) idols. In the Greek text both God and idols have the definite article. There is no definite article with the second "God." But that he is the one God is evident in *living and true*—as opposed to dead and false idols. Here one sees the positive and negative aspects of faith (Moffatt). Dead idols are helpless to save; false gods cannot lead to truth. God as "living and true" both saves and guides into all truth. Jesus is "the way, and the truth, and the life" (cf. John 14:6). No one comes to the

2 *The Interpreter's Bible* lists several uses of the verbal and noun forms (Joel 3:14 (LXX); Ecclus. 40:13; Luke 4:37; 21:25; 1 Cor. 13:1; Heb. 12:19).
3 William F. Arndt and F. Wilbur Gingrich, *A Greek-English Lexicon of the New Testament* (Chicago: Univ. of Chicago Press, 1960), p. 301, cites this verse to this effect.

Father except through him.

Obviously this refers to the Gentiles in the church, whether previously rank pagans or God-fearers. Originally both served idols; now they had turned to serve a living and true God. *To serve* means to serve as a slave. As they had once served as slaves of idols, now they were slaves of God (cf. Rom. 6:12 ff.).

And they served in hope. Note the two infinitives *to serve* and *to wait*. While they waited they served and vice versa. They were servants in waiting for the return of God's *Son from heaven*. This anticipates the problem of those who were waiting but idle (cf. 4:11–12). *Raised from the dead* refers to Jesus' bodily resurrection. Furthermore, he is *Jesus who delivers us from* (*ek*, out of) *the wrath to come*, the coming wrath upon all unbelievers. Here then are the resurrection, second coming, and final judgment. *Whom* and *Jesus* refer back to *his Son.* They looked for his Son whom God had raised in providing redemption for all who received him. This puts the crown upon the fact of the election of the Thessalonian Christians.

Wrath calls for brief emphasis. In the New Testament two words used most often for wrath are *thumos* and *orgē*. The former is used 18 times in the New Testament, ten times in Revelation (12:12; 14:8,10,19; 15:1,7; 16:1,19; 18:3; 19:15). *Orgē* is used 36 times in the New Testament, six times in Revelation (6:16,17; 11:18; 14:10; 16:19; 19:15). The former does not appear in the Thessalonian epistles; the latter is used three times in 1 Thessalonians (1:10; 2:16; 5:9).

Thumos means a sudden, intense expression of anger like the burning of straw. It is like the eruption of a volcano which soon subsides. Compare God's wrath in destroying Sodom. *Orgē* connotes something like God's abiding, universal wrath against evil (cf. Rom. 1:18). John the Baptist used this word (cf. Matt. 3:7). He saw this wrath as a desert fire, everywhere, before which snakes fled. This is the word used in 1 Thessalonians 1:10. Where may

one find safety from a desert fire? Where the fire has already burned. Where may one find safety from God's *orgē?* Where it has already done its worst, at Calvary. Paul's readers had done this. Thus at the judgment they would have been delivered from the coming *orgē*.

The deliverer is Jesus, the historic, crucified, risen, ascended, and returning Son of God. He is true to his name, Jesus, "Jehovah is salvation" (cf. Matt. 1:21). Such a gospel is needed today as it was then.

III. Reminders of the Past (2:1–16)

Having stated his assurance of their election, Paul recalled to the Thessalonians the circumstances under which they had heard the gospel and what had transpired since then. This chapter contains Paul's defense against the Jews who persecuted both him and the believers in Thessalonica. He expressed his abiding desire to visit them again and his continuing joy in their own faithfulness under persecution.

1. Difficulties in Witnessing (2:1–2)

¹ For you yourselves know, brethren, that our visit to you was not in vain; ² but though we had already suffered and been shamefully treated at Philippi, as you know, we had courage in our God to declare to you the gospel of God in the face of great opposition.

Again Paul used *know* (cf. 1:4). His readers knew with a certainty the history of his coming to Thessalonica. The emphasis is on *you yourselves.* Paul's motives had been questioned. So he appealed to what they themselves know. *Visit* (*eisodon* from *eis*, into, *hodon*, way) means a way into. *Was not in vain.* "Was" renders the perfect form of *ginomai* (to become), expressing completeness. The visit "has not become empty." It had borne fruit.

In Philippi the missionaries *had already suffered, and been shamefully treated.* This had happened at the hands of pagans before coming to Thessalonica (cf. Acts 16:16–40). "Shamefully treated" means to be treated insolently. More than the bodily suffering were the indignities inflicted upon

Paul and Silas as Roman citizens. Acts and this passage complement each other. Luke recorded it, and Paul tells how it remained as an unhappy memory. *As you know.* Note *oidate* again (see comment on 1:4).

Paul's unhappy introduction to Europe did not cause him to return to Asia. Rather he plunged deeper into the new mission field. To a fighter like Paul it was a challenge. So *we had courage in our God. Had courage* renders what Robertson calls an ingressive aorist. They came to have courage or boldness to go on to Thessalonica. This courage was in God, not in themselves alone. This entire passage forms a good manual for Christian workers, especially those who endure hardships for the Lord. Compare missionaries and pastors who find courage in danger through faith in God and his will. Today it probably takes more courage to be an honest pastor than to be a missionary in another land. Many pastors have suffered greatly for preaching New Testament truths about the dignity of every man and against the sin of discrimination.

This courage enabled Paul and his company to *declare* or speak *the gospel of God in the face of great opposition* (cf. Acts 17:1 ff.)—literally, "in the sphere of much conflict." *Opposition* renders *agōni* (note "agony"). This was an athletic term of striving in games. It could refer to both physical and mental agony, both of which Paul had in Thessalonica. Compare "the gospel of God" and "our gospel" in 1:5. Such determined boldness was evidence of his divine mission and of God's sustaining grace.

2. Paul's Defense of Conduct and Motives (2:3–12)

³ For our appeal does not spring from error or uncleanness, nor is it made with guile; ⁴ but just as we have been approved by God to be entrusted with the gospel, so we speak, not to please men, but to please God who tests our hearts. ⁵ For we never used either words of flattery, as you know, or a cloak for greed, as God is witness; ⁶ nor did we seek glory from men, whether from you or from others, though we might have made demands as apostles of

Christ. ⁷ But we were gentle among you, like a nurse taking care of her children. ⁸ So, being affectionately desirous of you, we were ready to share with you not only the gospel of God but also our own selves, because you had become very dear to us.

⁹ For you remember our labor and toil, brethren; we worked night and day, that we might not burden any of you, while we preached to you the gospel of God. ¹⁰ You are witnesses, and God also, how holy and righteous and blameless was our behavior to you believers; ¹¹ for you know how, like a father with his children, we exhorted each one of you and encouraged you and charged you ¹² to lead a life worthy of God, who calls you into his own kingdom and glory.

This passage reflects charges evidently made by the Jews against Paul and his associates after they left Thessalonica. But even more important it speaks of their manner of ministry and their tender love for the Christians there.

Appeal may read "exhortation" (cf. v. 11). Paul described that appeal or the manner in which it was presented. Note that throughout this passage he presented the negative, his opponents' charges, and the positive, his reply.

The appeal to their hearts had been not *from error or uncleanness nor, . . . with guile. From* denotes origin or source. In the Greek text it precedes both error and uncleanness. *With* means sphere or atmosphere. *Error* renders *planēs* (cf. planet). The ancients thought of the planets as wandering bodies, and so erratic. *Uncleanness* refers to immoral practices. Paul denied both charges. Their gospel was not based upon error or false beliefs. Neither were they guilty of gross, sensual living. Pagan religions abounded in such, but Paul was sensitive against such charges in connection with the Christian gospel. A preacher and any other Christian should realize that his character is his most precious asset in doing the Lord's work.

Guile comes from a verb meaning to catch with bait. They had been honest in their dealings with the Thessalonians. No effort had been made to catch them as fish on a hook. To the contrary, they were *approved by God.* "Approved" renders a verb meaning to test so as to determine genuineness as of a coin. They had been tested and found to be genuine. The result was that God had entrusted them with his gospel.

So we speak. They had been faithful to God's trust in making them stewards of the gospel (cf. 1 Cor. 4:1 ff.). *Not to please men, but . . . God who tests our hearts* (cf. Gal. 1:10). To please men is a preacher's subtlest temptation. This temptation is seen in many ways. It may be to tone down on the moral standards set forth in the Bible, even to living a life in keeping with the mores of the age. Or it may be to preach contrary to the clear teachings of the gospel as to God's redemptive purpose, work, and demands (see Gal. 1:10). Certainly it is evident in the temptation to avoid the social issues of the day such as racial prejudice. No preacher can avoid the social implications of the gospel and claim to preach all the gospel. His aim should be to please God, who tests the heart to see if it is genuine (Gk., same as for "approved"). Here it is a present participle, constant testing.

Morris notes that the verb translated *please* primarily means service in the interest of others. Compare James Hope Moulton, George Milligan [4] on *areskō.* Paul served God, not men. He delighted in being a servant or slave of Christ.

Continuing his defense Paul denied the use of *flattery . . . cloak for greed* (lit., in a cloak of covetousness or desire for more). Many teachers of that day relied upon flattery or fawning to win a hearing. Philodemus wrote a work *Peri Kolakeias* (*Concerning Flattery*). The word rendered *cloak* meant a pretext. They were not wolves in a sheep's clothing to satisfy their greed by catching men, or to fleece them of money in a pretense of service. Beware of the money motive in Christian service!

Note *as you know* and *God is witness.* The Thessalonians knew for a certainty that

[4] *The Vocabulary of the Greek New Testament,* (Grand Rapids: Eerdmans, 1949).

the apostles had not flattered them. And Paul called upon God as a witness as to their freedom from greed. *God is witness* may be seen as an oath taken by Paul (cf. Rom. 9:1; 2 Cor. 1:23; Phil. 1:8).

Denial of covetousness is naturally followed by denial of worldly ambition. Neither Paul nor his associates had sought *glory from* (*ek,* out of) *men, . . . from* (*apo*) either the Christians or others. As apostles of Christ they could have made demands, but did not. *Demands* means burdens. This could refer to dignity, authority, or finances. Westcott and Hort and Nestle make this phrase a part of v. 7. If this be correct, it refers to finances. But any of the above makes sense.

Rather than to be a burden they *were* (became) *gentle* (*ēpioi*). Some strong manuscripts use *nēpioi,* babes. The arguments are about even between the two readings. Later copyists would have more trouble with "babes" than "gentle." They may have changed from the former to the latter. The external evidence favors "babes." The same may be said for scribal evidence. The intrinsic evidence does not rule out either reading. It could read either way. Paul's point is the manner in which they had worked with the Thessalonian Christians. Rather than to get something for themselves they sought to give. *Taking care* means to cherish, to warm. *Affectionately desirous,* they were ready to share not only the gospel but their *own selves* (*psuchas*). This word may read "souls" or "lives." They held back nothing in their ministry. The Thessalonians had become *very dear* (beloved) to them—a tender note of love which should characterize every pastor or Christian worker.

In order not to burden the Thessalonians, they burdened themselves. *Labor and toil . . . night and day.* Labor means toil; toil is heavy labor. Perhaps they began before dawn (day) and labored into the night, probably at tentmaking (Acts 18:3), in order to be financially independent. They did this while they preached the gospel of God. *Preached* renders a word to herald.

It was used of a herald of the king who should be heard and obeyed as though the king spoke in person. They were heralds of the King.

In v. 11 Paul called upon his readers and God as witnesses to their *behavior.* They were *holy* toward God, *righteous* toward the *believers,* so that they were without blame before either. Here Paul changed his metaphor from a nurse (mother-nurse, Robertson) to a *father with his children.* Note the three phases of a minister's role: *exhorted, encouraged,* and *charged* (witnessed)—all of this with the aim, *to lead a life* (walk) *worthy of God.* They exhorted them to do so, encouraged or consoled them in their resultant trials, and witnessed concerning a life worthy of God, who is holy and righteous. "Worthy" carries the idea of weight. Their life should balance with the character of God, to walk worthily of God (cf. Eph. 4:1). Certainly this is a challenge to every Christian.

3. *Paul's Commendation of the Thessalonians (2:13–16)*

13 And we also thank God constantly for this, that when you received the word of God which you heard from us, you accepted it not as the word of men but as what it really is, the word of God, which is at work in you believers. 14 For you, brethren, became imitators of the churches of God in Christ Jesus which are in Judea; for you suffered the same things from your own countrymen as they did from the Jews, 15 who killed both the Lord Jesus and the prophets, and drove us out, and displease God and oppose all men 16 by hindering us from speaking to the Gentiles that they may be saved—so as always to fill up the measure of their sins. But God's wrath has come upon them at last!

Paul has been giving thanks for the election of his readers and the proofs of it (cf. 1:3 ff.). This has been developed up to this point. The Greek text of v. 13 begins with *kai dia touto kai hēmeis:* "And for this cause also we." Some see this *we also* as referring to a letter received from the Thessalonians. Probably Paul had only received a verbal report from Timothy as to their reaction to the gospel and to perse-

cution. *Dia touto* could refer back to 1:4—2:12 or even to 2:12, their response to Paul's exhorting, encouragement, and witness. At any rate it is the source of thanksgiving *constantly* or without leaving off being thankful.

Received refers to hearing the gospel. *Accepted* shows that they responded favorably to it, welcomed it to their hearts. Not as a *word of men but as what it really is, the word of God.* It came through men from God. It is the word *which is at work in you believers. Work* (*energeitai,* energizes) is a present tense. It keeps on working in them after Paul left Thessalonica.

For *imitators* see the comment on 1:6. Here they imitated *the churches of God in Christ Jesus . . . in Judea.* This pictures Paul's admiration for these churches, not antagonism against them and the other apostles as some suppose from Galatians 2. They are Christian churches in (in the sphere of) Christ Jesus. But their source is God. Geographically they are in Judea; spiritually they are in Christ Jesus. Note the plural "churches," not "church." He had in mind each individual church.

The Thessalonians imitated them in their suffering under persecution. *You suffered . . . as they did.* Judean churches suffered *from the Jews,* a well-known fact. In Thessalonica the suffering was related to their own *countrymen* stirred up by the Jews. Without the help of the Gentiles the Jews would have been ineffective. This passage does not justify anti-Semitism today. Both Jews and Gentiles had a part in Jesus' death. And both Jews and Gentiles persecuted the early church. The nation of Israel produced both prophets and bigots. With respect to Christ and his church, there were Jews on both sides. As a people largely they rejected Christ and brought him to his death. But many Jews received him as Saviour. Paul himself was a Jew—as was Jesus.

Verse 15 recites well-known history of what Jews rebellious to God had done to the prophets and Jesus (cf. Matt. 23:29 ff.; Acts 2:23). *Drove us out* refers primarily to Acts 17:5 ff., as does *hindering us.* This latter could refer also to the Judaizer controversy (cf. Acts 15; Gal. 2). The Jews rejected Christ and also hindered the preaching of the gospel to Gentiles. Refusing to enter the kingdom, they kept others out (cf. Matt. 23:13). Such continuous opposition to God's gospel had filled up their sins always. *To fill up* means to fill up full or to overflowing. Some see this as in God's purpose. But more likely it related to the natural result of the continual (always) sins of the Jews.

But God's wrath (see comment on 1:10) *has come upon them at last!* Paul apparently had no specific event in mind. He foresaw the final outcome of their conduct (see Matt. 23:33–36). Certainly subsequent history bore out Jesus' prophecy and Paul's words in A.D. 70. *At last* renders *eis telos.* *Telos* refers to a goal or an end. Perhaps Paul means to say that though they oppose God's work now, such will lead to an inevitable end—*God's wrath.* The writer prefers this idea. The destruction of Jerusalem was a *thumos* of God (cf. 1:10). But God's abiding, universal opposition to evil awaits all who stubbornly reject God and his Son. Paul clearly shows in Romans 1–3 that both Jews and Gentiles who reject Christ are under God's abiding wrath. But he also shows both may be saved by God's grace through faith in Jesus Christ. The gospel is to be preached to both Jews and Gentiles. God holds the door of hope open to Jews as well as Gentiles—open until the Lord's return (see Rom. 9–11).

IV. Present Relationships to the Thessalonians (2:17—3:13)

1. Paul's Desire to Visit Them (2:17–20)

¹⁷ But since we were bereft of you, brethren, for a short time, in person not in heart, we endeavored the more eagerly and with great desire to see you face to face; ¹⁸ because we wanted to come to you—I, Paul, again and again—but Satan hindered us. ¹⁹ For what is our hope or joy or crown of boasting before our Lord Jesus at his coming? Is it not you? ²⁰ For you are our glory and joy.

Evidently Paul's opponents had said that Paul's absence from Thessalonica meant that he had no concern for the Christians there. So the apostle poured out his heart of love to them. *Bereft* renders a verb *aporphanizō.* It is used only here in the New Testament, but is found in Aeschylus. Basically it means to be orphaned from someone. Note the change in metaphors from nurse (1:7) to father (1:11) to orphan (v. 17). This last refers to the period of separation since Paul left Thessalonica. His separation had been *in person not in heart.* Absent in body, but he was present in heart. In a sense he had left his heart with them. "Person" means face. They did not see his face, but they had his heart of love. Out of sight, not out of mind, as one says.

For that reason he *endeavored the more eagerly* or hastened with overflowing desire to see them *face to face* (lit., the face of you to see). He wanted his face before their faces in personal fellowship. He and his associates *wanted* or willed (wished) to come. Then Paul made it personal: *I, Paul, again and again.* (once and twice; cf. 2 Cor. 10:1; Gal. 5:2; Col. 1:23; Eph. 3:1; Philemon 19 for personal references). *But Satan hindered us.* "Hindering" (2:16) renders a different verb, to forbid. Here the verb *enkoptō,* to cut in or hinder, is used. Satan cut into Paul's plans. This verb was used of cutting into a road to make it impassable (cf. Rom. 15:22; Gal. 5:7; 1 Peter 3:7). How Satan hindered them Paul did not say. Perhaps it was the opposition of the Jews in Thessalonica. Robertson suggests illness or the Jews in Corinth or something else. Satan always seeks to make impassable the roads of service for Christ.

Then Paul poured out his heart to his readers. They are his *hope, joy,* and *crown of boasting before our Lord Jesus at his coming* (*parousiai*). *Parousia* basically means presence. Technically, as here, it refers to the return of Jesus (cf. 3:13; 4:15; 2 Thess. 2:1,8; 1 Cor. 15:23). Robertson cites Deissmann (*Light from the Ancient*

East, pp. 372 ff.) as noting that in the papyri it was used for the arrival of a king who expects to receive his "crown of coming." Paul's *crown of boasting* or glorying will be these Thessalonians. "Crown" (*stephanos*) was a laurel wreath given to the victor at the games. The royal crown is a "diadem" (*diadēma*). However, *stephanos* was sometimes used of the royal crown. Here it means a laurel wreath of victory. The Thessalonians will be his *glory and joy,* a crown which he will lay at the Lord's feet. Every Christian should have such a crown to lay at the Saviour's feet.

2. Timothy's Mission to Thessalonica (3: 1-5)

¹ Therefore when we could bear it no longer, we were willing to be left behind at Athens alone, ² and we sent Timothy, our brother and God's servant in the gospel of Christ, to establish you in your faith and to exhort you, ³ that no one be moved by these afflictions. You yourselves know that this is to be our lot. ⁴ For when we were with you, we told you beforehand that we were to suffer affliction; just as it has come to pass, and as you know. ⁵ For this reason, when I could bear it no longer, I sent that I might know your faith, for fear that somehow the tempter had tempted you and that our labor would be in vain.

In this passage Paul described his anxiety for his converts while in Athens (Acts 17:15). Timothy had come to him there. As much as he needed him, he denied himself for them. *Willing* means to think well of something. *We* may be editorial. But Robertson suggests that Silas also may have come to Athens. If so, it could include him and even Timothy. But note *I sent* in v. 5. Did he also send Silas back to Beroea? At any rate both came to Paul in Corinth (Acts 18:5).

To be left behind expresses desolation or a sense of abandonment. This is reinforced by *alone.* Paul felt abandoned in Athens as he faced the pagan idols and philosophers. Still he endured it willingly for the sake of the Thessalonians. Their need was greater than his.

Our brother and God's servant in the gospel of Christ. Note Paul's estimate of Timothy. He was not an underling but a Christian "brother" and "God's servant," Paul's companion in the work. *Servant* means fellow worker, one belonging to God (cf. 1 Cor. 3:9)—though some manuscripts read *diakonon* (minister). This shows why Paul entrusted to him so vital a mission. Compare "the gospel of Christ," "our gospel" (1:5), and "the gospel of God" (2:8); but they are the same gospel.

Timothy's mission was *to establish* and *to exhort* in the faith. Both infinitives precede *in your faith* (Gr. text). *Establish* means to fix firmly, confirm, strengthen. New converts need this, also to be encouraged (exhort) to continue resolutely in the faith once professed.

The aim of Timothy's mission was to the end *that no one be moved by these afflictions. Be moved* renders a verb meaning to wag the tail, to flatter, to beguile. The last meaning applies here. For "afflictions" see the comment on 1:6. Apparently the Jews had been telling the Christians that if they would reject Christ for Judaism they would escape persecution by the Gentiles. Note that they were not beguiled by the afflictions, but in (*en,* in the sphere of) these afflictions. This strengthens the idea that the Jews were doing as stated above.

You yourselves know that this is to be our lot. "Yourselves" is emphatic. For "know" see the comment on 1:4. "Be our lot" renders a verb meaning we are appointed or placed. By virtue of being a Christian one must expect both persecution and beguiling efforts. One should be prepared to resist in the power of the Holy Spirit.

Paul had told the Thessalonians while with them that this would be the case. *Told . . . beforehand* is an imperfect tense. Paul used to tell or told them repeatedly in the past. *Were to suffer affliction* may read "about to suffer affliction." It was not a prediction but a statement of imminent fact. It had come to pass, and they knew it well (cf. 1:4).

For this reason (because of this, v. 4),

when he could no longer stand the suspense and anxiety, Paul sent Timothy to Thessalonica *that I might know your faith.* To know is an infinitive of purpose. "Know" here renders *gnōnai,* aorist infinitive of *ginōskō,* to know by the experience of Timothy's report. "Faith" may refer to belief (3:2), or it may mean faithfulness, how they were standing up under adverse conditions. Erdman suggests "whether their faith was steadfast." However, if the reference is weighted in either direction it is not in terms of creedal belief. Paul's primary thought here is not orthodoxy. It is that this faith, trust that is bound up with what one believes, shall stand up under trial. Verse 8 clinches this point. Paul's assurance is that they stand firm in the Lord.

Paul's fear was that they being *tempted* might give in to the *tempter.* Thus his *labor* (wearisome toil) *would be in vain* or empty. The verb rendered "tempted" and "tempter" (the one tempting) means to test, to try. It may be in the good sense to prove genuine, or in the bad sense to prove false. God does the former (cf. Gen. 22:1); Satan does the latter (cf. Jas. 1:14 f.). James 1:12–15 has an interplay of these two ideas. Paul used the word in the evil sense here.

The tempter is obviously a reference to Satan working through the persecutors in Thessalonica. God would not do such. As Satan hindered Paul (2:18), so he sought to destroy his work.

3. Timothy's Report to Paul (3:6–8)

⁶ But now that Timothy has come to us from you, and has brought us the good news of your faith and love and reported that you always remember us kindly and long to see us, as we long to see you—⁷ for this reason, brethren, in all our distress and affliction we have been comforted about you through your faith; ⁸ for now we live, if you stand fast in the Lord.

This passage reads as if the sun came out on a gloomy day. *But now* introduces a new section of thought. Timothy had recently arrived in Corinth—*to us from you. He brought . . . good news.* This translates a participle of *euangelizomai,*

to evangelize or bear good news. He "gospelized" Paul as to conditions in Thessalonica. Morris (p. 65) points out that this is the only use of this verb in the New Testament other than with reference to the good news of God's saving work in Christ.⁵ It was a gospel indeed to Paul as he faced the wicked, pagan city of Corinth and the hostile Jews there.

The good news was twofold. The Thessalonians continued in *faith* toward Christ and *love* for Paul. Any doubts Paul had had about them were dispelled. They felt *kindly* toward him, and *longed* to see him. It formed a mutual bond between him and them.

For this reason he was *comforted* (and/ or encouraged) in *all our distress and affliction.* Robertson translates this as choking and crushing trouble. *For now we live, if you stand fast in the Lord.* "We" could mean Paul alone, or it could include Timothy and Silas. But the primary emphasis is upon Paul. "Live" is a present tense, keep on living. This renewed life was based upon their standing fast in the Lord, a condition which according to the Greek text Paul assumed was true.

Insofar as is known Paul had not been in danger of physical death in Corinth. But the "choking and crushing trouble" had almost killed him in spirit. All that was now of little significance as he applied himself with new life and vigor (cf. Acts 18:5 ff.).

No matter how hard one's task may be, it is made lighter to know that others in similar circumstances are standing by the faith and are remembering other Christians in love and fellowship.

4. Paul's Joy and Prayer (3:9–13)

⁹ For what thanksgiving can we render to God for you, for all the joy which we feel for your sake before our God, ¹⁰ praying earnestly night and day that we may see you face to face and supply what is lacking in your faith?
¹¹ Now may our God and Father himself,

⁵ Cf. J. B. Smith, *Greek-English Concordance to the New Testament* (Scottdale, Pa.: Herald Press, 1955), p. 156.

and our Lord Jesus, direct our way to you; [12] and may the Lord make you increase and abound in love to one another and to all men, as we do to you, [13] so that he may establish your hearts unblamable in holiness before our God and Father, at the coming of our Lord Jesus with all his saints.

At this point Paul almost shouted with a joy difficult to express. He might have taken pride in his work as shown by their steadfastness. Instead, he saw it as a work of God. So he wanted to utter *thanksgiving . . . to God.* But how? *Render* translates a compound infinitive *antapodounai* after *dunametha*, to be able or to have power. Literally, what thanksgiving can Paul give back to God because of the Thessalonians? Words would fail him to express *all the joy* he had because of them or through them.

But he continued to pray to God concerning their relationship. *Praying* renders *deomai*, which expresses a feeling of deep need, not merely a prayer of devotion (*proseuchomai*). *Night and day* shows how constantly he prayed (cf. 2:9). Even that was not enough. So he used the word *earnestly.* This translates *huperekperissou*, made up of *huper* (over, beyond), *ek* (out of), and *perrisou* (overflowing). His cup of prayer was filled to the brim and overflowed all the edges around. It appears in the New Testament only here and in 1 Thessalonians 5:13; Ephesians 3:20. Did Paul coin this word in an effort to express the impossible? Certainly he struggled for an expression too deep for words.

His prayer was that he might see his readers *face to face,* and that he might *supply what is lacking in your faith.* Supply means to put into unified and working condition (Bailey, p. 287). It is used for mending nets (cf. Matt. 4:21). But in the metaphorical sense, as here, it means to render complete. This thought is related to "lacking" or shortcomings, leftovers (Robertson; cf. Col. 1:24). Their faith needed strengthening and instruction. This pattern should be followed in dealing with all young Christians.

Paul concluded this discussion with a prayer to *our God and Father* and to *our Lord Jesus.* Note how "our Lord Jesus" and "our God and Father" are in such close relation. This is emphasized by the singular form of *direct* (to make a straight path). This plural subject with a singular verb makes God our Father and the Lord Jesus one, which stresses the lordship and deity of Jesus Christ. The early date for this letter shows how early the Christians accepted this concept without question. Morris (p. 69) notes that Paul would not have introduced a controversial question into a prayer. "Prayer is offered only to God; also, only One who was divine could be bracketed in this way with the Father." Compare 2 Thessalonians 2:16–17. So Paul prayed that God would make a straight path for him from Corinth to Thessalonica.

Furthermore, he prayed that *the Lord* (inclusive of Father and Son or referring to Christ as Lord, cf. Acts 2:36) would cause them to *increase and abound* (overflow, increase to overflowing) in Christian love to *one another* and to *all men.* This was Paul's attitude (*as we do to you*), and it should be theirs. Pagans might love each other. But Christian love should extend to all—Christian and non-Christian alike. This love is not natural to man; it is a gift of God's grace and transforming power. Hence Paul's prayer that it may be so.

In the Christian sense one does not need to agree with or even like someone in order to love him. Christian love, whose source is God, transcends all natural differences (cf. Rom. 5:8).

This to the end that the Lord *may establish* (support, make firm) *your hearts unblamable* (cf. Phil. 3:6) *in holiness. Holiness* refers to a state of dedication and sanctity or sanctification. Interpreters are not agreed as to whether sanctification is an instantaneous act or a process, a gradual development. Mullins (pp. 420 ff.) sees it as a "life process" beginning with regeneration and gradually developing or an "unfolding of the new life germ implanted in regeneration." Charles A. Trentham notes this position as "traditional theology."

However, he also notes that in a sense the believer is sanctified at the beginning of the Christian life.[6] W.T. Conner notes both positions, but sees the use of the term "sanctification" as largely referring to "a definite act at the beginning of the Christian life." Christians were called "saints" (1 Cor. 1:2) or "holy ones." The author sees sanctification as an instantaneous act at the beginning of the Christian life. But Christians should develop in the state of sanctification, not a process of becoming holy (*hagiōsunē*, not *hagiasmos*). It means the state of being regarded as holy by God. Substantives of this class (ending in *nē*) express a condition not necessarily true but which one (God) regards as true.

For instance, take *dikaiosunē*, righteousness (cf. Rom. 1:17). God is righteous in nature, and demands it in men. Since they cannot achieve it, God bestows it through Christ by grace through faith. A Christian is not perfectly righteous, but God regards him as such (justified before God) in Christ. In that state he should grow in righteous living.[7]

Likewise, *hagiōsunē* may be understood. By the indwelling Holy Spirit, God declares one who becomes a Christian as in a state of holiness, a saint, dedicated to God's service. Saints may be unsaintly, but they are "saints" (cf. 1 Cor. 1:2 and conditions described in that epistle). But God by grace chooses in Christ to regard them as in a state of *hagiōsunē*. In that state they are to grow and develop in holy living. This is seen in "in holiness" or in the state of being declared holy *before our God and Father*. In that state of being holy they grow until they become unblamable before God. This will be *at the coming* (see 2:19) *of our Lord Jesus with all his saints*, when the sanctified will be glorified.

---

6 "Sanctification," *Encyclopedia of Southern Baptists* (Nashville: Broadman, 1958), II, 1184.

7 On *dikaiosunē* see Joseph H. Thayer, pp. 149 ff.; Arndt and Gingrich, pp. 195 f.; *The Interpreter's Bible*, IX, 393 ff.; William Sanday, *Romans* ("The International Critical Commentary") (New York: Scribners, 1895), pp. 24-25.

In the New Testament "salvation" is used for regeneration, sanctification, and glorification. One is regenerated instantaneously. In that moment he is sanctified as he is indwelt by the Holy Spirit. He should grow in that state. At the Lord's return he will be glorified, including the bodily resurrection and the sum-total of rewards and glory in heaven. This is the full redemption mentioned in Ephesians 1:14. It is to this that Paul looked in 1 Thessalonians 3:13.

With all his saints. Some see the saints as angels who will accompany the Lord's return. In the Old Testament angels probably are called saints or the holy ones (Psalm 89:5; Dan. 4:13; 5:13). But the New Testament does not so denote them. It seems more likely that this refers to all the redeemed being associated with the Lord at his coming (cf. 4:16 f.).

V. *Practical Exhortations* (4:1–12)

A feature typical of Paul's epistles is that after the main body of thought he exhorted his readers on various matters. In this case he had finished the discussion of his own relation to the Thessalonians. Now he turned to the practical matters of their lives as Christians.

1. *Christian Example* (4:1–2)

1 Finally, brethren, we beseech and exhort you in the Lord Jesus, that as you learned from us how you ought to live and to please God, just as you are doing, you do so more and more. 2 For you know what instructions we gave you through the Lord Jesus.

Finally means "as for the rest." Bailey (p. 293) suggests "furthermore" since it comes so far from the end of the epistle. Paul was not introducing a conclusion, but was turning from his main point to other matters. *Brethren* adds a personal, tender note. He appealed to them as Christian brethren (cf. 1:4).

Beseech renders a word used in ancient Greek as a question. But Bailey notes that of 63 uses in the New Testament 45 percent carry the idea of a request or petition. In the papyri it is used for an urgent request. This seems to be the sense here. Added to Paul's request was an exhortation *in the Lord Jesus*. So his request was not only apostolic but in the Lord's name.

Learned (received alongside or from) refers to Paul's previous oral instruction. *Ought* expresses a moral and spiritual necessity. He had taught them how to live (walk) so as *to please God. Are doing* renders the same verb to walk, "just as you are walking." They should *do so more and more*. This renders a word for "more" preceded by the verb to abound or overflow. As Christians they were to continue living thus, to fill up and overflow in such a manner of life.

Verse 2 reads literally, "For you really know what instructions we gave to you through the Lord Jesus." Again Paul claimed divine authority. *Instructions* may also express charges (Acts 16:24), prohibitions (Acts 5:28), right living (1 Tim. 1:5). It was a military word found in Xenophon and Polybius. So Paul had charged them with respect to both negative and positive living. Simply to abstain from wrong is not enough. Christians should also do the right.

2. Moral Purity (4:3–8)

³ For this is the will of God, your sanctification: that you abstain from immorality; ⁴ that each one of you know how to take a wife for himself in holiness and honor, ⁵ not in the passion of lust like heathen who do not know God; ⁶ that no man transgress, and wrong his brother in this matter, because the Lord is an avenger in all these things, as we solemnly forewarned you. ⁷ For God has not called us for uncleanness, but in holiness. ⁸ Therefore whoever disregards this, disregards not man but God, who gives his Holy Spirit to you.

Paul now dealt with specifics. God's *will* is *your sanctification* (consecration). In Greek "will" is without the definite article, meaning that that which follows is not God's complete will but is contained in his will. Consecration (*hagiasmos*) is akin to holiness in 3:13 (which see). In the state of sanctification (3:13) God wills that Christians should grow in holiness and dedication to his will and way.

Robertson (p. 28) notes that the old Greek spelling of *hagizō, hagismos* was in the New Testament changed to *hagiazō, hagiasmos*. The former referred to dedication to a god or goddess with no thought of moral quality. The New Testament terms carry the idea of dedication to God's service, but also the added moral quality in keeping with God's nature.

The specific portion of God's will in mind deals with sex. So Paul urged them to *abstain from immorality. Immorality* refers to any kind of illicit sexual indulgence. Pagan religions regarded sexual freedom and promiscuous practice as natural and normal. Pagan gods and goddesses were grossly immoral; their worship involved the sex act, priestesses being provided for men who came to worship. Many Thessalonian Christians came out of paganism and still lived in that atmosphere. Christians should be sanctified to the opposite. That for Paul *hagiasmos* has taken on moral connotation is seen in that he contrasts it with *porneias*. The latter once stood for the sale of sex or prostitution. It came to be used at times interchangeably with *moicheia* (adultery). The original distinction is often preserved. Probably *porneias* here stands for prostitution, unless "to wrong a brother" (v. 6) implies the sin of adultery, sinning against a husband by taking his wife. God wills that each man *take a wife for himself in holiness* (holy living) *and honor*—monogamy. This in contrast to the *passion of lust like heathen who do not know God*. The verb "know" shows that they know gods but do not really know the true God. The rejection of God by many today is but a desire for sexual freedom.

That no man transgress, and wrong his brother in this matter. This apparently refers to the practice of one Christian either having sexual relations with another Christian's wife (husband) or divorce for the purpose of remarriage with such. Transgress means to go beyond. Wrong connotes to overreach, to take more. One should not go beyond Christian morality to take what belongs to another.

In vv. 3–6 the words abstain, know, take, transgress, and wrong are infinitives showing specific elements in God's will. These words are flaming swords guarding personal chastity and marriage, as much needed today as then. The Christian word *brother*, or course, does not open the gate of sexual laxness for non-Christians. Paul was simply dealing with Christian conduct here.

Because introduces a conclusion about these things. *Avenger* renders a word found in the papyri for a legal avenger. God occupies such a role. Sexual immorality is condemned throughout the Bible. Sexual freedom is forbidden by God, and carries its penalty both now and hereafter (cf. 1 Cor. 6:9).

Paul had warned against this in person, and repeated it now. Repeated warning was necessary. The "mysteries" of both Dionysus and Cabiri were in Thessalonica. So these believers were constantly exposed to their sexual abuses. They called men to do these things. But God called to consecration or holy dedication, not to *uncleanness* in illicit sexual living.

Verse 8 is a strong statement. Unclean living *disregards* (rejects) *not man but God*. While illicit sex is a sin against man, it is primarily against God *who gives his Holy Spirit to you*. The Christian's body is a temple of the Holy Spirit, and should not be joined to harlots (cf. 1 Cor. 6:13b ff.).

3. Brotherly Love (4:9–10a)

⁹ But concerning love of the brethren you have no need to have any one write to you, for you yourselves have been taught by God to love one another; ¹⁰ and indeed you do love all the brethren throughout Macedonia.

Paul felt that this thought was unnecessary except to commend and exhort to a growing expression of such love. *Love of the brethren* (*philadelphias*) is a combination of *philia* (warm, friendly love) and *adelphos* (brother), the root of which is *adelphus*, out of the same womb. *Philia*

and *agapē* are distinct words for love but are sometimes used interchangeably. Note *love* in this same verse. They had been "God-taught" to *love one another*. And they were doing this, not only in Thessalonica, but loved *all the brethren throughout Macedonia*. Paul needed only to *exhort* them *to do so more and more*, to do so until their love overflowed and continued to do so. What a challenge to all in Christian relationships!

4. Honest Endeavor (4:10b–12)

But we exhort you, brethren, to do so more and more, ¹¹ to aspire to live quietly, to mind your own affairs, and to work with your hands, as we charged you; ¹² so that you may command the respect of outsiders, and be dependent on nobody.

Paul continued his plea and exhortation. He had told them personally *to mind your own affairs*. Now he repeated it in writing. These exhortations are expressed in a series of present infinitives, to have the habit of doing certain things.

To aspire means to be fond of honor. Their ambition should be *to live quietly*. The verb means variously to be still, at peace, or silent. It is used of desisting from discussion (cf. Luke 14:4; Acts 11:18; 21:14) or to be silent. All of these meanings enrich the sense here. Evidently the church was restless and talkative about the second coming of Christ. And this disturbed the peace of the fellowship (cf. 2 Thess. 3:6 ff.).

To mind your own affairs—practice your own business or your own things. Nosy busybodies can disrupt the peace and quiet of any church (cf. 2 Thess. 3:11). *To work with your own hands.* Some had ceased working and had become gossiping troublemakers, thinking that the Lord's return was imminent. So why work? They were *to work* so as to *command the respect of outsiders* or non-Christians, and not to *be dependent* upon others for a livelihood. To do otherwise caused trouble in the church and brought scorn from their pagan neighbors. *Command the respect* means walk in a becoming manner, referring to one's manner of life.

The outside world watches the Christians. They should live above reproach in business, politics, and domestic and social life. At times the world scorns Christians without a reason. No believer should give it a legitimate reason to do so. Actually the world expects more of Christians than of non-Christians. No follower of Christ should live a life which denies his profession of faith in him.

VI. Problems Concerning the Lord's Return (4:13—5:11)

It would appear that in this section Paul was responding to a request brought by Timothy from the Christians in Thessalonica. Since Paul left, some believers had died. Some see this as evidence of an absence of Paul of a longer duration than a few weeks or months. However, one death would have been sufficient to raise the question. When Jesus returned, would the living go to him, leaving the dead behind? Paul assured them that both living and dead believers would share in the event. No mention is made of previous oral instruction about this, which may account for the problem.

1. Living and Dead (4:13–18)

13 But we would not have you ignorant, brethren, concerning those who are asleep, that you may not grieve as others do who have no hope. 14 For since we believe that Jesus died and rose again, even so, through Jesus, God will bring with him those who have fallen asleep. 15 For this we declare to you by the word of the Lord, that we who are alive, who are left until the coming of the Lord, shall not precede those who have fallen asleep. 16 For the Lord himself will descend from heaven with a cry of command, with the archangel's call, and with the sound of the trumpet of God. And the dead in Christ will rise first; 17 then we who are alive, who are left, shall be caught up together with them in the clouds to meet the Lord in the air; and so we shall always be with the Lord. 18 Therefore comfort one another with these words.

The negative *not* comes first in the sentence, so is emphatic. *Would* means will. He did not will or wish them to be *ignorant*

or without knowledge. *Concerning* means about. *Those who are asleep* are the ones sleeping. *Asleep* renders a present participle (*koimōmenōn*, note "cemetery"). The present tense means those who from time to time fall asleep, not a permanent sleeping.

The figure of sleep does not mean soul-sleeping or unconscious existence until the resurrection. It was a Greek and Roman term for death; they had no hope of the resurrection. Jesus used this term for death (John 11:11). Paul used it repeatedly in this sense (i.e., 1 Cor. 7:39; 15:6; 1 Thess. 4:13,15). Note that in John 11:11–12 it is used of death and of natural sleep. In the sense of death it suggests cessation of life's troubles, a rest from such. Bailey (pp. 301 f.) adds the expectation of the Lord's return as one sleeps expecting the new day.

Not grieve as others do who have no hope. There is always a sadness at parting. But for the Christian it is one of loneliness, not of despair for both the living and the dead. For he has the hope of the resurrection and reunion. "Others" refers to pagans (cf. 4:12, outsiders). Some pagan orators expressed hope for the future life. But as a whole they had no hope, as seen in their literature and inscriptions. Morris (p. 84 f.) cites from Frame two letters of the second century, one pagan and another Christian, which contrast the pagan hopelessness and the Christian assurance.

For since in Greek introduces a conditional statement assumed to be true. They shared with Paul, Silvanus, and Timothy a firm faith in Jesus' death and resurrection. *Even so* points forward to their faith in their own resurrection. The Greek text reads literally "God the ones sleeping through Jesus will bring with him." *Through Jesus* is amphibolous. It could mean those sleeping in Jesus, or God through Jesus will bring them with him at his return. Of course, Paul was talking only about Christians. But the RSV seems to be correct. Christians who sleep God through Jesus will bring with him (cf. 1 Cor. 15:20).

So God will bring them with Jesus at his return. This means that they are with him now, not lying in a lonely tomb.

A problem arises as one compares this idea with "the dead in Christ shall rise first" (v. 16). The body of flesh is in the grave. But Paul in 1 Corinthians 15:48 ff. shows the necessity of a heavenly body. Certainly he did not look forward to a disembodied state between his death and resurrection (see 2 Cor. 5:1–4). It is difficult to deal with all related passages in this context. But two things are clear. The Christian dead are with Christ now. At the Lord's return, they will be raised bodily with a spirit-controlled body (see 1 Cor. 15:42–44) infinitely more glorious than that which was planted in the bosom of the earth.

By the word of the Lord. There is no direct recorded saying to this effect (cf. Matt. 24:31). Was it some well known but unrecorded saying? Perhaps not. It was not something that Paul deduced. Most likely it was either the general tenor of Jesus' teachings or a direct revelation to Paul (cf. 1 Cor. 11:23). The latter seems to be the case.

We who are alive . . . until the coming (parousia) of the Lord. Did Paul expect to live until that time? Compare 1 Corinthians 15:51. But in 2 Corinthians 5:1 ff. he suggested the possibility as otherwise. Jesus had told his people to expect his return at any moment. Some generation would be alive then. Paul's was the only living generation at the time he wrote. So he held out the possibility that he would be alive, but also that he might not be. But he did not err about the matter. His should be the attitude of every Christian.

Shall not precede those who have fallen asleep. Precede is a better rendering than "prevent" (KJV). But even prevent once meant to come before. The Greek word means to come before, precede. The verb is preceded by a strong double negative, so is emphatic: "in no wise shall precede." So the fear of leaving dead loved ones behind was an empty one.

What then is the order? First, *the Lord himself will descend from heaven.* In the Greek text this comes at the end of the statement; so, climactic. *A cry of command.* This renders a word from the verb *keleuō,* to order or command, a military word used only here in the New Testament. But the verb is used 27 times as to command or give commandment. Moffatt (p. 38) sees this command as to muster the saints. *Archangel's call* (voice of an archangel). No definite article is used with either call or archangel. Michael is the only archangel mentioned by name in the New Testament (Jude 9). Moffatt (p. 38) sees this archangel as Michael, who according to Jewish tradition not only mustered the saints but also sounded a trumpet to herald God's approach for judgment. *Trumpet of God—* like the blowing of a trumpet. Paul was writing in eschatological language to picture the grandeur of the Lord's return. He will return in triumph and great glory. The fact that command, call, and trumpet are each preceded by *en* (in) shows that these will come in sequence.

Phillips' translation catches the picture. "One word of command, one shout from the Archangel, one blast from the trumpet of God and God in person will come down from heaven!" No other New Testament passage exceeds this in describing the Lord's return.

Second, *the dead in Christ will rise first. First* does not refer to one resurrection followed later by another. It means that the Christian dead will rise before the living will leave the earth. They definitely will share in the Parousia along with the living. Paul was not dealing with the unrighteous dead. But Jesus mentions the dead, righteous and unrighteous, in the same context (cf. John 5:24–25,28–29). Details are not given. Some will disagree, but the writer sees one resurrection and one judgment. Revelation 20:5 has a disputed meaning.

Paul here said nothing about the type of resurrection bodies (see 1 Cor. 15:35–37). Also note Jesus' resurrection body—

a real, recognizable body but not subject to the degrees of time, space, and density. This is a suggestion, but must not be pressed. Paul's point is that the dead believers will share in the Parousia with the living.

Third, *then we who are alive* (we the living ones). The Thessalonians feared that their dead loved ones would be left behind. Paul says that the living are the ones remaining. This verb may also mean the ones surviving death. They *together with them—shall be caught up . . . in the clouds to meet the Lord in the air*. It will be a simultaneous thing. The Greek reads *hama sun autois. Hama* denotes the coincidence of two actions (Arndt and Gingrich). This emphasizes *sun autois*, with them—so "together with them."

In the clouds . . . in the air. The majesty of the setting is seen in "in the clouds" (cf. Matt. 24:30; 26:64; Acts 1:9-11; Rev. 1:7). Moffatt (p. 38) says that in the clouds is "the ordinary method of sudden rapture or ascension to heaven." Since the air was regarded as the abode of "the prince of the power of the air," Satan (cf. Eph. 2:2), does meeting the saints in the air suggest the Lord's complete triumph over Satan? Morris (p. 89) calls in the air the meeting place. But he suggests on the basis of 1 Corinthians 6:2 that "the Lord proceeds to the earth with his people." However, this is an uncertain interpretation. For the saints to judge the world does not necessarily mean that they must be on the earth. The overall teachings of the New Testament suggest otherwise.

Paul simply says that *we shall always be with the Lord*. And this implies heaven, not the earth. A comforting note for the Christian bereaved is seen in "together with them . . . with the Lord." Certainly the Thessalonian Christians and all other believers can *comfort one another with these words*.

2. Times and Seasons (5:1-3)

¹ But as to the times and the seasons, brethren, you have no need to have anything written

to you. ² For you yourselves know well that the day of the Lord will come like a thief in the night. ³ When people say, "There is peace and security," then sudden destruction will come upon them as travail comes upon a woman with child, and there will be no escape.

Having stated the fact of the Lord's return, he said that it was not necessary to write of *the times and the seasons*. Apparently he had said nothing about this while in Thessalonica. Later he dealt with this somewhat (2 Thess. 2:1 ff.). But that was after the Thessalonians had disregarded his words in his first epistle.

Specifically *times* (*chronos*) referred to an extended period, and *seasons* (*kairos*) connoted a definite space of time (Robertson). In Acts 1:7 Jesus used these words without definite articles as used in 1 Thessalonians 5:1. It may be contended that Jesus spoke in Aramaic. Even if this be true, one may be certain that Luke has recorded in Greek the sense of Jesus' words. In Acts 1:7 Robertson notes the probable meaning as "points" and "periods" or the fine details with regard to the end of the age. Jesus said that these things "the Father has fixed by his own authority" (Acts 1:7). It is God's responsibility and should not overly concern his people. They are to prepare conditions for Jesus' return, not try to map out God's plans (cf. Matt. 24:14). Jesus never spoke of his return in terms of time but condition (cf. when [*hotan*] Matt. 25:31). *Hotan* refers primarily to condition. When the condition is right, that is the time (cf. Matt. 24:28).

Know well renders *akribōs oidate. Akribōs* may be rendered well, accurately, or perfectly. With *oidate* it suggests that if they would think through the matter, they would understand fully that one cannot foretell "the times and the seasons." For *the day of the Lord will come like a thief in the night,* or as a thief at night. This does not mean a secret coming before an open appearance. It means that as a thief comes unexpectedly, so will be the day of the Lord (cf. Matt. 24:43; Luke 12:39; 2 Peter 3:10). Paul may have given them

Jesus' words on this. If so, they knew well or accurately. No one will know in advance.

Peace and safety refers to a false sense of security, evidently on the part of pagans (cf. Ezek. 13:10; Matt. 24:37–39). *Sudden destruction*—not annihilation, but eternal separation from God on the part of the lost. It will come suddenly upon pagans and Christians alike, but only the former will be surprised and separated. Christians will be looking for it and will welcome it. As *travail* cannot be prevented or delayed, so this. *No escape.* In Greek there is a strong double negative. They most certainly will not flee out or escape. Christ's return will be known to all. Pagans will suffer judgment. Christians will receive vindication and bliss.

3. Children of Light (5:4–11)

⁴ But you are not in darkness, brethren, for that day to surprise you like a thief. ⁵ For you are all sons of light and sons of the day; we are not of the night or of darkness. ⁶ So then let us not sleep, as others do, but let us keep awake and be sober. ⁷ For those who sleep sleep at night, and those who get drunk are drunk at night. ⁸ But, since we belong to the day, let us be sober, and put on the breastplate of faith and love, and for a helmet the hope of salvation. ⁹ For God has not destined us for wrath, but to obtain salvation through our Lord Jesus Christ, ¹⁰ who died for us so that whether we wake or sleep we might live with him. ¹¹ Therefore encourage one another and build one another up, just as you are doing.

Not in darkness. Christians should not be surprised at the Lord's return. They are *sons of light . . . day . . . not of the night or of darkness.* As such they will not be separated from the Lord at his coming. But they should not *sleep* or have the habit of sleeping, but should have the habit of keeping *awake* and *sober.* All verbs in v. 7 are present active subjunctives, exhorting to a habitual practice. Awake means to be on guard. Sober means to be sober-minded or calm. Sleep and getting drunk are characteristic of night. Those of the day should be sober and *put on the breastplate.* They should be as a sentry (watch,

v. 6) protected by *faith* and *love* with a *helmet the hope of salvation.* In 1:3 the three graces (faith, hope, love) were qualities producing growth. In 5:8 they are for protection. Faith and love are a unit. Where faith goes love follows (Moffatt). Love of the brethren is one proof of genuine faith and its work (cf. 1 John 3:14). The breastplate protected vital organs of the body. The helmet protected the head, the coordinating center of the body. Faith in Christ produced both hope and love.

In Ephesians 6:10 ff. the soldier's armor was for conflict with evil. Here it is for guard duty as they awaited the Lord's return.

Christians are not *destined* for *wrath* (cf. 1:10) but to *obtain salvation* (cf. 2 Thess. 2:14) through Christ. At his return they, having been regenerated and sanctified, will be glorified. His atoning death avails for all believers, whether they *wake or sleep,* are alive or have previously died at his coming. The divine purpose is that *we might live with him.* The Greek text reads *hama sun autōi zēsōmen,* live together with him (cf. Rom. 6:4b–11).

Therefore refers back to the previous verses and introduces a conclusion. Verse 11 is similar to 4:18 but adds *build . . . up.* Such assurance will not only *encourage* (comfort; same verb in 4:18) but build up one another's faith, hope, and love—make strong Christians. They were already doing this, but should continue.

VII. General Matters (5:12–22)

¹² But we beseech you, brethren, to respect those who labor among you and are over you in the Lord and admonish you, ¹³ and to esteem them very highly in love because of their work. Be at peace among yourselves. ¹⁴ And we exhort you, brethren, admonish the idle, encourage the fainthearted, help the weak, be patient with them all. ¹⁵ See that none of you repays evil for evil, but always seek to do good to one another and to all. ¹⁶ Rejoice always, ¹⁷ pray constantly, ¹⁸ give thanks in all circumstances; for this is the will of God in Christ Jesus for you. ¹⁹ Do not quench the Spirit, ²⁰ do not despise prophesying, ²¹ but test everything;

hold fast what is good, 22 abstain from every form of evil.

Into his closing remarks Paul crammed a world of ideas. Apparently those who had been disturbed about the second coming were also unruly and/or weak, given to evil perhaps to escape persecution. It is a sad thing when outside enemies disrupt the fellowship within a church. So Paul, like a fighter or general, waded into the problem with blow after blow. He first begged and then commanded. Verses 13b–22 contain 15 imperatives.

To respect means to know (*eidenai* from *oida*, cf. 1:4). This means more than to know them as persons. Paul's thought is to have regard and understanding for those who labored unto weariness among them and who were *over* them or stood before them as leaders. While not using the terms bishop, pastor, or elder, he referred to those who occupied such a place (cf. Heb. 13:17). Some see this absence of titles as evidence of a primitive church organization, but it is not necessarily the case. *Admonish* means, literally, to put sense into them. Certainly some needed this. They were *to esteem* their leaders, hold them in high honor, and in *love because of their work.* The office should be honored even if they did not like the officeholder. Love included loyalty to its object.

Then Paul began his imperatives (v. 13b). *Be at peace.* No congregational strife should exist. Then Paul made an appeal or exhortation, followed by imperatives. *Admonish,* put sense into, *the idle* or those who had broken ranks. *Encourage* the *fainthearted* or little-souled who were tempted to quit. Three groups seem to be reflected here: (1) those who had quit work, talking only of the Lord's return; (2) those who had lost heart because some had died before that event; and (3) those who were morally weak, possibly converts from paganism. *Help* or support *the weak,* those tempted to immorality. *Be patient.* Such was needed in dealing with the unruly and weak. *See* that none pays back *evil for evil,* or no retaliation. This could apply to their relations with one another as Christians and also to their relations to outsiders, even those who were persecuting them. A follower of Christ should guard himself against a vindictive spirit. Jesus taught that his people should pray for those who abuse them and do good to such. No Christian should sink to the level of or even beneath those who do him evil. In the spirit of Christ he should rise above such. Only thus may he lift them to his level of Christian conduct.

Seek or chase after *good* to *one another* and *to all,* even to pagans. *Rejoice. Pray* without leaving off from such. *Give thanks* regardless of circumstances, even under hardships. Such is God's will. *Do not quench* the Holy Spirit, put out his fire, or despise his gifts for ministry (cf. v. 20). In v. 14 Paul had sought to calm down the wild enthusiasm of the idle troublemakers. But he did not want his readers to oppose the authentic work of the Holy Spirit. *Do not despise* or count as nothing *prophesying* or speaking forth (preaching) for God. *Test* or prove all things (cf. 1 Cor. 12:8–10; 14:29) to prevent error in teaching or practice. Verses 18–22 comprise a whole. Those who were caught up in the idea of the Lord's return evidently claimed a spirituality above that connected with preaching or prophesying. Paul wanted his readers to have fervor but also common sense. He exhorted them to "prove by testing" what is the true leading of the Holy Spirit. They were to have a true spirituality rather than a mere frothy enthusiasm. *Hold fast* the good or beautiful and noble in conduct. *Abstain,* hold away from, *evil* of any kind.

Pastors would do well to preach a series of sermons including each of these imperatives. They should seek to show that Paul is calling for true spirituality as seen in prophetic, inspired preaching as over against wild, proud, and meaningless claims to spirituality. Churches obeying Paul's commands will be happy, peaceful, effective churches.

VIII. *Conclusion* (5:23–28)

23 May the God of peace himself sanctify you wholly; and may your spirit and soul and body be kept sound and blameless at the coming of our Lord Jesus Christ. 24 He who calls you is faithful, and he will do it.

25 Brethren, pray for us.

26 Greet all the brethren with a holy kiss.

27 I adjure you by the Lord that this letter be read to all the brethren.

28 The grace of our Lord Jesus Christ be with you.

Paul prayed for his readers that *the God of peace* (peace in his nature and giving peace) would *sanctify* them *wholly* or set them apart from profane things and for divine service, and that this be done wholly or for all. That they *be kept sound* or kept in all parts—*spirit, soul,* and *body blameless* at the return of the Lord.

Did Paul here teach personal trichotomy as opposed to dichotomy as in other epistles? Robertson says, "Not necessarily." Moffatt (p. 38) sees this combination as untechnical. Erdman (p. 71) sees this not as "giving a scientific and technical division of the component parts of human nature . . . the reference is to the one indivisible personality, in its Godward relations, in its natural activities, and in its uses of the body." Morris agrees with this: "Paul is not here concerned to give a theoretical analysis of the nature of man, but is uttering a fervent prayer that the entire man may be preserved. Milligan thinks that the threefold petition is meant for 'man's whole being, whether its immortal, its personal, or its bodily side'" (p. 107). The fact is that man is a highly complex being. Aspects of his nature may be distinguished, but he cannot be divided up into parts. Man does not sin in either body or spirit irrespective of the other. The whole man is affected by sin, and the whole man is to be affected by salvation

(see 1 Cor. 6:19–20; "and in your spirit, which are God's," KJV, but not in the best manuscripts). Jesus came to save or make sound the whole man (John 7:23). "Spirit" precedes "soul" and "body." All men have a soul and a body—really, each person is both body and soul. The Christian is spiritual in both. His spirit indwells his body (*sōma*). The Holy Spirit indwells the Christian's spirit, thus permeating the whole of his life and soul or *psuchē*.

That to which God has called, he is *faithful* (trustworthy; cf. 2 Thess. 3:3) to perform. The Thessalonians can trust themselves to him.

Paul concluded the epistle with brief, pithy words. *Brethren, pray for us.* He used on imperative as a plea for them to keep on surrounding him with prayer, something he needed in Corinth and elsewhere. Billy Graham attributes the power of his work to the prayers of Christian people over the world. *Greet all the brethren with a holy kiss* (cf. 1 Cor. 16:20; 2 Cor. 13:12; Rom. 16:16)—a token of brotherly love, so it was holy. Many ancients greeted with a kiss on various parts of the body (cf. Luke 7:45; 22:48); Christians did so probably on the cheek (cf. 1 Peter 5:14). Little is known of the details of this practice. But probably men kissed men and women kissed women.

I adjure you by the Lord. This was a form of putting one on oath. Paul wanted this epistle read aloud to the entire church. This shows the importance that he attached to all his epistles.

The grace of our Lord Jesus Christ be with you. This is a fitting benediction, and richer than the customary "Farewell." Paul varied this in different epistles. He ended the epistle as he began it with grace (1:1; 5:28). This was one of Paul's great words, grace in redemption and in living.

Commentary on 2 Thessalonians

I. Signature and Address (1:1–2)

¹ Paul, Silvanus, and Timothy,
To the church of the Thessalonians in God our Father and the Lord Jesus Christ:
² Grace to you and peace from God the Father and the Lord Jesus Christ.

This salutation is the same as in 1 Thessalonians 1:1 except that here Paul added *our* before Father. He also used a longer statement in ascribing *grace* and *peace*. It is *from God the Father and the Lord Jesus Christ*. This phrase is found in some manuscripts of 1 Thessalonians 1:1 but is not genuine. Grace and peace appear in all other of Paul's epistles (but see Col. 1:2; "mercy" is added in 1 and 2 Tim.). "God our Father" and "Lord Jesus Christ" are equal but not identical; they are separate persons in the Godhead.

II. Present Situation in Thessalonica (1:3–12)

1. Paul's Thanksgiving (1:3–4)

³ We are bound to give thanks to God always for you, brethren, as is fitting, because your faith is growing abundantly, and the love of every one of you for one another is increasing. ⁴ Therefore we ourselves boast of you in the churches of God for your steadfastness and faith in all your persecutions and in the afflictions which you are enduring.

Paul usually began his epistles with a note of thanksgiving (but see Gal. and Titus). He had problems in Thessalonica, but in both epistles he began with thanksgiving for the believers there. In a sense he used good psychology, complimenting them before correcting them.

Bound renders a verb stating obligation. Perhaps some in Thessalonica had disclaimed any right to Paul's thanks in the first epistle. He insisted that there was much for which he was thankful. *Give thanks* (see comment on 1 Thess. 1:2). *Bound . . . fitting*—the former expresses obligation to God; the latter a proper attitude toward his readers.

In 1 Thessalonians Paul prayed for growth in faith, love, and hope (1:3). Now he thanked God that the Thessalonians had achieved this. In 2 Thessalonians he did not mention hope with *steadfastness,* but it is seen in 1:10.

Faith is growing abundantly (present tense of continuous action). It is like a tree growing beyond measure. Each one's *love* for others was *increasing,* flourishing as a tree. This is another present tense (cf. 1 Thess. 3:12).

Boast renders a present infinitive. As they kept on growing in faith and bearing abundant fruit in love, Paul kept on boasting about them in other *churches of God.* His boast was for their steadfastness (cf. 1 Thess. 1:3) and faith. Regardless of their trials, *persecutions* and *afflictions,* their faith was more than equal to them. "Persecutions" (*diōgmois*) is added to "afflictions" (1:6). *Diōgmos* was used only of religious persecution (Arndt and Gingrich; cf. Rom. 8:35; 2 Cor. 12:10; 2 Tim.

3:11). *Are enduring* means to be entangled in or to be held in (cf. Gal. 5:1, "submit"). It is a present tense, constantly are enduring. There had been no let up.

2. God's Judgment (1:5–10)

⁵ This is evidence of the righteous judgment of God, that you may be made worthy of the kingdom of God, for which you are suffering —⁶ since indeed God deems it just to repay with affliction those who afflict you, ⁷ and to grant rest with us to you who are afflicted, when the Lord Jesus is revealed from heaven with his mighty angels in flaming fire, ⁸ inflicting vengeance upon those who do not know God and upon those who do not obey the gospel of our Lord Jesus. ⁹ They shall suffer the punishment of eternal destruction and exclusion from the presence of the Lord and from the glory of his might, ¹⁰ when he comes on that day to be glorified in his saints, and to be marveled at in all who have believed, because our testimony to you was believed.

Paul pointed from the present to the future when present situations would be reversed insofar as the Christians and their persecutors were concerned.

Evidence renders *endeigma,* found only here in the New Testament. It means "proof." Without the definite article it means "an evidence." *Righteous judgment of God.* The Bible speaks of God's judgment within the context of history. But here it probably refers to the final judgment at the end of history. It will be righteous in accord with God's nature and wisdom. And it will be in keeping with the evidence or proof as found in the individual's life on earth and the subsequent results of that life in the lives of others.

Both the saved and unsaved will be judged (cf. Rom. 14:10; 2 Cor. 5:10; Rev. 20:11 ff.). This judgment will not be to decide whether one is saved or lost. That will have been determined beforehand (cf. John 3:18). Matthew 25:31–46 does see all men standing before the judgment seat of Christ with the separation of the "sheep" from the "goats." But this separation is the imitation of a condition already determined before death. It is based on their attitude toward Christ and whether he knows them or does not know them. The point is that men are not saved in heaven at last. They are either saved or lost determined by their relation to Christ at the time of death. The final judgment will make manifest this state one way or the other. The final judgment also relates to degrees of reward and punishment in heaven or hell. Deeds good and bad will be judged by the sum total of their fruits. All the evidence will be there. Small deeds done in Christ's name will bear great reward. Even so-called little sins will bear dire fruit in the judgment.

God's righteous judgment is seen with respect to both the persecuted and the persecutors. As for the former it is in their trials; for the believers it will be *that [eis] you may be made worthy of the kingdom of God. Eis* points to God's purpose in their trials. He did not cause them, but uses them to develop his people. "Be made worthy" renders *kataxioō, axioō* with *kata,* which intensifies its meaning (see 1 Thess. 2:12). The verb also carries the idea of a weight. The Thessalonians' Christian character is being made so as to balance off the kingdom of God. Thus they will become fit subjects for heaven. It is *for* (on behalf of) the kingdom that they *are suffering.* And they will be rewarded in the kingdom's final consummation.

Parenthetically Paul noted the other side of God's *righteous judgment, to repay with affliction those who afflict you.* Repay means recompense (cf. 1 Thess. 3:9). God will pay back in kind what the persecutors have given his people. In Greek there is a play on words. Literally, "to the ones afflicting you affliction." God's people may be in affliction now, but at the final judgment the ones afflicting them on earth will be in affliction. Some see v. 6 as the *lex talionis,* the law of retaliation, and so un-Christian. They regard it as perhaps a Jewish addition. But this is an untenable position. This punishment has to do with God's judgment rather than man's.

Resuming his main thought Paul says, *to grant rest with us to you who are afflicted.* This is another of God's purposes in their sufferings. Rest renders *anesin,* or ease. Along with Paul they may suffer now, but in the judgment all will have their pain eased (cf. Rev. 21:4).

This will be *when the Lord Jesus is revealed from heaven. Revealed* translates *tēi apokalupsei,* the unveiling or the apocalypse. Note that the book of Revelation is called in Greek *Apocalupsis.* The Greek text is literally, in (in the sphere of) the revelation. So the divine easing and retribution will not only take place when Christ returns but *in* his returning or as a part of the revelation: of blessing to his own and punishment to those who reject him. Of course, prior to the Lord's return, all suffering for the Christian ends at death.

In flaming fire. Gramatically this could go either with what precedes or with that which follows: *inflicting vengeance.* But it probably belongs with the former. It describes the glory and majesty of Christ's revelation. Literally, "in the revealing of the Lord Jesus from heaven with his mighty angels in flaming fire."

From the Lord's appearance Paul turned to his activity. It involves, first, the unsaved and, then, the saved. Inflicting vengeance literally means giving vengeance. It is a work of God only (cf. Deut. 32:35; Rom. 12:19; Heb. 10:30). That Paul pictures the Lord Jesus in this role attests to his essential deity.

Who do not know God. "Know" renders a perfect participle of *oida* (cf. 1 Thess. 1:4). This involves both Jews and Gentiles (cf. Rom. 1:16–31). They may know about God or gods, but they do not really know God. The perfect tense notes that at the point in time specified they were in a state of not knowing God. *Who do not obey the gospel.* This letter contains a Hebraistic flavor. So this may be a parallel to the previous thought. They do not really know God because they have rejected the gospel by which both Jew and Gentile may be saved (cf. Rom. 1:16). *Obey* renders a verb *hupakouō,* intensive form of *akouō.*

It means to hear under, and so to "obey."

Suffer . . . punishment means to pay a just penalty. It will not be an arbitrarily vindictive punishment but one in keeping with the sin of rejecting God and his good news of salvation in Jesus Christ. This penalty will be *eternal destruction.* Robertson (p. 44) notes that this phrase appears only here in the New Testament, but is found in IV Maccabees 10:15 of the eternal destruction of Antiochus Epiphanes.[1] Destruction does not mean annihilation but eternal separation from God (cf. 1 Thess. 5:3), as seen in *exclusion:* literally, "eternal destruction away from the face of the Lord and away from the glory of his might." Eternal separation from God is the second death, hell itself (cf. Rev. 20:14*b*).

From this awful thought Paul turned to the destiny of the saved. *When* (*hotan*) refers to condition primarily and not time. The time is when the condition is right (cf. Matt. 24:28). A. T. Robertson (p. 44) calls this a "future and indefinite temporal clause coincident with *en tēi apokalupsei* in v. 7." [2] *To be glorified in his saints.* His saints are the sphere in which Christ will find his glory at his revealing (cf. 1:7). Christ's highest glory is in his redemptive work (cf. Phil. 2:6–11). The Greek infinitive translated *to be glorified* is followed by *en tois hagios,* meaning in the sphere of the saints. Morris (p. 120) comments on this: "The saints will be, as it were, a mirror reflecting something of the greatness of the glory of their Lord (cf. 1 Jn. 3:2, 'when he shall appear, we shall be like him')." [3]

To be marveled at. Those who have believed in Christ will view Christ's glory. It will be so far beyond their expectations that they will be caught up in wonder and

---

[1] Antiochus Epiphanes (175–164 B.C.) persecuted the Jews terribly, trying to force them to renounce their faith for Greek religious customs.

[2] Cf. *A Grammar of the Greek New Testament in the Light of Historical Research* (New York: Doran, 1923), pp. 971 ff.

[3] Cf. John Lineberry, *Vital Word Studies in II Thessalonians* (Grand Rapids: Zondervan, 1961), pp. 30 f; also Erdman, p. 85.

admiration, lost in amazement. Phillips renders it, "It will be a breath-taking wonder." Christians will have *believed* in Christ. But the reality of him will show how he even exceeds their faith. No wonder that the believer's eyes, ears, and heart cannot begin to conceive the glory of heaven (cf. 1 Cor. 2:9)!

3. Paul's Prayer (1:11-12)

¹¹ To this end we always pray for you, that our God may make you worthy of his call, and may fulfil every good resolve and work of faith by his power, ¹² so that the name of our Lord Jesus may be glorified in you, and you in him, according to the grace of our God and the Lord Jesus Christ.

To this end refers back to vv. 5-10. Having set forth the fact of judgment, which will be one of reward and glory for the Christians, he prayed that this would be accomplished in his readers. The present tense of *pray* plus *always* adds to the constancy of prayer by Paul and his associates. He means, "We keep on praying always for you." They encircled them in constant prayer.

That our God may make you worthy of his call. Make worthy carries the idea of scales or balances. Their Christian lives should be as heavy as their call from God. This does not imply the possibility of the call being revoked. But having been called, they should show it in their lives.

Call refers to God's election or choice of the Thessalonian Christians (cf. 1 Thess. 1:4). "Call" in this sense is inclusive of the Christian life from its inception to its climax in heaven (cf. Rom. 11:29; 1 Cor. 1:26; Phil. 3:14).

Every good resolve may read "every good desire" or "desire of goodness." The KJV inserts "his" before "goodness" as though it was God's goodness. This word does not occur in the Greek text. It is coupled with *word of faith.* Both are related to the Christian, his resolve toward good and work inspired by faith. *By his power* translates in power or divine power. So Paul prayed that the aspirations and efforts of

his readers would in the Holy Spirit's power reach fruition.

Paul's prayer was to the end that *the name of our Lord Jesus may be glorified in you, and you in him. Name* stood for one's entire person, so here of the Lord Jesus. As Christians are glorified in Christ, so he is glorified in them (cf. Rom. 8:17).

According to the grace of our God and the Lord Jesus Christ. This grace is extended to all, but is effective only in believers in Christ. In the Greek text there is only one definite article with "God" and "Lord." Thus the syntax makes them one. Both are qualified by "Jesus Christ" (cf. Titus 2:13; 2 Peter 1:1).

Robertson (p. 46) so regards this.[4] But he notes that sometimes "Lord" is used without the article as a proper name: "So it has to be admitted that here Paul may mean 'according to the grace of our God and the Lord Jesus Christ,' though he may also mean 'according to the grace of our God and Lord, Jesus Christ.'" The writer prefers the reading "our God and Lord, Jesus Christ." But either links together in unity the distinct manifestations of the Godhead. The New Testament definitely teaches the full deity of Jesus Christ (cf. John 1:1,14; 10:30-33; Col. 2:9).

III. Problems of the Parousia (2:1-12)

This chapter contains the main purpose of the epistle. Paul had dealt somewhat with this matter in the first epistle (4:13—5:11). But since the problem persisted, he treated it more fully. William Barclay (p. 245) calls this "undoubtedly one of the most difficult passages in the whole New Testament; and it is so because it is using terms and thinking which were perfectly familiar to those to whom Paul was speaking but which are utterly strange to us. To those who read and heard it for the first time, it required no explanation at all; but to us, who have not their local knowledge, it is obscure."

Erdman (p. 88) notes the need for this

---

4 Cf. Lineberry, pp. 85 f.; Morris, p. 123.

passage today "as a test and corrective of much popular teaching concerning the Advent of Christ." [5] It should be noted that Paul used eschatological language which must be interpreted carefully. One must seek to discern the meaning behind his words.

1. Matters of Time (2:1–2)

[1] Now concerning the coming of our Lord Jesus Christ and our assembling to meet him, we beg you, brethren, [2] not to be quickly shaken in mind or excited, either by spirit or by word, or by letter purporting to be from us, to the effect that the day of the Lord has come.

We beg you is the first word in the Greek text (cf. 1 Thess. 4:1; 5:12). This shows how vital was this matter. *Concerning* basically means "on behalf of." But here it carries the idea of "in the interest of truth concerning" (Morris, p. 124). *Coming* is *parousias,* the presence *of our Lord Jesus Christ.* Mistaken ideas were abroad about this, so Paul was endeavoring to correct them.

Assembling renders *episunagōgēs* (cf. Heb. 10:25, gathering for Christian worship). Note the word "synagogue" in it. It was a gathering together, akin to *ekklēsia,* translated assembly or church (cf. 1:1). *To meet him,* in the Greek text, reads *ep' auton,* unto him. Paul had dealt with this idea in 1 Thessalonians 4:13–17. Now he touched upon other matters about the second coming.

Paul begged them *not to be quickly shaken in mind or excited.* Shaken means to agitate, to cause to totter like a reed. Morris notes the idea of the sea being tossed as by wind and wave. *Mind* refers to the mental aspect of a person. Paul did not want them to become mentally shaken or unbalanced over the Lord's return. *Shaken* refers to the initial shock; *excited* means a continuing state of agitation.

Three things could cause this: *spirit,*

5 Cf. Morris, p. 147; Bailey, p. 337; Lineberry, pp. 83 f.

word, and *letter,* one purported "to be from us" or as if through us. Some see "as through us" as related to all three items. More likely it refers only to letter. *Spirit* could be someone claiming a new revelation. *Word* probably refers to a reported private conversation with Paul (Lightfoot). *Letter* evidently is a forged letter purported to be from Paul.

The thing involved was the claim that *the day of the Lord has come.* "Has come" renders a perfect form of *enistēmi,* to place in, but could mean to stand in, at, or near. Some see it to mean "at hand" (KJV). Paul would hardly have denied this fact (cf. Rom. 13:12; Phil. 4:5). This perfect tense may be regarded as a present: has drawn near and is here or present. If this were the case then, what about Paul's words in his previous epistle? It meant that they and their dead loved ones had missed the Parousia. It is no wonder that the Thessalonians were shaken and troubled, or that Paul resented the forged letter and other false reports.

Christians can become shaken in mind and become as a restless sea, perhaps over this subject more than any other. For this reason Jesus warned against false signs of his coming (cf. Matt. 24:4–8).

2. Man of Lawlessness (2:3–10a)

[3] Let no one deceive you in any way; for that day will not come, unless the rebellion comes first, and the man of lawlessness is revealed, the son of perdition, [4] who opposes and exalts himself against every so-called god or object of worship, so that he takes his seat in the temple of God, proclaiming himself to be God. [5] Do you not remember that when I was still with you I told you this? [6] And you know what is restraining him now so that he may be revealed in his time. [7] For the mystery of lawlessness is already at work; only he who now restrains it will do so until he is out of the way. [8] And then the lawless one will be revealed, and the Lord Jesus will slay him with the breath of his mouth and destroy him by his appearing and his coming. [9] The coming of the lawless one by the activity of Satan will be with all power and with pretended signs and wonders, [10] and with all wicked deception for those who are to perish,

One should approach this passage humbly and with an admission of a lack of understanding. Doubtless Paul's language was understood by his readers. But the key to its full comprehension has been lost to modern people. In God's own time it may be disclosed. Or it may be evident as this passage is fulfilled. Man's natural curiosity will lead him ever to speculate. But it should be recognized as such.

However, that is no reason why men should not study this passage reverently, bringing prayer and all of their knowledge to bear upon it. The present purpose is to examine it in order to point out relevant truths.

Deceive you in any way. This includes items in v. 2 or any other effort to lead the Thessalonians astray. There have been many through the centuries (cf. Matt. 24:4 ff.). *Deceive* means to delude, deceive thoroughly, or to beguile. It is a different word from that used by Jesus in Matthew 24:4 (*planaō;* but see *planē,* 1 Thess. 2:3; 2 Thess. 2:11, "delusion"). Preceded by the negative particle *mē,* it means, "Do not begin to let any one deceive you." *In any way* renders another negative *mēdena.* So it is a strong warning.

The Thessalonians were in danger of being deceived on two accounts: that the Parousia surely would, not might, come any moment; that it had already taken place and was then present.

That day will not come translates one Greek word *hoti,* because or for. The translators have supplied the meaning: except or *unless.* Certain things must happen before that event. *The rebellion.* This statement is a negative condition of the third class, undetermined but with the prospect that it will be determined (Robertson). Paul recognized that he was speaking of an event yet in the future, how far he did not say. "Rebellion" with the definite article points to a definite event. This Greek word *apostasia* is transliterated into English as "apostasy." It is also called "falling away" (KJV). The Greek verb whence it comes means to stand off from. It was used in

classical Greek for revolt or rebellion. The papyri so uses it.[5] Such a rebellion must come *first* before the Lord's return.

What this rebellion is Paul did not say. Apparently it refers to a growing rebellion against God by unsaved men. "Paul's thought is that in the last times there will be an outstanding manifestation of the powers of evil arrayed against God. . . . It is as though Satan were throwing all his forces into one last despairing effort" (Morris, p. 126; cf. Rev. 19:19–20). This rebellion will not be by Christ's people but by those who oppose him.

As the climax to this rebellion *the man of lawlessness* (some mss. read sin) *is revealed* (cf. Orr, pp. 1975 ff.; M. N. Tod, pp. 2969 f.) "Revealed" is the same verb *apokaluptō* used of Christ (cf. 1:7). As Christ is unveiled, so will this man of lawlessness be unveiled. "Lawlessness" renders *anomias* (*nomos,* law, and the alpha privative, meaning no law). Whether sin or lawlessness, the meaning is the same. For sin is rebellion against God and his law.

Who is this man of lawlessness? That he is a definite individual is seen by the definite article used with both "man" and "lawlessness." Several positions have been taken: (1) that Paul was speculating and should not be taken seriously; (2) that it refers to some person then living, such as an emperor; (3) that it connotes the Roman pope and his system; (4) that it is some real person yet to be revealed.

One who believes that Paul was divinely inspired must reject the first position, as does the writer. In view of subsequent history one can hardly hold to either the second or third position. Christ has not yet come. The fourth position must then be true.

Of course, *the mystery of lawlessness* was already at work in Paul's day (v. 7). This may be identified with the Roman emperor and/or Rome's opposition to the

6 Herschel H. Hobbs, *Preaching Values From the Papyri* (Grand Rapids: Baker, 1964), pp. 25; cf. Lineberry, *Op. cit.,* pp. 41 f., who sees "falling away" (rebellion) as the "rapture of the church," 1 Thess. 4:13 ff.

Christian cause. In this sense it could refer to all opposition to it by whatever power, an opposition which works through the ages. But vv. 3–6, 8 seem to point to a definite person. It is difficult to distinguish clearly between "the mystery of lawlessness" and "the man of lawlessness." The former seems to be evident through the ages in any and all who oppose Christ. But before the Lord's return this lawlessness will be seen in a person so terrible as to embody all this opposition.

He will not be a false Christ (Matt. 24:5) but one opposed to Christ: Antichrist. John said that there were then and would be many antichrists or *antichristoi* (plural; cf. 1 John 2:18). But in the same verse he spoke of *antichristos*(singular), though without the definite article in the best manuscripts. However, it may read Antichrist, some person of great wickedness who will oppose Christ. Although Paul did not use the title, evidently he referred to the Antichrist.

The son of perdition (cf. John 17:12 of Judas, but here of the lawless one) is some person destined for perdition or for being destroyed. He will be revealed but will not prevail.

Then Paul described him. He *opposes;* he is the arch-rebel against Christ, so Antichrist. He *exalts himself,* lifts himself up above all others. Christ is exhalted by God (cf. Phil. 2:9–11), but the man of lawlessness exalts himself. He is *against every so-called god or object of worship.* "So-called god" may read "called God." It probably means all that is called God, whether the true God or pagan gods, above every form of deity. This is further extended to include *object of worship,* all kinds of objects of veneration (shrines, altars, or images).

Furthermore, *he takes his seat in the temple of God*—or "so that to sit" in the temple (*naos,* Holy of Holies) of God. Some see this as drawn from Caligula's claim to be God and his effort to have his image placed in the *naos* of the Jerusalem Temple (cf. Dan. 11:36). But the lawless one will take his seat personally, not place

an image of himself, in the *naos. Proclaiming himself to be God* or that he is God. Curiosity wishes that Paul had continued his description. But he left it there, possibly because his meaning was perfectly clear to his readers.

Do you not remember . . . I told you this? He had gone into this matter while in Thessalonica. Perhaps he explained it in more detail then. So he assumed their knowledge about it.

Know (see comment on 1 Thess. 1:4) *what is restraining him now. Restraining* renders a neuter participle of the verb to hold fast (1 Thess. 5:21), to hold back (Philemon 13), or to hold sway. The second applies here. In v. 7 *who . . . restrains* renders a masculine participle of the same verb. Was the restrainer a thing or a person? Evidently both. That which held back the lawless one at that time probably was the civil government of the Roman Empire (thing) personified in the emperor (person). This restraining power may be seen through the ages as constituted government and those who administer it. Rome passed away. But other governments followed. Paul apparently points to a time when such restraint will be removed. The man of lawlessness will exercise such tyrannical power as to do away with governmental limitations. He will act as he wills. God has ordained government to insure an orderly society. But in his own time he will permit this man of lawlessness to act without restraint. And the man of lawlessness will not be revealed until he who now restrains *is out of the way.* Then he will be revealed *in his time.* Not in the lawless one's time, but in God's time. Despite the rebellion God will still be in control of events. In his own time he will remove the restraint that the lawless one may be revealed in his true character.

Of the man of lawlessness Wilbur Smith commented, "He will be an arrogant, bitter enemy of God, blasphemous, contemptible person, who will honor the god of forces, the god of war, world ruler of the last days, the supreme enemy of God" (Lineberry,

p. 43). Moffatt (p. 49) said, "He is Satan's messiah, an infernal caricature of the true Messiah." As God will reveal his Messiah in glory, Satan's messiah will be revealed in shame.

Bailey insists that Paul was talking not about a principle but a person. Those who seek to identify the lawless one with some historical figure (Hitler, Mussolini, Stalin, the papacy) "are deplorably astray" (Bailey, p. 329). The man of lawlessness would be a personal figure who would have all the characteristics of these two historical figures (Antiochus Ephiphanes and Caligula) who had sought to destroy or desecrate the holy of holies in Judaism" (Bailey, p. 330).

The mystery of lawlessness is already at work. A mystery was something unknown to men, impossible of being discovered by human reason, but revealed by God in his due time (cf. Eph. 3:3–5). Evil forces opposed to God are already working in the world. But they cannot reach their consummation until the restraining power is removed.

And then the lawless one will be revealed, only to be slain by the Lord Jesus *with the breath of his mouth* (cf. Rev. 19:21)—not with swords of steel or nuclear weapons. This shows how easily Christ will consume the Antichrist (cf. Isa. 11:4; Job 4:8–9). In view of Ephesians 6:17*b;* Hebrews 4:12 f.; Revelation 19:21, does the breath of his mouth involve truth overcoming all that is false? At Christ's *appearing* and *coming,* words which here refer to the same thing, he will not only *slay* the lawless one but will *destroy* him. "Destroy" renders *katargeō,* to render inoperative or unworkable, like a machine that is shut off from its source of power. This is reflected in vv. 9–10. Not only will Christ slay the lawless one, but he will render inoperative his false works of wonder. In the presence of him who is truth the false will be revealed in its real nature and thus will become unworkable.

The lawless one is not *Satan* but works by the *activity,* the energizing power of Satan. He will work with all *power (dunamei), signs (sēmeiois,* cf. John 2:11), and *wonders (terasin).* These are the words used of Jesus' miracles. The first speaks of the power at work, the second connotes the significance of the work, and the third refers to the effect upon those who see it (Morris, p. 132). Only here these are qualified by lies, so *pretended.* Christ's miracles were true; those of the lawless one will be lies. He will work *with all wicked deception for those who are to perish* or the ones being *destroyed.* For this word see 1:9.

How may this passage be summarized? Lawlessness constantly works in the world, all of which is in reality rebellion against God. But it is restrained by civil government and power. In Paul's day it was the Roman Empire and the Caesar. But the principle applies throughout history. At some future time this lawlessness will become so great that God will remove the restraining power. Rebellion will be rampant and unfettered. In such a time the man of lawlessness will emerge. He will deceive men who have refused the truth of the gospel (cf. Matt. 24:24). He will do so by working false signs which are imitations of Jesus' miracles. He will defy all semblance of deity and divine worship, taking his seat in God's temple, seeking to replace God, and will proclaim himself to be God. When he shall have reached this extremity of lawlessness toward God, Christ will appear to consume him and render inoperative his work—and this by the breath of Christ's mouth!

There is a parallel to this in Jesus' earthly ministry. Through it all he was opposed by those against him and who were acting under Satan's power. When Jesus was arrested he said, "But this is your hour, and the power [*exousia,* here unrestrained power or tyranny] of darkness" (Luke 22:53). It was the hour of evil's unrestrained power. In a sense God said that evil was free to do its worst, even to killing the Son of God. How else can one explain what was done to Jesus from that point through his death? But God still would win, as he did in Jesus' resurrection.

So at the end of the age the unrestrained power of the man of lawlessness will be defeated by the breath of his (Christ's) mouth. God will win the final victory, and Jesus Christ will be "King of kings and Lord of lords" (Rev. 19:16).

3. Men of Delusion (2:10b–12)

because they refused to love the truth and so be saved. [11] Therefore God sends upon them a strong delusion, to make them believe what is false, [12] so that all may be condemned who did not believe the truth but had pleasure in unrighteousness.

Because introduces the reason why unbelievers will be deceived and so perish. *Refused* actually reads in the Greek text "they did not receive [welcome to themselves] the love of the truth." The love of the truth or the gospel is in contrast to the lying and deceit of Christ's enemies. They believed them rather than Christ (cf. John 8:44–47). *And so be saved.* They could be saved only by believing in and committing themselves to him who is truth. Truth brought salvation; falsehood resulted in eternal separation from God.

Therefore refers back to v. 10b. *God sends . . . strong delusion.* God will not arbitrarily do this. He will give them up to their own deliberate choice (cf. Rom. 1:24, 26, 28). In a sense he takes off the bridle when they reject the love of truth in favor of Satan's lie through the lawless one. Thus they rush to their own destruction. Sin bears its own fruit. In this case it will be a strong delusion or a working of deceit or error. Robertson (p. 53) comments, "Terrible result of wilful rejection of the truth of God"; also, "Here is the definite judicial act of God (Milligan) who gives the wicked over to the evil which they have deliberately chosen." The beginning of sin is to forsake God; the end of sin is to be God-forsaken. The result is *to make them believe what is false.* God does not will it, but it will be the natural outcome of the working of his moral and spiritual law.

Condemned is "may be judged" with the result being condemnation. Rejecting

the truth they *had pleasure in unrighteousness* (cf. Rom. 1:32). They rejoiced in evil. Instead of enjoying God, they enjoyed sin—but only for a season. Their end was/is to perish (cf. John 3:16; Rom. 6:23).

IV. Thanksgiving and Encouragement (2:13–17)

1. Gratitude for the Saints (2:13–14)

[13] But we are bound to give thanks to God always for you, brethren beloved by the Lord, because God chose you from the beginning to be saved, through sanctification by the Spirit and belief in the truth. [14] To this he called you through our gospel, so that you may obtain the glory of our Lord Jesus Christ.

On *bound to give thanks* see 1:3. On *brethren beloved* see 1 Thessalonians 1:4. Here it is of the Lord rather than of God, the Lord Jesus rather than God the Father. Note again the interchange of persons of the Godhead. *Chose* renders *haireō* (to take), used in the Septuagint of Israel (cf. Deut. 26:18). It refers to election (cf. 1 Thess. 1:4, where a different verb is used). *From the beginning to be saved* or unto salvation. This choice was in Christ, or all who believed in Christ. It was God's eternal choice (cf. 1 Cor. 2:7; Eph. 1:4). This was effected *through* (*en*, in the sphere of) *consecration* (sanctification, set apart to God's service) *by the Spirit and belief in the truth.* It was wrought by the Holy Spirit when the Thessalonians believed the truth of the gospel. Note *our gospel* (cf. 1 Thess. 1:5; 2:8; 3:2). God elected that Paul and his associates should preach the gospel and that the Thessalonians should believe it. *Obtain the glory of our Lord Jesus Christ.* In 1 Thessalonians 5:9 it was to obtain salvation, but here glory—but see v. 13. Glory is not something added to salvation, but it explains it. However, even though believers share in Christ's glory here, it will be fully realized in heaven (cf. John 17:22; Rom. 8:17).

2. Challenge to the Saints (2:15)

[15] So then, brethren, stand firm and hold to the traditions which you were taught by us, either by word of mouth or by letter.

From gratitude Paul turned to exhortation. *So then* or accordingly relates vv. 13–14 and 15. *Stand firm and hold to the traditions.* Both verbs are present imperatives or commands to have the habit of doing so. *Hold* renders *krateō*, to seize or to have a masterful hold on something. Traditions were the teachings handed down or over from one to another. The word might be used in a bad (cf. Mark 2:8; Col. 2:8) or good (cf. 1 Cor. 11:23) sense. Here it is the latter. With the definite article it refers to particular traditions or teachings, those of Paul and his associates, the gospel and other Christian teachings. *By word of mouth* or simply "by word" (while in Thessalonica) and by letter (1 Thess.). Despite persecution and false teachings, they were to stand firm in the truth.

3. Prayer for the Saints (2:16–17)

16 Now may our Lord Jesus Christ himself, and God our Father, who loved us and gave us eternal comfort and good hope through grace, 17 comfort your hearts and establish them in every good work and word.

Note *Lord Jesus Christ* before *God our Father.* Usually Paul mentioned the Father first (but see 2 Cor. 13:14). Here *himself* is first in the Greek sentence; so it is emphatic. Paul emphasized the Lord Jesus Christ due to his prominence in v. 14. God's call was in Christ. However, *loved* and *gave* are singular participles. Do they refer to God our Father only? Or to both persons of deity? Robertson (p. 55) sees them as referring to the Father. But he quotes Lightfoot: "Though it is difficult to see how St. Paul could otherwise have expressed his thought, if he had intended to refer to the Son, as well as to the Father. There is probably no instance in St. Paul of a plural adjective or verb, when the two persons of the Godhead are mentioned." Paul saw them as distinct but as one.

Comfort and *establish,* both aorists of point action, express a wish for the entire future (cf. 1 Thess. 3:2). As Timothy had done these things on his visit, Paul wishes

that God will do so in the future in *every* (or each) *good work and word.*

V. Exhortations to the Thessalonians (3: 1–15)

1. Appeal for Prayer (3:1–2)

1 Finally, brethren, pray for us, that the word of the Lord may speed on and triumph, as it did among you, 2 and that we may be delivered from wicked and evil men; for not all have faith.

Finally could be seen as introducing the close of the epistle. But it more likely introduces the remainder of the epistle (*to loipon,* the rest; cf. 1 Thess. 4:1). Several matters remained to be treated. *Pray* is a present tense, keep on praying. *For us* (*peri hēmōn*), surround us with an atmosphere of prayer. Paul asked prayer for two things introduced by *hina,* that. *That the word of the Lord may speed on and triumph.* The verbs *speed* and *triumph* reflect Greek games, where a runner outdistanced his opponents to win the race. The present subjunctive of both verbs means that God's word may keep on running and winning elsewhere as it had done in Thessalonica. Paul was fond of athletic terms (cf. 1 Cor. 9:24 ff.; Gal. 2:2; Phil. 2:16; 2 Tim. 4:7 f.).

That we may be delivered (rescued) *from wicked and evil men.* Note the order. Paul was more concerned about the success of the gospel than about his personal safety. He was in Corinth, a wicked and evil city where *not all* (indeed, few) *have faith* (cf. Acts 18:9–11). It is human to desire personal safety; it is divine to prefer the success of the gospel.

2. Faithfulness of God (3:3–5)

3 But the Lord is faithful; he will strengthen you and guard you from evil. 4 And we have confidence in the Lord about you, that you are doing and will do the things which we command. 5 May the Lord direct your hearts to the love of God and to the steadfastness of Christ.

The Lord is faithful (cf. 1 Cor. 1:9) or trustworthy. The Thessalonian Christians could depend upon him no matter how perverse men may be. He will *strengthen* and *guard* as a sentry *from evil.* "Evil" could refer to evil as found in evil men, or the evil one, Satan. Actually both ideas are true. They need have no fear what Satan through his servants may do to them. Paul had *confidence in the Lord* about them and their work which he had commanded by apostolic authority. His confidence is in the sphere of the Lord, who is *faithful. Direct* renders a verb to make smooth and straight (cf. 1 Thess. 3:11). *Steadfastness* renders *hupomonē* (cf. 1 Thess. 1:3). As Christ endured and overcame, so should they.

Paul wrote from Corinth. Of interest is what he later wrote to the Corinthians. 1 Corinthians 1:9 begins, "God is faithful." 1 Corinthians 15:58 reads, "Therefore . . . be steadfast, immovable, always abounding in the work of the Lord." These verses form parentheses enclosing the problems in Corinth. God is faithful in helping them in troubles. "Therefore. . . ." This is what Paul was saying in 2 Thessalonians 3:3-5.

3. Deal with the Disorderly (3:6-13)

⁶ Now we command you, brethren, in the name of our Lord Jesus Christ, that you keep away from any brother who is living in idleness and not in accord with the tradition that you received from us. ⁷ For you yourselves know how you ought to imitate us; we were not idle when we were with you, ⁸ we did not eat any one's bread without paying, but with toil and labor we worked night and day, that we might not burden any of you. ⁹ It was not because we have not that right, but to give you in our conduct an example to imitate. ¹⁰ For even when we were with you, we gave you this command: If any one will not work, let him not eat. ¹¹ For we hear that some of you are living in idleness, mere busybodies, not doing any work. ¹² Now such persons we command and exhort in the Lord Jesus Christ to do their work in quietness and to earn their own living. ¹³ Brethren, do not be weary in well-doing.

Paul saved these strong words until the last. From this epistle, as well as 1 Thessalonians, his readers could not doubt that he wrote them in love. But he wrote with apostolic authority (command) in the name or authority of *our Lord Jesus Christ* (cf.

1 Thess. 4:2).

Due to their confusion as to the time of the Lord's return, some, thinking that it would be immediately, had stopped working. They had become idle troublemakers. Paul ordered his readers *to keep away from* (withdraw from) *any brother* (fellow Christian) *who is living in idleness* contrary to Paul's *tradition* (cf. 2:15). *Living in idleness* should read "walking disorderly" or out of military ranks (cf. 1 Thess. 5:14) because of idleness or loafing. Paul still called such, "brother," but called for disapproval of his actions.

Know (cf. 1 Thess. 1:4). *Imitate* (cf. 1 Thess. 1:6). *Ought* states a moral and spiritual necessity. Paul referred to the example set by him and his associates while in Thessalonica. They were not idle or disorderly, they marched in ranks as true soldiers (cf. v. 6). *Not eat anyone's bread without paying* (cf. 2 Cor. 11:7 ff.). "Without paying" translates *dōrean*, a gift. Bailey (p. 336) renders it "gratuitously." Even though he stayed with Jason, apparently Paul paid for his meals. But the point is that he and his associates had pure motives in this regard. On *toil and labor . . . night and day . . . burden,* see 1 Thessalonians 2:9.

Not because we have not that right (cf. 1 Thess. 2:6; 2 Cor. 9:4). As the Lord's servants they could have expected support (cf. Luke 10:7; 1 Tim. 5:18). But they forewent that right in order to be *an example* which the Thessalonians could imitate. Paul was often charged with selfish motives. But his reply was the same (cf. 1 Cor. 9:3-27). This does not forbid a paid ministry. Rather it teaches such. At times Paul received gifts (cf. Phil. 4:14-17). But he followed his pattern in order to make groundless his enemies' charges.

In Thessalonica he had taught industriousness (v. 10). *If any one will not work* (does not will to work), *let him not eat.* Robertson (p. 59) suggests that this was a Jewish proverb based on Genesis 3:19. Through Timothy Paul had heard about *busybodies, not doing any work.* Although the present tense *hear* suggests more than one report. It could read "we hear from time to time." Three present participles describe such: *Living in idleness (peripatountas . . . ataktōs,* walking about . . . out of ranks); *not doing any work (mēden ergazomenous,* not working at all); *busybodies (periergazomenous,* working around). Note the similar Greek words in the second and third participles: "doing nothing at all but doing around." Moffatt (p. 53) notes that Paul's trouble there had been brought about through idlers (Acts 17:5). Now it was from those who were "not busy but busybodies." Robertson (p. 60) comments: "These theological deadbeats were too pious to work, but perfectly willing to eat at the hands of their neighbours while they piddled and frittered away the time in idleness." [6]

Command and exhort in the Lord Jesus Christ. Strong words by Paul the apostle based upon divine authority. What? Literally, "that with quietness" (inner tranquility as opposed to their excited state as busybodies) "keeping on working they keep on eating their own bread."

To the orderly Paul said, *Brethren, do not be weary in well-doing.* In the Greek text you (*humeis*) is written out, first in the sentence, and then present in the verb "be weary," so a double emphasis. You as opposed to the busybodies. The verb, an aorist subjunctive preceded by the negative *mē,* means "do not begin to be weary." *Weary* renders the verb *egkakeō* (from *en,* in, and *kakos,* evil), to become tired, weary, lose heart, despair, or behave badly. Except for Luke 18:1, it occurs only in Paul's writings (2 Cor. 4:1, 17; Gal. 6:9; Eph. 3:13; 2 Thess. 3:13). *Well-doing* renders a verb to do well, beautifully, honorably. It is found only here in the New Testament but is used in the Septuagint and a late papyrus (Robertson).[7] So do not behave badly in doing well. Whether rendered weary, behave badly, or lose

<hr>

[6] Cf. Morris, p. 147; Bailey, p. 337; Lineberry, pp. 83 f.

[7] Moulton and Milligan, p. 318.

heart, it makes good sense. This is a ever-needed exhortation.

4. Deal with the Disobedient (3:14–15)

14 If any one refuses to obey what we say in this letter, note that man, and have nothing to do with him, that he may be ashamed. 15 Do not look on him as an enemy, but warn him as a brother.

Robertson calls v. 14 an "ultimatum." Since these troublemakers had not heeded 1 Thessalonians, he threw out this challenge. *Note that man* means to put a sign on him, mark him, tag him as a troublemaker. It is found only here in the New Testament. The substantive *sēmeion* (sign) is used 27 times, 13 times in John's Gospel for Jesus' miracles (cf. also 2 Thess. 2:9). But the verb is found often in the papyri.

Have nothing to do with him, or have no company with him. The purpose is *that he may be ashamed.* The idea is that he may turn in his thoughts on himself to see what he is doing.

Do not look on him as an enemy, *but warn him as a brother.* He is not to be hated but regarded as a brother. On "warn" see 1 Thessalonians 5:12. Church discipline should be administered firmly but kindly. Within the Christian family the goal of discipline must always be to salvage, not to destroy or rid the fellowship of the undesirable person. Too often church people simply denounce and destroy those who seem not to do right. Every possible effort should be made to reclaim and strengthen the wrongdoer.

VI. Conclusion (3:16–18)

1. Prayer for the Saints (3:16)

16 Now may the Lord of peace himself give you peace at all times in all ways. The Lord be with you all.

On this v. see 1 Thessalonians 5:23. Here Paul used *Lord* instead of "God" but with the same sense. Paul's tender heart went out to his friends in prayer: *at all times in all ways,* for peace in heart and in the fellowship (cf. John 14:27).

2. Paul's Token of Authority (3:17)

17 I, Paul, write this greeting with my own hand. This is the mark in every letter of mine; it is the way I write.

Literally, "the greeting by the hand of me Paul." Paul dictated to an amanuensis. At this point he took the pen to write a closing greeting. *This is the mark in every letter of mine.* "Mark" (*sēmeion,* cf. 3:14). As Paul told his readers to put a tag on any troublemaker, so he put his tag of genuineness on this letter. It was to safeguard against forged letters (cf. 2:2). Some see this as evidence that this was his first epistle to the Thessalonians. It is more likely that his first epistle had been followed by a false one from a forger. So Paul adopted this method of proving his own letters genuine (cf. 1 Cor. 16:21; Gal. 6:11; Col. 4:18). Philemon may have been written entirely by Paul (v. 19). But he could have taken the pen to pledge payment to Philemon in his own handwriting.

Morris (p. 151) notes that the fact that Paul says nothing about it in other letters does not mean that he did not always do it, but that he did not emphasize it. He also cites an example by Deissmann of a letter written by one person, and with the final greeting by another.

It is the way I write. This was evidence that it was from Paul. They would recognize his handwriting. One shares the feeling of Robertson (p. 61): "If only the autograph copy could be found!"

3. Benediction (3:18)

18 The grace of our Lord Jesus Christ be with you all.

This is the same as 1 Thessalonians 5:28, except that here he added *all.* He did not exclude the troublesome ones. Though he disagreed with them, he still treated them "as a brother." This attitude would be a benediction on all in their relation to all Christians.

1-2 Timothy and Titus

E. GLENN HINSON

Introduction

First and Second Timothy and Titus, since 1703 usually called the "Pastoral epistles," confront students of the New Testament with one of their chief puzzles. On the one hand, they boast both strong external and internal support as the work of Paul. On the other hand, they manifest enough internal peculiarities in comparison with other letters bearing his name that many scholars have questioned whether Paul could have written them. Anyone seriously concerned to understand them must examine with some exactness the problems involved.

I. The Pastorals in Church History

External evidence favors the Pauline authorship of these letters. First Clement (*ca.* A.D. 96) and Ignatius (*ca.* 110–117) possibly alluded to them in several places.[1] In a letter to the Philippians (no later than A.D. 135, but probably about 115) Polycarp almost unquestionably quoted 1 Timothy and probably 2 Timothy and Titus. The spurious *Acts of Paul* (*ca.* 160), Irenaeus (185–189), Clement of Alexandria (190–200), Tertullian (*ca.* 200), and the Muratorian Canon (*ca.* 175–200) attributed them to Paul by name. The Syriac version of the New Testament, published *ca.* 150–200, contained all three. Eusebius of Caesarea,[2] a careful critic of such matters, listed them among the "universally acknowledged" and "undisputed" works of Paul.

Marcion, the would-be Paulinist from Pontus, did not include them in his canon, it is true. However, Tertullian[3] probably reported accurately that Marcion "rejected" them on account of their provision for church discipline. Basilides and Valentinus, the Gnostic princes, also rejected them; but Valentinus's successor, Heracleon, quoted 2 Timothy 2:13.[4] Tatian, founder of the conservative Encratite sect *ca.* 170, curiously rejected 1 and 2 Timothy but accepted Titus.[5] Though the recently discovered papyrus manuscript of Paul's letters, P[46] (dated *ca.* 250), lacks the Pastorals and Philemon, many scholars feel that their scribe's gradual compression of his letters toward the end would have allowed him to have included these writings on the seven missing leaves, even if the Pastorals alone would normally require eight leaves.[6]

From the second half of the second until the nineteenth century the authenticity of the Pastorals was acknowledged without demurrer. The first expressions of doubt, J. E. C. Schmidt's introduction to the New Testament (1804) and F. E. D. Schleiermacher's essay on 1 Timothy (1807), contested the genuineness of 1 Timothy alone. Subsequently, in view of the obvious simi-

[1] See *The New Testament in the Apostolic Fathers* (Oxford: Clarendon Press, 1905), pp. 50–51, 71–73.
[2] *Church History*, 3.3.5.

[3] *Against Marcion*, 5.21.
[4] Clement of Alexandria, *Stromateis*, 4.9.72.
[5] Jerome, Preface to *Commentary on Titus*.
[6] Cf. M.-J. Lagrange, *Critique textuelle* (Paris: J. Gabalda & Cie, 1935), II, 652 f.

larity of the letters, the genuineness of all three was questioned by J. G. Eichhorn (1812) and others. Contemporary scholars divide into three more or less well defined camps: (1) those who sustain Pauline authorship, (2) those who ascribe all three letters in their entirety to a later hand, and (3) those who ascribe the letters in their present form to a later writer or writers but admit genuine "fragments."

II. The Problem of the Pastorals

The problem of the Pastorals is an *internal* one. Five arguments have been advanced against Pauline authorship: (1) The vocabulary, grammar, and style vary decisively from those of Paul's other letters. (2) The doctrine, though Pauline, is post-Pauline, the reflection of second or third generation Christians upon Paul's thought. (3) The ecclesiastical organization depicted in them is more advanced and of necessity later than that presupposed by Paul's other writings. (4) The heresy attacked, probably Gnosticism, is late. (5) The historical data recorded in them cannot be fitted into the framework of Paul's lifetime as recorded in Acts.

Inasmuch as this commentary will presuppose the Pauline authorship of the letters, as posing fewer problems than the other views, it is necessary to give some answer to each of the five arguments.

1. *Vocabulary, Grammar, and Style.* The strongest argument against Pauline authorship is that from vocabulary, grammar, and style. P. N. Harrison [7] proved conclusively that, as they stand, the Pastorals contain a higher percentage of words not found in any other letter of Paul and of words not found in any other New Testament writing than the other ten letters which bear his name, fail to use some key Pauline words, and use some words in a different way. He also showed a number of peculiarities of grammar and style.

Several theories have been advanced to explain these peculiarities: (1) the use of

[7] *The Problem of the Pastoral Epistles* (London: Oxford University Press, 1921).

an amanuensis or secretary, (2) Paul's aging, and (3) natural variations in the vocabulary and style of any intelligent writer. While each of these may help to account for *minor* changes, they are inadequate to explain the radical character of the changes to the satisfaction of most scholars. A much stronger case can be made for Pauline authorship by recognizing the influence of preformulated materials upon vocabulary, style, and even thought. The fact is, the Pastorals contain a large number of quotations and near-quotations, some indicated by introductory formulas, taken from earlier sources. These traditional materials include hymns or confessions of faith, catalogues of virtues and vices, ethical codes, doxologies, popular proverbs, Scripture quotations, and other materials. (See the treatment of the text for those found in the Pastorals.) Paul's own vocabulary and style cannot be judged by these materials.

Now, if one first isolates the earlier materials used in all of Paul's letters and then compares the remaining portions, he will find that both the vocabulary and style of the remaining portions of the Pastorals coincide more closely with those of the other letters usually admitted to be Paul's —Romans, 1 and 2 Corinthians, Galatians, Philippians, 1 and 2 Thessalonians, and Philemon. Those portions of the Pastorals then have about the same percentage of unique words both for all the Pauline writings and for the New Testament and use them with similar nuances. They also have comparable grammar and style.[8]

On the positive side, it must be said further that the Pastorals share with the ten other Pauline letters 50 words found nowhere else in the New Testament and 492 words found in other New Testament writings. They use many Pauline favorite words with his distinctive meanings. They

[8] The reader will find the detailed evidence in E. Glenn Hinson, "A Source Analysis of the Pastoral Epistles with Reference to Pauline Authorship." Unpublished Th.D. thesis (Louisville, Kentucky: The Southern Baptist Theological Seminary, 1962).

contain certain of Paul's stylistic mannerisms and phrases which a forger would hardly seize upon to prove his Paulinity. Moreover, they include a large number of references to people, places, and events which ancient pseudonymous writers scrupulously avoided. This led Harrison to propose the "fragments hypothesis," which adjudged several parts of the letters authentic. However, the "fragments hypothesis" never explained how such small scraps of information could have survived and then been scattered throughout the letters.

Actually, the Pastorals lack all of the features of ancient pseudonymous writings: (1) The latter had to remain silent about names and places, for these easily gave them away.[9] Forgers normally avoided the letter form for this reason.[10] (2) An author had to have sufficient motivation to write in the name of a more famous person. In the Pastorals such motivation is lacking, both in the attack made on the heresy and in the sections concerning church organization. (3) If a pseudonymist, the writer failed to mention some of the most important considerations for proving his Paulinity—the trip to Spain referred to in Romans 15:24 and the stay in Colossae and Philippi alluded to in Philemon 22 and Philippians 2:24.[11] There is also some question about the acceptability of pseudonymity in the ancient world. Although some [12] have insisted that it did not bear the moral taint it now bears, the evidence from early Christianity proves that the church was neither undiscriminating nor undiscerning in respect of selecting canonical writings. Orthodox scholars quickly repudiated the Gnostic gospels and acts,

despite their use of pseudonyms of the apostles. They remonstrated with Marcion for editing Luke's Gospel and Paul's letters. For centuries some churches disputed, i.e., rejected for public worship, some writings which finally obtained a place in the New Testament canon and others which did not on account of their possible pseudonymous character. The priest who composed the *Acts of Paul and Thecla* "out of love for Paul" was defrocked.[13]

2. *Doctrine.* By and large the doctrine of the Pastorals agrees with that found in the undisputed letters of Paul. The differences which do appear can be attributed to the fact that much of the doctrinal material appears in the quoted sections and to the influence of the Roman situation upon Paul's thought at the time of writing. The theology is not *post*-Pauline but *pre*-Pauline, as Hans Windisch [14] demonstrated long ago for Christology, and shows a decisive Roman influence.

Two examples can be given. (1) The frequent application of the term Saviour (*sotēr*) to both God and Christ reflects the opposition of the church in Rome to the emperor cult which was burgeoning under Nero at the end of Paul's life. Correspondingly, Paul also used the term in his letter to the Philippians (3:20), which has traditionally been assigned to the Roman imprisonment. The commentary will show that most of these references belong to liturgical fragments. (2) The extensive use of the term godliness (*eusebeia*) is paralleled *only* in Roman writings, where Stoicism had a strong influence. Many times the word appears in quotations or allusions to the early catechism. Its use represents a deliberate attempt on Paul's part to accommodate his idiom to the Roman mode.

3. *Organization of the Church.* The ecclesiastical organization presupposed by the Pastorals is a twofold office—of presbyter-

9 See F. C. Burkitt, *Jewish and Christian Apocalypses* (London: Oxford University Press, 1914), p. 19.

10 M. R. James, *The Apocryphal New Testament* (Oxford: Clarendon Press, 1925), p. 476.

11 Cf. F. Torm, *Die Psychologie der Pseudonymität im Hinblick auf die Literatur des Urchristentums* (Gütersloh: C. Bertelsmann, 1932), pp. 49–53.

12 E.g., K. Aland, "The Problem of Anonymity and Pseudonymity in Christian Literature of the First Two Centuries," *Journal of Theological Studies*, new series, XII (1961), 39–49.

13 Tertullian, *On Baptism*, 17.

14 "Zur Christologie der Pastoralbriefe," *Zeitschrift für die neutestamentliche Wissenschaft*, XXXIV (1935), 213–38.

bishops and deacons (see comment on 1 Tim. 3:1 ff.; Tit. 1:5). While it is true that the undisputed letters of Paul contain no reference to presbyters, Philippians 1:1 proves that at least one church founded by Paul had the twofold office before he died. The use of the term *presbuteros* in both a nontechnical (older man; see comment on 1 Tim. 5:1,2,17,19) and a technical sense (presbyter; Tit. 1:5) proves that the Pastorals were composed at a primitive transitional period in the formation of the office. "Widows" in 1 Timothy 5:3–16 constituted no "order" as they did later. The function of an "evangelist" mentioned in 2 Timothy 4:5 (Acts 21:8; Eph. 4:11) is not referred to in second-century writings. Furthermore, the roles of Timothy and Titus in no way fit the character of the second-century episcopate. They are depicted in these letters as personal ambassadors of Paul, left behind to complete the mission work which he himself had begun. Laying on of hands in the sense of ordination (1 Tim. 4:14; 5:22; 2 Tim. 1:6) began quite early and related to the tasks of the mission (cf. Acts 13:3). The selection of persons for this work by the agency of prophets (1 Tim. 4:14) attests also an ancient practice (cf. Acts 13:2; 1 Clement 44:2).

4. *The Heresy.* The heresy attacked in the Pastorals was definitely not second-century Marcionism or Gnosticism. The quotation of 1 Timothy by Polycarp alone virtually eliminates the anti-Marcionite thesis. The reference to "antitheses of *gnosis* falsely so-called" in 1 Timothy 6:20 may be a later textual addition (see comment on this verse). If genuine, it represents the single allusion to *gnosis* in all three letters. Precise allusions show no sign of a docetic Christology, the Gnostic trademark. The rest of the evidence points to some kind of Judaistic inclination. At best we have a gnosticized Judaism involving still an opposition to the Gentile mission. The aberrants disrupted the community by "word battling" (1 Tim. 6:4; 2 Tim. 2:14,16,23; 3:8), defined more precisely as "quarrels over the law" in Titus 3:9. They wanted to be "teachers of the law" (1 Tim. 1:7) and fabricated "Jewish myths" (Titus 1:14) and "genealogies," all of which points to Jewish speculations about the Old Testament rather than Gnostic aeon-speculations.[15] They still had a connection with "the circumcision party" (Titus 1:10).

Their specific teachings included: (1) possible teachings about errant spirits and demons, (2) prohibition of marriage, (3) prohibition of certain foods (1 Tim. 4. 1–3), and (4) the belief that the resurrection had occurred already (2 Tim. 2:18). Belief in demons and malign spirits was universal in that day, so the doctrine does not provide a definite clue to the identity of the opposition. The Essenes prohibited marriage, and many Essenes could have joined the church in its inception. Prohibition of certain foods was a part of Jewish ritual law and one of the main points of contention in the Judaistic controversy (cf. Acts 15; 1 Cor. 10). The wording of their belief about the resurrection would incline one to guess that they believed that Christ had already returned cryptically, a Jewish approach to the question. Hellenistic Gnostics tended either (1) to deny resurrection altogether, or (2) to spiritualize it in terms of baptism (see comment on 2 Tim. 2:18). Paul may allude to the same theory in Philippians 3:9–11 when he admits that he has "not . . . already attained."

Further, they conducted an active campaign to lead people away from the Gentile mission. This campaign involved the sowing of doubt about Paul's apostolate, for he felt constrained to defend himself by citing his personal history (1 Tim. 1:11 ff.; 2:7). Above all, he reaffirmed his personal commission as an apostle "by command of God" (1 Tim. 1:1; Titus 1:1 f.). The sphere of the campaign was not restricted to Ephesus alone, but extended to Rome, where most supporters deserted him (2 Tim. 1:15–18;

15 Cf. G. Kittel, "Die *Genealogiai* der Pastoral-briefe," *ZNTW*, II (1921), 49–68; F. J. A. Hort, *Judaistic Christianity* (Cambridge & London: Macmillan & Co., 1894), pp. 135–8.

4:10,16-17).

5. *Historical Setting.* It must be conceded that the historical allusions of the Pastorals will not allow one to fit them easily into the framework of Paul's lifetime as outlined in Acts. Two observations can be made in reply, however: (1) Modern scholarship has proven that Luke did not give a complete picture.[16] (2) It is quite possible that Paul was released after a period of imprisonment in Rome, traveled extensively and then was reimprisoned, tried and executed by beheading sometime between A.D. 64 and 67.

Against the silence of Acts the tradition of two imprisonments is early and strong. First Clement 5.7 (A.D. 96) records that Paul reached "the limits of the West," which to a Roman writer could hardly have meant anything other than Spain. The apocryphal *Acts of Peter,* written by an Asian Christian (*ca.* 200-210), and the Roman Muratorian Canon both attest the journey to Spain. Origen and many later church Fathers knew the same tradition. Eusebius [17] explicitly stated that "the apostle was sent again upon the minstry of preaching" and suffered martyrdom after his return to Rome.

On the basis of this release-reimprisonment theory one may reconstruct Paul's activities mentioned in the Pastorals as follows: Upon his release in A.D. 63, he took his eagerly projected trip to Spain (Rom. 15:24,28). He probably had limited success there, for no traces have survived in Spanish tradition. After a brief stay he went to Ephesus, center of his work in Asia Minor, and stayed with Timothy, who had been his co-worker there earlier. In the meantime, accompanied by Titus, he went to Crete. Returning to Ephesus, he left Titus to continue the work of establishing order in the new mission field (Titus 1:5). After a very brief stay in Ephesus he transferred to Timothy the direction of the work there

and headed north through Troas to Macedonia, probably for a stay in Philippi (1 Tim. 1:3), where he may have composed 1 Timothy (so Spicq).

When he wrote the first letter to Timothy, Paul still intended to return to Ephesus (1 Tim. 3:14; 4:13), but he was not sure about it (3:15). He seems, at any rate, to have proceeded to Nicopolis to spend the winter (Titus 3:12), where he wrote the letter to Titus, dispatching it in the hands of Zenas and Apollos (Titus 3:13). When he wrote 2 Timothy, he was again a prisoner in Rome (2 Tim. 1:12,16,17; 2:9) and expected soon to be put to death. He may have realized his desire to return to Ephesus, and Spicq theorizes on the basis of 2 Timothy 1:15 that it was there that he was arrested for the last time. He certainly had plenty of enemies in Ephesus (cf. Acts 19:23—20:3; 21:27; 1 Cor. 1).

From Ephesus the party with Paul embarked at Miletus, leaving Trophimus behind on account of illness (2 Tim. 4:20), and crossed over the Aegean to Corinth. Leaving Erastus there, they probably proceeded by sea to Brundisium and then overland to Rome. Paul was imprisoned, tried according to Roman law under which a novel sect could be punished, and finally beheaded on the Ostian Way outside the city. During the period of his trial, many left him in the lurch. Demas abandoned him. Crescens went to Galatia, Titus to Dalmatia, apparently at Paul's bidding (4:10). Alexander the coppersmith did him much harm (4:14). Of the Asian companions Luke alone remained in his company (4:11), possibly serving as his amanuensis. So Paul wrote his second letter to Timothy to plead with his beloved son in the faith to come to Rome, bringing Mark (4:11), a cloak which he had left behind in Troas with Carpus, and certain books (4:13).

III. *The Purpose and Character of the Pastorals*

Acceptance of Pauline authorship of the Pastorals inevitably raises the question of

---

[16] Cf. 2 Cor. 11:23-33. See also John Knox, *Chapters in a Life of Paul* (New York & Nashville: Abingdon-Cokesbury, 1950).

[17] *Church History,* 2.22.2.

their purpose and character. Pseudonymity theories have never given a satisfactory explanation for the curious combination of personal allusions, references to Judaists, defense of apostleship, traditional materials, and denunciation of opponents we find here. To explain it, one must observe the deliberate emphasis on quotation and agreement with tradition. Several formulas accentuate this: "it is a true saying . . ." (1 Tim. 1:15; 3:1; 4:9; 2 Tim. 2:11; Titus 3:8); "and know this, that . . ." (1 Tim. 1:9; 2 Tim. 3:1 = Rom. 13:11; Eph. 5:5); "for the scripture says" (1 Tim. 5:18). A careful study of the traditional materials proves conclusively that the Roman tradition lay behind them—that is, materials representing the teaching and activities of the Roman church.[18]

The citation of the Roman tradition prompts one to ask: What historical situation could have prompted Paul to resort to this method of answering his opponents? *The only credible solution is Judaistic opposition to the Gentile mission.* The Jewish insistence and dependence upon tradition is, of course, too well known to require substantiation. The Roman church had a heavy Jewish contingent as both its theological and organizational tendencies in the first two centuries prove. (1) Mark, 1 Clement, and Hermas all lean toward an adoptionistic Christology, like the early Ebionites. (2) Organizationally Rome retained the synagogal pattern with presbyter-bishops and deacons until the late second century. It seems to me quite likely that Paul's opponents headquartered in Rome and tried to head off the Gentile mission as they recognized more precisely his strategy for evangelizing the Roman Empire. This may explain why Paul wrote Romans, including the conciliatory note regarding Judaism in chapters 9—11, how the Judaists finally secured his death, and why Christians first suffered persecution in Rome.

In writing these letters to Timothy and

18 See commentary on the text; see Hinson, *op. cit.*, ch. 8.

Titus regarding their roles in the Gentile mission, therefore, Paul buttressed his case by citing the tradition, now well known to him, of the one church (the Roman) whose authority the Judaists could not quibble with. Interpreted as non-Pauline and considered anti-Gnostic essays of the late first or early second century, they are merely a collection of unassorted pearls strung together without meaningful design. If, however, one interprets them as they project their own purpose, letters to aides who must establish churches and assure their orderly continuation in the face of opponents of the Gentile mission, they boast a thoughtful and intelligible arrangement. Rightly understood, they deserve the title of "missionary epistles" rather than "pastoral epistles." Whether written by Paul or a later author, they cast more light on the method of the early mission than any New Testament writing save the book of Acts.

Selected Bibliography

BARCLAY, WILLIAM. *The Letters to Timothy, Titus and Philemon.* ("The Daily Study Bible.") 2nd. ed. Philadelphia: Westminster Press, 1960.

BARRETT, C. K. *The Pastoral Epistles in the New English Bible.* Oxford: Clarendon Press, 1963.

DIBELIUS, MARTIN. *Die Pastoralbriefe.* 3 Aufl. Ed. HANS CONZELMANN. ("Handbuch zum Neuen Testament.") Vol. 13. Tübingen: J.C.B. Mohr (Paul Siebeck), 1955.

EASTON, BURTON SCOTT. *The Pastoral Epistles.* New York: Charles Scribner's Sons, 1947.

FALCONER, ROBERT. *The Pastoral Epistles.* Oxford: Clarendon Press, 1937.

GUTHRIE, DONALD. *The Pastoral Epistles.* Grand Rapids: William B. Eerdmans Publishing Co., 1957.

HANSON, ANTHONY TYRELL. *The Pastoral Letters.* Cambridge: University Press, 1966.

HARRISON, P. N. *The Problem of the Pastoral Epistles.* London: Oxford University Press, 1921.

HINSON, E. GLENN. "A Source Analysis of the Pastoral Epistles with Reference to Pauline Authorship." Unpublished Th.D. Thesis. Louisville, Kentucky: The Southern Baptist Theological Seminary, 1962.

JEREMIAS, JOACHIM. *Die Briefe an Timotheus und Titus.* ("Das Neue Testament Deutsch.")

Vol. 9. 4 Aufl. Göttingen: Vandenhoeck & Ruprecht, 1947.

KELLY, J. N. D. *A Commentary on the Pastoral Epistles.* ("Black's New Testament Commentaries.") Ed. HENRY CHADWICK. London: Adam & Charles Black, 1963.

LEANEY, A. R. C. *The Epistle to Timothy, Titus and Philemon.* ("Torch Bible Commentar-

ies.") Ed. JOHN MARSH and ALAN RICHARDSON. London: SCM Press Ltd., 1960.

SCOTT, E. F. *The Pastoral Epistles.* ("The Moffatt New Testament Commentary.") Ed. JAMES MOFFATT. New York & London: Harper & Brothers, Publishers, n.d.

SPICQ, C. *Les Epitres Pastorales.* ("Etudes bibliques.") Paris: J. Gabalda & Cie, 1947.

Commentary on 1 Timothy

Outline

Greeting and affirmation of apostolate (1: 1–2)
I. Paul's orders to a good soldier (1:3–20)
  1. Stop debating about the law and pursue love (1:3–7)
  2. The law has a place in Paul's gospel: to uncover sin (1:8–11)
  3. Paul's choice as apostle, a witness of God's grace to sinners (1:12–17)
  4. Fulfill your orders as a good soldier (1: 18–20)
II. Orders concerning public worship (2:1–15)
  1. Prayer for all (2:1–7)
  2. Tranquility in public worship (2:8–15)
    (1) Of men (2:8)
    (2) Of women (2:9–15)
III. Orders concerning the ministry (3:1–16)
  1. Presbyter-bishops (3:1–7)
  2. Deacons (3:8–13)
  3. Paul's reason for writing (3:14–16)
IV. Orders concerning behavior in the church (4:1–6:2a)
  1. False asceticism refuted (4:1–5)
  2. Timothy's conduct with reference to opponents (4:6–16)
  3. Conduct with reference to younger and older persons (5:1–2)
  4. Widows (5:3–16)
  5. Church discipline (5:17–25)
  6. Conduct of slaves toward their masters (6:1–2a)
V. Final orders (6:2b–19)
  1. Against the profit motive in religion (6: 2b–10)
  2. A personal charge to the man of God (6:11–16)
  3. A charge to the rich (6:17–19)
Closing charge and salutation (6:20–21)

Greeting and Affirmation of Apostolate (1:1–2)

¹ Paul, an apostle of Christ Jesus by command of God our Savior and of Christ Jesus

our hope,
² To Timothy, my true child in the faith:
Grace, mercy, and peace from God the Father and Christ Jesus our Lord.

Paul opens his letter with strong affirmation of his apostolate as in Galatians 1:1–5 and Romans 1:1–7. He is not an apostle by his own commission but by *command of God* our Saviour and *of Christ Jesus* our hope. The Greek word for *command* suggests a king or emperor commissioning someone as an officer in the army. The King of kings has imposed upon Paul his apostolic office (Spicq). The image is admirably suited to the overarching metaphor used to tie the entire letter together. An aged commander issues orders to a trusted soldier, expecting him to discharge his task faithfully. Paul had a great fondness for military language (cf. 1 Cor. 9:7). Moreover, like the Essenes at Qumran, early Christianity tended to conceive its mission in terms of a combat between Christ's army and Satan's. In the era of persecution, the first through the third centuries, the term "soldier" was used almost as a synonymn for Christians. The use of the metaphor in no way signified approval of war, however. The first several generations opposed military service and various forms of bloodshed. They battled not against "flesh and blood" but against the powers of evil.

Paul refers to God as *Savior* only in these three letters, although he applies the term to Christ in Philippians 3:20 and Ephesians 5:23. However, the ascription to either fits appropriately his belief that salvation is God's doing. The Old Testament provided ample precedent for calling God Savior, but Paul's use of the word here may have been directed also at the growth of the emperor cult in the Neronian era (Simpson). Our salvation depends equally upon God and Christ, for Christ's appearance has assured us that we have some hope of the glory of God (Col. 1:27). Appropriately, then, Paul calls him *our hope*, i.e., our hope of eternal life.

Paul addresses Timothy with deep affection when he calls him *my true child in the faith*. The words recall their long association through arduous trials—from Lystra to Ephesus to Corinth to Jerusalem to Rome. Paul had used Timothy as his "aide-de-camp" (Simpson) before, sending him, his "beloved and faithful child in the Lord," to Corinth to remind the Corinthians "of my ways in Christ, as I teach them everywhere in every church" (1 Cor. 4:17). The adjective *true* (Gk., *gnēsios*) actually means legitimate as opposed to adopted (cf. Phil. 2:20). Paul could hardly have stressed more strongly the intimate ties between himself and Timothy; he had many spiritual children, but none quite like Timothy.

The threefold salutation—*grace, mercy, and peace*—adds one member to Paul's usual greeting, grace and peace. All three terms bear Christian nuances. (1) In place of the customary Greek *chairein*, *charis* (*grace*) wishes for the recipient God's undeserved favor, shown in an exemplary way in Christ's sacrificial death and bestowed liberally by the Holy Spirit. (2) *Mercy* stands side by side with grace. It is God's loving-kindness toward men which forgives them their sins without any strings attached, as it were. (3) *Peace*, the common Hebrew greeting *shalom*, connotes security. By using it, Paul would remind Timothy of their common Jewish heritage (Acts 16:1). All three of these come *from God the Father and Christ Jesus our Lord*. All are grounded in God's fatherhood, i.e., his universal love out of which he creates and provides for mankind. Through Christ

he has extended these in a particular way to man, who had become estranged as a consequence of sin.

1. Paul's Orders to a Good Soldier (1:3–20)

Paul issues first certain general orders as to how Timothy is to counter the debaters.

1. Stop Debating About the Law and Pursue Love (1:3–7)

3 As I urged you when I was going to Macedonia, remain at Ephesus that you may charge certain persons not to teach any different doctrine, 4 nor to occupy themselves with myths and endless genealogies which promote speculations rather than the divine training that is in faith; 5 whereas the aim of our charge is love that issues from a pure heart and a good conscience and sincere faith. 6 Certain persons by swerving from these have wandered away into vain discussion, 7 desiring to be teachers of the law, without understanding either what they are saying or the things about which they make assertions.

Paul's first concern is to replace wrangling with love. Timothy evidently had written to him about the troublesome situation and perhaps hinted that he wanted to leave. This was not the first time he had shown some weakness, for Paul had had to send Titus to Corinth to bail him out of trouble (2 Cor. 8:6; 12:18). This time Paul will not allow him to leave.

As I urged you when I was going to Macedonia, remain at Ephesus would seem to refer to Paul's visit to Ephesus after his release from prison, for it does not fit the Acts scheme of Paul's journey (20:1). The passage is a bit difficult, however. We have here one of Paul's familiar anacolutha (cf. Rom. 2:17 ff.; 5:12 ff.; 9:22 f.; Eph. 3:1–14), leaving an incomplete thought. Apparently what Paul intended to say was, "As I urged you when I was going to Macedonia to remain at Ephesus, now I urge you again to remain, in order that . . ." The verb urge is a strong word, almost a command.

Timothy's first task is to *charge certain*

persons not to teach any different doctrine.
Paul does not name them, though he could
well have known who they were because
of his long association with Ephesus. He
frequently uses an indefinite reference for
opponents. The word *heterodidaskalein,*
translated *to teach any different doctrine,*
appears only here and in 6:3, but the forming of compounds with *heteros* ("any different") is characteristic of Paul (cf. *hetero-
zugein,* to yoke with another, in 2 Cor.
6:14).

This strange teaching involves *myths
and endless genealogies.* Some have explained these as Gnostic speculation about
the spheres (aeons) which surround the
earth and are guarded over by demonic
powers. However, the explicit reference to
"Jewish myths" in Titus 1:14, the reference
to their desire to be *teachers of the law*
in v. 7, and Paul's discussion of the law in
vv. 8–11 prove the essentially Judaistic
character of the debating. Jeremias has insisted that *myths* and *genealogies* refer to
speculations regarding the creation narra-
tives in Genesis, similar to those found in
Jubilees and in Philo of Alexandria. Spicq
conjectures along similar lines that their
interests probably focused upon "Jewish
apocryphal legends." Insofar as the church
is concerned, Paul concludes, they *promote
speculations* (cf. 6:4; 2 Tim. 2:23; Titus
3:9) *rather than the divine training that is
in faith.* The Greek word (*oikonomia*)
translated *training,* in Paul's writings, means
either stewardship (1 Cor. 9:17; Col. 1:25;
Eph. 3:2) or God's design for man (Eph.
1:10; 3:9). The latter nuance is probably
intended here.

Instead of such hurtful speculations
Paul wants to see *agapē*-love; this is the
aim (goal) of his set of orders. In Paul's
thought *agapē,* that love which places
the interest of the other person before
self-interest, provides the stackpole around
which all human relations must find proper
place (1 Cor. 13).

Where does *agapē* come from? *A pure
heart and a good conscience and sincere
faith.* (1) Purity of heart reflects the

Hebrew way of looking at life. The *heart*
signifies man's vital inner core, his self. The
saint sought from God a *pure* heart, one
without guile and deceit. "Blessed are the
pure in heart," Jesus himself had said, "for
they shall see God" (Matt. 5:8). (2) A
good (1 Tim. 1:19) or pure (3:9; 2 Tim.
1:3; Titus 1:15) *conscience* reflects the
Greek mode of thought. *Conscience* appears
only two or three times in the Greek Old
Testament. Apart from Paul's letters and
his speeches in Acts (23:1; 24:16), the
word appears only in Hebrews and 1 Peter.
In Stoic parlance conscience refers to the
center of rational and moral behavior. A
good conscience would be one free from
feelings of guilt (Kelly), in Paul's thought,
of course, as a consequence of God's grace.
(3) The phrase *sincere faith,* literally un-
hypocritical faith, appears only here and
in 2 Timothy 1:5. Certainly, as some critics
have said, Paul did not need to add such
a qualification. Interestingly enough, he
qualified love in the same way.

Those who have veered off the road
from these, Paul goes on to say, *have wandered away into vain discussion.* The opponents remind him of rabbinic debates over
trivia with their desires *to be teachers of
the law.* However, the Ephesian Judaists
were not like the Galatian Judaizers in
that they did not wish to impose the full
ceremonial law upon Christians (Kelly).
They not only do not understand the
subjects they discuss, Paul charges, they
do not even understand what they are
saying.

2. The Law Has a Place in Paul's Gospel: To Uncover Sin (1:8–11)

8 Now we know that the law is good, if any
one uses it lawfully, **9** understanding this, that
the law is not laid down for the just but for the
lawless and disobedient, for the ungodly and
sinners, for the unholy and profane, for murderers of fathers and murderers of mothers, for
manslayers, **10** immoral persons, sodomites, kidnapers, liars, perjurers, and whatever else is
contrary to sound doctrine, **11** in accordance
with the glorious gospel of the blessed God
with which I have been entrusted.

At this point Paul gives a pointed answer with the support of traditional materials to a major point of contention, evidently about his view of the law. His opponents were not antinomians, as Bauer once argued, but zealous defenders of the law. Paul concedes them a major point. *Now we know that the law is good* is his way of saying, Anyone would have to agree with you (cf. Rom. 2:2; 3:19; 8:28; 1 Cor. 8:1). This agrees with his admissions in Romans 7:12 that the law is "holy" and in 7:14 that it is "spiritual." But, and here he plays on the word law, it is good, *if any one uses it lawfully.* A catalogue of virtues and vices arranged on the plan of the Decalogue explains what "lawfully" means. Dibelius-Conzelmann and others have contended that in this conditional approval of law "the specific Pauline doctrine of the law is lacking." I think it more accurate to say that it is not fully developed. What Paul wants to say here, exactly as he argued in Romans 7:7–25 and Galatians 5:13–26, is that the law unmasks sin, that is, shows its sinfulness. The idea that *the law was not laid down for the just* was a common one in the Greek world; it probably belonged to the code which Paul quotes. The word *law* in this case, as Kelly points out, would be general, not alluding only to the Old Testament.

The first three pairs of vices recall negatively the first part of the Decalogue which dealt with man's obligations to God. The fourth pair sum up the negative side of the commandment, "Honor your father and your mother . . ." (Ex. 20:12). The rest of the catalogue alludes to breaches of the commandments regarding one's fellowman in the same order as the Decalogue. The latter forbade killing (*manslayers*), adultery (*immoral persons, sodomites*), stealing (*kidnapers*), and bearing false witness (*liars, perjurers*).

Paul concludes the catalogue with a characteristic catchall in vv. 9–10 (cf. Rom. 13:9; Gal. 5:21). *Sound doctrine* means healthy or wholesome teaching as opposed to the "sick" doctrine of the Judaists.

Such an understanding of the law is *in accordance with the glorious gospel* (lit. gospel of glory) *of the blessed God with which I have been entrusted.* Paul again reiterates his apostolic commission. Contrary to what the Judaists think, both he and his message are authentic. Paul could not forget the Damascus road experience. The *gospel* which he preached was a light in the darkness. It is not veiled, like Moses' face when he received the Ten Commandments, Paul told the Corinthians, except to those whose minds "the god of this world has blinded to the gospel of the glory of Christ" (2 Cor. 4:4). Paul normally speaks of "the gospel of Christ," but he also refers elsewhere to *the gospel of . . . God* (2 Cor. 11:7). The "good news" belongs equally to the Father and the One through whom he reveals himself. The reference to God as *blessed* here and in 6:15 undoubtedly draws from liturgical usage. God is called blessed because of his grace toward men.

3. Paul's Choice as Apostle, a Witness of God's Grace to Sinners (1:12–17)

12 I thank him who has given me strength for this, Christ Jesus our Lord, because he judged me faithful by appointing me to his service, 13 though I formerly blasphemed and persecuted and insulted him; but I received mercy because I had acted ignorantly in unbelief, 14 and the grace of our Lord overflowed for me with the faith and love that are in Christ Jesus. 15 The saying is sure and worthy of full acceptance that Christ Jesus came into the world to save sinners. And I am the foremost of sinners; 16 but I received mercy for this reason, that in me, as the foremost, Jesus Christ might display his perfect patience for an example to those who were to believe in him for eternal life. 17 To the King of ages, immortal, invisible, the only God, be honor and glory for ever and ever. Amen.

His recollection of his commission to proclaim the gospel causes Paul to make "a partial digression" (Easton). What he says, however, is intimately related to his argument. Not law, or debates about it, but God's grace saves sinners. Paul's apostolic appointment furnishes an unmistakable illustration of this central point in his message.

Paul first offers thanks to Christ (1) for choosing him, (2) for empowering him to discharge his commission, (3) for counting him trustworthy, and (4) for appointing him (Barclay). The phrase *I thank* used here and in 2 Timothy 1:3 is a Latinism (*charin echo*) which differs from Paul's normal expression (*eucharisteō*). Its usage could be ascribed to the influence of a lengthy stay in Rome, as Montgomery Hitchcock [19] has said, "in the company of an Italian who would not speak Greek, and with whom he would have to converse in Latin." The remaining thoughts accord remarkably well with those expressed in other letters.

Having chosen Paul, Christ gave him strength for his commission. The expression meaning to give strength is exclusively Pauline. Paul considered it the first qualification for an apostle (Gal. 2:8; Col. 1:29). The apostle has a special gift (*charisma*) from God (cf. Rom. 12:6; 1 Cor. 12:4 ff.). The presence of the risen Christ enabled Paul to endure any circumstances and to discharge any task required by his commission. "I can do all things in him who strengthens me" (Phil. 4:13). Paul also gives thanks to Christ *because he judged me faithful* (or trustworthy) *by appointing me to his service.* Essentially he repeats in different words his claim that "I have been entrusted" with the gospel (v. 11). He speaks where he does not have a direct word of the Lord, he tells the Corinthians, "as one who by the Lord's mercy is trustworthy" (1 Cor. 7:25). Paul's appointment as an apostle is to a *service.* He correctly interpreted the mind of Jesus that "whoever would be great among you must be your servant" (Mark 10:43-45).

What astonishes Paul, of course, is that Christ picked him despite and not because of what he had been. Paul had confronted

the Judaists with these facts before (Gal. 1:13 f.; 1 Cor. 15:9 f.) in confirming his apostolate. God granted him the forgiveness which comes from his *mercy because I had acted ignorantly in unbelief.* Paul here puts himself virtually in the category of a heathen prior to his conversion, not knowing God (1 Thess. 4:5). In the Old Testament sins of ignorance fell into a less serious category than intentional sins. But, though the statement is a bit vague, Paul does not mean to say that God forgave him on account of ignorance, a view which would conflict with what follows.

No, Paul was saved by God's abundant grace. God's grace is more than sufficient to cover our sins! This grace is undergirded *with the faith and love that are in Christ Jesus.* This addition could be interpreted in two ways: (1) Christ's faithfulness and love are an expression of God's saving grace. (2) Faith and love result from the action of God's grace, so that those who are "in Christ," a favorite Pauline phrase, manifest them in their lives. The second interpretation seemes preferable here. The phrase *in Christ Jesus* means both in the church and participating in the life of the risen Christ.

At this juncture Paul introduces a phrase from an early Christian hymn or instructional writing, using the formula of introduction found only in the Pastorals. By using the *saying is sure,* underlined by the addition of *and worthy of full acceptance,* Paul obviously intends to make a decisive point of quoting. The assertion *that Christ Jesus came into the world to save sinners* represents the heart not only of Paul's gospel but of all Christian teaching. It reflects the words of Jesus himself (Mark 2:17; Luke 19:10). Though we do not have the complete text of the hymn to help us interpret, the point which Paul makes is quite clear: the gospel is universal. Christ did not come only to save "the lost sheep of the house of Israel" (Matt. 15:24); he came to save all men.

Paul offers himself as the prime example of the working of God's grace. Though

[19] "The Latinity of the Pastorals," *The Expository Times,* XXXIX (1927-1928), 848.

the foremost of sinners, the prime example, God chose him to perform a ministry in his saving plan. By an act of mercy he chose him. The reason for this remarkable choice was *that in me, as the foremost, Jesus Christ might display his perfect patience for an example to those who were to believe in him for eternal life.* The word *display,* which except for Hebrews 6:10–11 (Gk.) in the New Testament appears only in Paul's writings, means "to give a clear demonstration or proof." In Romans 2:4 and 9:22 Paul has God as the source of *patience* or long-suffering. Elsewhere he lists it among virtues Christians must practice (Gal. 5:22; Eph. 4:2; Col. 1:11, 3:12; 2 Tim. 4:2). Obviously he does not distinguish between Christ and the Father as regards the act of salvation. *Perfect patience,* literally *all* patience, reflects a special Pauline idiom (cf. "all joy and peace" in Rom. 15:13; "with all joy" in Phil. 2:29). Christ chose Paul *for an example,* an outline sketch (Parry), which would help others believe in him and thus receive eternal life. Paul frequently puts himself forward as an example which would help others to imitate Christ and exhorts others to be examples. His whole narrative here reminds us that our own personal testimony is still the gospel's best witness.

Paul's reflection upon God's forgiving love toward him evokes from him a doxology, a customary reaction (cf. Rom. 11:36; 1 Tim. 6:15). The doxology appears to be a Jewish liturgical formula, adapted to the Hellenistic world (Spicq, Kelly). The title *King of the ages,* frequent in Jewish usage, appears in the Greek Old Testament in Tobit 13:6,10, in Revelation 15:3, and in 1 Clement 61:2, a community prayer! The similarity of this doxology with the prayer in 1 Clement 61:2 suggests a common, perhaps a Roman, origin. In this context *King of the ages* would imply both eternity (the Hebrew idea) and universality, King of the worlds (the Greek idea; Spicq). That God is *immortal* (Rom. 1:23; 1 Peter 1:4,23) and *invisible* (John 1:18; Col. 1:15; Heb. 11:27) is a common idea

in early Christian belief. The emphasis upon God as *the only God* probably has some reference to the imperial cult, just as does the use of the words Saviour and appearance. It was in Ephesus in 48 B.C. that Julius Caesar's epiphany was celebrated "as that of a God, son of Ares and Aphrodite, savior of all men" (Dibelius-Conzelmann). The half-mad Nero, whose pogrom was under way when these letters were composed, advanced the cult further. The adjective "wise" which appears in the KJV and in Walter C. Smith's hymn, "Immortal, Invisible," based on this text, has poor support in Greek manuscripts; it was probably a scribal insertion from the doxology in Romans 16:27. In ascribing *honor and glory* (cf. "honor and eternal dominion" in 6:16) to God, we are merely acknowledging what he already possesses.

Amen, the Hebrew "So be it!" was often spoken by the congregation in the service of worship (cf. 1 Cor. 14:16; Gal. 1:5). Jeremias has suggested that the reader of the letter would have paused to let the assembled people make an affirmative with *Amen.*

4. Fulfill Your Orders as a Good Soldier (1:18–20)

[18] This charge I commit to you, Timothy, my son, in accordance with the prophetic utterances which pointed to you, that inspired by them you may wage the good warfare, [19] holding faith and a good conscience. By rejecting conscience, certain persons have made shipwreck of their faith, [20] among them Hymenaeus and Alexander, whom I have delivered to Satan that they may learn not to blaspheme.

Paul now returns to his original charge (1:3,5) to the young Christian soldier. *This charge which I commit to you* refers backward to vv. 3 and 5 and forward to the remaining portion of the letter. The whole letter is structured on the military metaphor, as indicated above. The *charge* introduces new portions of the "orders issued" (4:11; 5:7; 6:14,17). The explication of the *charge* begins in 2:1.

Paul again addresses Timothy very affectionately—*my son* (lit., child Timothy). He undergirds his charge by reminding Timothy of *the prophetic utterances which pointed to you* (lit., came before you). The *prophetic utterances* could refer to Paul's original selection of Timothy to accompany him on his mission (Acts 16:1 ff.) or to his ordination for the ministry in Ephesus.

Paul here seems to envision Timothy's selection in much the same way Luke envisioned the selection of Paul and Barnabas for the mission to Asia Minor (Acts 13:2). A prophet, or prophets, inspired by the Holy Spirit, had received divine orders about Timothy and communicated them to Paul or to an early congregation. Timothy would then have hands laid on him by Paul (2 Tim. 1:6) and the elders of the church (of Ephesus?; 1 Tim. 4:14) in the manner in which Paul and Barnabas had hands laid on them (Acts 13:3). Paul himself placed great store by the prophetic, charismatic ministry. He believed his Gentile mission to be specially inspired and guided by the Holy Spirit in the manner depicted in the Pastorals. So his appeal to *prophetic utterances* as inspiration for Timothy's discharging of his missionary orders is quite in character for Paul.

The purpose of the charge is that Timothy *may wage the good warfare* (lit., war the good warfare). Paul again plays on his thematic metaphor. The adjective *kalos* (good or noble), employed so frequently in the Pastorals (16 times in 1 Tim. alone), is admirably suited to the metaphor. Timothy is to be the noble soldier who stands fast in the battle against the enemy, as 4 Maccabees 9:23 has it, "fighting a noble and holy fight for religion," to the point of martyrdom. The possibility of real martyrdom stands very much in the background, as 6:12 ff. and Paul's own impending death forecast in 2 Timothy show.

The equipment of the Christian soldier consists of *faith and a good conscience.* Though Paul fails to make an explicit connection between faith and conscience anywhere else, their conjunction is quite in place in a controversy with Judaists. The problem of eating certain foods (4:3), indicating a weak conscience, for instance, stemmed, in Paul's mind, from a faulty belief about God and the universe (4:4). In contradistinction to these Timothy needs a conscience fortified by proper trust in God.

Paul introduces a negative caution, therefore. *By rejecting conscience, certain persons have made shipwreck of their faith.* This reckless abandonment of conscience has led to *shipwreck* for the faith of some, a metaphor with much meaning to one who had been shipwrecked three times (2 Cor. 11:25).

Hymenaeus and Alexander are examples. Hymenaeus (2 Tim. 2:17) taught that the resurrection had already occurred. Alexander, possibly the coppersmith who did Paul much harm (2 Tim. 4:14), has been connected by some with the Alexander of Acts 19:33 who tried to make some defense of Paul, but the name was too common for certainty. Paul *delivered* (them) *to Satan that they may learn not to blaspheme.* What handing over to Satan meant both here and in 1 Corinthians 5:5, has received several explanations: (1) excommunication from the congregation, (2) casting out of the church into the realm ruled over by Satan, and (3) praying for physical affliction. Actually the three need not be seen as mutually exclusive.

The phrase was a formula of excommunication from the synagogue and church. Within the church, it was believed, the Holy Spirit protected the faithful against the demonic powers which caused physical as well as spiritual or moral affliction (cf. Job 2:1 ff.). By this action Paul means to deprive him of the Holy Spirit's power and to let Satan do what he would. Excommunication of some sort seems likely in view of Paul's plea to the Corinthians to "cleanse out the old leaven," i.e., the incestuous person (1 Cor. 5:7). However, even those not formally separated could suffer the effects of wrongdoing as the Ananias-Sapphira (Acts 5:1–11) and Elymas (13:11) stories confirm. Some at Corinth, Paul thought, experienced divine judgment in the form of illness and even death for their failure to "discern the body" (1 Cor. 11:30).

Paul's aim was not vindictive (Chrysostom), however, and Christian discipline should never be so. He wanted such discipline as would insure *that they may learn not to blaspheme,* i.e., speak hurtfully of God. The word *learn* in Greek is a strong one, which conveys the idea of stern treatment rather than simple instruction, so the idea of physical disability would be quite in line (Spicq; cf. Kelly). Titus 3:10–11 calls for gentler handling of the offenders perhaps.

II. Orders Concerning Public Worship (2:1–15)

Paul now turns to the first specific part of his orders to Timothy. Appropriately he deals first with prayer. Paul's instructions concerning prayer sound again the note of universality against the exclusiveness of the Judaists who oppose the Gentile mission.

1. Prayer for All (2:1–7)

¹ First of all, then, I urge that supplications, prayers, intercessions, and thanksgivings be made for all men, ² for kings and all who are in high positions, that we may lead a quiet and peaceable life, godly and respectful in every way. ³ This is good, and it is acceptable in the sight of God our Savior, ⁴ who desires all men to be saved and to come to the knowledge of the truth. ⁵ For there is one God, and there is one mediator between God and men, the man Christ Jesus, ⁶ who gave himself as a ransom for all, the testimony to which was borne at the proper time. ⁷ For this I was appointed a preacher and apostle (I am telling the truth, I am not lying), a teacher of the Gentiles in faith and truth.

Paul urges universal prayer on the basis of its desirability to God, who desires the salvation of all men, not just a select number. He sustains his charge (1) by citing a hymn which acknowledges only *one God,* the God of *all,* and *one mediator,* the mediator of all; and (2) by asserting

his own apostolic commission. His thought is logically connected with his argument in 1:12–17.

First of all, a classical formula in private correspondence, shows that Paul is ready to begin the main body of his letter. He proceeds to develop the charge alluded to in 1:3,5,18. *Supplications, prayers, intercessions, and thanksgivings* do not represent four clearly distinguished kinds of prayers. The word translated *prayers* has the most comprehensive meaning and is the commonest word for prayer in ancient thought. The words *supplications* and *intercessions* mean almost the same thing. However, the former appears often in Paul's letters, the latter only here and in 4:5. In legal papyri *intercession* appears frequently in statements addressing a superior, e.g., the king. In Christian writings apart from the New Testament it appears exclusively in Roman documents—1 Clement, Hermas, 2 Clement, and Justin's *Apology. Thanksgivings* may refer to eucharists as in 1 Corinthians 14:6 (Spicq), but this cannot be determined for sure.

The accent of the charge to pray is on universality (Spicq). *Intercessions* should be made *for all men.* This correctly draws out the implications of belief in one God, which the particularism of Judaism denied in practice.

The universality of prayer applies to *kings and all who are in high positions.* The word rendered *kings* was used in the East to designate the emperor. Because it is a plural, F. C. Baur and others have argued that the letters were composed after A.D. 136 when there were two emperors. In this context, however, the word has a more general application, including the emperor and various local monarchs who served as his lieges. Prayer for the emperor contrasted with worship of him. The practice reflected Christian fidelity to established institutions and the belief that power for orderly government came from God (cf. Rom. 13:1 ff.; John 19:11; 1 Peter 2:13 ff.; Tertullian, *Apol.* 40). The prayer would thus include *all who are in high positions*—senators, provincial governors, and a multitude of lesser officials.

The aim of the prayer would be not the conversion of the emperor but the welfare of the state, *that we may lead a quiet and peaceable life, godly and respectful in every way.* Paul has in mind "not only the danger of persecution, but also that of attacks by demonic powers" as mentioned in 2 Thessalonians 2:3–12 (Barrett). According to ancient psychology, demonic beings controlled the spheres around the earth and wreaked havoc on human life. In the Christian view, however, man need not despair because in the death and resurrection of Jesus Christ, God had overcome these hostile forces and equipped men to vanquish them. Prayer could put at one's disposal the divine aid.

The desire for a life which is *godly and respectful in every way* is the Graeco-Roman parallel for the Hebrew desire for a life "in holiness and righteousness" (Luke 1:75). The word translated *godly (eusebeia)* does not appear elsewhere in Paul's writings and the word translated *respectful (semnotes)* only in a cognate form. However, the change may be due to (1) a secretary, perhaps Luke (cf. Acts 3:12; 10:2,7), or (2) the influence of Paul's stay in Rome.

Universality in prayer *is good, and it is acceptable in the sight of God our Savior,* i.e., it pleases God. The fact is, God *desires all men to be saved and to come to the knowledge of the truth.* Scholars have attempted in various ways to obviate the universalism of the passage. John Chrysostom and many who have followed him have distinguished between God's antecedent and principal wills. By his antecedent will God desires the salvation of all, but by his principal or absolute will he allows some to be lost according to their free choice. Actually, Paul did not contemplate the problem; he simply opposed the narrowness of the Judaists (Kelly). God's desire for the salvation of all rebukes bigotry in any form. *To come to the knowledge*

of the truth appears nowhere else in Paul's letters except the Pastorals (2 Tim. 2:25; 3:7; Titus 1:1). It means essentially "to be converted to Christianity" (Dibelius-Conzelmann) and has its origin in Hellenistic Judaism (cf. Heb. 10:26; 2 John 1). However, *epignōsis* (knowledge) is a Pauline favorite.

Paul undergirds his argument by citing an extract from an ancient Christian hymn or instructional piece. Easton has called it "a Christian version of the Jewish *sh'ma*."

The fact that *there is one God* correlates with prayer for all. The Jews, Paul says in citing this hymn, did not correctly follow the logic of their monotheism.

Christian universalism is sustained further by the fact that *there is one mediator between God and men, the man Christ Jesus.* The idea of Christ as mediator does not appear in Paul's other writings, but the thought belongs to the hymn fragment and not Paul himself. At the center is the concept of covenant. Moses was mediator of the old covenant, Christ the mediator of the new. A close parallel of the concept appears in Paul's concept of reconciliation effected by Christ upon the cross (Rom. 3:24; 2 Cor. 5:19; Spicq). Its fullest development occurs in the anonymous letter to the Hebrews. One can only speculate about its implications in this hymn fragment.

The stress in Paul's quotation lies upon the nature of Christ's mediatorial role as a man *who gave himself as a ransom for all.* This understanding is built upon the words of Jesus found also in Mark 10:45 and Matthew 20:28. The style has been adapted to the poetic qualities of a hymn. The Hebraic "many" in the Gospels has been changed to its proper meaning, *all.* The key idea is that Christ, as a man, gave his life in exchange for the life of all men. This is the price paid for sin and its consequences. The figure of a *ransom* price suggests the buying of freedom for slaves or prisoners; it should not be pressed literally. Later penal substitutionary theories represent a gross development of the simple image implied in the hymn.

Scholars have debated whether *the testimony to which was borne at the proper time* belongs to the hymn fragment (Easton) or represents a Pauline addition (Kelly, Dibelius-Conzelmann). The style is possibly Paul's (cf. Rom. 12:1 f.; 2 Thess. 1:5), but its terseness (lit., "the witness to proper times") could be due to poetic abbreviation (Easton). Two interpretations are possible: (1) If interpreted in apposition with the immediately preceding proposition, *the testimony* would be synonymous with the gospel, the kerygma or the teaching of the early church. However, (2) if seen in apposition with the whole thought of vv. 4–6, it would connote the "proof" of God's will to save all (Spicq). *At the proper time* is a technical phrase in Paul (Rom. 5:6; Gal. 4:4; 1 Tim. 6:15; Titus 1:3) meaning "at an epoch fixed by God to achieve his promises," i.e., in the coming of Jesus.

The allusion to *the testimony* or the gospel evokes from Paul another affirmation of his apostolate, stronger than before. *For this* (testimony) *I was appointed a preacher and apostle . . . a teacher of the Gentiles in faith and truth.* Only here and in 2 Timothy 1:11 does Paul call himself a preacher and a teacher. However, he often refers to his preaching (e.g., Rom. 10:8; 1 Cor. 1:23) and teaching (1 Cor. 4:17; Eph. 4:21; 2 Thess. 2:15), particularly in the context of defending his apostolate. The introduction of the term *preacher* (*kērux*) at this point could be due to its common usage in Rome during his stay.[20] However that may be, the assertion that he is *a teacher of the Gentiles* leaves no doubt about his divine appointment. Christ has appointed him to a universal ministry.

In Greek the phrase *in faith and truth* has two possible interpretations. It may mean either (1) that Paul teaches faith and truth or (2) that he teaches faithfully and truthfully. Most commentators favor the first.

[20] 1 Clement, *Martyrdom of Polycarp; Justin;* and Tatian.

Within this strong affirmation of apostleship Paul has inserted a vigorous parenthetical defense of his honesty in making the claim. Some scholars have found such an insertion artificial (so Dibelius-Conzelmann). Whereas similar statements were quite suitable in other letters (Rom. 9:1; 2 Cor. 11:31; Gal. 1:20), they argue, this one is superfluous in a letter to his trusted colleague Timothy. Against this point one must remember that Timothy would probably have read the letter aloud to the Ephesian congregation (Jeremias). If so, as Scott has observed, "whether borrowed or not, the strong assertion of veracity is quite in place." The vehement statement highlights Paul's claims to the Gentile mission against the exclusivism of the Judaists, who "may well have been critical of evangelizing non-Jews" (Kelly).

2. Tranquility in Public Worship (2:8–15)

Having rebuked the narrowness of his opponents by insisting upon universality in prayer, Paul now rebukes their squabbling by giving orders concerning the proper conduct of public worship.

(1) Of Men (2:8)

⁸ I desire then that in every place the men should pray, lifting holy hands without anger or quarreling;

Paul the commander continues to issue orders to a young lieutenant. *I desire* is a euphemism for a binding command which bears the authority of a royal decree (Scott).

The universal note sounds again also. *In every place* is a Paulinism (1 Cor. 1:2; 2 Cor. 3:14; 1 Thess. 1:8), almost a technical phrase, meaning wherever Christians are joined in worship or wherever the gospel is preached.

Paul is not prescribing a form of prayer, *lifting holy hands;* he merely alludes to the commonest form of prayer in this day among pagans, Jews, and Christians (Jeremias, Kelly). The *Orantes* of the Roman catacombs depict Christians standing erect with eyes directed heavenward and palms turned upward in expectation of receiving the divine aid.

To stretch forth *holy hands* would mean to pray with pure intention (Barrett). In the Greek tragedians the phrase meant "liturgically pure" (Dibelius-Conzelmann), in Judaism and especially among the Essenes, "blameless frame of mind and conduct." [21] First Clement 29:1 gives an expanded parallel: "Let us then approach him in holiness of soul, raising pure and undefiled hands to him, loving our gracious and merciful Father, who has made us the portion of his choice for himself." Proper prayer would thus avert *anger or quarreling* (cf. Mark 11:25; Matt. 6:14), such as the Judaists engendered.

(2) Of Women (2:9–15)

9 also that women should adorn themselves modestly and sensibly in seemly apparel, not with braided hair or gold or pearls or costly attire 10 but by good deeds, as befits women who profess religion. 11 Let a woman learn in silence with all submissiveness. 12 I permit no woman to teach or to have authority over men; she is to keep silent. 13 For Adam was formed first, then Eve; 14 and Adam was not deceived, but the woman was deceived and became a transgressor. 15 Yet woman will be saved through bearing children, if she continues in faith and love and holiness, with modesty.

After this brief word concerning the conduct of men in the worship service, Paul turns to the conduct of women. His lengthier discussion of this matter would indicate that the latter posed a special problem, as they had at Corinth (1 Cor. 11:5 ff.; 14:33 ff.). In the Jewish synagogue, of course, women played no role in public worship; only men were permitted to pray aloud. However, Christianity broke down the male-female barrier and allowed women not only to participate but even to take leading roles. One thinks immediately, for example, of Priscilla (Acts 18:2,18,26; Rom. 16:3; 1 Cor. 16:9; 2 Tim. 4:19) at Rome and Ephesus, Lydia (Acts 16:14, 40) at Philippi, and Phoebe (Rom. 16:1) at Cenchreae. This newly won freedom

posed considerable problems regarding customs accepted in both pagan and Jewish society. The troublemakers must have encouraged women's freedom (2 Tim. 3:6 f.). Paul's instructions here reflect some of the difficulties which arose. For a part of his reply he borrows heavily from rules probably designed originally for women's conduct in general (Dibelius-Conzelmann). First Peter 3:3–6 is remarkably similar.

First, Paul urges adornment with *good deeds* rather than elaborate fashions. This teaching is predicated upon the typical early Christian instruction that each person should be content with necessary things. The majority in the early church probably possessed a minimum of the latter even. Consequently the flaunting of wealth offended. Paul, of course, does not inveigh against proper grooming. He condemns only the abuse of fashion—*braided hair or gold or pearls or costly attire,* the high and elegant apparel of pagan women. Christian women *should adorn themselves modestly and sensibly in seemly apparel . . . by good deeds.*

The good deeds suitable for *women who profess religion* are spelled out in various early Christian instructional pieces. They involve not merely avoidance of wrongdoing but a positive concern for the welfare of others. Early Christianity distinguished itself by its charities not merely toward its own constituents but even toward pagans. Among *good deeds* suitable for widows, which we must interpret as having general applicability, Paul lists rearing (orphaned) children, showing hospitality, washing the feet of the saints, relieving the afflicted, and doing every kind of good (5:10). The word translated *profess religion* appears only here in the New Testament, but often in Roman writings.[22]

In order to put a stop to some of the turmoil, Paul instructs women to *learn in silence with all submissiveness.* The solution is the same as that given in 1 Corin-

---

21 Cf. *Manual of Discipline* 9:1.

22 2 Clement, Diognetus; and *theosebes* in John, 1 Clement, and *Martyrdom of Polycarp.*

thians 14:34–35. However, because some early manuscripts place these verses after 1 Corinthians 14:40, some scholars have questioned their authenticity (Dibelius-Conzelmann). Against such a conclusion stands the fact that no manuscripts omit the verses entirely. *Submissiveness,* as Philip Carrington has shown, was a regular feature of the early catechism. Wives were enjoined to be submissive to their husbands, slaves to masters, children to parents, and citizens to rulers (cf. Rom. 13:1–7; Col. 3:18–4:1; Eph. 5:22–6:9). The injunction to silence seems to be Jewish (Dibelius-Conzelmann), but "the expectation that women can at least 'learn' is an advance on Judaism" (Easton). The prohibition of women teaching and assuming authority over men accords perfectly with Paul's Jewish background (cf. 1 Cor. 11:8). Circumstances did not allow the kind of freedom women have achieved in the last century or so.

Paul sustains his view that women voluntarily submit to their husbands by citing the creation stories of Genesis. He uses two arguments: (1) God created man before he created woman (Gen. 2:22). (2) Woman was deceived by the serpent; man was not (Gen. 3:1–6). In this second illustration Paul does not mean to deny Adam's transgression or "fall." His point is that the serpent deceived Eve alone, as the Genesis account says; it was she and not the serpent who gave the forbidden fruit to Adam.

The concluding statement is exceedingly obscure. With the rest of the section, vv. 11–15, it appears to oppose the troublemaker's prohibition of marriage (1 Tim. 4:3); hence the chief point would be, a woman should do what God intended for her to do—marry and bear children. The difficult statement that *woman will be saved through bearing children* has recieved a number of explanations, chief of which are (1) the ancient suggestion that Paul refers to the birth of Christ through Mary and (2) Moffatt's translation, "She will be brought safely through childbirth."

Neither really commends itself. Sir W. M. Ramsay has suggested that the statement does not imply the pain of childbearing, as in Genesis 3:16, but simply the natural role of motherhood.

Bearing children does not stand alone in a woman's taking her proper place in the plan of salvation. Women must also *continue in faith and love and holiness, with modesty.* The verb *continue* is plural and lacks a subject. Two possible subjects have been suggested here, either (1) the children or (2) women. The Greek favors the second rather than the first, for the word "children" does not actually appear. The word rendered *bearing children* in the RSV is one word, meaning literally childbearing. Previously the word *woman* has been used in the collective for women. The addition of *modesty* to the characteristic Pauline virtues of *faith and love and holiness* underlines once more the need for an attitude of moderation among women as well as men.

III. Orders Concerning the Ministry (3:1–16)

The disorder threatened by the Judaists at Ephesus requires Paul to issue directions also concerning the ministry. His instructions attest the early date of these letters in two ways: (1) There are prescriptions for only two offices—presbyter-bishops and deacons (cf. Phil. 1:1). The monarchical episcopate which arose in the second century is unknown, "one of the chief evidences of the early date of the Pastorals" (Scott). (2) The lists have a general character, depending heavily upon popular ethical lists for public offices.

1. Presbyter-Bishops (3:1–7)

[1] The saying is sure: If any one aspires to the office of bishop, he desires a noble task. [2] Now a bishop must be above reproach, the husband of one wife, temperate, sensible, dignified, hospitable, an apt teacher, [3] no drunkard, not violent but gentle, not quarrelsome, and no lover of money. [4] He must manage his own household well, keeping his children submissive and respectful in every way; [5] for if a man

does not know how to manage his own household, how can he care for God's church? 6 He must not be a recent convert, or he may be puffed up with conceit and fall into the condemnation of the devil; 7 moreover he must be well thought of by outsiders, or he may fall into reproach and the snare of the devil.

As a result of the general character of these lists, one cannot determine very exactly the role of presbyter-bishops or deacons in Paul's day. The similarity of the functional title *episcopos* to the Essene overseer or superintendent (*mebaqqer*) has led J. N. D. Kelly to theorize that "the term, and the administrative system it represented, passed into the Church from heterodox Judaism." The overseer's duties included examination of new members, direction of finance, teaching, disciplining, arbitration of disputes among members, conduct of public meetings, and rendering a general pastoral ministry.[23] Some of the same functions are at least hinted at in the Pastorals' lists of qualifications. Acts 20:17 ff. and 1 Peter 5:1 ff. both stress the pastoral or shepherding role of the elder-bishops. First Peter 2:25 depicts Christ himself as "the Shepherd and Guardian [Bishop] of your souls." The role evidently corresponds to the leaders mentioned in Romans 12:8 and 1 Thessalonians 5:12, the pastors of Ephesians 4:11, and the helpers and administrators of 1 Corinthians 12:28 (Kelly).

Paul defends the gift of administration by quoting a popular proverb. Though some have taken the formula *the saying is sure* with 2:15, it seems better to apply it to 3:1. The saying itself probably commends "ambition for office in general," not simply for the office of presbyter-bishop. A few manuscripts even read "popular" instead of "sure." Originally it probably meant, "If anyone aspires to public office (Gk., *episcope*) he desires a noble task." Paul thus plays on the words *episcope* and *episcopos*. The word rendered *aspires to* has a good connotation, implying inward intent rather than clever manipulation to

23 *Man. Disc.* 6:10 ff., 19 ff.; *Dam. Doc.*, 13:7–16; 14:8–12.

obtain a position.

Paul begins his list with a comprehensive qualification. The RSV rendering *above reproach* may be too strong. Easton has translated "chargeable with no misconduct." Both inside the church and outside, Paul intends to say, he should have a good reputation.

Exactly what *the husband of one wife* means here will remain in dispute. Five interpretations have been suggested: (1) faithful to his one wife (NEB, Barrett); (2) married to one wife at a time, i.e., monogamous; (3) married only once, i.e., not remarried after divorce or the death of his wife; (4) never divorced (A. T. Hanson); and (5) necessarily married. Though Paul opposed those who forbade marriage, the last interpretation would contradict his views in 1 Corinthians 7 where he discourages marriage "because of the times." The early tradition opposed to remarriages would tend to favor the third view, but Paul's encouragement of remarriage of widows in 5:14 would stand against it. The general nature of the instructions would probably make the first or the second view the most likely. Polygamy among both Jews and Gentiles was extremely common; unfaithfulness in marriage was almost a pagan habit. Paul insists upon faithfulness to the marriage bond.

The next three qualifications might be summed up with the words "a true Christian gentleman" (Kelly). The words *temperate* (cf. 3:11; Titus 2:2) and *sensible* (cf. Titus 1:8; 2:2,5) bear a similar nuance, implying not only soberness in regard to alcohol but in general attitudes and conduct. The word rendered *dignified* (cf. 1 Tim. 2:9), often associated with sensible in contemporary usage, is the opposite of disorderly, a characteristic of Paul's opponents. The problems posed for the leader of a diverse congregation requires someone with a cool head.

The requirements that the presbyter-bishop be *hospitable* and *an apt teacher* suggest two probable duties: (1) caring for the needy and travelers and (2) teaching. Hospitality to strangers brought distinction to the early church. Decent hostels were a rarity. The leaders of a local church had the responsibility of seeing that travelers had a place to stay (Titus 1:8). It may seem strange that Paul would have to mention the next items—*no drunkard, not violent but gentle, not quarrelsome*—but we must remember that Paul himself helped to convert some of the very dregs of humanity. Some of his Corinthians had been immoral, idolaters, adulterers, homosexuals, thieves, greedy, drunkards, revilers, and robbers (1 Cor. 6:9–11). The church often was chided by its chaste competitors for having an open-door policy.

But Paul had to do plenty of instructing and encouraging and cajoling to get his flocks to display an acceptable standard of morality. He does not prohibit drinking entirely (cf. 5:23), but he forbids excessive use—addiction (3:8) or enslavement (Titus 2:3) to it. Drunkenness, of course, often engenders violence and argumentativeness (lit., pugnatiousness) (cf. Rom. 13:13) and immorality. Instead of having these qualities, Paul wants his leaders to be *gentle* (Titus 3:2; cf. Phil. 4:5) or gracious in overlooking the faults of others, a quality which he ascribed to Jesus himself (2 Cor. 10:1).

It was important too that presbyter-bishops and deacons not be lovers of money or *greedy for gain* (cf. Titus 1:7). Perhaps already in Paul's day, and certainly later, the former directed the collection and distribution of offerings for orphans, widows, the poor, the imprisoned, and so on; the latter did the actual distribution. Much depended on their honesty and integrity even as it does today.

Paul now gives us our clearest hint regarding the function of presbyter-bishops and deacons. They are managers (3:4–5, 12) or stewards (Titus 1:7), as it were, of a local church, God's household. By analogy they must manage their own households well, if they would manage this larger household well. How their children behave furnishes an instructive test, that is,

whether they are *submissive and respectful in every way.* Early Christian codes of conduct taught submissiveness and obedience on the part of children (cf. Col. 3:20; Eph. 6:1 ff.). But Paul does not advocate bullying in order to keep them in line. He instructs fathers not to provoke their children, "lest they become discouraged" (Col. 3:21). Family discipline must be built on *agapē*-love. So also must church discipline!

A person who has such an important responsibility as managing a church *must not be a recent convert.* Elsewhere (5:22) Paul warns Timothy against hasty ordination. Scott has seen in this "an unguarded admission that the Pastorals are considerably later than the time of Paul." However, one need not conclude this in the case of the Ephesian church which would have been more than ten years old by the time Paul wrote. At any rate he does not make this same requirement for Crete, which was supposedly a new mission. The danger in a neophyte, Paul wisely notes, is that he may "get the bighead." The outcome would be that he would *fall into the condemnation of the devil.* This difficult phrase may mean either (1) that he would suffer the same judgment as the devil suffered when he was puffed up with conceit, i.e., expulsion from heaven, or (2) that he would be put in the hands of the devil for judgment like Job was, or (3) that he would be criticized by a slanderer, another meaning of the word devil. Favoring the first is the fact that Paul nowhere ascribes judgment to the devil (Barrett). Favoring the second is the clearer sense of the next sentence (v.7). The third interpretation is unlikely in the context.

Finally, presbyter-bishops *must be well thought of by outsiders,* a frequent Pauline admonition for all Christians (1 Thess. 4:12; 1 Cor. 10:32; Col. 4:5; Phil. 2:15). The church's mission depends upon the good reputation of its members, especially its leaders. A bad reputation leaves a leader open to *reproach and the snare of the devil.* Paul offers a similar warning concerning those grasping after money (6:9).

2. Deacons (3:8–13)

[8] Deacons likewise must be serious, not double-tongued, not addicted to much wine, not greedy for gain; [9] they must hold the mystery of the faith with a clear conscience. [10] And let them also be tested first; then if they prove themselves blameless let them serve as deacons. [11] The women likewise must be serious, no slanderers, but temperate, faithful in all things. [12] Let deacons be the husband of one wife, and let them manage their children and their households well; [13] for those who serve well as deacons gain a good standing for themselves and also great confidence in the faith which is in Christ Jesus.

The office of deacon has no specific parallel in Judaism. It seems to have originated more in the servant concept which Jesus held for his mission and which the early church inherited from him. The seven of Acts 6 were not the first deacons, for the term is not applied to them and they performed a very different function (Barrett, Kelly). Nevertheless, the idea of assistance to other church leaders has relevance for deacons. Actually, Paul uses the words *diakonos* (deacon or minister) and *diakonia* (ministry) in a variety of ways.

The diaconal list in 1 Timothy overlaps the episcopal list, revealing how closely interrelated the two offices were. Like the latter, it says little about duties; instead, the emphasis falls upon personal characteristics. *Deacons likewise,* i.e., like the presbyter-bishops, *must be serious.* In the good sense the word translated *serious,* found only in Paul (cf. Phil. 4:8; Titus 2:2), means worthy of respect or "men of high principle" (Barrett). Since his ministry to the needy would take him from house to house, he must *not* be *double-tongued* (lit., double-worded). Two meanings have been given for *double-tongued:* (1) someone who says one thing and thinks another, i.e., double-minded (Chrysostom), and (2) someone who says one thing to one person, another to another (Theodoret). Both have some application to the diaconate.

Like presbyter-bishops, deacons must avoid drinking to excess and greediness

(cf. comment on 3:3).

As sharers in the church's teaching ministry, *they must hold the mystery of the faith with a clear conscience.* The accent here falls upon purity of conscience (cf. comment on 1:5,19). The word *clear* or pure (*katharos*) appears 9 times in these three letters. Paul's only other use was in Romans 14:20 where he also dealt with questions of conscience in eating or not eating certain foods. Against the quibbling of the Judaists the teacher needed interior certainty regarding *the mystery of the faith.* *Mystery* means here what it usually does in Paul's letters, the eternal purpose of God which has been hidden but now is revealed in Jesus Christ. Paul believed himself a steward of God's "unveiled secret" (1 Cor. 4:1). *The faith* has the formal connotation here. Paul occasionally distinguished Christianity from Judaism in this way (cf. Gal. 1:23; Col. 2:7).

Paul advises a trial period for deacon candidates. No formal test is implied (Kelly). The statement would seem to have the same implication (note: *And let them also*) as his instruction that a bishop "must not be a recent convert" (3:6). Paul expected all Christians to perform a diaconate—caring for the needy, visiting the sick, comforting the bereaved, etc. If during this period *they prove themselves blameless,* of good reputation, let them be formally enrolled as deacons.

Verse 11 poses a major problem. Four interpretations of *the women* have been offered: (1) wives of deacons, (2) deaconesses, (3) wives of bishops and deacons, and (4) women in general. The third and fourth alternatives have received little support. Good arguments have been advanced for the first two positions. (1) The arguments used to support application to the wives of deacons are: (a) Since vv. 8 ff. and 12 f. deal with male deacons, it is unlikely that a reference to deaconesses would be introduced between them; (b) a reference to deaconesses would have been more detailed; (c) a more definite term than "women" would have been used;

and (d) the ministry of women is dealt with in 5:3–16, i.e., concerning widows.

(2) The arguments used to support the application to deaconesses are: (a) There is no feminine for *diakonos* in the New Testament; in Romans 16:1 Phoebe is referred to as a *diakonos*. (b) Grammatically this statement breaks the train of thought entirely. *Likewise* refers back to v. 2. (c) The virtues required are eminently applicable to ministers, not wives. (d) If Paul had meant wives, he would have been more explicit, *their* wives. The weight of argument favors the second interpretation slightly. By the end of the second century we have clear evidence for deaconesses. Certain duties would seem to have required women ministers, e.g., baptism, caring for sick women, and so on.

Either deaconesses or wives of deacons, sharing in their husband's ministry, would need diaconal qualifications. They must be women of high principles (see v. 8), *no slanderers* (cf. *not double-tongued*), *temperate,* and entirely trustworthy (cf. comment on 1:12). After this brief pause to speak concerning wives or deaconesses, Paul concludes his list of qualifications for deacons—*husband of one wife* (3:2) and good managers of their own homes (3:4–5). Good service as a deacon, he reminds us, earns *a good standing.* The word translated *standing,* found only here in the New Testament, originally meant step (on a stair or ladder) and from that degree or rank (e.g., of a soldier). Some have seen in the word the idea of advancement from deacon to presbyter, but this seems unlikely in view of the parallel statement. More likely, it connotes the position of respect one could attain by good service. This position of respect would lead in turn to *great confidence in the faith which is in Christ Jesus.* The phrase *great confidence* (lit., much boldness), used only by Paul in early Christian writings, refers to the Christian's confidence with reference to God's judging of him. The Greek has no article before *faith* and does not have the formal connotation implied by the RSV (cf. Eph.

3:12; 1 Thess. 2:2). Instead, Paul means to underline the *confidence* which arises from the Christian's commitment or trust *in Christ Jesus* (see comment on 1:14).

3. Paul's Reason for Writing (3:14–16)

[14] I hope to come to you soon, but I am writing these instructions to you so that, [15] if I am delayed, you may know how one ought to behave in the household of God, which is the church of the living God, the pillar and bulwark of the truth. [16] Great indeed, we confess, is the mystery of our religion:
He was manifested in the flesh,
vindicated in the Spirit,
    seen by angels,
preached among the nations,
believed on in the world,
    taken up in glory.

Having issued orders at some length regarding mundane matters, Paul pauses to assure Timothy of the significance of what he says. In these three verses he gives "the key to the inner meaning of the Pastoral Epistles" (Scott), building a bridge as it were between the two main parts of 1 Timothy.

Many scholars ask why Paul would need to have written the letter at all as stated here. Why did he not leave instructions with Timothy when he left for Macedonia (1:3), as a good businessman would (so Scott)? The answer perhaps lies in the fact that Paul's future was so uncertain and that Timothy, far more than Titus, whose instructions are rather limited, suffered his usual insecurity in Paul's absence. The letter would bolster him in shaky circumstances, saying more to the Ephesian congregation which heard the letter than to Timothy himself. This would agree with Paul's stated purpose. He writes in order that Timothy *may know how one ought to behave in the household of God.* The phrase translated *how one ought to behave* may apply both to the character and life of an individual (cf. Eph. 2:3; Heb. 13:18) and to relations between persons (2 Cor. 1:12; James 3:13). It could thus be translated "how *people* ought to behave."

Paul's reference to *the household of God,*

which picks up his thought in 3:4–5,12, furnishes an opportunity for expostulating on the church and its foundation Jesus Christ. The word translated "household" has no definite article with it, which means that Paul probably refers to each local congregation (Barrett, Kelly). Considered from this standpoint, Paul conceives of a local church as a Christian family (see above on vv. 4–5). Within each Christian household, he intends to say, harmony and concord must prevail as they do in a well-ordered family.

But the word *oikos* has another nuance, house (building), which Paul proceeds to develop metaphorically. Each congregation is a *church of the living God.* The word *church,* like *household,* lacks the article, so the RSV rendering fails to give a precise rendering. Paul has a strong preference for the phrase "the church of God" (cf. 1 Cor. 1:2; 10:32) but normally uses the article, so a local congregation seems clearly implied here. The reference to God as *the living God,* like the image of a *house,* is drawn from the Old Testament (cf. Rom. 9:26; 2 Cor. 3:3; 6:16).

Each local church, then, is a column and buttress of the truth. Once more the RSV fails to convey the correct image, for neither column (pillar) nor buttress (bulwark) has an article. Observe that Paul does not say foundation. Christ alone is the foundation (1 Cor. 3:11). A church performs the function of a column and a buttress, that is, it maintains the truth (synonymous with "the faith") and supports it against attack. The statement could have reference to the Essene claim, if Essene ideas lay behind the Judaists' views, "to establish in Israel a solid basis of truth." [24] In a letter to Ephesus it undoubtedly alludes also to the temple of Artemis and the powerful Artemis cult.

His allusion to *the truth* brings to Paul's mind a hymn, well chosen for its note of universalism. Several things prove the hymnic nature of the passage: (1) the

introduction, (2) Greek meter, (3) assonance, and (4) its lack of agreement with the context.

Early manuscripts give two possible readings for the introduction: (1) *Great indeed, we confess, is the mystery of our religion,* and (2) "By common consent (or confessedly) great indeed is the mystery of our religion." The manuscript evidence strongly favors the second reading, but the first is a more suitable way for Paul to introduce a quotation (cf. Rom. 10:9–10). *The mystery of our religion* is equivalent to "the mystery of the faith" (4:9) and an expanded transcription of *the truth* in v. 15. The phrasing parallels closely Ephesians 5:32. Paul could well have aimed it at the Ephesian cult's cry, "Great is Artemis of the Ephesians!"

The entire hymn stands in apposition with *mystery.* Quite clearly the subject of the hymn is Christ (cf. Col. 1:27; 2:2), though many early manuscripts have changed "who" (Gk., *hos*) either (1) to "which" (*ho*), thus making mystery the subject, or (2) to "God" (*theos*), which in an abbreviated form is barely distinguishable from "who."

The hymn itself has been arranged in two ways, either two stanzas of three lines each, or three couplets. The latter arrangement seems to account better for the Hebrew parallelism: (1) flesh-Spirit, (2) angels-nations, (3) world-glory. Joachim Jeremias has called to our attention the parallel between the progression of the three couplets and the Oriental enthronement ceremony: (1) elevation, (2) presentation, and (3) enthronement. Though this pattern probably lies in the background of early Christian hymnody, the hymn is best interpreted on the simple chronological order (cf. Phil. 2:6–11). The six stages would be: (1) incarnation, (2) resurrection, (3) ascension, (4) preaching of the gospel, (5) response to it, (6) Christ's final victory.

One or two items need further comment. Though some scholars have applied *vindicated* (justified) *in the Spirit* to the as-

24 *Man. Disc.,* 5:5; cf. *Dam. Doc.* 3:19.

cension, the chronological interpretation would favor the resurrection. Romans 1:4 and 1 Peter 3:18 would favor this. *Seen by angels* and *taken up in glory* might both be interpreted with reference to the ascension. To preserve the chronological sequence, some scholars have translated *angels* "messengers," a frequent nuance; others have applied the phrase to evil spiritual beings; still others have thought it referred to angels beholding the incarnation and resurrection (1 Peter 1:12). The most likely suggestion, however, is C. K. Barrett's, i.e., that *seen by angels* refers to the ascension (cf. Phil. 2:9 f.; Col. 2:15; Heb. 1:6) and *taken up in glory* to Christ's final victory, the judgment.

The universalism of the hymn should be noted. Christ's victory extends over all spheres of existence—angels, nations, and world. If one translated line 4 "preached among the Gentiles," he would detect a still stronger slap at the exclusivism of the Judaists. Christ has provided universal salvation. That is the "unveiled secret" of our religion, the truth which the churches everywhere must support and protect!

IV. Orders Concerning Behavior in the Church (4:1—6:2a)

Paul comes now to miscellaneous orders concerning behavior in the church at Ephesus. He refutes first the false asceticism of the Judaists with their prohibition of marriage and abstinence from certain foods (4:1-5). He then instructs Timothy to avoid debating and instead train himself in piety (4:6-10), taking care of Paul's own leadership ministry until he comes (4:11-16). He gives instructions about the proper behavior of certain groups who make up the constituency—younger and older persons (5:1-2), widows (5:3-16), elders (5:17-25), slaves and masters (6:1-2a).

1. False Asceticism Refuted (4:1-5)

[1] Now the Spirit expressly says that in later times some will depart from the faith by giving heed to deceitful spirits and doctrines of de-

mons, [2] through the pretensions of liars whose consciences are seared, [3] who forbid marriage and enjoin abstinence from foods which God created to be received with thanksgiving by those who believe and know the truth. [4] For everything created by God is good, and nothing is to be rejected if it is received with thanksgiving; [5] for then it is consecrated by the word of God and prayer.

For the first time Paul becomes rather specific about the Ephesian problem. He casts his refutation in the form of prophecy, a form "deeply imbedded in early Christian thought" (Kelly; cf. Mark 13:22, Acts 20:29-30; 2 Thess. 2:3,11 f.; 2 Tim. 3:1 ff.; Rev. 13). The Essenes, who may have been a channel for the Ephesian error, regularly used this style of commenting on contemporary events; and Paul obviously has an immediate and not a future problem in mind here, as his refutation in vv. 3–5 demonstrates (Dibelius-Conzelmann).

The word translated *expressly*, used only here in the New Testament, appears several times in Justin Martyr's *First Apology* (35:10, 63:11) to introduce an Old Testament prophecy. Paul undoubtedly alludes to a living prophet inspired by the Spirit, as in Acts 11:27 f.; 13:1 f.; 1 Corinthians 14. *In later times* means "in the last times," i.e., between the first and second comings of Christ, as in 2 Timothy 3:1.

Paul ascribes the deliberate departure of "some" (see comment on 1:3) to their *giving heed to deceitful spirits and doctrines of demons.* This could mean (1) that the erroneous teachers spent much time talking about evil spirits and demons. Colossians 2:8 ff. attests similar debates there. The Qumran War Scroll provides ample background in Judaism for such discussions. However, most scholars (2) interpret the reference to demons in the subjective sense. This would imply that, as in 2 Corinthians 2:11; 4:4, Paul believes that Satan and his demonic host have taken control of them with the result that their teachings are demonic (cf. Jeremias).

However that may be, as men they act *through the pretensions* (lit., in hypocrisy) *of liars whose consciences are seared.* Their problem has to do with a weak or defiled conscience (see comment on 1:5,19; 3:9). There is another way to interpret the verb translated *seared*. The devil has taken them captive (3:6–7) and put his brand on them in place of the brand of Christ.

Bad conscience leads to two errors: (1) prohibition of marriage and (2) abstinence from certain foods. Celibacy was practiced by the Essenes. Dietary laws formed a major part of ancient Jewish thought and figured heavily in the tensions between Jewish and Gentile Christians (cf. Gal. 2; Acts 15). Paul does not bother to refute the first view for he has already made his position clear in 2:15. He will reaffirm it again in 5:14 and in Titus 2:4. The dietary problem, perhaps the same as in Romans 14:1 f. and Colossians 2:20–23, is attacked by citing the Old Testament understanding of creation and the Christian concept of thanksgiving. (1) Foods are good if *God created* them, *for everything created by God is good* (Gen. 1:31). (2) They are good also when *received with thanksgiving by those who believe and know the truth,* i.e., Christians (cf. comment on 2:4), *and nothing is to be rejected if it is received with thanksgiving; for then it is consecrated by the word of God and prayer.* So Paul insists also in Romans 14:6, 1 Corinthians 10:30, and Philippians 4:6. *The word of God* may mean (1) the word spoken in creation in Genesis 1, (2) certain words of Scripture used in prayers of thanksgiving (e.g., Psalm 145:15–16), or (3) simply *prayer* itself. What Paul means is, when one offers *thanksgiving* at mealtimes, God himself consecrates the food anew, as if by a fresh act of creation. The fact is, he continues his creative activity always; in prayer we participate with him in this activity and enjoy its benefits.

2. Timothy's Conduct with Reference to Opponents (4:6–16)

⁶ If you put these instructions before the brethren, you will be a good minister of Christ Jesus, nourished on the words of the faith and of the good doctrine which you have followed.

⁷ Have nothing to do with godless and silly myths. Train yourself in godliness; ⁸ for while bodily training is of some value, godliness is of value in every way, as it holds promise for the present life and also for the life to come. ⁹ The saying is sure and worthy of full acceptance. ¹⁰ For to this end we toil and strive, because we have our hope set on the living God, who is the Savior of all men, especially of those who believe.

¹¹ Command and teach these things. ¹² Let no one despise your youth, but set the believers an example in speech and conduct, in love, in faith, in purity. ¹³ Till I come, attend to the public reading of scripture, to preaching, to teaching. ¹⁴ Do not neglect the gift you have, which was given you by prophetic utterance when the elders laid their hands upon you. ¹⁵ Practice these duties, devote yourself to them, so that all may see your progress. ¹⁶ Take heed to yourself and to your teaching; hold to that, for by so doing you will save both yourself and your hearers.

As he returns to these personal counsels, Paul thinks first of the community at Ephesus. Timothy is to *put these instructions,* i.e., all of the instructions which have preceded, *before the brethren.* In giving advice regarding the community, again Paul makes use of the family image. The verb translated *put before* contains "no note of authority or peremptory command" (Kelly). Timothy's charges are brothers (cf. 5:1; 6:2; 2 Tim. 4:21), a favorite Pauline address for his fellow Christians.

If Timothy passes on Paul's instructions properly, he *will be a good minister of Christ Jesus* (cf. 1 Thess. 3:2). The word *minister* (*diakonos*) is used in a general sense (see comment on 3:8,12), another evidence of the early date of the Pastorals. Effective Christian service, of course, derives from proper preparation. A good minister must be *nourished on the words of the faith and of the good doctrine which you have followed.* Accordingly, Paul had had to feed the Corinthians first milk, then solid food (1 Cor. 3:1 ff.), until they matured (cf. Heb. 5:12–14; Matt. 4:4). The diet in this instance would be *good* Christian doctrine, the opposite of the deceitful doctrines inspired by demons

(4:1). Timothy would know the distinction, for he had learned the message from Paul. Paul elsewhere claims to have taught a certain basic doctrine in all churches he reached in his mission (cf. Rom. 6:17; 16:17; 1 Cor. 4:17), and he insisted upon adherence to it. He was ready to anathematize either men or angels for proclaiming another gospel than he preached (Gal. 1:8 f.).

Thus he exhorts his son in the faith to *have nothing to do with godless and silly myths*. In his denunciation of the clever fabrications of the Judaists, Paul could hardly have chosen stronger terms. Avoid them entirely, he insists (cf. Titus 3:10). He calls the Judaistic *myths* (Titus 1:14) *godless* or profane and *silly*, a term used by philosophers to caricature views of opponents which means literally "old womanish." Such debates would be more suitable, he wants to say, for an old women's gossip circle!

On the positive side, Paul advises Timothy, *Train yourself in godliness*. In illustration of his point he introduces what appears to be a popular Stoic or Cynic maxim on the value of religion or godliness. The formula in v. 9 seems almost certainly to refer back to v. 8 and not to introduce a quotation in v. 10, since the latter (1) opens with *for* and (2) is written in the style of the Pastorals.

The point of the maxim is, if physical training has value, how much greater value has spiritual training. Paul often makes use of analogies drawn from athletics to make a similar point (cf. 1 Cor. 9:24–27; Phil. 3:12). If, as Easton says, "the virtual utilitarianism here is un-Pauline," this must be blamed on the quotation. In using it, Paul does not mean to imply that man's piety or pious exercises will save him, for he has insisted in 1:15 (cf. 2 Tim. 1:9, Titus 3:4 f.) that God's grace alone suffices. Instead, he wishes to argue that spiritual development has more importance than physical because it has farther reaching consequences, holding *promise for the present life and also for the life to come*.

Interpreting in this manner, v. 10 is seen as a commentary by Paul on his illustration. Paul and Timothy *toil and strive* in order to obtain the promise held forth by their faith (*to this end*). A number of early texts read "suffer reproach" instead of "toil." Since a scribe could have introduced the change because of Paul's use of toil and strive together in Colossians 1:29, this could be the correct reading (certainly following the rule of choosing the "harder" reading). However, *toil* fits the athletic imagery better; so most scholars favor it in view of the stronger support it has in early manuscripts.

Paul explains more precisely the basis of the missionary labor. It arises out of the fact that *we have our hope set on the living God, who is the Savior of all men*. The thought parallels closely what Paul has said in 1 Corinthians 15:13–19,30–34,58 (Jeremias). Once again, he comes down hard in opposition to the ascetic exclusivism of the Judaists. A heavy emphasis lies upon *all* as in 2:4,6 (Kelly). *The living God* (see comment on 3:15) is no exclusivist! He accepts men as they are. Their hope resides in his grace rather than in any special ritual or legal prescriptions they may set for themselves.

To this affirmation of universality, Paul appends a note of particularism which some scholars argue Paul would not have added. However, as Scott observes, the addition does not contradict the universal offer. It merely adds, "Since all men can look to God as their Saviour, the Christian may have absolute confidence." In a similar manner Paul urges the Galatians to "do good to all men, and especially to those who are of the household of faith" (6:10). Faith does make a difference in one's relationship to *the living God* and in one's assurance with reference to his salvation. *Those who believe*, almost a technical term meaning Christian, have laid claim to the relationship which God desires to establish and in this way contrast with unbelievers.

Paul becomes even more personal with Timothy. As was noted earlier (1:3), the latter had undoubtedly expressed misgivings about his role in Ephesus. This is apparently why Paul chose the old-commander-to-young-aide motif. In v. 11 he returns to this motif, commanding Timothy like a little child (Spicq). *Command and teach these things,* i.e., what Paul has discussed earlier. Those who doubt Pauline authorship have seen in the statement, *Let no one despise your youth,* a slip which confirms their judgment. Timothy, they insist, would have had to have been in his thirties by the time Paul wrote. The point is quite right, of course, but the Greek word for *youth* (*neotes*) covered anyone up to age forty. Paul evidently replied to a frequent complaint by Timothy, "I am too young!" (Spicq).

So Paul accepts no excuses. Timothy is bidden first to *set the believers an example,* "a truly Pauline touch" (Kelly). The mission of the church proceeds by *example* as much as by word (cf. Titus 2:7). Proper example involves both action—speech and conduct (cf. Rom. 15:18; 1 Cor. 4:20)—and character: *in love, in faith, in purity.* There is something peculiarly Pauline about this combination of actions and virtues (cf. 2 Cor. 6:1 ff.; 2 Tim. 3:10 ff.). They leave little to be added concerning proper moral character in a Christian.

With reference to his handling of the controversy at Ephesus, Paul directs Timothy secondly to go on with an instructional ministry until he returns (see comment on 3:15). The nature and brevity of his instructions indicate an early date (Kelly). A second-century document would almost certainly have referred to the Lord's Supper.[25] But this list includes only three functions, all a regular part of Jewish synagogue worship: (1) *The public reading of scripture* (lit., only reading) would involve primarily the Old Testament, the earliest Christian's Bible (cf. Luke 4:16; Acts 13:15; 2 Cor. 3:14; Justin, I *Apol.* 67). Paul's letter would probably be read at some point in the service also. (2)

[25] Cf. Didache; Justin, I *Apol.* 67.

Preaching (lit., exhortation), as in the synagogue, would involve comments on the Scripture texts (Acts 13:15; Rom. 12:8; 1 Cor. 14:3). Among Christians the sermon or homily probably emphasized messianic texts more than morality. (3) *Teaching* (Rom. 12:7) refers to the more extended instruction of new converts. Paul mentions a special spiritual gift for both preaching (Rom. 12:8) and teaching (1 Cor. 12:28–29; Eph. 4:11), but neither assumed the formal character of an office, like that of bishop, presbyter, and deacon.

Paul undergirds his two personal directives by reminding Timothy of his spiritual gift (*charisma*). In Paul this term usually designates an endowment by the Holy Spirit for a particular ministry (Rom. 1:11; 12:6; 1 Cor. 12:4,9,28,30–31; 2 Tim. 1:6); occasionally it is almost synonymous with grace (*charis*) (Rom. 5:15–16; 6:23).

The way in which Timothy received his gift, according to this passage, is somewhat unclear. The use of the passive verb *was given* means "God gave," not "prophecy gave" as might be suggested by the RSV rendering. As we have seen in 1:18, a prophecy inspired by the Spirit pointed Timothy out, the obvious meaning of the phrase *by* (or through) *prophetic* utterance. A problem also arises with reference to the laying on of hands by the *elders.* In 2 Timothy 1:6 Paul stirs Timothy with a reminder of "the gift of God that is within you through the laying on of my hands." This difference can perhaps be explained by the different character of the letters—a kind of community rule in the first, a personal testament in the second.

Following David Daube, however, J. N. D. Kelly has suggested another interpretation of the role of elders in Timothy's ordination which helps to solve the problem from another perspective. The usual view, represented in the RSV translation, is that the elders of the church at Ephesus (or Lystra) gathered around and one by one laid hands on him (cf. Acts 6:6; 13:3). Kelly notes that both 2 Timothy 1:6 and 1 Timothy 5:22 imply the laying on of hands by *one* person. The latter could of course refer to baptism and not ordination, the former only by assuming Paul's participation with others in the ordination. Daube has solved the problem by holding that the phrase "laying on of the hands of the presbytery" is a literal rendering of the Hebrew *semik-hath zeqenim,* a technical phrase for the ordination of an elder or rabbi in Judaism.[26] Kelly thus translates the verse, "Do not leave unused the special gift which is in you, which was bestowed upon you to the accompaniment of prophecy along with the laying on of hands for ordination as an elder." The chief problem with this view is whether Timothy actually filled the role of a presbyter.

Laying on of hands played an important role in Jewish practice; quite naturally, it also figured prominently in early Christianity. The rite was "an accompanying act —not a means" (Barrett) for conveying the Spirit, as some contend (cf. Dibelius-Conzelmann). Hands were laid on the sick for the purpose of healing; on children, the weak or unclean for the purpose of blessing (Mark 10:13 ff.); on those who had not received the Spirit for the purpose of imparting the gift (without connection with baptism in Acts 8:17; with baptism in Acts 19:6; Heb. 6:2); and on those commissioned to a special task (Acts 6:6; 13:3). The laying on of hands here and in 2 Timothy 1:6 belong to this last category.

Verses 15–16 resume the athlete metaphor of vv. 7–10 with special reference to the virtues of v. 12, the instruction of v. 13, and the charism of v. 14. Paul directs Timothy to *practice these duties* (lit., be concerned about these things) and to *devote yourself to them* (lit., be in them). The purpose of his faithful discharge of his duties is *that all may see your progress.* The word translated *progress* (only in Paul, Phil. 1:12,25) plays on the military motif; it means "promotion in rank." Timo-

thy has to establish his leadership position in the Ephesian church.

Paul sums up. Timothy should *take heed* to himself personally and to his *teaching.* In personal character and in sound doctrine he is to remain steadfast, for what he does affects his own relationship to God and that of his hearers. Easton has said that "the language could hardly be more un-Pauline." Admittedly, the statement is stronger than Paul has given elsewhere. Paul may have exaggerated a bit in order to leave Timothy in no doubt about the importance of his role. Actually, he seems to allude to his own fear, in which he struggled always to bring himself under control, "lest after preaching to others I myself should be disqualified" (1 Cor. 9:27).

3. Conduct with Reference to Younger and Older Persons (5:1–2)

[1] Do not rebuke an older man but exhort him as you would a father; treat younger men like brothers, [2] older women like mothers, younger women like sisters, in all purity.

At this point Paul begins to outline Timothy's conduct with reference to various groups in the church at Ephesus—older and younger persons (5:1–2), widows (3–16), presbyters (17–25), and slaves and masters (6:1–2). His advice concerning the first group agrees well with his image of a local congregation as a family. The counsel against harsh treatment (*Do not rebuke*) applies to all four groups mentioned. Far better, as was Paul's own custom, is exhortation or encouragement (cf. Rom. 16:13 f.). Positive discipline achieves far more than negative censure.

The use of the Greek *presbuteros* in the nontechnical sense of "older man" confirms again the primitiveness of these letters. The advice given has many parallels in contemporary documents and draws its schema "from popular moral philosophy."

4. Widows (5:3–16)

[3] Honor widows who are real widows. [4] If a widow has children or grandchildren, let them

[26] *The New Testament and Rabbinic Judaism* (London: University of London, Athlone Press, 1956), pp. 244–246.

first learn their religious duty to their own family and make some return to their parents; for this is acceptable in the sight of God. [5] She who is a real widow, and is left all alone, has set her hope on God and continues in supplications and prayers night and day; [6] whereas she who is self-indulgent is dead even while she lives. [7] Command this, so that they may be without reproach. [8] If any one does not provide for his relatives, and especially for his own family, he has disowned the faith and is worse than an unbeliever.

[9] Let a widow be enrolled if she is not less than sixty years of age, having been the wife of one husband; [10] and she must be well attested for her good deeds, as one who has brought up children, shown hospitality, washed the feet of the saints, relieved the afflicted, and devoted herself to doing good in every way. [11] But refuse to enrol younger widows; for when they grow wanton against Christ they desire to marry, [12] and so they incur condemnation for having violated their first pledge. [13] Besides that, they learn to be idlers, gadding about from house to house, and not only idlers but gossips and busybodies, saying what they should not. [14] So I would have younger widows marry, bear children, rule their households, and give the enemy no occasion to revile us. [15] For some have already strayed after Satan. [16] If any believing woman has relatives who are widows, let her assist them; let the church not be burdened, so that it may assist those who are real widows.

Widows and orphans were the object of special concern in early Christianity, as in Judaism (cf. Deut. 10:18; 24:17; Luke 2:37). Very early (cf. Acts 6:1; 9:39 ff.) the church made special provision for both. Since it appealed to the lower and poorer classes in its early years, the lists naturally grew at a rapid rate. By about the middle of the third century Cornelius of Rome reported 1500 widows and needy on the Roman dole.[27]

When Paul wrote these letters, the care of widows obviously constituted a heavy burden at Ephesus. His major aim was to enroll on the church's charitable list only those whose needs and manner of life demonstrated that they were genuine widows, i.e., without any family or relatives who could support them other than the church. With this in view he gives very

practical advice about narrowing the list and at the same time eliminating residual problems as well. Although some scholars (e.g., Jeremias, Scott) have tried to divide his advice into two sections—care of widows (vv. 3–8) and duties of widows (vv. 9–16)—the material lacks clear organization. Others (e.g., Parry arranges verses in the order 3, 4, 8, 7, 5, 6, 9) have offered rearrangements to solve the organizational problem. However, it seems best to treat the material in order, recognizing that Paul probably had no well formulated tradition from Judaism or early Christianity to draw from. As K. Weidinger [28] has shown, extra-Christian tables of duties lacked entirely any instructions concerning widows.

What is stated in this section does not require us to see here an "officially recognized order" of widows, like that of presbyter-bishops and deacons, though some scholars adopt that interpretation. Paul lists among qualifications only (1) need and (2) record of Christian service achieved *before* being widowed. The duties prescribed are those one would expect from persons who lived entirely from the subsistence provided by the church. Gradually widows' functions assumed a more clearly defined character, being merged with the office of virgins.

Paul first directs Timothy to *honor widows who are real widows*. *Honor* does not mean "officially recognize" (Kelly), but it does imply financial support as well as personal respect (Barrett, Dibelius-Conzelmann). Such respect and support should not be given indiscriminately, thus burdening the church's limited resources, but be reserved for "widows in real need" (Moffatt).

Where possible, Paul goes on to say, Christian families should care for their own. Instead of burdening the church, the *children* or *grandchildren* should *first learn their religious duty to their own family* (lit., to their household). In Greek the verb *learn* has no subject, so it is possible to

---

27 Eusebius, H. E., 6:43.

28 *Die Haustafeln* (Leipzig: J. C. Hinrichs, 1928), p. 68.

supply "widows" instead of *children or grandchildren.* The point would be, true widows demonstrate their widowhood by staying at home and taking care of their own family. However, this interpretation is made unlikely by the context, especially the reference to making *some return to their parents.* The better sense is that children or grandchildren will properly "practice their religion" (Kelly) and repay their parents by caring for widowed mothers or grandmothers. The reason is that *this is acceptable in the sight of God,* another allusion to the Fifth Commandment.

Paul now provides a test. His *real widow* comes strikingly close to Luke's picture of the prophetess Anna (Luke 2:37). Without visible means of support the genuine widow *has set her hope on God,* a Hebrew way of saying, She has taken refuge in God (cf. Psalm 91:2). Externally her commitment appears in continuous (*night and day*) involvement in private and public worship.

On the other hand, a spurious widow is *self-indulgent,* i.e., abandoned to pleasure and comfort (Kelly). The word translated *self-indulgent* has a broader nuance than "prostitution" (Easton). Such a person is spiritually dead. The only true life is life lived for God.

Paul underlines his command, for the church's reputation is at stake. Like bishops (3:2), those who represent the church by living off of its charity should be *without reproach.*

Verse 8 strengthens the directive in v. 4 (cf. Titus 1:16). Whoever fails to *provide for his own relatives,* in actions even if not formally, *has disowned the faith,* for Christianity teaches love. He is *worse than an unbeliever;* the pagan would take care of his own.

Paul now turns to enumerate more specific qualifications for *real widows.* In doing so, as Kelly observes, he perhaps "hints at the duties involved." The phrase *let a widow be enrolled* has a much more technical meaning than *honor* in v. 3. The verb was used with reference to placing names

(of officials, soldiers, etc.) on a recognized list or catalogue, but it does not make it "absolutely clear that there was a definite order of widows" (Kelly). Rather, the church's charity list is implied.

The major requirements are three: (1) over 60, (2) married only once, and (3) having a reputation for charitable works. Age 60 was the recognized old age in antiquity.

The wife of one husband must be interpreted in the light of 3:2,12 and Titus 1:6. Inscriptional evidence sustains the interpretation of one marriage (*monandria*).

As an object of charity, she *must be well attested for her good deeds,* i.e., those before applying. Paul spells out four specific items in this general test. (1) She should have reared children. Those who see an official order of widows here apply this reference to the children of other persons, particularly orphans. Barrett has correctly thought them "probably, but not necessarily, her own." Widows undoubtedly did aid in the rearing of orphans, a major care of the early church.[29] (2) She should have *shown hospitality,* i.e., entertained the numerous traveling missionaries, prophets, preachers, and teachers (cf. the Didache, chs. 11–12). (3) She should have *washed the feet of the saints,* i.e., Christians (a frequent usage in Paul's letters). Foot-washing was a courtesy for weary travelers performed by the menial slave of a household. It thus involves not only hospitality (Luke 7:44) but also preparation for self-denying, humble service (Jeremias), of which Jesus himself gave the example (John 13:14; Matt. 10:25). (4) She should have *relieved the afflicted.* Affliction here has a more general nuance than persecution, which the Pastorals do not mention directly (Hanson).

Paul sums up. She should have *devoted herself to doing good in every way* (cf. 2 Cor. 9:8). The phrase implies more than almsgiving, which the early church expected of its members also. It demands the

---

29 Cf. James 1:27; Hermas, *Mandates* 8:10; *Apostolic Constitutions* 3.3.2.

response of the whole person, arising out of the gratitude of a child of God (Jeremias), from which springs "a consistent habit of charity" (Scott).

In vv. 11–15 Paul proceeds to explain why younger widows must not be placed on the roll. The indiscretions of certain younger widows would appear to have been his second significant reason for composing the whole statement. He sets forth three major problems, the answers to which are to be found in remarriage: (1) sexual passion, (2) idleness, and (3) gossiping, or possibly even delving into sorcery.

His counsel against enrolling *younger widows* is phrased in very strong language. Shun them, he says, using the same word he had used about avoiding the sectarian's "godless and silly myths" (4:7; cf. 2 Tim. 2:23). This may imply more than the RSV rendering, *refuse to enrol younger widows,* suggests. Timothy, still young and unmarried, would need to exercise personal caution. Normally these youthful widows would have a strong sexual drive which would create a desire for marriage. Hence, they would act *against Christ,* the spiritual bridegroom (cf. 2 Cor. 11:2), violating *their first pledge.* This pledge may be either (1) the initial commitment of faith connected with baptism or (2) a vow of fidelity and chastity when placed on the roll of widows.

Of greater immediate consequence in view of the trouble at Ephesus is their idleness. Without homes and family to busy themselves with, young widows *learn to be idlers.* The Greek is a bit difficult, reading literally "idlers learn" (*manthanousin*). Some scholars have speculated that one letter was changed from the original which was "idlers escape notice" (*lanthanousin*). The latter has no early manuscript support, however; the RSV translation is entirely possible and preferred, fitting the context perfectly. In their idleness they gad about *from house to house.*

Vagabond habits open the way for gossip and meddling and all sorts of ill-advised talk. The word rendered *busybodies* in

the RSV may imply an involvement in some sort of magic. It figures prominently in the magical papyri. Luke uses it to describe certain Jewish sorcerers at Ephesus (Acts 19:19). If the word does hint at magical practices, *saying what they should not* may contain "an allusion to the spells and occult formulae used" by these widows with a view to curing the sick (Kelly).

So Paul issues a categorical order. *I would have* (cf. 2:8) is a euphemism for "I command" (Easton). Paul's strong stand here regarding marriage seems to conflict at first glance with 1 Corinthians 7:25 ff., where he strongly favors nonmarriage. Two factors, however, explain the differing positions: (1) Paul wrote 1 Corinthians 7 with a view to his expectation of Christ's immediate return. In later years he moderated this view. (2) In 1 Corinthians 7 he gives a general directive, in 1 Timothy 5 a directive addressed to a specific problem. Even in the former he advised marriage on account of sexual passion (vv. 9,36).

The church's reputation is at stake in the behavior of these women. The duties of marriage, rearing children, and taking care of a home will eliminate the problem of idleness, as any housewife knows. Accordingly, by different deportment the young women will *give the enemy no occasion to revile us.* To take or give occasion is a Pauline mannerism (cf. 2 Cor. 5:12). *The enemy* may be either (1) any opponent or detractor of the church (cf. 1 Cor. 16:9; Phil. 1:28) or (2) Satan. Paul is anxious to avoid scandal, for the mission depends heavily upon a good reputation (cf. 3:7; 6:1; Titus 2:5,8). Unfortunately, Paul laments, *some* (see comment on 1:3) *have already strayed after Satan,* i.e., have wandered away (the same verb as in 1:6) and fallen under Satan's control.

Paul concludes his statement regarding widows with a kind of appendix to vv. 4 and 8, which at the same time ties the whole discussion together. The main concern is clear: All should help to relieve the church's burden of charity *so that it may assist those who are real widows.* Another possible source of relief, besides immediate families, would be any Christian woman of means who could keep widows in her home. This seems to be the correct meaning of the text, but two others have been offered: (1) Several early Greek manuscripts read, "If any believing man (*pistos*) or believing woman (*pistē*) has widows." A few scholars have adopted this reading on the grounds that a woman could hardly head a household and care for others by herself. However, the manuscript evidence heavily favors the reading "If any believing woman." The example of Lydia (Acts 16:14,40) counters the other argument. (2) Some scholars have read the stronger text, "If any believing *widow* has widows," supplying the noun, which has been ellipted. This would imply that widows banded together for mutual support and encouragement. However, the most natural translation is the one given.

5. Church Discipline (5:17–25)

17 Let the elders who rule well be considered worthy of double honor, especially those who labor in preaching and teaching; 18 for the scripture says, "You shall not muzzle an ox when it is treading out the grain," and, "The laborer deserves his wages." 19 Never admit any charge against an elder except on the evidence of two or three witnesses. 20 As for those who persist in sin, rebuke them in the presence of all, so that the rest may stand in fear. 21 In the presence of God and of Christ Jesus and of the elect angels I charge you to keep these rules without favor, doing nothing from partiality. 22 Do not be hasty in the laying on of hands, nor participate in another man's sins; keep yourself pure.
23 No longer drink only water, but use a little wine for the sake of your stomach and your frequent ailments.
24 The sins of some men are conspicuous, pointing to judgment, but the sins of others appear later. 25 So also good deeds are conspicuous; and even when they are not, they cannot remain hidden.

This section of 1 Timothy has traditionally been applied to presbyters or elders in the official sense. Joachim Jeremias (supported by C. K. Barrett), however, has contested this interpretation and argued that the term *presbuteroi* should be given a non-formal meaning here, i.e., "older men." Though he probably errs in arguing the same for Titus 1:5, he does build a strong case for this passage. The chief problem with the official designation here is the opening statement. Would two salaries be set for two classes of presbyters—*those who rule well* and those who do not? Not likely! If, on the other hand, the statement applies to older men, as in 5:1, charged with certain leadership functions, then the meaning becomes quite clear.

Paul first deals with the matter of respect and pay due leaders. In accordance with the interpretation adopted above, *the elders* should read "the older men." The word translated *rule*, found only in Paul's letters, is not quite as strong as this rendering suggests. It was used in 3:4,12 with reference to fathers managing their households. It may also mean "be concerned about" (Titus 3:8,14). The church family image given in the Pastorals would suggest a rendering like "those elders who lead well" (cf. Rom. 12:8; 1 Thess. 5:12).

Effective leaders deserve *double honor.* The word *honor* commonly has a dual nuance; it means both (1) respect and (2) pay. The quotations in v. 18 show that Paul has primarily the latter in mind here (Easton). At this early stage (cf. *Didache* 13) the pay would involve gifts by the congregation, not salary (Hanson). In other letters Paul has insisted upon the right of ministers to receive such gifts (1 Thess. 2:9; 1 Cor. 9:7 ff.), but he stigmatizes those who use religion as a means of personal gain (1 Tim. 6:5 f.; Titus 1:11). Elders who lead well deserve *double* pay, probably meaning twice what widows and others on the church welfare list would receive.

Among the leaders Paul singles out *those who labor in preaching* (lit., in word) *and teaching.* The Greek word for *labor* is a technical Pauline term designating the apostolic ministry in general (cf. Rom. 16:12–13; 1 Cor. 15:10; Gal. 4:11; Phil.

2:16; Col. 1:29) and especially community leaders (1 Thess. 5:12). All presbyter-bishops were expected to share in teaching (3:2; Titus 1:8–9), but some had special spiritual gifts (see comment on 4:12 f.).

Paul supports his directive regarding pay for church leaders with two quotations—one from the Old Testament and one from oral tradition. *For the scripture says* is Paul's typical formula for quoting Old Testament texts (cf. Rom. 9:12; 10:11). He uses the same text (Deut. 25:4) in 1 Corinthians 9:9 with a similar application. The second quotation is found in Luke 10:7 as a word of Jesus. Paul has possibly already alluded to the same statement in 1 Corinthians 9:4. The agreement with the Lucan form of the quotation offers some support for the view that Luke was Paul's secretary. That a word of Jesus would be cited with the authority of Scripture should occasion no surprise. Paul elsewhere uses Jesus' teaching in a similar way (cf. 1 Cor. 7:25).

From his discussion of recompense for leaders Paul turns to consider discipline. He offers two rules to follow: (1) Consider an accusation against an older leader only when at least two or three persons confirm his fault. This would assure him the same fairness required by the Old Testament (Deut. 19:15; Matt. 18:16; 2 Cor. 13:1; John 8:17). No formal excommunication is implied; the case would be at the investigation stage. (2) If the charge is established and the accused persists (the present participle) in his sin, the offender should be rebuked publicly. Some have interpreted *in the presence of all* to refer to all the presbyters, but this seems to stand against the natural sense. *The rest* may refer to other leaders (Spicq, Dibelius-Conzelmann) or to the other members of the church.

Paul calls for a fair application of his rules with a solemn oath (Spicq). *I charge you* is more accurately rendered, I adjure you (2 Tim. 2:14; 4:1). He appeals to those who will take part in the final judgment—God, Christ, angels—an established

formula in Judaism (Dibelius-Conzelmann). The reference to *elect angels* (cf. "holy angels" in Luke 9:26; Rev. 14:10) shows the apocryphal influence on early Christianity (*Odes of Solomon* 4:8). Angels will accompany Christ when he returns to judge men (1 Cor. 11:10; Matt. 25:31; Mark 8:38; Luke 9:26). Paul is concerned chiefly that Timothy *keep these rules* (lit., only "these") *without favor, doing nothing from partiality*. The strong wording gives some hint of "a concrete case, or perhaps cases, of scandal arising out of the preferential treatment which erring elders have received" (Kelly). *Without favor* means without prejudice. *Partiality* refers to the personal inclinations which could lead to an unfair judgment.

We cannot be certain as to how vv. 22–25 relate to what precedes. *The laying on of hands* could refer to either of three usages: (1) in baptism (Acts 8:17), (2) in restoring penitent sinners (cf. Cyprian, *Epistle* 11), or (3) ordination. The context hardly favors the first. The second, while attractive from many points of view, has serious problems: (a) Elsewhere in the Pastorals (4:14; 2 Tim. 1:6), laying on of hands is related to ordination. (b) The evidence for the practice in restoring penitents comes from the third century. (c) In the first and second centuries assurance of sincere repentance sufficed for readmission. (d) The question here is of future, not past sins (Spicq, Scott). On the whole, the evidence favors the third option ordination.

Actually Paul deals here with preventive discipline. His advice against hasty ordination has the same thrust as his warning about neophytes in 3:6; there should be thorough investigation first. Since Timothy played such a strategic role in selecting leaders, unwise choices could cause him to fall under suspicion. He would be guilty —*participate in another man's sins*—by lack of care. So Paul adds a personal warning—*Keep yourself pure*.

Concern about Timothy's own reputation apparently evokes an aside. The statement emerges so abruptly that some (e.g., Moffatt) have treated it as a scribal gloss, but there is absolutely no manuscript evidence for doing so. It again confirms the authenticity of the letters, for what forger would have thought to break his train of thought in this manner?

The statement qualifies the word *pure*. It may have a polemical intent, i.e., opposing the extreme asceticism of the Judaists reflected in 4:1–5. With a tender disposition Timothy may have avoided wine even at the risk of his health. The medicinal value of wine was widely acknowledged in the ancient world. But both Jews and Greeks believed drinking water alone belonged to the pious man's regimen (cf. Dan. 1:12; *Pirke Aboth* 6:4; Epictetus 3.13.21). So Paul (cf. Rom. 14:2,21; Col. 2:21 f.) gives his instructions "not to advocate the use of wine, but to protest against a type of doctrine which would rule out the whole physical side of man's life as evil" (Scott).

After this brief aside Paul resumes his theme of discipline in more general terms. The two verses explain why hands should not be laid on anyone too hastily. The faults of some are easy to detect, those of others difficult, not visible until the judgment of God. In the same way good deeds are sometimes easy to see, sometimes difficult, but they too will be clearly visible in the final judgment.

6. Conduct of Slaves Toward Their Masters (6:1–2a)

¹ Let all who are under the yoke of slavery regard their masters as worthy of all honor, so that the name of God and the teaching may not be defamed. ² Those who have believing masters must not be disrespectful on the ground that they are brethren; rather they must serve all the better since those who benefit by their service are believers and beloved.

The fifth group concerning which Paul gives advice are the slaves. Slaves constituted a large and important element in the church's constituency and often received attention in early literature.

In this passage Paul distinguished two cases: (1) where slaves have heathen masters and (2) where they have Christian masters. Barrett has suggested that the statement is addressed "particularly to elders who are slaves." The reference to being *under the yoke* is redundant and does not set forth any special difficulty. Where slaves have pagan masters, Paul advises, they should give them full respect, i.e., they should not have ill feelings as a consequence of their servitude. As he had obviously advised Onesimus, service to Christ causes one to serve others better. The reason is missionary. If they serve well, their masters cannot speak hurtfully of (lit., blaspheme) *the name of God and the teaching* (cf. Rom. 2:24; Isa. 52:5).

Paul may have been more concerned about the potential difficulties of the second case. Converted slaves were undoubtedly tempted to take liberties with the equality of status in the church, refusing to pay deference to Christian masters, *on the ground that they are brethren.* Paul cautions against this. The common status of brothers in Christ should cause them to *serve all the better.* In Christ all are to "be servants of one another" (Gal. 5:13), so servitude should not irk a Christian. In the Greek *those who benefit by their service* may refer either to the masters or to the slaves. The former seems more likely. Slaves should serve with greater enthusiasm because believing and beloved masters rather than pagans would profit from their work.

V. Final Orders (6:2b–19)

In 6:2b Paul returns to the problem with which he began his orders to Timothy (1:3 ff.).

1. Against the Profit Motive in Religion (6:2b–10)

Teach and urge these duties. ³ If any one teaches otherwise and does not agree with the sound words of our Lord Jesus Christ and the teaching which accords with godliness, ⁴ he is puffed up with conceit, he knows nothing; he has a morbid craving for controversy and for disputes about words, which produce envy, dissension, slander, base suspicions, 5 and wrangling among men who are depraved in mind and bereft of the truth, imagining that godliness is a means of gain. 6 There is great gain in godliness with contentment; 7 for we brought nothing into the world, and we cannot take anything out of the world; 8 but if we have food and clothing, with these we shall be content. 9 But those who desire to be rich fall into temptation, into a snare, into many senseless and hurtful desires that plunge men into ruin and destruction. 10 For the love of money is the root of all evils; it is through this craving that some have wandered away from the faith and pierced their hearts with many pangs.

Christianity, like all religions, has from the first had some who adopted it for the wrong reasons. Simon the magician (Acts 8:18–24) has lent his name to all who have done so with a view to making money out of it. The Judaists apparently had some Simoniacs among them, who used their religion for pecuniary considerations. In denouncing them, Paul draws from popular proverbs which he intermingles so skillfully into his refutation that we have some difficulty following his points. The passage constitutes his harshest denunciation yet.

Teach and urge these duties has been applied to (1) the immediately preceding instructions regarding slaves, (2) the "whole epistle" (Easton), or (3) the words which follow (Scott). Spicq has perhaps given the best solution in interpreting it as a kind of transition statement.

The wording of the passage demonstrates that Paul resumes his initial attack on his opponents (1:3 ff.). The test for them would be Paul's own teachings (cf. Gal. 1—2), *the sound words of our Lord Jesus Christ and the teaching which accords with godliness. Words of our Lord* may refer either (1) to Jesus' teaching or (2) to instruction about him, perhaps to both. Paul considered the actual words of Jesus absolutely authoritative (cf. 1 Cor. 7), but he also counted Jesus, the risen Christ, the basis of Christian faith (cf. 1 Cor. 15:3 ff.). The addition of *the teaching which accords with godliness* emphasizes that doctrinal belief and manner of life go hand in hand.

Unfortunately the theorizing about the law did not produce proper piety. Instead it led to personal conceit and controversies. As was true in Corinth (1 Cor. 8:1), knowledge had "puffed up" rather than "built up." The one who strays from the *sound* or healthy *words*, Paul insists, becomes "spiritually sick" (Scott). While professing to have superior understanding, he comprehends nothing. Worse still, and Paul alludes again quite specifically to the erroneous teachers, *he has a morbid craving* (lit., is sick about) *for controversy and for disputes about words.* Luke uses the word *controversy* with reference to the debate over acceptance of Gentiles into the church (Acts 15:2,7; 25:20). The single Greek word (*logomachia*) translated *disputes about words* was apparently coined by Paul to describe the wrangling of the teachers of law (cf. 2 Tim. 2:14).

Such useless argument produces many other ills. Paul cites four from a traditional catalogue of vices. There would be an internal disruption by *envy* and *dissension* (cf. Phil. 1:15). There would be external criticism in *slander* (lit., blasphemies) and *base suspicions.* Early Christianity suffered a great deal from the follies of its own members, charged often with the grossest offenses against human decency. Though frequently untrue, the charges did illustrate the wisdom of Paul's counsel here.

Paul struggles for words sufficient to describe his contempt. *Wrangling* hardly does justice to the Greek word *diaparatribe* which Paul again coined. The latter is an intensive of *paratribe*, which means friction or irritation. Their debates are "extreme irritations" of *men who are depraved in mind and bereft of the truth.* Paul actually accuses them of being unable any longer to distinguish truth from falsehood, right from wrong.

Paul even attacks their motives (cf. Phil. 1:15). Some think *that godliness is a means of gain.* This statement may mean either (1) that they use their neighbors' piety to make money out of them (Kelly) or (2) that they act pious to make money and gain material advancement (Spicq). Titus 1:11 would suggest that they taught for pay, like many philosophers in the ancient world. Traveling teachers or preachers constituted a real problem in early Christianity, for they often used their "gifts" to exploit generous fellow Christians.

Lest his statement suggest that he sees no benefit in religion, Paul has to cover his tracks by expanding his thought. The Greek verb is in the emphatic position at the beginning of the sentence. Religion *is* indeed a means of *great gain* when pursued *with contentment.* The word translated *contentment* formed the very heart of Stoic doctrine. The true Stoic sought always to control his passions and to be contented with his lot. Though influenced by Stoicism, Paul has a much deeper understanding of the word contentment, which appears only in his writings in the New Testament (cf. 2 Cor. 9:8). Paul's feeling of contentment lay not in a resignation to circumstances, whatever they might be, but in his confidence in the risen Christ, who equipped him to surmount circumstances (cf. Phil. 4:13).

Verses 7–10 provide a commentary on the word *contentment* (Spicq). Paul borrows heavily from traditional teachings, probably of the Roman church where Stoicism was very influential. The standpoint of these materials is "a naive Eudaemonism" such as dominated popular philosophy, perhaps of Jewish-Hellenistic origin (Dibelius-Conzelmann). Yet one observes also some Old and New Testament parallels.

Paul argues for *contentment,* probably with a quotation, on the basis of the grim facts that we came into the world empty-handed and we leave it empty-handed (cf. Job 1:21; Luke 12:16–21). The text of the verse has caused considerable problem. The better manuscripts read, "for we brought nothing into the world, because, or that (*hoti*), we cannot take anything out of the world." The logical problem of this reading has led to a number of emendations: A few early texts have read (1)

"it is true that" or (2) "it is evident that" rather than "because," supposing an ellipsis. Modern scholars have suggested two other solutions: (3) that *oti* was added unintentionally in copying *on* in the word *kosmon* (world) and should be deleted, or (4) that *hoti* should be read as the neuter of *hostis,* thus translating, "for we brought nothing into the world which we are not able to take out." The RSV has adopted solution (3). However, there is no manuscript evidence of this reading, so the better solution is to suppose with (1) and (2) a kind of ellipsis or to leave the logical fallacy.

Food and clothing illustrate necessities. Paul says nothing here which would deny industry. However, the passage should certainly be taken as a warning against a reckless pursuit of material goods.

Paul now issues a warning. The pursuit of gain is sure to bring its own punishment (Scott). The antipathy to wealth reflected here and in 6:17–19 reflects the Lucan outlook. If Luke was Paul's amanuensis, he could well have composed rather freely. Apart from the specific problem here, wealth posed problems for the early church and often received the attention of Christian writers. Consisting preponderantly of the lower classes, during the first two centuries most Christians took a rather dim view of worldly goods. Clement of Alexandria (*ca.* 190–210) was the first to write more positively, offering some guidelines for a positive stewardship. Paul reflects here the earlier attitude.

Those who have money as their goal in life, Paul says, become easy prey for Satan, ruler of worldly things (see comment on 3:7; 2 Tim. 2:26). Falling under his control plunges men like sinking ships *into ruin and destruction,* i.e., of the final judgment. The words *ruin* (*olethros;* cf. 1 Cor. 5:5; 1 Thess. 5:3; 2 Thess. 1:9), and *destruction* (*apōleia;* cf. Rom. 9:22; Phil. 1:28, 3:19; 2 Thess. 2:3) emphasize the completeness of one's fall.

Not money per se, please note carefully, but obsession with money causes one's ruin.

The Midas story repeats itself over and over. "For the love of money is the root of all evils." Many have pointed out how sharply this thought contrasts with what Paul says elsewhere. Self-love, not love of money, lies at the root of the human problem. But Paul undoubtedly quotes here a current proverb which exaggerates his point. Having said it, he turns its thought back to the false teachers. It was their *craving* for money which caused them to stray *from the faith* (Christianity) and encounter many griefs (see comment on 1:19). Harsh words for the enemies of the Gentile mission, but ones of which Paul was quite capable.

2. A Personal Charge to the Man of God (6:11–16)

¹¹ But as for you, man of God, shun all this; aim at righteousness, godliness, faith, love, steadfastness, gentleness. ¹² Fight the good fight of the faith; take hold of the eternal life to which you were called when you made the good confession in the presence of many witnesses. ¹³ In the presence of God who gives life to all things, and of Christ Jesus who in his testimony before Pontius Pilate made the good confession, ¹⁴ I charge you to keep the commandment unstained and free from reproach until the appearing of our Lord Jesus Christ; ¹⁵ and this will be made manifest at the proper time by the blessed and only Sovereign, the King of kings and Lord of lords, ¹⁶ who alone has immortality and dwells in unapproachable light, whom no man has ever seen or can see. To him be honor and eternal dominion. Amen.

Paul seems to interrupt his warnings about avarice, continued in v. 17, with a final charge to Timothy. The character of the whole intervening parenthesis has led some scholars to suggest that we have here either a baptismal discourse (Hans Windisch) or an ordination address (Jeremias). More accurately, it appears to be a personal charge to Timothy sustained by an allusion to one or other of these.

As opposed to the unnamed persons of vv. 3 and 10, Paul enjoins Timothy to *shun all this*, i.e., contention and use of religion to make money. Instead, he should *aim at* the key virtues. The strong contrasting

commands (lit., flee and pursue) are peculiarly Pauline (cf. 1 Cor. 6:18; 10:4; 2 Tim. 2:22). The combination of *faith, love, steadfastness* are reminiscent also of Paul's triad of faith, hope, and love (1 Cor. 13:13). *Gentleness* is a rare word, but it is composed of the frequently used "meek" (*praus*). In this quality the *man of God* would emulate Christ himself (cf. Matt. 11:29; 5:5). The phrase *man of God* appears often in the Old Testament—of Moses, David, Samuel, Elijah, Elisha, and others—where it connotes especially one whom God has laid hold upon "for himself and for his service" (Barrett).

The pursuit of *godliness* will require discipline. Once again Paul resorts to an athletic or military metaphor. Timothy must *fight the good fight of the faith*, like the gladiator in the arena (Easton) or the soldier on the battlefield (Simpson), for the prize is worthy (cf. Phil. 3:14; 1 Cor. 9:25–26). It is not an earthly crown but *the eternal life to which you were called.* The last phrase eliminates any suggestion of a works righteousness. God himself invites us to *eternal life.*

The context of *the good confession* made by Timothy *in the presence of many witnesses* has been debated. Interpreting in light of v. 13, there are three possible alternatives: (1) confession made in persecution, (2) ordination (Meinertz, Jeremias, Barrett), or (3) baptism (Easton, Hanson, many others). The third suggestion has the strongest support. Persecution would not seem to have merited so formal a reference, and we have no record that Timothy experienced actual arrest and trial. Ordination seems unlikely because early ordination rites required no confession of faith.³⁰ Barrett has sustained this view on the grounds that it makes the best sense of "obey your orders" (v. 14), but, as we have seen, the military motif dominates the whole letter. The whole passage fits the early nuances of baptism perfectly. Baptism was an invitation to share in Christ's

³⁰ Cf. Hippolytus, *Apos. Trad.*

self-offering to God. Jesus himself referred to his impending death as a "baptism" (Mark 10:38) and evidently connected his baptism by John with the Servant role.

Paul undergirds his final orders with a solemn invoking of God and Christ Jesus as his witnesses. The content and structure of the passage would indicate that he is citing part of an early formula of confession, probably baptismal, as in 2:6. Two-part confessions such as this developed early in the Gentile setting. This particular fragment has an interesting resemblance to the Old Roman Symbol, forerunner of the Apostles' Creed, attesting again the Roman origin of the formal materials of the Pastorals.

The allusion to God should give Timothy courage, for it is he *who gives life to all things.* The RSV rendering takes the middle road between the two ancient readings —"who keeps alive" (the rare *zoogoneō* appearing only here and in Tatian) and "who makes alive or creates" (*zoopoieō*). The first reading has much stronger support and suits the context better. If God preserves life, Timothy has nothing to fear. Christ has given the supreme example of a worthy confession *in his testimony before Pontius Pilate.*

Before such unshakeable witnesses Paul charges Timothy to *keep the commandment unstained and free from reproach. The commandment* may be the baptismal charge (A. T. Hanson) or the charge of vv. 11–12 (Easton *et al.*). Actually both may be in Paul's mind. The adjectives *unstained and free from reproach* may apply either to Timothy or, more likely, *the commandment.* The orders are binding *until the appearing of our Lord Jesus Christ,* a clear indication that the return of Christ was still anticipated. Paul often uses *parousia* for the second coming (e.g., 1 Cor. 15:23; 1 Thess. 2:19), but he also uses *epiphaneia* (2 Thess. 2:8; Titus 2:13). The frequency of usage of the latter in the emperor cult may explain his preference in the Pastorals.

The mention of Christ's return brings to Paul's mind a hymn of praise, probably from the Hellenistic synagogue (Jeremias). The reference to the second coming as being *made manifest at the proper time* contrasts somewhat with earlier statements by Paul (Rom. 13:12; 1 Cor. 15:51 f.; Phil. 4:5; 1 Thess. 4:15 ff.), where he presses the imminence of the return. One must remember here that this phrase probably belongs to the hymn fragment. Paul also insisted elsewhere that God determines the appropriate time to consummate his purposes (cf. Gal. 6:9).

The hymn mixes Jewish and Hellenistic elements of praise. God is *the blessed and only Sovereign.* The Greek word rendered *Sovereign* appears in the Maccabean writings, which oppose sharply Seleucid claims to divine honors. In a similar way this hymn contests the Caesar cult. The one God is governor of all earthly princes— *King of kings and Lord of lords.* He alone possesses *immortality;* men receive their immortality from him. He *dwells in unapproachable light* not because he is obscure but because he is "too bright for mortal eye" (Barrett). In the Old Testament God is unapproachable because of man's sin (cf. Isa. 6:5; Heb. 12:14). God's invisibility was almost a truism in Greek thought (cf. John 1:18).

Characteristically of his Jewish heritage, Paul closes with a doxology. *Honor* and *eternal dominion* belong to God by right (cf. 1 Pet. 4:11).

3. A Charge to the Rich (6:17–19)

¹⁷ As for the rich in this world, charge them not to be haughty, nor to set their hopes on uncertain riches but on God who richly furnishes us with everything to enjoy. ¹⁸ They are to do good, to be rich in good deeds, liberal and generous, ¹⁹ thus laying up for themselves a good foundation for the future, so that they may take hold of the life which is life indeed.

Paul returns to his discussion of wealth, this time not remonstrating with those who use religion as a means of worldy gain but advising those who have substantial wealth. The abruptness of the change in context has caused Harnack and Falconer to suggest an interpolation. Several have thought the passage out of place. Von Soden located it after v. 2, Lock after v. 10. Actually digression is quite characteristic of Paul. The consideration of eternal life in vv. 11–16 could easily have aroused an after-thought about *this world.*

Paul does not denounce wealth per se. Instead, he teaches that Christians must use what they have for a right purpose (cf. Matt. 6:19; Luke 12:16–21; 16:9) and, more than likely, has the words of Jesus in mind (Scott).

First, the wealthy person must not *be haughty* or "purse-proud" (Simpson) by virtue of his material substance. The peculiar combination of Greek words (*hupselophroneō*) apparently was made by Paul (cf. Rom. 11:20; 12:16), for it does not appear in profane Greek. Haughtiness stands in antithesis to the humility which belongs to proper Christian character (cf. James 1:10). Paul makes a vice what many cultures have made a virtue.

Second, the wealthy person must not build his hopes on material wealth, the perishable, *but on God who richly furnishes us with everything to enjoy.* Mammon will let you down, Paul is saying. It makes sense, therefore, to put one's confidence only in the source of all things, God. But Paul does not subscribe to the ascetic views of his opponents, for, repeating his observations in 4:1–5, God has provided things for our enjoyment! One is not to be pitied simply because he has wealth, rather if he has hope only in this life.

Third, the wealthy person should consider his wealth a stewardship. That tiny minority within the primitive church who were blessed with property, the early chapters of Acts show, held a major responsibility. They had to share their material goods for the common welfare. True riches consist in generosity toward others. So Paul counsels that the wealthy *be rich in good deeds,* explained elsewhere as piety (2:10), care of widows, the poor, orphans, etc. (5:10; Titus 3:14). Liberality (cf. Rom. 12:8; Eph. 4:28) and generosity

(cf. Rom. 15:26; 2 Cor. 9:13) as habits of life would lay *a good foundation for the future,* i.e., for eternal life. *Generous* (*koinonikos*) recalls the *koinonia* of the Jerusalem church (Acts 2:42).

Paul has mixed his metaphors here, a practice not uncommon with him. *Laying up* is literally "treasuring up," which echoes Jesus' words (Matt. 6:19–20). The combining of "treasuring" with *foundation* may indicate that Paul had in mind the parable of the two houses (Luke 6:48) (Scott). At any rate, the meaning seems quite clear. Every Christian's ultimate goal should be *the life which is life indeed,* "quite a Pauline coinage" (Simpson).

4. Closing Charge and Salutation (6:20–21)

20 O Timothy, guard what has been entrusted to you. Avoid the godless chatter and contradictions of what is falsely called knowledge, 21 for by professing it some have missed the mark as regards the faith.
Grace be with you.

Paul concludes with a final plea, heightened by an affectionate addressing of Timothy. Again one may see the military imagery quite plainly. *Guard what has been entrusted to you,* like a faithful soldier. The accent falls on the aorist imperative which has a definitive nuance, "Guard with your life now!" *What has been entrusted to you* (cf. 2 Tim. 1:12,14) means sound doctrine, the truth of salvation, and the mystery of godliness, i.e., the whole Christian gospel, rather than spiritual endowment (Spicq, Barrett). In contrast to the usual Pauline *paradosis* (tradition), it connotes "what the individual Christian has received as a Christian" (Dibelius-Conzelmann).

Contrariwise, Timothy is to shun the emptiness of the erroneous teachers. Paul again speaks harshly of the latter. *Chatter* means literally "empty words." The word *contradictions* (*antitheseis*) has been the main prop on which Baur and others supported the anti-Marcionite origin of the Pastorals; however, such a late date is impossible (see Introduction). It is not impossible that we have in vv. 20–21a a later addition (Easton, Barrett). *Contradictions* is more precise than "disputes" in 6:4, characterizing the false teachers' methods of discussion or instruction (Spicq).

The claims to *knowledge* on the part of such persons were falsely named. Whatever knowledge they possessed led not to truth but to missing the mark regarding Christian faith.

The letter closes with a typical Pauline benediction (cf. Eph. 6:24; Col. 4:18; Philemon 25). The plural *you* is not the slip of a later hand, though some scribes changed it to the singular, but indicates a public reading.

Commentary on 2 Timothy

Outline

Greeting and affirmation of apostolate (1:1–2)
I. Recollections and personal encouragement (1:3—2:13)
  1. Paul's thanksgiving to God for Timothy (1:3–5)
  2. His confidence in God despite imprisonment an example for Timothy (1:6–14)
  3. The betrayal of the Asians, the faithfulness of Onesiphorus (1:15–18)
  4. Be faithful and endure suffering (2:1–7)
  5. Remember the faithfulness of Christ (2:8–13)
II. Counsels for Timothy (2:14—4:5)
  1. Avoid destructive debating and be a constructive workman (2:14–26)
  2. The destructive ones uncovered (3:1–9)
  3. Adhere to Paul's example and to your training (3:10–17)
  4. A final solemn appeal to preach the gospel (4:1–8)
III. Farewell (4:9–21)
  1. Come to Rome, but beware! (4:9–18)
  2. Mutual greetings (4:19–21)
  Concluding benedictions (4:22)

The second letter to Timothy, written after Paul's reimprisonment in Rome, has a decidedly different tone from the first. First Timothy is the orders of the old general of the Gentile mission to his aide-de-camp; 2 Timothy the last will and testament of one about to die (cf. 4:6–8). Second Timothy sounds two dominant notes, as the initial greeting already discloses: (1) Paul's affection for Timothy and (2) his choice of the latter as his successor to whom he has bequeathed the mission.

Greeting and Affirmation of Apostolate (1:1–2)

¹ Paul, an apostle of Christ Jesus by the will of God according to the promise of the life which is in Christ Jesus, ² To Timothy, my beloved child:
Grace, mercy, and peace from God the Father and Christ Jesus our Lord.

Paul's greeting here differs only slightly from that in 1 Timothy 1:1–2. As in 2 Corinthians 1:1 and Colossians 1:1, he declares himself an apostle *by the will of God,* undoubtedly an allusion to the Damascus road experience. The purpose of his special appointment is to make known *the promise of the life which is in Christ Jesus* (cf. 1 Tim. 4:8). Christ is the source of real life, which one obtains by union with him (cf. 1 Tim. 1:4; 3:13). Paul's "solemn formality" here is not so "unthinkable" as Easton maintains; Paul wants Timothy to be fully cognizant of the gravity of his bequest. His personal affection becomes perceptible in addressing Timothy as *my beloved child.*

The threefold salutation is the same as that in 1 Timothy 1:2.

I. Recollections and Personal Encouragement (1:3—2:13)

Paul begins his last will and testament with some remembrances with the intention of undergirding Timothy's self-confidence in discharging his task in the Gentile mission.

1. Paul's Thanksgiving to God for Timothy (1:3–5)

³ I thank God whom I serve with a clear conscience, as did my fathers, when I remember you constantly in my prayers. ⁴ As I remember your tears, I long night and day to see you, that I may be filled with joy. ⁵ I am reminded of your sincere faith, a faith that dwelt first in your grandmother Lois and your mother Eunice and now, I am sure, dwells in you.

The Greek style of Paul's thanksgiving, as in 1 Timothy 1:12, differs from his usage in other letters and may be ascribed either (1) to the change in his style under Roman influence or (2) to a different amanuensis. His thanksgiving is to God, who is the same for both Jews and Christians. This One, Paul has served or worshiped *as did my fathers.* His expression of pride in ancestry accords well with his statements in Romans 9:3–5 and Philippians 3:4–6. The apostle "thought of Judaism in such close connection with Christianity that his present worship of God is in a sense a continuation of his own Jewish worship" (Guthrie). *With a clear conscience* may refer to *serve* (as the RSV), but according to the order of the Greek it probably should be understood with the whole phrase. Both Paul and his fathers served God *with͵ a clear conscience.*

As often as he prays, Paul reminds Timothy, he remembers his child in the faith. Intercessions for intimate friends were a regular feature of Paul's prayer life (cf. Rom. 1:9; 1 Thess. 2:13), and he encouraged others to do the same (1 Thess. 5:17).

Remembrance of Timothy's tears at their parting aroused Paul's longing to see him and he later (4:9) bids him come to Rome. The tender parting scene referred to here may be the one mentioned in Acts 20:17–38, but it has "the air of being recent" (Spicq). It is perhaps better to theorize a separation after Paul's release from prison and just before his subsequent reimprison-

ment (see Introduction). *Night and day* stresses the intensity of Paul's longing, if we attach it to this clause. Some scholars have referred it to the *prayers* of v. 3, where it would strengthen *constantly* (cf. 1 Tim. 5:5).

Seeing Timothy again would fill Paul *with joy.*

Paul recalls specifically Timothy's *sincere faith* (cf. 1 Tim. 1:5). The aorist tense of the participle translated *I am reminded* has led some scholars (e.g., Spicq) to suggest that Paul had received a letter from Timothy. Timothy's grandmother and mother, Paul reveals further in an extremely intimate reference, were Timothy's forerunners in the faith. They testify, as have many others, to the importance of parental example in the instruction of children. From childhood they had taught Timothy from the Scriptures (3:15). The emphasis, however, falls heaviest upon the authenticity of their faith.

From Acts 16:1 ff. we learn that Timothy's mother was a Jewish convert to Christianity, his father a Greek. There is no mention of his grandmother. What seems probable is that Timothy's mother was the first Christian in his family. Paul could ascribe *sincere faith* to a devout Jewish grandmother even as he did to his own Jewish forebears in v. 3.

The conception of faith dwelling in the believer belongs exclusively to Paul among New Testament writers. He applies the image to the inhabitation of God (2 Cor. 6:16), the Spirit (Rom. 8:11; 2 Tim. 1:14), the word (Col. 3:16), and sin (Rom. 7:17). He expresses the same confidence about Timothy's faith that he could about that of Lois and Eunice. The expression *I am sure* is characteristically Pauline.

2. His Confidence in God Despite Imprisonment an Example for Timothy (1:6–14)

⁶ Hence I remind you to rekindle the gift of God that is within you through the laying on of my hands; ⁷ for God did not give us a spirit

of timidity but a spirit of power and love and self-control.

8 Do not be ashamed then of testifying to our Lord, nor of me his prisoner, but take your share of suffering for the gospel in the power of God, 9 who saved us and called us with a holy calling, not in virtue of our works but in virtue of his own purpose and the grace which he gave us in Christ Jesus ages ago, 10 and now has manifested through the appearing of our Savior Christ Jesus, who abolished death and brought life and immortality to light through the gospel. 11 For this gospel I was appointed a preacher and apostle and teacher, 12 and therefore I suffer as I do. But I am not ashamed, for I know whom I have believed, and I am sure that he is able to guard until that Day what has been entrusted to me. 13 Follow the pattern of the sound words which you have heard from me, in the faith and love which are in Christ Jesus; 14 guard the truth that has been entrusted to you by the Holy Spirit who dwells within us.

On account of his confidence in Timothy's inheritance of faith and his own solid faith Paul reminds him *to rekindle the gift of God that is within you through the laying on of my hands.* The challenge does not necessarily suggest a neglect of his spiritual *gift.* Rather the apostle plays on the analogy of fire with the suggestion that "the embers need constant stirring" (Kelly); Timothy's *charisma* does not operate *ex opere operato* (Barrett). The Spirit works through the minister's zeal (cf. 1 Thess. 5:19).

Laying on of my hands does not conflict with the laying on of hands by the elders in 1 Timothy 4:14. As noted in that connection Paul probably participated in the ordination ceremony.

Paul proceeds to generalize. The conferring of the Spirit should eliminate excessive fear. For the Christian spirit is not one of *timidity* (cf. Rom. 8:15) but of *power* (cf. 1 Cor. 2:4) *and love and self-control.* The connecting of the Spirit with *power,* inherited from the Old Testament, is frequent in the New Testament (cf. Luke 4:14; Acts 1:8; 1 Thess. 1:5). In Paul's writings *love* is the chief spiritual gift (cf. 1 Cor. 13:13). *Self-control (sophronismos,* only here in the New Testament,

but with cognates often in the Pastorals) conveys the idea of strength in the face of persecution. According to Hebrews 13:23, Timothy may have needed it when he suffered imprisonment.

In view of the spiritual strength at his disposal Paul exhorts his young aide not to be ashamed of *testifying to our Lord.* The Greek is probably best rendered as the RSV has it, but one may also translate "of our Lord's testimony" i.e., before Pontius Pilate (cf. 1 Tim. 6:13). The ignominy attaching to a crucified founder caused many to falter in their witness. But, as Paul declares to the Corinthians, God chose the ignoble in order to confound the worldly wise (1 Cor. 1:18 ff.).

Neither must Timothy be ashamed of Paul, as others had (cf. v. 15; 4:10–18). He is Christ's *prisoner,* not Caesar's, obvious appearances notwithstanding (cf. Eph. 3:1, 4:1; Philemon 1). Following Paul's example, then, Timothy is to *take your share of suffering for the gospel in the power of God.* The gospel in itself is a call to share Christ's cross.

Mention of the gospel evokes from Paul a hymn or confession. Several scholars (e.g., Kelly, Prat) have ascribed the passage to Paul himself on the basis of (1) its subordination to the preceding clause with no introductory formula, and (2) its strong Pauline ideas and vocabulary. However, Jeremias has arranged the hymn in three strophes of two lines each and conjectured a Pauline insertion in the words *not in virtue of our works but in virtue of his own purpose and (the) grace.* Titus 3:5 ff. reflects a similar insertion with the strong Pauline doctrine of grace. Both baptism (Easton) and the Lord's Supper (Hanson) have been proposed for the context of the hymn.

The first stanza praises God for his redemptive act in Christ (cf. 1 Tim. 1:15). Normally Paul himself uses the word "save" eschatologically, i.e., of the final purpose of God (Barrett). In this hymn it obviously parallels the Christian *calling.* Calling is a Pauline word. It refers to God's purposeful choice of Israel to carry out his mission, the reconciliation of mankind to himself. The *calling is holy* in that it proceeds from God and issues in a life dedicated to him (Barrett).

God's saving and calling does not stem from merit, a point argued at length in Galatians and Romans. On the contrary, it derives from *his own purpose* and grace. No one can earn what God gives freely.

The second stanza praises Jesus Christ as the one through whom God makes his gift. Here we have the true Pauline conception of predestination. Paul makes no suggestion of an irrevocable decree by which some were elected for salvation, some for damnation. Rather, he looks at God's redemptive activity in its totality— from beginning to end. *Ages ago* (lit., before eternal times) God established his eternal purpose. This plan has come to fruition *through the appearing of our Savior Christ Jesus. Appearing* refers here to Jesus' incarnate life; elsewhere (cf. 1 Tim. 6:14) to the second coming. The emphasis upon Christ (cf. Titus 2:13; 3:6) and God (1 Tim. 1:1; 2:3; 4:10; Titus 1:4, 2:10, 3:4) as Savior counters the emperor cult (cf. Phil. 3:20; Eph. 5:23). Salvation is God's gift, not man's.

The third stanza declares Christ's work. He *abolished death,* i.e., rendered it powerless. He *brought life and immortality to light. Life* refers to "new life made available in this world" and *immortality* to "its prolongation after death" (Barrett). In 1 Corinthians (15:24,50,53–54) Paul applies *immortality* to the resurrection body. Though the vocabulary reflects obvious similarities to the language of the Gnostics and mystery cults, the ideas are clearly Pauline (Kelly). Christ has conquered man's most feared enemy and laid a foundation for true life.

The entire hymn represents what God announces *through the gospel,* this phrase probably being Paul's addition. The bare mention of the word *gospel,* which the hymn summarized, strikes the same responsive chord it did in 1 Timothy 1:11

(cf. also 2:7). This gospel explains both Paul's ministry and his suffering. For the sake of the gospel God had appointed him a *preacher and apostle and teacher* (see comment on 1 Tim. 2:7). Those who deny Pauline authorship of the Pastorals contend that Paul would not have had to defend his commission in this way to Timothy. However, one must remember the wider audience Paul would expect to hear the letter and that Paul's mantle now falls upon Timothy. So the allusions are quite in place.

Paul's appointment to the gospel and discharge of this commission resulted in his imprisonment (cf. Phil. 1:12 ff.). His connecting of his ministry with suffering accords well with words of Jesus to the same effect. The disciple can expect what his master received (cf. Matt. 5:11–12; John 15:20).

But persecution does not deter Paul from doing Christ's commission. His strong personal faith will allow no other alternative. He does not name a definite object, so, in accordance with his thought elsewhere, he could mean either God or Christ. This faith is an abiding trust, as the perfect tense of the verb and the subsequent explanation show. God has sustained Paul in the past, he is sustaining him in the present, and, Paul is confident, he will sustain him even to the final consummation. Paul's personal confidence gives a basis also for confidence about the gospel, *what has been entrusted to me.* The word translated *what has been entrusted* may be taken to refer (1) to Paul's personal trust in God as well as (2) to the gospel message, but the latter is preferable in view of its usage in 1 Timothy 6:20 and in v. 14 below.

At this point Paul enjoins Timothy, *Follow the pattern of the sound words which you have heard from me* (cf. Phil. 4:9). Though the word *pattern* (*hupotuposis*) may conceivably refer to a creed or confession of faith (Easton), Paul undoubtedly has in mind the Christian tradition in general (cf. *tupos* in Rom. 6:17).

Ultimately Christian behavior should be

grounded *in the faith and love which are in Christ Jesus.* These words may be taken either with v. 13 (as in the RSV) or with v. 14 (Barrett). A similar usage of the phrase elsewhere (cf. 1 Tim. 2:15; 4:12) favors the traditional punctuation. *Faith* has no article and should probably not be given one in English. *Faith and love* ultimately have their foundation in a personal relationship with Christ Jesus. *In Christ Jesus* reflects Paul's dynamic understanding of salvation (see comment on 1 Tim. 1:14).

In accordance with Paul's example, Timothy is to *guard* the deposit—either (1) the gift of grace given at ordination or (2) the truth of the gospel committed to him (cf. 1 Tim. 6:20). The second meaning is probably the more accurate (Barrett). However, Easton and others have thought they detected here the succession theory of 1 Clement 42:2–4; 44:2. According to Clement, composed about A.D. 96, the apostles, knowing there would be contention for the episcopal office, appointed successors to themselves "and afterwards added the codicil that if they should die other approved men should succeed to their ministry" (44:2). The differences between 2 Timothy 1:14 and 1 Clement are clearly evident. Even if one may detect here a similarity, which is dubious, this would constitute no argument for a late date. (1) Paul himself placed tradition in a prominent place from the start. (2) At best, we have only the germ of succession and it applies to the preservation of truth, not to succession of ministers (Kelly).

The ultimate guardian of the gospel is *the Holy Spirit who dwells within us.* The plural, *us,* may refer (1) to Christians generally, all being partakers of the Spirit (cf. Rom. 8:9), or (2) to ministers in particular, who receive a special gift (cf. 1 Cor. 12:4 ff.). In the context Paul could well apply the words to Timothy and himself. In a special way God furnishes them for the task to which he has appointed them.

3. The Betrayal of the Asians, the Faithfulness of Onesiphorus (1:15–18)

15 You are aware that all who are in Asia turned away from me, and among them Phygelus and Hermogenes. 16 May the Lord grant mercy to the household of Onesiphorus, for he often refreshed me; he was not ashamed of my chains, 17 but when he arrived in Rome he searched for me eagerly and found me—18 may the Lord grant him to find mercy from the Lord on that Day—and you well know all the service he rendered at Ephesus.

Paul relates his own trials as something of a warning and encouragement to Timothy. The passage is usually counted among authentic Pauline notes even by those who deny Pauline authorship of the whole letter (e.g., Harrison). *You are aware that* is an emphatic idiom (cf. 1 Tim. 1:19), having the tone of an exhortation (Spicq). *All who are in Asia* (the Roman province in the western portion of Asia Minor) is hyperbolic surely. Exactly whom Paul meant has been debated. Among the possible alternatives it seems best to think he refers to the personal rejection of him by Ephesian (Asian) Christians when he was seized and taken to Rome for his second trial (Kelly). Otherwise one has to suppose (as Spicq proposes) that "who are in Asia" is a Hebraism for "who are *from* Asia." If the latter explanation is accurate, then some either (1) attacked Paul after accompanying him to Rome or (2) left him when they saw his cause lost and returned to Asia (4:16). The verb *turned away* suggests no theological apostasy (as in Titus 1:14) but personal abandonment (cf. Phil. 1:12–18).

Phygelus and Hermogenes, of whom we know nothing further, may have been the leaders in Paul's opposition (Guthrie). In singling them out, Paul obviously reveals strong personal disappointment.

By way of contrast, Onesiphorus offers Timothy a sterling example of trustworthiness. According to the apocryphal *Acts of Paul and Thecla,* Onesiphorus was converted in Iconium and aided Paul in the

Asian mission. The fact that the prayer and the salutation in 4:19 mention his "household" but not Onesiphorus personally suggests that he was already dead, possibly as a result of his zeal to aid Paul (Spicq).

Paul wishes divine *mercy,* i.e., in the day of Judgment, for Onesiphorus' household. *Lord* may refer either to Christ or God (see comment on v. 18). This good man *often refreshed me,* probably both physically and spiritually. Roman prison life quickly sapped a man's vitality. People of means could live fairly comfortably while undergoing trial, but someone like Paul, a Jew by birth, depended heavily on Christian friends. Onesiphorus, whose name means "bearer of profit," revived Paul's flagging spirit with a breath of fresh air. He did this too at some risk to himself, unashamed of Paul's *chains.* The reference to chains (cf. Eph. 6:20) offers a poignant witness to the apostle's plight.

The cost did not deter this faithful Asian. *When he arrived in Rome* he not only did not ignore the prisoner of the Lord, he took pains to *search* for him, a major task according to contemporary annals. But this accords well, Paul adds, with *all the service he rendered at Ephesus,* of which Timothy would be well aware.

In his prayer for Onesiphorus Paul plays on the word *found.* He *found me—may the Lord grant him to find mercy from the Lord on that Day.* The dual reference to *Lord* probably stems from a mixing of formulas: "The Lord [Christ] let him find mercy" and "May he find mercy with [God] the Lord" (Jeremias, Dibelius-Conzelmann). If Onesiphorus was deceased, Spicq and others have insisted, we have here "an example of prayer in favor of the dead absolutely unique in the New Testament." Second Maccabees 12:43–45 illustrates the currency of this practice in pre-Christian times. Easton cites 1 Corinthians 15:29 and 1 Peter 3:19–20 to demonstrate Christian belief in help for the departed. Others have seen in the passage "only the expression of a very

natural feeling" (Scott) or the expression of a wish for God's blessing (Jeremias).

4. Be Faithful and Endure Suffering (2:1–7)

> [1] You then, my son, be strong in the grace that is in Christ Jesus, [2] and what you have heard from me before many witnesses entrust to faithful men who will be able to teach others also. [3] Take your share of suffering as a good soldier of Christ Jesus. [4] No soldier on service gets entangled in civilian pursuits, since his aim is to satisfy the one who enlisted him. [5] An athlete is not crowned unless he competes according to the rules. [6] It is the hard-working farmer who ought to have the first share of the crops. [7] Think over what I say, for the Lord will grant you understanding in everything.

Having laid a considerable foundation in the preceding verses, with examples drawn from Timothy's grandmother and mother and his own experience, Paul turns decisively to Timothy. He commands him to continue in his footsteps as a faithful witness of the gospel. With three illustrations collected from everyday life he drives home his point—God will reward faithfulness.

You then is emphatic, the Greek ordinarily omitting the personal pronoun. *My son,* Paul's affectionate way of addressing Timothy, underlines the gravity of what follows.

Timothy must play the man now that the apostle has reached the end of his road. But like Paul himself, he can have confidence *in the grace that is in Christ Jesus. Be strong* is a typically Pauline verb (cf. Rom. 4:20; Eph. 6:10; Phil. 4:13; 1 Tim. 1:12). *Grace* is employed with it in the instrumental sense—"by means of" or "in the power of" (Kelly).

Timothy is also to prepare others as Paul has prepared him. *What you have heard from me* implies not general instruction but a summary of the gospel itself (cf. 1 Cor. 15:3 ff.; Rom. 6:17; see comment on 1: 13). *Before many witnesses* represents a free translation of the Greek *dia,* which, with the genitive, normally means "through" or "by." Those who contest the authenticity of the letters have seen in the phrase a proof for their theory of second or third generation authorship. However, *dia* has other nuances which seem to resolve the problem here. (1) It may be translated "with the attestation of." Spicq has proposed two possible references in line with this rendering: (a) the prophets, apostles, etc., as in 1 Corinthians 15:3–11; (b) other persons through whom Timothy has been able to check the authenticity of Paul's message—Barnabas, Lois, and Eunice. (2) Perhaps the most satisfactory rendering is that given in the RSV—"before," "in the presence of." From this perspective Paul would have the *witnesses* of Timothy's baptism or ordination in mind (cf. 1 Tim. 4:14; 6:12).

Paul thus instructs Timothy to place the apostolic message he received in the hands of *faithful men who will be able to teach others also.* The verb *entrust* (cf. 1 Tim. 1:18) comes from the same root as the deposit referred to in 1 Timothy 6:20 and 2 Timothy 1:12,14. We have in this statement an embryonic form of "succession." But it is a handing-on of the tradition of the original revelation through a succession of persons who would handle it responsibly, not "apostolic succession."

The apostle now brings from his treasure three figures which can serve as models for the fainthearted Timothy—the soldier, the athlete, and the farmer. All three illustrate perseverance, the quality Paul wants to inculcate in the younger man. He has employed the same three images in 1 Corinthians 9 to make an entirely different point. Here he seems to quote in part proverbs current in Stoic diatribes and in popular speech (see Easton, Dibelius-Conzelmann).

The soldier image conveys three points: (1) stalwart endurance of hardships, (2) avoidance of entanglements which might hinder dutiful service, and (3) desire to please the one who enlisted him. The Christian soldier, of course, owes all of these to Christ.

The athlete image apparently stresses the need for faithful discipline, although the proverb is not in itself entirely clear. *According to the rules* (lit., lawfully) may mean (1) according to the particular rules of the game in question or, more likely, (2) according to regulations which included prescriptions regarding preliminary training. In the Olympic games, which had particularly strenuous rules, each competitor had to take an oath that he had trained for at least ten months prior to the games. The thought here is, to attain the prize, the Christian has to accept the responsibility of discipline.

In the farmer image, used in 1 Corinthians 9:10 f. to sustain the right of a minister to material support, the accent lies on the adjective *hard-working*. This is "almost a technical term in Paul's vocabulary for ministerial work" (cf. 1 Tim. 5:17; Kelly). Paul reminds Timothy of the special blessing God will bestow on the faithful minister. As the farmer by right of his sweat and toil deserves the better part of his crop, so the faithful minister can expect a reward for his hard work.

At this point Paul pauses to interject a parenthetical "Are-you-listening?" comment. If Timothy has some difficulty comprehending all of these things, he should not give up trying, *for the Lord will grant you understanding in everything.* True comprehension, as opposed to human artifice, is a divine gift.

5. Remember the Faithfulness of Christ (2:8–13)

⁸ Remember Jesus Christ, risen from the dead, descended from David, as preached in my gospel, ⁹ the gospel for which I am suffering and wearing fetters like a criminal. But the word of God is not fettered. ¹⁰ Therefore I endure everything for the sake of the elect, that they also may obtain the salvation which in Christ Jesus goes with eternal glory. ¹¹ The saying is sure:
If we have died with him, we shall also live with him;
¹² if we endure, we shall also reign with him; if we deny him, he also will deny us;
¹³ if we are faithless, he remains faithful—for he cannot deny himself.

Paul's final encouragement for Timothy's faith comes from the gospel itself. Paul follows a brief summary of it with a personal testimony of its power. Though he is bound, the gospel cannot be. An early hymn reminds us that God will reward those who remain faithful to their commitment to Christ.

Timothy's confidence should be bolstered by remembering *Jesus Christ, risen from the dead, descended from David.* These words appear to be a kerygmatic formula similar to the one cited in Romans 1:3-4 (Dibelius-Conzelmann). The reference to Jesus' Davidic lineage would indicate a Jewish-Christian origin, as does the lack of an article with *risen* (Jeremias). The passive voice would agree with the early Christian view that God raised him (cf. Rom. 4:24-25). There is no reason for believing with Easton that "the Pastor has simply condensed Rom. 1:1-4." In both instances we have an earlier prototype.

It is for the sake of the gospel that Paul has to endure imprisonment. The Greek has only "my gospel, in which." "In which" may refer to *Jesus Christ* suggesting the Pauline Christ-mysticism (Simpson), but the RSV rendering seems more natural. Paul's *suffering and wearing fetters like a criminal* is analogous to Jesus' ignominious trial and execution, however.

Despite Paul's circumstances, *the word of God is not fettered* (observe the play on *fetters* and *fettered*). Here *the word of God* means the gospel (cf. Phil. 1:7,12-14; 2:17). God himself goes surety for it. *The word* is almost personified, as in 1 Thessalonians 2:13 and 2 Thessalonians 3:1.

Because of his confidence in the gospel (*therefore*), Paul endures whatever he has to *for the sake of the elect. The elect* (cf. Rom. 8:33) means not so much those already converted as "the potential Christians who have not yet been reached" (Scott). They would include the total number of those whom God has chosen and predestined to share in his eternal purpose. Regardless of the personal sacrifice, Paul expends himself that the full number of the elect *may obtain the sal-*

vation which in Christ Jesus goes with eternal glory. This *salvation* refers, as it does elsewhere in the apostle's writings, to the eschatological fulfillment of God's promises (Barrett).

Eternal glory contrasts with the *suffering* of v. 9. It represents the highest object of Christian hope, participation in incorruption and life (cf. 2 Tim. 1:10).

His reflections upon the assurances of God stir in Paul's memory a hymn of assurance for the faithful. He introduces it with the formula employed earlier (1 Tim. 1:15; 3:1; 4:9). Chrysostom's suggestion that the formula refers to the preceding words cannot be taken seriously. The parallelism and almost metrical quality of vv. 11-13a (through 12a according to Easton) easily prove the formal character of these verses. The Hebraic style of the hymn has led Jeremias to suggest Paul himself as the author, but most scholars consider it an early baptismal hymn.

The first stanza has an exact parallel in Romans 6:8. One may ascribe this (1) to Pauline creation of both, (2) to quotation of Romans in 2 Timothy, or more likely (3) to an allusion to a common hymn. The way in which Paul incorporates the saying in Romans, with the formula "we believe that," would sustain the third interpretation. If so, we have rather definite confirmation that 2 Timothy 2:11-13a was a baptismal hymn. Observe the past tense. Baptism entails a dying and rising with Christ in the sense of sharing in his Servant role. This death to self will be rewarded by participation in his resurrection.

The second stanza echoes words of Jesus repeated several times in the Gospels: "But he who endures to the end will be saved" (Matt. 10:22; 24:13; Mark 13:13). The hymn promises participation in Christ's messianic kingdom, i.e., that the saints would sit on thrones with him when he returns.

The third stanza issues a warning against denial; it is apparently based on the words of Jesus found in Matthew 10:33: "whoever denies me before men, I also will deny before my Father who is in heaven" (cf. Luke 9:26; 12:9). Though the hymn addresses itself to the problem of apostasy in persecution, we need not suppose an actual threat was present (Barrett).

Easton has questioned whether any of v. 13 belonged to the hymn. I would concur with Scott that it does, for "unchanging fidelity to Christ" seems to be the reason for quoting the hymn in the first place (cf. also Dibelius-Conzelmann). The concluding words, *for he cannot deny himself*, appear to be a Pauline addition to the hymn (Moffatt, RSV, Hanson), however. The last stanza thus corrects the harshness of the third. Whatever may be our steadfastness, God is true to his promises of mercy.

II. Counsels for Timothy (2:14—4:5)

In this next section of the letter Paul relates his directions more specifically to the Ephesian problem. He mixes personal counsels to Timothy (vv. 16,22) inextricably with instructions concerning the community. His chief advice is: Avoid getting entangled in meaningless squabbles, but handle those who need discipline with humility and gentleness in order that they may repent and become truly useful to God. The insight regarding church discipline makes this passage one of the most valuable in the New Testament.

1. Avoid Destructive Debating and Be a Constructive Workman (2:14–26)

14 Remind them of this, and charge them before the Lord to avoid disputing about words, which does no good, but only ruins the hearers. 15 Do your best to present yourself to God as one approved, a workman who has no need to be ashamed, rightly handling the word of truth. 16 Avoid such godless chatter, for it will lead people into more and more ungodliness, 17 and their talk will eat its way like gangrene. Among them are Hymenaeus and Philetus, 18 who have swerved from the truth by holding that the resurrection is past already. They are upsetting the faith of some. 19 But God's firm foundation stands, bearing this seal: "The Lord knows those who are his," and "Let every one who names the name of the Lord depart from iniquity."

20 In a great house there are not only vessels of gold and silver but also of wood and earthenware, and some for noble use, some for ignoble. 21 If any one purifies himself from what is ignoble, then he will be a vessel for noble use, consecrated and useful to the master of the house, ready for any good work. 22 So shun youthful passions and aim at righteousness, faith, love, and peace, along with those who call upon the Lord from a pure heart. 23 Have nothing to do with stupid, senseless controversies; you know that they breed quarrels. 24 And the Lord's servant must not be quarrelsome but kindly to every one, an apt teacher, forbearing, 25 correcting his opponents with gentleness. God may perhaps grant that they will repent and come to know the truth, 26 and they may escape from the snare of the devil, after being captured by him to do his will.

In Paul's mind the Ephesian problem was ominous. He directs Timothy to keep on reminding (present imperative) them of the gospel, summarized in the hymn of verses 11–13a. Indeed, Timothy should *charge them before the Lord*, i.e., have them take a solemn oath, *to avoid disputing about words.* The Greek manuscript evidence probably favors the marginal reading of the RSV, "charge them before God," rather than the text. *Before the Lord* was selected, however, as the harder reading, for Paul's letters invariably use *before God.*

To avoid disputing about words (lit., "not to word battle") has received two interpretations: (1) as a prohibition of any argument about doctrine (Moffatt) or (2) with reference to the kind of verbal battles going on at Ephesus. The second meaning is undoubtedly correct, being supported (a) by the use of the noun (*logomachia*) in 1 Timothy 6:4 and (b) by the seriousness with which Paul takes the problem, even enjoining a solemn oath to end it (Scott). Such wrangling *does no good* (lit., is useful for nothing, or makes for nothing useful), *but only ruins the hearers.*

Timothy must furnish the opposite example; his work should cause no embarrassment at all. Note again the Pauline emphasis upon example (see comment on

1:13; 1 Tim. 1:10). Paul urges his young successor to be zealous *to present yourself to God as one approved.* In the last analysis it is God, not other men, whom the minister must satisfy. The Greek word translated *approved* (*dokimos*), which in the New Testament appears exclusively in Paul's letters with the exception of James 1:12, bears a dual nuance of "tested" and "approved," like gold refined in the fire. Such a person will be a *workman* (laborer) *who has no need to be ashamed* of his work.

In the case of Timothy his work involves *rightly handling the word of truth,* i.e., the gospel. The Greek word translated *rightly handling* (lit., to cut straight) creates a metaphor problem. Used with *workman* (agricultural laborer), it may mean (1) to plow a straight furrow (Chrysostom). But mixed metaphors appear frequently in New Testament writings, and others have suggested (2) to hew a stone or to cut cloth (Scott). Another possibility (3) is suggested by Proverbs 3:6 and 11:5, where the verb is used with "road." Thus, the author would envisage the cutting of a straight road (Kelly). The emphasis falls decisively upon "straight."

As a tried and proven *workman,* then, Timothy should steer clear of *such godless chatter* (cf. the identical phrasing of 1 Tim. 6:20; also 4:7). The result can only be the advancement of *ungodliness.* The verb translated *will lead,* with the exception of Luke 2:52 used exclusively by Paul, means literally "to advance" and probably alludes to the Judaists' claims to superiority. Since it has no definite subject in Greek, the phrase may be translated: "for the (errorists) will only advance *un-godliness* more and more." The emphasis lies on *ungodliness* as a result of *godless chatter.*

This kind of *talk will eat its way* (lit., will have pasture) *like gangrene.* Little by little *gangrene* spreads until it infects the whole body.

Among the leaders Paul names Hymenaeus, undoubtedly the person he had "delivered to Satan" (1 Tim. 1:20), and Philetus, not mentioned elsewhere in the New Testament. There is no reason to suppose that 2 Timothy had to be written before 1 Timothy on account of the reference to Hymenaeus' "excommunication" in the latter; Hymenaeus could still have led the anti-Pauline opposition after exclusion from the fellowship of the church. These two have "shot wide of the truth" (NEB).

At this point Paul interjects a precise note concerning the teaching of his opponents. They said that the resurrection had already occurred. This statement is subject to differing interpretations, as noted in the Introduction: (1) Some millenarian movements have contended that Christ has already returned and the general resurrection taken place. (2) Menander, according to Irenaeus a disciple of Simon Magus, (*Against Heresies,* 1.23.5), connected the resurrection with Christian baptism. The more common Gnostic doctrine seems to be that ascribed to Demas and Hermogenes, with obvious allusion to 2 Timothy 2:18, in the *Acts of Paul and Thecla,* a second-century writing. These two insisted that the resurrection "has already taken place in the children whom we have, and that we are risen again in that we have come to know the true God" (ch. 14; Hennecke, II, 356 f.).

(3) If this passage alludes to a Menander type of thought, it definitely represents an early variety of Gnosticism (Jeremias). One finds no trace of docetism in the Pastorals. The spiritualizing may refer to Paul's own baptismal doctrine (cf. Rom. 6:4; Col. 2:12; 3:1–4; Eph. 2:6; 5:14). So the thought of this verse may be "best explained as a spiritualist doctrine of Gnostics, against whom Paul had already turned himself in 1 Corinthians 15" (Dibelius-Conzelmann). There is nothing here to contradict the theory of a gnosticized or Hellenized Judaism.

Such purportedly "advanced" teaching understandably did upset the "weaker" brethren. Paul himself insisted that the resurrection—Christ's and the general resurrection both—is a *sine qua non* for Christian faith (1 Cor. 15:16–17). He could exercise great flexibility on other doctrines and practices; on this one, he would not compromise.

Here too, therefore, the apostle draws a sharp line. In vv. 19–21 he uses two metaphors to drive home the contrast: (1) the solid foundation of a strong building and (2) the varied contents of a great household.

In contradistinction to the vacillations of the Hymenaeus and Philetus party, who have built on sand, God has laid a *firm foundation. Foundation* may refer to (1) Christ and his apostles (cf. 1 Cor. 3:11; Eph. 2:19 f.); (2) the truth of the gospel, the apostolic preaching, the deposit of faith; (3) the church as a whole (cf. 1 Tim. 3:15); or (4) the unshakable core of genuine Christians at Ephesus. In the context the fourth possibility seems most acceptable, understanding that the Ephesians would represent also the whole church.

The *seal* on the foundation, common on public buildings in Paul's day, would signify (1) security (cf. Matt. 27:66; Rom. 15:28), (2) authenticity and purpose (cf. 1 Cor. 9:2; Rom. 4:11), and (3) ownership (cf. 2 Cor. 1:22; Eph. 1:13; 4:30). Both inscriptions (v. 19) seem to have in mind the Korah rebellion against Moses and the divine punishment meted out in Numbers 16, but only the first inscription is specific. Jude 11 uses this incident also to issue a stern warning against rebellion.

In the first proverbial statement the accent falls on the verb *knows.* In Hebrew thought "to know" conveys a sense of intimacy—a man *knows* his wife in sexual union—which transcends the ordinary English usage. The word also has an ethical nuance—to know the Lord is to obey his will. So God draws a clear line between Korahites and *those who are his.*

Besides a possible allusion to Numbers 16:26–27, the second saying seems to have a number of references. It seems likely that we have here "an uncanonical text or a Jewish or Christian proverb" (Easton) or

an early Christian hymn fragment (Dı belius-Conzelmann, Hanson). The meaning is clear. Those who do not participate in the "rebellion" should distinguish themselves from it.

The foundation sayings naturally evoke the question: Why are such people in the church? Paul replies with a kind of parable. The two-pronged character of the metaphor may leave a bit of confusion, but the principal ideas are clear: (1) the church is a mixed body (v. 20); (2) individual members should strive to become the nobler kind of vessels (v. 21).

The imagery and manner of the parable are both Pauline, not copied (as Hanson holds) from 1 Corinthians 3:12; 12:23 f.; Romans 9:21–25 (Kelly). In Romans 9:21 ff. Paul uses the vessel imagery to illustrate an entirely different point—God's sovereignty in election. In 2 Timothy 2:20 he insists, possibly with allusion to Jesus' parable of the wheat and tares, that the church, like *a great house,* has all kinds of members. In v. 21, it should be noted, Paul uses the singular, *any one.* Discipline is seen here as self-administered and refers to "inward purification" (Scott). The faithful Christian in Ephesus must cleanse *himself* of unworthy uses, therefore, in order that he may serve worthy purposes. In this way, he will be *consecrated and useful to the master of the house,* i.e., God, *ready for any good work.* The stress falls on *any good work.*

At this juncture Paul again interjects a personal counsel to Timothy, employing once more his characteristic hortatory form, "flee" (*pheuge*) and "pursue" (*dioke*) (1 Tim. 6:11; 1 Cor. 6:18; 10:14). He urges him to *shun youthful passions,* i.e., uncontrolled impulses. *Youthful* probably has a general application, but it also suits Timothy, still under 40 (see comment on 1 Tim. 4:12). Positively, he should *aim at righteousness, faith* (fidelity), *love, and peace.* Paul has included the first three in the list given in 1 Timothy 6:11. *Peace* was added because the peace of the church was threatened (cf. the greetings of each letter). This would place him in the company of *those who call upon the Lord from a pure heart. From a pure heart* reflects Paul's Hebrew background; in modern idiom the phrase means "in complete sincerity."

Personal counsels open the way for advice concerning the handling of the disputants. The first directive is to stay out of any arguments which generate quarrels. The second is to handle the adversaries with patience and kindliness, seeking their restoration to God.

Paul employs strong language concerning the *controversies* or debates, as he did in 1 Timothy 4:7; 6:4,20. In themselves they are *stupid* and *senseless;* worse still, *they breed quarrels.*

Contrariwise, Timothy must display the character of *the Lord's servant.* Though common in the Old Testament, the phrase is normally "servant of God" or "servant of Christ" in the New. It may mean (1) any believer but designates here (2) someone specially endowed as a leader or minister (cf. Rom. 1:1; Rev. 15:3). It is analogous to "man of God" (1 Tim. 6:11; 2 Tim. 3:17). The one whom God has specially singled out for service, like Paul himself (cf. Phil. 1:1; Titus 1:1), will show a peaceful disposition, averting quarrels.

The accent falls on the characteristic of kindliness, a word used only by Paul in the New Testament (cf. 1 Thess. 2:7). Among other qualities required for such situations are the ability to teach (cf. 1 Tim. 3:2) and readiness to put up with malice (*forbearing*). These qualities will enable the minister to correct *his opponents with gentleness* (cf. 2 Thess. 3:15). Discipline, Paul knew, too easily assumes a vindictive character.

The aim of correction is the rescue of the offender, not his condemnation, by his repentance and return to the knowledge of the truth. The Greek reads literally: "that God might perchance grant them repentance to a knowledge of the truth." Repentance involves a change in the direction of one's will and manner of life, in this case, towards the knowledge of the truth, i.e., the authentic Christian message (see comment on 1 Tim. 2:4; 2 Tim. 3:7; Titus 1:1). This would mean rescue from the devil's snare (see comment on 1 Tim. 3:6–7).

Verse 26*b* has four possible interpretations by virtue of the Greek pronouns. (1) As in the RSV, where the devil is understood as the antecedent for both *him* and *his.* (2) Where the devil is understood as the antecedent of *by him,* God the antecedent of *his.* (3) Where *the Lord's servant* is understood as the antecedent of *by him,* God the antecedent of *his.* (4) Where God is understood as the antecedent for both *him* and *his.* The first alternative seems preferable, but one finds supporters for each of the others. The emphasis in the whole passage lies upon God's action in granting repentance.

2. The Destructive Ones Uncovered (3: 1–9)

[1] But understand this, that in the last days there will come times of stress. [2] For men will be lovers of self, lovers of money, proud, arrogant, abusive, disobedient to their parents, ungrateful, unholy, [3] inhuman, implacable, slanderers, profligates, fierce, haters of good, [4] treacherous, reckless, swollen with conceit, lovers of pleasure rather than lovers of God, [5] holding the form of religion but denying the power of it. Avoid such people. [6] For among them are those who make their way into households and capture weak women, burdened with sins and swayed by various impulses, [7] who will listen to anybody and can never arrive at a knowledge of the truth. [8] As Jannes and Jambres opposed Moses, so these men also oppose the truth, men of corrupt mind and counterfeit faith; [9] but they will not get very far, for their folly will be plain to all, as was that of those two men.

Having counseled Timothy regarding his handling of the opponents, the apostle issues a kind of apocalyptic warning against them. They represent to him the approach of *the last days,* i.e., of the return of Christ and final consummation.

But understand this, that is a Pauline formula (cf. Rom. 6:6) with the purpose of calling Timothy to attention rather than of referring backwards. *In the last days,* a common formula in Jewish apocalyptic writings (cf. Joel 3:1; Isa. 2:2), refers to the period immediately preceding the second coming. *Times of stress* (lit., harsh times) refers to the common expectation of overt criminality; physical "woes" such as eclipses, earthquakes, pestilences, etc.; and gross immorality (cf. 2 Thess. 2:3–12).

Despite the future tenses employed here, the catalogue of vices betrays that Paul describes perversions of his own day (cf. 1 John 2:18; 4:2–3). The catalogue is traditional, analogous to Romans 1:29–31 but not actually dependent upon it.

The opening and closing pairs of vices —*lovers of self, lovers of money*—give a key to the whole, insofar as we may find one. As Chrysostom commented long ago, self-love rather than love of God opens the way to all human faults.

The next three words have related meanings. Paul's catalogue in Romans (1:30) pairs the first two also. The word translated *proud* actually means boastful or pretentious, almost the equivalent of *arrogant* (cf. Luke 1:51; James 4:6). *Abusive* could be more accurately translated "slanderous" or "blasphemous."

The remaining words illustrate the essentially lawless and animal-like character of men who reject God's claim on their lives. They are *disobedient to parents* (cf. Rom. 1:30) and *ungrateful* to God or other men (cf. Luke 6:35). They are *unholy* or profane (cf. 1 Tim. 1:9) in the sense of being utterly without respect for the divine. The word translated *inhuman* means literally "without natural affection." Closely related is their *implacable* character (lit., without libation), i.e., unwillingness to effect a reconciliation with others. Not only do they resist efforts toward peace, they actively incite hatred. *Slanderers* is a mild translation of the Greek *diabolos,* which usually designates an adversary (cf. 1 Tim. 3:11; Titus 2:3). *Profligates* (lit., without self-control) and *fierce* depict the bestial quality of these persons.

Their lawlessness makes them *haters of good* (lit., without love of good), *treacherous* and *reckless* (cf. Acts 19:26).

Thus far the list has given a general picture of the lawlessness or amorality which apocalyptists believed would precede the end. Paul concludes with some words of his own which apply more directly to the Ephesian Judaists (cf. Jeremias). Puffed up *with conceit* (cf. 1 Tim. 3:6; 6:4), he accuses, they are *lovers of pleasure rather than lovers of God.* The accusation refers back to the opening charge—*lovers of self* and *lovers of money.* They are not really devout, as they pretend. What they have is *the form of religion,* not *the power of it.*

Timothy must *avoid such people,* literally "turn away from such people." The RSV has omitted the word "also" in its translation; this refers back to the false teachers described in 2:14–26.

Paul describes some of their activities. Some of these people are the ones *who make their way into households and capture weak women.* The verb translated *make their way* is a classical word for a furtive or stealthy entrance (Simpson); it might be better rendered "worm their way in" (Moffatt). By insinuation they manage to charm women with little resistive powers, literally "little women" (a diminutive of contempt).

What rendered these women so vulnerable was weak consciences, *burdened with sins and swayed by various impulses.* The word translated *burdened* means literally "heaped up" (cf. Rom. 12:20). In modern parlance we would say they had an extreme sense of guilt which made them liable to go off in any direction. Torn *by various impulses,* either good or bad, they *will listen to anybody.* The Greek reads "always (wanting to) learning." Whether serious or not, and many are, they *can never arrive at a knowledge of the truth,* i.e., of the gospel (see comment on 1 Tim. 2:4; 2 Tim. 2:25).

Paul draws on Jewish apocryphal lore to assure his young colleague that these charlatans will not succeed. According to popular legend, Jannes and Jambres were the Egyptian magicians who tried out their occult powers against Moses (Ex. 7:11,22). Both Jewish and early Christian sources allude to the story, the earliest being the recently discovered *Damascus Document* from Qumran (5:17–19). Origen referred to the story several times (e.g., *Commentary on Matthew*, 27:9; 23:37; *Against Celsus*, 4:51). These two magicians serve as a type of those who *oppose the truth* and fail; God establishes *the truth.*

As in other passages (cf. 1 Tim. 4:1 ff.), Paul deals severely with the troublemakers in Ephesus. They are *men of corrupt mind,* men whose minds have been completely destroyed. They possess a *counterfeit faith. Faith* here refers both (1) to Christianity and (2) to personal commitment (Scott).

With such evident self-condemnation Timothy need have no fears. They will not advance further in their deceit (see comment on 2:16), *for their folly* (lit., senselessness) *will be plain* (cf. 1 Tim. 5:24) *to all,* as was Jannes' and Jambres' (cf. Ex. 8:16–19).

3. Adhere to Pauls' Example and to Your Training (3:10–17)

10 Now you have observed my teaching, my conduct, my aim in life, my faith, my patience, my love, my steadfastness, 11 my persecutions, my sufferings, what befell me at Antioch, at Iconium, and at Lystra, what persecutions I endured; yet from them all the Lord rescued me. 12 Indeed all who desire to live a godly life in Christ Jesus will be persecuted, 13 while evil men and impostors will go on from bad to worse, deceivers and deceived. 14 But as for you, continue in what you have learned and have firmly believed, knowing from whom you learned it 15 and how from childhood you have been acquainted with the sacred writings which are able to instruct you for salvation through faith in Christ Jesus. 16 All scripture is inspired by God and profitable for teaching, for reproof, for correction, and for training in righteousness, 17 that the man of God may be complete, equipped for every good work.

Paul proceeds to contrast Timothy with the Ephesian charlatans. As Timothy had

shared Paul's missionary labors and trials, he knew already the cost of his discipleship. The charlatans would progress only in the direction of greater evil. Timothy, however, must stand fast with confident assurance by virtue of those who had taught him the gospel and by virtue of the gospel's foundation in the Scriptures of the Old Testament.

The apostle knows Timothy well enough to know that he may weaken in the face of harrassment and persecution. So once again (as in 1:13) he invokes his own example. Already, he reminds his long-time missionary associate, *you have observed my teaching, my conduct, my aim in life, my faith, my patience, my love, my steadfastness.* The Greek verb rendered *observed* actually has a more significant nuance than the translation may imply. In 1 Timothy 4:6 it was correctly rendered "you have followed." The Stoics gave it a technical application to disciples who "follow understandingly" (Easton).

The list of virtues, a combination of activities and ideals and characteristics, has a peculiarly Pauline stamp, being paralleled rather closely by the list in 2 Corinthians 6:4–6 (Hinson, pp. 349 f.). *Teaching* implies not only "what I teach" but "the way I teach" (Barrett). *Conduct* means literally "leading," i.e., either "training" or "course of life" (Simpson). Paul was Timothy's chief teacher and trail blazer. Though some have wanted to emend *aim in life* as interrupting the sequence of thought, it is quite appropriate in this catalogue. Paul wants to remind Timothy of his intense sense of purpose from which the missionary enterprise has sprung. *Faith* may mean fidelity (cf. 2:22; 1 Tim. 4:12) rather than belief. *Patience, love,* and *steadfastness* have an integral part in the missionary and teacher's role. Paul has already counseled gentleness in handling adversaries (2:24). *Patience* (lit., long-suffering) emulates God's attitude toward us (cf. Rom. 9:22; 1 Tim. 1:16). Longsuffering and *love* are essential in the building of a community composed of imperfect and sinful men (cf.

Eph. 4:2).

The mention of *steadfastness*, i.e., willingness to endure suffering (see comment on 1 Tim. 6:11), stirs Paul's memory concerning the personal cost of the Gentile mission. Some of those who contest the Pauline authorship of the Pastorals claim to find in this passage several un-Pauline characteristics: (1) the self-praise for endurance of suffering which Paul only indulges in comically in 2 Corinthians 10 and 11; (2) the mixture of different kinds of objects Timothy has followed; (3) vague references to past events; and (4) the fact that Paul refers to events before he met Timothy rather than those they would have shared (Hanson).

The first two objections overlook 2 Corinthians 6:1 ff. where Paul puts his experiences forward as an example in almost exactly this same manner. As to the third, Paul would not have needed greater precision to stir Timothy's memory; Lystra was Timothy's home city! Concerning the fourth, Jeremias has pointed out that Paul regularly mentions the *first* missionary journey regarding his sufferings (Gal. 4:13 f.; 2 Cor. 11:25); apparently these incidents fixed themselves ineradicably upon his memory. Besides, Scott has made the credible suggestion that "the intention may be to remind Timothy of how he had first been attracted to Paul by his *patience* under hardships."

Paul's *persecutions* and *sufferings* are delineated in Acts. At Antioch of Pisidia the Jews stirred up a persecution of Paul and Barnabas by inciting prominent devout women and city fathers (13:45). At Iconium mounting hostility of both Gentiles and Jews forced them to flee (14:5). At Lystra Paul was stoned and, in the belief that he was dead, dragged outside the city as a result of the subversive activities of Jews from Antioch and Iconium (14:9). The allusions to these three cities gives no basis for Easton's comment that this is "the first certain citation from Acts in Christian literature." There is no verbal similarity at all. The redundant *what persecutions I*

endured looks back to *steadfastness*, the quality which Paul wants Timothy endowed with. The faith which lay behind *steadfastness* in *persecutions* proved well grounded, for *from them all the Lord rescued me*, a parenthesis reminiscent of Psalm 34:17.

Persecution should occasion no surprise, however. *Indeed all who desire to live a godly life in Christ Jesus will be persecuted.* Paul here echoes a continuous refrain in early Christian thought. Jesus had taught the disciples to expect persecution. (Matt. 5:10–11; 10:22). Paul connected it with his own vocation (2 Cor. 11:23–29; 1 Thess. 3:4; Col. 1:24–25). First Peter (4:12 ff.) counted persecution a matter of rejoicing because it involved the sharing of Christ's sufferings. The frequency of this theme in traditional teaching[31] and the often noted un-Pauline phrasing (A. T. Hanson) of this statement suggests that Paul has taken over an early formula. Two Greek particles (*kai . . . de*) with similar meanings introduce the saying; one may have belonged to the original, the other being added by Paul. The truly Pauline note appears in the phrase *in Christ Jesus*. Paul often modified general sayings with *in the Lord* (cf. Col. 3:18). The phrase should bear the nuance Paul gives it elsewhere (see comment on 1:2; 1 Tim. 1:14). The Christian life is life in Christ, i.e., a life of personal commitment to him and within his body, the church.

The persecution of the righteous calls to mind again the signs of the end (3:1 ff.). The Greek wording implies a stronger contrast than the RSV rendering suggests. *Evil men and impostors will go from bad to worse. Evil men* means more than morally evil; they are utterly perverse (Spicq). *Impostors* means literally "magicians" (see comment on 1 Tim. 5:13), but may also bear the more general connotation. Luke seems to have blamed part of Paul's troubles at Ephesus on a group who made their living by magical arts (cf. Acts 19:19).

[31] Cf. Philip Carrington, *The Early Christian Catechism.*

The verb *will go* refers back to 3:9 (also 2:16). It involves no contradiction by a play on words. The charlatans will not "advance" further in influence (v. 9) but in greater evil (v. 13). They fool others, but they themselves are fooled, of course, by the devil and other charlatans.

Timothy must not fall prey to deceptions. Paul makes the contrast emphatic, *But as for you,* picking up v. 10 again. In the face of vacillation by others, another hint of Timothy's personal inclination, Paul directs him to plant his feet squarely upon *what you have learned and have firmly believed. What* is plural. It refers to the deposit of truth (1:12,14; 1 Tim. 6:20), the gospel as Paul taught it (1:8,10; 2:8; 1 Tim. 1:11), the "sound teaching" of Paul and others (3:10; 1 Tim. 1:10; 4:6,13,16; 6:1, 3), the basic apostolic message. The apostle gives the same counsel to others (cf. Rom. 16:17; 1 Cor. 4:6; Phil. 4:9). To this message Timothy has pledged himself already, i.e., at baptism and possibly again in his setting apart for missionary service.

Two things form the bedrock for the young missionary's commitment: (1) his personal knowledge of those *from whom* he learned the Christian faith and (2) the sure grounding of Scriptures. *From whom,* a plural, implies "no formal succession of ministers" (Barrett) but rather Timothy's mother and grandmother (1:5), Paul himself, and possibly others. *Their* fidelity to the truth should help to erase any doubts Timothy might have.

The Scriptures, however, furnish the ultimate grounds for assurance. Like every child of devout Jewish parents who were expected to teach their children the law from age 5 on, Timothy had come to know *the sacred writings.* Devout Christians evidently continued the practice. Sacred writings (lit., sacred letters) refers almost unquestionably to the Old Testament. Nothing in the context suggests Christian writings, and, even if the Pastorals were composed by a later writer, he would not likely make the slip of alluding to Christian works. The deliberate use of "letters," nor-mally used in the literal sense, perhaps plays on Timothy's early education—how he learned to read—"in a half-playful manner" (Scott). The accent may fall on the word *sacred,* however, in order to enforce the contrast between Timothy and the false teachers or to denote "sacred literature in its full extent" (Scott).

The Scriptures assume this importance because they *are able to instruct you for salvation through faith in Christ Jesus. Instruct,* the rarely used *sophizein,* denotes "the profound insight or grasp which the believer possesses" (Kelly). The Old Testament leads the way to *salvation through faith in Christ Jesus.* The early church adopted the Jewish Bible (in the Greek version called the Septuagint) for precisely this reason: they pointed to Christ. Christ is the key to the Scriptures.

The allusion to Scriptures evokes a more extensive comment, which again has the marks of an earlier formula, perhaps from the Hellenistic synagogue. The omission of a copulative in the statement has caused no small amount of debate. It is possible to translate either (1) *All scripture is inspired by God and profitable,* or (2) "Every scripture inspired by God is also profitable." In favor of the first rendering scholars advance the following arguments: (a) it is the most natural rendering of the Greek; (b) the construction is parallel to 1 Timothy 4:4; (c) if the second translation were intended, "inspired by God" would normally appear *before* "scripture"; and (d) the second translation "seems to contain a hint that certain passages of Scripture are not inspired" (Kelly). In favor of the second rendering are the following: (a) the absence of the article with *pas* (all, every) requires the translation "every"; (b) "scripture," which has a general application, needs an adjective. *Scripture,* in the singular (as here), may designate (1) a book of the Bible (in Hellenistic Judaism, not the New Testament); (2) the Old Testament as a whole (e.g., Gal. 3:8,22; Rom. 11:2; cf. 1 Tim. 5:18); or (3) a particular passage of Scripture (e.g., Mark

12:10; John 19:37; 20:9; Acts 8:35). Despite the irregularity in translating this way,
the second rendering seems preferable
(with the ERV, NEB, Scott, and others).

The doctrine of inspiration of Scripture
here agrees with the view of Jews in the
first century. Jeremias has insisted, however, that Jesus' and Paul's view paralleled
the Palestinian rather than the Hellenistic.
The latter tended toward verbal inspiration; [32] the former paid more attention to
the role of human transmission. We do not
have in this one verse a complete doctrine
of inspiration. It clearly supports the conviction, however, that the Scriptures are
uniquely inspired by God and offer the
one fully reliable revelation of the mind
and will of God in Christ.

Inspired *scripture is profitable for teaching, for reproof, for correction, and for
training in righteousness.* It is (1) a positive and unique source of Christian doctrine. (2) *Reproof* refers to the refutation
of error and rebuking of sin. Though Paul
did not use the noun (*elegmos*) elsewhere,
he used the verb several times (1 Cor.
14:24; Eph. 5:11,13). (3) *Correction*
(*epanorthosis*), another once-word in the
Pastorals, refers to the positive side of
discipline, the correcting of the erroneous
and setting them on the right path. (4)
Training in righteousness also points to the
positive, "constructive education in Christian life" (Kelly).

Easton considers the use of the Old
Testament as a moral guide propounded
in this statement opposed to Paul's use.
He rightly points out that Paul based his
moral code on Jesus' law of love (Rom.
13:8–10) and occasionally supplemented
it by other teachings of Jesus (1 Cor.
7:1 ff.). Paul, however, did not reject the
moral teachings of the Old Testament as
he did the ritual. He simply interpreted
in the light of Jesus' ethic.

The Scriptures serve in various ways to
prepare the man of God for his ministry.
As in 1 Timothy 6:11 *man of God* may

[32] Cf. Josephus, *Against Apion,* 1:37 ff.; Philo,
Special Laws, 1:65, 4:49; *Quis rerum divarum* 263 ff.

designate (1) any Christian but (2) more
likely, the religious leader, especially Timothy himself (cf. "the Lord's servant" in
2:24). In this clause *that* (Gk. *hina*) is
probably result rather than purpose (Barrett). The result of inspiration of Scripture
is the minister's equipping for his task.

4. A Final Solemn Appeal to Preach the Gospel (4:1–8)

[1] I charge you in the presence of God and of
Christ Jesus who is to judge the living and the
dead, and by his appearing and his kingdom:
[2] preach the word, be urgent in season and out
of season, convince, rebuke, and exhort, be
unfailing in patience and in teaching. [3] For the
time is coming when people will not endure
sound teaching, but having itching ears they
will accumulate for themselves teachers to suit
their own likings, [4] and will turn away from
listening to the truth and wander into myths.
[5] As for you, always be steady, endure suffering, do the work of an evangelist, fulfil your
ministry.
[6] For I am already on the point of being
sacrificed; the time of my departure has come.
[7] I have fought the good fight, I have finished
the race, I have kept the faith. [8] Henceforth
there is laid up for me the crown of righteousness, which the Lord, the righteous judge, will
award to me on that Day, and not only to me
but also to all who have loved his appearing.

Paul now reaches the summit of his
counsels to Timothy. Inspired by the perspective of his approaching death, the passage "sums up well the spirit and content
of the letter" (Spicq.) Timothy, like the
faithful soldier, must take his post and do
his duty no matter how intense the opposition may become. He will have to stand
alone, for the apostle himself will no longer
be at hand to lend his aid.

Paul begins "his last sacred charge"
(Scott) with a solemn oath (see comment
on 2:14; 1 Tim. 5:21; 1 Thess. 4:6). The
legal nuance would be conveyed better by
the word adjure rather than *charge.* The
apostle invokes three witnesses: *God,
Christ,* and Christ's *appearing* and *kingdom,* fulfilling the Jewish requirement for a
valid oath. He appears to draw from an
early two-part formula, perhaps employed
in baptism, in invoking *God* and *Christ*

Jesus who is to judge the living and the dead (cf. Acts 10:42 and 1 Peter 4:5). The third witness, *his appearing* and *his kingdom,* reinforces the entire oath. *Appearing* refers to the Parousia (cf. 2 Thess. 2:8; 1 Tim. 6:14; 2 Tim. 4:8; Titus 2:13), i.e., Christ's return in glory. *Kingdom* underlines the solemnity of the oathtaking further (cf. v. 18; 2 Thess. 1:5; Rom. 14:9; 1 Cor. 15:23–24).

The chief task is to proclaim the gospel. Paul spells this out with five imperatives. (1) *Preach the word.* Paul considered preaching one of his major tasks (cf. 1:11; 1 Tim. 2:7; Rom. 10:8,14–15). *The word* means the gospel (see comment on 2:9).

(2) *Be urgent in season and out of season.* The original nuance of the verb translated *be urgent* is "stand fast" or "stay at one's post." In v. 6 below, it means "be at hand." Paul is urging his sometimes timid colleague to stay on duty at all times. *In season and out of season,* in Greek a play on the words *eukairos, akairos,* can mean either (a) whether you feel like it or not or (b) in the face of opposition (Scott, A. T. Hanson), perhaps (c) both (Barrett).

(3) *Convince,* (4) *rebuke, and* (5) *exhort* apply respectively to the reason, conscience, and will. The verb translated *convince* is a technical term used in philosophy or law with reference to the cross-examining or questioning process. It thus has usually a negative connotation—"refute" or "prove wrong" (cf. 1 Cor. 14:24; Eph. 5:11,13). *Rebuke,* often employed in the Synoptics, refers to moral censure; Paul uses the noun in 2 Corinthians 2:6 to designate formal discipline by majority vote. *Exhort* has a double nuance—comfort (cf. 2 Cor. 1:4,6; 2:7; 7:6,7,13) and urge. Paul draws on the second sense to make a rather formal application to Christian preaching (cf. Rom. 12:8; 1 Tim. 6:2) or discipline (cf. 2 Cor. 9:5, etc.; 1 Tim. 5:1).

The whole ministry is to be done with complete *patience* and care in teaching, literally "in all patience and teaching." The Greek text has no verb (as in the RSV)

and the addition of one cuts off the relation of the qualifying clause with the preceding imperatives. *Patience* and *teaching* probably were meant to allude to all five imperatives, but especially to the last three. The exact nuance of *teaching* (cf. Titus 1:9) is not clear, but Paul undoubtedly means to stress the gentleness which should characterize instruction (cf. 2:24 f.).

Verse 3 explains *in season and out of season.* Preaching is so urgent because *the time is coming when people will not endure sound teaching.* The future tense sounds again the apocalyptic warning note (see comment on 3:1). *Endure* means literally "put up with." *Sound teaching* (see comment on 1 Tim. 1:10) is that which is based upon the truth, not fabrication. Novelty often has more followers than sanity! One can almost see the *people* Paul describes. They have a constant "itch" to find something new. So they pile teachers on top of teachers in order "to tickle their own fancies" (Moffatt), literally "according to their own desires." Both the Jews and the Gnostics majored on teaching. They are like the "silly women" described earlier, "swayed by various impulses" and "never able to arrive at a knowledge of the truth" (3:6–7).

Unfortunately such people turn their ear towards any sound except that of *the truth,* i.e., the genuine gospel. On the contrary, they *will turn* their ear *away from listening to the truth and wander into myths* (cf. 1 Tim. 1:6; 5:15, 6:20). The *myths* (Titus 1:14; 1 Tim. 1:4; 4:7) would be fables, etc., based on the law.

To counter such irresponsibility Timothy will need to exhibit an exemplary ministry. *As for you* (see 3:14) accents the contrast. *Always be steady* (lit., be sober in all things) might be rendered more accurately "Keep your eyes open all the time." The imperative (*nephein*) "hovers between the meaning of *sobriety* and *wakefulness*" (Simpson; cf. 1 Thess. 5:6). In the background stands the image of the athlete (v. 7) who abstains from wine in order to stay alert and vigilant (Spicq). Paul wants his colleague to avoid the nebulous world of fantasy in which his opponents live—"swollen with conceit" (3:4), "of corrupt mind" (3:8), foolish (3:9), "deceivers and deceived" (3:13).

The military motif turns up again in the command to *endure suffering.* Preaching the gospel will always evoke harrassment and persecution (cf. 2:9; Phil. 1:7,13–14, 17), for it involves participation in Christ's sufferings (see comment on 2:11–13).

Do the work of an evangelist means "preach the gospel." The primitive church had an office of *evangelist* (cf. Eph. 4:11; Acts 21:8), but the term has no formal connotation here (Kelly).

Fulfil your ministry sums up Timothy's total task. "Give full measure," as Paul himself has given (cf. 4:17; Luke 1:1; Acts 12:25). Timothy's *ministry* is the same as the apostle's; it is the ministry of the servant.

Paul now gives the reason why Timothy has to assume such an awesome burden. The apostle himself will no longer carry the message to the Gentiles; Timothy must act in Paul's place. *I* (*ego*) is emphatic, set sharply against *you* in v. 5. Many scholars who ascribe the Pastorals as a whole to a later hand regard this section as Paul's own (Harrison, Scott, Easton, others).

Paul depicts his approaching death with two metaphors, one drawn from Jewish sacrificial practice, the other from naval or military. *I am already on the point of being sacrificed* pictures the pouring of wine on the victim immediately before its immolation (Ex. 29:40; 30:9; Num. 28:7). As in Philippians 2:17, where the same word is used, Paul is himself the libation. Moffatt has translated beautifully, "The last drops of my own sacrifice are falling." The Greek word for *departure* designated the loosing of the ropes from their moorings in preparation for sailing on the high seas or the breaking of camp by soldiers.

Three additional metaphors sum up the apostle's labors. (1) *The good fight* (the Gk. term often used by Paul: Phil. 1:30; Col. 2:1; 1 Thess. 2:2; 1 Tim. 6:12) seems

to infer the wrestling or boxing match rather than the military motif (as Simpson would have it). (2) Both in the figure of the *fight* and of *the race* the emphasis lies on dedication. Paul has *finished the race,* never flagging in his efforts (cf. 1 Cor. 9:24; Phil. 3:14; Acts 20:24; 2 Tim. 2:5). (3) *I have kept the faith* is a stewardship metaphor. *The faith* (*pistis*) may mean (a) the Christian doctrinal message (cf. 1 Tim. 6:20; 2 Tim. 1:12,14); (b) the deposit entrusted to the minister or apostle (Kelly); or (c) the athlete's promise to keep the rules (cf. 2:5; Easton, Barrett).

The victory wreath will crown the faithful Christian contestant. A few have considered the suggestion of reward in this passage "very un-Pauline." However, they seem to overlook the sustained metaphor of vv. 7–8, one which accords well with Paul's boast in Philippians 3:14: "I press on toward the goal for the prize of the upward call of God in Christ Jesus."

Henceforth (*loipon*) has more of a final punctiliar sense than this translation implies, "Now, at this juncture." *There is laid up for me* is an idiomatic formula used in Paul's day to depict a monarch's rewarding of a loyal subject for faithful service. In this case Paul expects not the laurel crown of the victorious athlete but *the crown of righteousness.* In antiquity *the crown* adorned tombs or coffins, of both noble and ignoble, as a symbol of immortality. *The crown of righteousness* could conceivably refer (1) to the perfecting of the Christian in righteousness (cf. Gal. 5:5). However, as Kelly has pointed out, (a) Paul normally holds that the believer is already justified; and (b) righteousness can hardly be prepared already in heaven. Hence it seems best to consider it (2) as eternal life as a recompense (James 1:12; Rev. 2:10).

This eternal crown will be awarded by *the Lord* (Christ) on *that Day,* i.e., the day of judgment (cf. Matt. 25:31–46). Paul contrasts *the righteous judge* (cf. v. 1; Rom. 2:5–6) perhaps with the unjust tribunal of Rome (Spicq).

Not only to Paul, *but also to all who*

have loved his appearing God will award *the crown* of life. *Appearing* may refer to (1) the incarnation, but (2) the Parousia is more likely (Dibelius-Conzelmann). Those *who have loved* (*agapēkosi*) would thus be those "who have longed for" the consummation.

III. Farewell (4:9–21)

Paul has concluded the main part of his letter. He has placed upon the shoulders of his young colleague the burden of an apostle to the Gentiles which he has carried for many years. The remainder of the letter consists of personal notices and instructions, exchanges greetings, and closes with Paul's personal benediction. Scholars who adopt the "fragments hypothesis" consider all or most of this section authentic, composed of genuine earlier fragments but sharply conflicting with the earlier mood of the letter. Some of the details, e.g., the request for his cloak, books, and parchments, could hardly have been added simply to make a forgery credible. The character of the apostle shines through with a warm glow.

1. Come to Rome, but Beware! (4:9–18)

9 Do your best to come to me soon. 10 For Demas, in love with this present world, has deserted me and gone to Thessalonica; Crescens has gone to Galatia, Titus to Dalmatia. 11 Luke alone is with me. Get Mark and bring him with you; for he is very useful in serving me. 12 Tychicus I have sent to Ephesus. 13 When you come, bring the cloak that I left with Carpus at Troas, also the books, and above all the parchments. 14 Alexander the coppersmith did me great harm; the Lord will requite him for his deeds. 15 Beware of him yourself, for he strongly opposed our message. 16 At my first defense no one took my part; all deserted me. May it not be charged against them! 17 But the Lord stood by me and gave me strength to proclaim the word fully, that all the Gentiles might hear it. So I was rescued from the lion's mouth. 18 The Lord will rescue me from every evil and save me for his heavenly kingdom. To him be the glory for ever and ever. Amen.

Paul urges Timothy to join him in Rome as quickly as possible, which is probably his immediate motive in writing. The emphasis falls upon *soon,* an urgency explained by the approach of winter in v. 21. Many commentators (cf. Scott, Easton, Hanson) have insisted that this request conflicts with the earlier part of the letter, where Paul has painted a gloomy picture of his circumstances, and reveals an addition. The element of contrast may easily be overplayed, however. (1) Paul hints at his desire to see Timothy in 1:4. (2) While the outlook is gloomy, his formal trial has not yet taken place, and vv. 6–8 should not be taken to mean he expected immediate execution. (3) The earlier instructions are intended to equip Timothy for a long ministry, not suggesting (as 1 Tim. 1:3 did earlier) that he had to stay in Ephesus so long (Kelly, Spicq).

Paul explains why his circumstances warrant Timothy's making the long and arduous trip to Rome, bringing Mark with him. He is virtually alone, either because some have deserted him or because he has sent others away to fulfill the missionary task.

Demas, Paul's fellow worker during his first imprisonment (Col. 4:14, Philemon 24), *deserted* him and went to Thessalonica. Though once faithful, his motivation proved insufficient in a time of stress. Being *in love with the present age* contrasts with the motive of genuine Christians, those who have loved Christ's appearing (4:8). This does not imply apostasy in the formal sense but desire for ease and comfort (cf. 1 Tim. 6:17; Mark 10:21 f.) or perhaps fear of suffering.

Crescens and *Titus* apparently received mission assignments—Crescens to *Galatia,* Titus to *Dalmatia.* For Galatia a number of ancient manuscripts read Gallia (Gaul). Until the second century, Roman writers called Gaul (roughly equivalent to modern-day France) Galatia, so the alternate reading may interpret accurately what Paul meant. Later tradition [33] in fact, makes Crescens one of the founders of the church in Vienne (near Lyon). Paul had been to

33 *Pascal Chronicle:* PG, 92, 609.

Dalmatia (Rom. 15:19), so Titus probably was dispatched to check on the state of Christianity there. The reference confirms the authenticity of the letter (at least this fragment), for the letter to Titus was addressed to him on the island of Crete. One has to assume that that letter was written before 2 Timothy, during Paul's period of freedom. In that letter (3:12) Paul asked Titus to join him in Nicopolis, which was located in Epirus, south of Dalmatia. Titus would perhaps have proceeded to Rome with Paul.

Luke alone is with me does not mean that everyone had abandoned him, only that he was now shorthanded (Scott). Luke, "my well-loved doctor" (Col. 4:14; cf. Philemon 24), probably served the apostle both as a doctor and amanuensis.

Mark is almost certainly John Mark, companion of Paul and Barnabas on the so-called first missionary journey (Acts 12:25; 13:13). The rupture between Paul and John Mark (Acts 15:38) had been healed earlier, for Paul commends him to the Colossians (Col. 4:10). The young missionary may have been at Colossae when Paul gave these instructions. Thus Timothy would have to *get* him and *bring him* as he came to Rome. The ministry for which he would be *useful* may have a general nuance, but more likely it refers to personal service— letter writing, messenger service, etc. Mark would replace *Tychicus.*

A few scholars (e.g., A. T. Hanson) have interpreted the reference to *Tychicus* being *sent to Ephesus* as implying that Timothy was not in Ephesus when Paul wrote. The verb *have sent,* however, is probably an epistolary aorist, which means that Tychicus was the bearer of the letter. Tychicus had accompanied Paul to Jerusalem (Acts 20:4) and carried Colossians (4:7–9) and Ephesians (6:21 f.). Paul may well have intended for him to act as Timothy's deputy while the latter came to Rome (4:9, 21).

With winter approaching (4:21) Paul requests that Timothy *bring the cloak that I left with Carpus at Troas. The cloak*

referred to was a heavy, blanket-like garment with a hole in the middle to put the head through. Its weight would explain why Paul had *left* it behind in *Troas* with *Carpus,* a disciple not known from other references, presumably during his last journey to Rome. Paul had passed through Troas many times (cf. 2 Cor. 2:12; Acts 16:8; 20:6). Timothy would travel via Troas across Macedonia to the Adriatic and from thence to Brindisi on his way to Rome.

The books (*biblia*) Paul requested were probably papyrus rolls, containing perhaps copies of some Old Testament writings. The *parchments,* evidently the small and expensive leaves on which valuable documents were written, may have contained (1) Paul's certificate of citizenship and other personal papers (Moffatt, Scott, others). Kelly, however, has argued against this on the grounds that (a) we have no evidence of this use of the word in antiquity; and (b) Paul would probably have had such papers already in his immediate possession. More likely, the parchments composed (2) a paged notebook with valuable Christian writings.

The apostle inserts a warning about *Alexander the coppersmith.* The latter may be the Alexander whom Paul "delivered to Satan" (1 Tim. 1:20). There is no need to suppose from this fact that 2 Timothy was written before 1 Timothy, for Alexander could have caused Paul grief after his anathema against him. An Alexander, a Jew, tried unsuccessfully to quell the riot in Ephesus (Acts 19:33), but the commonness of the name forbids exact identification. Paul himself does not pronounce judgment, despite the harm done. Judgment belongs to God (cf. Rom. 2:6). Observe that Paul uses the future tense, not the optative (a few Greek manuscripts have changed the original). *The Lord will requite him for his deeds,* based on Psalm 62:12 (cf. 28:4), is "a prediction, not an imprecation" (Spicq). Timothy too must keep on his guard. Paul does not spell out the exact character of Alexander's opposition, but it was vigorous.

After the brief digression of vv. 14–15 Paul explains his situation more fully. *At my first defense (apologia) no one took my part; all deserted me.* From Chrysostom on, commentators have tended to interpret the *first defense* (1) with reference to the first imprisonment (Acts 28:30–31). Two other interpretations are possible: (2) Supporters of the "fragments hypothesis" ascribe this experience to the defense at Caesarea before Felix (Acts 24:1–23) or possibly at Jerusalem before the Sanhedrin (23:1–10). (3) Interpreting the letter as a whole in terms of Pauline authorship, it is reasonable to apply the event to the preliminary hearing (Latin *prima actio*) which would determine whether Paul would undergo a formal trial (Spicq, Kelly, others).

No one took my part refers to the lack of a witness or advocate standing forth in the prisoner's behalf. Cowardice or dissensions in the Roman church may have caused the desertion (cf. Phil. 1:15 ff.). Paul prays that this might *not be charged against them,* i.e., in the judgment of God (cf. 2 Cor. 5:19; Acts 7:60). At Ephesus friends had once stood by him (cf. Rom. 16:3–4).

Though deserted by men, the apostle to the Gentiles was not forsaken by God. *The Lord stood by me,* i.e., as an advocate. *The Lord* probably refers to God, as the doxology in v. 18 shows (Jeremias). Not only so, he also *gave me strength* (see comment on 2:1; 1 Tim. 1:12) *to proclaim the word fully* (lit., "in order that through me the proclamation may be completed"). Imprisonment did not bring the Pauline mission to a halt. Despite its evils, Paul was fully discharging (*plerophorein;* cf. 4:5) the task God had assigned, i.e, the preaching of the "good news" to all nations. God's purpose indeed is *that all the Gentiles might hear* the proclamation (see comment on 1 Tim. 2:7; 2 Tim. 1:11). *All the Gentiles* may allude (1) to Rome as the crown of the apostle's commission "to all the nations" (Rom. 1:5) or, more likely,

(2) to the cosmopolitan audience in the imperial court. Paul undoubtedly exploited the *prima actio* to proclaim the message, though some have applied the reference to preaching to the period between the first and second imprisonments.

Paul's rescue *from the lion's mouth* is probably figurative, *viz.* rescue from extreme danger. One need not refer it to a literal facing of wild animals in the amphitheater (which did actually occur under Nero), to the emperor Nero (Dibelius-Conzelmann), or to Satan (as 1 Pet. 5:8).

His allusion to rescue evokes from the great apostle a confession of faith in God. His confident boast does not conflict with his apprehension of approaching death (4:6–8). He thinks in terms of "spiritual rather than physical protection" (Kelly).

The *heavenly kingdom* is both present and the goal of Christians achieved in the return of Christ. *Heavenly,* employed almost exclusively by Paul in the New Testament (1 Cor. 15:40,48,49) is opposed to earthly. The future tense does not imply that Paul still expected to live to see the return of the Lord (as in 1 Thess. 4:15; 1 Cor. 15:51); this hope faded as the end drew near.

In his characteristic way Paul (cf. 1 Tim. 1:17; Rom. 9:5; Gal. 1:5; Phil. 4: 20) bursts into a doxology at the mention of God's saving work. As Easton notes, the implied verb is "is," not "be."

2. Mutual Greetings (4:19–21)

¹⁹ Greet Prisca and Aquila, and the household of Onesiphorus. ²⁰ Erastus remained at Corinth; Trophimus I left ill at Miletus. ²¹ Do your best to come before winter. Eubulus sends greetings to you, as do Pudens and Linus and Claudia and all the brethren.

The concluding paragraph exchanges personal greetings and supplies some additional information as a kind of afterthought. The personal references indicate that Timothy was still in Ephesus.

Prisca and Aquila were the husband and wife missionary team forced to leave Rome as a result of Claudius' edict expelling

Jews (Acts 18:2). They settled in Corinth and from there went to Ephesus with Paul (18:18). They joined Paul in sending greetings to Corinth (1 Cor. 16:19). Paul mentions both of them in Romans 16:3 f., which many scholars believe to be written to Ephesus, not Rome. The mention of Priscilla's name first indicates her great ability.

The greeting of Onesiphorus' *household* almost certainly indicates that he was now dead (see comment on 1:16).

Erastus seems to have been a dropout on the last journey of Paul to Rome. According to Romans 16:23, he was the city treasurer (*oikonomos*) of that city. He apparently joined Paul in Ephesus, for the apostle dispatched him and Timothy to Macedonia (Acts 19:22).

Trophimus was a Gentile Christian from Ephesus (Acts 21:29). With others he awaited Paul's return to Troas after his trip through Greece collecting the relief offering for the poor in Jerusalem (20:4). He accompanied Paul to Jerusalem; and Paul's Jewish opponents even thought he had gone past the forbidden areas of the Temple (21:29). Critics of Pauline authorship have questioned why Timothy, being at Ephesus, was unaware that Trophimus was ill in Miletus, only about 50 miles away. Supporters of the "fragments hypothesis" have used this to argue for the Caesarean origin of this section. One possible response is that Paul was telling Timothy *why* he had left Trophimus behind,

not simply giving information.

Paul urges Timothy to *come before winter.* During the winter the Adriatic was virtually closed to sea traffic. The letter was probably written in late summer or autumn, therefore.

Four friends join with Paul in sending greetings. Mention of their names does not conflict with the fact that no one stood beside Paul in his first defense (4:16). These persons, entirely unknown in other New Testament references, probably did not qualify for a formal defense (Kelly). The names of Pudens, Linus, and Claudia are Latin, confirming the Roman origin of the letter.

Concluding Benedictions (4:22)

[22] The Lord be with your spirit. Grace be with you.

Paul closes his second letter to Timothy with a twofold benediction, one addressed to Timothy himself, the other to the Ephesians. *The Lord* may be either God or Christ, but probably the latter (cf. Phil. 4:23). The *spirit* is that part of man which is an object of divine actions and influences, his obedient self (cf. Rom. 8:15–16). The singular *your* makes clear that Paul intends the benediction for Timothy alone.

Grace be with you is addressed to the community as the plural *you* demonstrates. A prayer for *grace* is Paul's common benediction (see 1 Tim. 6:21; Gal. 6:18; 1 Cor. 14:14).

Commentary on Titus

We know less about Titus than about Timothy. He is not mentioned in the Acts. Paul, however, supplies us with some information. He was of Greek ancestry (Gal. 2:3). Paul took him to Jerusalem with him a number of years after his conversion, refusing to allow his circumcision (Gal. 2: 1–3). After Timothy's failure to settle the Corinthian squabble the apostle dispatched Titus (2 Cor. 8:6; 12:18), who seems to have been successful in reconciling the Corinthians with Paul (7:5 ff.). Titus evidently served Paul in many ways subsequently. A major part of his mission work probably took place in Crete, where the apostle had left him following his own trip there in between imprisonments. According to Paul's request in this letter (3:12), Titus probably joined him in Nicopolis and subsequently accompanied him to Rome. During the second imprisonment, before the writing of 2 Timothy, Paul then sent him to Dalmatia (2 Tim. 4:10). Later

tradition, building on the account given here, counted him the first bishop of Gortyna, a city on the island of Crete, and located his death there.[34] Though these accounts cannot be trusted, the association of Titus' later activities with Crete is at least credible.

The letter to Titus is probably the oldest of the three pastoral letters. It has essentially the same aims as 1 Timothy: (1) the ordering of church life and (2) the defense of the mission against agitators. At one and the same time it is personal, to "my true child," and official, the word of the apostle. In response to those who question whether Paul would have written so formal a note to someone he knew as well as he did Titus, one will observe the general nature of the concluding greetings and benediction. Paul expected the letter to be heard by the whole church in Crete.

Greetings and Affirmation of Apostolate (1: 1–4)

¹ Paul, a servant of God and an apostle of Jesus Christ, to further the faith of God's elect and their knowledge of the truth which accords with godliness, ² in hope of eternal life which God, who never lies, promised ages ago ³ and at the proper time manifested in his word through the preaching with which I have been entrusted by command of God our Savior;
⁴ To Titus, my true child in a common faith:
Grace and peace from God the Father and Christ Jesus our Savior.

Paul begins his letter with a long and solemn greeting in which he affirms his apostolate (cf. Gal. 1:1–5; Rom. 1:1–7), another reminder that his Judaist opponents had not halted their attack on the Gentile mission. He holds credentials as *a servant of God and an apostle of Jesus*

³⁴ *Greek Acts of Titus,* ed. M. R. James, *Journal of Theological Studies,* VI (1905), 549–56.

Christ. The first title appears only here in Paul's letters; normally he calls himself "a servant of Jesus Christ" (Rom. 1:1). This designation is drawn from the Old Testament. For Paul it underlines his absolute commitment to God in being *an apostle of Jesus Christ.* Paul's servant role is identical with his apostolate to the Gentiles.

This servant-apostle commission has three aims: (1) *to further the faith of God's elect,* (2) to bring them *knowledge of the truth which accords with godliness,* and (3) ultimately to share with them the *hope of eternal life* promised and made available by God. The Greek text has been influenced strongly by liturgical language, so that the first purpose remains a bit uncertain. Literally, the Greek reads "according to (*kata*) the faith of God's elect," which could mean that Paul believed his apostolate was "constituted and determined by this *faith, knowledge,* and *hope*" (Barrett; cf. also Simpson). Such an interpretation hardly accords with his conviction, reiterated often in the Pastorals, that Christ himself had commissioned him. It seems better, therefore, to follow the RSV and most commentators in translating *kata* in the less frequently used sense, "in view of." Paul is thus talking about the advancement of *faith, knowledge,* and *hope* through his apostolate (cf. Rom. 1:5; Phil. 3:14).

So Paul's ministry expands the sphere of believers. He preaches for the salvation of all, but only the *elect* will believe (cf. 2 Tim. 2:10; Rom. 8:33; Col. 3:12; 1 Pet. 1:2). *God's elect,* a phrase used only by Paul (Rom. 8:33; Col. 3:12), means all whom God has enrolled and will enroll in his chosen people by virtue of their faith.

The second purpose merely elaborates on the first. To come to a *knowledge of the truth* means to become a Christian (see comment on 1 Tim. 2:4; 2 Tim. 2:25; 3:7). *Knowledge* alone may produce conceit; knowledge of oneself in light of God's self-revelation in Jesus Christ produces godly behavior, *godliness.*

In hope of eternal life may be attached to *godliness,* to *truth,* to *knowledge,* to

faith, or to *apostle,* but the last seems preferable. Paul's final aim as an apostle is that believers may obtain the hope of eternal life which God provides.

This hope never disappoints (cf. Rom. 5:5). First, because *God, who never lies, promised* it. God's veracity cannot be placed in question. *Who never lies* perhaps is placed here to contrast with the characterization of Cretans in v. 12. The words here recall the hymn or confession in 2 Timothy 1:9–10, which, according to Easton, "they seem to presuppose." *Ages ago* (lit., before times eternal) may also be translated "before creation" (so Chrysostom). By this interpretation God's promises existed even before time began.

Secondly, God *manifested* these promises *at the proper time,* that is, at a time established by himself, acceptable to him (cf. 1 Tim. 2:6, 6:15; Gal. 6:9). Paul is referring to the inbreaking of the eschatological age in Jesus, fulfiller of the Jewish messianic hope (cf. Gal. 4:4; Rom. 5:6; Eph. 1:9–10; Acts 17:26). This manifestation occurred *in his word. His word* probably does not mean "the Word" (Logos) in the technical sense but "the revealed truth, the message or Gospel which is expressed in the *proclamation* of apostles and evangelists" (Barrett). Thus it comes *through the preaching* (see comment on 2 Tim. 4:17) *with which I have been entrusted* (see comment on 1 Tim. 1:11–12; 2:7; 2 Tim. 1:11) *by command of God our Savior.*

Against his detractors the apostle again vigorously asserts the divine origin of his commission. *By command of God* may refer secondarily to *manifested* as Romans 16:26 shows (Spicq). Paul has an unbending command to preach (cf. 1 Cor. 9:16).

Paul addresses *Titus* as his *true child in a common faith* (cf. 1 Cor. 4:15). This agrees closely with his address to Timothy (1 Tim. 1:2). *True* means legitimate; Titus, too, was probably Paul's own convert. The term is, however, somewhat less tender than beloved (2 Tim. 1:2).

Grace and peace from God the Father is Paul's customary greeting (cf. e.g., Rom.

1:7). "Mercy" does not appear here as in the letters to Timothy (1 Tim. 1:2; 2 Tim. 1:2). The addressing of Christ as *Savior,* as in Philippians (3:20) and Ephesians (5:23), suggests again Christian opposition to the emperor cult.

I. Instructions for the Cretan Mission (1: 5—3:11)

The bulk of Paul's letter gives instructions regarding Titus's care for the Cretan mission. The apostle mixes instructions about the ordering of church life with warnings about the disturbers of the mission.

1. Qualifications of Elders-Bishops (1:5– 9)

5 This is why I left you in Crete, that you might amend what was defective, and appoint elders in every town as I directed you, **6** if any man is blameless, the husband of one wife, and his children are believers and not open to the charge of being profligate or insubordinate. **7** For a bishop, as God's steward, must be blameless; he must not be arrogant or quick-tempered or a drunkard or violent or greedy for gain, **8** but hospitable, a lover of goodness, master of himself, upright, holy, and self-controlled; **9** he must hold firm to the sure word as taught, so that he may be able to give instruction in sound doctrine and also to confute those who contradict it.

Paul first reminds Titus why he had *left* him *in Crete,* to *amend what was defective* and to *appoint elders in every town.* A number of Greek manuscripts read "why I am leaving you behind," but such a reading would hardly make sense. The statement cannot refer to Paul's brief stop recorded in Acts 27:7–9. The event probably occurred after Paul's release from prison.

The first reason for leaving Titus, plus the fact that Paul lists qualifications for only one office, indicates that the Cretan mission was in a primitive state. Titus had to set in order the things which Paul did not have time to take care of. To *amend what was defective* undoubtedly alludes to the gnosticizing Judaists, but it also implies incompleteness regarding the organization of Christian communities in Crete.

The second reason thus relates closely to the first. The appointment of properly qualified persons to direct the mission would help to overcome deficiencies. Since Titus himself would have remained only temporarily, others would have had to take charge of the mission. As B. H. Streeter has remarked, the appointment of elders city by city undoubtedly reflects accurately the practice of Paul himself.[35] The reference to *every town* does not suggest, as Scott holds, "that Christianity had now spread over the whole of the large island." It means rather appoint elders wherever there is a church. The first seed may have been planted by Cretan Jews who were present in Jerusalem at Pentecost (Acts 2:11). Hence Paul and Titus simply carried the work further.

This section proves that the terms *elders* and *bishops* were used interchangeably and substantiates the early date of the Pastorals. *Bishop (episkopos)* is used generically in v. 7, as in 1 Timothy 3:1, and describes the function of elders. It could be translated literally "the overseer" (see comment on 1 Tim. 3:1 ff.; 5:17).

Paul's ethical list corresponds rather closely with the one given in 1 Timothy 3:1 ff. for bishops and deacons. Presbyter-bishops should have an unimpeachable reputation (see comment on 1 Tim. 3:10; cf. also Col. 1:22), be married only once (see comment on 1 Tim. 3:2,12), and have believing and well-behaved children. These requirements, especially the third, illustrate again Paul's conception of the Christian community as a family. The presbyter-bishops will have the responsibility of a family larger than their own, so their success in regard to their immediate families provides a good measuring rod for their acceptability in the church. As in 1 Timothy 3:4–5,12, the apostle places much weight on the ability to control children. The children should not be open to *the charge of being profligate.* Their misbehavior could mar the reputation of their fathers. Similarly, if they are *insubordinate,*

85 *The Primitive Church,* pp. 218–219.

they give evidence that the latter have little to commend their leadership.

Such evidences of leadership are essential by virtue of the very character of the task of overseeing the community *as God's steward. For* in v. 7 offers conclusive proof that "elder" and "bishop" mean the same thing in the Pastorals (Scott, Barrett). The chief emphasis falls upon the phrase *as God's steward,* a role Paul assigned also to himself (cf. 1 Cor. 4:1-2). The church is God's household and thus requires the direction of a steward, not the domination of a tyrant (cf. 1 Tim. 1:5).

Paul expands the comprehensive requirement of a *blameless* reputation with five negatives and seven positives. A good *steward* should not be (1) stubborn (*arrogant*); (2) *quick-tempered,* i.e., grow angry easily; (3) *a drunkard* (cf. 1 Tim. 3:3); (4) *violent,* i.e., a brawler (cf. 1 Tim. 3:3); or (5) *greedy for gain* (a "money-grabber," NEB; see 1 Tim. 3:3,8; 6:10; 2 Tim. 3:2). The first two do not appear in the other letters, but they complement the three which do. Paul wants Titus to beware of the volatile, self-centered, and ambitious graspers after office who bring the church into disrepute.

Positively *God's steward* will be (1) *hospitable* (cf. 1 Tim. 3:2); (2) *a lover of goodness,* i.e., one who seeks to do good (cf. 1 Tim. 5:10); (3) *master of himself* (cf. 1 Tim. 3:2; Titus 2:2,5); (4) *upright* or just (cf. 1 Thess. 2:10), since he must arbitrate disputes between others; (5) *holy* or devout (cf. 1 Tim. 2:8; 1 Thess. 2:10), a genuinely religious man; (6) *self-controlled* (cf. Gal. 5:23); (7) a solid teacher. These virtues, all of which appear often in contemporary catalogues, round out the picture of the genuine candidate for leadership: mature, other-directed, and unselfish. A person endowed with these qualities will give a good account of himself in teaching.

The good pedagogical credentials of presbyter-bishops serve two purposes: (1) the preaching of *sound doctrine* and (2) the refutation of *those who contradict it.*

Throughout the Pastorals Paul stresses the importance of sound or wholesome teaching (see comments on 1 Tim. 1:10). Teaching always plays an essential role in the Christian mission. For the primitive church it was especially crucial in rescuing new converts from their "gods many and lords many" and bringing them under the rule of one Lord and God.

The competent preacher will also be able to *confute* opponents. The word translated *confute* means both "expose" and "convict" (see on 1 Tim. 5:20; 2 Tim. 4:2). The history of the church has shown the necessity both of positive *instruction* and defense. The better the former, the less need for the latter.

2. Refute the Gnosticizing Judaists (1:10–16)

10 For there are many insubordinate men, empty talkers and deceivers, especially the circumcision party; 11 they must be silenced, since they are upsetting whole families by teaching for base gain what they have no right to teach. 12 One of themselves, a prophet of their own, said, "Cretans are always liars, evil beasts, lazy gluttons." 13 This testimony is true. Therefore rebuke them sharply, that they may be sound in the faith, 14 instead of giving heed to Jewish myths or to commands of men who reject the truth. 15 To the pure all things are pure, but to the corrupt and unbelieving nothing is pure; their very minds and consciences are corrupted. 16 They profess to know God, but they deny him by their deeds; they are detestable, disobedient, unfit for any good deed.

Verses 10–16 spell out why solid teaching and defense of it are so important. For the young Cretan mission the presence of *many insubordinate men, empty talkers and deceivers* would present a special danger (cf. Jeremias). The three epithets define *those who contradict* sound teaching in v. 9. They refuse to acknowledge established authority (see v. 6; 1 Tim. 1:9). What they have to say contributes nothing to the building up of the church. They play tricks on others, *viz.,* like magicians. *Deceivers* (cf. Gal. 6:3) may hint at actual magic (see comment on 1 Tim. 5:13).

Paul identifies the troublemakers more specifically. A large portion of them were of *the circumcision party,* i.e., Christians of Jewish descent who still insisted on adherence to the ritual law (cf. Gal. 2:12; Col. 4:11). From Josephus we learn that there were numerous Jews on Crete.[36]

The threat posed by these gnosticizing Judaists calls for decisive action. With the mission in its infancy the apostle does not demand exclusion (as in 1 Tim. 1:20) but silencing. Their kind of chatter holds extremely harmful possibilities. *They are upsetting whole families* (households; see 2 Tim. 3:6). They teach not for honorable motives but *for base gain what they have no right to teach* (lit., what they ought not). This rather ambiguous statement may offer another hint of magical formulas (cf. 2 Tim. 3:13) and incantations (1 Tim. 5:13) in addition to the Jewish myths mentioned in v. 14. Such things were highly profitable in the credulous age of the primitive church; so the charge of profiteering comes as no surprise.

Paul backs up his warning with a quotation from the sixth-century B.C. Cretan poet Epimenides, *On Oracles.* Epimenides gained fame as a prophet because he predicted the failure of the Persian expedition against Greece ten years before it happened (490 B.C.). The apostle would not necessarily ascribe to him an authority comparable to the Old Testament prophets. He cites him as he did Menander in 1 Corinthians 15:33 (or Aratus in Acts 17:28?). A quotation achieves the purpose of sounding an alarm without leaving Paul himself open to a charge of nationalistic bigotry. The Cretan reputation was so bad that the Greeks coined the word *kretizein,* "to speak or play like the Cretan," i.e., to prevaricate. Paul accepts Epimenides' judgment. *This testimony is true.*

The baseness of the Cretan errorists requires decisive action. On this account Paul demands that Titus *rebuke them sharply.* The emphasis falls on *sharply.* The health of the young church depends on Titus's decisiveness. However, the aim

of discipline has the erroneous teachers themselves in mind, *that they may be sound in the faith.* The pastor's role is analogous to a doctor's; he desires the curing of the patient, never his loss.

The disease in this case has two elements: adherence (1) *to Jewish myths* and (2) *to commands of men who reject the truth.* The *myths* (see comment on 1 Tim. 1:3,6; Titus 3:9) undoubtedly involved some sort of speculations regarding the Old Testament (Jeremias). The commandments of human origin contrast with the commandments of God (1 Cor. 7:9) in Paul's writings. They probably refer to questions of food, drink, festivals, new moons, sabbaths, and so on referred to in Colossians 2:16 ff. In the latter document Paul seems to have been concerned with a gnosticizing Judaism. Dualistic asceticism, based on the erroneous view that matter is evil per se, led to various prohibitions.

These views are perversions of *the truth,* i.e., the gospel, the Christian faith (see comment on 1 Tim. 2:4; 4:3; 2 Tim. 4:4). Their authors have abandoned (cf. 2 Tim. 1:15) the right understanding. Paul takes time to explain. Purity depends on the inner man made right by faith. *To the pure all things are pure* may be a popular proverb, but it appears to derive from Jesus' words regarding Jewish dietary laws (Luke 11:41) referred to by Paul also in Romans 14:20; 1 Corinthians 6:12; 10:23 (cf. the negative phrasing in 1 Tim. 4:4). The apostle does not mean, as not a few have held mistakenly, "Anything goes!" *To the pure* means "to the pure of heart" (cf. Matt. 5:8; John 15:3; 1 Tim. 2:8). Ritual purity is superficial; it does not take care of the inner person.

In order to cut off any misunderstanding, Paul states the negative side. *To the corrupt,* i.e., the morally impure (cf. 1 Tim. 4:2; 6:5), *and unbelieving* (cf. 1 Tim. 5:8) *nothing is pure.* Such persons lack the capacity to distinguish between good and evil. No matter what kind of ritual ablutions or rites they undertake, they will not receive any of God's gifts to men with

---

[36] *Antiq.* 17.327; *Wars,* 2.103; *Legate to Gaius,* 282.

good conscience. The trouble is, *their very minds and consciences are corrupted.*

The Cretan troublemakers were probably sincere enough. *They profess to know God.* This claim to an experience of God may have been (1) "Judaistic pride in monotheism" (Guthrie), or (2) a gnosticizing tendency (Dibelius-Conzelmann, Easton, Barrett), or (3) both. The teachers Paul was concerned with had a kind of eclectic approach. Whatever their verbal claims, *they deny him by their deeds* (cf. 2:12; 1 Tim. 5:8; 2 Tim. 2:12–13; 3:5). All through his writings Paul has stressed the balance the Christian must maintain between his belief and his behavior. Confession of the mouth is not enough—deeds must match words!

The apostle can hardly find words strong enough to express his disgust. These master hypocrites *are detestable,* committing an abomination against God. Though claiming to be Christians, they act like *disobedient* pagans. They are utterly unqualified (*adokimos;* cf. 2 Tim. 3:8) for *any good deed* (see comment on 1 Tim. 5:10).

3. On Proper Behavior Within the Christian Community (2:1–10)

The antidote to bad behavior by the Cretan troublemakers is exemplary behavior by stable and faithful Christians, especially Titus himself. Adapting standard codes of conduct, somewhat as in Colossians 3:18—4:1 and Ephesians 5:22—6:9, Paul proceeds to set forth a brief model for older and younger men and women and for slaves. He interweaves with this some specific counsel for Titus, upon whom rests the difficult task of bringing order and harmony to the mission. Like other missions in their incipiency, the Cretan one had to struggle with low moral standards among pagans. Achieving even the level of ethics demanded by pagan sages, e.g., the Stoics, meant a big step upwards. Yet while the Christian code resembles the popular Stoic codes in many respects, it differs in motivation and sometimes in basic content.

The apostle places a distinct dividing line between Titus and the Cretan Judaists. *But as for you* is emphatic (see 1 Tim. 6:11). Paul wants his young aide to have no part of the Cretan "sickness." Rather, he insists upon wholesome teaching. "Teach" (lit., go on speaking) is a present tense in Greek. Titus' "sound doctrine," i.e., teaching, has no resemblance to the unhealthy teaching of Paul's opponents condemned in 1:10–16.

Specific instructions focus upon the family, for the erroneous teachers had apparently done the greatest damage there (cf. 1:11). The five groups for which Paul gives advice would constitute the principal members of a family, small children alone excepted. Older men and women should take the lead; their example will instruct others. The Greek has no verb, so one must supply one. "Speak" or "exhort" would fit naturally into the context.

(1) Of Older Men (2:1–2)

¹ But as for you, teach what befits sound doctrine. ² Bid the older men be temperate, serious, sensible, sound in faith, in love, and in steadfastness.

The older men, a different Greek word (cf. Luke 1:18; Philemon 9) clearly distinguished from "elder" (1:5; cf. 1 Tim. 5:1, 17,19), have the first duty. For them Paul lists essentially the same virtues he demands of elder-bishops (1:6; 1 Tim. 3:1 ff.) and deacons (1 Tim. 3:8 ff.). There are not two standards of conduct for Christians. The first three characteristics appear often in popular codes. *Temperate* (see comment on 1 Tim. 3:2,11) refers not only to alcohol but to all other desires as well; *serious* (see comment on 1 Tim. 3:8,11; Phil. 4:8) to a reverent attitude toward all of life; and *sensible* (see comment on 1:8; 1 Tim. 3:2) to the discreet and reasonable use of God's gifts. To these Paul adds three specifically Christian qualities. To offset the "sickness" (cf. 1 Tim. 6:4; Rom. 14:1) of the disturbers, *the older men* should be *sound* (healthy) *in faith, in love, and in steadfastness.*

(2) Of Older And Younger Women (2:3–5)

3 Bid the older women likewise to be reverent in behavior, not to be slanderers or slaves to drink; they are to teach what is good, 4 and so train the young women to love their husbands and children, 5 to be sensible, chaste, domestic, kind, and submissive to their husbands, that the word of God may not be discredited.

The apostle expects the same deportment of *the older women likewise,* but he adapts his list specifically to their station in life. The list is similar to that for deacon's wives or deaconesses in 1 Timothy 3:11. *Reverent* means literally "suitable for a sacred person, a priestess." The prohibition not to be *slanderers* hits hard at a common temptation for older women. So perhaps would the warning about enslavement to a wine bottle (lit., to much wine).

But *the older women* have a positive role to play too. By private example and word, not formal instruction (forbidden in 1 Tim. 2:22), they are to be teachers of good conduct (a single word in Greek) in order that they may teach *the young women.* Girls received little or no formal schooling in antiquity; they had to learn in the home. In this way they would learn primarily wifely and family duties. Paul's concern here is quite clearly strong and stable homes, and the young homemaker would play a major role in this.

A strong home begins with the love of a wife for her husband and the love of a mother for her children. Funerary inscriptions in Paul's day often mentioned these two virtues as the glory of womanhood. A wife and mother provides steadiness in the home—the bulwark against frustrations in a husband's work, against the disappointments of children, against the strain of daily living. Like the older men, then, she needs *to be sensible.* A sound marriage depends on keeping the marriage vows, to be *chaste* (cf. 2 Cor. 11:2). The family depends also on the mother's willingness to accept her *domestic* role, with all of its trivia and frustrations, without quibbling, doing the household chores with good

grace. Changing patterns of society today may necessitate an acceptance of domestic responsibility by either or both parents. A harmonious family will require also that the wife and mother be *kind* or good.

In a social structure dominated by males, such as Paul knew, family life was based upon dominance by the father. Both Jews and Greeks had no question about the inferior place assigned to women. But Christianity had broken down all gradations. Paul himself had said, "There is neither male nor female" (Gal. 3:28). This newly declared freedom for women created a number of problems, however (see comment on 1 Tim. 2:11), one of which is reflected here. The exercise of their freedom without restraint undoubtedly caused pagans and Jews alike to criticize the gospel as producing "loose women." So Paul, here and elsewhere (cf. 1 Cor. 14:35; Eph. 5:22; Col. 3:18), enjoins wives to be *submissive to their husbands, that the word of God may not be discredited* (lit., blasphemed). The initiative is to be with the wife. She is to relate properly her role as wife to that of her husband. Paul did not tell husbands to subdue their wives. Nothing in Christian life style must hinder *the word,* i.e., the good news of salvation in Jesus Christ.

(3) Of Younger Men (2:6–8)

6 Likewise urge the younger men to control themselves. 7 Show yourself in all respects a model of good deeds, and in your teaching show integrity, gravity, 8 and sound speech that cannot be censured, so that an opponent may be put to shame, having nothing evil to say of us.

Paul's directive concerning *the younger men* takes on a sharper tone as he introduces an imperative (*urge* or "exhort"). *Younger men* especially would be inclined toward a certain recklessness and impetuosity, so the apostle demands that they exercise self-control (cf. Rom. 12:3; 2 Cor. 5:13). According to the Greek text, *in all respects* (lit., concerning all things) may be read either (1) with *to control them-*

selves (so Spicq) or (2) with *show your-self* (RSV, Kelly, others). The second reading is perhaps to be preferred as giving *yourself* the emphasis it deserves (Kelly).

At any rate Titus, himself a young man, must set the right example for this group. He has to present himself as *a model* (cf. 1 Thess. 1:7). Again Paul reminds his associate that actions speak louder than words. One need not try to teach if his actions drown out what he says. The *teaching* itself must be backed up by personal *integrity, gravity,* and the kind of wholesome speech which others cannot fault. The noun translated *integrity* (*aph-thoria*) has two possible variants in early Greek texts—indifference (*adiaphthoria*) and liberality (*aphthonia*)—but neither has strong support. The integrity of Titus' *teaching* offers a reproof of the "sickness" of the opponents' teaching (1:10–16). *Gravity* or seriousness counters their flippant disregard for truth.

The reason for such caution is obvious— *so that an opponent may be put to shame, having nothing evil to say of us.* The Greek phrase translated *an opponent* is "deliberately vague" (Kelly). It may allude to (1) pagan critics (cf. vv. 5,10; 1 Tim. 5:14; 1 Peter 2:12–15), (2) the Christian opponents of the mission (cf. 1 Tim. 1:9; 2 Tim. 2:25), or (3), less likely, the devil (Chrysostom). Exemplary life and integrity go far toward refuting one's critics.

(4) Of Slaves (2:9–10)

⁹ Bid slaves to be submissive to their masters and to give satisfaction in every respect; they are not to be refractory, ¹⁰ nor to pilfer, but to show entire and true fidelity, so that in everything they may adorn the doctrine of God our Savior.

Just as the behavior of both old and young counted heavily in the church's mission, so also did that of the last group, the *slaves.* So here again (see on 1 Tim. 6:1–2; cf. 1 Cor. 7:20–24) the apostle has to reiterate his instructions regarding the conduct of slaves. The key, from the slaves' point of view, is voluntary sub-

mission and trying to please their masters *in every respect. In every respect* (lit., in all things) may go either (1) with *be submissive* (Jerome, Jeremias, Spicq) or (2) with *give satisfaction* (RSV). The parallel in Colossians 3:22 favors the former (cf. also 1 Peter 2:18). The Christian emphasis is evident in the positive directive to *give satisfaction, viz.,* as Christians rather than slaves.

The apostle spells out his concept of a proper attitude more fully. Slaves should not "talk back." They should not steal, a common practice in a Roman household (Spicq, Dibelius-Conzelmann). Paul even "inquires" whether the runaway Onesimus had stolen from his master Philemon (Philemon 18). On the contrary, they should *show entire and true fidelity* (lit., all good faith). The apostle wants no question about Christian trustworthiness (cf. 1 Tim. 5:12; Gal. 5:22).

Good behavior of slaves has the same aim as that of other members of a Christian family, *so that in everything they may adorn the doctrine of God our Savior.* In other words, their faithful and willing discharge of their tasks will make the Christian message attractive and noble to others. The Christian adorns himself with purity of heart rather than external finery (cf. 1 Tim. 2:9; 1 Pet. 3:5). He has nothing stronger to commend what he says about God's saving act in Jesus Christ.

4. God's Grace the Foundation of Godliness (2:11–14)

¹¹ For the grace of God has appeared for the salvation of all men, ¹² training us to renounce irreligion and worldly passions, and to live sober, upright, and godly lives in this world, ¹³ awaiting our blessed hope, the appearing of the glory of our great God and Savior Jesus Christ, ¹⁴ who gave himself for us to redeem us from all iniquity and to purify for himself a people of his own who are zealous for good deeds.

His allusion to God as Savior (see comment on 1 Tim. 1:1) strikes a responsive chord in Paul's brain. The apostle briefly recounts the basis for Christian behavior,

God's saving grace. The passage has a liturgical ring which has led some scholars to propose dependence on traditional materials—perhaps "a citation from a Greek Christian credal formula or hymn" (Easton) or "an extract from a prayer used at the eucharist or at baptism" (Hanson). Both the style and language, especially use of Old Testament and Hellenistic liturgical phrases, would support such a conclusion. If this conclusion is correct, it would help to explain why some scholars (e.g., Barrett, Scott, Easton) have detected un-Pauline features—in the idea that God's grace *appeared* suddenly, in the view that grace "instructs," and in the sharp distinction of the present age from the future.

This summary of the gospel gives the basis not only for the good conduct of slaves but for the entire code which precedes (2:2–10). The basis is, of course, God's free and unmerited favor, as elsewhere in Paul (cf. Eph. 2:8). This *grace . . . appeared* at a definite moment in history, i.e., in the birth of Jesus of Nazareth. In doing so, it made deliverance from sin and death available *for . . . all men.* Paul again (as in 1 Tim. 2:4) accents the universality of God's soteriological act in Christ. Both the order of the Greek and the dative case prove that *for . . . all men* should go with the adjective *sotērios* (translated *for the salvation of*) and not the verb *has appeared.* Christ did not simply appear to all—he brought salvation to all!

This *grace* has instructional value. *Training* here bears the Greek sense of education (cf. Acts 7:22; 22:3) rather than the usual Pauline sense of chastise or correct (cf. 1 Cor. 11:32). Admittedly, the thought clashes with Paul's usual emphasis on grace as a gift of freedom, acquittal, and reconciliation on the basis of faith. However, Kelly has rightly pointed out that Paul also connects *grace* with the work of the Holy Spirit in the Christian life. So he would not necessarily have found it essential to correct the traditional formulation.

The reasons God supplied his instructive grace are (1) that we may live devout lives in the present and (2) await eagerly the consummation of the Christian hope. The first purpose is expressed in terms of the strong contrast between the former pagan life and the present Christian life. The Christian life began with a renunciation. The allusion may possibly be to baptism, which entails a decisive break with the past—its impiety (cf. Rom. 1:18) *and worldly passions.* By the second century at least the baptized person made a formal renunciation. Prior to baptism, Satan held sway; after baptism, Christ rules. *Worldly passions* (cf. 2 Clement 17:3) refer to desires which Satan controls, that part of life which is not consecrated to God.

The positive aim of Christians *in this world* is *to live sober, upright, and godly lives.* Three adverbs describe the Christian's relationship to himself, to his fellow men, and to God. Personally he takes life seriously, controlling his *passions* and desires. With reference to others he is just, trustworthy. With reference to God he is genuinely devout.

For the earliest Christians, however, the present life only foreshadowed what life would be. They awaited the *blessed hope* (cf. Rom. 8:19,23) which is connected with the return of Christ. In Greek the absence of the article with *appearing* demonstrates the intimate connection between *hope* and *appearing. Hope* is the object hoped for, *viz.,* Christ himself.

Awaiting our blessed hope (cf. Luke 2:25,38; 12:36; 24:15) and the circumlocution in *the appearing of the glory of our great God and Savior Jesus Christ* reflect Hebrew thought patterns and indicate further that we are dealing here with traditional materials. *Appearing,* like *Savior,* a technical term drawn from Hellenistic cultic language (see comment on 2 Tim. 1:10), was applied to the birth, assumption of power, or enthronement of both gods and emperors. *Great* also was often applied to God, kings, divinities, and heroes in profane literature.

The Greek will allow two translations of this last clause: (1) as found in the RSV text or (2) the appearing of the glory of "the great God and our Saviour Jesus Christ" (KJV, RV, Jeremias, Kelly). In favor of (2) exegetes cite (a) the infrequent description of Christ as God in the New Testament (possibly Rom. 9:5; John 1:1; Heb. 1:8); (b) the fact that the Pastorals regularly distinguish Christ and God (1 Tim. 1:1; 5:21); (c) the fact that the Pastorals' Christology stresses the dependence of Christ and the uniqueness of God (cf. 1 Tim. 6:16); and (d) the support of some early scribes.

Slightly stronger arguments appear to be given for the first rendering: (a) the fact that Christ's Parousia is in mind; (b) the fact that the Greek clause has only one article (with *God*); (c) the regular combination of "God and Savior" in Hellenistic religions; and (d) the support of most Greek Fathers (Spicq, Barrett, others).

The theological summary concludes with a statement of Christ's work. He *gave himself for us* (cf. 1 Tim. 2:6; Gal. 1:4), an "entirely Pauline" statement (Spicq) based on words of Jesus (Mark 10:45), for two purposes: (1) to liberate us from sin and (2) to prepare us to be God's own people.

First, Christ's self-offering frees us. Sin or *iniquity* is thought of not as guilt but as power (cf. Gal. 2:20; 1 Tim. 2:6). His death supplies the ransom price necessary for our freedom (cf. Rom. 5:6,8).

Second, his self-offering lays the foundation for the church. Paul and his contemporaries believed that the church was the true Israel, not a new one, and that the covenant promises applied to them. By his death Christ purifies *for himself a people of his own*. The phrase rendered *a people of his own* based on Exodus 19:5 (cf. Deut. 4; 14:2), is literally "a wealthy or peculiar people." Paul adds a brief qualifying phrase explaining what this special relationship to God implies. They will be zealous not for the law (Acts 21:20) or for the ancestral traditions (Gal.

1:14; cf. Eph. 2:10), but rather *zealous for good works* (see 1 Tim. 2:10).

5. A Charge to Titus (2:15)

15 Declare these things; exhort and reprove with all authority. Let no one disregard you.

A general charge to Titus interrupts Paul's instructions momentarily, accenting what has been said and preparing the way for what follows (cf. 1 Tim. 1:18-20; 4:12). The apostle will have Titus show no timidity. The combination of imperatives bears much the same force as 2 Timothy 4:2: "convince, rebuke, and exhort." *Declare* (lit., speak) *these things* refers to vv. 1 ff. *Exhort* (cf. v. 6; 2 Tim. 4:2) means urge strongly, almost command. *Reprove* (cf. 1:9,13; 2 Tim. 4:2) *with all authority* applies to the obstinate sinners and opponents. *With all authority*, a phrase used only by Paul (1 Cor. 7:6; 2 Cor. 8:8), may conceivably refer to all three preceding verbs, but it goes more naturally with the last (Jerome, Spicq). Titus has been invested with apostolic authority, Paul's own. Therefore, Paul urges, *let no one disregard you*. There is no mention of his youthfulness, as in Timothy's case (1 Tim. 4:12), but Titus would perhaps have been about the same age as Timothy.

6. Proper Attitudes Toward Non-Christians Based on God's Kindness and Generosity (3:1-8a)

1 Remind them to be submissive to rulers and authorities, to be obedient, to be ready for any honest work, 2 to speak evil of no one, to avoid quarreling, to be gentle, and to show perfect courtesy toward all men. 3 For we ourselves were once foolish, disobedient, led astray, slaves to various passions and pleasures, passing our days in malice and envy, hated by men and hating one another; 4 but when the goodness and loving kindness of God our Savior appeared, 5 he saved us, not because of deeds done by us in righteousness, but in virtue of his own mercy, by the washing of regeneration and renewal in the Holy Spirit, 6 which he poured out upon us richly through Jesus Christ our Savior, 7 so that we might be justified by his grace and become heirs in hope of eternal life. 8 The saying is sure.

In chapter 2 Paul has given prescriptions concerning conduct within the Christian community. In chapter 3 he offers instructions concerning the larger community in which Christians live. Verses 1–2 urge the Cretan faithful to be models of good citizenship. The basis for such conduct, Paul says in vv. 3–7, is the new life which they have begun as a result of their having received the Holy Spirit, an event which has put them in a new relationship to God and their fellow men.

Paul directs his aide first to *remind them* (see comment on 2 Tim. 2:14) *to be submissive to rulers and authorities.* Submission was a regular part of the early teaching for new converts—submission of wives to husbands (1 Cor. 14:34; Eph. 5:22,24; Col. 3:18; Titus 2:5; 1 Peter 3:1,5), of Christians to their leaders (1 Cor. 16:16; 1 Peter 5:5), of slaves to their masters (Eph. 6:5; Col. 3:22; 1 Tim. 6:1–2; Titus 2:9–10; 1 Peter 2:18), of children to their parents (Eph. 6:1; Col. 3:20), of citizens to their rulers (Rom. 13:1,5; 1 Tim. 2:1 f.; Titus 3:1; 1 Peter 2:13), even of Christians to one another (Eph. 5:21). Paul's directive here, therefore, draws directly from the common fund. The statement could have direct application also to the Cretans, who were notorious for their turbulence (cf. Kelly, Scott). This would clarify the explanatory addition *to be obedient,* which would seem to imply that the state was not at this time commanding the worship of the emperor (Barrett). *Rulers and authorities,* virtually synonymous words in common parlance, would cover all persons in positions of authority (cf. Rom. 13:1; 1 Peter 2:13 f.). Christians accept established authority, unless it conflicts directly with God's revealed will (cf. Acts 5:29), as given by God himself (cf. Rom. 13:1–2; 1 Peter 2:15–16). This general principle would not rule out protest and dissent regarding unjust and ungodly forms of government.

Good citizenship extends further than civil obedience. It has a positive character, involving a readiness to do *any honest work. Any honest* (lit., good) *work* involves not only charity, a major arm of the Christian mission (see comment on 2:14), but whatever goes with good citizenship.

The apostle gives four other prescriptions for a well ordered and healthy citizen's role, the key to which is the last, *perfect courtesy toward all men.* The word translated *courtesy* (meekness) appears often in Paul's lists of Christian virtues (e.g., 2 Cor. 10:1). For him it plays an essential role in maintaining harmony within the Christian community. Christ himself taught (Matt. 5:5) and gave the supreme example (Matt. 11:29; 21:5; 2 Cor. 10:1) of meekness. Here the spirit of meekness, born of humility (see comment on 2 Tim. 2:25), must go out *toward all men.* Such a spirit will overcome the common tendency to slander others (lit., to blaspheme). A spirit of gentleness will take the place of a tendency to quarrel.

The rationale for good citizenship is the new life in Christ. Paul employs the familiar "Once . . . now" scheme (cf. Rom. 6:17 f.; 1 Cor. 6:9–11) to drive home his point. In v. 3 he gives a catalogue of vices, similar to 2 Timothy 3:2–4 (cf. also Rom. 1:21–31), which depict the pre-Christian life in dark colors; then in vv. 4–7 he incorporates an early Christian (baptismal) hymn (Jeremias) to mark the point of departure to the Christian life.

The catalogue of vices in v. 3 perhaps portrays the more unseemly aspects of contemporary Roman morality, but it does not misrepresent it. Roman moralists like Seneca (54 B.C.—A.D. 39) used some of the same terms to describe the ethics of their fellows. Paul takes pains to include himself (*we ourselves*) in the same category with Titus and other Christians. All men, both Jews and Greeks, he has argued in Romans (cf. 3:23), fail to live up to God's law.

The whole list illustrates the character of those who do not know God (see comment on 2 Tim. 3:2–4). In such a state they are *foolish,* i.e., blind to the reality of God and his law (see comment on 1 Tim. 6:9; cf. Luke 24:25), and *disobedient,* i.e., contemptuous of God's will and impatient of all authority (see comment on 1:16; cf. Rom. 1:30; 2 Tim. 3:2). Worse still, while presuming to be wise, they are *led astray,* becoming dupes of false guides. The result is that they become *slaves to various passions and desires,* given over to purely material things (cf. Gal. 4:3). The Stoics frequently combined *passions* and *desires,* but they would add to these grief and fear. Paul, however, goes on to indicate how such utter self-indulgence accumulates, with men living thoroughly antisocial lives, *in malice* (cf. Rom. 1:29; 1 Cor. 5:8; Col. 3:8) *and envy* (cf. Rom. 1:29; Gal. 5:21; Phil. 1:15). The final consequence is a society torn apart by mutual hatred, an observation every human generation can make for itself. Where *malice* and *envy* prevail, men are *hated by men* (or "are hateful") and they hate.

As far as Christians are concerned, this situation should no longer prevail. God has done something about it, as Paul shows in citing a hymn or confessional statement. That vv. 4–7 contain pre-formulated traditional materials is proven (1) by the formula of citation in v. 8; (2) by the rhythmic quality and heightened tone of the Greek; and (3) by the awkward placing of "saved" and the lack of an expressed subject, which would suggest bodily insertion. Scholars have proposed various theories regarding the extent of the hymn: vv. 3–6a (Dibelius-Conzelmann), 4–6 (Lock), 4–7 (Scott, Jeremias), 5b–7 (Easton), 5b–6 (Kelly). This writer prefers to see the whole as a unit with Pauline additions in v. 5 (see comments below). The clear allusions to baptism in vv. 5–6 sustain Jeremias' view that the fragment had something to do with baptism.

Whatever man's lot in the pre-Christian era, God decisively altered it in the incarnation of Jesus Christ. It was in this event that *the goodness and loving kindness of God our Savior appeared.* The verb *appeared* marks a definite event in history (see comment on 2:11; cf. 2 Tim. 1:10; 1 Tim. 6:14). The coming of Christ makes openly manifest to us the goodness and loving kindness of God. *Goodness (chrestotes)* is an exclusively Pauline word, which he applies both to men (2 Cor. 6:6; Gal. 5:22; Col. 3:12) and to God (Rom. 2:4; 11:22; Eph. 2:7). In the ancient world it was often coupled with *loving kindness* or "generosity" (*philanthropia*) as a designation for the supreme quality of a ruler. Applied here to *God our Savior,* they again smite the emperor cult. *God our Savior* may refer either (1) to the Father, or (2) to Christ, probably the former.

In this dramatic act, entirely unmerited by men, God *saved us.* The aorist tense of the verb *saved* here underlines the once-for-allness of the act. This emphasis would not conflict with Paul's understanding of salvation as a process. The hymn is looking at the act from God's point of view. In one decisive intervention in human history God accomplished what was needed for man's salvation. Man, however, participates in this once-for-all act as a process—past, present, and future. From his point of view it will be completed in the consummation of God's whole purpose for mankind.

To avoid any misunderstanding, Paul inserts a parenthetical statement which qualifies the verb *saved.* God *saved us, not because of deeds done by us in righteousness, but in virtue of his own mercy.* Heavy emphasis falls on the contrast between what we do and what God does in securing man's salvation. The Greek accents *we* and *his.*

Paul's phrasing here differs somewhat from that found in other letters, but, as Barrett comments, it "has a Pauline sound, and conveys accurately enough Pauline doctrine." Against the critics, it may be urged (1) that though faith is not mentioned, it is implied. (2) Though Paul does not use the phrase "not from works in righteousness" (cf. 1 Tim. 6:11; 2 Tim.

2:22; 3:16), it represents accurately his view. Actually, the passage should be translated "not from works which we have done with a view to obtaining justification," which rightly interprets Paul's "not from works of the law" (Rom. 3:20,28; Gal. 2:16; 3:2,5,10). (3) Paul does normally use "grace" rather than *mercy,* but he occasionally interchanges them (cf. Rom. 9:23; 11:31; 15:9; Eph. 2:4).

The hymn resumes. God *saved us . . . by the washing of regeneration and renewal in the Holy Spirit. Washing* (*loutron*) clearly refers to baptism (cf. Eph. 5:26; 1 Cor. 6:11)—as I see it. The Greek can be translated in two ways: (1) "by the washing of regeneration and by the renewal of the Holy Spirit" or (2) as in the RSV text. The former would imply a distinction between water baptism and Spirit baptism, a distinction which did occur by the third century in Christian history. Acts (e.g., 10:44) records the reception of the Holy Spirit *before* baptism. If a separation of *washing* and *renewal of the Holy Spirit* had been intended, however, the preposition (*dia,* through) would probably have been repeated before *renewal* (Barrett). Moreover, early Christian writers normally connect the action of the Holy Spirit with water baptism. The Holy Spirit is the efficient cause in baptism, not the washing. So the RSV rendering is perhaps preferable. Neither translation implies that baptism is essential to salvation.

Regeneration translates a Greek word found only here in Paul's writings. The Stoics used the term to describe periodic restorations of the world. In Matthew 19:28 it is applied to the eschatological restoration in the second coming. The mystery religions applied the word to the mystical rebirth of initiates. Possibly with a variety of these nuances the concept of a new birth in baptism, without any suggestion of magical efficacy, appears in early Christian thought (cf. 1 Peter 1:3,23; John 3:3–8).

Renewal (*anakainosis*) appears only in Paul. In Romans 12:2 it depicts the complete transformation or elevation of the Christian to a new order of being. In Colossians 3:10 Paul uses the verb with a possible allusion to baptism under the rubrics of putting off the old man and putting on the new, "which is being renewed in knowledge after the image of its creator." The point is the same as Paul argues here. Symbolically in baptism but actually through the action of the Holy Spirit, man again receives the divine image which makes him a new creation.

The *Holy Spirit* is the one which God *poured out upon us richly through Jesus Christ our Savior.* The statement probably refers both (1) to Pentecost (cf. Acts 2:17, in fulfillment of Joel 2:28) and (2) to the baptism of each Christian (Hanson). On the one hand, the gift of the Holy Spirit is what sets the messianic Israel, Christianity, apart from the old Israel, Judaism. With the dawning of the messianic era in Christ's resurrection all believers receive the Spirit. Thus in Ephesians 5:25–26 the whole church is "cleansed," i.e., set apart for God's purpose, "by the washing of water with the word."

On the other hand, Paul also believes that the Spirit was imparted at baptism (cf. 1 Cor. 6:11; 12:13). The Spirit bears fruit within the believer and confirms in him the Christian hope (cf. Gal. 5:22 ff.). He supplies in abundance, *richly,* what the Christian requires for faithfulness to God.

The Spirit is mediated to Christians by their faith union with Christ, *through Jesus Christ our Savior.* Both *God* the Father and *Christ* are addressed as *Savior* (see comment on 2 Tim. 1:10) without particular distinction, for salvation comes from God *through Jesus Christ.*

The purpose (*hina*) clause in v. 7 may refer back to the verb *saved* (v. 5) or to *poured out* (v. 6). Pauline theology, especially of Romans 5 and 6, favors the former; the sequence of the Greek the latter. Actually salvation and the gift of the Spirit stand in such close connection that one might solve the problem by accepting both verbs as references. The purpose of the whole divine act is, literally rendered, "that, having been justified by his grace, we might become heirs according to the hope of eternal life."

The RSV rendering, distinguishing two purposes, does not do full justice to the sequential implication of the Greek. By virtue of God's *grace* in Christ we "have been justified" (an aorist participle). The verb, a causal, perhaps means both to make righteous and to declare righteous in Paul's letters. God's "rightwising" puts us in a new relationship vis-à-vis himself (see Rom. 5:1,9; Gal. 3:8 ff.). We are no longer slaves, but sons and, as sons, *heirs* (cf. Rom. 4:13,14; Gal. 3:29). The inheritance, of which we have only a foretaste now, belongs to the future. So the believer lives *in hope of eternal life* (see comment on 1:2).

The apostle underlines his quotation with the recurrent formula, *the saying is sure* (1 Tim. 1:16; 3:1; 4:9; 2 Tim. 2:11). There can be little doubt that the formula looks backwards (cf. 1 Tim. 4:9, which is less certain). It is difficult to decide, however, whether *I desire you to insist on these things* belongs with the formula or, as in the RSV text, with what follows. The difficulty lies with the conjunction (*kai*), which the translators simply delete. The statement would appear to glance both backwards and forwards.

7. Avoid Harmful Disputes (3:8b–11)

I desire you to insist on these things, so that those who have believed in God may be careful to apply themselves to good deeds; these are excellent and profitable to men. ⁹ But avoid stupid controversies, genealogies, dissensions, and quarrels over the law, for they are unprofitable and futile. ¹⁰ As for a man who is factious, after admonishing him once or twice, have nothing more to do with him, ¹¹ knowing that such a person is perverted and sinful; he is self-condemned.

In concluding the main body of his letter, Paul takes a parting shot at the troublemakers.

His purpose in writing *these things*, i.e., what has gone before, is *that those who have believed in God* (Christians) *may be careful to apply themselves to good deeds.* The Greek idiom will permit the translation "that they engage in honourable occupations" (NEB). However, the more general nuance is supported (1) by the normal meaning of the verb and (2) by the meaning of "good deeds" elsewhere in the Pastorals (1 Tim. 2:10; 5:10; 6:18; 2 Tim. 2:21; 3:17; Titus 1:16; 2:7,14; 3:14). Though the church did place certain strictures on occupations in the late second or early third centuries,[37] nothing in the context here would suggest as much. The chief concern here is with exemplary Christian behavior, including charity, by which the gospel would advance.

Paul accentuates his statement further. *These are excellent and profitable to men.* *These* may refer to *good deeds* (RSV, NEB), the whole of the preceding statements in vv. 4–7 (Spicq), or even "baptism and its consecration" (Easton). Since the apostle has contrasted good deeds with the behavior of the Cretan Judaists throughout the letter (see especially 1:16; 2:7,14), the first, sustained also by the word order, would appear to be the most natural referent. Such good deeds are not only good but also profitable to men.

By way of complete contrast the *stupid controversies* (see comment on 1 Tim. 1:4; 6:4; 2 Tim. 2:23), *genealogies* (see comment on 1 Tim. 1:4), *dissensions* (cf. 1 Tim. 6:4; 2 Tim. 2:23), *and quarrels over the law* (see comment on 1 Tim. 1:8 f.) are *unprofitable and futile. Unprofitable* plays on the word *profitable* in v. 8, another reminder that "they profess to know God, but they deny him by their deeds" (1:16). Paul urges Titus to *avoid* (see comment on 2 Tim. 2:16) this kind of religion.

Even if the latter would avoid a futile way, the community of faith might suffer from factious persons. In this case Titus ought to *have nothing more to do with* someone *who is factious* after one or two warnings. The Greek for *factious* is *hairetikos*, which appears only here in the New

37 Cf. Hippolytus, *Apos. Trad.*, 16.

Testament. The word does not bear the second-century connotation of doctrinal error. Paul himself elsewhere uses the noun *hairesis* to designate partisan cliques (1 Cor. 11:19; Gal. 5:20). Factionalism is the problem in Crete also. So the apostle counsels Titus to have nothing more to do with a *factious* person. The verb, used in the letters to Timothy in reference to avoiding disputes (1 Tim. 4:7; 2 Tim. 2:23) and refusing to enroll young widows (1 Tim. 5:11), has a stronger nuance than "avoid," but is not a technical term for excommunication (Barrett).

The practice of *admonishing him once or twice* originated in Judaism. Presumably the warnings would be private rather than public. Matthew 18:15-17, possibly reflecting the same procedure in the missionary situation, prescribes three stages: (1) private confrontation, (2) confrontation before two or three witnesses, and (3), as a last resort, public confrontation. Shunning would occur when there remained no hope of reconciliation.

If a *factious* person refuses attempts at reconciliation, one need have no qualms about shunning him. No one condemns him but himself, for he has passed up ample occasions for correction. The sin rests upon him for his refusal to reform.

II. Some Final Instructions (3:12-14)

[12] When I send Artemas or Tychicus to you, do your best to come to me at Nicopolis, for I have decided to spend the winter there. [13] Do your best to speed Zenas the lawyer and Apollos on their way; see that they lack nothing. [14] And let our people learn to apply themselves to good deeds, so as to help cases of urgent need, and not to be unfruitful.

The apostle has concluded the principal portion of the letter. He now intersperses personal notes with his final instructions to Titus. A number of scholars who hold the "fragments' hypothesis" regard part or all of the remaining verses as genuine—some vv. 12-13 only (e.g., Barrett, Hanson); others, vv. 12-13, 15 (e.g., Scott); others, vv. 12-15 (Harrison, Easton with reser-

vations). In support of authenticity one may cite (1) references to people and to a place not mentioned in Acts or other letters and (2) the lifelike touch in v. 12. With reference to the "fragments' hypothesis" it is hard to believe that such a tiny fragment could have survived at all.

When he wrote, sending the letter by Zenas and Apollos apparently, Paul had not quite made up his mind whether he would send *Artemas or Tychicus* to take Titus' place. *Artemas*, an abbreviation of Artemidoras (gift of Artemis, whose cult centered on Ephesus; cf. Acts 19:23-41), is not mentioned elsewhere in the New Testament. Later tradition listed him as one of the seventy (Luke 10:1 ff.) and the first bishop of Lystra. *Tychicus* (see comment on 2 Tim. 4:12; cf. Acts 20:4; Eph. 6:21; Col. 4:7) apparently did yeoman service for the apostle in his twilight years. The fact that Titus was replaceable shows that Paul did not consider his position indispensable (Barrett).

Paul bids Titus to *do your best* (see 2 Tim. 4:9,21) *to come to me at Nicopolis*, where he planned to spend the winter. There were several towns which bore this name ("city of victory") in Paul's day. The most likely one would be Nicopolis in Epirus, founded by Octavian in 31 B.C. in honor of his triumph over Anthony and Cleopatra at Actium.

Paul had evidently sent *Zenas* and *Apollos* via Crete, bearing his letter, to an unknown destination. *Zenas the lawyer*, so identified to distinguish him from some other Zenas, is not mentioned elsewhere. In other New Testament references (Matt. 22:35; Luke 7:30; 10:25; 11:45,52; 14:3) *lawyer* designates an expert in Jewish law, but here the word must have the broader secular sense. The name *Zenas*, an abbreviation of Zenodorus (gift of Zeus), is Greek.

Apollos is probably, though not positively, the well-known Alexandrian Jew who had worked in Corinth (cf. Acts 18:24; 19:1; 1 Cor. 1:12; 3:4-6,22; 4:6; 16:12). Later writers have sometimes identified him as the author of the letter to the Hebrews.

Paul urges Titus *to speed* them *on their way* amply provided for. The early church manifested a generous concern for travelers. In the late first or early second century the composer of the Didache had to delineate safeguards for this generosity. Traveling missionaries may stay only one or two days; if one stays three, "he is a false prophet." They should go on their way with nothing but bread until they arrive at their next stopping place. Anyone who asks for money "is a false prophet" (11:3–6). Travelers would carry letters of recommendation such as Paul includes in this one (cf. 2 Cor. 3:1 ff.).

Paul's mention of help for Christian travelers gives an opening for urging once more the theme of practical Christianity. *And* (a double conjunction in Greek) *let our people* (i.e., genuine Christians and those who represent his and Titus' way of thinking in Crete) *learn to apply themselves to good deeds* (exactly as in v. 8), *so as to help cases of urgent need.* The last clause means literally "the things necessary for life," a phrase used technically by the Stoics (Easton). Charity goes with Christianity like heat goes with the sun. Those who do not practice it, the opponents (vv. 8–9), are *unfruitful;* this, followers of Paul and Titus must not be.

Concluding Salutations and Benediction (3:15)

15 All who are with me send greetings to you. Greet those who love us in the faith.
Grace be with you all.

The apostle closes with an exchange of greetings and his usual benediction. *All who are with me send greetings to you* suggests a rosier picture than 2 Timothy 4:9 ff. (cf. 1 Cor. 16:19 f.; 2 Cor. 13:12). *Those who love us in the faith* would be all true friends and true Christians. *In the faith,* which lacks the article in Greek, may be translated "loyally."

The final benediction uses a plural *you* (cf. 1 Tim. 6:21; 2 Tim. 4:22). Paul expected the whole community to hear his letter.

Philemon

RAY F. ROBBINS

Introduction

A little more than 100 miles east of Ephesus, in the valley of the Lycus River, the tri-cities of Laodicea, Hierapolis, and Colossae were located. Only a few miles separated them from each other. In pre-Hellenistic times these cities were located in the extreme southwest part of the country known as Phrygia.

These cities formed a center of early Christianity (Col. 4:13). It appears that Paul was not personally acquainted with the churches in these cities which had been founded by others (Col. 1:4,7–8; 2:1). However, he kept in touch with them and regarded himself as their apostle. He wrote at least one letter to the church in Laodicea (Col. 4:16), and probably two letters to the church in Colossae (i.e., Colossians and Philemon). It is evident that the two extant letters to Colossae were written while Paul was in prison (Col. 4:3,10,18; Philemon 1,9 f.).

I. Genuineness

The genuineness of the letter to Philemon has seldom been doubted. Some of the patristic writers questioned its place in the canon because its subject matter appeared too private and commonplace. These doubters supposed either that it did not proceed from Paul or that he wrote it in his private, unapostolic capacity.

F. C. Baur (1792–1860) questioned its authenticity and supplied several arguments in support of his opinion. He claimed that the language was un-Pauline. He in-

terpreted it as the "embryo of a Christian work of fiction" by some later writer to illustrate the idea that Christianity unites and equalizes in a higher sense those whom outward circumstances have separated. Baur's thesis is more ingenious than convincing, and it has found scant acceptance.

II. Occasion

All that we know about the occasion of the writing is gathered from this brief letter. Because the evidence is so meager and ambiguous many questions are not answerable with complete assurance. It is generally assumed that the owner of Onesimus and of the house in which the church met was Philemon.

Many scholars are convinced that the owner of both the slave and the house was Archippus, who is mentioned in closest connection with the church (v. 1). This view was probably first stated by Karl G. Wieseler (1813–1883), a German theologian. Wieseler held the opinion that Philemon was a Laodicean, and he also identified the epistle to Laodicea (Col. 4:16) with the letter to Philemon. Wieseler's theses have been adopted, with certain modifications, by many scholars. In America, E. J. Goodspeed [1] and John Knox (see bibliography) are both influenced by Wieseler's theory. In Knox's opinion Philemon was a letter within a letter. He thinks it was an appeal to Archippus within the

[1] *An Introduction to the New Testament* (Chicago: University of Chicago Press, 1937).

framework of a greeting to Philemon. Knox argues that since Paul did not know Archippus personally, he sought the help of his friend Philemon. These theses, though supported by some plausible arguments, are not without difficulties. A consensus of critical opinion opposes them.

It has generally been assumed that Onesimus was a runaway slave; however, the letter does not say that he was a slave. Albert Barnes [2] argues that Onesimus was not a slave but an apprentice. His arguments are strong; however, this thesis has gained little support.

From the meager information found in this letter it seems that Philemon had been won to faith in Christ through the efforts of Paul because he owed his very self to the apostle. He was probably from Colossae (Col. 4:9) and was possibly an officer in the church there. He was Paul's "beloved fellow worker" in the cause to which the apostle had devoted his life. His house served as the meeting-place for the local church. He was able to refresh the hearts of the saints probably by temporal as well as spiritual gifts. He was noted for his generosity toward his fellow Christians in distress. Also his house was large enough to accommodate Paul and his traveling companions, if the apostle should visit Colossae. He had a good reputation among his fellow Christians for faith in Christ and love for the saints. He was probably a dedicated layman of considerable wealth.

Onesimus, one of Philemon's slaves, had previously wronged, perhaps robbed, his master and run away. He made his way to Rome (or Caesarea or Ephesus) where Paul was imprisoned. Somehow he came into contact with Paul, who led him to exercise faith in Christ. He attached himself to Paul and rendered him personal service. Paul greatly appreciated his service and became deeply attached to him. Paul would have retained him as his attendant but was unwilling to presume upon Philemon's favor. Paul persuaded Onesimus to

2 *Barnes Notes on the New Testament* (Grand Rapids: Kregel Publications, 1962), pp. ccxci–ccxcvi.

perform the dangerous act of voluntarily returning to his master's house.

An occasion arose which afforded an opportunity for Onesimus' return to Colossae. Epaphras, possibly a pastor in the church in Colossae, visited Paul and shared his imprisonment (Philemon 23). Probably from him Paul learned about the serious doctrinal difficulties in the church in Colossae. To correct these false teachings Paul wrote a letter (i.e., Colossians) to the church which he sent by Tychicus (Col. 4:7–8). At the same time Paul wrote a letter to Philemon on behalf of Onesimus, whom he sent with Tychicus back to Colossae. The purpose of the letter was to beg forgiveness for the slave and at the same time to insure that he would be received as a Christian brother. Paul not only sent the letter to Philemon but also recommended Onesimus to the whole church (Col. 4:9).

III. Authorship

Three times the writer calls himself Paul (vv. 1,9,19). Since the second century the letter's existence and authenticity have been acknowledged. Both internal and external evidence for the Pauline authorship is very strong. Timothy is associated with Paul in the address (v. 1), but there is no further reference to Timothy. Paul possibly made Timothy a joint author of the letter because of Timothy's personal acquaintance with Philemon. It is also possible that Timothy was included because the matter in question was of a somewhat legal nature. For the signing of the bond and the recommendation concerning the runaway slave, Paul had a witness (Zahn, p. 456). However, it was Paul who was the real author of the letter (notice the frequency of "I," "me," and "my"), not Paul and Timothy.

IV. Date

Where Paul was when he wrote this letter we can only guess. It was probably written from Rome while Paul was a prisoner there (Acts 28:16–31). However, many scholars think that it was written from Caesarea, and others think that it was written from Ephesus. Likely it was written about the same time that the epistle to the Colossians was written. It seems certain from Colossians 4:7,9, as compared with Philemon, that Paul wrote the two epistles at the same time and sent them to Colossae by Tychicus and Onesimus. If this be so, and if it was written in Rome, then it is not difficult to fix the date with some degree of accuracy—about A.D. 62.

V. Roman Slavery in the First Century

Slavery was a universal institution in the ancient world. In Judaism a slave was a member of the family, a person with rights and dignity.[3] However, among the Greeks and Romans a slave had no rights in law; he was not considered a person but a thing. There were some notable exceptions, but on the whole the lot of the slaves was pitiful. They were absolutely under the master's control. Offenses were mercilessly punished. Runaways were branded on their foreheads with the letter F (for *fugitivus*, i.e., runaway) with a hot iron. Slaves were their master's property, and they were bought and sold like cattle. They were bred like cattle. Their offspring were their master's property. When they were sold, they were stripped and exposed so that their intended purchasers might inspect them. They were trotted around like horses to prove their agility (Smith, p. 570).

There were some 60,000,000 slaves in the Roman Empire about the middle of the first century (Barclay, p. 310). This large number of slaves was a constant menace to free people in the Roman world. There was a common proverb: "So many slaves, just so many enemies." The slaves were held down by strong hands and intimidated by terrible examples. Roman law decreed that if a master had been murdered by a slave, the whole of his fellow slaves in the household should be put to

death. In A.D. 61, probably just a few months before Paul wrote Philemon on behalf of Onesimus, a case occurred which shocked Rome. The prefect of the city, Pedanius Secundus, was murdered by one of his slaves. The Roman Senate voted to enforce the law. Four hundred slaves composing his household, men, women, and children, though well known to be innocent of the crime, were led forth to death. Such examples were thought necessary to repress the slaves and protect the masters (Smith, pp. 569–574).

In Philemon Paul was pleading for one for whom the Roman world offered no word of sympathy, understanding, love, or hope. He had committed a serious offense according to Roman law. Paul's intercession for the runaway slave brought the love of Christ to bear upon the whole institution of slavery and other institutions of society which violate the rights of persons (Johnson, p. 82).

The younger Pliny (A.D. 62-*ca.* 113), a Roman author and orator, who was born about the year in which the letter to Philemon was written, wrote another letter pleading for a runaway slave. Pliny interceded for the slave, who was anxious to return to his master but dreaded the effects of his master's anger. This celebrated letter has often been compared with that of Paul's in behalf of Onesimus.[4] It is the twenty-first letter in Pliny's ninth book and has been translated as follows:

Your freedman, whom you lately mentioned as having displeased you, has been with me; he threw himself at my feet and clung there with as much submission as he could have done at yours. He earnestly requested me with many tears, and even with the eloquence of silent sorrow, to intercede for him; in short, he convinced me by his whole behaviour, that he sincerely repents of his fault. And I am persuaded he is thoroughly reformed, because he seems entirely sensible of his delinquency.

I know you are angry with him, and I know too, it is not without reason; but clemency can never exert itself with more applause, than

---

[3] Frank Stagg, *New Testament Theology* (Nashville: Broadman Press, 1962), p. 52.

[4] *Pliny Letters*, II, tr. William Melmoth; rev. W. M. L. Hutchinson. "The Loeb Classical Library." (London: William Heinemann, Ltd., 1958).

when there is the justest cause for resentment. You once had an affection for this man, and, I hope, will have again: in the meanwhile, let me only prevail with you to pardon him. If he should incur your displeasure hereafter, you will have so much the stronger plea in excuse for your anger, as you shew yourself more exorable to him now. Allow something to his youth, to his tears, and to your own natural mildness of temper: do not make him uneasy any longer, and I will add too, do not make yourself so; for a man of your benevolence of heart cannot be angry without feeling great uneasiness.

I am afraid, were I to join my entreaties with his, I should seem rather to compel, than request you to forgive him. Yet I will not scruple to do so; and so much the more fully and freely as I have very sharply and severely reproved him, positively threatening never to interpose again in his behalf. But though it was proper to say this to him, in order to make him more fearful of offending, I do not say it to you. I may, perhaps, again have occasion to entreat you upon his account, and again obtain your forgiveness; supposing, I mean, his error should be such as may become me to intercede for, and you to pardon. Farewell.

Outline

Selected Bibliography

BARCLAY, WILLIAM. *The Letters to Timothy, Titus and Philemon.* ("The Daily Study Bible.") Philadelphia: Westminster Press, 1960.

ERDMAN, CHARLES R. *The Epistles of Paul to the Colossians and to Philemon.* Philadelphia: Westminster Press, 1933.

HENDRIKSEN, WILLIAM. *The Epistles to Colossians and Philemon.* ("New Testament Commentary.") Grand Rapids: Baker Book House, 1964.

JOHNSON, PHILIP C. *The Epistles to Titus and Philemon.* ("Shield Bible Study Outlines.") Grand Rapids: Baker Book House, 1966.

KNOX, JOHN. *Philemon Among the Letters of Paul* (rev. ed.) Nashville: Abingdon Press, 1959.

MOULE, HANDLEY C. G. *Colossian and Philemon Studies.* London: Pickering and Inglis, Ltd., n.d.

MOULTON, HAROLD K. *Colossians, Philemon and Ephesians.* ("Epworth Preacher's Commentaries.") ed. GREVILLE P. LEWIS. London: The Epworth Press, 1963.

ROLSTON, H. *Thessalonians to Philemon.* ("Layman's Bible Commentary.") London: SCM Press, Ltd., 1963.

SCOTT, ERNEST F. *The Epistles of Paul to the Colossians, to Philemon and to the Ephesians.* ("The Moffatt Commentary.") ed. JAMES MOFFATT. New York: Harper and Brothers Publishers, 1930.

SMITH, DAVID. *The Life and Letters of St. Paul.* New York: Harper and Brothers Publishers, n.d.

ZAHN, THEODOR. *Introduction to the New Testament,* Vol. I. Grand Rapids: Kregel Publications, 1953.

Commentary on the Text

I. Introduction (1–7)

1. Address and Salutation (1–3)

¹ Paul, a prisoner for Christ Jesus, and Timothy our brother,
To Philemon our beloved fellow worker
² and Apphia our sister and Archippus our fellow soldier, and the church in your house:

³ Grace to you and peace from God our Father and the Lord Jesus Christ.

The writer begins by naming himself as Paul, which was customary in the writings of the apostle.

This is the only salutation in which Paul designates himself as *prisoner.* The purpose of the letter is to ask a favor, and he knew that his request would be more appealing if Philemon remembered that he was suffering hardship in the cause that was dear to them both (Scott, p. 101). Five times in this brief letter he refers to his imprisonment (vv. 1,9–10,13,23). He was asking for a sacrifice from Philemon, as one who knew something of sacrifice.

When writing to churches, the usual title which he used for himself was "apostle." This title emphasized his authority. However, in this private letter to a friend he does not claim his official title of apostle ". . . to command . . . what is required, yet for love's sake . . . to appeal . . ." He was trying to persuade his friend to act as a Christian in a way that was entirely different from the customs of his time.

Paul goes behind all secondary causes and sees Christ Jesus as the author and reason for his imprisonment. It was through his life and work for Christ that he had come into the plight in which he found himself. He had suffered the loss of liberty and the shame and suffering of imprisonment because of loyalty to Christ. He had received the shackles because of his faithfulness to Christ; therefore, they were a badge of office or a decoration of honor. It was not Jewish hatred or Roman policy that had sent him to prison. He was not Nero's prisoner, but the prisoner of Christ Jesus.

Timothy was included in the salutation probably because he and Philemon were acquainted. He was called *our brother* because Paul wanted to emphasize the brotherhood of all Christians. It was upon this spirit of brotherhood that Paul was depending as he asked for a kindly reception to be given to the runaway slave (Erdman, p. 128). However this letter is emphatically the letter of Paul alone. After the salutation, Timothy's name disappears from the letter.

The letter was addressed primarily to Philemon (or according to Knox to Archippus). Philemon was greatly beloved by Paul (vv. 1,7,9) and was an active Christian worker. However, since the request was for a master to restore a slave to his household, it was natural to direct the letter to the wife or a close relative, the pastor, and the other Christians who regularly gathered in the home as well as the master himself. In Colossians, sent at the same time, Paul commended Onesimus to the whole church (Col. 4:9).

However, the final decision about the request for the kind reception of the slave would be made by Philemon. In spite of this fact, Paul wanted the others to hear the letter. Their friendly reception of the runaway slave would be important. If Philemon received Onesimus back as Paul asked him to, Onesimus would naturally become a member of the group. Paul also wanted the church to assist Philemon in doing his duty (Hendriksen, pp. 210–211). In a way, Paul was appealing to the "authority" of the church to reinforce his request concerning Onesimus.

Philemon is called *beloved*. This probably expresses Paul's and Timothy's general sentiment toward him. He is also called a fellow worker of Paul and Timothy. This probably means that he assisted in some way in spreading the gospel in his vicinity.

The name Apphia was probably a Phrygian designation of endearment. It has been found many times in Phrygian inscriptions. Apphia may have been the wife or some close relative of Philemon. The way she is mentioned in the letter and also tradition support the idea that she was his wife. She also may have occupied some position in the church. She is called *our sister*, which meant that she belonged to the family of faith. Throughout the epistle the appeal is based on the reality of the love of Christ which makes all Christians one family (Johnson, p. 86).

It has been supposed, and tradition supports the idea, that Archippus was a son of Philemon, but there is nothing in the letter to indicate this. The fact that he is mentioned in a private letter is evidence that he bore some relation to Philemon other than membership in the church

(Knox claims that he was the owner of Onesimus). He is mentioned in the New Testament only here and in Colossians 4:17. He seems to have occupied an important ministry in the church in Colossae. He may have been serving as the pastor of the church in the absence of Epaphras (Col. 4:17).

Paul called Archippus a *fellow soldier.* This title in the New Testament is used only of one other person, Epaphroditus (Phil. 2:25). These two men shared the apostle's labors and hardships. They took part in the common cause and common perils of service in the gospel.

Paul also addressed *the church in your house.* In the absence of regular church buildings, the houses of particular members were used for that purpose (1 Cor. 16:19; Rom. 16:5,23; Col. 4:15; Acts 2:46; 5:42; 20:20). The family, slaves, and dependents formed the nucleus of the gatherings. The oldest known church building which has been discovered by archeologists was built in A.D. 232–233 at Dura Europas in eastern Syria on the Euphrates. This was a modified once-private dwelling. During the first and second centuries Christian families held worship in their own homes. If the house was large enough to accommodate others they were invited. If the number of Christians in any city was large, many house-churches would be necessary (Hendriksen, p. 211). The church which met in Philemon's house was also addressed because it would have an interest in the contents of the letter. The members would need to receive Onesimus into their fellowship. It probably included Philemon's family, his slaves, friends, and the other believers who met for instruction and worship.

The two main points to be observed in the salutation of v. 3 are the comprehensiveness of the expressed wish and the source to which the apostle looks for its fulfillment. This salutation may be regarded as a prayer, a wish, or a promise. The word *grace* stresses the self-motivated actions of God, the spontaneous and loving disposition from which his kindly acts

proceed. It stresses God's free, self-originating, benevolent favor. God is a gracious being. This word grace emphasizes that God is not motivated by anything that man thinks, feels, or does. God's gracious action to man should produce a sense of gratitude, a realization of unmerited favor, or thanksgiving.

Peace conveys the primary idea of reconciliation with God, but also the inner serenity which flowed from that reconciliation. It conveys the idea of concord, safety, and pleasure. It is used to express the spiritual state of the redeemed. Through God's grace the redeemed man has the right relationship with God, with himself, with his fellowmen, and with the created order.

Paul pronounces upon Philemon, Apphia, Archippus, and the church the two blessings of grace and peace *from God our Father and the Lord Jesus Christ.* Only God's grace could make Philemon sufficient to meet the situation before him. Only God's grace in Philemon and the Colossian Christians could produce the reconciliation and mutual acceptance that was desired. With that grace, peace would fill the hearts of all (Johnson, p. 87).

2. Recognition of the Christian Character and Service of Philemon (4–7)

⁴ I thank my God always when I remember you in my prayers, ⁵ because I hear of your love and of the faith which you have toward the Lord Jesus and all the saints, ⁶ and I pray that the sharing of your faith may promote the knowledge of all the good that is ours in Christ. ⁷ For I have derived much joy and comfort from your love, my brother, because the hearts of the saints have been refreshed through you.

According to his custom when writing to churches, Paul follows his salutation with thankful commendations and prayer for the continued welfare of those whom he addressed (Knox, pp. 21 f.). In this letter, however, after the salutation only Philemon (or according to Knox, only Archippus) is addressed. Paul thanked God that he remained strong in faith and displayed his faith in a life of practical goodness. As often as the name of Philemon came to his mind as he waited before God, he gave thanks. Verse 4 reveals much about the habit of the apostle's private devotions. He often stated that he mentioned individuals and churches by name.

Paul's reason for giving thanks is explained in v. 5. This verse should be read in parenthesis. The apostle was constantly hearing, probably from Epaphras, Onesimus, and others, of Philemon's generosity and hospitality and in his prayers thanked God as the ultimate giver of these blessings. He praised Philemon for the way he had helped his fellow Christians. His love for all saints (i.e., all Christians) was demonstrated by his willingness to share his blessings with others (Hendriksen, p. 213). Faith in Jesus Christ was the source from which his love for all saints came (cf. Eph. 1:15; Col. 1:4). Notice the tact with which Paul refers to a well-known feature of Philemon's character, and one on which he was about to draw so largely. This liberality on the part of Philemon is emphasized so strongly because Paul is about to make a further demand upon his generosity. Since Philemon had been so kind and generous, surely he would be glad to show one further deed of Christian love. Paul did not make his request at this time, but he persuasively prepared the mind of Philemon for the request later.

Verse 6 refers back to v. 4 and gives the content of Paul's prayers for Philemon. The meaning of this passage is not clear. It seems that Paul gave thanks for Philemon, but also asked God on his behalf, that Philemon's labors in spreading the gospel might be blessed with fruitfulness. Paul also asked God to cause those with whom Philemon labored, not only to recognize all that was good in him, but also to attribute it to the grace of God. It seems that Paul says that he prayed for him in order that his fellowship in the faith would further show its power in his relation to others, by exhibiting every grace which is in Christians to the glory of Christ. Paul,

while he encouraged his friend, was careful not to puff him up with spiritual pride.

Paul stated that his own heart had been gladdened and comforted by the way Philemon had refreshed the hearts of the saints. Verse 7 seems to indicate that it was by some signal act of goodwill that Philemon had brought encouragement to the Christian community. This may have been some unusual act of beneficence, possibly in connection with a recent earthquake. However, it may have been his usual acts of kindness which he had shown to Christians. His fellow Christians had been refreshed by his infectious Christian life among them. He again addressed Philemon as *brother*, a word of affection. Also this word would prepare the way for the appeal which follows. Philemon must have been moved by these complimentary references to himself from Paul.

II. The Request (8-20)

1. Appeal by Entreaty Rather Than Command (8-11)

8 Accordingly, though I am bold enough in Christ to command you to do what is required, 9 yet for love's sake I prefer to appeal to you—I, Paul, an ambassador and now a prisoner also for Christ Jesus—10 I appeal to you for my child, Onesimus, whose father I have become in my imprisonment. 11 (Formerly he was useless to you, but now he is indeed useful to you and to me.)

The word *accordingly* refers to the preceding thought. Philemon's faith in Christ and love shown to all the saints were the cause of such joy to Paul (v. 7) and were the reasons why he was now being requested to demonstrate the same kind of love toward Onesimus. Paul stated that his apostolic authority gave him the right to command Philemon to do what was right in the matter. He reminded him of this in order to suggest that the request he was about to make was in accord with Philemon's Christian profession. Since Philemon owned Christ as his absolute Master, he must recognize Onesimus as his spiritual brother. Instead of Paul commanding, he preferred to rely on Philemon's own sense of moral fitness which had its basis in his faith in Christ and his love for the saints (Rolston, p. 129). He puts away command, and in words of deep affection and gentle persuasion he entreats for love's sake, the bond which unites all Christians. "It is not Philemon's love nor St. Paul's own love, but love absolutely, love regarded as a principle which demands a deferential respect." [5] Paul—as an apostle—could have commanded Philemon and the Colossian church to receive Onesimus as a member, but he chose to appeal to them in love to receive him as a brother.

Paul then brought personal considerations to bear on his appeal by presenting his own circumstances as adding persuasiveness to his request. He was an old man (or ambassador?) and he was a prisoner. The word for "old man" in Greek is usually spelled *presbutēs* and the word for "ambassador," *presbeutēs*. However, Lightfoot [6] and others have shown that ambassador was sometimes spelled *presbutēs*, which appears here. An old servant of Christ, and one who was in prison for the sake of his Master, would surely not be denied a request from a Christian man with faith in Christ and love for the saints.

With great caution and almost timidity Paul at length introduced his request. Moreover, when he finally came to his request he did not name Onesimus at once, but prepared the way by an affectionate reference and a favorable description of him. He withheld the name until he had favorably disposed Philemon to his request. (In the Greek the name Onesimus comes last in v. 10.) Philemon's former unprofitable slave was now Paul's spiritual child, begotten under the hardships and hindrances of his imprisonment (cf. 1 Cor. 4:15; Gal. 4:19). This means, of course, that Onesimus had become a Christian through the witness of Paul.

When Paul finally mentioned the name

[5] R. H. Lightfoot, *The Epistles of St. Paul: Colossians and Philemon* (London: Macmillan, Ltd., 1912), p. 335.

[6] *Op. cit.*, pp. 335–337.

of Onesimus, he immediately declared that a change had taken place in Onesimus. In Greek "Onesimus" means profitable, gainful, helpful, or useful. This was a common name for slaves. With a sensitive appreciation for well-chosen words Paul makes a play on words in describing the change in the slave. The meaning is something like this: "Profitable he is named, but in times past he was (I confess) not profitable, but unprofitable; in the future, however, he will be profitable to both of us." Paul seemed to say that Onesimus had not previously lived up to the meaning of his own name, but now he would do so.

2. Explanation of Paul's Conduct and Motives (12–16)

12 I am sending him back to you, sending my very heart. 13 I would have been glad to keep him with me, in order that he might serve me on your behalf during my imprisonment for the gospel; 14 but I preferred to do nothing without your consent in order that your goodness might not be by compulsion but of your own free will.

15 Perhaps this is why he was parted from you for a while, that you might have him back for ever, 16 no longer as a slave but more than a slave, as a beloved brother, especially to me but how much more to you, both in the flesh and in the Lord.

The words of v. 12 indicate that in all probability Onesimus was the bearer of the letter (together with Tychicus, Col. 4:7–9) as his own passport to his master's welcome. The words *I am sending . . . back* is the translation of only one word in the Greek. That word was used when sending someone to a higher court. In this case, Philemon was to give a verdict that was consistent with his Christian profession.

There is no indication that Paul sent Onesimus to Colossae against his own inclination, or that he would have sent him at all unless he himself had requested it. Onesimus belonged to Philemon, being a part of his property. However, Onesimus was very dear to the apostle; in sending him back to his master Paul was parting with his *very heart* (i.e., part of himself). He was very eager for Philemon to receive

Onesimus in the right manner (Moule, p. 298).

Paul was confident that if Philemon had been personally present with him he would have gladly rendered him whatever service he could. A slave was his master's property, and his slave could only act by his master's consent and on his master's behalf. Therefore in a real sense Onesimus had performed service to Paul for Philemon. Paul made it seem almost as though Philemon had sent Onesimus to serve him, instead of having lost him as a runaway.

Paul stated that he had even considered the possibility of keeping Onesimus with him. He made it clear, however, that without Philemon's knowledge and consent he would not keep Onesimus any longer. He did not want Philemon to offer such service from a sense of duty. He refused to control in anyway his friend's liberty of action. Philemon's decision had to be made entirely of his own free will and not forced upon him (Moulton, p. 74).

Paul suggested that perhaps through the slave's misconduct the providence of God was somehow working to bring good out of evil and to turn sorrow into joy (cf. Gen. 45:4–8). What appeared to Philemon to be an unprofitable experience and a temporary loss might have been permitted to occur in order that he might receive a higher benefit and a greater good. This thought would mitigate Philemon's wrath. He avoided the blunt words "run away" in favor of one which suggests overruling providence. In this divine providence he could receive Onesimus not only as a "profitable" slave but as a *beloved brother.*

Paul did not ask Philemon to set Onesimus free but to love him as a brother. Lest Philemon should dislike calling a slave brother, Paul had already recognized him as his brother and son. Earthly relationships become eternal if they are grounded in a common surrender to Jesus Christ. At work and in worship the new relationship between master and servant, and brother and brother, would assert itself (Hendriksen, p. 221).

The word *brother* was used by the Hebrews to describe not only members of their families, but also all other Hebrews. This word was also used in some religious communities among the Greeks when the members addressed each other. Among the early Christians this word was widely used to refer to fellow Christians. This practice arose because they all acknowledged God as their own Father. If God was Father to each one of them, then in a real sense, they all were brothers.

The actuating force which has destroyed slavery and can destroy the exploitation in any form of other human beings is found in this principle. *Any* man who has been redeemed by Jesus Christ, made a son of God, is, therefore, a beloved brother to all who are members of the family of God. For Paul those "in Christ" can be "neither Jew nor Greek . . . neither slave nor free . . . neither male nor female" (Gal. 3:28). In this realm the world's relationships have become altered. This realm annihilates all man-made distinctions.

3. *Plea in Behalf of Onesimus* (17)

17 So if you consider me your partner, receive him as you would receive me.

All the preceding verses of the letter have been written in preparation for the request. In this verse Paul finally makes his request in behalf of Onesimus. It is that the runaway slave shall be given a kind reception and complete pardon. Paul distinctly makes the case of Onesimus his own. In the Greek text he literally says: "If therefore me you are having (or holding) a partner receive him as me." In the Greek Paul assumes that Philemon counts him a partner. *Partner* translates a Greek word from the same root that is translated "sharing" in v. 6—also often translated "fellowship." The word partner as used here indicates some peculiar bond of fellowship between Paul and Philemon. It seems that Paul was appealing both to his friendship with Philemon and to his fellowship in the Christian life. If Philemon would receive Paul as a partner in the spiritual fellowship, he should receive Onesimus in the same way. In fact, in a real sense Paul would be present in Onesimus (cf. Matt. 25:31–46; Rom. 12:5; 1 Cor. 12:20,27; Eph. 4:12,25). To refuse Onesimus a place in the Christian fellowship would be to put the apostle himself out of the fellowship of faith. Onesimus believed in the same Jesus Christ, was living by the same principles, and had the same hopes; therefore, he was a member of the body of Christ. Paul was insisting on a unity of Christian brotherhood.

4. Acceptance of Responsibility for Onesimus (18–19)

18 If he has wronged you at all, or owes you anything, charge that to my account. 19 I, Paul, write this with my own hand, I will repay it—to say nothing of your owing me even your own self.

Verse 18 assumes that the statement is true. There is little doubt in Paul's mind that Onesimus has wronged Philemon. However, the hypothetical form avoids discussion of the details of the offenses of Onesimus. Probably Onesimus had related these to Paul. Paul offered compensation for all the loss which Philemon had suffered. With a sensitive appreciation of the well-chosen and expressive word Paul makes the letter into a bond. He says in effect, "Here is my promissory note, with my signature attached to it." With this statement Paul obligated himself to repay whatever Onesimus owed Philemon, even though he may have guessed that Philemon would not hold him to it. In fact, Paul wrote the statement in this way in order delicately to give Philemon to understand that he ought not to demand *any* compensation for the damages. These words seem to indicate that Paul wrote all of this letter himself; this was quite exceptional. He wanted to make this letter as personal as he could.

Paul was now in debt to Philemon for all the loss caused by Onesimus' actions. However, Philemon owed Paul a debt which outweighed every other. He owed what money could never repay. Paul had been used of the Lord either directly or indirectly in winning Philemon to Christ. For this reason Philemon owed him not money but his own self besides, i.e., every personal sacrifice. Therefore, both Philemon and Onesimus were Paul's spiritual children.

5. Plea for Personal Consideration (20)

20 Yes, brother, I want some benefit from you in the Lord. Refresh my heart in Christ.

Philemon was addressed with the same word which Paul used in v. 16 to refer to Onesimus: *brother*. If Philemon and Onesimus are both Paul's brothers, then they must be brothers to each other. Paul stated that the real plea was not for Onesimus but for himself. He had such a deep affection for Onesimus as to give him deep concern about his welfare. If Philemon would receive Onesimus as a beloved brother, then Paul's anxious feelings would cease. As Philemon had "refreshed" the hearts of the saints (v. 7), should he not refresh Paul's heart and relieve his anxiety about Onesimus.

The Greek for *benefit* is akin to Onesimus and may have been chosen for that reason as a play upon the slave's name. Paul says in effect: "May I find you (as I have found him) a true Onesimus (i.e., my profitable one).

The phrase *in Christ* means the sphere of fellowship of which Christ is the head and the inspiration. Paul meant that if his request was granted he would recognize the hand of the Lord in it, and would receive it as a blessing from him. Only the Lord could enable his servant to act in such a magnanimous way.

III. Conclusion (21–25)

1. Confidence in Philemon's Obedience (21)

21 Confident of your obedience, I write to you, knowing that you will do even more than I say.

There is no hint in the word *obedience* of Paul's apostolic authority, but an expression of Paul's confidence in Philemon's willingness to obey Christ in the matter. He trusted Philemon's obedience to Christian duty because he knew his faith in Christ and his love to the saints (v. 5). He never really doubted that Philemon would grant his request. Genuine faith and obedience are inseparable. Paul had requested Philemon to forgive Onesimus for all the wrong which he had done to him and to welcome him back as a beloved brother as if he were Paul visiting him. What *even more* could Philemon do? He did not specifically say. Knox concluded that the fullness of Paul's request would be that Onesimus be released to Paul for Christian service.

Paul did not tell Philemon that because he was a Christian he was compelled to free Onesimus. He has often been criticized because he never denounced the institution of slavery as unchristian or unlawful. In his extant epistles (e.g., 1 Cor. 7:21-24; Eph. 6:5-8; Col. 3:22—4:1; Titus 2:9-14; 1 Tim. 6:1) he was content to accept slavery as a part of the existing order, and required that slaves should submit to their lot and do their duty faithfully as unto Christ (Scott, p. 99). Paul rightly called each person to be Christian in the actual situation which he faced in life. However, the Christian conscience must also call in question all the institutions of society which violate the rights of persons.

In Paul's extant epistles, there is no open protest against any social or political institution of his time. Paul took the position that all real change must be effected from within. This is the position of the whole New Testament. Brotherly love practiced between master and slave ultimately made slavery meaningless. This indirect attack upon the institution of slavery asserted the principle of spiritual equality and unity in Christ, a principle that eventually ended the system of slavery. The principle of Christian love and unity made it impossible for the Christian to regard another man as chattel.

Christianity has overcome social evils, not by military force, not by insurrection and rebellion, not by revolution and violence, but by changed men governed by Christian principles. By their prayer, faith, and hard work institutions of inhumanity and cruelty have been undermined and overthrown (Erdman, p. 121).

2. Request for Lodging (22)

22 At the same time, prepare a guest room for me, for I am hoping through your prayers to be granted to you.

Paul was expecting a speedy release from prison. His original plan of going from Rome to Spain (Rom. 15:24,28) had apparently been postponed or altered. This request for lodging may have been an additional inducement for Philemon to do more than Paul had asked him to do. If this release from prison developed, Paul would like to visit Philemon. He did not take his release for granted, but he hoped that in answer to the prayers of the church he would be allowed to visit them. This expectation of a visit from Paul would tend to secure compliance with his request. This is an incidental mention of what Paul had planned but it carries a gentle compulsion to Philemon. As he receives Onesimus, let him also prepare for the coming of Paul!

According to Knox, Onesimus was returned to Paul as a helper and became in time the bishop of Ephesus (ca. A.D. 107–117). Goodspeed thinks that Onesimus, who was concerned with the fuller use of Paul's writings, made a collection of Paul's letters. These suggestions are possible, though not demonstrable.

3. Salutations (23-24)

23 Epaphras, my fellow prisoner in Christ Jesus, sends greetings to you, 24 and so do Mark, Aristarchus, Demas, and Luke, my fellow workers.

The salutations here are very similar to the ones given in Colossians 4:10. All of the people mentioned were probably well known to Philemon, especially Epaphras, who was probably Philemon's pastor. In Colossians he is spoken of as being a resident in Colossae; he may have been the founder of the church there (Col. 1:7–8; 4:12).

4. Benediction (25)

25 The grace of the Lord Jesus Christ be with your spirit.

In the address and salutation Paul addressed the entire "church in his [Philemon's] house." Here again the plural indicates the same group is intended. This benediction is a prayer to Christ or an earnest wish expressed on behalf of the church in Philemon's house.